Additional Praise for

PUTIN'S KLEPTOCRACY:

"[A] copiously researched account . . . the most persuasive account we have of corruption in contemporary Russia. Dawisha won't be getting a Russian visa anytime soon. Her indictment—even if it wouldn't stand up in a court of law—hits Putin where it really hurts."

—*New York Times Book Review*

"[An] unblinking scholarly exposé."

—*Forbes*

"An important and valuable work because it provides the most exhaustive investigation into the patterns of Russian government corruption to date."

—*The Wall Street Journal*

"Dawisha's book stands as the most detailed indictment of the venality that she argues has marked every step of Putin's career."

—*Foreign Affairs*

"[Dawisha] makes extensive use of the work of others, both fellow political scientists as well as journalists working across the US and Europe. . . . The resulting work has a certain admirable relentlessness. For by tying all of these disparate investigations together so thoroughly, so pedantically, and with so many extended footnotes—and by tracking down Western copies of documents that vanished from Russia long ago—the extent of what has always been a murky story suddenly becomes more clear. . . . [Dawisha] turns a relentless focus on the financial story of Putin's rise to power: page after page contains the gritty details of criminal operation after criminal operation, including names, dates, and figures. Many of these details had never been put together before."

—Anne Applebaum for the *New York Review of Books*

"[A] who's who of the people on the sanctions lists drawn up by America and the EU. It is also a guide to the crony capitalism that grew out of the nexus of Mr. Putin's plutocratic interests, his shady past and authoritarian rule."

—*The Economist*

"*Putin's Kleptocracy* should be on the reading list of anyone who wishes to understand the true nature of Putin's regime, which, as Dawisha correctly states, is 'committed to a life of looting without parallel.'"

—*Washington Free Beacon*

"A rich and exhaustive account of Putin and his regime . . . Among Dawisha's many contributions to our understanding of post-Soviet politics, this book may be the most significant, as the author combines an analysis of such politics and a biography of Russian president Vladimir Putin in unrivaled detail. . . . The notes in this volume represent one of the finest and most imaginative uses of published source materials that this reviewer has ever seen in a book on post-Soviet politics."

—*Library Journal*, starred review

"A damning account of Vladimir Putin's rise to power and of the vast dimensions of the corruption—political and economic—that both reigns and rots in Russia. . . . Dawisha's research is extremely impressive. . . . The light of Dawisha's research penetrates a deep moral darkness, revealing something ugly—and dangerous."

—*Kirkus Reviews*, starred review

"[A] devastating dossier on what history may recognize as a state system that served mainly as a cover for the criminal looting and victimization of the people whose self-sacrificing patriotism it so cynically and shamelessly manipulated."

—*The Washington Times*

"[An] important new book . . . [Dawisha] has compiled an extraordinary dossier of malfeasance and political corruption on an epic scale. . . . Dawisha is the first Western author to have pieced together all the relevant material. . . . Above all, she charts the extraordinary accumulation of wealth and power by Putin's associates and friends over a period of two decades. . . . Dawisha has done us all a service in her meticulous account. . . . *Putin's Kleptocracy* is a courageous and scrupulously judicious investigation into the sinews of wealth and power in Vladimir Putin's Russia."

—*The Times Literary Supplement*

"A long-time Russia scholar . . . Dawisha spent almost eight years researching her book. . . . In studying high-level corruption under the Putin regime, Dawisha does a thorough job of analysing the relevant material in the historical archives and court records, and collating reports in the Russian and western press. The power of her argument is amplified by the coolness of her prose."

—*Financial Times*

ALSO BY KAREN DAWISHA

Russia and the New States of Eurasia:
The Politics of Upheaval (with Bruce Parrott)

Eastern Europe, Gorbachev, and Reform:
The Great Challenge

The Kremlin and the Prague Spring

Soviet Foreign Policy towards Egypt

PUTIN'S KLEPTOCRACY

Who Owns Russia?

KAREN DAWISHA

Simon & Schuster Paperbacks

New York   London   Toronto   Sydney   New Delhi

Simon & Schuster Paperbacks
An Imprint of Simon & Schuster, Inc.
1230 Avenue of the Americas
New York, NY 10020

First Simon & Schuster paperback edition September 2015

SIMON & SCHUSTER PAPERBACKS and colophon are
registered trademarks of Simon & Schuster, Inc.

For information about special discounts for bulk purchases,
please contact Simon & Schuster Special Sales at
1-866-506-1949 or business@simonandschuster.com

The Simon & Schuster Speakers Bureau can bring authors to your live event.
For more information or to book an event contact the Simon & Schuster Speakers
Bureau at 1-866-248-3049 or visit our website at www.simonspeakers.com.

Cover design by Flag Tonuzi

Manufactured in the United States of America

5 7 9 10 8 6

Library of Congress Control Number: 2014948969

ISBN 978-1-4767-9519-5
ISBN 978-1-4767-9520-1 (pbk)
ISBN 978-1-4767-9521-8 (ebook)

To free Russian journalism
and the memory of Boris Nemtsov (1959–2015),
whose struggle against Kremlin corruption will not be forgotten

CONTENTS

GLOSSARY OF ACRONYMS AND KEY POLITICAL LEADERS

Connection to Vladimir Putin; 2015 position

Abramovich, Roman: oligarch, early supporter of Putin; owner, Millhouse LLC, Chelsea football club

Akimov, Andrey: KGB, Donau Bank, Vienna Austria; Gazprom Board

Aleksandrov, Aleksey: St. Petersburg Company Rus', co-founder, Bank Rossiya; Federation Council

Aven, Pyotr: Minister Foreign Economic Relations 1991–92, authorized Putin contracts during Food Scandal; president, Alfa bank

Baltik-Eskort: private security firm guarding Putin in St. Petersburg, headed by Roman Tsepov and Viktor Zolotov

Bank Rossiya: St. Petersburg bank established 1990, connected to Putin Ozero Circle

Bastrykin, Aleksandr: classmate of Putin; head of Investigative Committee

Berezovskiy, Boris: Yeltsin-era oligarch who supported Putin's rise; lived in exile in London until his death in 2013

BND: German Federal Intelligence Agency, Bundesnachrichtendienst

Borodin, Pavel: head, PPMD, 1993–2000, Putin was his deputy 1996–97; head of the Union of Russia and Belarus

CEC: Central Electoral Commission, Russia

Chemezov, Sergey: Dresden KGB with Putin; boards of many major banks and arms makers

Cherkesov, Viktor: head of Leningrad/St. Petersburg KGB and successor organizations, FSB First Deputy Director when Putin head; chair, Duma Security and Anti-corruption Committee

CPRF: Communist Party of the Russian Federation

CPSU: Communist Party of the Soviet Union

FSB: Federal Security Service, Federal'naya Sluzhba Bezopasnosti

Fursenko, Andrey: Ozero cooperative with Putin; presidential aide

Fursenko, Sergey: Ozero cooperative with Putin; director, Lentransgaz

Gazprom: Russia's major gas producer, headed by Miller

GDR: East Germany, German Democratic Republic

GKU: Main Control Directorate, Kremlin, Putin worked at GKU 1997–98

Golubev, Valeriy: KGB; mayor's office, St. Petersburg; board of Gazprom

Gorelov, Dmitriy: Bank Rossiya and Petromed

Gref, German: legal advisor to mayor's office, St. Petersburg; CEO, Sberbank

Grigor'yev, Aleksandr: childhood friends; KGB/FSB; head, Gosrezerv until death, 2008

Ivanov, Sergey: KGB; head of Presidential Administration

Ivanov, Viktor: mayor's office, St. Petersburg; head, Federal Narcotics Control Service

KGB: Committee for State Security, predecessor to FSB, Komitet gosudarstvennoy bezopasnosti

Kogan, Vladimir: CEO, Promstroybank

Kolesnikov, Sergey: Petromed; whistleblower on "Putin's Palace"; in exile

Komsomol: All-Union Leninist Communist League of Youth, Vsesoyuznyy Leninskiy Kommunisticheskiy Soyuz Molodyozhi

Koval'chuk, Yuriy: Ozero Cooperative with Putin; Bank Rossiya

Kozak, Dmitriy: mayor's office, St. Petersburg; Deputy Prime Minister

Kozhin, Vladimir: mayor's office, St. Petersburg; Presidential Aide, Military-Technical Cooperation

Kudrin, Aleksey: mayor's office, St. Petersburg; former Finance Minister; confidant of Putin

KVS: Committee for Foreign Liaison

LDPR: Liberal Democratic Party of Russia

Medvedev, Aleksandr: KGB, Donau Bank Vienna Austria; Boards Gazprombank, Gazprom

Medvedev, Dmitriy: mayor's office, St. Petersburg; Prime Minister

Miller, Aleksey: mayor's office, St. Petersburg; chairman, Gazprom

MVD: Ministry of Internal Affairs

Myachin, Viktor: Bank Rossiya, Ozero; CEO "Abros," a subsidiary of Bank Rossiya

Naryshkin, Sergey: KGB; chairman, State Duma

Nurgaliyev, Rashid: KGB; Deputy Secretary of the Security Council

OVR: Fatherland–All Russia, Otechestvo–Vsya Rossiya

Ozero Dacha Consumer Cooperative: lakeside dacha community and joint bank account shared by Putin, Smirnov, Shamalov, Fursenko brothers, Yuriy Koval'chuk, Yakunin, and Myachin

Patrushev, Nikolay: KGB; Secretary of the Security Council

Petromed: medical supply company established by Sergey Kolesnikov, initially as joint venture with Putin's KVS, became major national medical infrastructure company. Later used as vehicle to skim funds, according to Kolesnikov, for building "Putin's Palace."

PPMD: Presidential Property Management Department

PTK: Petersburg Fuel Company, Peterburgskaya Toplivnaya Kompaniya

Reyman, Leonid: head of telephone system, St. Petersburg; chairman of board, Syazinvest, Russia's largest telecommunications holding company

Reznik, Vladislav: St. Petersburg businessman, Bank Rossiya; chairman, State Duma Committee on Finances

Rosneft: Russia's major oil producing company, headed by Sechin

Rotenberg, Arkadiy: childhood friend of Putin; Stroygazmontazh, major recipient of Kremlin contracts

Rotenberg, Boris: childhood friend of Putin; Stroygazmontazh, major recipient of Kremlin contracts

SPAG: St. Petersburg Real Estate Holding Company

Sechin, Igor: St. Petersburg government with Putin; head of Rosneft

Shamalov, Nikolay: Ozero cooperative with Putin; Bank Rossiya

Siloviki: generic Russian term for those who have backgrounds and employment in security services, military, and police

Sistema: Russian term for the way the Russian political system really works, as opposed to formal state institutions

Smirnov, Vladimir: Ozero cooperative with Putin, SPAG; head of TENEX until 2007

Sobchak, Anatoliy: mayor of St. Petersburg, 1991–96; died 2000

Surkov, Vladislav: deputy head, Presidential Administration under Putin; Putin advisor on Ukraine

SVR: Foreign Intelligence Service, Sluzhba Vneshney Razvedki

Timchenko, Gennadiy: St. Petersburg oil business; head of Volga group and many major Russian companies

Tokarev, Nikolay: Dresden KGB with Putin; Sovcomflot and Transneft

Tsepov, Roman: co-founder, Baltik-Eskort; died of possible polonium poisoning, St. Petersburg, 2004

Twentieth Trust (Dvadtsatyy Trest): construction company suspected of siphoning funds from St. Petersburg city budget during Putin tenure

Warnig, Matthias: East German secret police (Stasi) when Putin in KGB; director, Nord Stream, board of many Russian corporations

Yakunin, Vladimir: Ozero cooperative with Putin; Russian Railways chief

Zhirinovskiy, Vladimir: head of Liberal Democratic Party of Russia (LDPR)

Zolotov, Viktor: co-founder, Baltik-Eskort, St. Petersburg; Deputy Minister of Interior

Zubkov, Viktor: mayor's office, St. Petersburg; chairman of board, Gazprom

Zyuganov, Gennadiy: head of the Communist Party of the Russian Federation (CPRF)

PUTIN'S KLEPTOCRACY

INTRODUCTION

IN REACTING to Russia's annexation of Crimea and support for pro-Russian separatists in Ukraine in early 2014, the U.S. government announced an unprecedented response: not the Russian state but individual Russian citizens would be subjected to asset seizures and visa bans. The Sixth Fleet was not called into action; exports to Russia as a whole were not banned; cultural and educational exchanges were not stopped. Rather, individual elites close to "a senior Russian Government official"—Vladimir Putin—were targeted.

Probably the most serious international crisis since the end of the Cold War, and the White House targets individuals. Why this response? Because at last, after fourteen years of dealing with President Vladimir Putin as a legitimate head of state, the U.S. government has finally acknowledged publicly what successive administrations have known privately—that he has built a system based on massive predation on a level not seen in Russia since the tsars. Transparency International estimates the annual cost of bribery to Russia at $300 billion, roughly equal to the entire gross domestic product of Denmark, or thirty-seven times higher than the $8 billion Russia expended in 2007 on "national priority projects" in health, education, and agriculture.[1] Capital flight, which officially has totaled approximately $335 billion since 2005,[2] or about 5 percent of GDP, reaching over $50 billion in the first quarter of 2014 alone, has swollen Western bank coffers but made Russia the most unequal of all developed and emerging economies (BRIC: Brazil, Russia, India, China), in which 110 billionaires control 35 percent of the country's wealth.[3]

And these billionaires, far from being titans of industry motoring the modernization of the Russian economy, have secured and increased their wealth by relying on and bolstering the centralized power of the state. The wealth of the oligarchs and political elites who came to power with Putin in 2000 has been more stable than in any other G7 country; they have made millions, though some have also lost as much. Political leaders close to Putin have become multimillionaires, and the oligarchs around them, according to *Forbes* Russia, have become billionaires. They are able to maintain that power and wealth as long as they don't challenge Putin politically. Under this system, the state absorbs the risk, provides state funds for investment, and gives those close to the Kremlin massive monetary rewards. With the return under Putin to state capitalism, the state nationalizes the risk but continues to privatize the rewards to those closest to the president in return for their loyalty.

Within weeks of Putin's coming to power, the Kremlin began to erode the basic individual freedoms guaranteed under the 1993 Russian Constitution. This pattern of gradually closing the public space and denying citizens the rights of free press, assembly, and speech was present and planned from the very beginning, as will be shown in my discussion of a document, never before published outside Russia, detailing the plans made in late 1999 and early 2000 to reshape the entire Presidential Administration to achieve these ends. In Russia, the Presidential Administration is the true locus of power, particularly under Putin's "vertical of power." Its offices and departments shadow and supervise the work of the government ministries, the two houses of the legislature, the courts, regional government, the media, and societal movements like youth groups and trade unions. It is from here that policy is made in all sectors of domestic and foreign policy, to be implemented by the government or passed into law by the Duma and the Federation Council. Putin was enormously assisted by very favorable global economic conditions in which the price of oil shot up to over \$140 per barrel, allowing the Kremlin to provide an increased standard of living for ordinary Russians and the emerging middle class while also creating greater social stability.

But Putin also benefited from the existence of a tight-knit circle that came with him from St. Petersburg and with whom he had worked for over a decade. In this book I lay out the case for the existence of a cabal to establish a regime that would control privatization, restrict democracy, and return Russia to Great Power (if not superpower) status. I also detail the Putin circle's use of public positions for personal gain even before Putin became president in 2000. The trail leads to the establishment of Bank Rossiya, now sanctioned by the United States; the rise of the Ozero Dacha Consumer Cooperative, founded by Putin and other members now subject to visa bans and asset seizures; the links between Putin and Petromed, the medical supply company that diverted millions in state funds to build "Putin's Palace" near Sochi; and the role of security officials from Putin's KGB days in Leningrad and Dresden, many of whom have maintained their contacts with Russian organized crime.

Elections in all new democracies suffer from certain problems of weak party stability; poor, loose, and fluid electoral laws; and voter manipulation and fraud. However, these problems should decrease over time, leading to the consolidation of democratic institutions. In Russia, however, they have only increased, until in the 2011–12 electoral cycle the fraud and abuse were so widespread that popular demonstrations broke out. By the end of 2011, having come through a thoroughly fraudulent and publicly documented sham election for the Duma (the lower house of the Federal Assembly, Russia's Parliament), it became crystal clear that the ability of activists in Moscow and St. Petersburg to seek democratic change was significantly inferior to the regime's ability to suppress change.

After Putin publicly wept, possibly from relief, when he was declared the winner of the 2012 presidential elections, increased targeted repressions began again, reminiscent of the early 1930s or the late 1960s in the USSR. Nonviolent demonstrators were once again sentenced to either prison or indefinite psychiatric treatment. With the economy suffering a downturn—mainly because of elite plundering—the crony regime's inner logic seemed clear: Putin was willing to use force to maintain his potentially indefinite hold on power so that his group could continue to loot the country without limit. In response, Russian websites held endless discussions of the reign of *bespredel*—the limitless and total lack of accountability of the elites—under the façade of "restoring Russian greatness."

It is this kleptocratic tribute system underlying Russia's authoritarian regime that the U.S. government sought to expose and punish beginning in March 2014. The names on the sanctions list read like a Who's Who of Team Putin. For the first time the White House explicitly talked about Putin's circle as his "cronies" and targeted their money abroad, exposing the fact that Western governments have known for some time the broad details of where this group's money is, what their private rules are, and what high crimes and misdemeanors they have committed to establish and maintain their *sistema*—and that Western governments are no longer willing to keep silent.

How was this group formed? What were its origins? And why did it take Western policy and academic communities so long to embrace this view of the Russian political system as a steel hand in an initially velvet glove? We may never know precisely when the current regime decided to do what they have clearly done, any more than we know on which day Stalin stopped being a pencil pusher and decided to imprison millions in the gulag, or even when Hitler hit on the idea of exterminating the Jewish population of Europe. Horrifying details such as these are not something one reads about in dictators' memoirs after they start receiving their pension. It is a pity (purely from a historian's point of view) that there is usually so little time between the collapse of dictators' regimes and their own ultimate demise.

Because we can see that there is a complex and clever system in Russia, quite opaque and full of interesting details and inner rules, we should conclude that the system came about by intelligent design. But how? The evidence strongly suggests that it did not come about by chance. This book firmly rejects the ideas often promulgated in Western academic circles that Putin is an "accidental autocrat" or a "good tsar surrounded by bad boyars." Of course, the boyars—now called oligarchs—are indeed mainly bad. And of course, not every detail of their ascent could have been worked out in advance. Not everything went as planned; certainly they met with deep resistance from other rivals, in both St. Petersburg and Moscow. But I believe that Putin's group could never have predicted how successful they would be and how little their acquisition of power would be resisted by Russians and the West. The contention of this book is that the group around Putin today is the same as the one that brought him to power from St. Petersburg in the 1990s and that the purpose of that project was never to embed Western-style democratic institutions and values. The group did not get lost on the path to democracy. They never took that path.

Why did the West not firmly resist "Putin's project" until now? In the process of interviewing for this book, it became clear that many Western officials stationed in Russia certainly knew from the early 1990s what kind of operative Putin was and whom he depended upon to get things done. But he was regarded as a relatively low-level person in one city in one very turbulent country. And so the eyes of Western intelligence were wide shut until, in the course of less than two years, Putin rose from being an out-of-work deputy mayor, whose boss had just lost his bid for reelection, to the head of the Federal Security Service (Federal'naya Sluzhba Bezopasnosti, FSB), the modern-day KGB. One year later Putin was prime minister; six months after that he was president. Jobless to president in three and a half years. Only then did Western journalists and policymakers focus closely on his background and his circle, but by then it was too late. According to government leaks to *Newsweek*, U.S. government analysis of Putin's personal involvement in a money-laundering scheme through a German-based company, SPAG, led in 2000 to Russia's being placed on an international money-laundering blacklist: "A key reason, said a former top U.S. official, was a sheaf of intelligence reports linking Putin to SPAG," including documents showing he "signed important St. Petersburg city documents for the company's benefit."[4] The pattern of helping his friends to the detriment of his people was set early.

Then, at the Slovenia summit in June 2001, President George W. Bush looked into Putin's eyes and saw his soul, and when Putin quickly joined with the United States in the "war on terror," analysts report that the primary focus of Western intelligence gathering shifted away from Russia and toward the Muslim world. Putin was regarded as a reliable partner in helping the West target Islamic extremists, especially in Afghanistan, since there were Chechen fighters in al Qaeda camps too. Only slowly did Putin's malevolence dawn on Western governments, especially in light of the Kremlin's transparently predatory actions in taking apart Russia's largest private oil company, Yukos, and imprisoning its independently minded owner, Mikhayl Khodorkovskiy, in 2005. The following year, at the G8 meeting in St. Petersburg, President Bush called for "strengthened international efforts to deny kleptocrats access to our financial system," but he still did not mention Russia by name.[5] Western newspapers now report that in 2007 a CIA assessment of Putin's personal wealth "largely tracked" with assertions made by the Russian political analyst Stanislav Belkovskiy, who claimed that Putin had holdings totaling about $40 billion in the commodity-trading company Gunvor, the publicly traded state-majority-owned gas giant Gazprom, and the oil and gas company Surgutneftegaz.[6]* At last, one thought, the West might start to stand up against this vast scheme, with its potential to undermine not only Russia's development but Western financial institutions, the banks, equity markets, real estate markets, and insurance companies that were showing signs of being undermined internally by employees eager to receive their commissions from these illicit transactions.

But then President Barack Obama, as have all new U.S. presidents, announced he was going to "reset" relations with Russia. As a result, Putin spent only minutes in the penalty box for the 2008 invasion of Georgia before being embraced at the 2009 G8 meeting of the world's leading industrial nations. The meeting was hosted in Italy by Putin's personal friend, Prime Minister Silvio Berlusconi, even as U.S. government cables reported allegations circling in Rome that he was "profiting personally and handsomely" from secret deals with Putin that included the "exchange of lavish gifts."[7] From 2008 to 2014 six more years were lost while low-level government officials gathered materials on Putin's wealth and high-level political appointees ignored them.

In the academic world, there was a similar trend in writing about Russia. Books continued to frame Russia as a democracy, albeit one that was failing

---

*U.S. government anonymous leaks in 2014 claimed that Putin had spent illicit funds since the early 2000s on the unrivaled acquisition of luxury items, including his twenty presidential residences; that he had siphoned off cash from Gazprom to the tune of 70 percent of its capital expenditures; and that he controlled an estimated 4.5 percent of Gazprom, 37 percent of shares in Surgutneftegaz, and 50 percent of Gunvor. See Bill Gertz. "Putin Corruption Network Revealed," *Washington (DC) Free Beacon,* April 7, 2014, http://freebeacon.com/national-security/putin-corruption-network-revealed/.

or in crisis. Like other scholars of Russia, I have spent a significant portion of my career thinking and writing about how the post-Communist states might make a transition toward democracy.* Initially Western government and academic circles† believed that institutions could be established in practically any country that would guide it along a democratic path. Most of the new central European countries had early elections, established non-Communist governments, and never looked back. Our uncurbed enthusiasm even extended to Russia. But then the quality of democracy in Putin's Russia just kept getting worse.

Still there was little shift in academic direction, as much of the literature approached the Putin era as a democracy in the process of failing rather than as an authoritarian project in the process of succeeding.‡ Clearly in the 1990s democracy was in fact both being built and failing, but when the success or failure of democracy building is the central telos of the narrative, one loses track of the counternarrative, which is that there were elites

---

*This redirection in my research was particularly reflected in several earlier works, including *Eastern Europe, Gorbachev and Reform* (1990); *Russia and the New States of Eurasia: The Politics of Upheaval* (1994), coauthored with Bruce Parrott; and two series coedited with Bruce Parrott, the four-volume *Democratization and Authoritarianism in Postcommunist Societies* (1997) and the ten-volume *The International Politics of Eurasia* (1994–97).[8]

† Most books in this genre were influenced by the writings of Samuel Huntington, *The Third Wave: Democratization in the Late Twentieth Century* (1991). But in addition to these institutional perspectives, theories derived from economics and public choice also were used to bolster the claim that over time, democracy would emerge in Russia, as in Mancur Olson's *Power and Prosperity* (2000).[9]

‡ The field has a rich collection of books on democracy in Russia (e.g., McFaul 2001; Fish 2005; Sakwa 2011), and all of them are full of foreboding about democracy's limits and failings. But there are no Western academic accounts of the origins and development of authoritarianism as an elite project in Russia. Henry Hale's early discussion of stalled party development, *Why Not Parties in Russia* (2007), Regina Smyth's (2006) book on the impact on democracy's "grand strategy" of rational actor microchoices made by candidates in Russia's mixed electoral system, Brian Taylor's study of the power ministries, *State Building in Putin's Russia* (2011), the books by Gulnaz Sharafutdinova (2011) and Thomas Remington (2011) on the political economy of Russia's regions, and Michael Urban's book on elite discourse, *Cultures of Power* (2010), are notable exceptions, although they each deal with only one aspect of the building of authoritarianism in Russia. The serious contributions by Russian analysts on this subject are too numerous to mention and are discussed in depth throughout this book. Wider works on competitive authoritarianism certainly exist, including excellent contributions by Levitsky and Way (2010), Gandhi (2008), and Brownlee (2007).[10]

(centered on Putin and his security cabal, the so-called *siloviki*) who sought from the beginning to establish an authoritarian regime in Russia, not perhaps for its own sake but because controlling the political and economic development of the country was for them a greater ambition than building any democracy that would inevitably force them to surrender power at some point. When they came to see themselves as the personal guardians and guarantors of Russia's future, this only increased the possibility that they would not only resist the rotation of elites, critical to a democracy, but actively seek to stymie it. And they used many methods to achieve this, including engaging in criminal behavior, controlling the legal system and the media, and, above all, maintaining group cohesion through combinations of threats and rewards.

Instead of seeing Russian politics as an inchoate democratic system being pulled down by history, accidental autocrats, popular inertia, bureaucratic incompetence, or poor Western advice, I conclude that from the beginning Putin and his circle sought to create an authoritarian regime ruled by a close-knit cabal with embedded interests, plans, and capabilities, who used democracy for decoration rather than direction. In other words, Russia is both a democratic failure and a resounding success—that is, a success for Putin and his cronies and a success on their terms.

Of course, in this system, there is robust political contestation, there is great uncertainty and instability, and there are still democrats and democratic aspirations. There is also popular support for Putin beyond Russia's intellectual classes—support bolstered by high oil prices and state control over almost the entire media space. The internal logic of this system has strengthened the power of Putin over the rest; of "manual control" over institutions; of instructions and "understandings" (*ponyatiya*) over law; and of money over everything.

Putin and his circle could have passed and upheld laws to protect, promote, cement, and sustain democratic institutions, but they chose not to. On the contrary, they have established what they themselves internally call a *sistema* that undermines, mocks, and mimics democracy but that actually serves the purpose of creating a unified and stable authoritarian state that allows individuals close to Putin and his associates to benefit personally from the unparalleled despoliation of Russia's vast natural resources. The evidence I present suggests that, from the moment Putin took power in 2000, Russia ceased to be a place where democratic dreamers could flourish. To be sure, Putin has built a legalistic system, but this system serves to control, channel, and coerce the middle class and the broader elite while at the same time allowing the inner core to act with impunity along what has been called Putin's "vertical of power," according to the adage "For my friends, anything. For my enemies, the law!" [11]

This is not to say that the Russian ruling elite does not see the benefits of a robust rule-of-law system. On the contrary, their behavior in parking their money in Western banks suggests they are very interested in it—just not in their own country. The American economist Mancur Olson was right to posit that in the transition from dictatorship to democracy, "roving bandits" will over time gain an interest in laws to vouchsafe their gains and will settle down, and from this interest in the stability and predictability of gains, democracy will emerge. Under Putin, as the regime made the transition from what Olson called "roving" to "stationary" bandits, interelite violence did decrease, and the streets became safer, as Olson predicted. [12] But Olson failed to foresee the extent to which globalization would allow Russian elites to continue to maximize their gains by keeping domestic markets open for their predation while minimizing their own personal risk by depositing profits in secure offshore accounts.

This book does not look in detail at what is happening in Russia today; instead I seek to ascertain the authoritarian moment in Russia. The story starts with the collapse of the USSR, when, as the archives of the Communist Party of the Soviet Union (CPSU) reveal, the KGB moved the CPSU's vast financial reserves offshore, out from under President Mikhayl Gorbachev's control, thus further crippling his regime. The August 1991 coup by Communist and KGB hardliners failed, but aspirations for revanche remained. One of the chief PR strategists of Putin's 2000 victory, Gleb Pavlovskiy, subsequently put it like this, after he had been sacked by the Kremlin: "Putin belongs to a very extensive but politically invisible layer of people who after the end of the 1980s were looking for a 'revanche' in connection with the fall of the Soviet Union."[13] The 1990s was spent preparing for that moment.

Vladimir Putin spent his entire early life yearning to join and was finally accepted into the KGB. By his own account, his favorite songs are Soviet standards, not Western rock. He has been deeply conservative his whole life. Yet he has also been a keen collector of every possible trapping of material wealth. When he was stationed in East Germany, he had the leaders of the German Red Army Faction (also known as the Baader-Meinhof Group) steal speaker systems for him when they had a moment free from their terror campaigns. Back in Russia in the early 1990s, Putin acquired a substantial country house, or dacha, and an apartment in the most prestigious section of St. Petersburg within his first years of working in the city; neither of these could have been purchased with his meager official salary.

This pattern of uncontrollable greed, of wanting what rightfully belongs to others, which Masha Gessen calls *pleonexia*,[14] has resulted in over twenty official residences, fifty-eight planes, and four yachts. Sadly for Russians, Putin does not "own" any of these, except his St. Petersburg properties and perhaps his first yacht, the *Olympia*, which was presented to him as a gift by a group of oligarchs headed by Roman Abramovich just prior to Putin's becoming president in 2000 and delivered in 2002. Without the presidency Putin theoretically would not be allowed to keep any of these accoutrements of power, except perhaps for the $700,000 in watches that he routinely sports—six times his declared annual income, a subject of constant Russian journalistic interest.[15] Thus his motivation to leave power is reduced to zero. Those who say politicians can't be called corrupt unless the police find $20,000 in small bills in their freezer, or who say "But the U.S. presidents have Camp David," should contemplate how much has been spent from public funds on the construction, maintenance, furnishing, and round-the-clock staffing of these twenty residences, most of which did not exist, or at least not in their current gilded state, prior to Putin's rule.

The demands of this tribute system have meant that the cost of doing business in Russia has escalated to such an extent that Russian and foreign businesses alike wonder whether they can even turn a profit. The global Swedish furniture chain Ikea threatened to call it quits after years of trying to run a clean business in Russia. When the head of Ikea Russia, Lennart Dahlgren, left the company in 2006, he revealed that they had been subjected to years of legal traps that they sought to solve by meeting personally with Putin. But a high-ranking official told them that a meeting with Putin would cost $5 million to $10 million. Stating that he didn't know whether they were speaking seriously or joking, Dahlgren told reporters: "I sensed that it would be better not to get into that discussion any deeper." [16]

A democracy is easier to research than a dictatorship. Even so, non-democratic actions in a democracy, like corruption, are less easy to research than candidates' public speeches, for example. When the subject of study is how, when, and why Russian elites decided to take the country away from democracy, obviously no one from this group is giving public interviews, and if they do, as happened with Aleksandr Litvinenko, they suffer a cruel death.

More difficult to research are Russian elites' private financial motivations for taking certain actions and the clan conflicts within the elite that produce sometimes contradictory public results. I spent almost eight years studying archival sources, the accounts of Russian insiders, the results of investigative journalism in the United States, Britain, Germany, Finland, France, and Italy, and all of this was backed by extensive interviews with Western officials who served in Moscow and St. Petersburg and were consulted on background. Based on all this, I believe it is possible to construct a credible picture of Putin's rise. I also consulted with and used many accounts by opposition figures, Russian analysts, and exiled figures who used to be part of the Kremlin elite. These have become an increasingly credible source of information, particularly as the number of émigrés increases.

Above all I have relied on the work of Russian journalists who wrote this story when the Russian media was still free. Many of them died for this story, and their work has largely been scrubbed from the Internet, or (as I discovered several times) infected with viruses attached to online documents, leading to computer crashes. Whole runs of critical newspapers have disappeared from Russian libraries. But "they" always forget to remove them all, and many Russians still keep clippings, reminiscent of a previous era when the state similarly ended press freedoms.

Finally, the dump of nonredacted cables from Wikileaks is very regrettable but also a completely fascinating source of information. For example, a 2010 cable from America's ambassador in Moscow John Beyrle to the U.S. secretary of state provided the following description of how money, elections, criminal activity, and the Kremlin interact:

> XXX [name redacted by author] stated that everything depends on the Kremlin and he thought that . . . many mayors and governors pay off key insiders in the Kremlin. XXX argued that the vertical works because people are paying bribes all the way to the top. He told us that people often witness officials going into the Kremlin with large suitcases and bodyguards full of money. The governors also collect money based on bribes, almost resembling a tax system, throughout their regions. He described how there are parallel structures in the regions in which people are able to pay their leaders. For instance, the FSB, MVD [Ministry of Internal Affairs], and militia all have distinct money collection systems. Further, XXX told us that deputies generally have to buy their seats in the government. They need money to get to the top, but once they are there, their positions become quite lucrative money making opportunities.[17]

Vladimir Putin is both a product and a producer of this pervasive system of corruption. Of course, he is not the only Eurasian or Western leader to have collected gifts and tributes. But to have created with this clique an entire system that spans eleven time zones is by any account an impressive achievement. I argue that the outlines of the authoritarian and kleptocratic system were clear by the end of Putin's first one hundred days in 2000. It is a story that begins even before the collapse of the USSR.

Chapter One

———◦◉◦———

The USSR at the Moment of Collapse

I N DECEMBER 2012, in a judicial hearing in London into the death of Aleksandr Litvinenko, a former operative for the Russian FSB who for some time had been a virulent critic of President Vladimir Putin, Hugh Davies, the counsel to the inquest, stated that evidence possessed by the British government established "a prima facie case in the culpability of the Russian state in the death of Alexander Litvinenko."[1] In July 2014, as relations with Russia deteriorated, British prime minister David Cameron announced he would let the public inquest proceed. At the center of the inquiry was a claim by Litvinenko's widow that, at the time of his 2006 death by polonium-210 poisoning, he was providing evidence to Spanish authorities about "Russian mafia links to the Kremlin and Vladimir Putin."[2]

The inquest pointed to the tangled web of relations between the Russian state and the mafia, relations that were known to Western governments and much discussed in U.S. cables released by Wikileaks. In particular, a series of events in Spain underlined what had become an interlocking network of associations and clan-based politics centered on Putin. First there was the arrest in Spain in 2008 of the reputed leaders of the St. Petersburg–based Tambov-Malyshev organized crime group,* including Gennadiy Petrov and Aleksandr Malyshev. Then there was the warrant for the arrest

———

* The Tambov and Malyshev groups had often been rivals but united forces in Spain. They had also sometimes united in St. Petersburg in fights against other outside rivals, including the Kazantsy from Tatarstan. For the best account of their early, and fluid, relationship, see Konstantinov (1995), 147–55.

of Vladislav Reznik, who was the cochairman of the ruling United Russia Party and chairman of the Duma's Finance Committee.[3]* Finally, there was the revelation that Communications Minister Leonid Reyman owned a beachfront house in the same resort in Majorca as Petrov, who introduced him to potential Spanish partners, and that Reyman himself was under investigation by Spanish authorities.[5]

All those under investigation in Spain came from St. Petersburg, and all were close associates of Putin, as they rose up together from the early 1990s onward. This incident goes to the heart of whether, as Spanish prosecutors stated in classified briefings to U.S. and other Western governments, made public via Wikileaks, Russia under Putin had become a virtual "mafia state"[6] in which state structures operate hand in glove with criminal structures to their mutual benefit, with the mafia operating within guidelines established by top Kremlin elites for the purpose of strengthening Putin's hold on power, silencing critics, and maximizing mutual economic benefits.

Briefing U.S. officials behind closed doors, the Spanish prosecutor called Russia, Chechnya, and Belarus "mafia states" and stated that in such countries "one cannot differentiate between the activities of the government and OC [organized crime] groups." Further, the security services "control OC in Russia. . . . The FSB is 'absorbing' the Russia mafia" and using them

---

* In a revealing 2011 article in *Novaya gazeta*[4] that was translated and included in a U.S. government document released as part of Wikileaks, the author, Sergey Makarov, drew the following conclusions about Reznik and the way he did business as head of the Finance Committee based on an extensive survey of Moscow experts: "After United Russia started establishing its 70 per cent dictatorship in the State Duma in 2004, the deputies lost the opportunity to introduce amendments to the budget in the second reading (including in the interests of their own business); in the opinion of the experts, 'Now in order to lobby for some line of the budget in the interests of their own business, a deputy must "win over" Reznik so that he will "drop off" the sum of the deputies' "proposals" to the Ministry of Finance.'" As for what happens to these considerations once they arrive in the Ministry of Finance, where the budget is put together and disbursed, Makarov notably points out that while there were many in the Ministry who were seen as corrupt, its chief, Aleksey Kudrin, was generally seen as "not of this world": "As compared with what he could get out of the budget inventories, he takes very little, and perhaps he does not take any at all. From that standpoint Kudrin in Putin's eyes is the kind of 'keeper of the treasury' who opens it up only for Putin, while he sends other influential people away since one cannot lay away enough for everybody."

for black operations as a price for operating on Russian territory. But at the same time, the prosecutor told U.S. officials, Russian organized crime responds to pressure by taking advantage of "the corruption of high-level ministers." Extensive wiretaps showed that these Russian organized crime leaders had a " 'dangerously close' level of contact with senior Russian officials."[7] The secret cable reported Spanish press allegations that the Spanish government had compiled a list of Russian procurators, senior military officers, and politicians, including current and former ministers, who were involved with Petrov and Russian organized crime. The list included at least four sitting ministers, including the Russian minister of defense at that time, Anatoliy Serdyukov, who was notable for his "very close ties" to Petrov.[8] The cable that was released also referenced other classified lists of compromised officials that were not part of the Wikileaks documents but indicate that the U.S. government has had a very specific idea of the officials involved in links between the Russian government and Russian organized crime since at least 2008.*

The questions arising from this fascinating story are many: What kind of system has Putin created? When did these plans emerge? Who is at the center of them along with Putin? What kind of control does Putin have over the plans themselves? I suggest that the antidemocratic and politically illiberal aspects of the plans were present from the beginning, as were the efforts to create a liberal economic system that would allow Russians to enjoy the fruits of their labors more than at any time in their history. The plan was always that those closest to power would be in a position to enjoy those fruits on an unprecedented scale. The story starts when the Soviet Union was still standing, if declining, in the 1970s and 1980s.

Beginning in the 1970s, when the Soviet leadership started to enter the world economy to sell oil in exchange for technology (some of it bought illegally at high prices) and grain to offset the structural problems in their own economy, they began to accumulate funds in hard currency abroad. Conflicts in the Middle East quadrupled the price of oil in the 1970s,

---

*By early 2010, the Spanish prosecutor had been reassigned and the investigation appears to have gone dormant.

thus massively increasing the amounts in Soviet overseas accounts. These accounts were under the strict day-to-day control of the KGB and were used to fund foreign operations, underwrite friendly parties and movements, and purchase goods for import. The strategic decisions about how the money would be spent were made by the Communist Party hierarchy, while the KGB was in charge of implementation. However, under Soviet president Mikhayl Gorbachev there is reason to think that the KGB declined to repatriate funds and only increased the economic crisis of a leadership in which they had no confidence. Indeed even more funds began to flood out of the USSR in the late 1980s for safekeeping abroad. As one well-placed Russian cooperative owner observed in 1989, "The West thinks the KGB is gone. They [the KGB] are no longer concerned with investigating *people*, but they are very involved in destabilizing *perestroika*. Last week the KGB created a new division of forty agents to do nothing but start joint ventures with Western firms. This is their experimental sociological work. If the crowds rush in tomorrow to kill Gorbachev, the KGB will do nothing because they are concentrating on their scientific experiments." [9]

When the newly elected Russian president Boris Yel'tsin banned the CPSU after the failed 1991 August coup against Gorbachev, the CPSU's guidance ceased, and the control over this vast mountain of foreign money fell to KGB agents who had access to foreign operations and accounts. Some of the money stayed abroad and disappeared, but when the USSR collapsed and assets became available for purchase inside the country, this money was available for investment to those who controlled the accounts. Thus were born, it is estimated, most of Russia's oligarchs and commercial banks. By the early 1990s KGB veterans who knew the details of these accounts needed like-minded officials in key positions who could help control who would get to invest in Russia and who would not. [10] For this they found willing allies among the KGB and Party veterans who flooded into the new cooperative movement in the late 1980s [11] and who then sought to build capitalism, enrich themselves, and control market entry. Among these was the rather more junior KGB official Vladimir Putin. And in trying to control what kind of economy would emerge, they were up against a formidable and historic collapse.

Some people visualize Russia in the late 1990s as a country that went through a "Wild West" period, or something similar to Al Capone's reign in Chicago. But in 1999 a prominent expert stated in testimony before the U.S. Congress:

For the U.S. to be like Russia is today, it would be necessary to have massive corruption by the majority of the members of Congress as well as by the Departments of Justice and Treasury, and agents of the FBI, CIA, DIA [Defense Intelligence Agency], IRS, Marshal Service, Border Patrol, state and local police officers, the Federal Reserve Bank, Supreme Court justices, U.S. District court judges, support of the varied Organized Crime families, the leadership of the Fortune 500 companies, at least half of the banks in the U.S., and the New York Stock Exchange. This cabal would then have to seize the gold at Fort Knox and the federal assets deposited in the entire banking system. It would have to take control of the key industries such as oil, natural gas, mining, precious and semi-precious metals, forestry, cotton, construction, insurance, and banking industries—and then claim these items to be their private property. The legal system would have to nullify most of the key provisions against corruption, conflict of interest, criminal conspiracy, money laundering, economic fraud and weaken tax evasion laws. This unholy alliance would then have to spend about 50% of its billions in profits to bribe officials that remained in government and be the primary supporters of all of the political candidates. Then, most of the stolen funds, excess profits and bribes would have to be sent to off-shore banks for safekeeping. Finally, while claiming that the country was literally bankrupt and needed vast infusions of foreign aid to survive, this conspiratorial group would invest billions in spreading illegal activities to developed foreign countries. . . . The President would not only be aware of all these activities but would support them.[12]

This statement was made in testimony to the U.S. House Committee on Banking and Financial Services by Richard L. Palmer, who had been CIA chief of base and chief of station in countries of the former Soviet Union. When Palmer gave his testimony in September 1999, Putin was not yet president, but he was prime minister, he had been head of the successor organization to the KGB, the Federal Security Service, and he had been investigated on a number of occasions for high-level corruption and criminal activity.

Of course, there were those in the Russian government who were aware of the problem and had tried to correct it. On February 18, 1992, for example, the Yel'tsin-Gaidar government signed an agreement with an American corporate private investigation firm, Kroll Associates, to track down and help repatriate money illegally held or taken abroad by former Communist Party and Soviet government agencies, including the KGB. The money had allegedly left the country prior to the August 1991 attempted coup against the reformist-oriented Gorbachev by conservatives in the highest echelons of the ruling Communist Party and the KGB.[13] A group of Central Committee officials, including the head of the Party department dealing with the defense industry, the head of state television and radio, and the deputy head of the committee in charge of privatizing state property, were all dismissed after revelations about their involvement in embezzlement and capital flight. Several of them had also been involved in efforts during the Gorbachev period by a so-called patriotic wing of the special services to organize various provocations to undermine Gorbachev and prove that his reforms needed to be halted. Yegor Gaidar, who at that time was the minister of finance, stated that this kind of activity was not only illegal but constituted continued political resistance to the government's economic reform efforts: "Last year saw large-scale privatization by the nomenklatura [the high-ranking elite], privatization by officials for their own personal benefit."[14] The *New York Times* reported that the office of the Russian procurator general had been "unable to penetrate the maze of hidden bank accounts and secret investments, left behind by party officials acting in some cases . . . with the cooperation of the K.G.B. . . . One estimate for the party's hidden assets is $50 billion."[15] Kroll, which had also led the hunt for stolen funds from the Marcos regime in the Philippines and Saddam Hussein's invasion of Kuwait, was reported to have "found that thousands of mostly offshore bank accounts, real estate holdings and offshore companies had been set up to launder and shelter these funds and what had been the Soviet Union's gold reserves." [16]*

In response to this report and their own investigations, the Yel'tsin government passed a law giving it the right to confiscate funds taken abroad illegally. Yel'tsin was receiving monthly updates from Kroll; the lower house of the Russian Supreme Soviet, the Council of Nationalities (as it was called until December 1993), demanded that the Foreign Intelligence Service[†] provide a report on Kroll's progress, which *Izvestiya* reported was provided in a closed session by First Deputy Director Vyacheslav Trubnikov. [18] The Supreme Soviet Presidium had decreed that a special commission be established by the procurator general to investigate corruption, abuse of power, and economic offenses. Its report was presented to the Supreme Soviet in September 1993. In it Kroll's efforts were noted; the document recounted widespread instances of "bribery of officials, blackmail, and the illegal transfer of currency resources to foreign banks," with specific ministers sanctioned by name, including Minister of Foreign Economic Relations Pyotr Aven (whose activities in approving Putin's early contracts as

---

* Joseph Serio, an American seconded to the Organized Crime Control Department of the Soviet Interior Ministry in 1990–91 who went on to head Kroll's operations in Moscow, reached similar conclusions. On this subject and the global spread of Russian organized crime that occurred in parallel at this time, see Handelman (1995), Klebnikov (2000), Friedman (2002), Varese (2001), Gerber (2000), Williams (1997), and Shelly (2004). [17]

† When the KGB was broken up after its involvement in the 1991 coup attempt against Gorbachev, several separate security institutions emerged with different functions: The Foreign Intelligence Service (Sluzhba Vneshney Razvedki, SVR) was formed out of the First Directorate of the KGB and was responsible for external intelligence. The Federal Agency of Government Communications and Information (Federal'noye Agentstvo Pravitel'stvennoy Svyazi i Informatsii, FAPSI) was made responsible for electronic surveillance. FAPSI was the rough equivalent to the National Security Agency in the United States. It existed until 2003, when Putin reunited it with the FSB. The Main Administration for the Protection of the Russian Federation (Glavnoye Upravleniye Okhrany, GUO) came out of the Ninth Directorate of the KGB. It was renamed the Federal Protective Service (Federal'naya Sluzhba Okhrany, FSO) in 1996. It is roughly equivalent to the U.S. Secret Service and is responsible for the protection of high-ranking officials, including the president. The Ministry of Security was formed out of the internal security functions of the KGB and was responsible for domestic and border security. It was reorganized in December 1993 into the Federal Counter-Intelligence Service (Federal'naya Sluzhba Kontrrazvedki, FSK). The FSK was then reorganized into the current-day Federal Security Service (FSB) in April 1995, and it was the FSB that Putin took over as director in 1998.

head of the St. Petersburg Committee for Foreign Liaison* are dealt with below). The report also criticized the Ministry of Security (the precursor of the FSB) for the fact that while it had opened three hundred investigations in the first six months of 1993 alone, only "two criminal cases had been instituted in practice."[19] In theory, in both Yel'tsin's camp and in the Communist-dominated legislature, everyone was seeking to stanch the flow. But nothing happened in practice. As one of Kroll's investigators stated, the report raised "suspicions about certain players and institutions [in the former Soviet Union]. Our problem is that when we sent it to Moscow, it was never followed up."[20]

This image of high-level culpability was reinforced when U.S. law enforcement intercepted telephone calls in the United States from the highest officials in President Yel'tsin's office, Prime Minister Viktor Chernomyrdin's staff, and other ministers to and from the head of the Russian firm Golden ADA, established in San Francisco, linking the firm to various scams that collectively added up to almost $1 billion.[21] The size of the scams is suggested by the fact that in 1994 Golden ADA had a *declared* taxable income in the United States of $111,485,984, according to U.S. court documents.[22] FBI records show that the FBI turned over to Russia information linking Golden ADA with Yevgeniy Bychkov, the chairman of the Russian Committee for Precious Gems and Metals, and Igor Moskovskiy, a deputy minister of finance. Eventually, in 2001, with documents provided by FBI wiretaps, as the FBI website wryly states, both "were convicted of abusing their state positions and immediately granted State Duma amnesties."[23] At an Aspen Conference in St. Petersburg in the early 1990s, I asked a high-ranking U.S. government official, "How many Russian government ministers have bank accounts abroad in excess of $1 million?" The reply came back immediately and without hesitation: "All of them. Every last one." This was the general view of what was going on throughout the entire country at the time, a view reaffirmed by subsequent Russian journalistic investigations.[24]

---

* Komitet vneshnikh svyazey—KVS, also sometimes referred to as the Committee on Foreign Economic Relations, or External Relations.

While capital flight quickly became a broader problem involving economic entrepreneurs and industrial enterprises, the problem began with the privileged access to Soviet state reserves by insider KGB and CPSU elites. The story began when KGB chairman Vladimir Kryuchkov convinced Gorbachev to use KGB-trained economists to stimulate and control an opening for Western investors in the USSR and increased Soviet investments abroad.[25] Kryuchkov and the top leadership in the KGB distrusted Gorbachev and his policies and feared that he would lose control of the country.* Having received permission from the leader of the CPSU to control the process of opening up to the West, the top KGB leaders lost no time in ensuring that their institutional interests were secured. Russian and foreign journalists worked to put together the story of what had happened to the USSR's reserves, and all signs pointed to efforts beginning in 1990, if not earlier, to prepare for the possible collapse of power. Looking at the situation in eastern Europe, where Communist regimes had fallen without so much as a whimper, these investigative accounts suggest that Soviet KGB hardliners clearly acted to resist any similar assault. And they did this in collaboration with hardliners in the Party and with the support of Politburo decisions, specifically an August 23, 1990, Central Committee decree that authorized "urgent measures on the organization of commercial and foreign economic activities of the Party."

Issued over the signature of Vladimir Ivashko, the deputy general secretary of the CPSU at the time, the memo expressed the need to develop an "autonomous channel into the party's cash box," in preparation for the time when the CPSU might not be the only party in the USSR. The memo called for specific measures to protect the Party's "economic interests": form new economic structures abroad to provide the basis for "invisible party economics"; establish a foreign bank for the Central Committee that would "conduct currency operations"; and consult with the relevant state

---

* According to the account provided by a Kryuchkov loyalist in the KGB, General Yuriy Drozdov, they also believed that the pro-perestroika leadership around Gorbachev had among them "agents of influence" from the CIA. Such was the certainty of their belief that subsequent to the collapse of the USSR, conservative "patriots" even instituted proceedings against the architect of perestroika, Aleksandr Yakovlev, on these charges.

institutions to use "national property for the foreign economic work of the Party, [including] the property left after the Soviet armies left Czechoslovakia, Hungary and the German Democratic Republic." To achieve these ends, "there must be a strict observance of discreet confidentiality and the use of anonymous facades to disguise the direct use of money to the CPSU. The final objective is to build a structure of 'invisible' party economics. . . ; a very narrow circle of people have been allowed access to this structure. . . . All this is confirmed by the experiences of many parties, working for decades within a framework of multiparty cooperation and market economics." [26]*

To this end, a colonel in the KGB First Chief Directorate,† Leonid Veselovskiy, was transferred to the Central Committee's Administrative Department. A memo attributed to him was later uncovered by Paul Klebnikov, the American editor of *Forbes* Russia, assassinated in Moscow in 2004, and reads in part:

> The earnings which are accumulated in the Party treasury and are not reflected in the financial reports can be used to purchase the shares of various companies, enterprises, and banks. On the one hand, this will create a stable source of revenue, irrespective of what may happen to the Party. On the other hand, these shares can be sold on the security exchanges at any time and the capital transferred to other spheres, allowing the Party to keep its participation anonymous and still retain control. . . . In order to avoid mistakes in the course of this operation during the "period of emergency," it is essential to orga-

---

*The existence of this document became known when it was submitted by Richard Palmer, the former CIA station chief, as an appendix to his testimony before a U.S. House Banking Committee investigation into Russian money laundering. It was not included in the *Fond 89* documents used in the trial of the CPSU, nor is there any indication of Gorbachev's knowledge or complicity in the movement of these funds, although the fact that they were being moved by a small group of hard-line Party and KGB officials suggests their aim was to conceal what they hoped would be the death knell for the perestroika regime.

† Sometimes also referred to in English as the First Main (from the Russian *glavnoye*) Directorate. The terms used in the organizational charts provided by Andrew and Mitrokhin are used throughout this text.[27]

nize, both in the USSR and abroad, special rapid response groups, staffed by specially trained instructors from the "active reserve" of the KGB of the USSR, as well as by trusted individuals volunteering their cooperation and by individuals who, for one reason or another, have lost their job in the field units or administrative departments of the KGB of the USSR.[28]

He later stated, "The reason for my transfer was the urgent need of the directors of the Administrative Department to create a division capable of coordinating the economic activity of the Party's management structures in the changing climate.... The choice fell to me, since by education I am an international economist [and] I have experience working abroad."[29] Having been transferred to the Central Committee, Veselovskiy worked under the supervision of a small group that consisted of Ivashko; Nikolay Kruchina, the CPSU Central Committee chief of the Administrative Department; and KGB chairman Kryuchkov and his deputy director, Filipp Bobkov, who sent a directive to overseas residences that they should immediately submit proposals for the creation of covert KGB commercial firms and financial establishments.[30]

Those in the International Department of the Central Committee and the First Chief Directorate of the KGB, dealing with foreign operations, already had a standard operating procedure for transferring secret funds abroad as a result of their support of foreign Communist parties. For example, General Nikolay Leonov, who was the deputy chief of the First Chief Directorate, had been in charge of money flows to Latin American countries (as well as having had contact with Che Guevara and interpreting for Khrushchev and Castro). He described the procedure in a subsequent interview: "Technically it was done in a very simple way. The Central Bank of the State of the Soviet Union handed the money directly to the Central Committee, to the International Relations Department which was responsible for relations with communist parties and national liberation movements. The money was physically taken to the Central Committee and as the final paragraph of these resolutions always said '... the KGB is entrusted with carrying out the decision,' we received the order to collect the money, send it to the corresponding countries and deliver it to its destination."[31] The only thing that changed in 1991 was that the KGB and CPSU Central Committee were using this procedure to ensure their own future, not the future of some Latin American Communist party.

Under the supervision of this group, Veselovskiy created a capitalist economy within the CPSU apparatus, establishing joint ventures and bank accounts abroad, both to make money and to hide money. According to a 1991 report, Veselovskiy, who "was assigned to manage Communist Party commercial affairs overseas, told his masters that he had found ways to funnel party money abroad. The stated goal: to ensure the financial well-being of party leaders after they lost power."[32] After the August coup Veselovskiy fled the country, first to Canada to link up with a Canadian subsidiary of a Swiss-based firm, Seabeco, and then to Zurich to begin a banking career at one of the very banks he had helped to establish.[33] Kryuchkov was briefly jailed; Kruchina died during the coup after a fall from his apartment window;* and Ivashko was briefly general secretary of the CPSU during the August coup but retired in 1992 and died soon after.

However, most of the KGB operatives who had been involved in forming cooperatives at home (many from the KGB's Fifth Chief Directorate, headed by Filipp Bobkov, or the Sixth Chief Directorate, in charge of economic security and controlling the mafia) or joint ventures abroad (the function of the First Chief Directorate) formed the backbone of the new caste of KGB entrepreneurs who not only set up their own firms but provided security for emerging oligarchs, some of whose greatest profits came from this period. Bobkov, who joined the KGB during the reign of Lavrentiy Beria in the Stalin period, reportedly took about three hundred of the top operatives of the KGB Fifth Chief Directorate who were responsible for

---

*After the August 1991 coup failed, Kruchina was one of the officials who died, when he fell, jumped, or was pushed from a window. The extent of his efforts to move and hide CPSU money will never be fully known. Six weeks later his predecessor, Georgiy Pavlov, also fell to his death. In April 1991 *Time* magazine reported that Dmitriy Lisovolik had also leaped to his death, "after investigators found $600,000 in U.S. dollars in the office of Lisovolik's boss, Valentin Falin, at Central Committee headquarters." Veselovskiy named International Department deputy chief Karen Brutents as also having access to knowledge of the accounts, as well as three Politburo members, who were unnamed.

internal order to form the security services for Vladimir Gusinskiy's Media-Most company. He also is reported to have taken many of the KGB's personnel files with him.[34]

Aleksey Kondaurov, also a general in the Fifth Chief Directorate, became the head of analysis for Bank Menatep, owned by the Russian oligarch Mikhayl Khodorkovskiy. He conceded that "leaders from all levels of power, from the party nomenklatura to the red directors, were looking for people who would help them deal with the new economic realities. . . . Khodorkovskiy and his group were these new young wolves."[35] Khodorkovskiy moved to establish links with the West, but those financial circles recall that when they first met him and his team, the Russians didn't know how to use a credit card, they didn't know how to write a check, and they didn't have money enough to stay even in a hostel. They were quick learners, but as Anton Surikov, an independent security expert who had previously served in Soviet military intelligence and who knew Khodorkovskiy and those like him in the late 1980s, stated, "It was impossible to work in the black market without KGB connections and without protection from the KGB. Without them, no shadow business was possible. . . . The creation of the oligarchs was a revolution engineered by the KGB, but then they lost control."[36] As to whether Khodorkovskiy's Bank Menatep was indeed one of the many vehicles used to launder CPSU money, as the legend goes, one of the five major initial shareholders, Mikhayl Brudno, who fled to Israel when Khodorkovskiy was arrested under Putin in 2003, simply said, "It can't be ruled out that some companies that belonged somehow to the Communist Party were clients, but we were not able to identify them as such."[37]

Bobkov and Kondaurov were not the only Party or KGB officials who moved to take advantage of the new law on cooperatives and the easing of foreign trade regulations. In November 1991 the magazine *Stolitsa* reported that two-thirds of the employees of the nascent Russian stock exchange center were ex-KGB officials who were using their new position to launder KGB and CPSU money abroad.[38] On June 24, 1992, *Literaturnaya gazeta* published excerpts from a telegram dated January 5, 1991 (No. 174033), which said that in December 1990 KGB chairman Vladimir

Kryuchkov had authorized "provisional regulations of a secret operating structure within the organs of the KGB." The purpose was to "provide reliable protection for leaders and the most valuable [KGB] operatives, in case the internal political situation develops along East German lines; obtain funding for the organization of underground work if 'destructive elements' come to power; and create conditions for the effective use of foreign and domestic agents during increased political instability."[39]* Both General Oleg Kalugin, who had been head of Soviet counterintelligence until 1990, and the Russian journalist Yevgeniya Al'bats have underlined that the KGB really struggled to control the privatization process against the mafia on one side and the "destructive elements" (democrats) on the other.[40] Kalugin subsequently stated that even before Gorbachev came to power, the KGB had placed its people in most Soviet banks abroad, in line with KGB chief Yuriy Andropov's policy of maneuvering the KGB to promote economic reforms while controlling the process by greater political repression.[41] Conveniently Kryuchkov's own son was reported to be the KGB *rezident* (head of station) in Switzerland.[42]

The Russian government lead procurator from the Procurator General's Office, Sergey Aristov, responsible for Criminal Case No. 18/6220–91, brought against those top officials who carried out the August 1991 coup, claimed that at the beginning of 1991 the CPSU Property Management Department alone had 7 billion rubles ($3.92 billion)[†] in assets. By the autumn of that year, after the coup had failed and the investigation had begun, this 7 billion had largely been disbursed to commercial banks at home and abroad and to 516 businesses established using the Gorbachev-era law on cooperatives. Of these 516, the largest, according to Aristov, was a "loan" of 300 million rubles ($168 million) to a cooperative society of

---

*When the article's author, Mark Deych, drowned many years later, the "patriotic" blogosphere exploded with denunciations of his work particularly in the perestroika period. As one vile example, see "Mark Deych: Shit sinks," at http://www.liveinternet.ru/users/prozorovsky /post218488816/.

† Annual average ruble-to-dollar exchange rates are used throughout, derived from Central Bank of Russia data.

former KGB officers called Galaktika, or Galaxy.* [43] CIA station chief Richard Palmer claims that Galaktika and other KGB-fronted firms received almost 1 billion rubles ($560 million) from Party funds. [44] Further, Aristov claimed, more than ten commercial banks were established using 3 billion rubles ($1.68 billion) of Party money. He asked, "In the summer of 1991, a giant, finely tuned 'invisible' Party economy, corruptly involved to the necessary degree with the current government, went underground. . . . How much did they manage to hide?" Yel'tsin's own press secretary, Pavel Voshchanov, similarly charged that the Communists had set up an "invisible party economy" that allowed them to hide money abroad. He also claimed that the Party had used Western credit to support "debt-ridden friendly companies" outside Russia rather than use the money for its intended purpose: to purchase food to prevent shortages during the coming winter. [45] In another example, Aristov found that a cooperative venture called ANT, which was established by KGB officers reporting to the Council of Ministers and under the protection of Politburo member Yegor Ligachev, had received 30 billion rubles' ($18.3 billion) worth of bartered materials from a French company in the first half of 1989 alone. [46] The ANT cooperative was the subject of a four-part investigative series by *Novaya gazeta* in 2008 in which the authors concluded that the ANT deal was one in which, "long before the August coup, the security forces had set out to stop perestroika with tanks." The investigation confirmed what was found in the 1992 investigations following the failed August coup: that the KGB had used various means to stymie the emerging democratic movement in Russia. [47] *Novaya gazeta* concluded that ANT "employees," who were in fact KGB officials, put modern battle tanks on flatbeds without proper authorization from the Ministry of Defense, labeled as "means of transportation unsorted." [48] At the last minute these cooperative workers were to be "caught" trying to illegally export the export-restricted tanks from the country, in this way

---

* General Leonov of the KGB stated that the free-for-all grabbing of CPSU properties began as early as August 23, 1991: "There was a massive seizure of party property: Office buildings, educational institutions, publishers, printing houses, holiday homes, villas and offices, etc." Leonov (2002), p. 51.

giving conservative opponents to Gorbachev the ability to hold up these reforms and say, "Look. Admire—Gorbachev's reforms will destroy Russia."[49] Anatoliy Sobchak, who spoke about the scandal in the Congress of People's Deputies, accused ANT employees not only of planning to provoke a crisis with the "sale" of tanks but also of trying to organize the sale of rough-cut diamonds from the state and of trying to export strategic raw materials worth tens of billions of rubles.[50] Sobchak's intervention further bolstered his public persona as a leader of the democratic movement and someone ruthlessly opposed to such KGB tactics. It probably also alerted KGB officials that Sobchak was someone who would, in the future, need to be brought under control, which is where Putin would come in.

As for the money abroad, Procurator Aristov's team received numerous reports of money flooding out of the country in advance of the August coup, including, for example, $70 million to Finland in one transfer alone. But his investigative efforts were hampered by the reluctance of foreign banks to provide account information without proof of a crime and the unwillingness of "certain circles" within the Russian government to allow investigators carte blanche.[51]

Carlo Bonini and Giuseppe d'Avanzo, the two Italian reporters who later broke the Mabetex story revealing Yel'tsin's corruption, reported that during this period KGB operatives in particular were working to keep the core of their institution together, since it constituted, in their opinion, the backbone of the entire country. [52]* By their own accounts, top KGB officials felt that unless they coalesced around each other, the country would fall apart. General Leonov, who had been the deputy head of the KGB's First Chief Directorate in charge of foreign operations, lamented in a 1998 interview that lack of leadership had doomed the USSR from the mid-1970s onward: "Brezhnev dies, and Andropov takes over, already sick. He is followed by Chernenko, also ill. Then Gorbachev takes office, but he is

* Bonini and d'Avanzo have covered Russian politics and misdeeds as well as those of Western intelligence agencies, including the role of the Italian intelligence service SISMI in planting evidence they knew to be false of Saddam Hussein's supposed efforts to obtain uranium to make nuclear bombs from Niger. The story is recounted in their 2007 book.[53]

not a leader, and finally Yel'tsin, the destroyer. In other words, we did not have a leader of national stature." [54]

While some of these "state people" from the KGB, including Vladimir Putin, according to his own account,[55] may have had a high opinion of Gorbachev's plans to reform a system they certainly realized was moribund, their highest respect evidently went to Andropov, who as KGB chief and then as Leonid Brezhnev's successor, had encouraged economic liberalization even as he cracked down on dissent. Now in 1990, with as many as 30 percent of those KGB employees stationed abroad, including Putin, they suddenly found themselves without a job and forced into the "active reserves," waiting for their next assignment.

A definition of the role, rights, and duties of those members of the active reserves was provided by Valery Shchukin, the deputy governor of Perm *oblast'*, one of Russia's regions, in 2000, when Putin's own status as a member of the active reserves in St. Petersburg also became known. To be a member of the active reserves "means that a person is not receiving a salary but continues to be on the staff list, has access to operational information, is eligible for promotion, and is obligated to carry out orders from superiors, including secret, confidential orders, without notifying his superiors at the place of civil service." [56] These were agents with knowledge of foreign languages and cultures and also black banking and black methods; it is not surprising that they sought to establish networks of mutual support.[57]

Many members of the active reserves went into the private sector, setting up banks and security firms. Others, it would appear, formed the backbone of the coup attempt in August 1991. They did this less for their Communist ideals per se than for the Motherland, for the institution of Chekism (loyalty to the idea of an unbroken chain of security services, from Lenin's Cheka through the KGB to Russia's new FSB), and for themselves.* As General Kalugin stated, "The KGB is the most stable part of the integrated structure. . . . The structure created to work under any conditions continues to work automatically. Although the processes of peeling away and dis-

---

*For a very sympathetic account of the coup from the former KGB chief of its Analytical Department, see Leonov (2002).[58]

integration are also at work there, for the KGB authorities it is a question of preserving not only the system itself, but themselves. It's a question of self-defense and survival. The KGB will be one of those structures that will struggle until the end. And that's the danger."[59] But when the August coup failed, the money stayed abroad, where the KGB had easy access to it. And because the CPSU was banned after the coup, the KGB alone now controlled it.[60]

The KGB also established commercial banks in what would soon become the newly independent states of the former Soviet Union, as when a memo authorized Kruchina to transfer 100 million rubles ($56 million) to the new Kompartbank commercial bank in Kazakhstan, possibly with the idea that it would be easier to extract the money from Almaty than from Moscow if the regime collapsed.[61]

Inside Russia, authorities were struggling to put goods in the stores in the absence of old administrative command mechanisms. Gavriil Popov, the mayor of Moscow, freely admitted that this was done by relying on the traditional "trade mafias," which had previously worked for the Party but now started to function on their own. They came to be known mainly by their ethnic or by their district or regional affiliation—the Azeris, the Chechens, the Solntsevo group in Moscow, the Tambov group in St. Petersburg—and they seized the opportunity to use the new laws permitting commercial activity to legalize their actions and capture market share.[62] But in the absence of the Party and with the collapse of the state, these groups had to provide their own security. Without state-backed law enforcement, violence became the means of enforcing contracts.[63]

At the same time, the trade mafias came into conflict with Party and state officials who were themselves entering the private economy. A former chief procurator who was responsible for bringing dozens of top officials to court for corruption explained, "Former bureaucrats, those who used to run the administrative economic system, have poured into this milieu. They instantly used their connections, spreading metastases in this new fabric. They do everything in order to come more closely and definitively to property. Before, they possessed it indirectly, but now they have the opportunity to possess it directly."[64] The trade mafias that were not associated with or protected by former KGB or Party bureaucrats had to provide their own security. This intense competition between former officials and elements from the previous black market was a critical feature of Russian economic transition throughout the 1990s.

Thus Gorbachev's encouragement to form cooperatives and joint ventures inside the country, combined with the urgent establishment of off-the-books banking structures abroad, created a situation in which cooperatives legally funneled state funds into the private sector, and commercial banks were established abroad to receive these funds. The comparative advantage of being part of this early cohort cannot be overestimated. In a February 2000 interview with Boris Berezovskiy, one of the major oligarchs close to the Kremlin at that time, I asked whether the billions he was reported to have collected would withstand legal scrutiny, as some in Russia were demanding. His response was intriguing: "Absolutely. I would submit all of my wealth to legal scrutiny. Except for the first million." [65] The oligarchs depended on both the ex-KGB and organized crime groups to use targeted violence to control market entry, market share, and border control. The situation was the same in St. Petersburg, Putin's home city. When the CPSU was legally banned after the August coup, the Leningrad (and then St. Petersburg) Association of Joint Ventures stepped in and took over its controlling shares in the newly formed Bank Rossiya. Thus the comparative economic advantage of these elites as the transition to democracy began.

As I stated previously, after the collapse of the USSR and the failure of the August coup, the Yel'tsin government launched an urgent hunt for the CPSU's money. They stood little chance of recovering the money; in fact much more started to flow abroad on the established financial pathways, sometimes, but not always, quite discreetly. The government and Parliament actively aided and abetted capital flight, as when, in February 1992, the Presidium of the Russian Parliament (under the Speaker Ruslan Khasbulatov) passed the resolution On Measures to Stabilize the Financial Situation of Foreign Banks Set Up with Capital of the Former USSR, authorizing the Central Bank to take over all the shares in Western banks set up with Soviet capital and to provide funds as required to stabilize those banks. (The Russian Parliament was able to order the printing of money until after 1993.) These included Moskovskiy Narodniy Bank in London, Donau Bank in Vienna, and branches of Vneshekonombank, among others.[66] Among those involved in this effort were Aleksandr Medvedev and Andrey Akimov, both of whom were associated with the Donau (Danube) Bank, and both reputed to be KGB officers.[67] Medvedev later became deputy chairman of the Management Committee and director general of Gazprom Export; a member of the Coordination Committee of RosUkrEnergo, an intermediary company that bought gas from Gazprom and sold it after a price increase to Ukraine; and a member of the Shareholders' Committee of Nord Stream, a joint-stock energy company. Akimov also became a member of RosUkrEnergo's Coordination Committee and chairman of the board of Gazprombank.[68] In 2005 VTB, Russia's largest commercial bank, acquired Donau. By 2011 Akimov was a member of the board of Gazprom.

As Procurator General Yuriy Skuratov was to reveal in 1999, in November 1990 the Paris branch of the Soviet State Bank (the predecessor to the Central Bank) had set up an offshore company called Financial Management Company Ltd. (FIMACO) based in the Channel Island of Jersey.[69] According to a 1991 report, Leonid Veselovskiy, the former KGB colonel, had been assigned to funnel the CPSU money abroad.[70] It was as if European Central Bankers, rather than trying to bolster and save the euro, decided to open dollar accounts in the Bahamas using EU funds. Over the next six years, according to documents provided to *Newsweek* and in congressional testimony by the former CIA station chief Richard Palmer, the Russian government moved billions of dollars into FIMACO, sometimes also moving the money back to Russia. It was essentially a slush fund for the Kremlin and was used for off-the-books political purposes, including Yel'tsin's 1996 presidential campaign.[71]

Simultaneously in the early 1990s, trading firms appeared that acted as intermediaries for selling Russian raw materials abroad, receiving materials at state-subsidized "internal prices" but selling them abroad at world market prices. The Russian Parliament established committees to document and stanch this unprecedented outflow of raw material wealth, reported to include "60 tons of gold, 8 of platinum, 150 of silver," plus an unknown amount of oil, variously estimated between $15 billion and $50 billion.[72] Some estimates were even starker: former prime minister Nikolay Ryzhkov claimed that the gold reserves in January 1990 were 784 tons, but by autumn of that year, Grigoriy Yavlinskiy, Gorbachev's economic advisor, claimed that number had fallen to 240 tons. After the attempted coup, officials admitted, "A certain amount of gold is missing,"[73] but they were unable to verify the exact amount.

In investigating the loss, the Duma found that hundreds of KGB accounts had been established to transfer assets abroad, flowing from the Politburo decision referred to earlier.[74] The Duma further concluded that at that time no company in partnership with the West would have been able to succeed without a deputy director or local manager from the security services.[75] Certainly cooperatives that were established quickly came to rely on other cooperatives that were formed of former KGB or MVD* personnel who provided security.[76] These new banks also relied on the knowledge of and connections to Russian and international organized crime,[77] as well as former KGB operatives who had knowledge of foreign banking operations and rules. As this discussion has shown, it can generally be concluded that *anyone* who was establishing cooperatives and succeeding at it in the late Gorbachev period had either KGB or Komsomol cover or *krysha*.†

The irony is not that KGB officials sought to become rich or to keep others from entering the market and gaining a foothold. The irony is that such officials sought to establish and maintain control of the process of privatization for the purpose of keeping unconnected and unauthorized people, whether mafia or democrat, from entering the market, in order to implement Andropov's dream of establishing an economically freer but politically still controlled and conservative regime, like Pinochet's Chile

---

*Ministry of Internal Affairs (Ministerstvo Vnutrennikh Del, MVD), which supervises all police, public order militias, and prisons.

† The All-Union Leninist Communist League of Youth (Vsesoyuznyy Leninskiy Kommunisticheskiy Soyuz Molodyozhi, Komsomol) was an organization for those fourteen to twenty-eight. For a detailed analysis of the Komsomol roots of one such successful early entrepreneur, Mikhayl Khodorkovskiy, see Sakwa (2014).

or post-Mao's China. Gleb Pavlovskiy subsequently also concurred that he had been "one of them. My friends couldn't accept what had happened. There were thousands of people like that in the elite, who were not communists—I was never a member of the communist party. They were people who just didn't like how things had been done in 1991. By revanche I mean the resurrection of the great state. Not a totalitarian one, of course, but a state that could be respected. And the state of the 1990s was impossible to respect." [78] The writings of ex-KGB officers like Yuriy Drozdov and Nikolay Leonov bring home the same point: the West won the Cold War; the collapse of the USSR objectively deprived Russia of historic allies and strategic depth; and Yel'tsin almost brought about internal collapse. Only with the beginning of the Putin era were the conditions created for Russia to return to the global stage. [79]

The Soviet dissident Lev Timofeev presciently argued more or less the same point, but from a different perspective, in the early 1990s: "The danger isn't that yesterday's district Party committee secretary will become a factory owner or a bank manager. Let him. The trouble is, rather, that this person *is* yesterday's man, an unfree person linked to the conspiracy, bound hand and foot to his social class—that very apparat, military-industrial complex, and KGB. He is dependent on that trinity in everything he does, because he obtains his property rights from them for a price: a silent oath of loyalty. If he breaks that oath, he will not remain a property owner for long." [80]

Putin himself often harks back to the experience of being a KGB officer, when he was allowed more freedom of thought than others in Soviet society and was allowed to travel to Germany. One of the conclusions he reached from that experience was that it was obvious that a market economy could outperform a planned one. As he said in 2012, a planned economy "is less efficient than a market economy. History has staged two experiments that are very well known in the world: East Germany and West Germany, North Korea and South Korea." [81] But what kind of hybrid controlled-market regime can be established by KGB-trained cadres, who subsequently justified their moves by saying that they alone saw the writing on the wall in the late 1980s and, as Chief Kryuchkov of the KGB stated in a closed speech to the Supreme Soviet in June 1991, saw that Western intelligence services were using high-ranking politicians as "agents of influence" to bring about the collapse of the USSR?* How better to safeguard the CPSU's funding from Western plots than to bury it deep in secret accounts in Western banks? Rather than fight to keep the USSR going, risking a Yugoslav-style breakup, this group preferred to beat a strategic retreat, while keeping the hopes for revanche alive through the next generation of Chekists—including the FSB's next generation coming of age with Vladimir Putin. In the meantime, if that doesn't work out, perhaps they will all at least get rich. The deep history of this hope for political revanche and the money machine that runs it is the story of this book.

---

*Major General Vyacheslav Shironin was once head of KGB counterintelligence. He also was involved in the massive KGB crackdown in Azerbaijan in the dying days of the USSR. He represented one of the main voices who supported the view that perestroika had itself been guided by Western intelligence agencies through "agents of influence" like Eduard Shevardnadze and Aleksandr Yakovlev.[82]

Chapter Two

The Making of Money and Power

The Establishment of Putin's Circle, from the KGB to St. Petersburg, 1985–1996

I t became clear to Russian and Western observers long before Putin started his third full term as president in 2012 that he operated a complex informal system in which subgroups were constantly balanced against each other, with Putin alone as the ultimate arbiter. His power derived less from the institutional legitimacy conferred by being head of state than from the successful operation of a tribute system that obliged all participants to recognize his authority. In the words of American economists Clifford Gaddy from the Brookings Institution and Barry Ickes from Pennsylvania State University, Putin operates a "protection racket" [1] dependent on a code of behavior that severely punishes disloyalty while allowing access to economic predation on a world-historic scale for the inner core of his elite. By his third term, he had created a highly controlled security system able to use the laws, the media, and the security forces as a means of intimidating, and critically balancing, rival economic elites. Others have called it a "corporation," [2] "Kremlin, Inc.," [3] "a *sistema*," [4] or a "corporatist-kleptocratic regime." [5]

No one trying to analyze the locus of power in Russia in 2014 was calling it a normally functioning, democratizing, or even developing state. The Russian political analyst Yevgeniy Gontmakher, the deputy director of Moscow's Institute of World Economy and International Relations, made the astute observation that "there is no state in Russia." There is "a certain structure in which millions of people who call themselves bureaucrats work," but they do not perform the function that a state is supposed to perform: "Instead of the state as an institution implementing the course of a developing country, we have a huge and uncontrolled private structure which is successfully diverting profits for its own use." In present-day Russia, he continues, "there isn't even a pale copy of this mechanism of the formation of the state." The Parliament had become "yet another department of the Presidential Administration," along with the entire legal system, and bureaucrats who thought they worked for the state in fact serve only the interests of an "extremely large monopolistic business structure which can do anything it likes" and which controls "not less than 50 percent of the economy." [6]

Profits are diverted on the whole not to assist the population but to line the pockets of bureaucrats and the political elite. By 2013 the gap between rich and poor in Russia was larger than in any other major country, and twice that of Western Europe.[7] A report on global wealth by Credit Suisse stated in 2013, "Of the 26 Russian billionaires in 2005, 25 of them were still on the list in 2010—a higher survival rate than any other BRIC or G7 country," possibly reflecting "state protection of billionaire interests." The report went on to say that, whereas across the world billionaires account for 1 to 2 percent of total household wealth, "in Russia today 110 billionaires own 35% of all wealth," giving it practically the highest level of wealth inequality in the world.[8] Irrespective of what term we use to describe Putin's regime, most commentators in 2014 were agreed that its inner logic was focused on the protection of the wealth of those closest to the Russian president.

This chapter examines the interlocking networks that Putin built beginning in the 1990s. It is not just the story of how Russia descended into uncontrolled corruption and violence, the trope that Putin himself now often repeats to compare his period of stability to Yel'tsin's period of chaos. For Putin the 1990s was the period when "everything came true." It was a time when a group of former KGB, mafia, and political and economic elites joined forces, combining their money, connections, and position to create the basis for Putin's spectacular success in building an authoritarian and kleptocratic regime.

The key to Putin's political authority is thus not the law but rather *vlast'*, or power. Courses of action must be taken not because there are strict rules and regulations but because there is an unwritten understanding, or *ponyatiya*, about how things must be done. It is clear that even before his presidency, Putin sought to be at the center of a tribute system that would determine which Russian elites would get a seat at the privatization table and on what terms. Even before his inauguration in 2000, he said that he intended to bring into the Kremlin people who were connected to him personally. Defending why so many ex-KGB from St. Petersburg were given key positions in Moscow, he told ABC *Nightline* anchor Ted Koppel, "I've brought some of them to the Kremlin in staff positions—people who I've known for many years—and people whom I trust. So that is the reason why I've brought them in. Not because they worked in the KGB and follow some specific ideology. It has nothing to do with ideology—it has to do with their professional qualities and personal relationships."[9] Anton Surikov, a former military intelligence specialist who became an outspoken critic of Putin, was more candid in speaking to a Western journalist: "To tell you the truth . . . all Russian politicians are bandits from St. Petersburg."[10] One of the persistent features of Putin's circle is that they promote their friends and do not forget to punish their enemies. Surikov—who had served as a go-between in relations between Chechen rebels and the Kremlin in 1999 but who then made many enemies within the establishment—was dead within several months of this 2009 interview, although no link was ever proven between his views and his death.

Russia in the early 1990s was indeed a gangsters' paradise. Some of the gangsters were mafia, some were ex-security people now in the private sector. The former sought to keep the state weak; the latter hoped to rebuild it as its new leaders. A lengthy analysis of the overall situation in Russia's regions concluded, "Robbers are leaving the 'highway' more and more frequently to make themselves comfortable in offices, where a criminal business concludes transactions with a legal free enterprise. . . . [There is] a reorientation of the 'crime boss' into a respectable gentleman who gathers tribute from legal free enterprise without losing his coloration as a thief. . . . The criminal organizations are obviously gaining the upper hand over the state structures in their degree of organization." [11] The establishment of this tribute system occurred as Putin was becoming the linchpin in Russia's main "window to the West," responsible for all foreign economic relations in St. Petersburg.

Putin's St. Petersburg days underline this style of work, building overlapping networks of people in which he is at the center, relying on them to promote privatization while supporting the state, and assisting each other in personal gain. Putin occupied one position after another that regulated and controlled the privatization process, becoming indispensable in legalizing what otherwise would have been illicit activities. He relied not only on friends and coworkers in the former KGB, but also on those who shared his desire to develop capitalism in Russia, including both economists and businessmen who were willing to take the extraordinary risks required to build something from nothing in post-Soviet Russia. For this they needed and initially relied on criminal elements from the Russian underworld. Gradually private security firms headed by ex-KGB and -MVD officials appeared. Over time these officials formed the security team around Deputy Mayor Putin and then formed the core of his security team when he became president. But the story starts before Putin arrived back in his hometown of Leningrad, when he was stationed in the East German provincial city of Dresden; there he was part of a core of associates with whom he would build lifelong ties.

Putin in the KGB: Dresden and the Founding of Putin's Circle

It is generally accepted that Putin joined the KGB in 1975, that he had at least a year of training both in Moscow and in Leningrad (where he met Sergey Ivanov, who has been part of his inner circle from the beginning and who became, under Putin, minister of defense, deputy prime minister, and head of the Presidential Administration, among other assignments), and that he was stationed from at least 1985 until 1990 in Dresden. Other aspects of his KGB career are highly contested, however. Putin's own statements provide little clue. Some claim that before his 1985 posting abroad, he worked for the Fifth Chief Directorate in Leningrad, which was responsible for internal order and suppression of dissent.[12] Others claim he worked as a rank-and-file Line VKR (foreign counterintelligence) officer of the KGB in Leningrad, responsible for preventing defections or recruitment of Soviet citizens by foreign intelligence agencies.[13] Leaks from German intelligence services to journalists in 2000 suggest that Putin was given the cover of a TASS reporter in Bonn in 1975 but botched the operation and was asked to leave West Germany in the late 1970s.[14] Others claim that he was photographed by Western intelligence in front of the West Berlin department store KaDeWe (in other words, a place he was not supposed to be as a Soviet citizen accredited to East Germany, not West Germany nor West Berlin). Andreas Förster, the editor of the *Berliner Zeitung*, claimed that Putin was accredited in the GDR from 1982 to 1986 under the false name Aleksandr Rybin, born February 9, 1947, according to the Diplomatisches Protokoll Fremde Missionen (Diplomatic List of Foreign Missions) of the GDR Foreign Ministry, in which there was allegedly a photo of Rybin that Förster claims bore a "striking resemblance to Putin."[15]

This confusion about whether Dresden was Putin's first German posting led his German biographer Alexander Rahr to conclude that "forces of the so-called 'invisible front' in Moscow today try to put a thick fog of silence over this section of Putin's biography."[16] Rahr himself has always had a high-level and close association with the Kremlin, receiving honorary degrees from the Moscow State Institute for International Relations and the Higher School of Economics. At the same time, he worked for Radio Free Europe, as well as being part of the negotiations that brought Mikhayl Khodorkovskiy out of Russia in 2013. For Putin's most important German biographer to recognize that Putin's German period was subjected to what one might call a significant scrubbing only combines with other details to indicate that Putin's time there was probably not filled with routine paper-pushing. Certainly he could have had more success in covert operations than anyone would ever subsequently admit.

It is also conceivable that one of the reasons his circle was so interested in that "thick fog of silence" was a 2011 allegation that the Putin household had itself been infiltrated by a West German agent, a woman who became a confidante of his wife, Lyudmila Putina. A German journalist who covered intelligence matters claimed he had received confirmation from highly placed sources in both the BND (Bundesnachrichtendienst, the German Federal Intelligence Agency) and the Verfassungsschutz (the Office for the Protection of the Constitution) that this woman was a West German posing as a Baltic German with fluent Russian and German and that she operated under the names Lenchen and Lenochka. She was employed as an interpreter in the Dresden office, and she became close to Putina, who confided in her. "Lyudmila told her that Vladimir frequently beat her, and often cheated on her, that he had had trysts with other women."[17] This account of their relationship is roughly shared by Irene Pietsch, a German official's wife who befriended Putina and subsequently wrote a book about it.[18] But it is at odds with the remembrance of Putin's biographer and coworker Vladimir Usol'tsev, who describes Putin as a devoted family man.[19]

The German journalist who researched this story, Erich Schmidt-

Putin and his wife, Lyudmila, at Easter service in April 2011. They had rarely been seen in public for several years and announced their decision to divorce in 2013. Photo by Sasha Mordovets, Getty Images

Eenboom, noted for his extensive work on German intelligence activities, also stated that one of the activities of the KGB in East Germany after 1985 was to "take revenge" for the BND's successful running of a KGB colonel codenamed Viktor who spied for the BND from the early 1970s to 1985 and who apparently was stationed in Dresden until 1985. Schmidt-Eenboom claims that Yuriy Drozdov and others were personally involved in the "cleanup" from this failure.[20] Usol'tsev also claimed that Putin worked for counterintelligence in Dresden, recruiting future "illegals." If so, this would certainly have put him in direct touch with Drozdov, who headed this directorate.[21]

As to what Putin did on official business during the period when he clearly was in Dresden, from 1985 to 1990, there are also questions. On January 10, 2000, the German newspaper *Welt am Sonntag* published an interview with Günther Köhler, a former Stasi* officer who knew Putin. Köhler said Putin called himself Adamov, spoke excellent German, and traveled frequently to West Germany, and that he was part of Operation Luch, designed to encourage the reformist movement in the East German regime.[24] Köhler claimed that Putin tried to recruit Western businessmen and East Germans traveling to the West and that "he kept a book on East Germans who supported economic reform."[25] Other journalists who investigated Putin agree that he indeed worked as a recruiter[26] and that he used the name Adamov in his dealings with non–East German citizens.[27]†

---

* Ministry for State Security (Ministerium für Staatssicherheit, Stasi). Historians estimate that almost one in fifty East Germans collaborated with the Stasi, surpassing both the KGB's infiltration of Soviet society at any time except the late 1930s and Nazi penetration of German society.[22] Putin's coworker Usol'tsev described the relationship between the Stasi and the KGB as "an expedition in which recent graduates of the secret service met with dogged old Chekists."[23]

† Putin himself gives a very interesting and specific answer to the question of whether he traveled into West Germany at this time: "No, not once while I was working in the GDR."[28] The answer does not exclude several possibilities: that he traveled to West Germany as an illegal before being formally stationed in the GDR; that he traveled to West Berlin, which in international law was still under formal Allied military occupation until German reunification on October 3, 1990. While the West treated West Berlin as part of the Federal Republic, the Soviet Bloc countries certainly did not, treating it as the "third" German jurisdiction, or a *selbstständige politische Einheit* (independent political entity). Thus saying that he did not travel to West Germany certainly does not mean he did not travel to West Berlin. Nor is it excluded that he was infiltrated into

Irrespective of his activities before arriving in Dresden, it is agreed that he spent the better part of five years in Dresden, until 1990, several months after the collapse of the Berlin Wall. In Dresden it appears that he was involved in espionage designed to steal as many of the West's technological secrets as possible; in fact by the time the USSR collapsed, approximately 50 percent of all Soviet weapons systems were based on stolen Western designs. The success rate was lower in other areas of the economy, not because KGB operatives were not successfully stealing secrets but because the economy no longer had the capacity to respond. In a 2010 speech at the Russian Academy of Sciences, Putin recollected that in the late 1980s he realized, "The results of our own research, and the results of your foreign colleagues' research that were obtained by 'special means,' were not actually introduced into the Soviet Union's economy. We did not even have the equipment to introduce them. And so there we were, working away, gathering away, essentially for nothing." [29]

But the greatest speculation about Putin's activities in Dresden concerns whether he was part of the mysterious Operation Luch, which means "ray" or "sunbeam" in Russian. Much is not known about Luch. It is referred to in the Mitrokhin Archive* as a long-running operation to monitor opinion within the GDR leadership and population and to examine the efforts of the West to "harm the building of socialism" inside the GDR. Particularly after the 1968 invasion of Czechoslovakia, where a large number of KGB operatives had been sent in advance,[30] the Soviets did not restrict their operations in Eastern Europe to formal state-to-state intelligence operations. While the formal purpose of intelligence cooperation was to coordinate actions against the West—Putin himself described his work as gathering information about NATO, the "main opponent"[31]—the KGB also had an interest in monitoring the political situation inside the Socialist Bloc, which

---

West Germany before receiving an open assignment in Dresden. And of course, he could simply not be telling the truth.

* The Mitrokhin Archive is a vast collection of documents and handwritten notes collected and brought to the West by the KGB First Chief Directorate archivist, Vasiliy Mitrokhin, in 1992. It detailed the most important KGB spies working in the West, the KGB's role in a wide range of events, and the extent of KGB penetration of Western intelligence services.

had only become more fragile after the 1968 invasion. For this purpose, in East Germany sometime in 1973 they established Operation Luch.[32] By 1974 the KGB was so focused on the need to monitor events not only in the West but also in the Soviet Bloc that "the section of the Karlshorst KGB responsible for Luch was raised in status to a directorate."[33]

In conception Luch appears to have been an extension of Operation Progress, started by Andropov after the invasion of Czechoslovakia, in which Soviet illegals were infiltrated into Bloc countries to test public opinion, monitor allied intelligence capability, provide an independent source of intelligence to the Soviet leadership, and engage in active operations—including the kidnapping of dissidents.[34] Naturally the knowledge that KGB operatives were active within an allied and sovereign country created a delicate situation. In 1978, for example, Andropov and Stasi chief Erich Mielke signed an agreement acknowledging that the Soviets could "recruit GDR citizens for secret collaboration" but only for "solving tasks of intelligence and counterintelligence work in capitalist states and in West Berlin" and only with the knowledge of the Stasi, strongly indicating that the Stasi did not approve of the KGB's secretly recruiting their own officials. The 1978 protocol put strict limits on the number of KGB liaison officers who could be placed alongside their Stasi counterparts, limiting the "overall number of liaison officers from the Representation of the KGB with the MfS [Ministerium für Staatssicherheit, Stasi] of the GDR" to thirty, "of which 15 are assigned to District Administrations of the MfS of the GDR."[35]

This laughably small number was undoubtedly never adhered to, but the fact that it would be included in a protocol shows the East Germans' sensitivity to the issue. The GDR foreign intelligence chief Markus Wolf later estimated that by 1989 there were about a thousand "pure" KGB intelligence operatives, including liaison officers in the GDR, excluding military and signals intelligence, for a total of five to seven thousand.[36] In a 1981 meeting, Mielke and Andropov discussed extensive measures that would have to be taken to ensure that the nascent Solidarity movement in Poland did not spill over and affect the populations in their two countries. Both agreed that the key was close cooperation and the use of "party methods" to maintain control of the working class. Additionally at this meeting,

Andropov recognized the role of the Stasi in stealing high-tech and defense secrets from the West, thanking Mielke for "all your information provided, especially on West German tank production, defense technology, and the NATO manual." He promised that the East Germans would also receive information from the KGB, at which point Mielke chimed in, "The quality is crucial!" Mielke wanted in particular to cooperate to "acquire even more new technology for our economy." [37] Clearly Mielke was making every effort to maintain East Germany's status as first among equals in its relationship with Moscow.

As Gorbachev's reforms of *glasnost'* and perestroika began to unleash further protest movements throughout the Communist world, the KGB leadership became more and more alarmed by the situation both in Eastern Europe and inside the USSR. A meeting between Mielke and General Ivan Abramov of the KGB's Fifth Chief Directorate* took place in 1987 in which Abramov openly admitted that in the view of KGB senior staff, Gorbachev's reform agenda was unworkable and destabilizing, and concluded that in the USSR "perestroika itself proceeds anything but smoothly and easily." Mielke was direct in his response, noting that while a plan for dealing with threats to socialism may be passed, "at the end, nothing comes out of it. You talk, and they sign a good resolution. . . . Bobkov [director of the Fifth Chief Directorate] will give a good speech tomorrow at your [KGB] conference in Moscow. . . . Yet when he does not tell his people what they are actually supposed to do, the entire ideological explanation will not be of much value." [38] The situation in East Germany clearly became worse after Communist regimes in neighboring Bloc states came under pressure from wide-scale social movements like Solidarity in Poland and Charter 77 in Czechoslovakia. After 1989, when the Hungarians opened their border with Austria, the mass and uncontrolled exodus of East Germans began, which ultimately led to the collapse of the regime after the Berlin Wall fell in November 1989. [39]

---

*The document lists him as head of the Fifth Chief Directorate, but he was deputy head, in charge of monitoring and suppressing domestic dissent. Filipp Bobkov was the head of the Fifth Chief Directorate at this time.

While Putin acknowledged that Operation Luch did have the objective of "working with the political leadership of the GDR," he denied having any involvement with it.[40] As the Soviet KGB leadership became more and more worried about the collapse of the GDR, especially after 1988, speculation arose that Luch was used not only to monitor the political mood of the country but also to recruit a set of agents who would "live on," reporting to Moscow if a united Germany came to pass. On the Soviet side, this group was reputed to consist at the top level of twenty or so KGB operatives in East Germany, who reported directly to KGB chief Kryuchkov. Kryuchkov admitted both to visiting Dresden in 1986 to evaluate the readiness of Hans Modrow to succeed Erich Honecker, as Markus Wolf confirms, and to the existence of Luch, but he wasn't sure of Putin's involvement, saying elusively that he remembered faces but forgot names.[41] Major General Vladimir A. Shirokov, who headed the Dresden office, also confirmed that their function was to work as the liaison between the KGB and GDR institutions, including the Stasi, the police, the border guards, the Customs Office, and the local party organs, "in particular the 1st Secretary of the Dresden district committee of the SED [East Germany's ruling Socialist Unity Party] Modrow."[42]

Luch, and Putin's role in it, became the subject of an investigation by the German Verfassungsschutz (Federal Office for the Protection of the Constitution) when Putin came to power in 2000. The Germans were concerned that Putin had recruited a network that lived on in united Germany. According to the London *Sunday Times*, "Several high-ranking officers of the former East German Stasi secret service who knew Putin personally were questioned recently in an effort to identify some of those he is believed to have recruited."[43] Horst Jemlich, the personal assistant to Dresden's Stasi chief Horst Böhm and a Stasi agent for thirty years, knew Putin and was one of those questioned. He told the *Sunday Times*, "They questioned me about it for hours. But we in the Stasi knew nothing about the operation. The KGB mounted it behind our backs, recruiting in utmost secrecy. The plan was to prepare one day to let us fall and have new guys supply them with information. I only found out about Luch recently and felt betrayed. The Russians were playing a double game."[44] The list of agents recruited as part of Luch was never revealed in the West, either because it was burned or, more likely, because it was removed back to the USSR as the Berlin Wall was falling.

Putin indirectly admitted to running some of these agents himself when he spoke about the times after November 1989 when crowds threatened to storm the KGB building in Dresden after the collapse of the Wall. He decided to go out to calm down the protesters so that they would not break through, thus "saving the lives of the people whose files were lying on my desk."[45] Inside the KGB offices, staff members were busy burning all the files. Putin later stated, "We burned so much stuff that the furnace exploded."[46] He recounts that despite the local office's efforts to get the Soviet military to come to their rescue, and in general to defend their positions in East Germany, "Moscow was silent. . . . I only really regretted that the Soviet Union had lost its position in Europe, although intellectually I understood that a position built on walls . . . cannot last. But I wanted something different to rise in its place. And nothing different was proposed. That's what hurt. They just dropped everything and went away. . . . We would have avoided a lot of problems if the Soviets had not made such a hasty exit from Eastern Europe."[47]

The head of the Dresden office, Major-General Shirokov, confirmed Putin's story that the furnace had exploded. In his memoirs he provided more details about the evacuation, saying that after the furnace exploded, they decided to place all the documents in a massive pit and use napalm to burn them. But when the soldiers responsible for delivering the chemical incendiary were delayed, Shirokov instead poured gasoline into the pit and set it on fire. This too was insufficient for dealing with all the documents, so ultimately they loaded what remained on twelve Soviet army trucks and repatriated all of it to Russia.[48]

Putin's normal duties focused on obtaining high-tech secrets from the West. He certainly admits to recruiting agents who traveled to or were from the West.[49] He also is said to have assumed the identity of Mr. Adamov, the director of a German-Soviet friendship society in Leipzig, where he kept a close eye on foreign visitors for possible recruits.[50] The *Sunday Times* reported that Putin used his agents to penetrate the Siemens electronics giant via agents in its East German partner, Robotron, a state company that was one of only five mainframe and personal computer companies in the Soviet Bloc, providing computers to the KGB itself.[51] The BND's fear was that because it was believed that both the Stasi and the KGB had infiltrated Siemens via Robotron during this period, these links would live on after German reunification. This concern was heightened when Siemens received many favorable contracts early in the post-Soviet period, including those approved by Putin when he was head of the Committee for Foreign Liaison (Komitet vneshnikh svyazey—or KVS—also sometimes referred to as the Committee for Foreign Economic Relations, or External Relations) in St. Petersburg. The Western company that received the first contract for medical equipment in post-Communist St. Petersburg was Siemens. And one of Putin's closest collaborators and a cofounder of the Ozero Cooperative,* Nikolay Shamalov, was the Siemens representative in northwestern Russia. Additionally whistleblower documents brought out of Russia in 2011[52] detail a multiyear scam involving funds that should have gone to building health clinics all over Russia but instead helped build what is called "Putin's Palace" in the southern Russian town of Gelendzhik; these too involved contracts from Siemens.† Still, there is no direct evidence that the KGB infiltrated Siemens or that Shamalov's subsequent appointment as Siemens's representative in the Russian northwestern region grew out of the KGB's early interest.

In East Germany, Kalugin states, in response to complaints by East German leaders about the overly large size of the KGB presence (450 agents in East Berlin alone, he claims), agents, "particularly in the provinces," as was Putin, were moved into joint ventures and trade missions, giving them a head start in learning about economic processes when privatization

---

* The Ozero Cooperative, which is dealt with extensively below, was a gated compound of businessmen, including Putin, who shared lakefront properties and a common bank account. Their mutual connections and loyalties form the base of the political system built by Putin beginning in the 2000s, but their connections go back to the early 1990s.

† In 2008 Siemens AG paid $1.6 billion in penalties to the U.S. and German governments after admitting to 4,200 illegal payments totaling $1.4 billion over six years to various countries, including specifically for the supply of medical devices to Russia.[53]

began in Russia in the 1990s.[54] Given the ability of embassy staff and KGB agents in East Germany to buy goods in the West, they became highly involved in smuggling goods back to Russia in the 1980s.[55] The USSR's own long-standing ambassador to East Germany, Pyotr Abrasimov (who held the post of Soviet high commissioner in Germany), ambassador extraordinary and plenipotentiary to the GDR since 1962,[56] was evidently himself implicated in supplying smuggled Western goods to the Central Committee,[57] but because of his friendship with Brezhnev, according to Kalugin, the affair was hushed up until Andropov came to power, at which point he was recalled.[58]

As for Putin, many authors have written about his role in these activities and his acquiring coveted Western consumer goods. Masha Gessen recounts an interview with a former member of the radical West German group the Red Army Faction,* who had regular meetings with Putin. He told her, "He [Putin] always wanted to have things. He mentioned to several people wishes that he wanted from the West." Gessen writes that the Faction leader gave Putin a Grundig Satellite shortwave radio and a Blaupunkt stereo for his car. The Faction member particularly remembered Putin's attitude toward paying for these items, an attitude that would reappear in the years to come: "The East Germans did not expect us to pay for it, so they would at least make an effort to say, 'What do I owe you?' And we would say, 'Nothing.' And Vova [diminutive for Vladimir, i.e., Putin] never even started asking, 'What do I owe you?'"†

---

*During this period East Germany had become what its non-Communist interior minister, Peter-Michael Diestel, called "an Eldorado for terrorists."[59] Terrorist groups, including the Red Army Faction (RAF), Libyan-sponsored Arab terrorists, and Carlos the Jackal, operated from East Germany under Stasi and KGB control. During the time that Putin was in Dresden, the RAF was implicated in bombings at the USAF Rhein-Main Air Base and the assassinations of the chief of technology at Siemens and the chairman of Deutsche Bank.[60]

† Putin's interest in acquiring personal consumer goods, which Gessen describes as "pleonexia," has continued into his presidency.[61] Robert Kraft, the owner of the New England Patriots, recounted at an after-dinner speech at a public ceremony in the Waldorf-Astoria in 2013 that in 2005, while on a business trip to Russia with a group of top executives, Kraft had shown Putin his Super Bowl ring, encrusted with over four carats of diamonds, a fact confirmed by many pictures taken at the time: "I took out the ring and showed it to [Putin], and he put it on and he goes, 'I can kill someone with this ring.' I put my hand out and he put it in his pocket, and

President Putin sizes up Robert Kraft's 2005 Super Bowl Ring at Konstantin Palace outside St. Petersburg, Russia, June 25, 2005. AP Photo/ Alexander Zemlianichenko

In 1989–91, after the Berlin Wall came down and before the USSR collapsed, Putin, like all KGB officers, capitalized on his contacts with Stasi officials in East Germany who were themselves entering private business for the first time. They had also established dummy companies in the West through which they laundered funds and ran operations. The East German Ministry of Foreign Trade's Commercial Coordination Division cooperated closely with the Stasi, and between 1987 and 1990 alone, 400 million West German marks left the country through dummy front companies.[64]

---

three KGB guys got around him and walked out." Kraft made it known he wanted the ring back, but he claims that he got a call from the George W. Bush White House saying, "It would *really* be in the best interests of U.S.-Soviet [*sic*] relations if you meant to give the ring as a present."[62] So Kraft released a statement saying he decided to gift the ring to Putin. But by 2013 he had changed his mind, and in response to this new story, Putin's spokesman Dmitry Peskov said Putin would not return the ring but would be happy to buy Mr. Kraft another one and advised that anyone who believes the story should "talk with psychoanalysts."[63]

In the immediate aftermath of the collapse of the Berlin Wall, West German and U.S. intelligence services both rushed into East Germany to take over as many files and agent networks as possible. It is claimed that the CIA managed to acquire the complete card catalogue of all of East Germany's foreign intelligence agents.[65] But it would appear that at least some of the agents were willing to work for the KGB, and Putin seems to have been involved in trying to keep many of the die-hard loyalists on the payroll. One was Klaus Zuchold, a Stasi officer from Dresden who, in an interview with the *Sunday Times* in 2000, claimed he had known Putin since 1985 and admitted to having been recruited by him in January 1990.[66]* Eleven months later, as reunification was taking place, he claimed to have turned himself over to German intelligence and at the same time revealed not only the names of four East German police who had spied for the KGB for years but also a detailed biography of Putin's time in Dresden. Stasi archives do confirm that the GDR authorities complained formally and directly to the Soviets about the unauthorized Soviet recruitment of police and radio specialists, and they were given assurances that such recruitment would go through proper channels in the future.[68] Putin was involved in the recruitment of GDR police, and documents show that he requested that Dresden Stasi chief Horst Böhm intervene to have a telephone line installed in the apartment of one of his main informers.[†69] Zuchold said of Putin, "He showed me his wristwatch, which had an inscription from some KGB bigwig. He loved patriotic stories of Russia's great past and popular heroes." Zuchold also revealed that when visiting Putin in his apartment, Putin had showed off a new stereo bought during a trip to KaDeWe in West Berlin.[70]

The opening of the Stasi archives following German reunification allows a closer look into Putin's German colleagues than into his KGB circle. Among the members of Putin's inner circle who got their start with him in Dresden, the most notable example is Matthias Warnig, a former Stasi

---

* Zuchold's file in the Stasi archive confirms his employment by the Stasi in Dresden from 1982 to 1989, coinciding with the years Putin worked there.[67]

† A leading unofficial informer (Führungs-Inoffizieller Mitarbeiter) knows the identity of other informers and leads them.

operative. Warnig worked in the Sector for Science and Technology (Sektor Wissenschaft und Technik, SWT), of the Hauptverwaltung Aufklärung, the foreign intelligence arm of the Stasi from the Department for Rocket Science and Technology (XV/3). Stasi archives indicate that Warnig was recruited as an informer by the Stasi in 1974 and adopted the cover name Hans-Detlef.[71] In hiring him, the Stasi district office noted, "The IM [Inoffizieller Mitarbeiter, unofficial informer] candidate is willing and able to support our body. From the outset, the high level of commitment exhibited by the IM candidate in the solution of our organ's orders should be emphasized."[72] The following year, 1975, he was hired full time by the Stasi, where his codenames were listed first as Arthur and then Ökonom, the Economist, given to him after he earned a degree in economics.[73]

Warnig distinguished himself in the Stasi, receiving a silver medal in October 1984 and the title Honored Activist, one of only thirty-seven from the 1974 intake class so recognized by the leadership that year.[74] In 1985 he was assigned to the group to establish residencies in the West (SWT/AG1, Working Group 1), and he was sent to Düsseldorf in 1988 to recruit new agents. He became acting head of SWT's Department for Rocket Science and Technology in 1989 and was then sent to Dresden in October to cooperate with the KGB.[75]

It is not known exactly when Putin and Warnig met, especially since Warnig long denied his Stasi past. They both received awards at the same GDR National People's Army ceremony on February 8, 1988, when Warnig received a bronze Medal of Merit of the National People's Army. While many have commented that Putin "only" received a bronze, it is worth noting that he was one of only fifteen Soviets who received a medal that day from Stasi chief Mielke, and he was only thirty-six, as compared with the average age of fifty-four for the rest.[76] Warnig and Putin were again pictured together in a group to commemorate the seventy-first anniversary of the Cheka (precursor to the KGB), along with Sergey Chemezov, Putin's co-worker and neighbor in Dresden who has risen to be the head of Rosoboroneksport—in charge of Russian arms exports.

The problem with developing capitalism in Russia was that, in contrast with Eastern European states, almost no Russians had any experience of working in legitimate business enterprises in the West. Thus those like Putin, who worked close to the West or were stationed as KGB operatives to study the West, had an advantage, however skewed. Warnig's job had been industrial espionage, and he is said to have worked with Putin to recruit West German agents.[77] The *Wall Street Journal* interviewed Frank Weigelt, who claimed to be Warnig's supervisor at the time; Weigelt said that Warnig had recruited twenty agents in the 1980s in West Germany to steal military rocket and aircraft technology. The *Journal* also interviewed Vladimir Usol'tsev, a coworker of Putin with whom he shared an office, who claimed that Putin's task was the same kind of recruitment, but for the KGB. The two men's paths crossed when Warnig was stationed in Dresden in October 1989—one month before the Berlin Wall came down—to start cooperating with the KGB, which "was running an operation in the city to recruit key Stasi members, with an eye toward getting its hands on their West German spies." According to Zuchold, "Mr. Warnig was in one of the several KGB cells Mr. Putin organized in Dresden." Zuchold further claimed that Warnig's cell operated "under the guise of a business consultancy" but was actually recruiting agents for the KGB.[78] The close relationship between Warnig and Putin was also affirmed by Irene Pietsch.[79] Pietsch told the *Wall Street Journal* that Lyudmila Putina had once commented that it was easier to talk to East Germans than West Germans. When Pietsch asked what she meant, she used Warnig as an example: "She said we all grew up in the same system, and that Volodya [diminutive of Vladimir, i.e., Putin] worked for the same firm. I asked her what she meant. She said Matthias was in the Stasi, and Volodya the KGB," and that they had worked together in Dresden in the 1980s. Moreover Pietsch showed the *Wall Street Journal* faxes that Putina had sent her not only from the St. Petersburg mayor's office and the Kremlin, but also from Dresdner Bank, or Dresden Bank, which Warnig headed.[80]

In the atmosphere of postunification Germany, no one wanted to admit that he had hired an ex-Stasi officer, and the CEO of Dresdner Bank later insisted that "he would not have hired Warnig had he known of his Stasi past."[81] Warnig was hired by Dresdner in March 1990 and was sent to open their first branch in Russia in St. Petersburg in 1991. By 2002 he was heading all their operations in Russia. Initially his Stasi past was career suicide.

This picture was taken January 24, 1989 on the occasion of the joint visit
of Stasi, KGB, and military forces to the 1st Guards Tank Army Museum
to "commemorate the 71st anniversary of the formation of the Cheka
and the 70th anniversary of the formation of the Soviet military defense
organs." Putin is pictured second from the left; Matthias Warnig, third
from the left in the back row; and Sergey Chemezov, seventh from the
left in the back row. Stasi Archives, BStU MfS-BV-Ddn-AKG-10852-Seite-
0002-Bild-0001. www.miamioh.edu/havighurstcenter/putins-russia.

But as Putin's power became consolidated around a state filled with officials from the former KGB and other so-called power ministries, known
as *siloviki*, Warnig's background became, if anything, an asset. So much so
that his public biography on the Russian bank VTB's website, on whose
board he sat, stated that Warnig had been an "officer at the Ministry for
Foreign Trade and Cabinet Council of the German Democratic Republic,
and Main Intelligence Directorate; in 1989 retired as major." [82]

Therefore, when it was time for St. Petersburg to set up branches of
foreign banks, Putin chose from among the many applicants his friend
and Dresden coworker Matthias Warnig. Warnig opened Dresdner's first
branch in Russia in St. Petersburg in 1991, located on Malaya Morskaya,
just steps away from St. Isaac's Square, where the city parliament building

is located, in the building of the former Imperial German Embassy. Soon after the formal opening in September 1993, Russia imposed a moratorium on the registration of foreign-owned banks.[83] Warnig then became deputy director of the Moscow branch, and in 2000 he became the chief coordinator of the Dresdner Bank Group in Russia. Some reported that he was an early shareholder in Bank Rossiya, established in 1990 by Leningrad Communist Party insiders and then reregistered in December 1991 under Mayor Anatoliy Sobchak and Deputy Mayor Putin, who had become the city's supervisor in charge of foreign economic relations.* Warnig became a member of the board of directors of Bank Rossiya in 2012.[84]

Warnig was always available to assist Putin personally and professionally, stepping in to pay for Lludymila Putina's surgeries and lengthy medical treatment in Germany after a serious car accident in 1993, as well as several of Putin's trips to Hamburg and traveling expenses for Putin's two daughters, Maria and Ekaterina, to attend public schools in Hamburg— this according to Pietsch and Dieter Mankowski, who was head of the German Industry and Trade Association's Petersburg office in the early 1990s.[85] His bank also provided St. Petersburg with $10 million in low-interest (7.8 percent) credits—at a time when inflation officially was running at 200 percent—to equip a children's hospital.[86] In 2003, when Putin needed help in taking apart Yukos, the oil company owned by the oligarch Mikhayl Khodorkovskiy, Warnig and Dresdner Bank were instrumental.† By 2014 Warnig had been named a trustee or member of the boards of Bank Rossiya,

---

* Sobchak was head of the Leningrad City Council from May 1990 until June 1991, when the new position of mayor was established and he was chosen to become St. Petersburg's first mayor. Putin was his advisor until June 1991 and then became deputy mayor in June 1991 and first deputy mayor in March 1994. Throughout the period, irrespective of his title, Putin was responsible for supervising St. Petersburg's foreign economic relations.

† Dresdner was involved in the Kremlin's attack on Yukos when the Ministry of Justice commissioned the bank's investment arm, Dresdner Kleinwort Wasserstein, which Warnig oversaw in Russia after the local DrKW office was merged into Dresdner Bank ZAO in Russia, to value Yukos's core asset, Yuganskneftegaz, before it was sold by the court. The tender was awarded without competitive bidding. DrKW stated that Yugansk was worth between $15 billion and $17 billion, a figure generally supported by Western investors. The company was sold to a shell company, Baikal Finance Group, for $9.3 billion, and then several days later was resold to state-owned Rosneft, whose chairman of the board was Igor Sechin.[87]

Rosneft, Verbundnetz Gas, and VTB Bank, as well as chairman of the board of Rusal (the world's largest aluminum producer) and Transneft, chairman of the administrative board of Gazprom Schweiz AG, and managing director of the $10 billion Nord Stream project bringing Russian gas to Germany via an entirely offshore pipeline.[88] Dmitriy Medvedev's decree in 2011 that state officials could not serve on boards of directors only elevated Warnig's position: Putin loyalists Warnig, Chemezov, and Akimov all moved in to take over positions held by state officials.[89] Many of these companies are the subject of a high level of speculation about Putin's personal corruption.[90]

Nikolay Tokarev is another person with whom Putin worked in Dresden, according to Russian newspapers. *Vedomosti*'s Roman Shleynov ran a biography of Tokarev in 2013, stating that after graduating from college, he had gone to the KGB Higher School in Moscow and was in the same class as fellow KGB member and, beginning in late 2011, chairman of the State Duma Sergey Naryshkin. After completing the course, he was posted to Dresden, where he became Putin's boss. A mutual colleague told Shleynov, "Nearly all the KGB residency in Dresden lived in the same apartment block. The front doors were not closed. We constantly visited each other's homes. Once we were sitting with Tokarev in a group. Someone comes in who is pale, quiet and shy. 'That's Vova [Putin].' Someone invites him: 'Vova, sit down have a drink. . . .' 'No,' Tokarev answers for him, 'Vova does not drink with us.' "[91] The quote implies that Tokarev was responsible for Putin's actions in every respect.

After Dresden, Putin went back to Leningrad and Tokarev to Berlin, returning to the USSR after German reunification in 1990. In 1996, when Putin went to Moscow, he hired Tokarev as his deputy in the Presidential Property Management Department. Tokarev acknowledged working in the PPMD but was characteristically reticent when he described working with Putin. In a 2008 interview in *Vedomosti* he said simply that "their work there had been full, but after that life demanded we deal with different themes."[92] When Putin became president, Tokarev became the CEO of Zarubezhneft, a state-owned oil company that in Soviet days had provided oil to client states such as Vietnam, Syria, and Cuba. In 2007 he became the CEO of Transneft.[93] In 2010 the opposition activist and corruption blogger Aleksey Navalnyy charged that Transneft's construction costs for the East Siberian–Pacific Ocean Oil Pipeline were inflated and had led to the embezzlement of over $4 billion in state funds. While Navalnyy appeared to be focusing on the actions of Tokarev's predecessor, with the implication that Tokarev had been put there to get the project back on track, the Kremlin clearly signaled there would be no investigation. Hours after Navalnyy's post, Putin issued an order praising Transneft "for the great contribution to the development of the energy partnership between Russia and China." [94]

Sergey Chemezov also claims to have met Putin while the two were with the KGB in Dresden, where they were neighbors and friends, often gathered for social occasions, and drank beer together, a detail also noted in the Usol'tsev biography. [95] Chemezov told the magazine *Itogi* in 2005, and later posted on his Web page for the Novikombank board of directors, that he had worked there from 1983 to 1988. [96] In one of the few interviews he gave, Chemezov admitted that he had worked in the GDR, not just anywhere but in Dresden, and lived in the same apartment building as Putin and all the other KGB and Soviet representatives: "We worked in East Germany at the same time. From 1983 to 1988, I was the lead representative of 'Luch' in Dresden,* and Vladimir Vladimirovich [Putin] arrived there in 1985. We lived in the same house, and were associated with each other both in the service [*obshchalis' i po sluzhbe*], and as neighbors." [98] When Usol'tsev was interviewed about Chemezov and his role in Luch, whether it was intelligence, counterintelligence, or control of the East German Party nomenklatura, he certainly did not deny that Luch existed, but he would not be drawn on anyone's exact assignment, simply responding, "Let's just leave this question without an answer." [99] Chemezov admits to having worked with Putin occasionally when he was in Moscow as the deputy director general of Sovintersport,† and so "their professional interests sometimes intersected" and they maintained their personal friendship. [104]

---

*Chemezov did not say that Luch was a KGB operation. Rather he described his work as "heading the Experimental Industrial Association Luch in the GDR" ("Ya vozglavlyal predstavitel'stvo ob'edineniya 'Luch' v Drezdene"). [97]

† Sovintersport was the agency responsible for handling commercial ventures involving Soviet sports and was reputed to be controlled by the KGB. But it was also clearly filled with people

Chemezov followed Putin into the Presidential Property Management Department as head of the External Economic Relations Department. He admitted, "I do not hide that Vladimir Vladimirovich recommended me for the post. I was committed to trying to regulate the use of Russian foreign property, restoring to the state that which it once owned but was lost as a result of incompetent management."[105] He rose through the ranks with Putin, becoming in September 1999 the head of the state company Promeksport and in 2004 the head of the main Russian arms exporter, Rosoboroneksport, for which he traveled with Putin to reopen the market for Russian arms after a lull in the 1990s.

Also part of the Dresden team while Putin was stationed there was Yevgeniy Mikhaylovich Shkolov, who was born in Dresden, reportedly the son of a Soviet spy. Shkolov was trained by the KGB in the USSR before returning to Dresden at the same time as Putin, where the two of them shared an office. While not from St. Petersburg and not part of his inner team, Shkolov had a career path that paralleled Putin's, becoming the head of the department for foreign economic relations in the city of Ivanovo after the collapse of the USSR and rising to work in the Kremlin as assistant to the head of the Presidential Administration under Aleksandr Voloshin and then Dmitriy Medvedev. He was a member of the board of directors of both Transneft and Aeroflot and in 2006 was named deputy minister

---

who the athletes felt were interested in padding their own wallets. In 1989, for example, U.S. boxing promoters provided Sovintersport $200,000 per boxer for six fighters who would be managed by U.S. promoters. But Uri Vaulin, the Russian heavyweight champion, claimed that Sovintersport was paying him only $900 per month.[100] In other sports, like ice hockey and cycling, Sovintersport acted as the intermediary for Soviet athletes. Star ice hockey players bristled against continuing to give Sovintersport a reported 97 percent of their contracts. After negotiations, the amount was reduced to 90 percent, then 80 percent. In the end the top players received contracts in the West that paid $300,000 each a year, with slightly less going back to Sovintersport.[101] Chemezov claims to have been part of the creation at Sovintersport in 1989 of the first professional cycling team to feature Russian cyclists, Alfa Lum, and has remained active as the chairman of the supervisory boards of the Russian Cycling Federation and Team Katyusha, Russia's premier cycling team.[102] Working with him as head of the Russian Cycling Federation is Igor Makarov, who, according to Harvard economist Marshall Goldman, founded ITERA, a trading company that at one point became the second-largest producer of natural gas in Russia, with headquarters in Jacksonville, Florida.[103] Chemezov's extensive links to Ukraine are also explored in http://www.foreignpolicy.com/articles/2014/03/19/dmytro_firtash_ukraine_billionaire_corruption_arrest.

of interior and head of the department of economic security in the MVD. In 2013 Putin appointed him to "take decisions on the implementation of the checks provided for legal acts of the Russian Federation on combating corruption." [106]

With Ivanov, Tokarev, Chemezov, Shkolov, and Warnig, Putin had the beginning of an inner circle. He met others when he was stationed in Leningrad in the 1970s, and when he returned there in 1990 the core team would take shape.

Putin in Leningrad prior to the Attempted Coup

There is no solid evidence about Putin's roles either in moving KGB and CPSU money abroad or in preparing for the August 1991 coup, and what evidence there is happens to be highly circumstantial. Putin did receive promotions while in Germany, rising to the rank of lieutenant colonel and, according to Stasi documents, Party secretary of the local Dresden office.* Putin himself acknowledges that he was a member of the Party Committee for the KGB for the whole GDR. [108] Masha Gessen interviewed a defector in Germany, Sergey Bezrukov, who claims that in February 1990 "Putin had a meeting with Major General Yuriy Drozdov, head of the KGB illegal-intelligence Directorate 'S' within the First Chief Directorate, when the major general visited Berlin. 'The only possible purpose of the meeting could have been giving Putin his next assignment. . . . Why else would the head of the directorate be meeting with an agent who was scheduled to be going home? That sort of thing just did not happen.'" [109] † Gessen's conclusion, that Putin remained an

---

* Stasi files list Putin in a December 1988 list of birthdays of the Soviet officers in Dresden as "OSL Putin Wladimir Wladimirowitsch (Parteisekretär), 7.10.1952." OSL is an abbreviation for Oberstleutnant, or lieutenant colonel. [107]

† Drozdov (1925–) is the modern version of the real live Stierlitz, the undercover agent in the Soviet drama *Seventeen Moments of Spring*, which had motivated Putin to join the KGB. As an illegal in Germany, Drozdov posed as the cousin of the condemned Soviet spy Rudolf Abel, who was imprisoned in the United States and swapped for Gary Powers across the fabled Glienicke Bridge in Potsdam between East and West Germany in 1962. [110] He headed the KGB's Directorate "S," [111] in charge of illegals. As such, he was involved in several other fabled operations: he

employee of the KGB until after the attempted coup and received instructions, assignments, and a salary from them, is supported by other Putin biographers,[118] and Putin readily admits that he continued to have contact with the KGB in St. Petersburg until the coup attempt, that he was on their payroll, and that they relied on him for support in the mayor's office, although he implies that the support was mainly for their business ventures.[119]

Drozdov's presence in Dresden was confirmed by Major General Shirokov in his memoirs when he stated that Drozdov came to Dresden when they were trying to organize the withdrawal of all their forces, documents, and equipment while at the same time simulating a normal workday. Evidently Drozdov arrived under the cover of a vacation with his wife and children, and he and Shirokov put the most secret machines, presumably those for cryptography, into compartments in two cars, placed their children and families on top of these, and drove through the night via Poland to return them to the USSR. Under such conditions it is more than likely that Putin was involved.[120]

There has never been any other direct evidence, however, that Putin met with Drozdov, although Drozdov was in and out of the Dresden office over the years and is said to have attended Putin's inauguration in 2000. One possibility was raised by Yevgeniya Al'bats, whose work on the KGB in the

---

headed an elite unit of special forces in charge of the Soviet attack on Afghan president Hafizullah Amin's palace that killed Amin as a precursor to the Soviet invasion in 1979,[112] and in 1981, when the KGB formed Vympel, an elite unit composed only of officers to carry out "deep penetration, sabotage and liquidations in times of war," [113] Drozdov was its first head. A photo of him taken in 2011 (at the age of eighty-five) shows him under a bust of the Napoleonic war hero Kutuzov.[114] Vympel was a victim of all the reorganizations that took place after the collapse of the USSR, but on October 8, 1998, less than three months after Putin was named director of the FSB, Vympel was reintegrated into the FSB and became one of the elite units in the Special Operations Center (known by the umbrella term Spetsnaz units) under General Aleksandr Tikhonov. In 1999 it became part of the Service to Protect the Constitutional System and Combat Terrorism within the FSB, combining political investigations and antiterrorism work. It has been involved in all the most deadly, secret, and controversial operations of the Russian state under Putin, including the Nord-Ost and Beslan hostage crises, assassinations of Chechen leaders at home and abroad, and, some say, Aleksandr Litvinenko's murder.[115] *Sovershenno sekretno* maintained that operatives of this unit who reported directly to Tikhonov were responsible for placing the explosives in the basement of the apartment in Ryazan in September 1999.[116] This was confirmed by other in-depth investigations.[117]

early 1990s focused on the transformation of the security services from the old KGB to the new FSB and their continuing efforts to remain "the state within a state."[121] She underlines the role of KGB foreign intelligence officers, of which Putin was one, in infiltrating *domestic* democratic movements prior to the attempted coup against Gorbachev. She quotes testimony published afterward from Lieutenant Colonel V. Aksyonov from the First Chief Directorate: "The First Chief Directorate has begun to interfere actively in internal domestic processes. Intelligence officers and illegal agents are being recalled from abroad to the territory of the Union, primarily to the areas of maximum tension (the Baltics, Azerbaijan, Moldavia), for the purpose of gathering information and conducting active measures."[122] What is not known is the extent to which Putin personally was part of an active core of KGB officers who placed their people (or were themselves placed) into the offices of democratic leaders in the late Gorbachev period for the purpose of preparing for a coup, although the clear view among writers is that the highest levels of the KGB did struggle to maintain group cohesion and promote the power of the security services over time.[123] What is known for certain is that when Putin became president, Drozdov did what he could to promote him as a worthy successor to Andropov by publishing a biography called *Yuriy Andropov and Vladimir Putin: On the Path to Re-Birth*.[124]

Certainly a rich but hybrid combination of Chekists, mobsters, and officials in bureaucratic positions of power existed throughout the USSR at this time, and Leningrad was no exception. Putin was at the nexus of these three worlds: the two well-known Italian investigative journalists Carlo Bonini and Giuseppe d'Avanzo, who conducted an investigation of Putin, interviewed a former KGB First Directorate employee, "Nikolay," who claims that he was approached by his superior in the spring of 1990 to be part of the following scheme:

[You will be part of a] new clandestine structure where you will work with the best of the best. Your personnel files will be removed from the archives. No one will ever know your past. You will become a clandestine agent; you will begin to work for the Fatherland. Against

those who want to destroy it. . . . I agreed. . . . I worked directly on
cleaning up the archives of the KGB. Together with my files, hundreds of others were removed. Including that of Vladimir Vladimirovich Putin. After the failed coup of '91, I found myself working
as the chief financial officer of a major joint venture on behalf of the
KGB. My life is divided between Moscow, St. Petersburg, Stockholm,
Vienna, and Geneva. Money, money and more money. I took care
of nothing except running their affairs, in one offshore paradise or
another. We, the patriots of the KGB, were moving millions and millions of dollars into bank vaults. And along those same channels also
moved the money from organized crime, to the point that I would
not be able to tell which monies belonged to the KGB and which to
the mafia. In response to my timid questions, they responded: just
move the damn money. And I did.[125]

As the KGB *rezident* at Leningrad State University and as an employee
of the Leningrad Fifth Chief Directorate, where he worked as a member
of the active reserves after returning from East Germany, Putin would certainly have had access to the lists of agents and informants who worked
for the KGB during the Soviet period. He also would have been tasked
to monitor political activity among faculty and students at the university. Lieutenant Colonel Andrey Zykov,* the lead Russian investigator in
St. Petersburg for especially important cases, who was assigned to examine
Putin's activities for criminal behavior, even went so far as to allege that two
of Putin's later associates, Anatoliy Sobchak and Dmitriy Medvedev, both
of whom were teaching law at Leningrad State University at the time, had
provided Putin with information ("I Anatoliy Sobchak, i Dmitriy Medvedev byli ego stykachkami").[127] Thus Putin would not have been the only
person interested in "cleansing" his own file of damaging materials. Eastern Europe at this time was awash with exposés as high-ranking politicians

---

* Formally Zykov was the senior investigator for particularly important cases of the Criminal
Investigation Department of the Investigative Committee of the Ministry of Internal Affairs
of the Russian Federation's Northwest Federal District based in St. Petersburg, according to his
statement on his nine-part YouTube testimonial.[126]

were unmasked as agents of either the KGB or local security services. No one in Russia wanted a repeat of this, and indeed there has never been such a period in post-Soviet Russia. Clearly the KGB got there first, and files, lots of files, were burned. As mentioned earlier, Putin himself admits that in Dresden, after the Berlin Wall came down in November 1989, he burned so many files that the furnace exploded. But also the entire mood in Russia, the heart of the Soviet Empire, was quite different compared to the rest of the Soviet Bloc—it was one thing to unmask someone in Poland who had worked for the Russians; it was quite another to reveal that a Russian son had been spying on his father, for example.[128] Russians as a whole sensed that such a settling of accounts would be divisive, ruinous, and pointless. And those tens of thousands of people coming out of the collapsed CPSU and KGB had other tasks in mind—most notably making a living in new conditions. The elites from these two organizations knew where the money was and how to use it. They had more lucrative assignments in mind than revenge.

In the Beginning: Bank Rossiya

While spontaneous privatization was occurring throughout Russia, with the KGB and the mafia getting a head start, it also occurred in Leningrad, where, at the request of the local *oblast'* (regional) Party committee, a new bank was established that would be closely associated with the circle around Putin. On June 27, 1990, the Aktsionernyy Kommercheskiy (Joint-Stock Commercial) Bank Rossiya, or OAO AB 'Rossiya,' known simply as Bank Rossiya ever since, was established in Leningrad.[129] An initial 1.5 million rubles ($840,000) was received from Nikolay Kruchina, the CPSU Central Committee chief of the Administrative Department, in July 1990 to capitalize the new bank.[130] The veteran Russian journalist Vladimir Pribylovskiy claims that in a letter to Kruchina (who died by defenestration following the attempted coup) dated September 27, 1990, Leningrad's Party secretary Boris Gidaspov asked for a further transfer of 500 million rubles ($280 million) "to finance the activities of the Central Party structure" in Leningrad.[131] It is not known whether any of this money was ever transferred, but a further 50 million rubles ($28 million) was deposited from the Central Committee's insurance trust in April 1991.[132] The Leningrad *oblast'* Party committee held 48.4 percent of the shares in the new bank, but these shares were frozen after the attempted coup, when the CPSU was legally disbanded. The remaining shares, according to Pribylovskiy, were held by the insurance company Rus' and the media company Russkoye Video. Rus' was owned by Arkadiy Krutikhin, formerly head of the Property Management Department of the Leningrad *oblast'* Party committee, Vladislav Reznik, and Aleksey Aleksandrov. Reznik and Aleksandrov would rise to become Duma members and founding members of United Russia, the ruling political party, under Putin. Russkoye Video was headed by Andrey Balyasnikov, who had worked in the city's Ideology Department. Pribylovskiy claims that Russkoye Video's founding capital of 13 million rubles ($7.3 million) also came from the Leningrad regional (*oblast'*) Party committee.[133]

Twenty-three years later, in March 2014, in response to Russia's annexation of Crimea, the Obama administration introduced sanctions against officials close to Putin and against one lone entity, Bank Rossiya. This move was justified by a White House official's description of Bank Rossiya as a "crony bank—this is a bank that provides services to senior Russian government officials." One of the bank's owners and founders, Yuriy Koval'chuk, was described as "essentially the personal banker for many senior government officials of the Russian Federation, including President Putin."[134] So how did Bank Rossiya emerge, and what is Putin's relationship to it?

Putin's involvement in helping Bank Rossiya began in his first week of office, when, on July 4, 1991, his newly formed Committee for Foreign Liaison took a 5 percent interest in the new St. Petersburg World Trade Center, with Bank Rossiya also purchasing 5 percent of the initial shares, putting St. Petersburg city money into a joint venture with Bank Rossiya, along with ten other cofounders, including foreign firms. The coordination and registration of this new venture went through Putin's office, and it was the first of several dozens of new firms that his committee would help found and, on behalf of the St. Petersburg municipal government, would co-own with private ventures. Pribylovskiy, who had access to all the registration documents for the period 1991–94, states that it was Putin's legal advisor Dmitriy Medvedev who developed the legal case for city ownership.[135]*

When, in December 1991, Bank Rossiya was allowed to resume operations, the CPSU had been dissolved and the shares held by the Leningrad *oblast'* Party committee were thus up for grabs. Records show, as confirmed by the subsequent director general of Bank Rossiya,[136] that the Leningrad regional party executive committee (*obkom*) share was redeemed by a certain Leningrad Association of Joint Ventures,† which consisted of five of the founding members of the Ozero Cooperative: Andrey Fursenko, Yuriy Koval'chuk, Vladimir Yakunin, Nikolay Shamalov, and Sergey Fursenko.‡ Of these, the first three ended up on the U.S. government's March 2014 visa ban and asset seizure list. Koval'chuk was described in the U.S. Treasury Department's list as a "personal banker for senior officials of the Russian Federation including Putin."[143] He became a member of the St. Petersburg municipal commission on enterprises with foreign investment, headed by

---

*Throughout the years Pribylovskiy has been a major and reliable source of documentation on the Russian elite through his writing and his website, Anticompromat.org. He had access to the entire database for Putin's Committee for Foreign Liaison, listing all the companies the committee registered.

† The association was formed in 1990 from four joint ventures: two from Germany, one from Finland, and one from the United States. The Finnish joint venture, Filco, was formed from Finland's largest construction company, Haka OY, and the city of St. Petersburg, to redevelop the site on the Moyka Canal that subsequently housed the South African and then the Netherlands Chancery.[137] So from the very beginning, the city of St. Petersburg was a partner in joint ventures with foreign companies. The city provided the site as its contribution to this unusual joint venture, relocating the communal apartment residents who were in it at the time.[138] Interviews I conducted suggest that during the construction, which was not completed until 1993, Sobchak and Putin used the building's courtyard to garage their Mercedes, rumored to have been gifts from the Chechen security for the new Mercedes dealership established in St. Petersburg in 1994. When Western officials called the mayor's office to inquire where they had purchased the cars, Putin is said to have immediately stopped driving his Mercedes, but not Sobchak. At this time Boris Berezovskiy and Badri Patarkatsishvili were working together in Logovaz, which involved the importing of used German cars and had proven to be extremely lucrative in St. Petersburg, where they stated that Putin provided them with *krysha* (a roof).[139] Berezovskiy later reported that Putin had neither demanded nor accepted a bribe,[140] which is at odds with the otherwise unsubstantiated story relayed by Western officials.

‡ Also members of the original ownership team of Bank Rossiya were Mikhayl Markov and Yuriy Nikolayev.[141] Matthias Warnig became a member of the board of directors in 2012, and some have suggested that he too was an early shareholder.[142]

Putin, in 1995. Bank Rossiya became the primary funding vehicle (into which city funds for new companies approved by Putin were channeled) for Putin's Committee for Foreign Liaison when the city became a cofounder of enterprises.[144]

Koval'chuk remained a major shareholder throughout the history of the bank, owning about 30 percent.[145] He would become a cofounder of the Ozero Cooperative, which established a common bank account for its members, one of whom was Putin. Also among those close to Putin who were involved in Bank Rossiya were Nikolay Shamalov and Dmitriy Gorelov, who consistently held about 10 percent each of Bank Rossiya shares, and Viktor Myachin, another original shareholder. At the beginning of 1992, in addition to individual shareholders, a number of other joint ventures also held shares, but given that these joint ventures were themselves owned, according to Pribylovskiy,[146] by Ozero members connected to Putin, the ownership of Bank Rossiya stayed within a tight circle.* Subsequently another of Putin's close circle, Gennadiy Timchenko, would invest in Bank Rossiya; by 2013 he was listed as owning 8 percent of the shares, and Gazprom 16 percent.[147]

Putin benefited directly from Bank Rossiya early on, when a film about him was funded by the bank in 1992. The documentary filmmaker Igor Shadkhan recounts that he was called in to Putin's office in 1992 to make a series called *Vlast'* (Power) on St. Petersburg's new government, and which would include one whole episode on Putin. Shadkhan ended up making only one forty-five-minute show, the one about Putin, portraying him as smart, savvy, trustworthy, and having a KGB background. In his autobiography, *First Person*, Putin admitted that he used Shadkhan's film to reveal his KGB past so that he wouldn't be blackmailed for it.[148] Shad-

---

*NPP Quark (18.27 percent; Vladimir Yakunin, Yuriy Koval'chuk, Mikhayl Markov, Viktor Myachin, Andrey Fursenko, Sergey Fursenko, Yuriy Nikolayev). In September 1992 NPP Quark changed its name to Stream Corporation. JSC Bikfin (15.87 percent; Mikhayl Markov, Vladimir Yakunin, Sergey Fursenko). JV JSC Agency for Technical Development (11.3 percent; Viktor Myachin). JSC TEMP (7 percent; Sergey Fursenko, Vladimir Yakunin, Mikhayl Markov). JV CJSC Bikar (5.61 percent; Vladimir Yakunin, Sergey Fursenko).

khan, whose previous well-regarded works were on the gulag, admits that Putin "recruited" him.[149] The piece opened with the haunting and popular theme from Putin's favorite Soviet TV series, *Seventeen Moments of Spring*, a series that continues to have enormous resonance for Putin and for Russians nostalgic for the Soviet era.* In the film Putin says that totalitarianism isn't something that can be imposed from above—it's "embedded in our own people's mentality." The filmmaker subsequently said he would like to ask Putin who is to "blame for the resurrection of the authoritarian regime—the people?"[150] Putin's effort to shine a favorable PR light on his background, and to use Bank Rossiya money to do it, indicates his early ambition for a bright political future and his methods.

Bank Rossiya was not, however, just a vehicle for investment by members of what would become Putin's Ozero circle. It was also one of the many places where this circle came in contact with, and collaborated with, Russian organized crime. Marina Litvinovich, a Kremlin spin doctor turned whistleblower, provided the following detailed account of this tangled web, from which she concluded that 18.6 percent of the original shares in Bank Rossiya were owned by Gennadiy Petrov:

> In 1992, Quark NPP, Bikfin CHC and other companies owned by the Fursenko brothers, Yuriy Koval'chuk, Mikhayl Markov, Vladimir Yakunin and Viktor Myachin, became shareholders of Bank Rossiya. Their partner in the Bank was mob boss Gennadiy Petrov (arrested by Spanish police in 2008 as head of the Tambov-Malyshev crime group). Petrov is Vladimir Kumarin's neighbor; earlier Petrov was one of the actual shareholders of Petersburg Fuel Company. Petrov used to be partners with Sergey Kuzmin, whom Petrov met in a Soviet prison where both were serving criminal sentences. The company was represented by Bank Rossiya's board of directors member Andrey Shumkov. Shumkov, employed at Ergen company and Fuel Investment Company (where Kuzmin and Petrov held shares), controlled

---

*The main theme can be heard at http://www.youtube.com/watch?v=cY5QtEw_VTc.

14.2% of the Bank's shares. Kuzmin and Petrov also personally held a 2.2% share each. Overall, companies affiliated with Gennady Petrov held 18.6% of the Bank.[151]

Novaya gazeta reported that investigations into Russian mafia corruption by Spanish police had concluded that 2.2 percent of the shares of Bank Rossiya were held by Gennadiy Petrov and Sergey Kuzmin directly, and 14.2 percent belonged to three St. Petersburg companies Ergen, Forward Limited, and Fuel Investment Co., associated with Andrey Shumkov, Kuzmin, and Petrov.[152] All were involved in various activities in St. Petersburg associated with Russian organized crime in the 1990s and were part of the investigation and arrests made by Spanish police as part of Operation Troika in the 2000s.

Another connection between Putin and Bank Rossiya was through the trio who headed up St. Petersburg's oil refinery in Kirishi in the late 1980s: Andrey Katkov, Yevgeniy Malov, and Gennadiy Timchenko. They were the original owners of Kinex, short for Kirishineftekhimexport (Kirishi Petroleum Chemical Export). Putin gave them preferential treatment during the so-called food crisis in 1991, when he signed contracts allowing them to export oil at depressed domestic prices from St. Petersburg's Kirishi refinery in exchange for food that the Sal'ye Commission concluded never arrived. Katkov and Malov each owned 3.17 percent of Bank Rossiya's shares.

Timchenko had a long-standing personal relationship with Putin. He not only became a shareholder of Bank Rossiya but established and was the co-owner of Gunvor, a global commodity trading company. The announcement of the U.S. government sanctions directly linked Putin and Timchenko: "Timchenko is one of the founders of Gunvor, one of the world's largest independent commodity trading companies involved in the oil and energy markets. Timchenko's activities in the energy sector have been directly linked to Putin. *Putin has investments in Gunvor and may have access to Gunvor funds*" (italics added).[153]

Timchenko's stake in Bank Rossiya grew over time. In 2010 he was revealed to have a 7 percent share.[154] Also disclosed at that time was the fact that the cellist Sergey Roldugin, who provided many adulatory quotes about Putin in *First Person* and who is the godfather of Putin's elder daughter, owns 3.9 percent of the bank.[155]

Doing the day-to-day work at Bank Rossiya at its inception was its founding CEO, Arkadiy Krutikhin, and his deputy, Vladislav Reznik.* Both were also associated with the insurance company Rus', and Reznik had also been deputy director general of Russkoye Video. Krutikhin told the *New York Times* in October 1990 that the bank would start with a capital base of 3 million rubles ($1.83 million) and would finance restoration projects in Leningrad.[156] Aleksandrov and Reznik would rise to become Duma representatives and founding members of United Russia, as previously mentioned. Reznik was the main sponsor of a 2006 bill on preventing money laundering. This activity occurred before he was investigated by Spanish authorities, according to a U.S. cable leaked by Wikileaks, for ties to the Tambov crime family and Gennadiy Petrov, described in the cable as the leader of "one of the four largest OC [organized crime] networks in the world." Spanish government officials evidently raided Reznik's and Petrov's houses in Spain,[157] having intercepted what the Spanish conservative daily *ABC*, as repeated in Wikileaks, called "hundreds" of phone calls that would "make your hair stand on end" for their revelations about Petrov's "immense power and political connections, as well as the range of criminal activity in Russia that the Troika defendants directed from Spain. . . . Troika mafia leaders invoked the names of senior GOR [government of Russia] officials to assure partners that their illicit deals would proceed as planned."[158] Spanish investigators said the entire operation started in 1990 with the purchase for 15 million euros of the Palmira Beach Hotel in Peguera, Majorca, by Petrov with Leningrad Communist Party and KGB funds. According to the investigators, having bought the hotel, Petrov was able to host St. Petersburg notables, including the city's new mayor, Anatoliy Sobchak, Putin's boss.[159] Reznik's name would be found on numerous documents showing that

---

*Krutikhin was followed as CEO by Vitaliy Savel'ev (1993–95), Viktor Myachin (1995–98, 1999–2004), Mikhayl Markov (1998–99), Mikhayl Klishin (2004–6), and Dmitriy Lebedev (2006–).

he and his wife* were co-owners of various companies with both Petrov and Aleksandr Malyshev, also arrested on suspicion of money laundering, tax evasion, and the establishment of a criminal structure that traded in contraband, arms trafficking, and murder, and which, according to Spanish authorities, could be traced back to St. Petersburg and the monopoly position given by the St. Petersburg government to the Tambov criminal organization in the supply of gasoline in the 1990s.[160]

The bank not only united elites close to Putin; it became a vehicle for investment in the Russian economy. By 2005 it had gained 51 percent control over SOGAZ (Gas Industry Insurance Company), one of the largest insurance companies, which had belonged initially to Gazprom. A report on corruption by key members of the Russian opposition, including those with past ministerial positions in the energy industry, claimed that Bank Rossiya received these shares for $58 million, despite their estimated value of $2 billion.[161] The company has provided insurance for all of Gazprom's major schemes, including all its pipeline and exploration projects. SOGAZ is controlled through Abros, a subsidiary of Bank Rossiya. Kirill Koval'chuk, the nephew of Yuriy Koval'chuk, is on the board of directors of Abros. Abros was one of the companies sanctioned in the second round of U.S. Treasury sanctions in April 2014.[162]

By the time the White House sanctioned Bank Rossiya, it had become the seventeenth-largest bank in Russia, with over $10 billion in assets, including U.S. dollar accounts with U.S. and European institutions that would be frozen as a result of the sanctions. Putin responded by announcing that he would henceforth open a ruble-only account with them and would make them the primary bank in the newly annexed Crimea as well as giving them the right to service payments on Russia's $36 billion wholesale electricity market—assuring the bank $112 million annually from commission charges alone.[163] Clearly he would do what he could to make sure that the financial well-being of this inner core would not suffer. After all, their loyalty to each other began in the very early 1990s.

---

*Diana Gindin, the Russian American Swiss banker, at that time the president of the First Boston Bank in Russia and representative in Spain of Credit Suisse, according to *El País*.

The Establishment of Putin's Security Circle: The *Siloviki*

Putin's experience put him in touch with a close group of security service personnel with whom he had studied, trained, or served in Leningrad and abroad. They would form the backbone of his personal security team as he rose through the ranks.

Sergey Ivanov, Nikolay Patrushev, Aleksandr Grigor'yev, Vladimir Strzhelkovskiy, and Viktor Cherkesov were all contemporaries of Putin in the Leningrad KGB in the 1980s. Of this group, Patrushev and Ivanov have remained the closest to him. Patrushev has headed Russia's Security Council since 2008, and Ivanov has been Putin's chief of staff in the Presidential Administration, a position that singled him out for inclusion on the White House sanctions list.

Grigor'yev was close to Putin from an early age; they studied together at university,[164] and the two are pictured together in *First Person*. Grigor'yev graduated from the KGB's Higher School in 1975 and went on to serve with Viktor Ivanov in Afghanistan (1983–85) and then under Cherkesov in the St. Petersburg security services in the mid-1990s. He received awards for his "service to the Orthodox Church" and was named to the advisory board of the Center for the National Glory of Russia, a project that united Putin's inner circle of *siloviki*, including Yakunin, Viktor Ivanov, Sergey Ivanov, Cherkesov, and Chemezov.[165] Sergey Ivanov and Putin both graduated from Leningrad State University in 1975, but from different departments and, according to Ivanov, did not know each other then. However, they became acquainted in 1976 when they received specialized training in the Leningrad region's counterintelligence department of the KGB from "experienced intelligence officers" who had worked as "sleeper agents" (i.e., illegals) abroad and were their Teachers "with a capital letter."[166] Patrushev had been slightly ahead of them at university; he was in the Leningrad counterintelligence section of the KGB in 1975 and had risen to become the region's chief for combating contraband and corruption.

All had careers that have flourished under Putin. In 1998 Putin, who was then director of the FSB, appointed Sergey Ivanov as one of his deputy directors.[167] Patrushev preceded Putin to Moscow and there became chief of the Federal Counter-Intelligence Service Directorate of Internal Security, and in 1998 followed Putin as chief of the GKU, the Control Directorate of the Presidential Staff, and then deputy chief of the Presidential Staff. He moved over to the FSB the same year, rising to become director in 1999, replacing Putin, and then becoming secretary of the Security Council in 2008. Strzhelkovskiy, who never rose to the level of political importance the other Putin-connected *siloviki* achieved, worked in the Leningrad KGB from 1980 to 1991, rising to the rank of lieutenant colonel. In November 1990 he created the travel agency Neva, which became the official travel agency of the St. Petersburg administration. When Putin was named prime minister in 1999, he named Strzhelkovskiy deputy minister in charge of physical training, sports, and tourism, and after 2000 he became the deputy minister of economic development and trade and head of its State Tourism Committee.[168] In 2008 this "longtime friend" of Putin was named CEO of the privately held mining company Norilsk Nickel, the world's largest producer of nickel and palladium. He had the support not only of Putin but also of one of the three major shareholders, the billionaire Vladimir Potanin. He was appointed over the objections of other oligarch board members and major shareholders, including Oleg Deripaska, who cited his lack of managerial and metals industry experience.[169] When he eventually resigned in 2012 with a $100 million cash golden parachute, the *New York Times* summarized the significance of the unprecedentedly large payout by noting that "it is likely to be remembered most as another data point in the shift of corporate wealth and influence away from the first generation of former Soviet businessmen—known as the oligarchs—and toward a coterie of well-connected former security service agents who made their mark under President Vladimir V. Putin." [170]

Some accounts claim that Putin met Cherkesov in the 1980s, when the latter was a top official in the Leningrad KGB.[171] Cherkesov graduated from Leningrad State University's Law School in 1973, two years earlier than Putin. He was the director of the St. Petersburg FSB from 1992 to 1998, and apparently he and Putin were friends there, even going to the bathhouse together.[172] Cherkesov in particular was reviled by the democratic opposition as someone who was actively and personally involved in the suppression and interrogation of dissidents in Leningrad in the 1970s and 1980s. He was infamous in St. Petersburg as the last KGB officer to arrest anyone (under Article 70) for political crimes, the future Yabloko Party Duma deputy Yuliy Rybakov. The case was closed by Gorbachev, who in 1991 rehabilitated all the Leningrad intellectuals who had been repressed under the harsh regime imposed in that city by Cherkesov and others in the local office of the KGB's Fifth Main Directorate.[173] It was a cruel irony, therefore, when in 1992, only months after the collapse of the USSR, Cherkesov was appointed head of the Ministry of Security (the successor to the KGB and precursor to the FSB) in St. Petersburg over the protests of horrified democratic activists and lawmakers in the city. He followed Putin to Moscow, becoming one of his deputies at the FSB and moving into other top federal positions under Putin's protection. Putin's appointment of Cherkesov as his deputy at the FSB prompted a group of human rights campaigners, including Yelena Bonner (the widow of the nuclear physicist and dissident Andrey Sakharov and a human rights activist in her own right), to write an open letter warning, "Under Putin, we see a new stage in the introduction of modernized Stalinism."[174]

This clarion call from Russian activists went unheeded, and the *siloviki* continued to gain influence. Grigor'yev was Cherkesov's deputy at the FSB until 2001, when the two had a falling-out, allegedly over how many of the contract murders in St. Petersburg should be blamed on the Tambov crime family and how many on Yuriy Shutov (an early assistant in Sobchak's administration who was fired after accusing the mayor's office of being mired in corruption). Cherkesov wanted to lay the blame exclusively on Shutov, and Grigor'yev is said to have wanted to go after Tambov, in particular Aleksandr Malyshev and Vladimir Kumarin. Grigor'yev also contended that Cherkesov had appointed two officials with known connections to Tambov, according to *Segodnya*.[175] Patrushev, who by 2001 was director of the FSB, announced Grigor'yev's resignation "due to the transition to other work."[176] The incident underlined the tensions between the FSB and their colleagues in the organized crime world. Grigor'yev went

on to become head of the Agency for State Reserves, Gosrezerv, responsible for maintaining state reserves of raw materials to prevent the kind of
chronic shortages of foodstuffs, oil and gas, medicines, and other hard-
currency exports that had become dangerously low in the early 1990s.
Fiona Hill and Clifford Gaddy of the Brookings Institution are right to
underline the importance to Putin and his team of this unique agency and
his circle's control over it, since it gave them the ability to dispense favors
via the selected "release" of raw materials from the strategic reserves for
sale abroad.[177]

Yevgeniy Murov and Viktor Zolotov have been critical to Putin's personal security since the 1990s. With the former Ministry of Interior officer
Roman Tsepov, Zolotov cofounded a security company called Baltik-Eskort
(License No. 020004)[178] in St. Petersburg in 1992, which provided security
for both Sobchak's family and Putin. Zolotov had been in the Ninth Chief
Directorate of the KGB (which provided bodyguards to the Soviet elite)
and was photographed next to Yel'tsin when the latter spoke atop a tank
during the attempted August 1991 coup.[179] As an officer like Putin in the
KGB's active reserves, he was able to establish and run a private security
agency while receiving KGB cover and support. As mayor Sobchak had the
right to Federal Protection Service (FSO) security, yet even though Zolotov
was an officer in the FSO, his family did not have that right, and neither
did Putin or his family. They therefore employed the services of Baltik-
Eskort, where Zolotov also happened to work "on the side."[180]

Zolotov had worked for General Yevgeniy Murov, who had served in the
First Chief Directorate of the KGB (foreign intelligence) in Southeast Asia
during the Soviet period. Murov served in 1997–98 as deputy director of
the FSB in St. Petersburg and Leningrad *oblast'*. From 1998 to 2000 he was
first deputy head of the Department for Economic Security of the central
FSB.[181] On May 18, 2000, Putin named Murov director of the FSO, the
agency that provides overall security for political leaders.[182] He remained in
this position until at least 2014. He was put on the 2014 U.S. sanctions list.
From 1992 to 2000 Zolotov served in the St. Petersburg FSB, including as
deputy chief of their Department of Economic Security. He was reputed
to be one of Putin's sparring partners in boxing and judo and provided

him with personal security. Zolotov followed Putin to Moscow and became head of the Presidential Security Service in 2000, where he was elevated to lead what has essentially become a Praetorian Guard to protect Putin and his regime.[183] He was added to the U.S. government visa ban and asset seizure list in April 2014.[184]

Connected with Zolotov and Putin was Roman Tsepov, who was reputed to have been closely involved in running Putin's tribute system while in St. Petersburg. Investigator Andrey Zykov stated in 2012 that in the 1990s "Putin had become the main person involved in many criminal cases, as he participated in the criminal privatization, in particular of BMW; Baltic Shipping Company, helping to arrange the sale of Russian ships at low prices; with all the actions carried out by the criminal authority Traber;* purchasing the alcohol distillery 'San Trust' through the criminal authority Misha Kutaisi [real name Mikhayl Mirilashvili]; and even the privatization of the Hotel Astoria" in St. Petersburg, about which Zykov made the following claim based on the results of the police investigation: "In the autumn of 1998, in St. Petersburg a tender was held for the sale of a 40% stake of the hotel Astoria. Putin had tried to increase his own stake in the company which owns the hotel,† in order to win the tender. But he did not succeed. The tender was awarded to the manager of the plant for the production of alcoholic beverages, [Aleksandr] Sabadash. Putin threatened that he will crush the plant and finish its chief. At the end of 1998, the parties reached a compromise—Sabadash paid Putin compensation of about

---

*For his part Il'ya Traber maintains that his success was due to his close and legitimate connections with political figures. He stated in an interview that when he established his antiquarian business in St. Petersburg, he decided, "Antiques—this is the kind of business that should be a merger of state power and the money of honest businessmen. The system is simple—we create a joint venture with the city—33% belongs to City Hall, the remaining 67% to me and my staff. But no one wants to play by these rules. Because then you cannot steal." On the occasion of Sobchak's inauguration as mayor, he presented him with a bust of Catherine the Great.[185] Traber's business interests expanded in the 1990s to include a significant role in developing the St. Petersburg port. *Novaya gazeta* also reported that he had been named as communicating with Petrov and Reznik while they were in Spain.[186]

†This sensational charge by Zykov, who had access to official documents, is not found elsewhere, and it has not been possible to substantiate it further.

$800,000." [187]* Peter Reddaway provides the following detailed description of Tsepov and Baltik-Eskort:

> While Tsepov's company charged Putin only a nominal $400–500 a month for guarding him, he had Tsepov collect tribute from city businesses for the use of the city's Committee [for Foreign Liaison], which Putin headed. He also had Tsepov take part in major commercial operations like the privatization of the Baltic Shipping Company. In addition, he helped Baltik-Eskort to become the biggest security agency in St. Petersburg. It expanded its remarkably efficient business to include the supply of enforcement services and the transportation of the cash needed for illegal deals. Also, Tsepov was allowed to become a nominal officer of the MVD's unit for combating organized crime (RUBOP),[†] to wear the insignia of various security agencies, and to display a special VIP pass on his car.[189]

Tsepov himself admitted that he started working as Putin's bodyguard only after the privatization process at the Baltic Shipping Company had produced several killings and threats to Putin's life. As a result, he was asked by the city to enter into a contract for "the maintenance of public order in places of stay of V. V. Putin."[190‡]

Both Zolotov and Tsepov had been supporters of the conservatives in the failed coup against Gorbachev, and Tsepov apparently sought to go to the

---

*Aleksandr Sabadash became the owner not only of the distillery (producing both Smirnoff and Russian Standard vodkas in Russia) but also of Vyborg pulp and paper mill. In 2003 he was appointed a representative of the Nenetsk Autonomous Region in the Federation Council, a position from which he resigned in 2006.

† The Regional Directorate for Combating Organized Crime (Regional'noye Upravleniye po Bor'be s Organizovannoy Prestupnost'yu, RUBOP) was a division of the Ministry of Internal Affairs created to suppress organized crime in 1988, reorganized in 2001, and finally disbanded in 2008. During its twenty years of existence it was tasked with fighting drug and arms trafficking and corruption. In the 2000s Putin used it increasingly to fight terrorism and "extremism." Throughout the 1990s it was widely considered in the Russian press to be "acting on behalf of the highest bidder in political and business disputes."[188]

‡ Western intelligence agencies were said to have even investigated the 1993 car accident in which Lyudmila Putina was seriously injured as a misplaced attempt on her husband's life.

defense of the Supreme Soviet when Yel'tsin attacked the White House in 1993.[191] Leonid Nikitinskiy's research suggests that while Zolotov provided the muscle for Putin and the mayor's office, Tsepov had "the more difficult part of the job: construction of the balance and the spheres of influence between Petersburg representatives of the Central Government, the power structure, the Mayor's Office, business (which in those years was seldom transparent) and outright criminal structures. There is evidence that Baltik-Eskort provided high security transportation for the 'black cash' [*chyornyy nal*] needed for such operations."[192] Other sources also talk about Baltik-Eskort's role in St. Petersburg; one source stated that "Baltik-Eskort prior to 1996 actively worked with the mayor's office to fulfill orders that could not be put in the hands of official law enforcement agencies, including relations with many foreign business partners."[193] Baltik-Eskort's offices were reportedly subjected to over thirty searches by various federal regulatory bodies, all to no avail; Tsepov, according to Andrey Konstantinov, was the subject of several murder plots.[194]

All this supports the argument not just about the level of criminality in Petersburg at the time but also about the direct involvement of Putin and his circle. Tsepov stayed in St. Petersburg after Putin went to Moscow but continued to be subjected to assassination attempts and criminal investigations as late as 1999, when he was charged with large-scale extortion and inflicting grievous bodily harm, under Section 3 of Article 163 of the Russian Criminal Code.[195] But he was not convicted, due to what the press described as his "complicated relationship with law enforcement."[196]

Some reports allege that after Putin became president, Tsepov continued to be involved in the day-to-day running of the Kremlin's tribute system, in which the "administrative resources" of the Kremlin were provided to those who paid the largest tribute and presented the best prospect for providing stability of leadership for the Kremlin in various regions.[197] In other words, in this scheme, tribute payments to get on the electoral roll went to the highest state officials whose approval was necessary for anyone to be registered as a candidate. Once a person was accepted as the candidate, payments from the Kremlin's public funds were disbursed for the campaign. In this way governors were chosen who responded to central interests irrespective "of their success in promoting the welfare of the inhabitants of the region." [198] Days before Tsepov died, the newspaper *Russkiy Kur'er* wrote that he had operated a price list for promotion to governor that included charges of $3 million to $5 million to be included on the "presidential candidate list" (i.e., those candidates whom Putin would favor with visits to their regions, for example) and additional sums for "verbal praise in the presence of the President." [199]

Tsepov died as a result of a mysterious poisoning in 2004, said by some to be a "radioactive element," [200] and the local procurators opened a criminal investigation of murder. [201] The case was quickly closed, however, "in the absence of any suspects," despite the fact that many of the careful analyses of Tsepov's last weeks showed there was an abundance of suspects. [202] *Kommersant* speculated about who might have killed Tsepov:

> Despite the modest post of Director of a security company, Roman Tsepov was considered a highly influential businessman. His main influence was very broad, ranging from the pharmaceutical and security business to port, tourism, transport, insurance and even the media. According to sources in law enforcement, Roman Tsepov maintained close contacts with many security officials from Interior Minister Rashid Nurgaliyev to the head of the presidential guard Viktor Zolotov. They say that he was the entree to Deputy Chief of the Presidential Administration Igor Sechin and even to Vladimir Putin. The MVD's unit for combating organized crime (RUBOP) [203] claimed that Mr. Tsepov actively used his connections to lobby for the appointment of officers to the Ministry of Internal Affairs and FSB. This, incidentally, is why he was known in certain quarters as "The Producer." [204]

It was also reported that he overstepped his limits when he was commissioned by Sechin, Zolotov, and even Putin to "negotiate" with the embattled Yukos oil company executives, including Mikhayl Khodorkovskiy, during which he apparently demanded a place on the Yukos board along with Gennadiy Timchenko. The Russian commentator Yuliya Latynina stated on the radio station Ekho Moskvy on September 25, 2004, that when she was told this story, "I had the impression that Mr. Tsepov . . . didn't understand that this [deal] is for others, and that, in essence, these people didn't need a representative in the person of Mr. Tsepov."[205] The myriad stories about Tsepov's lists and how he overstepped his boundaries may well have been the Kremlin signaling to others that they should not similarly transgress.[206]

Irrespective of whether or not Tsepov exceeded his authority, his funeral provided an opportunity to observe the interlocking relationships between *siloviki* and mafia at the heart of the Putin regime. He was given a three-gun salute and buried next to the submariners who died in the *Kursk* accident, and mourners included numerous Interior Ministry officials, as well as Vladimir Kumarin (also called Vladimir Barsukov), the alleged head of the Tambov crime family; Aleksandr Sabadash, to whom Putin had given the monopoly on distilling vodka in the early years in Petersburg and who was now a member of the Federation Council (the upper house of Parliament); and the head of President Putin's FSO, General Viktor Zolotov.

Arkadi Vaksberg, a highly respected forensic and legal writer for *Literaturnaya gazeta*, who authored many books on the hidden secrets of the Stalin regime, wrote a book from his home in Paris on the renewed use of poisonous toxins in post-Soviet Russia. He had the following to say about Tsepov's death: "The circumstances surrounding his death . . . demanded some clarification. Things were complicated by the fact that the pathologist's finding and the autopsy report were never published and the history of the illness was classified. . . . [However] Tsepov's own doctor, Pyotr Perumov, leaked some details. The patient fell ill on the evening of September 11 [2004]. That morning he had drunk some tea in the office of one of the heads of the St. Petersburg office of the FSB. During the day he had a business lunch and later ate an ice cream that one of the agents had brought him. His state suddenly worsened with unusual symptoms appearing. The doctors could not explain what was happening and he asked them to get him ready for an air-lift to Germany where he also had a family doctor. But the problem could no longer be treated. It was affecting the brain. It later became known (unofficially of course) that Tsepov had died of colchicine poisoning. . . . Tsepov had been taking pills to prevent cardiac problems. . . . Quite likely someone had swapped the tablets. Or perhaps he was killed using an unknown poison based on heavy metal salts that introduce radioactive isotopes into the body. This is quite likely since they found a level of radiation in his body that was a million times the normal level! . . . Everyone agrees that for some very influential people their connection with Tsepov had become a source of embarrassment. His self-assurance and the amount of information he possessed had reached dangerous proportions. Everyone also realized that his killers were present at their victim's ceremonial funeral." [207]

Putin associates were key players in establishing business in Russia from the very earliest days, and their relationship with Putin has been richly rewarded. But others from the early Putin era have also made their mark during his subsequent terms, particularly those with whom he worked in the mayor's office as head of the Committee for Foreign Liaison and the group around the Ozero Cooperative. Putin's story is not just the story of cowboy capitalism. It is the story of how an extremely adept political figure was able to gather around himself a group of varied individuals who were devoted to Russia, to be sure, but also, and indeed even more so, to their personal survival and prosperity. It is the story of law enforcement's continuous efforts to stop the accruing of ill-gotten wealth by this group, and its ultimate failure.

Putin and His Circle in the St. Petersburg Mayor's Office

Putin began his political career in St. Petersburg in May 1990, as advisor to the City Council leader and then to Mayor Anatoliy Sobchak, and later as the deputy (and then first deputy) mayor under Sobchak. From June 28, 1991, to June 1996, he was also the chairman of the Committee for Foreign Liaison (KVS), responsible for encouraging, regulating, and licensing foreign investment in St. Petersburg and Russian investment through St. Petersburg abroad. This committee was uniquely positioned to regulate the movement of money, goods, and services into and out of Russia's largest trading city, whose ports and rail and pipeline terminals controlled 20 percent of all Russian imports and exports.

Sobchak himself was the most nationally visible of St. Petersburg's leaders; he had become prominent when he chaired the commission that investigated the deaths of nineteen peaceful demonstrators in Tbilisi, Georgia, when KGB and MVD troops put down demonstrations there. The commission assigned blame to top generals and implied that KGB provocateurs had infiltrated the crowd. So Sobchak's role as a preeminent democrat and someone who was reviled by KGB leaders was firmly established by 1990 and was reflected in their subsequent writings about him.[208]

When Putin went to work for Sobchak, he immediately began to gather around himself the core group of people who would work with him throughout the 1990s and into his presidency. They came from varied backgrounds in the KGB, the Main Intelligence Directorate (Glavnoye Razvedyvatel'noye Upravleniye, GRU), Komsomol, and legal and business circles. Among these, the inner core consisted of Dmitriy Medvedev, Igor Sechin, Viktor Zubkov, Viktor Ivanov, Aleksey Kudrin, German Gref, Sergey Naryshkin, Dmitriy Kozak, Aleksey Miller, Vladimir Kozhin, and Nikolay Shamalov. Medvedev would be president in 2008–12 and prime minister after 2012; Sechin and Miller eventually became chiefs of the state-owned companies used as two key instruments of Putin's foreign policy, oil and gas; Zubkov has stood astride the tax inspectorate as well as serving as prime minister for a time; Gref and Kudrin controlled the largest bank and the Ministry of Finance, respectively; and Ivanov, Kozak, Kozhin, Naryshkin, and Shamalov have served in various capacities. Of this group, Ivanov, Kozak, Kozhin, Naryshkin, and Sechin were targeted as part of the 2014 U.S. sanctions.

The newspaper *Vechernyy Leningrad* interviewed Putin about his responsibilities as the new chairman of the Committee for Foreign Liaison in August 1991, two weeks before the attempted coup. He already anticipated that his committee would have "a hard currency–economic department, an administration to service foreign representatives and registration chambers, and an administration for humanitarian connections." He called for eliminating restrictions on travel abroad but also underlined the importance of vetting would-be foreign investors and preventing Gorbachev's *kooperativy* (cooperatives) from having links with foreign investors without proper supervision: "Anarchy in this area is impermissible. Representation of the city's interests in the international arena must be centralized and meticulously prepared."[209]

In his role as deputy mayor he was responsible for oversight of all law enforcement, the Administrative Directorate of the city, the Hotel Directorate, the Justice Department, the Registration Chamber, and the Public Relations Directorate. He was also still in the KGB's active reserves until at least August 1991, and it seems clear that initially he was placed with Sobchak by the KGB, which was trying to monitor the emergence of democratic leaders—a fact that Sobchak himself was evidently aware of.[210] Interviews with foreigners who did business in Russia universally reported that if you wanted to get something done in the city, you worked through Putin, not Sobchak.

As a former KGB operative in East Germany, with dealings in East-West German economic relations, Putin had more experience than most Russians in foreign economic relations. And he started using those connections as soon as he returned to St. Petersburg from Dresden, when he helped Leningrad State University form a joint partnership with the city and Procter & Gamble. As the CEO of Procter & Gamble subsequently noted, "Years later, in 1999, in the course of preparing for a tax audit, we discovered that Vladimir Putin, who by then was prime minister of Russia and later became president, had signed the Joint Venture P&G USSR registration document while he was chairman of the Committee for Foreign Liaison."[211] So Putin helped establish the relationship while he was at the university but then expanded it to include the city when he started working at the mayor's office.

In the mayor's office, Putin dealt with literally thousands of foreign and native investors, from Coca-Cola to organized crime bosses. Because foreign exchange controls were draconian in the early 1990s, money could not go abroad without the approval of his KVS. Businesses that wanted to be established legally in St. Petersburg had to be licensed and registered, not least so that any profits could be taxed. The KVS became an early co-investor in numerous financial projects, buying shares in new companies, presumably with access to the Mayor's Contingency Fund, a virtual slush fund under Sobchak's control that his deputies presumably had access to in order, like in any city, to make the trains run on time. His activities came under scrutiny when money started to disappear abroad. To be sure, he was operating in an environment that was rife for exploitation by organized crime. A well-known Russian specialist on criminal activity in St. Petersburg estimated that the main areas for organized crime at the time were "bank speculation (shady transactions); fictitious real estate transactions; stealing and reselling cars; illegal export of non-ferrous metals; black-market transactions relating to humanitarian aid (bribing city functionaries for a wholesale purchase); production of and traffic in fake hard liquor; arms sales; and counterfeiting money."[212] These actions were evidently more significant financially than the usual mafia activities related to gambling, the sex trade, and narcotics.

Putin relied on his core group to aid him in his extensive efforts. Medvedev, who kept a desk outside Putin's office,[213] provided the KVS, and Putin, with legal counsel throughout. He also maintained a private practice, serving as a lawyer for clients that included the insurance company Rus', headed by Vladislav Reznik, the influential St. Petersburg businessman who has been a Duma deputy since the late 1990s. Medvedev is said to have been the cofounder and 50 percent shareholder of a company called Fintsel.[214]* The St. Petersburg procurators who were looking into Putin's own corruption evidently also gathered information on Medvedev, subsequently concluding, "According to a statement of the Audit Chamber

---

*Co-owners were believed to be Zakhar Smushkin (21.25 percent) and the brothers Boris (21.25 percent) and Mikhayl (7.5 percent) Zingarevich.[215] In April 1992 Fintsel founded and registered with Putin's committee the Ilim Pulp Enterprises, a Russian-Swedish joint venture and the biggest producer of pulp and paper in the country. By September 1994 Fintsel owned 40 percent of Ilim, along with the Swiss company Intertsez (40 percent), the Ust Ilim works (10 percent), and the Kotlasskiy Cellulose and Paper Combine (10 percent). Because Medvedev owned a 50 percent stake in Fintsel, most observers believe he acquired a 20 percent stake in Ilim Pulp. Medvedev worked as Ilim's legal director from 1994 to 1999.[216] It is not known how he acquired these stocks, which were worth approximately $80 million in 1999, when he claims he sold them.[217]

[Schyotnaya palata] of the Russian Federation, already in 1994, the humble clerk Medvedev owned 10% of Europe's largest pulp and paper mill. Even then he was a millionaire. And this was only Medvedev, Putin's advisor. Can you imagine what kind of money was already owned by his boss?"[218] Irrespective of the percentage, there is general agreement with Medvedev's own statements that he owned the shares but subsequently sold them when he entered public service.

Igor Sechin had worked abroad with Soviet forces in Mozambique before joining the sister cities department of the Leningrad KVS.* Sechin and Putin are said to have met in 1990 on an official visit to Brazil, where Sechin worked as Putin's translator. He started working with Putin in June 1991 as head of the administrative apparatus of KVS and went on to become one of the heads of the *silovik* faction in the Kremlin and deputy prime minister. Putin has always relied on Sechin as his personal adjutant. In 1993, when Putina had had a serious car accident and couldn't reach her husband, it was Sechin who was called to collect one of their daughters who was also in the car.[220] Putin would take Sechin with him when he went to Moscow in 1996, and Sechin has worked alongside him since then, advancing as Putin advanced. One cabinet minister is reputed to have said in 2004, "Sechin is not just Putin's sounding board, Sechin is part of his brain cells."[221]

Viktor Zubkov had been a state farm director and regional Party official in the Priozersk district northeast of Leningrad in the Soviet period.[222] As chair of the Priozersk Municipal Executive Committee in the early 1990s, he was said to have secured the land where the Ozero dachas for Putin and his circle were ultimately built.[223] He went on to become first deputy chairman of the Leningrad Oblast' Executive Committee of the CPSU as the USSR collapsed, an important position given its role as the incubator for Bank Rossiya. In January 1992 he joined the KVS as deputy chairman, with a special focus on agriculture; he stood side by side with Putin dur-

---

* According to Hill and Gaddy, Sechin worked for the GRU as a military interpreter in Mozambique and Angola but never worked for intelligence, despite his fantasies of doing so. Presidential Administration insiders told them that Putin made Sechin an "honorary" colonel as an "inside joke."[219]

ing the food scandal, in which tenders were provided for exporting Russian raw materials to barter for food that never arrived.[224] Having survived this scandal, from November 1993 to November 1998 he was chief of the St. Petersburg Department of State Tax Inspection and simultaneously deputy chairman of state tax inspection for the city. He was well placed to shape the policy that emerged in the early 1990s of using tax inspections as a vehicle to push unwelcome competition from the Russian market, as occurred when the Swedish owners of the Grand Hotel Europa were forced to withdraw from the city.[225] Zubkov would later be prime minister under Putin and chairman of the board of directors of Gazprom.

Viktor Ivanov also had a background in the KGB, beginning in 1977 with unknown assignments for the first seven years, then serving for a year in Afghanistan and then in Leningrad/St. Petersburg from 1988 to 1994, where he headed the local KGB's anticontraband unit. It was reported that on Putin's recommendation, Ivanov was hired to head the administrative staff at the mayor's office as well as heading the city hall office in charge of liaison with police and security agencies. When Sobchak lost reelection in 1996, Ivanov worked locally in Petersburg for two years, and in 1998, when Putin became head of the FSB, Ivanov became head of the department for internal security at the FSB and then in 2000 became the deputy head of the Presidential Staff responsible for all personnel. He has a reputation for being "authoritarian" both in his personal style and in his philosophical outlook.[226] In the Kremlin he was widely associated with the most authoritarian group, coalescing around Sechin, whose position could not have been cemented without Putin's blessing and general philosophical alignment. As the veteran analyst Andrey Piontkovskiy commented, "It's no secret that Putin's political philosophy and favorite concepts—managed democracy, administrative vertical, dictatorship of law, a 'control' shot to the back of the head, etc.—are close to this group."[227]

Ivanov also has a reputation for closely controlling access to Putin and vetting all appointments for loyalty to the system's core objectives. In 2001 he was also appointed to represent the state interest on the boards of the Antey Corporation and Almaz Scientific Industrial Corporation (later merged to become Almaz-Antey and one of the country's largest arms exporters), developing and producing air defense systems, including the S-300 and S-400 antimissile systems. In 2008 he was made chief of the Federal Drug Control Service and a member of the Security Council.[228] His role as the gatekeeper to Putin since 1994 earned him a place on the U.S. government sanctions list.

Aleksey Kudrin was head of St. Petersburg's Committee for Economy and Finance until 1996. He was also a deputy mayor until 1996, when he moved to Moscow, becoming first deputy chief of the Presidential Administration, then deputy minister of finance under Yel'tsin, and then minister of finance and deputy prime minister in 2000, staying in the government until 2011.

Along with him rose another economist from Petersburg, German Gref, who served as deputy director of the city's Committee for Property Management before going to Moscow as first deputy minister of state property and then as minister of economic development and trade in the first Putin government. In 2007 he became the new president of Russia's largest bank, Sberbank. Both Gref and Kudrin appeared to be drawn to Putin less because of his KGB past than because of his embrace of liberal economic policies and his clear ability to move the paper and get things done in St. Petersburg at a time when most people were paralyzed by the "alegal" political situation and the total eruption of criminal activity at all levels.

Sergey Naryshkin was another native of Leningrad/St. Petersburg, who, according to Gazeta.ru, studied at the KGB Red Banner Institute in the same group as Putin.[229] He was attached to the Soviet Embassy in Brussels in the late 1980s and early 1990s as a third secretary, though some reports claim he was stationed there as a KGB officer.[230] Upon returning, he headed the foreign economic relations subdepartment of the Committee for Economy and Finance in the mayor's office. In 1995 he left to head the foreign investments department of the Promstroybank, owned by Vladimir Kogan, known at that time as Putin's personal banker, insofar as in the 1990s "Kogan was president of a bank in which Putin was a client and a shareholder."[231] A biography of Naryshkin in the *Moscow Times* notes, "The bank attracted major clients as multinational firms quickly learned that connections were key to winning privileged contracts in a city slow to adapt to the country's new capitalist spirit."[232] Naryshkin became chief of the Presidential Administration and speaker of the State Duma. Kogan stayed behind the scenes but continued to have a close relationship with Putin throughout his presidency. Describing this relationship, head of Moscow's Center for Political Information Aleksey Mukhin observed, "Since 2000, Kogan has been meeting regularly with Putin in the Kremlin. These meetings have not been publicized, but as a result of them Kogan has implemented various 'social projects.'"[233]*

Dmitriy Kozak graduated with a degree in law from Leningrad State University and served in the GRU from 1976 to 1978.[234] He was deputy head of the St. Petersburg City Hall's legal department in 1990–91 and subsequently headed that department. He stayed on in St. Petersburg, working in the office of Sobchak's rival and successor until 1999, when he went to Moscow to become head of the government staff when Putin was named prime minister. When Putin became president, Kozak was named deputy chief and then, in 2003, first deputy chief of the Presidential Administration. He has a reputation as a technocrat and as someone people want to work with—which is not something normally said of others in Putin's circle. He has had a number of substantive appointments: plenipotentiary to the Southern Federal District, regional development minister, and deputy prime minister in charge of the Sochi Olympics. In 2014 Putin gave his Ukrainian-born ally responsibility for the incorporation of the newly annexed Crimean Federal District's social, political, and economic institutions into Russia's.[235] In April 2014, he was added to the U.S. government's sanction list.[236]

Aleksey Miller, trained in Leningrad as an economist, replaced Aleksandr Anikin as Putin's deputy in the KVS, where he served from 1991 to 1996. When Putin went to Moscow, Miller stayed on in St. Petersburg, first as director for development in the Port of St. Petersburg and then as direc-

---

*A reference to the Kremlin's "invitation" to oligarchs to make charitable contributions to various worthy causes as a way of keeping in good stead with those authorities who are in a position to grant them state contracts.

tor general of the Baltic Pipeline System. He became deputy minister of energy and then head of Gazprom under Putin.

Vladimir Kozhin came up through Leningrad Komsomol circles and established an early Russian-Polish joint venture called Azimut International, evidently agreeing to bring in Putin's Committee for Foreign Liaison as a partner when it was registered.[237] He then worked for Putin as assistant to the deputy mayor and in March 1993 became the director general of the St. Petersburg Association of Joint Ventures, which had earlier secured the shares from the CPSU's Leningrad *oblast'* bank to create Bank Rossiya, and then transferred those shares to the Ozero Cooperative founders. From 1994 to 1999 he was the chief of the Northwestern Center of the Federal Directorate for Currency and Export Control of Russia. While he was there, according to *Novaya gazeta*, the office of the procurator in St. Petersburg started a criminal case against Kozhin under Articles 170 and 293 of the Criminal Code for buying a holiday in Bulgaria for himself and his wife from the tourist agency St. Petersburg Holidays, paid from the accounts of the Northwest Center. The newspaper reports that according to their information in 2001, this case was never closed.[238]*

Kozhin's ability to control the movement of money across borders made him a key part of what he called "Team President." He became the head of the Presidential Property Management Department under Putin in 2000 and has remained in that position ever since. All state-owned or -supervised property, including the Kremlin and all the official and unofficial residences of high government officials, including "Putin's Palace" in Gelenzhik, are under his authority. As such, Kozhin has been part of what he himself has described as "a small informal club of people who can be called team president in the narrow sense—who came in 1999–2000, from St. Petersburg, and who are now working in various capacities. We try to get together at least once a month, just to see each other, have a beer, play pool, and talk like a human being, without bringing up politics. We always emphasize

---

* The author of this article, Oleg Lur'ye, had a long career as an investigative journalist, working at the beginning of the Putin period at the opposition newspaper *Novaya gazeta*. This came to an abrupt end in 2008, when he was convicted in Moscow of extorting money from a politician in return for keeping a story about him from going to press.

that we are there not on the basis of the position we occupy, but on the basis of our relationship to each other. And as far as I can judge, for eight years, these relationships have not changed." [239] Kozhin's wife, Alla, was the Putin family dentist and was also close to them. [240] Kozhin admitted to having a close relationship with Gennadiy Timchenko for a long time, "when St. Petersburg was Leningrad, the country was different and he and I were both other people." [241]*

Nikolay Shamalov, who was originally trained as a dentist, worked for Putin's KVS in 1993–95 and became the representative of Siemens in Russia's northwest. He was a cofounder of the Ozero Cooperative and was listed as the legal owner of "Putin's Palace." [244] But before this, he and Putin had established a relationship through Petromed. *Kommersant* reported on November 21, 1992, that Putin himself, as deputy mayor of St. Petersburg, had "signed a decree authorizing the City's Finance Committee to transfer to Vneshekonombank loans and guarantees in the sum of 450 million rubles [$1.6 million] for the purchase in Germany of medical equipment for City Hospital No. 2. The sum was to be covered by a commensurate reduction in city expenditures." [245]

To carry out this project, Putin turned to a newly formed medical equipment company, Petromed. It was formed by Dmitriy Gorelov, who had studied with the future minister of health Yuriy Shevchenko at the Military Medical Academy in St. Petersburg, and Andrey Kolesnikov, a biophysicist from the Polytechnic Institute who had previously established a cooperative to manufacture medical devices for sale to the city's health department. But then Putin had a bigger idea: to import much larger amounts of equipment from abroad. Thus this small start-up co-op linked up with the city. Putin's Committee for Foreign Liaison got 51 percent of the shares; 10 percent went to the city's Committee on Health, and 39 percent to the newly

---

*The size of the Presidential Property Management Department grew exponentially under Putin, although figures vary. An investigation by *Sovershenno sekretno* in 2010 reported that in October 2000 the department employed over 120,000 people in its hundreds of state properties, including twenty-seven resorts for top officials, with an annual budget in 2001 of 4.6 billion rubles, a figure that grew to 60 billion by 2009. [242] The U.S. government, in its press release sanctioning Kozhin, stated that he had a staff of sixty thousand, over a hundred enterprises and institutions, including the Kremlin itself, and over four thousand vehicles. [243]

formed Center for International Cooperation, headed by Gorelov. In January 1992 the same team founded Petromed. Kolesnikov subsequently confirmed that the renovation of Hospital No. 2 was Petromed's first big project, involving 95 million Deutschmarks of imported equipment. On the German side was Siemens, and the representative of Siemens to the northwest region of Russia, including St. Petersburg, was Shamalov, who was hired by Putin in 1993.

The conflict of interest was massive. Kolesnikov subsequently described the working relationships: Gorelov was the director of Petromed, ordering medical equipment; Shamalov was the representative of Siemens, delivering the equipment; and Shamalov in particular was a good friend of Putin, with whom he went on to found the Ozero Cooperative. Kolesnikov said, "When Shamalov came to us with a proposal for Vladimir Vladimirovich, we understood that this was in reality a proposal directly from Vladimir Vladimirovich."[246] Gorelov believed that the relationship with Putin's KVS was beneficial because it provided the "roof" to protect against demands from organized crime. When Vladimir Yakovlev became governor of St. Petersburg (the mayor's position was changed to governor), the relationship between Petromed and the city soured, and Gorelov and Kolesnikov bought out the city's stake, making Petromed a closed company owned equally between the two of them. They became major shareholders in Bank Rossiya, purchased a stake in Vyborg Shipyards, and by the mid-2000s were included in the *Forbes* Russia list of the richest Russians. Kolesnikov continued to run Petromed but ultimately became a whistleblower against what he maintained was a massive diversion of funds by the Kremlin to build "Putin's Palace."[247]

Vladimir Churov claims to have worked for an experimental design bureau at Leningrad State University before joining Putin in the KVS, where he worked until 2003.[248] Marina Sal'ye, a leading democrat and deputy in both the St. Petersburg and Russian parliaments, stated that an investigation by the city legislature in 1990 concluded that Churov had worked for the KGB.[249] Clearly Putin and Sal'ye had diverging views of the value of a KGB background, and Putin continued to promote Churov. After working for the KVS, he became a member of the Duma for the Liberal Democratic Party of Russia, and led the Central Electoral Commission during the 2007–8 and 2011–12 successor operations that the Russian state insisted on calling elections.

Aleksandr Bastrykin had also been a classmate of Putin in the law faculty of Leningrad State University.[250] After 2011 he led the increasingly powerful Investigative Committee of the Procurator General's Office* when it became independent of the Procuracy, began reporting directly to Putin, and became a vehicle for many politically based cases,[251] including investigations that led to the arrests of Pussy Riot, Aleksey Navalnyy, and the leaders of the 2011–12 Bolotnaya demonstrations against electoral fraud. Bastrykin was accused of "unscrupulous borrowing" of large parts of a book on J. Edgar Hoover for his own 2004 book.[252] Navalnyy published evidence on his website of Bastrykin's ownership of property and a residence permit in the Czech Republic that led him to charge that "the man responsible for all investigations and the entire struggle against corruption is a swindler, a fraud and a foreign agent."[253] *Novaya gazeta* accused him of personally threatening the life of its deputy editor.[254] He was invited to give a lecture at the Sorbonne in 2013, but when he started speaking to a nearly empty hall about his medals, noble origins, and French wines, he was interrupted by questions about Greenpeace detentions, torture, his plagiarism, and political arrests. In a video posted online, one attendee can be heard loudly shouting in Russian, *"Vy prestupnik!"* (You're a criminal).[255]

Such is the quality of the group that Putin has gathered around him from his days in the St. Petersburg mayor's office. From these sketches it is easy to see why Viktor Ivanov, Sechin, Kozak, Kozhin, and Naryshkin were singled out by U.S. sanctions, and it is easy to imagine that others of this group could be added if relations between Russia and the United States were to deteriorate further.

---

*There was an Investigative Committee of the Procurator General's Office that became an independent agency reporting directly to the Kremlin as well as an Investigative Committee of the Ministry of Internal Affairs.

The Rotenberg Brothers

Boris and Arkadiy Rotenberg grew up with Putin and have known him longer than perhaps anyone else from his inner circle.[256] Both were placed on the U.S. sanctions list, not because they are government officials but for "acting for or on behalf of or materially assisting, sponsoring, or providing financial, material, or technological support for, or goods or services to or in support of a senior official of the Government of the Russian Federation"[257]—a clear reference to Putin. They admit to running around together on the rough streets of Leningrad in their teenage years and sparring together as judo partners. When Putin became president, their businesses seemed to flourish. Speculating on the impact of knowing Putin, Arkadiy, who studied at the Leningrad Institute of Physical Culture, told the *Financial Times*, "Friendship never hurt anyone. But I have great respect for this person and I consider that this is a person sent to our country from God. He does a great deal for Russia. Therefore, you can't just go to him and ask for something. . . . Firstly, this is not my style and secondly, he wouldn't even let me through the door. When we meet, we are training—

Putin and Arkadiy Rotenberg at funeral of their judo trainer, August 2013. Photo by Sasha Mordovets, Getty Images

now we play ice hockey—or we are speaking about sport and remembering the days when we did sport. . . . He is a great person and I really do value these relations more than anything else. For me, friendship with this person is most of all a responsibility."[258] Boris also sparred with Putin as a teen and remained close.

The brothers worked together to gain access to Gazprom subsidiaries and emerged as major figures in pipeline construction and drilling, as well as road construction. They are the main owners of the Severnyy Morskoy Put' (Northern Sea Route) Bank.[259] In addition, they received from Gazprom many of the intermediate companies that purchase gas pipes and sell them to Gazprom. In other words, they acted as middlemen producing neither the pipes nor the gas but simply sold one to the other—a situation that led Bill Browder of Hermitage Capital Management (which had $3.5 billion in Western investments in Gazprom) to express concern as early as 2005 that these intermediary companies were driving up prices, diminishing profits to Gazprom (which is a publicly traded company in the West, with billions of dollars of Western investments from pension funds alone), and receiving unfair preferences.[260] The U.S. Treasury Department announced that between the two of them, the brothers had received approximately $7 billion in contracts for the 2014 Sochi Olympics,[261] or more than the total cost of the Vancouver Winter Olympics. According to Boris Nemtsov, a political opponent of Putin, the Rotenbergs' twenty-one no-bid contracts accounted for 15 percent of the total budget for the Sochi Games.[262] They were both in the 2013 annual *Forbes* Russia list of billionaires,[263] their personal wealth increasing by $2.5 billion in the past two years alone. Both have remained in touch with Putin through their sponsorship of the premier judo club in Russia, the Yawara-Neva Judo Club in St. Petersburg, where Putin is the honorary president, and through work with the Russian Judo Federation. In defending his close personal relationship with the president and the cost of the Sochi Games, Arkadiy stated that those projects were "big, difficult, and responsible projects that had to be completed within tight schedules. . . . Unlike my friends, I am not entitled to make a mistake, because it is not only a question of my reputation. . . . Vladimir Vladimirovich does not protect me. If I were to involve myself not in business but in some other practices, he would not say: 'He must not be touched, he is a good guy!' "[264] Hill and Gaddy observe, "In other words, in Rotenberg's and Putin's views of how the crony oligarch system works, it is not 'corruption' when your friends get lucrative contracts *if* they get the job done. . . . From Vladimir Putin's perspective, the reason you give the contracts to your friends, the crony oligarchs, is because you can make them understand that very crucial point."[265]

The Pièce de Résistance: The Ozero Dacha Consumer Cooperative

Putin and his circle started to gain power and privilege from the moment Bank Rossiya was established and Putin became head of the Committee for Foreign Liaison. Five years later, when Anatoliy Sobchak lost his 1996 bid to be reelected St. Petersburg's mayor, outsiders may have believed that the efforts of this group to dominate St. Petersburg politics had been wasted. Sobchak and Putin would once again be under investigation by federal and local authorities, and Sobchak would soon flee abroad. Surely it would be the end of the road for Putin and his team too. But nothing could have been further from the truth. Putin almost immediately received a top job in Moscow, from where he continued to exert influence in Petersburg. Several of his group moved to Moscow with him, though many stayed to shape events in their home city. But without access to the Mayor's Contingency Fund, how were investments going to be shared, and what would be the mechanism for bringing together the tribute system that had been established by political and economic elites around the future president? One of the answers was the Ozero Dacha Cooperative Society. Three of its founders (Vladimir Yakunin, Yuriy Koval'chuk, and Andrey Fursenko) found themselves on the 2014 U.S. sanctions list that specifically mentioned their roles as cofounders with Putin of the cooperative. How did the Ozero Cooperative come about, and what has been its influence?

Putin had already acquired property on the banks of Lake Komsomol'skoye before Ozero was established. Investigator Andrey Zykov asserted publicly, "We investigated and found out that the Twentieth Trust corporation built a house for Vladimir Vladimirovich Putin on the shores of Lake Komsomol'skoye as well as a villa in Spain." [266] This is a reference to Putin's dacha on the site of the Ozero Cooperative. In 2012 Zykov reiterated his belief that based on the investigation of Twentieth Trust that he had participated in, Putin had used Trust money to pay for his Ozero dacha. Zykov also stated that "the person who bought the land, scared the local residents, burning down their little houses if they refused to sell them, was a St. Petersburg officer who turned out to be none other than Vladimir Vladimirovich Putin. . . . At the end of 1992, Putin bought two adjacent plots of land—3,302 by 3,484 square meters [.85 acre]. . . . A public official in 1992–3 could not afford to buy an apartment and a cottage unless there was 'excess' income. And Putin, of course, had that income. In the summer of 1996 on this site they completed a 2-storey villa, like a palace. This house was estimated at about $500,000." [267] When the house burned down in August 1996, Putin prevailed on the builders to rebuild it for free, as their installation of a faulty sauna had caused the fire in the first place: "When the firemen later analyzed the fire, they concluded that the sauna builders were to blame for everything—they hadn't put the stove in the banya properly. And if they were to blame they had to compensate us for the damage. . . . Everything was as it had been before the fire, and even better." [268] Zykov also claimed that the building of the houses in the gated community violated a law guaranteeing free access to protected shoreline, which he claims they had illegally privatized. [269]

No action was more symbolic of the intention of the group around Putin to support, promote, and fund his political ambitions and be supported by him in turn than the registration on November 10, 1996, of the Ozero Dacha Consumer Cooperative (Ozero Dachnyy Potrebitel'skiy Kooperativ). The legal document establishing the cooperative lists Vladimir Smirnov as its leader. Its other members, listed in the order they appear on the document, are Nikolay Shamalov, Vladimir Putin, Vladimir Yakunin, Yuriy Koval'chuk, Viktor Myachin, and Sergey Fursenko and his brother Andrey Fursenko. [270]

The group built a number of dachas, actually small mansions, next door

Founding Registration document of the Ozero Dacha Consumer Cooperative, with its founding members and bank account number listed. http://www.anticompromat.org/putin/ozero.html

to each other on the shores of Lake Komsomol'skoye in Priozersk District, northeast of St. Petersburg.[271] Critically they also established a cooperative association, with a bank account (Settlement Account No. 180461008)*

---

*The settlement account, or *raschetnyi schyot*, was introduced in the late Soviet period by organizations and cooperatives practicing *khozraschyot*, or economic self-sufficiency. They became standard with privatization. Soviet and then Russian law allowed such accounts to be used without restrictions for payment for wages, repairs, and capital purchases as required by the account

The Ozero Consumer Dacha Cooperative
Address: 643, 188760, Russia, Leningrad Oblast', Priozersk city,
    Lenin st. 34,68
Telephone 279 22058
Date of registration: November 10, 1996

Leader: Smirnov, Vladimir Alekseyevich

Members:
Smirnov, Vladimir Alekseyevich
Shamalov, Nikolay Terent'yevich
Putin, Vladimir Vladimirovich
Address: St. Petersburg, 2nd line, Vasil'yevskiy Oblast', 17, 24
Yakunin, Vladimir Ivanovich
Koval'chuk, Yuriy Valentinovich
Myachin, Viktor Evgen'yevich
Fursenko, Sergey Aleksandrovich
Fursenko, Andrey Aleksandrovich

Account No. 180461008
Leningrad Oblast' Bank
Type of Account: Settlement (Raschetnyy) Account
Date Opened: April 2, 1997

in Leningrad Oblast' Bank, where money could be deposited and used by all account holders, cooperatively, in accordance with the Russian law on cooperatives.* This group has stayed by Putin throughout his entire

---

holders. In the 1990 law governing cooperatives, all members have equal rights, and the cooperative may receive loans from banks.[272] The specific financial transactions of the Ozero Cooperative have never been explored, and details of transactions are unknown. However, by law, any of the members would be able to deposit and withdraw funds for his own use.

* The 1988 Law on Cooperatives legalized private economic cooperatives and allowed shares to be issued, free from state supervision, and the formation of joint ventures with foreign companies. Cooperatives were indistinguishable from private enterprises in Western countries.[273]

period in office, and they have all made hundreds of millions and even billions of dollars.[274] In Russia a cooperative arrangement is another way for Putin to avoid being given money directly, while enjoying the wealth shared among co-owners. Where Putin got the money to acquire the land and build the dacha within the settlement in the first place is disputed. Zykov claims that the Ministry of Internal Affairs had documentation proving Putin's money for the dacha came from the Mayor's Contingency Fund.[275]

This group of men around Putin promoted his interests, and in return he promoted theirs. The choice of Smirnov as the registered leader of the cooperative is most revealing; to quote from a paper by former Russian government officials who became Putin opposition members, Smirnov had long been "closely linked with the well-known 'mafia' businessman Vladimir Barsukov (Kumarin)."[276] Smirnov met Putin in 1990 in Germany when the first decisions were made to invest in St. Petersburg. He then headed one of the companies involved in the food scandal of the early 1990s that resulted in millions being stolen; he and Putin sat together on the board of the St. Petersburg Real Estate Holding Co. (SPAG) beginning in 1994, which the German police accused of laundering money for Russian and Columbian organized crime; and he signed over a monopoly position to the Petersburg Fuel Company, which he co-owned with Barsukov-Kumarin. And after all this, Putin not only joined him in the Ozero Cooperative, but when he became president he appointed Smirnov head of Tekhsnabeksport, one of the world's largest suppliers of nuclear goods and services to foreign governments, including Iran.[277]

Sergey Fursenko became head of Lentransgaz, which then became Gazprom Transgaz Sankt-Peterburg, one of Gazprom's largest subsidiaries, with an annual turnover of 50 billion rubles.[278] He also became chairman of the board of directors and president of St. Petersburg's premier soccer club, Zenit,[279] and president of the Russian Football Union, before being forced out after Russia's poor showing in the European Cup. Andrey Fursenko was appointed deputy minister, then first deputy minister, then acting minister of industry, science, and technology; after 2004 he became minister of education and science, with a federal budget of 800 billion rubles in 2011.[280]

Of all the members of Putin's inner circle, Andrey Fursenko is the only one to have risen through the ministerial ranks to become minister.

Vladimir Yakunin, who had been first secretary at the Soviet mission to the UN, a post normally reserved for KGB officers,[281] returned to St. Petersburg and in early 1991 went into the export business with Yuriy Koval'chuk, Andrey Fursenko, and Viktor Myachin, all of whom he had known from the Ioffe Institute, where he had served as head of the International Relations Department when they worked there.[282] Yakunin has said that he and the other members of the Ozero Cooperative visited Putin in his dacha before it burned down and put the idea of creating a cooperative to him.[283] When Putin went to work for the Presidential Property Management Department in Moscow, Yakunin became the federal representative for that office in the Northwest Region.[284] He moved on to become deputy minister of transportation in charge of the country's seaports in 2000 and then in 2005 became head of Russian Railways. In June 2013 Putin announced that $43 billion of stimulus money—controversially to be borrowed from Russia's pension fund—would be used to stimulate the economy, including $14 billion to build three infrastructure projects, two of them by Russian Railways.[285] This occurred over the objections of economic authorities such as Aleksey Kudrin, who questioned its financial basis as inflationary, unlikely to produce growth, and likely to undercut the country's pension system.[286] The Russian free media also forecast that such a move would only stimulate further corruption, particularly given the publication by the Russian press and the anticorruption crusader Aleksey Navalnyy of pictures and property maps of a massive marble-clad seventy-hectare compound they claimed was owned by Yakunin. Navalnyy bitterly criticized Yakunin's entry to the ranks of Russia's billionaires, given that, as the head of a state-owned firm, Yakunin is a salaried employee and nothing more. He lambasted the Kremlin for allowing this to happen: "In all other countries, the railways are used for movement, but we use them for stealing."[287]

Summary

So what is the significance of all these inner circles? Putin formed them, chose them, could have excluded some, could have set down different rules. Of course, in some circles, he was not the leading figure from the beginning. But he created an interlocking web of personal connections in which he was the linchpin. He wasn't the only strong person in these groups, but he was the only one who stood astride all of them. And they would be allowed to make money and come to power with him, and only because of him. This included members of organized crime circles, who roared out of the Soviet period fully prepared to benefit from and contribute to general lawlessness. Putin's approach was never to shut them out completely but rather to allow those who were willing to cooperate with him to thrive, as long as they recognized his authority and the authority of the "new nobility." In a 2008 article titled "Grease My Palm," the *Economist* outlined the essential truths of the Putin era that he set out to establish in St. Petersburg:

> The job of Russian law enforcers is to protect the interests of the state, personified by their particular boss, against the people. This psychology is particularly developed among former (and not so former) KGB members who have gained huge political and economic power in the country since Mr. Putin came to office. Indeed, the top ranks in the Federal Security Service (FSB) describe themselves as the country's new nobility—a class of people personally loyal to the monarch and entitled to an estate with people to serve them. As Russia's former Procurator General, who is now the Kremlin's representative in the north Caucasus, said in front of Mr. Putin: "We are the people of the sovereign." Thus they do not see a redistribution of property from private hands into their own as theft but as their right.[288]

By 2013 the *Forbes* Russia list of the wealthiest businessmen in Russia[289] was replete with friends of Putin, many of whom have been discussed in this chapter: Roman Abramovich (estimated to have a net worth of

$10.2 billion),* Vladimir Kogan ($.95 billion), Yuriy Koval'chuk ($1.1 bil-lion), Arkadiy Rotenberg ($3.3 billion), Boris Rotenberg ($1.4 billion), and Gennadiy Timchenko ($14.1 billion). Shamalov and Gorelov were both estimated to be worth $.5 billion. Among the *Forbes* Russia list of the total incomes of families of federal officials for 2012,[292] there are also many Putin friends: Sergey Chemezov ($.5 billion), Igor Shuvalov ($.4 billion), Vladislav Reznik ($.3 billion), and Viktor Ivanov ($.1 billion).

A third list from *Forbes* Russia[293] reveals the alleged annual compensa-tion, including payments made abroad, for state corporation managers in 2012: Aleksey Miller ($25 million), Igor Sechin ($25 million), German Gref ($15 million), Vladimir Strzhelkovskiy ($10 million), Nikolay Toka-rev ($5 million), and Vladimir Yakunin ($4 million). These figures do not include these officials' unofficial access to other resources of their compa-nies. Russia's *Finance* magazine in 2011[294] also listed Vladimir Smirnov's worth at $.6 billion and Pyotr Aven at $3.8 billion.

Vladimir Litvinenko was the rector of the Mining Institute from which Putin received a degree in 1996 after writing a dissertation that proposed increased state control. In 2004 he received shares in PhosAgro, one of the companies captured from the breakup of Khodorkovskiy's Yukos, in com-pensation for consulting work. The company's 2011 annual report listed Litvinenko's ownership stake as 10 percent, with a total capitalization of $5.23 billion. Litvinenko insisted that the arrangement "did not contra-dict any laws."[295] He served as the St. Petersburg chairman of Putin's 2000, 2004, and 2012 presidential campaigns. It was revealed that large sections of Putin's dissertation were plagiarized from other sources, though it has never been determined whether he was responsible for this plagiarism or whether the dissertation was written by others who included plagiarized

---

* Abramovich, regarded as one of the oligarchs under Yel'tsin, does not owe his start to the rela-tionship with Putin. However, he was certainly able to stay in the game as a result of throwing his lot in with Putin in the late 1990s. As a sign of his loyalty, he helped to fund the purchase for $50 million of Putin's first new presidential yacht, the *Olympia*, fundraising for which preceded Putin's being elected president.[290] He also became the source of the first funds that were diverted to the construction of "Putin's Palace" in Gelendzhik, according to Petromed's owner, Sergey Kolesnikov, although Abramovich has consistently claimed that he provided this money for the building of medical facilities.[291]

portions. Either way, Putin still received the *kandidat ekonomicheskikh nauk* degree (an advanced degree somewhere between a Western MA and a PhD), and Litvinenko's career certainly did not suffer.[296]

Putin's cellist friend became a multimillionaire, and the sons of his nephews and myriad other relatives became fabulously rich as well. In the meantime, Putin's own reported income remained meager while his life-style kept pace with the richest of the rich. The presidential security services were in charge of no fewer than five luxury yachts and speedboats, which an analytical study by opposition figures[297] estimated were worth not less than $110 million, excluding their full-time crews. The head of the state enterprise that managed all Russian commercial vessels, Dmitriy Skarga, admitted in open court in London that he was responsible for managing a "yacht which had been presented to Mr. Putin and was being managed by Unicom,"[298] the 100 percent state-owned subsidiary of the state-owned agency Sovcomflot, headed at that time by Presidential Aide Igor Shuvalov, who had amassed a fortune of $.4 billion by 2012.[299]

The study by opposition activists, three of whom, Vladimir Milov, Boris Nemtsov, and Vladimir Ryzhkov, had served in Yel'tsin's government, addi-tionally found that the Russian president and prime minister have access to twenty-six official residences—a number that expanded considerably after Putin came to power.[300] In addition Putin's Petersburg friends built palaces that had presidential offices available for his use. Shamalov's formal owner-ship of the palace in Gelendzhik did not conceal that it was in fact "Putin's Palace," given that it had the Russian state seal on the office chairs and over the main gate, its construction was supervised according to signed docu-ments by Kozhin's Presidential Property Management Department, it was guarded by Zolotov's Federal Protection Service, and federal budget funds were diverted for its construction.

Putin's relationship with his friends was one of reciprocity: he gave them access to the state's largesse in the form of supporting their raids on pri-vate businesses, providing their companies with no-bid state contracts, and allowing the courts to legalize their activities and criminalize those of their opponents. In return they supported his continuation in power; they became the bulwark of his base; they helped finance and secure his electoral victories; they didn't criticize him in public; they removed his enemies from the scene; and they paid him tribute. All this began in St. Petersburg in the early 1990s, when he started to promote his comrades from the Leningrad and Dresden KGB offices. "The basic point is that these guys have benefited and made their fortunes through deals which involved state-controlled companies, which were operating under the direct control of government and the president," said Vladimir S. Milov, a former deputy energy minister and now political opposition leader who has written several reports alleging corruption. "Certain personal close friends of Putin who were people of relatively moderate means before Putin came to power all of a sudden turned out to be billionaires."[301] And this occurred at the same time that studies showed income disparity in Russia had never been worse, with the superrich doubling their wealth and the bottom fifth of the population in 2011 making only 55 percent of their 1991 earnings in real terms.[302] All this despite Putin's electoral claims that his rule had brought prosperity to Russians in comparison to the stagnant 1980s and the turbulent 1990s.

Returning to Petersburg in the early 1990s, Putin had become deputy mayor alongside Vladimir Yakovlev. Putin ultimately became the first deputy mayor and had control over all private and foreign economic activity. Yakovlev held the portfolio for housing, transportation, and infrastructure. They would quickly become bitter rivals. Putin attached his loyalties firmly to Sobchak, whom Yakovlev defeated in the 1996 mayoral race. From 1996 to 2003 Yakovlev controlled everything in St. Petersburg and was well poised to make life difficult for Putin by proceeding with criminal investigations of his activities and allying himself with other governors, such as Moscow's mayor Yuriy Luzhkov, to try to defeat the Kremlin "party of power" and then Putin in the 1999–2000 elections. But even leaving aside Yakovlev's political motivation to undermine Putin, Putin's behavior while he was in Petersburg left a lot to be desired.

Chapter Three

———◦◎◦———

Putin in St. Petersburg, 1990–1996

Accusations of Illicit Activities

THE RUSSIAN and foreign press, as well as internal and external investigative services, have associated Putin with many incidences of corruption. The opposition press is replete with charges and innuendos. Roman Shleynov of *Novaya gazeta*'s investigative department led an analytical piece in 2005 on Putin's connection to criminal cases with the following observation: "At a recent meeting . . . President Vladimir Putin laughed at an abstract question about corruption in the Kremlin. . . . No one asked him about specific cases. There are a lot of these. We made a list. You can call it 'Antiforbes': leading figures of the Russian Federation and criminal cases in which they are mentioned. A simple comparison showed that the Russian president is the one most often mentioned in connection with criminal cases."[1] The point of the story was to underline that one can't understand the logic behind Putin's personnel policy—who is appointed and to what job—without understanding that key personnel are connected by this common corrupt activity from the St. Petersburg days.

Several cases have been the subject of serious investigation by Russian and international law enforcement. In the 1990s Western agencies in particular monitored Putin's extensive travels to Germany, Finland, and Spain, where St. Petersburg investigators also alleged that he traveled numerous times on false papers. Certainly Putin went back and forth between Russia and Germany, and Russia and Finland dozens of times on official business after he started working in St. Petersburg, as would be expected of anyone who headed a city committee in charge of foreign trade. But after interviewing four senior Finnish diplomats, Anders Åslund reported that "Putin visited Finland 60 to 70 times during his five years as deputy mayor, and the Finns investigated his links with organized crime in Turku, Finland."[2] Officials in Turku conceded publicly that Putin was often there not only on government trips but also on "private visits to businessmen in the area," which included the celebration of his fortieth birthday.[3]

Putin's role in securing a monopoly position for select firms was a feature of his style while deputy mayor. While he professed an interest in economic liberalization and private property, he also acted to reduce competition, structure the market, and maximize profits for his friends. In St. Petersburg, Åslund reported, "both Swedish and Finnish businessmen complained about Putin squeezing out their companies, mainly through persecution by the lawless tax police, to the advantage of companies with which Putin was friendly"—as happened with the Grand Hotel Europa, where, using the tax police, Putin squeezed out the Swedish management that had already made a multimillion-dollar investment in favor of German and Russian investors closer to him.[4] Putin also allegedly favored a takeover of the St. Petersburg port by the Tambov organized crime group.[5]

Other sources indicate that Putin chose to go abroad because, as he told friends, he couldn't talk without fear of being bugged anywhere inside Russia. Lyudmila Putina's friend from East Germany, Irene Pietsch, similarly reported that Putin regularly went abroad for business during this period. Putina told her that her husband "always goes to Finland when he has something important to say. He says that in all of Russia, there is no place where you can speak without being overheard."[6]

A short list of the best-known legal investigations and cases related to his work in St. Petersburg city government includes the following:

1. Censure by the St. Petersburg legislature over illegal actions in the assigning of licenses and contracts by Putin as head of the Committee for Foreign Liaison.

2. Collaboration with criminal organizations in the regulation of the gambling industry in St. Petersburg.

3. German police raids on a money-laundering operation by the St. Petersburg Real Estate Holding Company, of which Putin was a member of the advisory board.

4. His role in providing a monopoly for the Petersburg Fuel Company, then controlled by the Tambov criminal organization.

5. His role in Dvadtsatyy Trest, or Twentieth Trust, which produced a criminal prosecution (Criminal Case No. 144128), dropped only when he became president.

6. His involvement in obtaining, along with Mayor Sobchak, an apartment in St. Petersburg, and charges of his unauthorized use of funds from the Mayor's Contingency Fund (Criminal Case No. 18/238278–95), which was also closed down after his election.

The Food Scandal and Censure
by the St. Petersburg Legislature

Putin's interest in becoming the linchpin between government operations and private business began almost immediately in 1991 upon starting work at the mayor's office. There had not been a more uncertain time in St. Petersburg since World War II. In the midst of the collapse of the Soviet system, there was dire need for food, and money was in short supply, with hyperinflation increasing the desirability of barter arrangements. The head of the Lensovet, the local city council, Aleksandr Belyayev, described the context of those days: "In November 1991, the Congress of People's Deputies of Russia formed the Gaidar government. Reforms had already been declared—the forthcoming liberalization of prices. The situation was ambiguous. . . . When the Gaidar government allocated a license for the export of raw materials for food, business entities that managed these resources were not eager to bring in food. They were waiting for the liberalization of prices. This was the situation."[7] Belyayev does not state that Putin himself was more or less corrupt than any of the other politicians of that time, but that "this was the very beginning of the corrupt system."[8]

Others were much less generous and targeted Putin as corrupt from the very beginning.[9]*

Putin was in a very important position—in charge of licensing imports and exports in conditions where food was scarce, the political center was in disarray, and the value of money was collapsing. Under those circumstances, he acted first and received permission later. Legislators in the St. Petersburg Parliament were immediately concerned about him because they had negotiated a contract in summer 1991 through a German company called Kontinent to purchase 90 million Deutschmarks of meat from Germany; when Marina Sal'ye, as head of the legislature's food committee, arrived in Germany to sign the contract, she was told that it had already been signed by Putin as head of a delegation, and the meat had been delivered. But it did not arrive in St. Petersburg. Masha Gessen cites Sal'ye's view that the meat was paid for out of St. Petersburg's budget but delivered to freezers in Moscow as part of the reserve being established by the KGB in preparation for the August coup.[11] While the meat undoubtedly did not arrive in St. Petersburg, it is not definitively known what happened to it since an investigation never took place. But when Putin started to act in a similar way in the late autumn of 1991, legislators were already skeptical. When more shipments of food had not arrived by winter, a commission was formed by the Leningrad, and then St. Petersburg, parliament that was headed by Sal'ye and fellow parliamentarian Yuriy Gladkov.

Marina Sal'ye was a Russian geologist who worked for the Academy of Sciences Institute of Geology and a politician, a long-standing and highly respected leader of the democratic movement who, like Sobchak, had been elected both to the Leningrad City Assembly and the Russian Congress of People's Deputies. She was a key member of the Interregional Group of Deputies who threw their support to Yel'tsin as the USSR collapsed, and she participated in the 1993 Constitutional Council to prepare a draft of

---

* The journalist Vladimir Ivanidze was working in 2000 for *Vedomosti* and tried, unsuccessfully, to get his editor to publish an exposé on Putin's role in the St. Petersburg food scandal, which he thought showed Putin's early involvement in corruption. He eventually left the country, writing from Paris. The allegations in Ivanidze's original 2000 article were taken up by Oleg Lur'ye in *Novaya gazeta*.[10]

the new Russian Constitution. Sal'ye was a founding member of the Free
Democratic Party of Russia and the Democratic Party of Russia, and, after
coming out of hiding in 2011, she joined the anti-Putin Party of National
Freedom. When she died in 2012, newspapers called her the "grandmother
of Russian democracy." [12] She was also an early and vehement opponent of
Putin. The Sal'ye Commission established by the St. Petersburg legislature
clearly documented that Putin signed licenses more than a month before
he had permission from Moscow to do so. Before that, the legal authority
from the prime minister went to the minister for foreign economic relations and from him to his representative in the northwest federal region,
A. P. Pakhomov. So Putin himself had no legal authority to grant licenses
and simply issued them over his own signature. This began, it appears, on
December 4, 1991, and by the time Deputy Prime Minister Yegor Gaidar got wind of it, goods—mainly raw materials, as detailed below—had
already left the country, theoretically to be exchanged for food. [13] Meanwhile Sobchak was trying to get the authority transferred to his office to
legalize the situation. But in the meantime Putin continued to issue licenses
and contracts. Gaidar gave written permission only on January 28, 1992,
authorizing Putin personally (no one else was named in the decree) to set
quotas, issue licenses, and work with suppliers directly, without having to
pay export duties, and in the name of the Ministry, for the sale or barter of
natural resources in exchange for food. [14] In terms of the scope of the operation that Putin was to launch, Gessen, after interviewing Sal'ye, asserts that
"Moscow had actually given St. Petersburg permission to export a billion
dollars' worth of commodities." [15] Putin initially resisted handing over the
documents to the Sal'ye Commission, claiming that doing so would compromise business secrets. Ultimately, under the duress of a subpoena, he
handed over documents for twelve contracts and licenses amounting to
about $122 million in exports. But the scope of the operation was thought
to be ten times larger.

The Sal'ye Commission found Putin very uncooperative; [16] according
to the Lensovet's former chair, Belyayev, when Putin appeared before the
deputies, he challenged their authority to call someone to account who had

not been appointed by them,[17] and he refused to provide the full set of licenses and contracts, citing, according to the official report, "commercial confidentiality." Nevertheless the Commission conducted an investigation and submitted its report to the City Council. On that basis, the Council prepared its own nineteen-page report, signed by head of the City Council, Belyayev, in which it concluded in Section 2.2 that Putin's actions were "flagrantly and repeatedly in violation of the law."[18]

Further the Council report made a number of specific charges. First, most of the contracts contained no or low penalties for nondelivery—in the range of 1 to 5 percent only.[19] "Such an approach toward penalties shows that the Committee for Foreign Liaison of the Mayor 'distributed' them in the interests of the licensees and not the city,"[20] a situation that "from a legal point of view allows firms and intermediaries to evade commitments."[21] The report stated that many of the companies had vanished after they had taken their materials out of the country, sold them, and deposited their profits in offshore banks.

Second, most of the licenses and contracts were prepared incorrectly, from a legal standpoint, and were not therefore capable of being upheld in court. That is, the city had no legal recourse to sue for nonfulfillment of contracts because the contracts were not legally binding. Putin and his deputy, Aleksandr Anikin, both lawyers, were specifically accused of providing unilateral concessions and preferences that "ignored the interests of the city" and intentionally doing shoddy work so that firms could "evade their commitments without damage to themselves."[22] The contracts and licenses lacked a proper signature, stamps, and legal details that rendered them illegal.[23] More than half lacked the signature and stamp of one of the two parties.

Third, while large penalties were not charged for nonreceipt of foods, the commissions charged for licenses by the KVS were exorbitant, ranging from 25 to 50 percent.[24] What was done with the money the KVS earned in this way was not revealed. However, it is clear that some of it went into the Mayor's Contingency Fund, which Putin had access to for funding projects in St. Petersburg and abroad, thus making it another vehicle for corruption and capital flight. The total KVS commission fees for twelve contracts exceeded $34 million.[25]*

Fourth, the Council report concluded that several of the firms chosen had "close ties with officials of the Mayor's Office ('Kompleks,' 'Interkomtsentr,' the Foreign Economic Agency of Lenoblispolkom, etc.) or were created not long before the signing of the agreements."[27] The company Interkomtsentr Formula-7 already had a storied history. In an agreement with this firm,[28] Putin gave them the right to trade 150,000 tons of oil products to the West (given to them at a contracted internal rate of 450,000 rubles, officially about $270,000, but worth on the world market at that time $112,500,000), in return for delivering 300,000 tons each of butter, sugar, and potatoes to St. Petersburg (valued according to the contract at 4.215 billion rubles, or $2.5 billion), with a penalty of only 2 percent for nondelivery. The contract was signed by Putin and G. M. Miroshnik, president of Interkomtsentr Formula-7. Miroshnik had already served two jail sentences and was alleged to have been involved in the misappropriation of 20 million Deutschmarks earmarked for the relocation of the USSR's Western Group of Forces when it withdrew from East Germany. A parliamentary investigation into Interkomtsentr Formula-7 concluded, "The operations involving the duty-free importing of goods (under the guise of military property) owned by the [Interkomtsentr] Formula-7 Firm are criminal, and in their actions one can see the qualification of crimes under the heading of smuggling."[29] Observers maintained that for much of his previous professional life, Putin "could not have remained uninformed about Miroshnik's exploits."[30] Miroshnik evidently worked with a circle of Germans from the east who Irene Pietsch claimed were also connected to Putin. When Putin and his wife went to Moscow in 1996, Lyudmila Putina used to send faxes to her friend Pietsch from the Interkomtsentr Formula-7

---

*Western businessmen also reported being asked directly by Putin for a 25 percent commission, including an American firm that was permitted to donate free butter to the city of St. Petersburg only if it allowed the city to take 25 percent off the top, and it was Putin who did the asking, according to the American Richard Torrence, who worked as an advisor to Sobchak for International Projects at the time.[26]

offices in Moscow: "These were East Germans whom Putin had met in Dresden and who were now living in Moscow, where the husband occupied a managing position in one of the large German banks."[31] Miroshnik was not only connected to the Western Group of Forces deal but also became the advisor to General (and at that time Vice President) Aleksandr Rutskoy prior to the 1993 parliamentary showdown with Yel'tsin.[32] Miroshnik is said to have flown on Rutskoy's plane to Spain to escape prosecution, going briefly to the U.S. on forged documents, and returning to Greece, where he claimed citizenship based on his father's Greek ethnicity. He returned to Russia after Putin was elected, and the fraud case against him was dropped for "insufficient evidence."[33]

Of particular interest at the time and subsequently was the contract signed with the foreign trade branch of the Kirishinefteorgsintez refinery, also called Kinef, based in Kirishi near Leningrad. Gennadiy Timchenko had worked in its foreign trade branch, Kirishineftekhimexport, since at least the early 1990s.[34] Timchenko and Putin were said to have collaborated on this deal,[35] setting the stage for their reported subsequent association in the oil trading company Gunvor,[36] which was confirmed by the U.S. Treasury in announcing sanctions against Timchenko.[37]

A rare interview given by Timchenko to the *Wall Street Journal* in 2008 provides a glimpse of his background and connection to Putin. The authors of the article provide the following information:

> When Mikhayl Gorbachev came to power in 1985 and began relaxing the government's monopoly on trade, Mr. Katkov says he and Mr. Timchenko hatched a plan with Yevgeniy Malov, who worked in a state trading agency in the same office block. The three lobbied a state-owned refinery in nearby Kirishi to set up an in-house operation to trade oil, Mr. Katkov says. In 1987, several refineries, including Kirishi, were given the right to set up trading branches to export a limited range of products. The refinery set up a trading arm and hired the trio. "My luck started there," Mr. Timchenko said. . . . Mr. Putin, meanwhile, returned from his. . . . KGB stint in East

Germany to his hometown of St. Petersburg. There, as head of the city's Committee [for Foreign Liaison], he handed an early piece of business to Mr. Timchenko and his colleagues. The 1991 collapse of the Soviet Union and its command economy had left St. Petersburg dangerously short of food. To help the city raise money, Moscow granted oil-export quotas to local authorities. Mr. Putin's committee passed these to Mr. Timchenko and his crew at the refinery trading company, which used the proceeds from foreign sales to buy herring from Iceland and other foodstuffs. Some of the barter deals supervised by Mr. Putin drew an investigation by St. Petersburg's city council.*[38]

Both Timchenko and Putin initially denied that they had a close relationship, and indeed Timchenko sued Britain's *Economist* magazine for libel for a 2008 article that contained the following passage about Rosneft, Russia's largest oil company that is majority owned by the state:

> Rosneft sells the bulk of its oil through a Dutch-registered trading firm, Gunvor, whose ownership structure looks like a Chinese puzzle. The rise in Gunvor's fortunes coincided with the fall of Yukos. A little-known company before 2003, Gunvor has grown into the world's third-largest oil trader, which ships a third of Russia's seaborne oil exports and has estimated revenues of $70 billion a year. One of Gunvor's founders is Gennady Timchenko, who sponsored a judo club of which Mr. Putin was honorary president and worked in an oil company that was given a large export quota as part of a controversial oil-for-food scheme set up by Mr. Putin during his time in St Petersburg. Mr. Timchenko says he was not involved in the deal and his success is not built on favours.[39]

---

* A subsequent investigation by the Russian weekly *Ogonek* claimed that Timchenko began work in Leningrad's branch of the Ministry of Foreign Trade in 1982, not 1985, but doesn't suggest that Timchenko and Putin met each other until the early 1990s.

The *Economist* subsequently cut this passage from the online version of the article and issued a statement: "We accept Gunvor's assurances that neither Vladimir Putin nor other senior Russian political figures have any ownership interest in Gunvor." [40] The British weekly *Private Eye* noted that despite the *Economist*'s statement, there had been no apology, no settlement, and that Timchenko's "people," having seen the *Economist*'s long defense document and realizing that "fresh revelations" might be made, simply abandoned the case. [41]

Likewise the British *Guardian* quoted *Vedomosti* as suggesting that Timchenko "abandoned" his libel case after realizing that he might have to "reveal potentially embarrassing details of his private bank accounts and the ownership and asset structure of his Swiss-based oil trading company, Gunvor." [42] The newspaper also reported on an interview with the Russian political analyst Stanislav Belkovskiy in December 2007: "Putin had secretly amassed a $40 billion fortune. Putin was the beneficial owner of '75% of Gunvor,' [Belkovskiy] claimed, adding that Putin's ownership structure was concealed through a 'non-transparent network of offshore companies.' Putin denied the claim three months later." Alluding to the pressures that might have been exerted on Timchenko to drop the suit, the *Guardian* quoted an anonymous source familiar with the case saying that Timchenko may not have understood the high-status role of the *Economist* in Britain: "He thought he was suing some tabloid. He didn't realise he was suing the British establishment." [43]

Possibly emboldened by Timchenko's retreat, Russian newspapers also started to investigate the extent of his business dealings and favorable treatment from the Kremlin. [44] In 2011 Putin did finally admit publicly that he had known Timchenko since the beginning of the privatization process in St. Petersburg, when "he [Timchenko] worked with my [Putin's] friends and colleagues in Kirishinefteorgsintez." [45]

Timchenko was the subject of what the *Wall Street Journal* described as "persistent whispers" about a KGB background, which Timchenko dismissed as a "fairy tale." [46] He graduated from the same Mechanical Institute as other members of the Putin inner elite, including Ozero cofounder Vladimir Yakunin and both Aleksandr Grigor'yev and Sergey Naryshkin.[47] As noted earlier and confirmed in other sources, he linked up with two other colleagues, Andrey Katkov and Yevgeniy Malov, to set up an in-house foreign trade operation called Kirishineftekhim-export within the state-owned Kirishi refinery to export a limited range of products after Gorbachev changed foreign trade laws in 1987.[48] They partnered with Andrey Pannikov, who admits to still being on the KGB bankroll at this time,[49] setting up SP Urals, a joint venture with a Swedish company and several Russian partners, including Timchenko's Kirishineftekhimexport, where by then Timchenko had become head of the export division.[50] Putin's very first application to export materials was with Kirishinefteorgsintez, signed on December 20, 1991,[51] citing authorization from Deputy Prime Minister Gaidar on December 4, 1991.[52] The final report from the St. Petersburg legislature supported the Sal'ye Commission's finding that the fuel left the country, but the proceeds were not repatriated.[53]

Trading in oil was particularly lucrative because the domestic whole-sale price for a ton of oil in early 1990 had dipped to 30 rubles (just over a dollar at the unofficial exchange rate)—the price of a pack of Marlboros on the streets of Moscow. At this time the world market price exceeded $100 a ton.[54] When trade was completely controlled by the state, individuals could not legally sell oil abroad at domestic prices. But once the foreign trade rules were relaxed and private cooperatives were formed in the late Gorbachev period, there was a short period when vast fortunes were made this way.[55] Raw materials were "purchased" at domestic prices by cooperatives, which were given an export license by Putin's KVS or by other legal authorities, and sold abroad at world market prices. In these transactions, sometimes an authorized local government official, like Putin, was part of a joint venture, and sometimes he simply licensed and regulated this newly emerging private enterprise. No one would have objected to Putin's KVS being listed as a contracted party if a fully transparent and documented exchange had actually taken place in which oil was either sold for sums that went back to the city coffers or full shipments of food arrived. But when the oil left the country and the food didn't arrive, that was another story: as a

Financial Times investigation showed, Timchenko's company "was a beneficiary of a large export quota under a scandal-tainted oil-for-food scheme set up by Mr. Putin when he worked as head of the city administration's foreign economic relations committee in 1991, local parliament records show."[56] Timchenko and his colleagues were never prosecuted, and indeed he went on to establish Gunvor.

Charges of Putin's connection to Gunvor and Timchenko were long-standing among Russian analysts, including the presidential candidate and former deputy prime minister Ivan Rybkin, who in 2004 maintained, "I—and not just me—have lots of concrete evidence of Putin's participation in business. [Roman] Abramovich, as is known, but also Timchenko, the Koval'chuk brothers* and others are responsible for Putin's business."[59] Shortly after making this statement, Rybkin disappeared from Moscow, and upon returning accused the Kremlin of having kidnapped him. He subsequently withdrew from the race. Stanislav Belkovskiy became the director of the National Strategy Institute, a think tank that at one time was politically aligned with Putin, and made similar claims about the link between Timchenko and Putin.[60] Putin himself has consistently denied having any interest in Gunvor. Timchenko did say only that 20 percent of the company is owned by an associate in St. Petersburg, whom he declines to name.[61] Repeated investigations in the Russian and Western press asserted the close relationship between Putin and Timchenko and insinuated that Putin is a hidden beneficial owner of Timchenko's Gunvor but did not produce concrete evidence of that ownership.[62] Then in 2014, the U.S. government's sanctions announcement claimed a direct connection

---

*Yuriy Koval'chuk's brother, Mikhayl, was a physicist from the prestigious Ioffe Institute of Physics and Technology who, beginning in 2001, served as the Kremlin's scientific secretary of the Council for Science and High Technologies. In 2007 he was appointed acting vice president of the Russian Academy of Sciences for Nanotechnology and was made a corresponding (not full) member of the RAS. The RAS Charter states that vice presidents must be full members, but in 2008 RAS members rejected his application for full membership, so he remained an acting VP.[57] In 2013, having failed to pressure the RAS to promote Koval'chuk, the Duma passed a law handed down by the Kremlin, stating that henceforth all corresponding members would now be listed as full members. In addition RAS institutes' control over their own property was transferred to a newly created government agency, a move regarded by some as a "personal vendetta" by Putin in defense of Koval'chuk.[58]

between Putin, Timchenko, and Gunvor: "Timchenko's activities in the
energy sector have been directly linked to Putin. Putin has investments in
Gunvor and may have access to Gunvor funds."[63]

In January 1992 Putin also registered a company called Golden Gates, in
which, as reported in the *Financial Times*, he and Timchenko both participated. It was reportedly set up to build an oil terminal in St. Petersburg, but
according to a banker involved with Golden Gate, the plans fell apart when
organized crime blocked the deal, leading, the *Financial Times* claimed, to
Putin's having to send his daughters to Germany for safety.[64] But it was
Gunvor International, with Timchenko as co-owner, that brought Timchenko into the ranks of the world's ultrarich. The oil trading firm, which
grew out of and benefited from the Russian state's dismantling of Yukos in
2003, eventually gained control of over 5 percent of Russia's total economic
output[65] and revenues of over $70 billion annually.[66] Forbes.ru estimated
Timchenko's personal worth at $14.1 billion.[67]

Another of Putin's personal friends stood behind this first transaction.
This license for 150,000 tons of petroleum products went to Nevskiy
Dom, which was owned by Putin's friend Vladimir Smirnov, who went
on to cofound the Ozero Cooperative with Putin. Nevskiy Dom was subject to only a 5 percent penalty for nondelivery, and Smirnov provided a
25 percent fee to Putin's KVS in return for the license.[68] Smirnov would be
involved with Putin in the St. Petersburg Real Estate Holding Company
and ultimately would follow him to Moscow, where he worked in the Presidential Property Management Department and then became chief of the
Russian Federal Atomic Energy Agency.

Prices in the contracts were either absent altogether, making it impossible to assess the economic efficiency of the transaction, or were so under-
stated that the Sal'ye report accused Putin's KVS of sanctioning "dumping."
The difference between the amounts charged for eight rare earth minerals
and their value on world markets was almost 14.2 million Deutschmarks,
or $9.4 million.[69] The company involved, Dzhikop (or Jikop in German),
registered only at the end of October 1991 with capital of only 100,000
rubles, was evidently owned by a front man, an unknown German sub-

sequently identified as Peter Bachmann.[70] Dzhikop received a tender for rare earth metals in which the sale price was up to two thousand times lower than world market prices, leading to condemnation by the St. Petersburg City Council of the "criminal nature of the terms and conditions of the agreement" and to the conclusion that it was not surprising that the company "self-dissolved" and put the "total revenue in accounts of foreign banks."[71]

Vladimir Pribylovskiy subsequently stated that Dzhangir Rahimov was behind the company and he was the brother of one of Putin's classmates from Azerbaijan and closest friends, Ilham Rahimov.[72] Putin's coworker in Dresden and biographer claimed that while in Dresden Putin had found a way to visit "his lawyer friend (and possible classmate)" in Azerbaijan and had come back horrified at the complete failure of Soviet policy there—instead, Putin reported, "nepotism among clans was just like the nepotism in the Party's higher ranks, so evident within the 'civilized' part of the USSR—in Russia."[73] A 2012 *Forbes* Russia investigation into the relationship between Putin and Ilham Rahimov confirmed that they had been classmates and friends in the Law Faculty at Leningrad State University; Putin often stayed in Rahimov's dorm room and they shared a love of judo. Presidential spokesman Dmitriy Peskov confirmed to *Forbes* Russia that the two had indeed been friends at university. *Forbes* Russia listed Rahimov's net worth in 2012 at $2.5 billion.[74]

The documents used by the Sal'ye Commission show Putin's guiding hand in these activities. He signed contracts at below-market rates; he intervened with Moscow to gain the authority to sign export licenses; he intervened to override the objections of the head of customs, who had refused to open the border because the paperwork was not in order.[75] His signature is on all of these documents.

After all of this feverish activity, according to the Sal'ye Commission report, the $122 million of quotas that Gaidar had granted Putin's KVS translated into two tankers of cooking oil delivered by a company called Tamigo, registered in Germany, with a Petersburg-domiciled general director, G. N. Misikov.[76] As the press subsequently reported, the tanker "trundled into St. Petersburg on February 3, 1992. The arrival of this cooking oil was a sufficient triumph for Putin to write Gaidar on February 6 to inform him of it."[77]

In acting on the results of the investigative report by the Sal'ye Commission, the St. Petersburg City Council could not have been clearer in assigning blame and suggesting remediation. In a paragraph that Investigator Andrey Zykov was subsequently to call "the control shot to the head,"[78] the Council recommended that the documents be turned over to the Procurator General's Office for prosecution: Putin was accused of "showing complete incompetence, bordering on bad faith in drafting contracts . . . and an unprecedented negligence and irresponsibility in the submission of documents to the parliamentary group."[79] The Council recommended that Putin and his deputy be "removed from their posts"[80] and that the "right of the Committee for Foreign Liaison to conduct business be withdrawn."[81] Procurator Vladimir Yeremenko sent a representation to the mayor proposing that he start an investigation of "the Committee for Foreign Liaison's improperly drawn-up contracts and false registration of some licenses."[82]

The report was passed on to Moscow, to fellow Petersburger and corruption crusader Yuriy Boldyrev, chief of the Main Control Directorate of the Presidential Administration, who investigated the matter. He issued a statement on March 31, 1992: "The Main Control Directorate has received documents from St. Petersburg city council representatives attesting to the necessity of removing the head of the city's Committee for Foreign Liaison Vladimir Vladimirovich Putin from his post. I request that the question of appointing him to any other post not be raised before the Main Control Directorate reaches its final decision regarding this issue."[83] He called to Moscow Sobchak and all his deputies, including Putin, and they wrote down their version of events. Boldyrev recalled, "There were enough material facts that checked out."[84] He requested of Minister of Foreign Economic Relations Pyotr Aven, who had already reinstated Putin's right to issue licenses, that Putin not be given any further authority until the case was finally settled.[85] As part of the investigation, Yel'tsin's federal representative to the St. Petersburg and Leningrad *oblast'* was asked to assist. Boldyrev also requested documents from Putin and his KVS and found the level of cooperation so lacking that he wrote Putin on February 12, 1992, "I have been sent documents that are incomplete, and are not relevant to my request to the point that it is not possible to draw any conclusions. I was not even sent a copy of the licenses or copies of the contracts, which should be at least thirteen. I have been delivered only two documents, one of which is in Finnish, which at the very least is unjust on your part. I demand the presentation of a full set of documents by February 17." [86] Boldyrev also reported the entire case to Yel'tsin, who, like Minister of Foreign Economic Relations Pyotr Aven, ultimately did nothing.*

No one was able to unseat Putin or oblige Mayor Sobchak to discipline his own deputy. The local procurator general also declined to take up the case. The KVS continued to function as before, and even after Putin was promoted to first deputy mayor in March 1994, he held on to his function as chairman of this committee. The Council's report asked Sobchak to consider the position of both Putin and Putin's deputy, Aleksandr Anikin. In response Sobchak didn't fire Putin, but Anikin did lose his job. Anikin's own deputy, Aleksey Miller, was promoted to take his place. [89] In 2000 Putin would appoint Miller as deputy minister of energy, and then in 2001 as head of Gazprom, a position in which he was widely reported to have acquired vast wealth. [90]

While Putin temporarily lost the right to grant contracts, this authority was once again reinstated by Minister Aven later in 1992. [91] Once he regained his authority, he granted licenses to those, like Vladimir Yakunin and Andrey Fursenko, with whom he would ultimately be associated as co-owners of the Ozero Cooperative. [92] Yel'tsin disbanded the national leg-

---

*Aven left the government in 1994 and has risen to be first president and then chairman of the board of Russia's largest private bank, Alfa-Bank. In 2014 *Forbes* estimated his net worth as $6.2 billion. [87] As for Boldyrev, who had been a key democrat in the early 1990s and an initial ally of Sobchak, he lost his position in the Main Control Directorate of the Presidential Administration and went on to fight against corruption as a member of the Federation Council and a member of the Federal Audit Chamber. He became a founding member of the liberal Yabloko Party and fell out with Sobchak after 1993. Despite the fact that he represented St. Petersburg, by his own testimony Sobchak and Putin worked against him: "In 1994–5 when I was one of two representatives of St. Petersburg in the Federation Council, I never got the chance to speak live on St. Petersburg television." [88]

islature in October 1993, and the local legislature in St. Petersburg, which was elected to serve until 1995, was also disbanded when Sobchak had Yel'tsin sign a decree dissolving it, leaving the city without a counterbalance to the mayor's office until a legislature was finally seated in the fall of 1994. Sal'ye and the other deputies had to either run again for the new assembly, over which the mayor now had tremendous powers (mirroring the national situation under the new presidential system), or find other work—and in any case already by this time the legislature had been limited to one meeting on Wednesday afternoons, with the mayor's office providing only the most scant information, like budgets of only two to three pages.[93]

Despite the investigations that swirled around him, Putin was promoted to first deputy mayor in March 1994, only fueling the view that Sobchak was also involved in this corrupt business. Indeed Sobchak was implicated in handing out apartments on Vasil'yevskiy Island to his friends and family, including Putin. Around this time Putin's address changed to the one that would be listed as his personal address on the document establishing the Ozero Cooperative.[94] Andrey Zykov, a lead investigator in the case against Sobchak and Putin (Criminal Case No. 18/238278–95), subsequently stated quite categorically that the procurator's

> dossier had material on the purchase of Putin's apartments on the 2nd "line" of Vasil'yevskiy Island in St. Petersburg. In 1993, the City had resettled and refurbished some apartments there, and it turned out that Putin, then the deputy mayor, had the desire to live in that neighborhood. So a scheme was hatched. A joint stock company called Liniks owned some apartments in Vsevolozhsk, it's not clear how. The Head of the administration for the Vasileostrovskiy District, Valeriy Golubev,* proposed that these apartments be exchanged

---

*Valeriy Golubev reportedly served in the Leningrad KGB with Putin, who made him head of the Secretariat of the Mayor's Office in July 1991, and then head of the Vasil'yevskiy Island district administration in April 1993. In that capacity Golubev assisted in obtaining for Putin an apartment—on the 2nd line, Building 17, apt. no. 24—on this island.[95] He became a member of the Federation Council in 2002 and in 2003 a member of the Management Committee of

for the ones on Vasil'yevskiy. . . . The settlement of this issue could not be achieved without a scandal . . . and it took the personal intervention of Mayor Anatoliy Sobchak. At market prices this was a decidedly unequal exchange as the flats on Vasil'yevskiy Island were much more expensive than apartments in Vsevolozhsk. The units were then distributed to Golubev [and others], and apartment 24 in building 17 on Second Line Avenue went to Putin.[98]

After his electoral loss in 1996, Sobchak was charged by the procurator general with corruption for his role in this apartment exchange, and he had to flee the country in an operation widely reported as masterminded by Putin. Thus getting Sobchak out of the country not only saved the former mayor but also protected those, like Putin, about whom there was a lot of incriminating information. As Sal'ye stated, "Before, Putin was under Sobchak's protection, and now Sobchak was under Putin's protection [*krysha*]."[99]

When Putin went to Moscow in 1996, one of the first positions he took was in the Main Control Directorate, where he would have had access to all the documents that Boldyrev and others had gathered. Boldyrev had been one of the original founders of the Yabloko Party, and it is worth considering that Putin's particularly harsh treatment of Yabloko has stemmed from their leader's early involvement in investigating his corruption.

Marina Sal'ye continued to follow Putin and to seek his removal. In 2000, just as Putin became acting president, the opposition and international media got wind of this long-forgotten episode and began to publicize it widely. In an interview with the London *Sunday Times* in 2000, Sal'ye once again summarized what her commission had uncovered:[100] "When we compared the original contracts with the table [Putin] had first given us we discovered a discrepancy of $11m which he had tried to conceal. To this day we have no idea what happened to that sum."[101] The contract with Dzhikop alone deprived the city of $7 million in potential earnings.

Gazprom, then deputy chairman of its governing board[96] and director general of Gazkomplektimpex.[97]

"Most of the contracts signed were fraudulent," Sal'ye asserted. "The companies were highly dubious; the contracts were riddled with mistakes, fictitious sums and irregularities that meant in practice they were legally non-binding. Millions of dollars [an estimated $92 million] were earned, and millions of dollars vanished. Whereto remains a mystery." [102] Sal'ye summed up the operation and Putin's ambition this way: "The whole point of the operation was the following: Cook up a legally defective contract with a person, take a license to the Customs Office, on the basis of this license open the border and send the goods abroad, sell the goods and put the money in your pocket. That is what happened. It was therefore not put out to tender. They needed their 'partners,' 'partners' of the shadow economy, criminal and mafia structures, front companies that could ensure this ambitious scam. These were Putin's 'partners.' He chose them himself and that's why his daily lamentations about the disappearing firms deserve nothing but contempt." [103] She claims that in 2000 she went to the Moscow offices of State Duma deputy Sergey Nikolayevich Yushenkov (who was an ex-military man, member of the Liberal Russia Party, and head of the Duma's defense committee for a time), with whom she was going to cooperate politically. Standing behind Yushenkov, obviously uninvited, there was another person: "I saw a person there who I didn't want to see any time, any place, under any circumstances. I'm not going to reveal his name. But I then understood it was time to go. And Sergey Nikolayevich was soon killed." [104]*

As for Putin's own view of the earliest period in his political career, he has a very different take. In his autobiography, *First Person*, he relates the following exchange with three journalists, answering their questions in ways that are often at odds with the documented facts:

---

* Sergey Yushenkov believed that Putin was the one person who would have benefited personally from the apartment bombings in summer 1999 that marked the beginning of his ascent to the presidency,[105] and it was reported by *Izvestiya* after his death that he frequently urged reporters to write about the involvement of "power structures" in the bombings, saying, "It's all obvious, but no one will write about it." [106] Anti-Putin sources—including Anna Politkovskaya, Boris Berezovskiy, Aleksandr Litvinenko, and Chechen separatist groups—alleged that Yushenkov received information shortly before his death linking the FSB to the attack by Chechens on the Dubrovka musical theater complex in Moscow.[107]

Much has been written in the St. Petersburg press about the food delivery scandal. What was that?

In 1992, there was a food crisis in the country. . . . Our businessmen presented us with a scheme: if they were allowed to sell goods— mainly raw materials—abroad, they would deliver food to Russia. We had no other options. So the Committee for Foreign Liaison, which I headed, agreed to their offer. We obtained permission from the head of the government and signed the relevant contracts. The firms filled out all the necessary paperwork, obtained export licenses, and began exporting raw materials. The customs agency would not have let anything out of the country without the correct paperwork and accompanying documents. At the same time, a lot of people were saying that they were exporting certain rare earth metals. Not a single gram of any metal was exported. Anything that needed special permission was not passed through customs.

The scheme began to work. However, some of the firms did not uphold the main condition of the contract—they didn't deliver food from abroad, or at least they didn't import full loads. They reneged on their commitments to the city.

A deputies' commission was created, headed by Marina Sal'ye, who conducted a special investigation.

No, there wasn't any real investigation. How could there be? There was no criminal offense.

Then where does this whole corruption story come from?

I think that some of the deputies exploited this story in order to pressure Sobchak into firing me.

Why?

For being a former KGB agent. Although they probably had other motives too. Some of the deputies wanted to make money off those deals, and they wound up with nothing but a meddlesome KGB agent. . . . I think the city didn't do everything it could have done.

They should have worked more closely with law enforcement agencies. But it would have been pointless to take the exploiters to court—they would have dissolved immediately and stopped exporting goods. . . . You have to understand: we weren't involved in trade. The Committee for Foreign Liaison did not trade in anything itself. . . .

But the granting of licenses?
We did not have the right to grant licenses. That's just it: A division of the Ministry for Foreign Economic Relations issued the licenses. They were a federal structure and had nothing to do with the municipal administration.[108]

These statements are simply factually incorrect: the Sal'ye Commission certainly did exist, it did report, it did censure Putin by name, recommend his removal, and recommend that the matter be handed over to the Procuracy. The St. Petersburg legislature concurred and also called on Sobchak to remove Putin. The matter went all the way to Moscow, where the chief of the Main Control Directorate, Boldyrev, also specifically recommended that Putin's KVS not be allowed to work until the investigation was completed. This was not a small matter, nor was Putin "just like" everyone else at that time. Putin was given permission to issue licenses and contracts, and his personal signature is on many of the deals. His KVS made over $34 million in commissions alone for just the licenses and contracts he submitted to the parliamentary commission. This figure is reliably estimated to be about one-tenth of the total amount of business the KVS licensed during this period; this figure also excludes the income from those businesses, including gambling, in which the KVS owned a share of the company.

Moreover Putin was not a victim of the wiles and whims of anonymous businessmen. Among those with whom he signed the first agreements were his personal friends and acquaintances: Rahimov, Warnig, Timchenko, and Smirnov. The gap between the documents of the case and Putin's account brilliantly demonstrates his ability to deflect criticism, to admit that something happened but that he was on the sidelines, or even himself a victim of others' venal or politically motivated actions. Additionally, despite what must have been a huge effort to find concrete evidence of Putin's own bribe taking, there is none. Any cuts Putin took, any favors he received in return for favors he gave were not documented, did not occur in Russia, or were "commissions" for the Mayor's Contingency Fund. If he is the owner or partial owner of any of these companies, they must be registered abroad, not in Russia. This Teflon ability to deflect criticism and to not give his critics an easy win with evidence of bribe taking would stand him in good stead throughout his career.

As for Sal'ye, she went into hiding in 2000, spending over ten years living in a remote settlement of twenty-five dachas on the border with Latvia. She reemerged only in 2010 to give a series of interviews in a desperate attempt to prevent Putin from running for a third presidential term. In an interview with Radio Free Europe, she stated, "Putin wrote in his book and I almost quote: 'There were not any licenses at all.' But I have everything in my files. [After a pause] They're going to kill me."[109] Following the demonstrations to protest the theft of the 2011 Duma elections, she joined the protest rallies in St. Petersburg in February 2012 and announced she would work with the anti-Putin and anticorruption Party of National Freedom, led by Boris Nemtsov, Vladimir Milov, Vladimir Ryzhkov, and others. But on March 21, 2012, she died of a massive coronary at the age of seventy-seven. Critically, four days after her death, unnamed supporters exercised her "nuclear option" by uploading all of the documents, including all those cited above, onto her public Facebook page.[110] Based on the evidence provided in those documents, it is impossible to avoid the conclusion that Putin was directly involved in the food scandal. The public investigations at the time that resulted in the St. Petersburg legislature censuring him, recommending his removal, and advising the mayor to forward the case to prosecutors for criminal prosecution showed his culpability. Putin's subsequent denial of the evidentiary basis of these acts, saying "there wasn't any real investigation,"[111] represented a massive cover-up.

46113

811111111111111

Putin, the Gambling Industry, Organized Crime, and Baltik-Eskort

Not only was Putin involved in licensing all foreign economic activity, but beginning on December 24, 1991, by Order No. 753-r of Mayor Sobchak, he was made head of the supervisory council overseeing the entire gambling industry in St. Petersburg. He was given the authority to license all activities, to allocate city property for casinos, to work with tax collection agencies, and to oversee compliance.[112] In public he adopted a tough no-nonsense approach to criminality. Speaking at a public meeting in 1991, he threatened, "If criminals attack the authorities, there must be an appropriate punishment. It's the duty of the militia to be severe and even cruel if necessary. It is the only way to reduce criminality, the only way. We hope to eliminate ten criminals for each officer killed, within the law of course."[113] In his book *First Person* Putin writes:

> At that time we were trying to bring order to the gambling business in St. Petersburg. . . . We created a municipal enterprise that did not own any casinos but controlled 51 percent of the stock of the gaming businesses in the city. Various representatives of the basic oversight organizations—the FSB, the tax police, and the tax inspectorate—were assigned to supervise this enterprise. The basic idea was that the state, as a stockholder, would receive dividends from its 51 percent of the stock. In fact, this was a mistake, because you can own tons of stock and still not really control something. All the money coming from the tables was cash and could be diverted. The casino owners showed us only losses on the books. While we were counting up the profits and deciding where to allocate the funds—to develop the city's businesses or support the social sector—they were laughing at us and showing us their losses. Ours was a classic mistake made by people encountering the free market for the first time. Later, particularly during Anatoliy Sobchak's 1996 election campaign, our political opponents tried to find something criminal in our actions and accuse us of corruption.[114]

But how did the city become a majority owner in the gaming industry in St. Petersburg? Putin, the head of the Committee for Foreign Liaison, turned to the legal advisor to the committee, Dmitriy Medvedev, who reportedly came up with the formula: "by relinquishing the right to collect rent for the facilities that the casinos occupied," the city could claim 51 percent ownership of all gambling activity. They did this by establishing a joint stock company called Neva Chance,[115] which was officially housed at the same address as Putin's KVS—6 Antonenko Pereulok (lane).[116] Neva Chance went on to create over twenty-five different companies, all in the gambling industry and many of them headed by ex-FSB officials, including Valeriy Polomarchuk, who later became the representative in St. Petersburg of Lukoil.[117] Also alleged to have been involved was Roman Tsepov, a former officer in the Ministry of Internal Affairs, who cofounded with Viktor Zolotov the private security company Baltik-Eskort.[118]*

Baltik-Eskort operated openly as a private security service to protect Putin, Sobchak, and other high-ranking officials. It also allegedly acted as a liaison with the criminal underworld in St. Petersburg, including both Aleksandr Malyshev, reputed head of the Malyshev criminal organization, and Vladimir Kumarin, the reputed head of the Tambov crime organization. Some of the agency's employees were members of criminal groups and, like Aleksandr Tkachenko, the alleged leader of the Perm organized crime group, were accused of being involved in the assassinations of political figures at this time and subsequently, including the "death by Mercedes" of a Duma member and head of the rival Christian Democratic Union on December 9, 1995. ITAR-TASS reported that Vitaly Savitskiy was riding in a car that "belonged to the St. Petersburg mayor's office" when its driver made an inexplicable U-turn, allowing a Mercedes owned by Baltik-Eskort and driven by Tkachenko to ram the back passenger side of the car at full

---

*Olesia Yakhno's article, on which this information is based, is well-informed, at least partly because she was the wife of Stanislav Belkovskiy, the director of the National Strategy Institute, who most notably led a campaign against Mikhayl Khodorkovskiy in the early 2000s, prior to the latter's arrest for fraud. He also revealed details of the relationship between Putin and the oligarchs, including the alleged extent of Putin's own personal wealth, which in 2007 Belkovskiy claimed included 37 percent of the shares in Surgutneftegaz and 4.5 percent of Gazprom.[119]

speed, killing Savitskiy immediately. The driver, who suffered only minor injuries, was taken to St. Petersburg's military hospital, where inexplicably he died "of shock" a week later, prompting the police to close the case for lack of witnesses, despite widespread coverage from the Russian and foreign press.[120]

Some but by no means all of these gambling companies were controlled by ex-KGB, and as such they pushed hard to get the Russian mafia to submit to their authority. They shared common interests in legitimizing gambling in St. Petersburg while also benefiting from it financially. On June 26, 1991, while the USSR still existed, the Council of Ministers had issued a decree requiring firms engaged in gambling to be licensed by the Ministry of Finance.[121] In St. Petersburg only one casino had complied, the Admiral; in the 1993 opinion of the St. Petersburg Procuracy, all the rest were running illegally, under the cover either of Putin's licensing, via a special permit, No. 274 of May 27, 1992, signed by Putin, or of Neva Chance.[122] Putin also clearly interacted with certain leaders of organized crime, including reportedly the leaders of the Tambov and Malyshev gangs. Such cooperation among new entrepreneurs, mafia, and political elites was typical of Russian society more widely at that time.[123]

Several reputed members of the Tambov and Malyshev gangs became acquainted with Putin at this time. Gennadiy Petrov and Aleksandr Malyshev, *Novaya gazeta* reported, were sent abroad by Putin's KVS, along with Vladimir Kiselyev, who headed the White Nights Festival Association of St. Petersburg, which was registered in January 1992. Reputed crime bosses who might not have easily received visas to Western countries now arrived as members of official cultural delegations and did their business abroad under the protection of these delegations. They proceeded to sit on the board of these festivals along with the city's cultural elites.[124] Kiselyev's association claimed to be the result of two founding joint ventures, the Music Center of Kiselyev, whose "commercial director" was Aleksandr Malyshev, and Petrodin, whose head was Sergey Kuzmin. Kuzmin was an associate of Gennady Petrov, and was until 2007 listed as one of the owners of the house on Stone Island where Petrov held court as one of the leaders of the St. Petersburg mafia. Kiselyev was the nominal head of the White Nights

Festival Association, but it was widely reported that he worked for Petrov.[125] Their KVS travel documents could have been obtained from Putin himself or the head of the administrative apparatus for the KVS, Igor Sechin, or Vladimir Kozhin, who in March 1993 became the director general of the St. Petersburg Association of Joint Ventures, and then from 1994 to 1999 (after Putin had gone to Moscow) the chief of the Northwestern Center of the Federal Directorate for Currency and Export Control of Russia. As discussed previously, Kozhin went on to become the head of the Presidential Property Management Department under Putin, and Sechin became the deputy prime minister and head of the *silovik* faction in the Putin regime. The journalist Vladimir Ivanidze, who said he had seen Malyshev's travel application, asked him whether he had ever been found guilty of a crime. Malyshev answered, "Not prosecuted," despite having served two sentences for murder.[126] As an annual event, the festival served the city leaders' purpose of showcasing the city and the mafia's purpose of allowing them to travel abroad on "cultural business," mixing city money, cultural money, and illicit money at the same time.[127]

The breadth of Petrov's reach into city affairs was such that one member of the Japanese mafia, known as Kinishi, claimed with great respect that Petrov had told him that his influence in the city government was sufficient that he was able to "change any contract, particularly contracts with foreign investors."[128]* Kinishi stated that his friend in one of the casinos

---

*Kinishi invested in a joint stock company with Petrov called Petrodin, which sold the gaming slots to the casinos in St. Petersburg. In 2012 he gave a very respectful interview in which he fondly remembered Putin's efforts to control gambling and prevent the overt violence that had so scared Kinishi that he started to carry a pistol when he went to St. Petersburg. He recounts his many visits to the house and hotel controlled by Petrov on Kamennyy Ostrov (Stone Island, Pervaya Berezovaya Alleya, 7): "The house was in a posh address. . . . Putin also had a building nearby. Gena [Gennadiy] was there every day. Each day there were people outside the gate waiting to meet with Gena. It was like in a movie about the mafia. Security guards with Kalashnikovs opened the gate and closely examined who came in. A boss from another region arrives to talk to Gena and must wait his turn. Gena is sitting there every morning. He often said to me: 'Kinishi, I'm so tired of this, people talk to me about their problems, and I sometimes just do not have time to deal with these problems.' . . . In 1991, men with assault rifles stood at the subways and shopping centers, and we made good money. In 1992, authorities make a very large step toward legalizing casinos. Doors were open. And when the exhibition of equipment was hosted, Putin spoke to us and said 'Welcome to foreign investors.' After the exhibition we had evening cock-

was denied all the money from his investment because Petrov was able to get access to the contract in the tax authorities' office and change it to exclude him, even though he was an original investor.[130] During much of this period Viktor Zubkov was head of the St. Petersburg Department of State Tax Inspection, and Putin as deputy mayor oversaw the Registration Chamber, supervising all licenses, contracts, and registrations. It was therefore within their power to bring charges on behalf of foreign investors, but none were brought, except, for example, when the legitimate owners were pushed out in favor of those connected to Putin. This occurred in the transfer of ownership of the Grand Hotel Europa from Swedish owners to Germans connected to Putin, after the tax authorities levied a bill greater than the total cost of the structure and forced the owners to sell.[131]

Thus these changes became legal because the St. Petersburg authorities provided a fig leaf of legal respectability through their joint stock and licensing activities. It is astonishing that Putin would claim that the city didn't receive any benefit from this extraordinary windfall of partnership with criminal elements. However, no one has discovered where the money went. All efforts to investigate the situation after Sobchak lost power in 1996 resulted in people dying or in prosecutions being shut down, since Putin and the others were now in Moscow and in a position to suppress investigations, according to the chief investigator involved.[132]

It is worth restating that in 2008, when Spanish officials arrested Petrov and Malyshev on allegations of money laundering, racketeering, and tax evasion (in Operation Troika), they stated that these elements began to set up a permanent presence in Spain beginning in 1996—the year Putin went to Moscow. They became so influential in Spain that Petrov owned a house next door to the sister of King Juan Carlos and near Russian ministers and politicians, including the minister of communication and a long-standing Putin friend, Leonid Reyman, and Duma deputy Vladislav Reznik.[133]

---

tails at the house on Stone Island. Not in our building, but very close. Literally steps away." In 1992 the house on Stone Island was taken over by a group of ex-KGB operatives who were moving into the casino business themselves. Both Petrov and members of the Malyshev gang had to leave St. Petersburg temporarily.[129]

While Petrov and Malyshev were under arrest in Spain, Kiselyev continued to play a central role as a "Kremlin entertainment entrepreneur." Despite his association with those who were under investigation by Interpol, he was appointed by Vladimir Kozhin, head of the Presidential Property Management Department, to head a new company, the Federal State Unitary Enterprise, which Kozhin described as maximizing the use of Kremlin palace performance spaces that were underutilized. Kozhin talked about the St. Petersburg roots of his relationship with Kiselyev and their subsequent falling-out: "I knew Vladimir for a long time. . . . He organized the White Nights festival in St. Petersburg. . . . Overall his work with us started well, but then some unacceptable things happened. They started working largely for themselves. . . . He can do anything he likes, . . . but not under the umbrella of my department. The enterprise was liquidated . . . , and he was launched into the open sea [*pustilsya v svobodnoye plavaniye*]." [134]

But Putin did not abandon him. Kiselyev emerged as the key figure behind the Federation Fund concert, where Putin was introduced to such Hollywood celebrities as Goldie Hawn and Sharon Stone. And he was responsible for the famous fundraiser for cancer on December 10, 2010, at which Putin sang "Blueberry Hill." It turned out that the Fund was legally registered only eighteen days later, on December 28,[135] and that the funds raised were distributed only after mothers of sick children complained of fraud, leading the Russian media to take up the case.[136] A very sheepish Kiselyev appeared in a press conference protesting about misunderstandings. Again Putin did not abandon him, appearing at a subsequent antinarcotics rally Kiselyev organized in Kaliningrad and another Hollywood-star-studded event in Moscow.[137]

As quoted earlier, Putin regarded his experience regulating the casinos in St. Petersburg as a mistake: "While we were counting up the profits and deciding where to allocate the funds—to develop the city's businesses or support the social sector—they were laughing at us and showing us their losses." [138] Undoubtedly the casino owners made money in St. Petersburg as they do everywhere, including by skimming their profits in cash and declaring losses to avoid taxes. But Russian journalists who investigated

these affairs also pointed to the role of Baltik-Eskort, the *private* security
company that provided armed security for Putin and Sobchak and was
said to be involved in collecting the *chyornyy nal* (black cash) that "make[s]
the world go round" in St. Petersburg.[139] Baltik-Eskort was believed to
be the cut-out that dealt with organized crime for the mayor's office. The
company's owners, Roman Tsepov and Viktor Zolotov, "worked with the
mayor's office to fulfill orders that could not be put in the hands of official
law enforcement agencies."[140] The fact that Putin has kept Zolotov by his
side ever since—raising him in May 2014 from head of his personal security detail to first deputy minister of interior and commander of the Internal Troops—underlines his view of Zolotov as someone who is absolutely
loyal to him personally.

Putin and the St. Petersburg Real Estate Holding Co.

In April 1999 the German Federal Intelligence Agency, BND, completed
an investigation and issued a report on money laundering in Liechtenstein
in which it was alleged that a previously unknown Russian-German firm,
the St. Petersburg Real Estate Holding Co. (SPAG), was heavily involved
both in laundering Russian money and in laundering money from other
sources, including the Cali drug cartel. Putin was listed as a member of
the advisory board of SPAG. On May 13, 2000, only four days after his
inauguration, police in Liechtenstein, acting on the BND report and working with their Austrian colleagues, arrested the Liechtenstein founder and
leader of SPAG, Rudolf Ritter. Ritter also happened to be the brother of
the economy minister of the principality, population thirty-five thousand.
Copies of the report were obtained first by *Le Monde* and then by *Der
Spiegel* and other European, American, and Russian newspapers. Only on
May 23 did the SPAG website state that in anticipation of his inauguration, Putin had stepped down from the board.[141] So what was SPAG, and
what did it do for and with Vladimir Putin?

From the beginning SPAG connected Putin with Vladimir Smirnov,
and through Smirnov, with Vladimir Kumarin. Putin had already had
business dealings with Smirnov in 1991, when he signed a contract with

Smirnov's Nevskiy Dom for the export of raw materials, as discussed earlier. Smirnov claims they had actually met before that, in Frankfurt in 1991, "where the question of attracting the first private investors to our city was decided."[142] In 1992 Putin and Smirnov were part of a trade delegation to Frankfurt, as a result of which, on August 4, 1992, they, along with partners from Germany and Liechtenstein, registered the St. Petersburg Real Estate Holding Co.[143] From the beginning, according to German commercial registry documents obtained by *Newsweek*, Putin was listed as a member of the advisory board,[144] along with three other St. Petersburg city officials, including German Gref.[145] Mayor Sobchak wrote a letter to SPAG, saying, "We support you politically and administratively," that was posted on the SPAG website.[146] The company issued an IPO in Frankfurt in 1998 (WKN 724440, ISIN: DE0007244402) and sold shares for almost 500 euros per share before they plunged to 35 euros in 1999 and then to .64 euros[147] when German and Liechtenstein police raided the company offices as part of a money-laundering investigation.[148]

As far as can be determined, the money-laundering scheme at SPAG worked in the following way: Money from all kinds of licit and illicit sources flooded out of Russia into a variety of Western banks and offshore accounts in the early 1990s. But these Russians also wanted to use this money to attract other money into Russia, so the question was how to launder it, use it as a honeypot to gather more investors, and then repatriate it so that it could be used to make legitimate property purchases inside Russia that would secure and legalize the wealth of the originators. The possibility also existed of purely scamming Western investors. As head of the Committee for Foreign Liaison, Putin could issue licenses for export that would allow foreign currency and commodities to pass through the border and issue import licenses for newly clean money to come back in. There were many who agreed with Boris Berezovskiy's claim that "as stated in the press, the 'roof' [*krysha*] of SPAG and Ritter personally in Petersburg was Vladimir Putin,"[149] and it is entirely reasonable to assume that, at a minimum, Putin lent his name to SPAG in order to increase money flows into SPAG and then into St. Petersburg and to lend the whole exercise respectability. Putin and Yuriy L'vov, the founder and president of the Bank of St. Petersburg, set up the first foreign currency exchange bureau—evidently inside the mayor's administration offices at Smolny itself—in 1991 to facilitate these transactions, but also to garner further huge commissions.[150]* And as the Sal'ye Commission documented, there was hard evidence that the city attached a fee, ranging from 25 to 50 percent, in return for granting licenses. The KVS could also serve as a co-contractor, so that dividends and profits would be paid directly to the KVS for use by the city and its officials on an ongoing basis. Putin's KVS managed a massive flow of money, since in Russia in the early 1990s there were still severe foreign exchange controls. And given St. Petersburg's position as a port and frontier city, it played a very significant role in the overall exodus of money—foreign trade licensing being a key first step in capital flight at this time.[153]

The reputed head of the Tambov crime gang, Vladimir Kumarin, known throughout Petersburg at this time as "the Night Governor," got involved in two subsidiaries of SPAG, called Znamenskaya and Inform-Future. Both were licensed by Putin's KVS in July 1994,[154] and in both of them Smirnov was listed as a co-owner. Kumarin himself estimated that Putin had signed between eight hundred and eighteen hundred contracts during the early 1990s.[155]

The city of St. Petersburg was reported to have an initial 20 percent stake in SPAG,[156] and in December 1994 Putin signed an order giving Smirnov the right to vote "our" (the city's) shares. This was revealed in BND records leaked to *Newsweek*,[157] reprinted in Jürgen Roth's account of the role of Russian dirty money in Germany,[158] and reconfirmed in market analyses of the company, which shows that by 2000 the city's share had grown to 27.58 percent.[159] To safeguard and guarantee the deals, St. Petersburg officials were put on the advisory board. At least two German directors of the company confirmed that they had met Putin at least seven times

---

* L'vov's bank served as the preferred bank for most of the public institutions in St. Petersburg and was so successful that in 1993 it paid its shareholders over 1,000 percent dividends. L'vov became deputy minister of finance in the first Putin government.[151] St. Petersburg governor and Putin ally Valentina Matvienko also had an interest in the bank when her son Sergey became vice president, despite his having been charged in 1994 with robbery and infliction of bodily harm (Criminal Case No. 187898).[152]

in Frankfurt or Russia in the early 1990s.[160] But apparently, and perhaps unknown to the German banks that were involved, the company was used from the beginning as a vehicle for significant money laundering by Kumarin and the Tambov crime gang.[161] Writing for the *St. Petersburg Times*, Catherine Belton comments on the international press coverage of SPAG and on a book published in Germany by the investigative journalist Jürgen Roth: "Roth traces the German investigators' probe to two individuals, Boris Grinshtein and Peter Haberlach, both of whom are under suspicion of being the Tambov group's point men in Germany, according to his sources in German law enforcement. Investigators believe that one of the ways funds were laundered through SPAG was via share issues in the company. At least two companies connected to Grinshtein and Haberlach are pinpointed by Roth as having taken part in such deals. In December 1994, a firm called E. C. Experts Ltd., which was then headed by Grinshtein, bought shares in SPAG for 500,000 German marks. . . . Then in July 1995, it took part in another share issue, buying up 13,000 shares for 110 Deutschmarks each. . . . In October of that year, again according to Roth, [Rudolf] Ritter signed off on the sale of 10,000 shares for 140 marks each to a firm called ICI International Consulting Investments. Haberlach is a director of E. C. Experts and is also under investigation in Hamburg on allegations of human trafficking and running a prostitution ring. Haberlach's brother, Roth writes, is married to the former wife of Kumarin. Roth cites the BundesKriminalAmt (BKA), or German police, as saying it suspects 'ICI International Consulting Investment to have played a central role in founding SPAG and its affiliated companies and that through this company certain people also wielded influence over the chain of money flows into SPAG. The firm Euro-Finanz also appears to have played a similar role.' In what could be a vital link between the SPAG case and the case against Ritter for laundering Colombian drug money, Euro-Finanz is also identified in a Liechtenstein prosecutors' indictment against Ritter, a copy of which has been obtained by the *Moscow Times*."[162] At 1.6 Deutschmarks to the U.S. dollar, these total share purchases were worth about $1.7 million.

In 2000 SPAG's website proclaimed that the company had been

given the right to be the only foreign investor in the real estate sector in St. Petersburg that could take the profits from its investments out of the country ("habilitée à récolter des investissements").[163] Such a move would have needed political capital and approval by the board, including Putin. Even in 2012 the website still maintained that SPAG was the only Western company authorized to invest in real estate and development projects in key strategic areas of St. Petersburg. So if someone wanted to invest in St. Petersburg and take his profits out of the country, SPAG would be the ideal vehicle. The investigators charged that deals were put together in which money from Russian organized crime was commingled with Western money, some of which was also being laundered from illicit activities, including from Colombia's Cali cartel. But some of it was legitimate investment from Western sources impressed with the fact that Putin was on the company's advisory board. German bankers were quoted as saying that they had agreed to work with SPAG in the 1990s and had handled its IPO partly because Putin was on its advisory board. The spokesman for the head of the German Baader Bank, which by 2003 owned 30 percent of SPAG, claimed that it had organized the firm's initial IPO in 1998 because "we thought it was good business if there was someone like Putin on the board."[164]

Putin's good friend and Ozero neighbor Smirnov was involved in every step of the process. He received contracts signed by Putin; he was one of the directors of SPAG; and he was the head of the two subsidiaries of SPAG in Russia, Znamenskaya and Inform-Future, in both of which Kumarin was also involved.[165] Kumarin and Smirnov, whose Rif-Security is said to have provided security for the properties of the Ozero Cooperative,[166] were listed as lead developers of two real estate ventures supported by SPAG. The Tambovskaya Business Center, which became the Inform-Future Business Center (located on Tambovskaya str., 12), advertised itself as the first business center built to Western standards—"24 hour security, fiber optic telephone system, internet"—with three thousand square meters of rentable office space and client support.[167]

The second property being developed by Znamenskaya was the Nevskiy International Center, on Nevskiy Prospect at Vosstaniya Square in a prime location across from the train station. Documents showed that the

St. Petersburg city government loaned Znamenskaya 1.5 billion rubles to resettle residents of communal apartments occupying that building, but when Yakovlev became mayor, he came after Znamenskaya for not repaying the loan, leading journalists to conclude that Smirnov had not been obliged to repay the loan as long as Sobchak and Putin were in office.[168] Kumarin confirmed that he had worked on the SPAG project and had worked to relocate the residents, but when he received the monopoly of the sale of gasoline in St. Petersburg (a monopoly granted by Putin), "we decided that we could make more money building gas stations, and I left the project."[169] The Nevskiy building stood empty for fifteen years, and yet SPAG company records show that SPAG continued to transfer funds to Znamenskaya for reconstruction of the building. Thus between October 1997 and July 2000 documents reproduced by *Novaya gazeta* show that 63.83 million Deutschmarks ($35 million) was transferred to Znamenskaya in twenty payments, over Smirnov's signature. This was self-service in the extreme in that he was signing for SPAG as a member of the board, authorized by Putin to vote the city's shares, and giving money to Znamenskaya, which he headed, for a project that was not being built.[170]

Putin's price for doing real estate deals generally was that 25 percent had to go into the city's coffers for infrastructural and social projects, but there is no evidence of his seeking any commission for this deal. But since the city was itself a co-owner, and he had a position on the board, he certainly did not need to extract a commission as a means to gain access to profits. The BND reports about Putin and SPAG circulated widely. U.S. government analysis of SPAG found clear evidence of Putin's involvement in money laundering, and in 2000, according to a *Newsweek* report, "U.S. officials . . . successfully lobbied for Russia to be placed on an international money-laundering blacklist. A key reason, said a former top U.S. official, was a sheaf of intelligence reports linking Putin to SPAG," including reports showing he "signed important St. Petersburg city documents for the company's benefit."[171]

The Ukrainian president Leonid Kuchma claimed he too was given the SPAG documents. (One can only speculate about why the BND would spread the good word about Putin at a time when its own investigations were reportedly stalling under political pressure at home as the new German chancellor Gerhard Schröder took office.)[172] Kuchma then had to decide whether to turn them over to Putin, whose security chief, Nikolay Patrushev, was furiously trying to manage the fallout from Putin's name being linked to criminal money-laundering charges in Germany. We know all this because Kuchma's presidential guard famously made audio recordings that implicated Kuchma in many illegal actions, including the death of a journalist. But the recordings also reveal interesting details about Putin's role in SPAG and, more important, the role of his security services in handling matters behind the scene. The first conversation, between Kuchma and his security chief Leonid Derkach, took place in Kyiv on June 2, 2000:

> **Derkach:** Leonid Danilovich [Kuchma]. We've got some interesting material here from the Germans. One of them has been arrested.
>
> **Kuchma** (reading aloud): Ritter, Rudolf Ritter.
>
> **Derkach:** Yes and about that affair, the drug smuggling. Here are the documents. They gave them all out. Here's Vova Putin, too.
>
> **Kuchma:** There's something about Putin there?
>
> **Derkach:** The Russians have already been buying everything up. Here are all the documents. We're the only ones that still have them now. I think that [FSB chief] Nikolay Patrushev is coming from the 15th to the 17th. This will give him something to work with. This is what we'll keep. They want to shove the whole affair under the carpet.[173]

The second conversation took place two days later, when Kuchma and Derkach decided to keep the documents, clearly to use as leverage at some future time:

> **Kuchma:** The handover should only take place with the signature of Patrushev. This really is valuable material, isn't it?

Derkach: About Putin?

Kuchma: About Putin.

Derkach: Yes. There is some really valuable stuff. This really is a firm, which . . .

Kuchma: No, tell me, should we give this to Putin, or should we just tell him that we have this material?

Derkach: Yes, we could. But he's going to be able to tell where we got the material from.

Kuchma: I will say the security services; I will say that our security service has some interesting material.

Derkach: And we should say that we got it from Germany, and that everything that exists is now in our hands. Otherwise, no one else has it, yes? Now, I got all the documents about Putin prepared to give them to you [Putin].

Kuchma: Probably, if that's necessary. I'm not saying that I will personally hand them over. Maybe you'll give them to Patrushev?

Derkach: No. I'll just . . . when we make a decision we'll have to hand them over anyhow because they've bought up all these documents throughout Europe and only the remaining ones are in our hands.

Kuchma: Or perhaps I will say that we have documents, genuine facts from Germany. I won't go into details.

Derkach: Hmm.

Kuchma: I will say, "Give your people the order to connect with our security service." And when they get in touch with you, you say, "I gave it to the president, damn it. And I can't get it from him now."

Derkach: Good.

Kuchma: We need to play with this one.[174]

In July 2001 two of SPAG's founders, Eugene von Hoffer and Ritter, were indicted in Liechtenstein of money laundering and using shares in SPAG to scam foreign investors, including Americans—Ritter received one year probation and von Hoffer eight years on this and an additional charge.[175] Meanwhile in Russia, Putin named Gref his economic development minister and Smirnov head of the Presidential Property Management Department and then director general of Tekhsnabeksport (Tenex), which is responsible for all Russian state exports of goods and services for the nuclear power industry, including the U.S.-Russian Megatons to Megawatts program and the building of the Bushehr nuclear reactor in Iran.[176]*

Given the political sensitivity of the investigation, the Germans moved slowly and cautiously. German newspapers stated that Chancellor Schröder personally kept Putin informed about the investigation.[178] Three years after Putin was elected president and his name had disappeared from the company's roster, the Germans finally raided twenty-seven offices and banks associated with SPAG in Germany alone. Sources in the investigation said that the raids were "in connection with people who worked at [SPAG] in the '90s" suspected of laundering "tens of millions of euros" for "one of the biggest and most powerful" Russian organized crime groups involved in "numerous crimes, including vehicle smuggling, human trafficking, alcohol smuggling, extortion and confidence trickstering."[179] Putin's name did not appear in the indictments, and Ritter pled guilty on a lesser count. German observers concluded that as long as Schröder was chancellor, even at one point calling Putin a "flawless democrat,"[180] Putin would not face another hostile investigation.[181] Even more, intelligence experts claim that Schröder handed Putin a BND file during his trip to Berlin on February 10, 2003, containing the results of a BND investigation into the company IWR, which had been involved in the disappearance of East German Communist Party funds prior to reunification. They found that Bank Menatep, owned by Mikhayl Khodorkovskiy, had possibly been involved, giving Putin the information needed to charge Menatep leaders with money laundering.[182]

---

* In 2005 *Novaya gazeta* came into possession of documents purporting to show that Tenex had set up a subsidiary in Germany for the purpose of representing Tenex interests in selling nuclear fuel and nuclear technology but also for the purpose of continuing to launder money.[177]

Schröder was made head of the shareholders' committee of Nord Stream within months of leaving office. Nord Stream was headed by Putin's long-time friend, the ex-Stasi officer Matthias Warnig. Schröder and former Italian prime minister Silvio Berlusconi were the only Western leaders prominently present at Putin's 2012 inauguration.

The massive SPAG site at 114–6 Nevskiy Prospekt on Vosstaniya Square was renovated and then sold to the Finnish company Stockmann only in 2005,[183] and a luxury mall opened there in 2010. In 2012 SPAG's website still insisted that "the Company is the only Western company authorized to invest in real estate and development projects in key strategic areas of the municipality of St. Petersburg, northwestern Russia."[184] The stock's volatility continued, as when, on February 1, 2007, the stock collapsed, plunging from 412 euros to 44 euros the next day, despite gains in the European markets. Investors rebelled, calling an emergency general meeting to prevent the board from using company funds to launch a legal defense.[185]

As for Putin, his involvement in SPAG was public, and even leaving aside whether he benefited personally from his association, his presence on the advisory board had the multiple effect of allowing Russian money to flow into SPAG, attracting licit and illicit Western money through the surety of his association with the company, supporting the provision of properties for investment, and providing the use of St. Petersburg city funds for the relocation of residents. He resigned from his position on the board only on May 23, 2000, well after becoming president. German investigators did not pursue the link with Putin, and the case against him fizzled.

Putin and the Petersburg Fuel Company

As with Putin's connection to SPAG, his involvement in the establishment of the Petersburg Fuel Company (Peterburgskaya Toplivnaya Kompaniya, PTK) features his tight circle of collaborators from the mayor's office, organized crime, Ozero Cooperative members, and former KGB members. PTK was licensed by Putin in August 1994 when he was first deputy mayor. Vladimir Smirnov and Vladimir Kumarin were partners in the company, along with Vadim Glazkov, a Leningrad native who knew Putin from the KGB and the mayor's office,[186] and Viktor Khmarin,[187] a St. Petersburg lawyer who was a friend of Putin and the brother of Putin's first fiancée.[188] Company records indicate that founding shares were held by twenty-one different companies and government agencies, including Bank Rossiya, the insurance company Rus' (which included Arkadiy Krutikhin, the former head of the property management department of the Leningrad *oblast'* committee, Vladislav Reznik, and Aleksey Aleksandrov—all of whom had also been involved in the founding in 1991 of Bank Rossiya), and both the St. Petersburg and Leningrad *oblast'* committees for property management.[189]

In January 1995 the city signed a series of agreements with PTK giving it the exclusive right to supply gasoline to the city's entire fleet of vehicles, from ambulances to buses and cars,[190] to build a chain of gasoline stations throughout the city, and to "participate in the formulation of policies of the St. Petersburg Mayor's Office in the area of [gasoline] supply."[191] Russian media sources reported that the PTK brought together the city administration and the Tambov and Malyshev criminal groups.[192] Il'ya Traber, who controlled both the antiquarian market in the city and held a major interest in the St. Petersburg port, also was involved, and the Tambovs' Kumarin returned to Petersburg in early 1996 after being badly wounded in a turf battle there. It appears this was one area where rival groups ultimately cooperated for their mutual benefit, which allowed them to fix prices, evade taxation, and skim deliveries,[193] against the interests of St. Petersburg citizens who suffered from higher prices and poorer quality. In this way the city administration allowed itself to be captured by criminal elements, presumably as in such cases worldwide, for their mutual benefit. Thane Gustafson, whose book *Wheel of Fortune* provides an extensive study of Russian oil, summed up the political forces at work in St. Petersburg: "The local fuels business was a rich source of off-the-books cash, and therefore it was quickly penetrated by organized crime, typically with the behind-the-scenes backing of city officials and local law-enforcement agencies."[194] The Russian investigative reporter Roman Shleynov states:

The PTK was the nexus of the interests of those described as members of the Tambov group and the pool of Vladimir Putin's cronies who today control the country's key assets. At the time the PTK was set up in 1994, the shareholders included Bank Rossiya, whose co-owners were [Putin's] long-time cronies, who had founded the Ozero cooperative together with him: Yuriy Koval'chuk and Nikolay Shamalov. Interestingly, Gennadiy Petrov, who has since been arrested in Spain, was a shareholder of Bank Rossiya in 1998–1999. Another shareholder in PTK was the Piter Information and Legal Office, in which Il'ya Traber had a stake. The structure of PTK's assets and management had changed by 1998. According to the company's records, another mate of Putin's, Vladimir Smirnov (co-founder of the Ozero cooperative) became chairman of the Board of Directors, while Vladimir Kumarin, who is now under investigation, became a vice president.[195]*

Novaya gazeta's investigative reporter Roman Anin concluded in 2011, "Although the city's Property Management Committee had the biggest (14%) stake in the PTK, if the shares owned through various entities by Gennadiy Petrov, through various structures together with Vladimir Kumarin (even though Kumarin was not officially a shareholder) are aggregated, they owned the petrol monopoly, which enjoyed serious protection from the St. Petersburg mayor's office and Vladimir Putin himself."[197]

This group held wide sway in St. Petersburg while Putin worked there and after he left. To be sure, it might not have been possible to establish a more competitive market given the propensity by rival groups to use violence. It is, however, notable that the city authorities, including Putin, worked with, strengthened, and ultimately legitimized the crime families

---

*A further 5 percent of the PTK went to Viktor Khmarin, Putin's close associate and friend, through the company Vita-X. Bigger stakes went to ZAO Petroleum (12 percent), affiliated with Gennadiy Petrov, and the Baltic Bunker Company (12 percent), which had links with Petrov, Traber, and Dmitriy Skigin, who was expelled from Monaco in 2000, according to police officials there, for links to the Tambov crime family.[196]

in their midst. It is not surprising that Kumarin was not arrested in Russia until after Petrov was under arrest without bail in Spain in 2008.* Spanish officials told the U.S. Embassy that their extensive phone taps and seized documents led them to the conclusion that Russia had become a "virtual mafia state." There were two reasons to worry about the Russian mafia, they said. One was its "tremendous control" over certain strategic sectors, like aluminum. "The second reason is the unanswered question regarding the extent to which Russian PM Putin is implicated in the Russian mafia and whether he controls the mafia's actions. Grinda [José Grinda González, the chief Spanish prosecutor in charge of the case] cited a 'thesis' . . . that the Russian intelligence and security services . . . control OC [organized crime] in Russia. Grinda stated that he believes this thesis is accurate." [200]

Kumarin was finally arrested in Russia in 2007 and in November 2009 received a fourteen-year sentence for fraud and money laundering, having presided as head of one of the last remaining organized crime groups in St. Petersburg for the first two Putin terms. Some reports concluded that the Russians wanted to demonstrate to the Spanish officials that they were going to get tough on organized crime by actually imprisoning him. The thinking was that this paved the way for Petrov and Malyshev to be freed on bail in February 2010, allowing them to return to their Majorca villas. [201] Others contend that Kumarin had lost a battle for market share against a government minister. [202]

The tight connection between Putin, his Ozero friends, his KGB collaborators, and the criminal world was significantly illustrated in the PTK case. Boris Gryzlov, who had come from Petersburg with Putin and was his first interior minister, confirmed the relationship between PTK and Tambov when he stated in 2001 that whole sectors of the economy in St. Petersburg

---

* Spanish prosecutors were said to have had incriminating evidence not only against Petrov but against two other St. Petersburg friends of Putin: Leonid Reyman, who became Putin's first minister of communications, and Vladislav Reznik, who followed Putin to Moscow and became head of Rosgosstrakh (the Russian State Insurance Company) before being dismissed in 1998 for "violations committed in the course of the company's privatization." [198] Putin nevertheless picked Reznik to be deputy chairman of United Russia, in charge of its economic program in 2001. Reznik was also picked to be the main author in 2006 of the law On Preventing Laundering of the Income from Criminal Activities and Financing of Terrorism. [199]

during this period were under the control of organized crime, including commercial seaports in the northwest, the fuel and energy complex, and timber exports.[203]

Putin and Twentieth Trust: Another Criminal Case

When discussing what personal use Putin himself made of the funds that went into the city's coffers, most often at the top of the list is Criminal Case No. 144128, relating to the investigation initiated by the Ministry of Internal Affairs' Investigative Committee on February 4, 1999.* The case charged Putin with authorizing the transfer in the early 1990s of almost 23 billion rubles (almost $28 million) from the city budget to Twentieth Trust as advances and loans that were never paid back.[204] According to Lieutenant Colonel Zykov, the investigation concluded that "the Corporation, as a commercial firm, was receiving loans from the city, through channels and from special funds on favorable terms, it did not return them; it put the money into deposit accounts at commercial banks; it was then rerouted to other companies for purposes not related to the original submission; and it charged for other frivolous expenses."[205]

The Twentieth Trust was registered on October 20, 1992, by Putin's Committee for Foreign Liaison as a company devoted to "construction, reconstruction and repair of industrial, domestic and cultural sites in Russia *and abroad.*"[206] In 1993 alone, Zykov claimed, the Trust had a budget of over $4.5 million and received about 80 percent of its funds from the city of St. Petersburg, even though it was a private company and not a public corporation that needed to meet a payroll, like many others that received public assistance at the time.[207]

---

*Leading the investigation were Lieutenant Colonel Andrey Zykov, the senior investigator for particularly important cases of the Criminal Investigation Department of the Investigative Committee of the Ministry of Internal Affairs of the Russian Federation's Northwest Federal District, based in St. Petersburg, and Oleg Kalinichenko, a senior operative officer in the St. Petersburg branch of the Anti-Corruption Department of the Ministry of Internal Affairs. Although these documents have not been made public, quite a lot of the information that fueled the investigation is available and has been the subject of journalistic investigations by both *New Times* and *Novaya gazeta,* as quoted in the text.

According to the charges, Putin appears to have used his connection with Twentieth Trust to make many transfers of funds to his friends, and for his own benefit, both in Russia and abroad. The investigation found that Twentieth Trust transferred money to other companies in eight countries, mainly Spain and Finland.[208] *Novaya gazeta*'s investigation, in which they had access to case documents, concluded that Putin flew to Finland with Sergey Nikeshin, the head of the Trust, charging their expenses to a Twentieth Trust American Express card, and leading the investigators to ask, "Why is a private corporation paying for St. Petersburg City Hall officials?"[209] Zykov said that money was used to build thirty houses near Torrevieja, including "cottages for Putin and Sobchak," and he repeated the charge made in Spanish newspapers that Putin had crossed into Spain thirty-seven times on forged documents, "including when he was Director of the FSB."[210] Other investigators found that Nikeshin and "Putin banker" Vladimir Kogan had villas built for them; according to locals and Russian laborers in Spain interviewed by *Novaya gazeta*, the villas were built by Spanish contractors using Russian Army labor. After escaping to Portugal, one former colonel told a Russian reporter that they had not been paid, their passports had been confiscated, and they were constantly subjected to threats and blackmail: "I felt like a Russian prostitute in Turkey."[211] As I discuss in the next chapter, there were also separate allegations that Putin visited Spain on forged documents during the period 1996–2000 in connection with business meetings between himself, Boris Berezovskiy, and Russian crime figures. Both these sets of allegations would follow him into the presidency.[212]

Money was evidently also used to build a hotel in Spain under the cover of reserving it for veterans, and on one occasion at least, on February 9, 1996, Putin authorized $2,000 per person to be allocated "for recreation for veterans" and their families to stay in the hotel. It was alleged that city officials and their families and the leadership of Twentieth Trust instead took over the hotel on holiday in May 1996. The *Novaya gazeta* investigation quoted Case No. 144128 documents that concluded, "In a breach of contract . . . the list of persons traveling on holiday to Spain . . . included citizens who have relations neither to veterans nor to those active in science and art: Head of the Federal Treasury V. N. Karetin and two members of his family, . . . Chairman of the Board of Directors of Twentieth Trust R. V. Kamaletdinov and two members of his family." [213] Spanish intelligence (Superior Center of Defense Information, Centro Superior de Información de la Defensa, CESID) monitored Putin's comings and goings from Spain and subsequently provided the information to Spanish newspapers in 2000, which revealed that "the CESID already knew about [Putin's] earlier presence in Alicante where the current President spent some of his summers. In Torrevieja, they believe he participated in the development of apartments for Russian officials to spend vacation time in Spain when he was vice-mayor of St. Petersburg." [214]*

In November 1995 Twentieth Trust received from Putin 415 million rubles (more than $90,000) for reconstruction of the Russian Orthodox Gornenskiy Convent in Jerusalem, which had already received funding the previous year. Security service personnel were dispatched to look at the convent; they did no work (according to Zykov) but submitted expense claims for $20,000. [218] In thanking Putin "for providing financial assistance for the 1994–95 biennium," the head of Twentieth Trust, Sergey Nikeshin, "respectfully asks you to provide us with financial assistance from the Mayor's Contingency Fund for the continuation of the work." At the top of the letter Putin simply wrote, "Agreed." [219]

Here we have evidence, as shown in documents reproduced by *Novaya gazeta* and *New Times*, [220] that the mayor's money was being distributed without documentation, without proof that the reconstruction was on any kind of schedule or subject to any kind of contract—it was essentially used

---

*In addition to the charges against Putin, Zykov alleges that other Putin associates were under investigation. He claimed to have documents related to an apartment that Aleksey Kudrin, the deputy mayor and future minister of finance under Putin, purchased in Italy. [215] The investigators evidently also made a request to the Central Bank of Russia (N 17/sch-8005) in connection with Case No. 144128, seeking information about Kudrin's personal checking accounts and safety deposit boxes, but *Novaya gazeta* claimed that the request was rejected because data on Kudrin was "not relevant to the case under investigation." [216] German Gref, who became Putin's minister of economic development, was alleged to have approved a contract for $470,000 to Twentieth Trust for renovating a one-thousand-square-meter building in St. Petersburg, with money going to firms in Germany, Finland, and the United States. Investigators stated that the work was never done. [217]

as a slush fund for city officials. In an interview with the Mother Superior of the convent, she confirmed that after the collapse of the USSR, the convent was in dire need of repairs, not having had any done since prerevolutionary times. It lacked running water, a telephone, and an inn for pilgrims, and the cathedral was unfinished. Only in 1997, when Patriarch Aleksey II visited the convent, was substantial restoration work done, according to her account.[221] Not only is there no indication that any work was done at this time on the Gornenskiy Convent by Twentieth Trust, but *Novaya gazeta*'s conclusion is that the convent's money was actually diverted to build two thirty-two-apartment hotels called La Paloma in the Spanish resort of Torrevieja, near Alicante, for which Nikeshin received more than half a million dollars for the design and documentation stage alone.[222]

Local Spanish company registries show that the Twentieth Trust Company, SL (Sociedad Limitada), was incorporated in Torrevieja on July 21, 1994 (company code B03959467, address 20 2 Glorieta Ramón Gallud, 03180 Torrevieja, Alicante, Spain), and operated until at least 2004.[223] Company reports show that funds were transferred by Nikeshin into Twentieth Trust each year from 1994 to 1997. *Novaya gazeta* subsequently summed up the amounts that had been transferred from St. Petersburg city coffers to Twentieth Trust and concluded that while only $3 million had found its way into the property market in Spain, "$22.5 million in total had been 'stolen' from St. Petersburg by Anatoly Sobchak's team."[224] Shleynov puts the estimate as high as $28 million (see the chart on page 149). Investigator Zykov, whose own account is in accordance with this, concludes with this chilling—for Putin—statement: "All documents on this fraudulent affair are safely hidden in the 117 secret volumes. However, copies of the documents, tracking who had endorsed the allocation of money, and for what purpose, . . . I have passed to 'Radio Liberty.'"[225] I confirmed that Radio Liberty did receive these volumes.

In another case, at the end of 1993, *Novaya gazeta* claimed that Putin granted a loan "as an exception" of 2.5 billion rubles to Twentieth Trust for construction in St. Petersburg of a business center called Peter the Great at the unusually favorable rate of 6 percent APR (the average rate then was

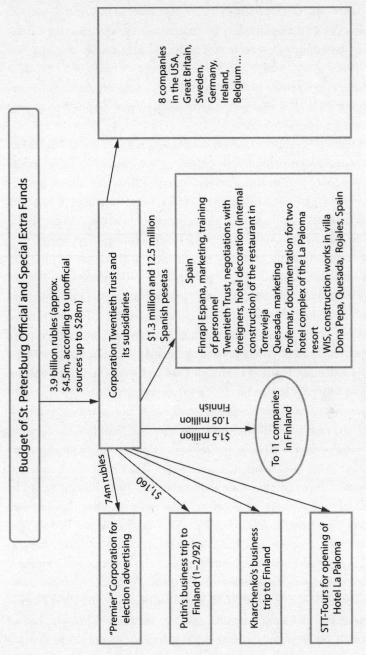

Twentieth Trust: How Did the Money Flow?
Source: Roman Shleynov, *Novaya gazeta*, October 3, 2005.

Budget of St. Petersburg Official and Special Extra Funds

3.9 billion rubles (approx. $4.5m, according to unofficial sources up to $28m)

Corporation Twentieth Trust and its subsidiaries

8 companies in the USA, Great Britain, Sweden, Germany, Ireland, Belgium…

$1.3 million and 12.5 million Spanish pesetas

Spain
Finrapl Espana, marketing, training of personnel
Twentieth Trust, negotiations with foreigners, hotel decoration (internal construction) of the restaurant in Torrevieja
Quesada, marketing
Profemar, documentation for two hotel complex of the La Paloma resort
WIS, construction works in villa
Dona Pepa, Quesada, Rojales, Spain

$1.5 million
1.05 million Finnish

To 11 companies in Finland

74m rubles

"Premier" Corporation for election advertising

$1,160

Putin's business trip to Finland (1–2/92)

Kharchenko's business trip to Finland

STT-Tours for opening of Hotel La Paloma

200 percent), despite the fact that the only collateral the Trust posted was fifty-five cars of various models. Investigators found that the loan was not repaid, the business center was not built, and only twenty-two cars were now offered as collateral![226] Nikeshin also received a credit of $1.3 million from the mayor's office in 1993 toward the construction of a forty-story skyscraper in St. Petersburg that never came to pass despite having been approved by the mayor's office.[227]

Twentieth Trust also was an official cosponsor of the White Nights Festival, but investigators found that the money was used to buy more Spanish real estate and purchase Finnish prefab homes.[228] The chief controller of the Ministry of Finance of the Russian Federation in St. Petersburg, V. Kabachinov, concluded, "On January 1, 1997, the debt of the corporation [Twentieth Trust] to the city stands at 28,455,700,000 rubles" ($1.1 billion).[229]

Matt Bivens of the *Moscow Times*, in writing about Twentieth Trust, interviewed the Yabloko Party's Igor Artem'yev, who came in as head of the city's finances after Sobchak (and Putin as his campaign manager) lost the 1996 mayoral elections. Bivens quotes Artem'yev: " 'The city suffered an enormous loss here. . . . This was a criminal story or at least a story of dishonest intentions.' Artem'yev was aghast at the shape in which he found the city's finances. He sued Twentieth Trust and won. (But, he complains, for some reason Governor Yakovlev won't go collect the money.)"[230]

Moscow's *New Times* investigation added, "CEO Nikeshin could easily call the next president of Russia and report to him the need to transfer several million dollars for the reconstruction of an Orthodox church in Greece. Medvedev controlled this transfer. The future of the money is unknown. The money went through the famous Bank Rossiya owned by the Koval'chuk brothers. [Yuriy Koval'chuk was a founding member with Putin of the Ozero Cooperative.] The office was located on the first floor of the Smolny Institute [city hall], and as sources tell *New Times*, investors could get approval from Vladimir Putin for their project on one condition: everything had to be done through Bank Rossiya."[231] *New Times* drew attention to the fact that "in 1999, in connection with the activities of the corporation [Twentieth Trust] a criminal case No. 144128 was brought, but on August 30, 2000 (after the arrival of Vladimir Putin in the Kremlin) it was closed. Soon, one of the investigators who worked on the case of this corporation Oleg Kalinichenko retired to a monastery. Another, Andrey Zykov, was sent into retirement."[232] Other investigators also have asserted that Medvedev was involved in the flow of money out of the country, with Putin working with Nikeshin through Twentieth Trust and Medvedev responsible for organizing the financial flows from the Mayor's Contingency Fund. Having said that, it is remarkable how seldom Medvedev is mentioned in these schemes compared with others, particularly Putin.[233] The chart on page 149, prepared as a result of extensive investigation by *Novaya gazeta*'s Roman Shleynov,[234] indicates what he believed to be the flow of money.

Even after Putin went to Moscow, this case would have to be dealt with and would continue to haunt both Putin and Kudrin. Marina Litvinovich, who had been one of Putin's Kremlin image-makers and who worked on his 2000 campaign, wrote in 2012:

> Economics and Finance committee head Kudrin and deputy mayor Vladimir Putin are also named in criminal case No. 144128 initiated in 1999 in connection with *Dvadtsatyy Trest* (20th Trust) Construction company operations (Trust head Sergey Nikeshin was a member of the St. Petersburg Legislative Assembly). The investigation used documents from a 20th Trust audit by the RF Ministry of Finance Audit Department, which was conducted on the instruction of the municipal administration for combating economic crime. According to audit documentation, Kudrin signed agreements in order to secure several million dollars in government loans for 20th Trust, which were then wired to over 20 companies in Spain, Finland, Sweden, Germany, Belgium, Ireland and the U.S. The investigation ended when Vladimir Putin was inaugurated President of Russia, with lead investigators saying they experienced unprecedented pressure [to close the case].[235]

These charges were very serious. Between Sobchak's involvement in the corruption scandal and Putin's own exposure in yet other cases, it must have occupied a lot of Putin's time to get the investigations stopped. But stopped they were. Criminal Case No. 144128 was terminated by order of the procurator general on August 30, 2000, but not before Kalinichenko came under "very serious pressure," according to Zykov, so serious that he abandoned all his files and joined a monastery, telling Zykov that "he had got tired of all those things; the materials in which such surnames were mentioned were doomed anyway."[236] Zykov was also forced to retire, and then sued Putin. But the court received a letter from the Presidential Administration asserting that a sitting president could not be a party to a suit. Ultimately Zykov gave the lengthy interview cited earlier and also provided an extensive nine-part commentary that was posted on both the Russian and English versions of YouTube.[237]*

Putin and "the Sobchak Case": Criminal Case No. 18/238278–95

Knowledge about the charging of commissions in St. Petersburg and other instances of gross malfeasance had reached Moscow and was considered "so serious," according to Zykov,[238] that in December 1995 FSB director Mikhayl Barsukov and Interior Minister Anatoliy Kulikov joined with Procurator General Yuriy Skuratov in the creation of "an inter-ministerial operational investigative group for the investigation of kickbacks by officials at the City Hall of St. Petersburg," which resulted in Criminal Case No. 18/238278–95.[239] Underlining the gravity of the charges, the twenty-person team was led by Leonid Proshkin, deputy chief of the Investigation Department of the Procurator General's Office in Moscow and a renowned investigator.

Many in the top leadership in St. Petersburg were under investigation for "taking bribes" and "abuse of power,"[240] including Sobchak, Putin, Kudrin, and Oleg Kharchenko, chief architect of the city and head of its urban planning committee, who was also on the advisory board of SPAG

---

* The transcription of Zykov's testimonials is available in Russian on the author's Web page at www.miamioh.edu/havighurstcenter/putins-russia.

and would go on to be the chief architect of the Sochi Olympics.*[241] The allegation was that Sobchak had signed Executive Order No. 825-r giving 350 million rubles of support from the city budget and other benefits to the real estate company Renaissance, which in turn gave apartments to city officials, including Sobchak, Putin, Kharchenko, and others.† Despite the investigations that swirled around him, Putin was promoted to first deputy mayor in March 1994, only fueling the view that Sobchak was also involved in this corrupt business.

I have already discussed how Sobchak was implicated in handing out apartments on Vasil'yevskiy Island to his friends and family, including Putin. The procurator general charged Sobchak with corruption for his role in this apartment exchange; when he was being questioned he suffered a health crisis, had to be taken to the hospital, and from there fled the country, apparently with Putin's assistance. The prosecutors did not pursue the case, and once Putin became prime minister (and succeeded in getting rid of Skuratov), he was in a position to squash the case. When he was acting president, Putin acknowledged that the heads of these three agencies—the FSB, MVD, and Procurator General's Office—had appointed the commission that came to St. Petersburg and "opened up several criminal cases," although he contended that Sobchak was at least initially only a witness and not under investigation.[244]

---

*Oleg Kharchenko was the head of the City Property Management Committee from 1991 to 2004 and rose to become the chief architect of the Sochi Olympic construction company Olympstroy. He and Putin were linked in the German-registered company SPAG. Also being investigated were Sergey Tarasevich (head of the Federal Migration Service's St. Petersburg office), G. A. Filippova (head of the Housing Renewal Department), V. A. Dryakhlov (head of the Vasil'yevskiy Island Militia), Vladimir Yeremenko, a procurator (investigated for providing forged documents that retroactively registered apartments acquired for the main participants, including Putin and Sobchak), and Yuriy Kravtsov (chairman of the St. Petersburg Legislative Assembly and member of the Federation Council).[242]

† The details were published in several sources, including a "documentary narrative" written as a thinly disguised fictional account by Andrey Evdokimov, which Investigator Zykov claims was based on inside knowledge of the criminal corruption scandals of the period.[243]

Other Cases against Putin

One of the most persistent contradictions in statements about Putin is the view that he never directly took a bribe but that he surrounded himself with many figures from the criminal, business, and governmental world who did. Of course, Russia was full of people at the highest level who were immersed in the corrupt politics of the 1990s, and it is hard to imagine anyone surviving and getting ahead without taking a bribe. Since much of our view of Putin's incorruptibility comes from Boris Berezovskiy, who testified that this was the feature about Putin that most struck him, it should be taken with a grain of salt, given that the British High Court judgment against Berezovskiy in his lawsuit with Roman Abramovich characterized him as someone who regards "truth as a transitory, flexible concept."[245] It is far more likely that Berezovskiy was impressed with the lengths to which Putin would go to get Sobchak out of Russia, saving both Sobchak and himself at the same time.

More impressive still is the list of close Putin allies who were mired in one corruption scandal after another. Many of them are mentioned above. In addition there is the case of Leonid Reyman. Reyman would come to be identified as one of the most corrupt ministers in Putin's government not only by Russian and Western investigative journalists[246] but also in Western legal circles. Yet he remained a close associate of both Putin and his wife, Lyudmila.

In Germany both civil and criminal probes were launched against a Danish lawyer and four executives of a German bank, Commerzbank,‡ alleging they had participated in laundering more than $150 million of suspicious funds. According to the *Wall Street Journal*, they were alleged to have "assisted former Russian telecommunications minister Leonid Reyman in selling telecommunications assets he allegedly controlled in offshore companies, while concealing who the true owner was. From 1996 to 2001, the German bank held the telecom assets in trust for the Danish law-

---

‡ Dresdner Bank, which had employed Matthias Warnig, was taken over by Commerzbank in 2009.

yer, Jeffrey Galmond. Prosecutors contend Mr. Galmond acted as a front for Mr. Reyman, who, they say, had converted telecom businesses from state ownership to that of a number of foreign companies that Mr. Reyman allegedly set up and controlled after the collapse of communism in the 1990s." [247] German prosecutors, having started the investigation in 2005, ultimately had to drop the case, with the German executives paying nominal fines. The statute of limitations had run out, and the Russian procurator general had written a letter concluding that no violation of Russian laws had taken place. As such, according to a German court spokesman, under German law at that time, Reyman could have been convicted of money laundering only if he had committed a crime in Russia. [248]

In Switzerland the International Court of Arbitration of the International Chamber of Commerce, in a case featured on the World Bank's Stolen Assets Recovery website, "found that Minister Reyman of the Russian Government was the beneficial owner of IPOC [International Growth Fund Limited (Bermuda)] and that he committed criminal acts under Russian law." [249] A court in the British Virgin Islands deemed that IPOC documents had been faked, and IPOC and its associated firms "pleaded guilty and were convicted of two counts of perverting the course of justice" and ordered to pay $45 million in costs and fines. [250] Reyman sought to avoid paying the fine by claiming that his lawyer was the actual owner, but the BVI courts agreed with the Swiss arbitration that in fact "IPOC's beneficial owner was Mr. Reyman and IPOC was [the] center of a scheme to conceal Mr. Reyman's diversion of Russian state assets." [251] This activity started as early as 1994, when Telecominvest was formed in St. Petersburg, when the state owned 95 percent and Reyman's lawyer owned 5 percent. By 1995, according to the World Bank summary of the arbitration, the state share had shrunk to 49 percent and a Luxembourg company named First National Holding owned 51 percent. First National Holding's stake grew to 85 percent, and Reyman rejected claims that he owned this stake and continued to assert that it was in fact owned by his lawyer.

Lyudmila Putina was said to have worked for Reyman's Telecominvest in 1998–99, although German investigators were quick to point out that "it would have been impossible to call the Moscow branch an office. It was more likely a place where communication specialists who came from St. Petersburg held their meetings. . . . Lyudmila Putina was the only employee. She answered phone calls and organized meetings. There wasn't any political background in her work."[252] Nevertheless it is extraordinary that she would work in the office of someone under such scrutiny since she would have had many other choices of places to work. And Putina would continue to do joint public events with Reyman, opening communications fairs and the like as late as 2007, long after these investigations had been launched and had become public.*

In 2006, for example, the *Financial Times* published the following transcription of a videotaped conversation that took place in London's Ritz Hotel, which was submitted in evidence to the U.K.'s Privy Council, where the British Virgin Islands case was on appeal. In it, Galmond is heard speaking to James Hatt, who had worked with Galmond and Reyman in St. Petersburg in the 1990s and now was working for Mikhayl Fridman, chairman of Alfa Group, who was trying to secure a 25 percent stake in the mobile phone company Megafon, linked to Reyman and IPOC. In the transcription, Hatt asks Galmond whether Mr. Reyman wants a settlement with Fridman and Alfa, to which Galmond replies, "He doesn't want fucking Alfa in Megafon. That's it. And if Fridman doesn't understand the music he should have a word with Mr. Khodorkovskiy, and he should have a word with Mr. [Vladimir] Potanin and he should have a word with some of the other guys sitting outside Russia. One who owns a football club [Roman Abramovich] and another who is sitting in Marbella enjoying the sun [Vladimir Gusinskiy], not coming back to Russia and another one sitting here in London playing the political clown [Boris Berezovskiy]. Fridman and Potanin are the last two oligarchs in place and if they don't understand the music, then they will have to face the music. They don't want Alfa in Megafon." Hatt tries to sum up: "So my question to Uncle Leonid [Reyman] is very simple: do you want me to take Alfa's money?" To which Galmond replies, "No, I simply, we don't. Neither Leonid nor I want you to take Alfa's money." Galmond subsequently maintained that his

* For example, at InfoCom-2002[253] and BibliObraz—2007.[254]

references to Reyman in this conversation were to the minister as a regulator of the industry, not as a beneficial owner of IPOC. He did concede that Reyman was named as the primary beneficiary of a Liechtenstein trust that held a stake in First National Holdings, which in turn held the Telecominvest shares, from 1997.[255]

While initially Reyman's activities offshore were not prosecuted in Germany because they had not violated Russian law, in 2009 the German Supreme Court ruled that it had the right to pursue cases if crimes were committed on German soil, and the cases against Reyman were reopened. This move clearly indicated that Russian officials could not avoid the risk of being prosecuted for money laundering even when using offshore accounts. Vadim Volkov of the European University in St. Petersburg commented, "Obviously, this story could become a precedent. . . . Officials and businessmen who built their companies on dubious schemes are not immune from prosecution of law enforcement officers from other countries."[256]

The Reyman case is only one of many cases of Russian political leaders close to Putin accused of corruption. This includes not only businessmen around him, from his Ozero circle, for example, but also ministers in his government, like Reyman. Yet even those who are pursued by international courts for corruption rarely, if ever, are extradited or prosecuted in Russia. Nor do they fall from Putin's favor. On the contrary, those who were accused of corruption in St. Petersburg in the 1990s went on to spectacularly successful careers as recipients of state contracts once Putin became president.

Why Focus on Putin's Corruption?

In the West it might seem remarkable that anyone whose whole career is marked by allegations of corruption should rise to become a three-term president of any country. In Russia it is less surprising. Russia of the 1990s was awash with criminal activity, and elites were barely separate from the mafia underworld. Putin, who was always known in St. Petersburg as the person who could get things done, had a practical approach to the criminal world. The mafia and the KGB had always had points of intersection and conflict—the 1990s were no different, and the mafia had its uses. It was global, it could move money, it could hide money, and in any case, some of that money would come back to St. Petersburg for investment.

So how did Putin operate? First and foremost, he made illegal activity legal. On the surface there is nothing wrong with this, except that the banker in the West who knowingly launders drug money is as guilty of a felony as the drug cartel that supplied his bank with the cash. Additionally Putin was not even-handed: he controlled who got access, and he had strong views about giving his friends market share and pushing his enemies from the scene. He certainly favored joint ventures with the state, in the form of his Committee for Foreign Liaison or other committees of the St. Petersburg mayor's office, from the beginning. He was also vengeful: those who criticized him or his patron Sobchak did not, to put it mildly, get career advancement. Some examples:

1. Yuriy Shutov was an early assistant to Sobchak who saw the first shoots of corruption in the mayor's office in 1990. He wrote about Sobchak in the most negative terms in a 1991 book that made him an early target for dismissal.[257]* He also charged that Putin had used compromising material on Sobchak to obtain and maintain his positions.[259] Shutov was arrested a number of times and remains imprisoned in 2014, despite successful appeals to the European Court of Human Rights.

2. Pavel Koshelev, a KGB colonel from Leningrad, had gone to school with Putin, had written a recommendation for him to enter the KGB,[260] and was Putin's judo partner in the KGB. While this would have been a perfect beginning to a successful career, he leveled a number of corruption charges against Sobchak and his team in the mid-1990s and was dismissed, only to be rehired

---

* His subsequent writings from prison were restatements of these basic views, along with broader analyses of the basic forces shaping international politics, with long quotes from the discredited *Protocols of the Elders of Zion*. They certainly indicate that prison did nothing to soften his views of either Sobchak or Putin.[258]

by Mayor Yakovlev in the Petrograd district of St. Petersburg in 1996. He declared, "My first job will be to locate the money taken out of the Petrograd budget by the city administration," referring to $250,000 he alleges disappeared rather than being used for restoration of the Petrograd district's Austrian Square.[261] Koshelev stated that after his dismissal he started to receive threatening phone calls. He gave friends a dossier incriminating Sobchak, instructing them to publicize it in the event of his death.[262]*

3. On August 24, 1998, the journalist Anatoliy Levin-Utkin was beaten to death outside his apartment. He had worked as deputy editor for the newly established newspaper *Yuridicheskiy Peterburg Segodnya*. After his death, during which the documents and photos inside his briefcase were stolen, journalists investigated and publicized his stories. He had written an article on Putin's activities as chairman of the KVS, his connections to Sobchak, and his participation in getting Sobchak abroad, all of this leading to an article in the next issue entitled "Vladimir Putin Became Head of the FSB Illegally." The article provides a picture of Putin as a rank careerist from his KGB days onward who used KGB methods to suppress market competition in Petersburg.[265] Evidently after this article appeared, "Putin's people had called the newspaper and were very upset."[266] The editor of *Yuridicheskiy Peterburg Segodnya*, Aleksey Domnin, gave a news conference in which he said, according to the accounts, that "Levin-Utkin's murder could be connected with stories the paper had run about the State Customs Committee, Bank Rossiiskiy Kredit and St. Petersburg native Vladimir Putin, who was recently appointed head of the Federal Security Service, the KGB's main successor agency. 'People from the northwestern customs department and from Bank Rossiiskiy Kredit called us and demanded that we reveal the sources and the

---

* Koshelev's efforts to publicize the wrongdoings of the Sobchak administration were the subject of journalist Andrey Evdokimov's book *Austrian Square*.[263] The factual correctness of Evdokimov's book was affirmed by Petersburg procurator Andrey Zykov.[264]

authors of the articles,' Domnin said. He also said that 'Putin's friends,' whom he refused to name, met with him after the second issue of the paper came out. Domnin said 'the meeting was of an obviously political nature.'"[267] A car carrying the last issue (no. 3) that Levin-Utkin had worked on was detained by the militia under false pretenses, according to the Moscow-based Committee for Journalism in Extreme Situations.[268]* Soon afterward the newspaper stopped publishing altogether.

Mancur Olson writes that over time in emerging democracies, the rule of law will be established by those entrepreneurs who no longer want to use violence and absorb its costs.[269] Clearly in St. Petersburg and in Russia as a whole, entrepreneurs fought to capture and maintain market share. Putin could have legitimized this by using his legal position to allow the market itself to decide who would win and who would lose. Instead he hired private security to decide who would get market share. Despite his training as a lawyer, he eschewed transparency and legal norms to make it clear that he himself could make or break a transaction. From the very beginning he promoted ex-KGB officials, cooperated with mafia interests, and worked in a style that was reminiscent of the Soviet era and not called for in the Yel'tsin period. The chair of the St. Petersburg legislature, Aleksandr Belyayev, tried other methods to rein in Putin's behavior as head of the KVS, but largely failed. He accused Putin of using KGB methods in running his office, spying on contacts and rival elites not to help Russian firms but to help his own friends, including foreign business partners.[270]

Sadly left unexplored by investigators was the evidence of significant Russian involvement in money laundering, including documents, according to *Der Spiegel*, showing that from 1993 to 1998 huge amounts of gold from St. Petersburg were melted down in Lugano, Switzerland, each year.[271]

Oleg Kalugin, the KGB general who denounced the failure of that

---

*Issues of the newspaper, which ceased to exist soon after, have disappeared from the Internet and from local, state, and university libraries in Russia, although individual copies are in the author's possession and have been scanned into the author's website at www.miamioh.edu /havighurstcenter/putins-russia.

organization to reform after the fall of the USSR, had been a senior officer in Leningrad with a rank above Putin's. Kalugin subsequently left the country and settled in the United States, prompting Putin, in *First Person,* to call him a "traitor." [272] This produced a blistering open letter from Kalugin with the following passage: "If I were of your frame of mind, I could very well brand you as a thief, bribe-taker and even war criminal, the more so as you have left behind in Leningrad a foul smell of corruption, and some of your former associates are now on the run outside Russia's borders." [273]

When Russia was placed on the Financial Action Task Force (FATF) black list of states involved in money laundering,[274] it was widely stated that one of the reasons the action had been taken was Putin's clear involvement in SPAG. However, in truth, SPAG was a typical, not exceptional, example of Russia's general pattern of noncompliance. The broader claims against Russia are a litany of challenges the country faced in 2000, as Yel'tsin's era gave way to Putin's. Yet in 1996, as Putin made his way toward Moscow, it is clear that the general features the FATF identified certainly applied to his own behavior while in St. Petersburg:

- Absence of or ineffective regulations and supervision for all financial institutions.
- Existence of anonymous accounts or accounts in obviously fictitious names.
- Absence of an efficient mandatory system for reporting suspicious or unusual transactions to a competent authority.
- Lack of monitoring and criminal or administrative sanctions in respect to the obligation to report suspicious or unusual transactions.
- Obvious unwillingness to respond constructively to requests.
- Inadequate or corrupt professional staff in either governmental, judicial or supervisory authorities.
- Lack of a centralized unit or of an equivalent mechanism for the collection, analysis, and dissemination of suspicious transactions information to competent authorities.[275]

In considering the balance of Putin's contribution to the transition to democracy in St. Petersburg, it is worth noting that he, and he alone, was responsible for regulating foreign economic activity into and out of Russia's "window to the West." All accounts of Putin in this period, whether favorable or critical, agree that he was the "gray cardinal" who ran the mayor's office. He represented a unique vortex of power, drawing everything toward him in this otherwise turbulent period. The city's geographic situation on the Gulf of Finland and its talented population could have combined to make St. Petersburg a leader among Russian cities in relations with the outside world. And yet, based on calculations made by Hill and Gaddy, in St. Petersburg during this period, "on a per capita basis, foreign trade was 26 percent of Moscow's, foreign investment was 55 percent, the number of small businesses set up with foreign participation was 38 percent, and the number of people employed by foreign-owned small businesses was 30 percent of the capital's." [276] Putin's style was a failure for the city because it suppressed initiative. But it was a victory for his clan. He would now bring that style and set of priorities to the country at large as he moved to Moscow.

Chapter Four

——◈——

Putin in Moscow, 1996–1999

P UTIN LEFT St. Petersburg for Moscow after Anatoliy Sobchak lost the
May 1996 mayoral election to Vladimir Yakovlev, another first deputy
mayor, whom Putin had publicly and unapologetically branded a "Judas"
both during the campaign and subsequently.[1] During much of the time
he was in St. Petersburg, Putin was under investigation by the St. Petersburg legislature and the Procuracy for many of the activities previously discussed. The arrival on the political scene of an opponent only accelerated
those investigations and added new ones, with the result that he would
spend considerable effort over the next few years "controlling" the situation
in his home city.

While in St. Petersburg, Putin had become head of the local office of
Our Home Is Russia, the first of many Kremlin "parties of power," a post
he held until June 1997, despite the fact that the party lost the 1995 Duma
elections in Petersburg.[2] He also worked for Yel'tsin's reelection campaign,
even while managing Sobchak's failed campaign. A falling-out between
Yel'tsin and Sobchak had created a conflict of interest of sorts for Putin and
led some to believe that he had run a lackluster campaign for Sobchak on
purpose. Nevertheless being on the losing side in these electoral campaigns
evidently did nothing to strengthen his support for truly democratic elections, and thus when he decided to leave St. Petersburg and go to Moscow, he did not seek a position in the ruling party or Duma. Rather he
sought a post that would allow his strengths to come to the fore, shaping
events behind the scene.[3] Why was Putin able to secure a series of key posi-

tions in Moscow beginning in 1996? Hill and Gaddy provide the answer: "The people who brought Vladimir Putin from St. Petersburg to Moscow never cared about his credentials as a specialist in *developing* business. For them he was an expert in *controlling* business. All the time Putin worked in St. Petersburg, he played an official role as deputy mayor and chairman of the Committee [for Foreign Liaison], but, behind the scenes, Mr. Putin operated in his most important identity—the Case Officer. In St. Petersburg, Vladimir Putin was an 'operative.' Businessmen were not partners but targets."[4] Putin demonstrated that it was he who would select those who would become and remain wealthy. Those who stood against him and his circle would face a very tough uphill battle. While Putin came to power in 2000 with the pledge to stop the oligarchs' plundering of the Russian state, he had essentially been involved in the same kind of activity in St. Petersburg, as the Sal'ye Commission demonstrated. He and his circle also used the state as a vehicle for their own vision and their own personal interests.

While he may have left St. Petersburg physically, Putin certainly remained very involved in the politics of the city, not least because of the many close political associations he maintained and depended upon there. And of course he maintained his home in the Ozero Cooperative, north of St. Petersburg. The Russian press wrote that in 1996, when they interviewed St. Petersburg politicians and asked about Putin, who had just been offered a position in Moscow, "one could see concern and even horror in their eyes: 'I will not say anything about him to the press.' And after a moment of nervous silence they would add something totally frightening: 'Please don't write that I didn't want to talk about Putin!' "[5] Putin certainly continued to cast a long shadow in his native city, surrounded as he was by the St. Petersburg–based circle of ex-KGB politicians and friends who helped cement his political base as he rose to power. But it would also seem that he depended on those who remained in St. Petersburg to ensure that the activities he had been involved in during the early 1990s did not result in any successful criminal prosecutions.

The year 1996 saw a lot of changes for Putin. His wife too started a new job, working in the office of Telecominvest, established by Putin's friend and future minister of communications Leonid Reyman.[6] Putin himself started work in Moscow in July. That same summer, in St. Petersburg, evidently while he was there on summer holiday in August, his dacha burned down, and several months later he, along with his closest friends, formally established the Ozero Cooperative. According to his own account, he was able to "force them [the sauna builders who had installed the faulty sauna oven that Putin claimed had caused the fire] to rebuild the house," which they did, "and even better" than the original.[7] Security for the Ozero Cooperative was said to have been provided by Rif-Security, a firm owned by Tambov head Vladimir Kumarin and Vladimir Smirnov.[8]

Most of Putin's closest circle would eventually find their way to Moscow, but the one person he took with him at the beginning was Igor Sechin. He noted in *First Person*, "I liked Sechin. When I moved to Moscow, he asked to go along. I took him."[9] Of all Putin's lieutenants, Sechin was the one with the reputation for the greatest loyalty, a trait that Putin values above all. Sechin would rise with Putin, accompanying him at every stage, until becoming head of the world's largest oil company, Rosneft, in 2012.

The Presidential Property Management Department, July 1996–March 1997

Putin's first job in Moscow was as deputy head of the Presidential Property Management Department.[10] He claims the PPMD wasn't his first choice, that he wanted to work for Yel'tsin's personal staff and had been offered the post of deputy chief of staff. But then fellow Petersburger Anatoliy Chubays became chief of staff and, evidently having grave doubts about Putin's liberal credentials,* eliminated the position to avoid hiring Putin. Putin reports in *First Person* that Pavel Borodin, the head of the PPMD,

---

* Chubays was the linchpin in a circle of liberal economists from St. Petersburg who had formed discussion clubs during the perestroika period, establishing the intellectual agenda for privatization. The group included Aleksey Kudrin, Andrey Illarionov, Alfred Kokh, Sergey Vasil'yev, Dmitriy Vasil'yev, Mikhayl Dmitriev, Vladimir Kogan, and Mikhayl Manevich (who was murdered in 1997). All rose to prominent positions in business and government around Chubays. They were not in the same circle as the staff around Sobchak, which included more personnel from the former Communist Party apparatus and the security services.[11]

had promised him this appointment, and when confronted with the fact that Putin was still waiting for the call, Borodin had retorted, "I didn't drop [Putin]. It was our little pal Chubays who ruined it." [12]

The enmity expressed in this statement and repeated by Putin in *First Person* is symptomatic of the broader antagonism between the KGB elites and the liberal reformers. In one account of the early 1990s era of privatization, former KGB general Nikolay Leonov described Chubays as "the executioner of the [Soviet] economic system. To perform the role of executioner, special talents are required. One needs to be insensitive to others' pain and have the ability to coolly perform these acts as prescribed by certain ideological doctrines or strangers' recommendation." In explaining why Chubays would be involved in this "execution," Leonov put the blame squarely on Chubays's Jewish roots: "Many researchers have noted that every work of destruction of the state is charged to non-indigenous nationalities. Their conscience is not bound to the genetic ties binding the titular nation [i.e., the Russians], they are alien to its history and spirituality." [13] Leonov concluded that "Boris Yel'tsin was wrong in predicting that Anatoly Chubays was the face of a new generation. No, this [new generation] has the face of another person—it is the face of Putin." [14] Thus for this older generation of KGB veterans who suffered a temporary setback when the August 1991 coup failed, Putin represented the culmination of their ideological, ethnic, and institutional desire for revanche.

Hill and Gaddy underscore that it was the connection between Chubays, chief of Yel'tsin's Presidential Administration, and Aleksey Kudrin, who was head of the Main Control Directorate at this point, that led to Putin's placement in the PPMD, and Putin certainly concedes that Kudrin helped him obtain the position. But they point to a "confidential memorandum" Chubays wrote after the 1996 election, proposing not only that the Communist Party needed to be eliminated as a political force but that disloyal cadres needed to be removed from the Presidential Administration and replaced by liberal economists who were committed to privatization but willing to fight oligarchic rule. Chubays points a finger at the oligarchs who controlled most of Russia's wealth, had weakened the state, were avoiding paying taxes, and had operated in a nontransparent fashion.

Chubays turned to Kudrin: "Chubays's memo specifically recommended bringing Kudrin in from St. Petersburg. It did not mention Vladimir Putin, but Putin nonetheless came along."[15]

Kudrin intervened for Putin with Chubays, but all Chubays would offer was a position as head of the Directorate for Public Liaison, the public relations arm of the Kremlin. In a clear if ironic understatement, given his career trajectory, the future president lamented, "That really wasn't my cup of tea, but what could I do? If I had to work with the public, then I would work with the public."[16] He agreed to take the job, but then Kudrin was able to intervene with Prime Minister Viktor Chernomyrdin's first deputy, Aleksey Bolshakov, who had been the first deputy of the Leningrad City Council's executive committee.[17] And so Borodin took Putin on personally in the PPMD. Kudrin's role in helping Putin to improve his chances in Moscow and going to bat for him is typical of Putin's career, as Viktor Talanov observes. Talanov was a member of the Leningrad and then St. Petersburg legislature and a trained psychologist and wrote a psychological study of Putin, whom he knew, in which he concluded that Putin had two key characteristics: a very high tolerance for risk and an ability to make close friendships with influential and forceful patrons who were able to "extract" (*vytyanut'*) him from any difficulties.[18]

Kudrin became head of the Main Control Directorate (GKU), whose powers had been strengthened by a presidential decree (*ukaz*) on March 16, 1996, which gave the GKU logistical support, under Article 9, from the PPMD. While Chubays had not sought to appoint Putin, it was the tandem of Kudrin and Putin that strengthened the effectiveness of their work. Chubays himself became a victim of the oligarchs' revenge when he was forced out of his leadership position in the Presidential Administration by a *kompromat* attack (a slanderous attack using real or faked compromising materials) involving the receipt of book advances alleged to be veiled bribes. This was the beginning of the Bankers War, and the beginning of the end for Chubays's unimpeachable power.

Putin and Borodin knew each other when Putin was St. Petersburg's deputy mayor. In 1994 the PPMD was involved in expropriating a property that the Kremlin wanted for hosting foreign dignitaries at 6 Polovaya

Alleya on Kamennyy Ostrov, an elite island housing summer dachas built by the tsars in St. Petersburg on the northernmost branch of the Neva River. The leaseholder of the mansion was a German national, Franz Sedelmayer, who lived in the house and also used it as the office of a U.S.-registered security firm, Kamennyy Ostrov Co. He established the U.S.-Russian joint stock company in 1991 with the St. Petersburg branch of the Ministry of Internal Affairs to provide security equipment and counterterrorist training for those guarding foreign diplomats and businessmen, especially in advance of the 1994 Goodwill Games.[19] He claimed to have sunk $4 million into the business before Yel'tsin issued a 1994 decree nationalizing the holdings without compensation, on the grounds that the company had not been properly registered in the first place. Sedelmayer turned to the U.S. consulate in St. Petersburg for help, and Consul General John Evans protested, "In every country there are occasions when the state needs to take private property for public use. We understand that. But it is an internationally recognized principle that when this happens there should be prompt and adequate compensation of the private party."[20] But neither the consulate nor the U.S. Embassy in Moscow was able to help. So Sedelmayer looked to Putin, who offered that the city could take over Sedelmayer's share in the venture and assist in finding him an alternative space but could not compensate him for the expropriation. Together they wrote Borodin, "asking him to compensate us for our leasehold improvements for around $800,000. To our surprise, Borodin wrote back to us stating that the company had been established illegally, and thereby the Russian state had no duty to pay us any compensation."[21]

Sedelmayer had to leave the country, but he successfully sued Borodin and the Russian government in courts in Sweden and Germany and was awarded $2.3 million plus interest. When the Russian state, now headed by Putin, refused to pay, Sedelmayer sought to sequester Russian state property in both Sweden and Germany. The cases dragged on for more than twenty years[22] until, in 2013–14, Sedelmayer was able to obtain the foreclosure and sale of Russian government properties in both countries, despite interference and threats of retaliation by the Russians.[23] In the meantime, the St. Petersburg mayor's office became partial owner of one of the most prestigious addresses in the country, which happened to be only steps away from the house used by Gennadiy Petrov.

According to Borodin, when his daughter became ill he called Putin for help getting her treatment at an elite hospital.[24] So Putin was by no means unknown to Borodin or to officials in the Kremlin. And his position in the PPMD, in charge of foreign property, was perfect for him.

When the Soviet Union collapsed and the CPSU was banned, President Yel'tsin seized the property of the Communist Party for the Russian state. And just as under the old *nomenklatura* system, the PPMD took control of distributing the perks of loyalty. So, as Anders Åslund writes, "a Minister might earn about $200 a month, while he or she could obtain an apartment from the Kremlin property management worth up to $1 million. . . . About 2,000 such apartments were being distributed on personal fiat each year."[25] Under a 1996 presidential order, the rights of this office had been expanded. In August 1995 Yel'tsin issued a decree, which was amended and entered into force on December 11, 1996,[26] stating that all USSR and CPSU foreign property would be registered and controlled from this office, putting billions of dollars' worth of real estate (715 properties in seventy-eight different countries, totaling a reported 550,000 square meters— about 6 million square feet) under its control.[27] Putin brought with him as his deputy a long-standing friend with whom he had been a coworker and neighbor in Dresden, Sergey Chemezov.[28] In 1999 Chemezov became head of the state company Promeksport and then, beginning in 2004, oversaw all Russian military exports as head of Rosoboroneksport.

The PPMD became involved in high Kremlin politics when it was revealed that members of Yel'tsin's circle were being investigated for embezzling $62.5 million for refurbishments in the Kremlin that the PPMD was in charge of. The scandal involved the payment of kickbacks for the provision of contracts to the Swiss-based company Mabetex, and Borodin was personally charged by Swiss authorities.[29] By then Yel'tsin was losing control, and corruption was creeping up to the very top reaches of power. After Yel'tsin's 1996 election he still had a rather broad circle of advisors; only in the late 1990s would this circle shrink as more and more elites defected to opposition positions. They became alarmed at Yel'tsin's heavy drinking bouts, his loss of physical and mental ability as his heart condition worsened, and the growth of influence of a few top advisors, family members, and confidants, which would collectively eventually be called "the Family." At its innermost core, this group consisted of his daughter Tat'yana D'yachenko; the oligarch Boris Berezovskiy; two successive chiefs of the Presidential Administration, Valentin Yumashev and Aleksandr Voloshin; and ultimately Putin as their instrument. Yumashev became an advisor to Yel'tsin in 1996 and then succeeded Chubays as head of the Presidential Administration in 1997. Evidently during this period, Borodin introduced Putin to Yumashev, and he was slowly drawn into the inner circle. *Moskovskiy Komsomolets* quoted "a Kremlin courtier" recalling, "Whenever I went to Yumashev, Tat'yana and Putin were sure to be sitting there."[30] Voloshin rose from Yumashev's assistant to head of the Presidential Administration in 1999 and stayed on after Putin became president.

Felipe Turover* was the person who allegedly provided over four thousand pages of evidence, divided into forty-nine sets of documents, to Swiss courts and Russian procurators in 1998 about Kremlin corruption involving Mabetex. He was a junior official of the Banca del Gottardo, where, the Swiss alleged, accounts had been opened in 1995 in the names of Yel'tsin, Borodin, and some of their family members. The Swiss shared this information with and requested assistance in their prosecutions from Yuriy Skuratov, the Russian procurator general. Skuratov confirmed that Turover's documents were legitimate: "Turover is a great archivist. He gathered some very serious documents and filed them in the greatest detail. His archive is something unique." Skuratov also confirmed that the documents covered not only Yel'tsin's activities but also the corrupt activities of many members of the political elite, including Putin.[31] In September 1998 Skuratov flew to Switzerland for a meeting with the Swiss prosecutor general Carla

---

*Turover came from a Republican Spanish family who fled Spain to the USSR after Franco's victory. He returned to Spain after Franco's death and then in the late 1980s began working for the Swiss Banca del Gottardo, where he handled accounts of the Swiss construction firm Mabetex and provided advice to members of the Yel'tsin government about managing debts with Western creditor banks. For more on Turover's life after he was "outed" by Del Ponte, see his interview (Elsässer 2002).

Del Ponte, who was pursuing her own prosecution of corruption in the Russian elite based on Turover's documents.[32] On October 8, 1998, Skuratov initiated criminal proceedings against Borodin as chief of the PPMD on charges of corruption.[33] Not surprisingly, therefore, from this moment on, priority number one for the Kremlin was to dismiss Skuratov and find Turover.

When interviewed in 2000, Turover had quite a lot to say about Putin's role in the PPMD, but he did not believe Putin was a central member of the Family: "Most likely Putin willingly or unwillingly provides cover for the activities of the band that is called the 'Family,' probably out of a false sense of gratitude to those who made him president. You understand that I know him and I think that sooner or later Putin will have to choose between Voloshin, [Mikhayl] Kas'yanov [members of the Yel'tsin regime whom Putin put in his first government] and Russia. . . . But he should know that [the amounts stolen] run to tens of billions of dollars. We need to understand that the 'Family' is a formidable system . . . which continues to operate."[34] The following comments on Putin, in an interview Turover gave to *Novaya gazeta*'s Oleg Lur'ye in December 1999, shortly before Turover went into hiding, indicate that he was afraid if he traveled to Russia there would be a "probable assassination attempt right at the airport:"*

Lur'ye:	Can you name the high-ranking Russians implicated in corruption whose names feature in your archive which is at the Procurator General's Office?
Turover:	Chernomyrdin, Stepashin, Shokhin, Luzhkov, Abramovich, Shantsev, Fedorov,† Orekhov, Golovatyy, Berezovskiy, Ilyushenko, Silayev, Yaroshenko.
Lur'ye:	Putin?

---

*When subsequently interviewed by the Moscow English-language newspaper *The eXile*, Turover insisted that Lur'ye had not interviewed him, but then conceded that the interview had in fact taken place. However, he denied that he had said anything about Putin.[35] *Novaya gazeta* did not retract the story.

† It is unclear which of the many Fedorovs this is a reference to.

Turover: Volodya Putin is a separate long story. I have run up
against him, but that is not the point. The point is that for
the eight months of his work at the President's Administration of Affairs in 1996–1997, Putin was responsible
for Soviet property abroad. Let me explain. In addition to
debts, Russia also inherited from the former USSR property abroad worth many billions, including property that
belonged to the CPSU. Various organizations laid claim
to it in 1995–1996—the Foreign Ministry, the Ministry
of the Maritime Fleet, and many others. But in late 1996
Yel'tsin issued an edict ordering that all USSR and CPSU
property abroad be transferred not to the Ministry for the
Management of State Property but for some reason to
the President's Administration of Affairs. And Mr. Putin
immediately got his paws on it. On orders from above,
of course. When he embarked on the so-called classifi-
cation of former USSR and CPSU property abroad in
1997, all sorts of front companies, joint-stock companies,
and limited companies were immediately set up. Much of
the most expensive property and other assets abroad was
registered in the name of these structures. Thus property
abroad was very thoroughly plucked before the state got
its hands on it. And it was the current premier [Putin]
who did the plucking. He gained his first experience
of theft during his time in Germany. Back then Putin,
together with Shokhin and Poltoranin,* contrived to
"steal" the huge building of the Russian cultural center
in Germany. They leased it out for a purely symbolic sum
for 50 years to a German firm with a tiny incorporation
capital. Of course, this firm immediately sublet the build-

---

* Mikhayl Poltoranin, who became head of the Federal Information Center, was accused by
Deputy Prime Minister Aleksandr Shokhin and former procurator general Valentin Stepankov
of an attempt to sell army property to a German firm. All charges were dropped in October
1993.[36]

ing, but for very substantial sums at normal German
prices. Where did the difference end up? I think there is
no need to explain.

Lur'ye: Was this information about Putin also in your archive
that is now in the hands of the Procurator General's
Office?

Turover: For the present I am not going to answer that question. I
think both you and I want to live a while longer on this
earth.[37]

Putin was already prime minister when the Swiss issued the arrest warrant for Borodin. Swiss officials indicated that two more arrest warrants
would be issued. Putin had quietly dismissed Borodin from the PPMD
weeks before the warrant was issued, underlining that he most likely had
been following the matter closely and was acting to control damage from
these investigations not only to the Yel'tsin Family but to himself.[38] A
twelve-page document leaked by the Swiss in September 2000 specifically
named Borodin as having transferred funds in four installments between
March 1997 and August 1998—in other words, *after* Putin had left the
office.[39] The U.S. government arrested Borodin on a Swiss warrant as he
entered the country in 2001 and in the process of extraditing him provided
details of the Swiss charges: Borodin was charged with extracting $30 mil-
lion in kickbacks from Swiss companies for the reconstruction of parts of
the Kremlin.[40] Despite what the Swiss believed was clear evidence of corruption, Russian authorities refused to be pressured or coaxed to deliver
any of their state officials.

Twenty-six months after the case was opened, it was closed by Russian
investigators in December 2000 for "lack of evidence"—with nineteen
thousand pages of documents consigned to the Kremlin's secret archives.[41]
Shortly thereafter the Russians issued an international arrest warrant for
Turover on suspicion of stealing a $16,000 watch, failing to pay $8,000
in rent for his Moscow apartment, and accepting a $3,000 bribe. Russian
journalists concluded that all this was an effort to ensure that he did not
testify against Borodin in the latter's trial in Switzerland.[42] But Turover

warned that he could testify against Putin in any such trial: "If they want to turn the Yel'tsin-gate into Putin-gate, one can do that."[43] But he did not expand on this remark; later he quietly sought witness protection in Switzerland and disappeared from view.[44]

When Putin left the PPMD, he was replaced as head of the External Economic Relations Department by his deputy, Sergey Chemezov.[45] As was Putin's practice, he took Igor Sechin with him to the GKU, where he was listed as working in the Administrative Directorate under Putin.[46]

The Main Control Directorate, March 1997–May 1998

Putin has not disclosed his reasons for leaving the PPMD, although the brewing storm over Borodin clearly had the potential to expose him personally and politically. In March 1997 he once again relied on the political clout of Aleksey Kudrin, who was leaving the Main Control Directorate to become first deputy finance minister. Putin took over as chief of the GKU and simultaneously became deputy head of the Presidential Administration.

The GKU, equivalent to the Inspector General's Office in the United States, was responsible for overseeing the implementation of federal laws, executive orders, and presidential instructions.[47] Under Kudrin, the GKU had become what journalist Andrey Kolesnikov called "a formidable structure"—using the Russian word *groznaya*, which can also mean "terrifying."[48] On November 6, 1996, another presidential *ukaz* increased the power of the GKU even further, extending its authority to strengthen fiscal and budgetary discipline and to monitor the work of all federal regions and officials.[49] Putin claimed to find the work boring, saying in *First Person* that he had even thought about leaving the Presidential Administration and setting up in private practice as a lawyer because the work at the GKU "was not very creative work. It was important, it was necessary, and I understood all that. But it simply wasn't interesting to me."[50]

That is not to say that he did not have, once more, a valuable time, again involving himself in covering up various scandals. Before Kudrin, the head of the GKU was another Petersburger, Yuriy Boldyrev, who had uncovered "significant violations" in his own investigation of the Sal'ye Commission's allegations against Putin[51] and had recommended that Putin not be given any further authority until the case of corrupt use of budget funds was solved.[52] Now Putin was in charge not only of this office but also of all the files against him that had been collected by Sal'ye and Boldyrev, which some charged had "disappeared." Boldyrev, while not confirming or denying that they may no longer be available, stated in 2004 that when he was at the GKU, all the archives were in perfect order and that the documents should still be available.[53]* After Putin became chief of the GKU, there were no more investigations of the Sal'ye affair, and in 2012, after Sal'ye died and Radio Free Europe sought to discover whether her documents were in the presidential archives, they received a written reply that "the documents are no longer stored in the archives."[55]

The most significant effort Putin made during this period was in securing Sobchak's escape abroad, and in so doing saving not only Sobchak but also himself from possible criminal charges. As stated previously, when Sobchak lost the 1996 mayoral elections, not only did this put Putin and Sobchak, and others, out of a job, but it left them open to prosecutions for alleged illegal activity during the 1991–96 period. Both worked all their connections to try to get beyond the reach of the law, but Putin was more successful than Sobchak, who was called for questioning in connection with the illegal acquisition of an apartment on Vasil'yevskiy Island. In the summer of 1997 the investigation accelerated, and three of Sobchak's staff were arrested: the head of the Planning and Economic Department of St. Petersburg, B. Lubin; the head of the Committee for City Planning and Architecture, Oleg Kharchenko; and Sobchak's chief of staff, V. Kruchinin. The noose was tightening.[56]

Sobchak was evidently so concerned that he appealed to U.S. President Bill Clinton and the mayor of Paris Jacques Chirac during their trips to St. Petersburg to put in a good word on his behalf with Yel'tsin; he also asked

---

* Boldyrev, who was one of the founders of the liberal Yabloko Party from St. Petersburg, had moved on to the Federation Council and had become a member of the Federal Audit Chamber. Within months of Putin's becoming president, Boldyrev lost his position in the Chamber and denounced it as "Putin's tool."[54]

Chirac to help him move to Paris.[57] On October 3, 1997, while Sobchak was being questioned by Moscow procurators, he complained of "heart problems" and was taken to the hospital, where he stayed for a month. The head of the investigation became so suspicious that he asked for a medical team in Moscow to come to St. Petersburg to determine whether Sobchak was fit to give evidence. But before they could arrive, Sobchak was transferred on November 3 to the St. Petersburg Military Academy Hospital, where he was put under the care of the hospital's chief, Yuriy Shevchenko, a friend of Putin's, who would become minister of health in 1999.

Four days later, during the November Revolution Day holidays, Sobchak was taken by ambulance onto the tarmac of Pulkovo Airport, where eyewitnesses reported that he "literally jumped out, accompanied by his wife Lyudmila Narusova and almost jogged up the stairs into a small private aircraft owned by the Finnish company 'Jetflite OY.'" The flight to Paris was apparently ordered by "an unnamed person from Moscow" at a cost of $25,000 to $30,000.[58] Putin, who by this time was chief of the GKU, was alleged to have arranged all the medical paperwork, obtained travel documents, and secured the aircraft, reportedly without consulting Yel'tsin.[59] In his autobiography Putin conceded that he had been in St. Petersburg and had gone to visit Sobchak in the hospital but denied that the escape was his operation, saying only that "[Sobchak's] friends" had sent him a medevac plane. He also denied that Sobchak had been "whisked out, without even going through customs. That's not true; he passed through customs and passport control at the border. Everything was as it was supposed to be. They put stamps in his passport. They put him on the airplane." Of course, VIPs the world over can have border officials come onto a departing plane to handle these matters, so there is no real inconsistency between these accounts. Putin's pride in the operation's success was evident when he said, "Since it was November 7—a national holiday—his [Sobchak's] absence from St. Petersburg was not noticed until November 10."[60] Sobchak's wife, Lyudmila Narusova, who had been elected to the Duma on the Our Home Is Russia ticket in 1995 and who became a member of the Federation Council after 2002, later confirmed Putin's involvement in making all the arrangements:[61] "Vladimir Vladimirovich had helped me organize the plane. . . . He told me how to do it. . . . He risked everything."[62]

While Sobchak was in Paris, he was out of the reach of the law, but he was still actively being investigated, including by journalists. An exposé in *Izvestiya* in April 1998 targeted not only Sobchak and Narusova for illegally taking over an apartment* and using force to move the residents of a communal apartment next door so that he could expand his space, but also obtaining two other apartments illegally in Petersburg for relatives.[63] The article also referred to *Izvestiya*'s possession of a tape recording of someone "whose voice sounds like the voice of Narusova," who at that time was a Duma representative. In the tape, whose authenticity *Novaya gazeta* also believed in, a woman is talking to Mikhayl Mirilashvili, known in the criminal underworld as Misha Kutaisi. They are talking about the latest charges of corruption in the mayor's office, announced by Yuriy Shutov on a radio program in St. Petersburg. Shutov had been Sobchak's assistant in 1990 and was one of the first to write and speak openly about corruption there. His first book, published in 1991, was extremely dismissive of the "democratic credentials" of both Sobchak and his wife.[64] In the tape, alleged to have been made in May 1995, while Sobchak was still mayor, Narusova urges, even orders Mirilashvili to "act through Kumarin" to "shut Shutov up." *Novaya gazeta* printed the following transcript, justifying doing so because it was Narusova herself who had been leading the campaign criticizing the "gestapo methods" being used to investigate her husband:

Narusova:	I'm listening.
Mirilashvili:	Well, can you wait?
Narusova:	So I can't say anything right now. At ten, I told you . . . Mikhayl Mikhaylovich! Again today on the radio there was a live broadcast. Shutov (former assistant of Sobchak.—Ed.) again went on about corruption, about

---

*At Naberezhnaya Reki Moyki, 31 in St. Petersburg. Sobchak's occupation of this apartment is confirmed by the memorial to his living at that address placed directly outside.

apartments (or cashiers? Inaudible.—Ed.).* You know,
we must act through Kumarin (Kumarin, according to
law enforcement authorities is one of the leaders of the
Tambov criminal group.—Ed.). With him, everything
is possible. . . . He simply has to be shut up.†

Mirilashvili: Well, you know, it's necessary to talk this out.

Narusova (interrupting): There I go, I'm sorry, I'm acting like a
gangster.‡

Mirilashvili: We need to talk today. We will not use the telephone . . .

Narusova (interrupting): . . . It is already becoming simply inde-
cent . . .§

Mirilashvili (calming): I understand, let's talk about it today . . .

Narusova (interrupting): We have to act very hard . . .¶

Mirilashvili: OK, but to me . . .

Narusova: Call today at ten.[65]**

---

* "O kvartirakh (ili kassirakh?)"

† Ego nado prosto zatknut'.

‡ Zdes' uzhe, izvinite, ya deystvuyu kak gangster.

§ Eto uzhe stanovitsya prosto neprilichnym

¶ Nado deystvovat' ochen' zhestko.

** Shutov was elected to the St. Petersburg Legislature in December 1998. At the time, he alleged that Putin had used *kompromat* against Sobchak in 1990 to obtain a position in the mayor's office.[66] In February 1999 Shutov was stripped of his parliamentary immunity and arrested for involvement in the murder of Mikhayl Manevich and Galina Starovoytova. In November he was freed in the courtroom, and within minutes an OMON (Otryad Mobilniy Osobogo Naznacheniya) detachment of the Ministry of the Interior paramilitary riot police from Moscow descended on the courtroom, beat him up, and detained him once again, this time charging him with other murders. In 2002 he was elected again to the city parliament, and the Russian Supreme Court ruled his detention illegal. Only in 2006 was he finally convicted of a murder, previous murder charges having not been proved. He spent seven years in pretrial detention, which was the subject of a complaint by his lawyers to the European Court of Human Rights in *Shutov (III) v. Russia*, Application No. 20922/08.[67] He was never convicted of the murder of either Manevich or Starovoytova. In 2006 Anatoliy Chubays hinted that Shutov had been behind Manevich's murder, saying after Shutov had received a life sentence, but without men-tioning Shutov's name, "I have carried out everything I promised word for word: All the organiz-ers of this murder are sitting in prison for life, and not one of them will ever come out."[68] For more on the Shutov case and the chronicle of criminal activities in St. Petersburg during the 1990s, see Mikhaylov (2005).

Putin's apparent loyalty to Sobchak and Narusova would be remembered by those in the Yel'tsin Family who were similarly coming under investigation,[69] but Putin was able to deal with his own problems with Skuratov by getting Sobchak abroad. Without Sobchak, Skuratov was unable to pursue the case, and it was dropped.[70] As Putin himself reflected, Sobchak "had been implicated in this murky story of the apartment. A case was opened up, but it fell apart in the end."[71] What Putin fails to mention is that he also was charged with receiving an apartment in return for city contracts; indeed he also acquired an apartment on the prestigious Vasil'yevskiy Island at this time, the address that would be listed as his personal address—apartment 24 in building 17 on Second Line Avenue—on the document establishing the Ozero Cooperative.[72]

This was not the only St. Petersburg scandal that Putin was alleged to have been involved in during this period. Russkoye Video was one of the original shareholders in Bank Rossiya. Vladimir Pribylovskiy claims that, as with Bank Rossiya, Russkoye Video's founding capital of 13 million rubles also came from the Leningrad regional executive committee (*obkom*).[73] It was headed by Andrey Balyasnikov, who had worked in the city's Ideology Department during the Soviet period. Vladislav Reznik was his deputy—another cofounder of Bank Rossiya and a founding member of United Russia, whose house in Spain was next door to Gennadiy Petrov's, described as the leader of "one of the four largest OC [organized crime] networks in the world."[74]

Further commentary is provided by Chief Investigator Andrey Zykov, who claims that "during privatization of the St. Petersburg Channel Eleven and its sale to 'Russkoye Video,' which involved Putin, the law on privatization was violated. Given the evidence, a criminal case was opened on 'Russkoye Video' which was under the supervision of a senior investigator for particularly important cases of the Procurator General's office, Yuriy M. Vanyushin. On the basis of the evidence, D. Rozhdestvenskiy was arrested—he was the General Director of 'Russkoye Video' and had funded trips abroad by Putin's wife."[75] According to the materials of the case, Pribylovskiy and the Russian historian Yuriy Felshtinskiy quote from a document that additionally claims not only that Russkoye Video paid for

Lyudmila Putina's foreign trips but also that "the Russkoye Video Company illegally produced pornographic movies. The work was handled by D. Rozhdestvenskiy. . . . The materials of the case are in the possession of V. A. Lyseiko, deputy head of the Directorate for the Investigation of Cases of Special Importance at the General Procurator's Office and the head of the investigative team. Deputy General Procurator Katyshev is acquainted with the facts of the Russkoye Video case. Putin is trying . . . to influence the outcome of the investigation."[76] Roughly the same charges were laid out in an article by Oleg Lur'ye and Inga Savel'eva in a *Versiya* piece in 1999 titled "Four Questions for the Heir to the Throne."[77] Masha Gessen claims that the procurator in charge of the case, Yuriy Vanyushin, was also a classmate of Putin. Rozhdestvenskiy was subjected to audits, daily interrogations, and periods of imprisonment beginning in 1997. He was charged with a variety of economic crimes, none of which stuck. He was eventually released from prison but died at the age of forty-eight, his health broken. Most commentators conclude that Russkoye Video's secrets somehow involve Putin. When Gessen called Procurator Vanyushin to interview him about the case in February 2000, he warned, "Leave it alone. Believe me, Masha; you don't want to get any deeper into this. Or you'll be sorry." Surveillance of her apartment began soon after, and Gessen took a vacation abroad and dropped the story.[78]

Novaya gazeta investigated eyewitness allegations that on December 12, 1997, the SUV Jeep in which Putin was traveling, with the typical rooftop flashing blue *migalka* used by high government officials, and much resented by the population, was involved in a high-speed traffic accident at kilometer 17 along the Moscow-to-Minsk highway that killed five-year-old Denis Lapshin, who died shortly after the accident in Moscow's Hospital No. 71.[79] Journalist David Satter, who investigated the case, reported, "According to eyewitnesses, in the aftermath of the crash, plainclothesmen not only removed Denis's body from the area without the permission of his relatives, they also tried to alter the accident scene to make it look as if Putin's car had not been responsible."[80] Initially Putin's driver, Boris Zykov, was not arrested, but when the boy's family took up the case, he was eventually charged under Article 264.2 of the Criminal Code, on Violation of the Rules for Traffic Safety and Operation of Transport Vehicle, resulting in death, which is punishable by up to five years in prison.[81] But Zykov did not even appear in court and was in fact subsequently amnestied, although never convicted.[82] He also apparently did not appear in a subsequent civil court case that the enraged family brought in February 2000, after Putin was already acting president.[83] Despite the fact that *Novaya gazeta* took up the case and submitted materials to the procurator general,[84] ultimately they were forced to issue a retraction, stating that the use of the term *killer* to describe Zykov was "incorrect from any point of view" and that Putin's presence in the car "had not been confirmed" by investigative agencies.[85] The fact that more than three years passed between the incident and the retraction, filled with both a criminal and a civil case, certainly underlined the amount of effort that would have been required to make such claims go away.

First Deputy Chief of Staff in Charge of Russian Regions: May 25, 1998–July 25, 1998

After Chubays moved on to become head of the Russian state power utility RAO UES, Valentin Yumashev replaced him as chief of staff in the Presidential Administration. Putin too received a promotion, becoming first deputy chief of the presidential staff with special responsibility for the regions, a position he used to reassert central control.[86] In this new position, Putin replaced Sergey Shakhray, who had used his considerable knowledge of interethnic relations to sign forty-two bilateral compacts between Moscow and the regions designed to demarcate federal jurisdictions and give the regions a legal basis for the trend toward decentralization. Putin would sign none during his short tenure, reportedly believing that the process had gone too far.[87] This is the post that he found most interesting prior to becoming president: "To this day I think that was the most interesting job. I developed relationships with many of the governors at that time. It was clear to me that work with the regional leaders was one of the most important lines of work in the country. Everyone was saying that the *vertikal*, the vertical chain of government, had been destroyed and that it had to be restored." He conceded that not all the governors agreed with this approach, but "you can't please everybody."[88] Yel'tsin had encouraged the emergence of a federation in which regions would take the kind of independence they could handle within the framework of the Constitution; in contrast, Putin's view was that only because of the weakness of central authority, regional independence would have to be tolerated for the time being. The contacts Putin established with governors during this period would come in handy in the summer of 1999, when twenty-four of them sent appeals to Yel'tsin to step down in favor of Putin.[89]

Head of the FSB, July 25, 1998–August 9, 1999, and Secretary of the Kremlin Security Council, March 29, 1999–August 9, 1999

Though Putin said he didn't know that he was being considered for FSB chief,[90] it is hard to imagine that any appointment of this magnitude—in any country—would not have its backstory. Some reported that he came to Yel'tsin's attention because of his straightforward and professional reports about the situation in the regions. Other Russian reporters at the time noted that "knowledgeable people say that Putin stubbornly cherished the dream to become the director of the FSB. The first rumors of his possible arrival began to circulate in the summer of '97. The authors well remember talk in the Lubyanka corridors about a certain presidential crony who is dreaming of becoming the director."[91]

When Putin arrived at the FSB on July 25, 1998, replacing the professional KGB appointee Nikolay Kovalev, he was the fifth head of this agency in as many years. One estimate stated that the FSB had lost more top leaders to forced retirements during the Yel'tsin period than the security organs had during World War II.[92] Nevertheless Yel'tsin is on record as saying that it needed more such retirements.[93] Kovalev had come under criticism for losing control of the FSB's Directorate for Combating the Activities of Organized Crime Groups (URPO), whose chief had been accused of graft and of ordering a special unit to take an oath that they would carry out any order, including illegal ones, up to and including murder—the charge was made by journalist and opposition parliamentarian Yuriy Shchekochikhin, who himself died of what appeared to be deliberate radioactive poisoning in 2003.[94] Noted Russian security specialist Andrey Soldatov called URPO an example of "Russian death squads."[95] It was members of this unit, which included Aleksandr Litvinenko, who later in 1998 held a press conference stating that they had refused an order to assassinate Boris Berezovskiy. And it was Putin, according to Mikhayl Trepashkin, a KGB and then FSB investigator who later broke with Putin, who personally fired and then ordered the prosecution of Litvinenko for going public with the scandal and provoking the URPO dismissals. Litvinenko served nine months in prison for "abuse of authority" and then escaped to England after his release.[96]

Putin used his time at the FSB to completely restructure the agency and bring in his cohort of KGB classmates from Petersburg, the so-called *piterskiy* echelon,[97] who would help support his ascendancy, while at the same time promoting their own.[98] Specifically two key agencies within the FSB were eliminated by Putin: the Directorate for Economic Counter-Intelligence and the Directorate for Counter-Intelligence Protection of Strategic Sites. These were the agencies charged with investigation of high-level economic crimes, such as those surrounding the oligarchs and the Family, including the allegations of kickbacks from the Swiss company Mabetex and other investigations of Berezovskiy taking place at that time associated with his takeover of Aeroflot and his running of AvtoVAZ, as well as the protection of strategic sites, including all nuclear facilities and closed labs. Russian political commentator and politician Aleksandr Khinshteyn notes that they and many other long-serving professional "*chekisty* of the old echelon, persons not accustomed to vacillating with the course of the dollar,"[99] were obliged to retire. These two directorates were replaced with six new ones, filled with Putin loyalists from Petersburg, including Viktor Cherkesov, Aleksandr Grigor'yev, Sergey Chemezov, Sergey Ivanov, and Nikolay Patrushev. Cherkesov became first deputy director in August 1998; Grigor'yev took one of the deputy directorships while maintaining his position as head of the FSB in St. Petersburg.[100] Ivanov was named deputy director in charge of the Department for Analysis, Prognosis and Strategic Planning, given the role of preparing the daily briefings for the

Kremlin.[101] And Patrushev followed Putin out of the GKU in July 1998 and became head of the Directorate for Economic Security; he became first deputy director under Putin in April 1999 and then succeeded him as director when Putin became prime minister in August of that year. Patrushev brought along Rashid Nurgaliyev, who had been his deputy in Karelia, to the north of St. Petersburg. Nurgaliyev would rise to become minister of internal affairs after 2003.[102] Some sources say that Igor Sechin accompanied Putin into the FSB[103] as his factotum prior to being named as head of Putin's secretariat at the office of the prime minister, but his biographies, official and online, are silent on this episode. In the process the FSB deputy directors in charge of these directorates were forced out, and similar changes occurred in the Ministry of Internal Affairs and the Office of the Procurator General (where Mikhayl Katyshev, who had opened many of the cases against Berezovskiy, was forced out).[104]

There are many other examples of Putin associates making their way to Moscow at this time. Their unity was critical as they faced the beginning of a decisive period for them and for Russia. In May 1999 Dmitriy Kozak joined the Presidential Administration working on legal affairs, having been deputy governor of St. Petersburg.[105] In July 1999 Viktor Zubkov was named chief of the State Tax Inspectorate for St. Petersburg and simultaneously deputy chief of the federal-level Russian State Tax Service.[106] Leonid Reyman became deputy chairman of the State Committee for Telecommunications in July 1999, and then its chairman in August. Putin subsequently admitted to meeting with the former KGB chief Kryuchkov at this time, and once he became president he conceded, "I was working rather actively with the long-time veterans."[107] So while he put his own people into line positions, he also was carefully proceeding with the support of the former senior KGB leadership.[108]

At this time Yel'tsin claimed that the "inner circle" consisted of himself, his daughter, the head of the Presidential Administration (until December 1998) Valentin Yumashev, and Aleksandr Voloshin, who became head of the Presidential Administration in March 1999.[109] Nikolay Bordyuzha, a onetime chief of the federal border guards who most recently had been secretary of the Security Council, stepped in to head the Presidential Administration briefly in early 1999 but was never part of the inner circle. There were other key players, mentioned in every chronicle of the divisive politics of this period. But the key issues facing Yel'tsin in what the *New York Times* called the "bleeding away of his political authority"[110] were the protection of his legacy amid persistent rumors of his own physical incapacity and corruption within his circle, and the need to strengthen this inner core and either keep them in power after the planned 2000 elections or secure immunity for them and for him so as to avoid arrest. These aims had to be achieved without the benefit of public support, given the generalized collapse in sympathy for Yel'tsin after the August 1998 banking crisis, which led to an estimated $25 billion in capital flight, a 64 percent drop in the value of the ruble, and a 41 percent increase in consumer prices.[111] As a result, in the critical year between the August banking crisis and the appointment of Putin as prime minister a year later, Yel'tsin had to defeat his opponents despite the fact that his ratings in the public opinion polls had virtually collapsed.* As such, politics left the public sphere and went into the backrooms. In this behind-the-scenes struggle, Putin would be invaluable.

In the wake of the August 1998 financial crisis, Yel'tsin was obliged to appoint as prime minister Yevgeniy Primakov, the only candidate deemed acceptable to the Duma, which, even before the financial meltdown, had instituted impeachment proceedings against Yel'tsin. These proceedings would continue until May 1999 and would serve as a continuing backdrop to the poisoned relationship among the Duma, the prime minister, and the president.[113] Primakov was persuaded to take the position after Viktor Chernomyrdin was turned down twice by the Duma and it faced dissolution if they voted against Yel'tsin's choice a third time. According to Yel'tsin's

---

*The annual polls conducted by the Levada Center going back to the 1990s show that the period following the August 1998 banking crisis produced the single greatest increase in popular pessimism, fear about the future, and distrust of authorities: 82 percent reported that 1998 had been harder than the previous year; in 1999, of people's feelings about the past year, the greatest percentage reported tiredness, fear, confusion, and bitterness. In response to the question of where Russian political life was going, 62 percent chose "escalating chaos and anarchy." Consequently general indices of confidence in public institutions showed an unprecedented decline in confidence in the president; his numbers in 1998 and 1999 dipped for the first time below the already low numbers for the government, the Duma, and regional officials as a group.[112]

daughter, except for Primakov, many felt that only Moscow's mayor Yuriy Luzhkov, who was known throughout the country, would be acceptable to the Duma.

But the Family had grave reservations about Luzhkov's credentials and loyalty.[114] Berezovskiy still had tremendous influence in the Kremlin, and he and the other oligarchs still had enormous power in financial and media circles. But with the appointment of Primakov and the resultant increase in the power of the Communists in the Duma, they were struggling to find top-level officials who would conform to their own interests. They too used this period to find good candidates who would represent them in the post-Yel'tsin period, including at this time General Aleksandr Lebed, and they were determined to avoid a presidency by either Primakov or Luzhkov. In the post-Soviet period, Primakov had been director of the Foreign Intelligence Service (SVR) from 1991 to 1996 and had had two years as foreign minister, during which time he rallied public opinion against the buildup of NATO pressure on Serbian forces in the Yugoslav war. Thus he had a real support base not only among professional intelligence elites but also among the nationalists and the Communists, and indeed among many sectors of society simply exhausted from reading daily accounts about the untrammeled influence of the oligarchs over Kremlin policy. The day after his confirmation, Primakov gathered the heads of law enforcement agencies and announced a sweeping fight against crime and corruption. This created the atmosphere that allowed Yuriy Skuratov in the Procurator General's Office to proceed with investigations into the corruption within the Family.

Primakov evidently fought against Putin's appointment from the very beginning. Yel'tsin's daughter later related in her blog that Primakov didn't like Putin, intervened with Yel'tsin to have him replaced, and blamed him in particular for "the defeat of professional cadres in the FSB."[115] She also said that Putin refused to use his position as FSB director to aid Primakov politically, including going to Yel'tsin to report that he had refused Primakov's request to eavesdrop on Yabloko Party chief Grigoriy Yavlinskiy.[116] In Primakov's larger struggle with the Family, and with Berezovskiy above all, Putin clearly sided with Berezovskiy from the beginning.

Putin was also dragged into a controversy when, in November 1998, Berezovskiy alleged in an open letter to Putin published in *Kommersant* that the FSB senior leadership had conspired to have him assassinated. The letter went on to state that this information had come out when the group tasked with carrying out the operation refused to do so and instead informed Berezovskiy. Among those allegedly assigned to be in the "hit squad" was Lieutenant Colonel Aleksandr Litvinenko, who had previously moonlighted as Berezovskiy's bodyguard. *Kommersant* observed that when the FSB refused to "prosecute people in high places who ordered a murder that never took place," Berezovskiy decided to go public and publish the allegations in an open letter to Putin.[117] This was the first time that Litvinenko, who would die from polonium-210 poisoning in London in November 2006, made public allegations about the misdeeds at the highest reaches of the FSB. *Kommersant* reported that while his statements were investigated and generally regarded as valid, "the Chief Military Procurator's Office, after hearing witnesses' testimony, decided that telling someone to murder Berezovskiy is not a crime."[118] In an article released two days after his death, Litvinenko stated that while Berezovskiy had sought to pressure Putin to clean out the highest ranks of the FSB, unbeknown to Berezovskiy, Putin had his own obligations to some of the senior FSB officers who had been involved in working with organized crime in the early 1990s to smuggle rare metals out of Russia via St. Petersburg. As head of the Committee for Foreign Liaison, Putin had the task of licensing this activity so that the goods could legally cross the border. According to Litvinenko, Putin worked with the mafia and top KGB officials in taking these metals out of Russia, and, according to his informant in St. Petersburg city hall, "all his licenses were mob fronts." Litvinenko claimed that when Berezovskiy asked him to produce all the information on corruption in the top levels of the FSB, Berezovskiy did not know that Putin was connected with some of their schemes, and that this was the reason Putin did not pursue any of these investigations and also made sure that Litvinenko was himself investigated, hounded out of the agency, and ultimately forced to flee abroad.[119]

Berezovskiy relates that in February 1999, while Primakov was trying to open legal proceeding against the oligarch, Putin appeared uninvited at a birthday party at Berezovskiy's house and assured him that "he [didn't] care what Primakov thinks." [120] Putin's public display of loyalty occurred at the same time that he was actively involved in trying to suppress the Mabetex investigations by Procurator General Skuratov. Skuratov was continuing to work with the Swiss prosecutor Carla Del Ponte on the goings-on within Pavel Borodin's Presidential Property Management Department, where Putin had previously worked. On February 1, Skuratov maintains, he was called into the office of the head of the Presidential Administration, who was at that time General Nikolay Bordyuzha, and encouraged to drop the Mabetex investigation. When he demurred, he claims, he was shown a sex tape containing a person "resembling" him cavorting naked with two prostitutes in a small bedroom. Skuratov subsequently admitted he was "in shock. . . . The chief of staff said 'the President no longer wants to work with you. You have to resign.'" [121] But when Skuratov refused to go, the Kremlin showed the video to legislators in the upper house, the Federation Council, who had previously shown their support for Skuratov; once again they sided with him, expressing doubts that he was actually the person in the video.[122]

Skuratov intensified the pressure on Yel'tsin. He called Yel'tsin's daughters in for questioning about Mabetex and announced that he was opening proceedings on FIMACO, the offshore company organized by the Central Bank and sponsored by the Kremlin, for channeling billions of state funds abroad. In documents obtained by *Newsweek*, including an internal audit of the Central Bank, just in advance of Primakov's visit to Washington to ask for more IMF funding, it was alleged that $500 million of an $800 million installment of its first loan to Moscow in late 1993 had gone "straight to FIMACO for safekeeping," even though it was stated that the funds were later returned and disbursed as intended by the IMF.[123] There is no suggestion that Putin was involved with FIMACO, but his interest in curtailing the investigations of him by the St. Petersburg procurators and by Skuratov over his own possible involvement in Mabetex certainly coincided with the Family's own desire to avoid prosecution. Thus there is strong evidence that Putin's personal interests could have cemented his decision to throw his loyalties firmly behind Yel'tsin and the Family. At a minimum, the rapidity with which he moved his own people into top positions and ousted opponents in the FSB, while emerging as a strong player in favor of the oligarchs and the Kremlin against Primakov, Luzhkov, and Yakovlev, suggests he was a consummate inside player able to act decisively to protect his interests and ensure his political survival.

On March 16, 1999, when Skuratov did not budge, the incriminating sex tape was aired on RTR state television nationwide and immediately became a sensation.[124] But Skuratov still didn't give in, and on March 23 Carla Del Ponte herself flew to Moscow with new documents on the Mabetex affair. Minister of Interior Sergey Stepashin also sided with Yel'tsin and tried to squash the investigation. Del Ponte says that Stepashin asked her to hand over all the documents, but she declined.[125] At this point the pressure on Skuratov intensified. In the face of widespread debate about the authenticity of the video, Putin himself led the inquest into its origins and announced unequivocally, "Today the identity of the man resembling Skuratov in the infamous video has been verified as the Procurator General."[126] The Kremlin's demands for Skuratov to resign increased. Skuratov states that Putin became the go-between between him and Yel'tsin's daughter Tat'yana D'yachenko: "Putin came several times to me and, opening up, said to me that the 'Family' was satisfied with my conduct. He said that they wanted to name me ambassador to Finland, to send me, so to speak, into honorable exile. 'I won't go,' I said firmly. . . . In this situation contacts with Putin were important for me because they were also contacts with Tat'yana. . . . She herself did not enter into contact [with me] but for that purpose chose Putin."[127] Skuratov reports that Putin tried to be philosophical about the bold attempt at *kompromat* by the authorities, telling Skuratov, "Alas, Yuriy Il'ich, they say that there is a similar film [*plyonka*] about me."[128]

There is little doubt that the secret services and their special talents for surveillance were involved in entrapping Skuratov. Retired KGB general Leonov is circumspect: "Virtually all state and business 'elites' in Russia live a lax and immoral life. Mutual peeping into bedrooms, the creation of situations to create compromising material is commonplace. Involvement of the secret services is commonplace. . . . [In the Skuratov case], evidence suggests that behind this venture were the special services. Maybe Putin's career started here."[129]

Putin's efforts to mediate continued; evidently he was at the meeting in March with Yel'tsin and Primakov in which Skuratov finally agreed to resign.[130] Soon after, on March 29, Putin was named secretary of the Kremlin's Security Council, while maintaining his FSB post, thus ensuring that all the information reaching Yel'tsin about foreign and domestic threats would go through him.[131]

In the midst of the storm over the Skuratov affair, Putin was given a more pronounced role in handling the deteriorating situation in the North Caucasus, beginning with the federal response to a morning blast in the market in Vladikavkaz on March 19 that killed fifty-three people. This was the first bombing in Russia since the end of the First Chechen War in 1996.[132] Putin and Stepashin, then the interior minister, rushed to the scene, and Putin headed the federal response.[133] The blast derailed planned talks between the Chechen leadership and Prime Minister Primakov on regional cooperation in combating crime and kidnapping.[134] Despite the fact that Primakov was reported to be strongly opposed to any increased expenditures for a new war in the Caucasus,[135] Stepashin later reported that planning for a limited operation in Chechnya began in March 1999, to take the territory up to, but not beyond, the Terek River on the plains north of the capital Grozny, and that these actions were to be taken "even if there had been no explosions in Moscow."[136] Stepashin confirmed that Putin had been involved in this planning and that he himself, unlike Putin, had not been in favor of the ultimate plan to expand operations south of the Terek.

While the Russians blamed the Vladikavkaz bombings on the Chechens, this was the first of many incidents in the summer of 1999 in which investigative Russian journalists and opposition leaders blamed the Russian government for their possible culpability. Stepashin would later declare that his own opposition to an expanded operation—and his failure to prevent the rise of an alliance between Primakov and Luzhkov that produced a unified party—were the main reasons why he lost the prime ministership to Putin in May 1999.[137] From March 1999 forward, Putin would be associated with the hawks' camp in promoting a strong military response to events in the North Caucasus, while also blocking any increase in the role of the Ministry of Internal Affairs, something that might have been expected given the evident rivalry between the two men.

It was at this time, in March 1999, that rumors began to circulate about the introduction of emergency rule, possibly a last-ditch effort to stop the multiple threats to Yel'tsin's presidency arising from the growing popularity of Primakov; the institution of impeachment proceedings against Yel'tsin by the Communists, who held 35 percent of the seats in the Duma; and the appearance of Luzhkov's Otechestvo (Fatherland) Party. The Duma's Impeachment Commission had announced in February that it had finished its work and was prepared to start hearings on the floor of the Duma on five charges beginning on April 15.[138] Yel'tsin was in and out of the hospital during this period, and his team worked overtime to prevent the hearings from coming to a vote, which they feared they would lose. On April 12 the hearings were rescheduled for May 13, the date that would drive both the sacking of Primakov on May 12 and the preparation of contingency arrangements in case he refused to go quietly. Aleksandr Khinshteyn, a journalist known for his strong dislike of Berezovskiy, charges that Pavel Maslov, the commander of the MVD's Internal Troops, resigned at this time because he "refused to develop a plan for declaring a state of emergency in the country and wrote an extremely sharp report [Maslov otkazalsya razrabatyvat' plan vvedeniya v stranye chrezvychaynogo polozheniya i napisal kraynye rezkiy raport]."[139] On March 27, as Primakov's enemies started to close around him, Maslov gave an interview to *Krasnaya zvezda* praising Primakov's "courageous stand" on "the long-suffering Serbian lands."[140] Maslov was replaced on April 5 by Colonel General Vyacheslav Ovchinnikov, who had been the commandant of MVD forces in Grozny.

Along with Maslov, General Bordyuzha lost his position at this time. Yel'tsin sought to diminish the power of Bordyuzha, who was another supporter of Primakov. Bordyuzha taped one such conversation with Yel'tsin, and it later appeared in Primakov's own book. In the transcript of the conversation, Yel'tsin asks Bordyuzha to step down as head of the Presidential Administration but stay on as secretary of the Security Council, which

Bordyuzha declines, saying the campaign to "undermine Primakov" was "imposed on you by D'yachenko, Yumashev, Abramovich, Berezovskiy and Voloshin. . . . The country is not ruled by the president but in the name of the president by a small group of unscrupulous people. It is ruled in their interests and not those of the state." Yel'tsin responds, "I had not expected that they had accumulated such strength." When Bordyuzha insists that he will stay on only if D'yachenko and her circle leave the Kremlin, Yel'tsin signs the decree dismissing him that very evening.[141] It was under such circumstances that Voloshin became head of the Presidential Administration and Putin found his way in as Bordyuzha's replacement as head of the Security Council on March 29.

On May 12, the day before impeachment proceedings were due to begin in the Duma, Primakov was finally fired, and Sergey Stepashin became prime minister. With Primakov out, the political alignments in the Duma shifted; the hearings lasted only two days and resulted in Yel'tsin's being acquitted on all five charges on May 15—although the fifth charge, unleashing the First Chechen War as a political ploy to increase his electoral chances, fell only seventeen votes short of the necessary three hundred. Yel'tsin had once again narrowly avoided impeachment, but there was no doubt that the opposition forces were immeasurably stronger as they went into the summer and fall electoral season. The draft of a presidential order (Decree 1999) released by Duma deputy Yuriy Shchekochikhin and published in July in *Novaya gazeta* along with his commentary revealed that had the impeachment vote passed, the Kremlin planned to introduce emergency rule, to be administered by Stepashin and General Lebed (who Berezovskiy and the oligarchs believed was sympathetic to their interests, even though he presented a gruff pro-nationalist image).[142] Articles by two well-placed Western correspondents in Moscow in early June repeated these concerns: Jan Blomgren of *Svenska Dagbladet* reported on June 6, 1999, that a group of powerful Kremlin figures was planning bombings in Moscow that could be blamed on the Chechens.[143] And Giulietto Chiesa, the highly respected Moscow correspondent of the Italian newspaper *La Stampa*, who was later to become a member of the European Parliament, wrote a piece in *Literaturnaya gazeta* in mid-June in which he analyzed the logic behind the generalized increase in tensions. He provided the following analysis of the Vladikavkaz bombings:

> That criminal act was conceived and carried out not simply by a group of criminals. As a rule the question here concerns broad-scale and multiple actions, the goal of which is to sow panic and fear among citizens. . . . Actions of this type have a very powerful political and organizational base. Often, terrorist acts that stem from a "strategy of building up tension," are the work of the secret service, both foreign but also national. . . . With a high degree of certitude, one can say that the explosions of bombs killing innocent people are always planned by people with political minds. They are not fanatics; rather they are killers pursuing political goals. One should look around [in Russia] and try to understand who is interested in destabilizing the situation in a country.[144]

Writing later about the purpose of these bombings and possible Kremlin culpability, Chiesa was more specific, stating that his earlier piece had been a "veiled warning" and that he had "received information concerning the preparation of a series of terrorist acts in Russia which had the goal of canceling the future elections."[145]

Having been fired by Yel'tsin, Primakov was now free to pursue his political ambitions, and he decided to lead the Vsya Rossiya (All Russia) electoral faction in the Duma elections and in his own run for president. Joining him was Yuriy Luzhkov, the powerful mayor of Moscow, who had formed the political party Otechestvo (Fatherland) in December 1998 to launch his own presidential campaign. He had particular support not only among Muscovites but also among nationalists and populists who admired his stand on reincorporating Crimea. Once Primakov was no longer prime minister, his favorable rating in the country rose from 20 to 30 percent, and thus his alliance with Luzhkov, which occurred when they merged their two factions into Fatherland–All Russia (Otechestvo–Vsya Rossiya, OVR), became the single most viable threat to Yel'tsin electorally. Allied with them as one of the leaders of OVR was Vladimir Yakovlev, Sobchak's replacement as governor of St. Petersburg. Yakovlev, whom Putin had openly called a "Judas" both during the 1996 electoral campaign and in *First Person*, was of particular concern to Putin because of his detailed knowledge of Putin's activities as deputy mayor and Yakovlev's apparent encouragement of legal proceedings against Sobchak and his deputies, including Putin.

On May 19, within days of the failed Duma vote to impeach Yel'tsin and on Stepashin's first day in office as prime minister, Yel'tsin met with Putin not on their normal meeting day but on a day packed with working meetings to sign a decree that Putin himself had drafted and, according to his own account, already put through the Security Council. According to news reports, the decree On Additional Measures to Fight Terrorism in Russia's North Caucasus gave the FSB increased funding and authority to assume a greater role in the "coordination of all forces and resources that are at the disposal of federal government agencies." [146] In the press report of the meeting, one journalist used an ironic touch to describe how Putin briefed Yel'tsin on two recent FSB achievements, "the Leningrad Military District military court's conviction of six especially dangerous criminals, and the elimination of a channel through which food products were being smuggled (the affair involved corrupt customs officials). Undoubtedly, this well-timed report of successes achieved by Vladimir Putin's agency was meant to affect the President's mood when he signed the decree redistributing powers and resources in the North Caucasus in the FSB's favor." [147] Putin himself concedes that he understood that the country's stability and his own political future went through the Caucasus. [148]

No one among the oligarchs or in the Family, including Putin, could doubt that an OVR victory would spell, at a minimum, the end of their political careers. Stanislav Belkovskiy, the founding director of the National Strategy Institute and a political conservative, stated in an important interview in 2007 with *Die Welt* that it was the oligarchs Berezovskiy, Gusinskiy, Abramovich, and Khodorkovskiy who were running Russia after Yel'tsin's 1996 election, and it was they who "made him president in order to fulfill the task of guaranteeing the results of privatization by ensuring the transformation of the privatized companies into 'living money' [*lebendes Geld*] that was legal and could be circulated openly in Russia and abroad." [149]

But Putin had his own interests to promote and should not be seen as a simple puppet of oligarchic forces. In June 1999 a criminal case (No. 144128) with a fifty-two-page report was sent to the Federal Procuracy branch in St. Petersburg recommending an indictment of Putin and Kudrin on charges of abuse of office under Articles 285 and 286 of the Criminal Code. The investigation had been conducted by a twenty-man team drawn largely from outside St. Petersburg.[150] It is hard to imagine that Putin was not warned of this investigation by any of his colleagues still in Petersburg, such as Dmitriy Kozak, who was deputy governor; Viktor Ivanov, who until 1999 was the head of the St. Petersburg city government Administrative Staff, first under Mayor Sobchak and then under Governor Yakovlev; or Aleksey Anichin, who was in the northwest division of the Procurator General's Office. Anichin had been a classmate of Putin in the law faculty of LGU[151] and initially worked in the Military Procurator's Office. He found his way to become the deputy and then chief of the Investigative Committee of the MVD's Northwestern Region, where he was able to supervise, and reportedly then squelch, investigations into Putin's corruption in the late 1990s and early 2000s.[152]*

Putin could have been under no illusions that if OVR won, their plan had to include putting him in jail, along with other members of the Family.

---

*Anichin went on to become deputy minister of internal affairs and head of its Investigative Committee. He was accused of involvement in the Magnitskiy case and calls were made in the West to place him on a visa ban list. Magnitskiy was a Russian citizen who represented the U.S.-based investment firm Hermitage Capital, which alleged that Russian companies were engaged in corrupt and fraudulent practices and was itself raided by the police and charged with tax evasion. Magnitskiy was employed to investigate the case but was arrested and held for eleven months in pretrial detention, where he died after being beaten and tortured and denied medical treatment. One of the commissioners of the Moscow Public Oversight Commission who released a study of the death described it as a "premeditated murder."[153] According to Lyudmila Alekseyeva, a human rights activist in Moscow and head of Russia's Helsinki Group, Magnitskiy had been subjected not only to "willful torture" but also to false claims by Anichin that he was guilty of committing the alleged crimes despite the fact that he was never put on trial.[154] She made these claims in a formal letter to Aleksandr Bastrykin, who had replaced Anichin as head of the Investigative Committee at the same time that the committee ceased to report to the procurator general and started reporting directly to the president in January 2011. International reaction led in December 2012 to the passage of a law in the United States that subjected those who were directly involved in Magnitskiy's detention to denial of visas and seizure of foreign assets.[155] Medvedev subsequently "released" Anichin from his position on June 11, 2011.[156]

Primakov had already called for "freeing places in the prisons and camps for those we will be sending there."[157] In a subsequent interview, Putin's PR chief, Gleb Pavlovskiy, developed this theme: "Putin always said, we know ourselves . . . we know that as soon as we move aside, you will destroy us. He said that directly, you'll put us to the wall and execute us. And we don't want to go to the wall. . . . That was a very deep belief and was based on [the] very tough confrontations of 1993 when Yel'tsin fired on the Supreme Soviet [Parliament] and killed a lot more people—Putin knows—than was officially announced."[158]

That summer Kremlin insiders started to court the country's human rights community and liberal elites, seeking support for Putin. Pyotr Aven, who had a strong relationship with Putin from the very beginning, hosted one such dinner at his palatial estate with Putin and Igor Malashenko, one of the founders of NTV, who had been Yel'tsin's campaign manager in 1996. In a subsequent interview, Malashenko stated that he thought the evening was going to end without his getting a real feeling for who Putin was. But then Malashenko's wife received a call from her daughter in London complaining that the private school she was attending had failed to send a car to pick her up from the airport. "Our daughter is a strange girl," she sighed. "I would certainly take a taxi instead of waiting at the airport so long." Putin immediately responded, "Listen, your daughter is correct and you are not." Malashenko's wife was slightly irritated. "Why do you say that?" "You could never be confident it's really a cab." Not long afterward Yumashev asked Malashenko to support Putin as Yel'tsin's successor, saying, "He didn't give up Sobchak. He won't give us up." But Malashenko declined Yumashev's request, insisting, "He's KGB and KGB can't be trusted."[159] Andrey Kolesnikov similarly described the veteran human rights campaigner Sergey Kovalev's hesitation as liberal and human rights circles debated the issue "Who is Mr. Putin?"[160]*

---

* In July Putin's situation was made a little more delicate by the return to Petersburg of his erstwhile mentor, Anatoliy Sobchak, whose plane touched down at Pulkovo Airport to great fanfare. Sobchak announced to the hundreds of waiting journalists that he was going to stand in the December 1999 Duma elections, which Putin presumably would have supported. In response to questions about the status of corruption charges against him, he defiantly declared,

At the end of the summer of 1999, Putin was named prime minister. What happened that made him so indispensable to the Family? What did he have to do to maneuver himself to avoid prosecution in Petersburg? What evidence is there, if any, that he was part of a plan to escalate the conflict with the Chechens as a way of increasing his own chances of taking power? In May, Berezovskiy and the Family, with Putin's help, were shaping Stepashin's cabinet and limiting his choices. Chubays, who had evidently tried to block Putin's rise, suffered a major defeat at this time, when neither the IMF nor the World Bank would intervene with Yel'tsin to prevent his ouster.[166] Chubays was said to favor Stepashin over Putin as Yel'tsin's successor,[167] and Yel'tsin himself had initially been taken with Stepashin's "naïve optimism."[168] But in his own memoirs he reveals why, during the summer of 1999, he decided that Putin was the better choice to deal with the very real threat of an OVR victory: "It was clear to me that the final round of a pitched political battle was approaching. . . . Stepashin was able to reconcile some people for a time, but he wasn't going to become a political leader,

---

"If there are any complaints against me, I am ready to testify openly in court about the whole affair," a statement that could hardly have been welcomed by Putin, who had worked to have the investigation suppressed. Sobchak immediately went to lay flowers on the graves of two political allies who had been murdered since he had fled to Paris, the federal parliamentarian, human rights campaigner, and possible presidential contender Galina Starovoytova, and the former Petersburg deputy governor Mikhayl Manevich, neither of whom was ever specifically linked to corruption scandals in Petersburg. Sobchak pointedly declared, "If today those working in our law enforcement bodies are unable or unwilling to solve these murders, sooner or later there will be people there who will."[161] When Sobchak's efforts to win a Duma seat failed, he threw himself into campaigning for Putin's presidential run. Putin was campaigning about the need for democracy while still keeping a hard line on Chechnya, and Sobchak declared that Putin was "a new Stalin, not as bloodthirsty but no less brutal and firm because that is the only way to get Russians to do any work."[162] This was hardly the message that Putin wanted to get out to the West. Sobchak also told a reporter from *El País* that he was independent of Putin and did not need his help, suggesting there had been a falling-out.[163] While in Kaliningrad *oblast'*, Sobchak died in disputed circumstances. Officially he was said to have suffered a heart attack, but reports swirled that he had not been alone in the room when he became ill and that he had had two autopsies, one in Kaliningrad that suggested foul play and one in St. Petersburg that concluded he had had a heart attack. He was buried the next day, February 24, 2000.[164] Arkadi Vaksberg, an investigative journalist with forensic experience who lived in Paris and was a friend of Sobchak, claimed that Sobchak's bodyguards had also become ill, suggesting foul play. Vaksberg suggested that an old KGB technique had been revived: putting poison on the lightbulb of a bedside lamp that released deadly toxins when the lamp was turned on.[165]

a fighter, or a real ideological opponent to Luzhkov and Primakov. . . . The Prime Minister had to be changed. I was prepared for battle." [169]

What kind of "battle" was being contemplated? In two articles in *Moskovskaya Pravda*, in July and August, the military correspondent Aleksandr Zhilin claimed that "sources in the Kremlin" had confirmed that plans included declaring a state of emergency and canceling elections for five years after creating a "Hungarian version of events" in Moscow that would simultaneously discredit Luzhkov and create the conditions for declaring the state of emergency. The plan, allegedly called "Storm in Moscow" by the Kremlin planners, was laid out in a document dated June 26, 1999,[170] and involved "high-profile terrorist attacks (or attempted attacks) against a number of public buildings of the FSB, MVD, Federation Council; . . . the kidnapping of a number of famous people and ordinary citizens by 'Chechen fighters'; . . . criminal-enforcement actions against companies and businesses who support Luzhkov; . . . provoking a war between criminal groups in Moscow, creating an unbearable crime situation in the capital on the one hand and providing a cover for the planned terrorist attacks against State institutions on the other." [171] Zhilin also quoted Kremlin sources justifying Stepashin's removal because he "rejected all these adventurist plans . . . that could have led to civil war" and because he was becoming popular and could make an independent run for the presidency without requiring the backing of the Family. "Stepashin was educated, fairly strong, intelligent, ready for tough decisions while at the same time rejecting dictatorship. . . . After another couple of months he would have developed a solid political base and it would have been difficult to force his resignation." [172]

Concerned about the imminent collapse of Yel'tsin's physical and psychological well-being, which would force his resignation, the Family pushed to shape a team that would be completely reliable. According to Zhilin's Kremlin sources, reportedly Deputy Head of the Presidential Administration Sergey Zverev, who was fired on July 29,[173] this team included Putin as acting president, a Putin appointee in the FSB, and pro-Berezovskiy appointees as prime minister and minister of internal affairs.[174] On August 9, Putin had been named prime minister and designated presidential successor; also on August 9 his Petersburg colleague Patrushev had taken over as head of the FSB; and Stepashin, who wouldn't do Berezovskiy's bidding when it came to declaring a state of emergency and ratcheting up the conflict in Chechnya, had been replaced by Vladimir Rushaylo as minister of interior on May 21. Rushaylo would famously declare in 2001, "You should not confuse corruption with bribe taking." [175] In the Soviet period, he had risen through the ranks of the Ministry of Internal Affairs to supervise the foreign-currency-only Beryozka stores popular with expats and dollar-possessing Soviet citizens. He then headed the Moscow branch of the Organized Crime Unit in 1992–96, before becoming deputy minister and then minister of interior. Stepashin would run for the Duma as an opposition Yabloko candidate and win a seat in December. Chubays, discovering that Yel'tsin was about to name Putin as his successor, feverishly tried to prevent it; he attempted to talk Putin out of accepting the promotion and then appealed directly to the Family. [176] Others claim that Chubays supported Putin in principle but felt he could not get acceptance from the Duma. [177]

Other evidence of Kremlin intrigue emerged publicly when, on August 3, Yel'tsin signed a decree releasing Deputy Head of the Presidential Administration Sergey Zverev from his position. Zverev responded by calling a news conference the same day, blasting Chief of Staff Voloshin for forcing him out, saying Voloshin's actions were "harmful to the country and harmful to the president." He continued, "The [Presidential] Administration has turned into a body that has actually wreaked havoc." [178] Using a chess analogy, he did not rule out that the Kremlin was developing contingencies to cancel the elections: "Perhaps these kinds of plans are hatched in the Kremlin, if the situation is getting out of control, or if there are no 'free moves.'" [179] Zverev sharply condemned the influence of both Berezovskiy and Abramovich, who had pushed the Presidential Administration into serving "corporate not state interests." [180] He declared that the Kremlin did not make decisions without consulting with them. In blunting the rise of OVR, Zverev stated, the government "in the conflict with regional leaders needed an effective instrument of struggle. . . . Stepashin is a reasonable person and will not participate in such activities. He understands what might be the results. This means it might be necessary to find another instrument and another man who will do this." [181]

In August and September, Chechen and Dagestani militants, numbering into the hundreds or even low thousands, according to some reports, and led by Shamil Basayev and Movladi Udugov, seized several villages in Dagestan and triggered a Russian military response. Investigative reports suggested that the raid may have been planned at the very top. According to transcripts that were published (allegedly recorded and leaked by a Dagestani FSB official) in mid-June, someone who sounded like Berezovskiy had a series of conversations with two people who sounded like Udugov and Kazbek Makhashev, representing Basayev and his radical Chechen wing, in which he promised them money for preparing a raid. [182] In July more meetings were allegedly held at a private house on the French Riviera, where Basayev met with a man "resembling Kremlin chief of staff Voloshin" in a deal in which Basayev would come to power in Chechnya while Russian forces would suppress the conflict, giving them "a small war, a border conflict, a big performance with fireworks" that could be exploited for political gain. [183] Stanford University's Hoover Institution historian John Dunlop writes that both French and Israeli intelligence monitored and verified the meeting, [184] and Boris Kagarlitskiy reports that French intelligence was able to eavesdrop on the entire conversation. [185] General Ovchinnikov, the head of MVD Internal Forces, warned on July 30 that "shelling, attacks and other acts of provocation . . . launched from Chechen territory were increasing." [186] He subsequently stated in an interview that he had raised concerns at the time with Interior Minister Rushaylo about MVD forces along the Dagestan-Chechen border being withdrawn at the same time that warnings about an imminent invasion were increasing, giving the Basayev forces complete access to two villages the MVD had seized. [187] The local MVD commander in Dagestan also subsequently reported, "That there would be a war in August was spoken of as early as the spring [of 1999] starting from operatives from the power structures and ending with women at the bazaars." [188] The Chechen deputy prime minister and national security minister Turpal-Ali Atgeriev claimed that he had twice told FSB chief Putin in July 1999 of Basayev's plans, knowing full well that

Basayev could be playing into the hands of those who wanted a second Chechen war. Atgeriev was captured in October 2000 and sentenced to one year in prison, where he died of leukemia on August 22, 2002, according to Moscow's Interfax. His parents and Chechen authorities, however, insist he was tortured to death.[189]

Dunlop's extensive research of this episode lends significant credibility to the argument that the Chechen incursion into Dagestan was the beginning of an extended "false flag" operation in which specific Chechen leaders, paid by the Family, acted to create a state of panic in the country that would justify putting the government on a war footing and declaring a state of emergency if needed. The Chechen incursion into Dagestan was unimpeded by federal forces. During the fight to capture the villages, where the Chechens faced stiffer than expected resistance from local villagers, the Russians came to the "aid" of the Dagestanis by razing the villages through bombardment, in the process killing hundreds of Russian soldiers and an unknown number of innocent Dagestani civilians. Then, despite the carnage, the Chechens were allowed to withdraw unimpeded.[190]

Prime Minister, August 9, 1999

Two days after Basayev's initial incursion into Dagestan, Yel'tsin announced that he had fired Stepashin and replaced him with Putin. Not only was he naming Putin to be yet another prime minister, but Yel'tsin also named him as his preferred successor, the first of his five prime ministers to be so designated. In the transcript of his remarks, Yel'tsin stated, "I have decided to now name the person who is, in my opinion, able to consolidate society and, drawing support from the broadest political forces, to ensure the continuation of reforms in Russia. He will be able to unite around himself those who are to renew Great Russia in the new 21st Century. He is the Secretary of the Security Council and the Director of the FSB of Russia, Vladimir Vladimirovich Putin."[191] Discussing his dismissal on that day, Stepashin pointedly stated, "The main thing now is that we should act in a constitutionally legal way. The elections must take place on time."[192] Chubays reportedly once again tried to block the move, without success.[193]

Yel'tsin frankly admitted that Putin had expressed some reluctance about accepting this position, less due to lack of willingness to do the day-to-day work than from distaste for campaigning and being in the public eye. Yel'tsin said Putin told him, "Electoral campaigns—I don't like them. I really don't like them. I don't know how to fight them and I don't like them."[194] Yel'tsin also conceded that Chubays fought against the appointment, that he complained both to Yel'tsin personally and to the Family, saying that Yel'tsin had "lost his mind" (*soshol s uma*) and that the Duma should step in to stop the appointment. Yel'tsin also maintained that Chubays warned Putin that he wasn't ready for the attacks he would sustain in the public eye. But Putin told him this was Yel'tsin's decision and Chubays should abide by it.[195]

Over the next week the still largely unknown Putin made his first forays onto the public stage. In a speech before the Duma on August 16, as part of the confirmation process, he laid out his priorities. In his very first sentence he stated what would become the trademark of his rule: "The first thing that ought to concern us all equally right now is the stability and reliability of authority." On the issue of elections, he clearly did not close the door to emergency rule since elections require "calm and order," but neither did he suggest he was leaning in that direction: "Second, one of the government's main tasks is to ensure calm and order in the country and the holding of honest and just elections, both State Duma elections and presidential elections." He repeatedly returned to the need to strengthen the state: "The weakness of state institutions . . . is the bait for unscrupulous entrepreneurs and a reason for blackmail and pressure on the authorities in the pursuit of selfish interests. The result of this is the proliferation of crime throughout our economy. This is particularly dangerous against a background of attempts to privatize law-enforcement bodies and to turn them into an instrument of war among clans and groups. In its fight against this phenomenon, the government will avail itself of all of its potential. . . . Laws on the market are only truly effective when there is no disorder in the united mechanism of state management, when the work of all branches of power is aimed at one thing—preserving the unity and integrity of our state." On the instability in the North Caucasus he was more forthcoming about the potential for introducing emergency rule: "Regional leaders are looking to the executive authorities for the most resolute measures against the terrorists. The possibility of imposing a state of emergency there was discussed. Today, this morning, right up to now, we have been discussing this issue in detail, and demands have been made in this house for a quicker decision, within the law, on a state of emergency. I think that we can contain the conflict and remove its root causes without resorting to that extreme measure." His concluding words summed up his main point: "I do know one thing for sure: not one of these tasks can be performed without imposing basic order and discipline in this country, without strengthening the vertical chain of command in the executive authorities."[196]

Although Putin was confirmed, he received only 233 votes—only seven votes more than the minimum of 226 required for passage.[197] It was clearly not yet the case that the future of the Family was secure. And the announcement the following day, August 17, that Yevgeniy Primakov, universally rated in public opinion polls the country's most respected leader, and Mayor Yuriy Luzhkov, rated number two in the polls, would "unite all healthy, centrist forces"[198] around OVR to fight for victory in the December Duma elections was a lightning bolt to the Family. A furious campaign would be required by the Kremlin to prevent their victory. It seems likely that Yel'tsin's personal preference was for proceeding with the elections, but given his physical incapacity, those around him were willing to explore all options to keep their potential jailers from coming to power. Of course, they were able to use the "administrative resources" of the Kremlin to help bring to power a group that would secure their future. The spinmeister of the Putin project, and the PR guru for the Family since 1996, Gleb Pavlovskiy, subsequently explained, "In 1999, when Putin was pulled into project 'Successor,' there was always a certain amount of physical fear for the existence of the 'Family.'" When the interviewer asked Pavlovskiy whether this extended to Putin, he replied, "Yes. Maybe back then [in 1999], internally he [Putin] was skeptical about all that, but now [after the 2011 election demonstrations], probably, not anymore. Now there is fear."[199]

The public didn't know Putin, and if the Family was going to secure their future through legal immunity granted by Putin as the next president, Putin needed to be "created." This was Pavlovskiy's job. As part of the Family's brain trust, Pavlovskiy had a significant task: to create an image of Putin out of thin air. Beginning in August, Pavlovskiy arranged for Putin to speak at various venues to build alliances and to show the Moscow elite in particular that he was more than a lowly officer from the KGB. Pavlovskiy relates that Putin was so effective at a meeting at the end of August at Moscow's elite PEN Club with leading Russian writers, an ordinarily extremely skeptical group, that after an hour they practically became his proxies. The image that Pavlovskiy worked on was of Putin as someone who, through everything, remained "on his post," protecting the "true" interests of the nation against all enemies. He was to be the latter-day Stierlitz, the mythologized Soviet spy portrayed in the famous Soviet series *Seventeen Moments of Spring* who won World War II by serving undercover deep inside the SS regime. As discussed earlier, Putin himself had already shaped the 1992 documentary by Igor Shadkhan that made the connection between Stirlitz and himself, with both men portrayed as having sacrificed their personal happiness to protect the motherland. Similarly the message Pavlovskiy helped convey through Putin (and Pavlovskiy clearly admits that he initially underestimated Putin's ability) was "I am still on my post amidst these corrupt oligarchs. Just wait. I will deliver." Pavlovskiy's task was made easier, he admits, by the huge contrast between Yel'tsin's feebleness and Putin's youth. The fact that Putin's main opponents, Primakov and Luzhkov, were of the Yel'tsin generation also helped—as did Pavlovskiy's carefully constructed leaks of details about Primakov's supposed failing health and Luzhkov's alleged corruption.[200]

Berezovskiy would provide the funding and the access to ORT, the state-run channel that he had a minority stake in, as well as possibly helping to fund off-the-books operations, as Dunlop suggests, including Basayev's raid into Dagestan that acted as the tripwire for this era. It was widely reported that Putin and Berezovskiy had many clandestine meetings before Putin became prime minister, both in Moscow, in the elevator shaft of the FSB building, which, according to Masha Gessen, was the only place in FSB headquarters that Putin believed was safe from bugs;[201] in a holiday flat Putin rented in the south of France;[202] and in the Sotogrande resort in southern Spain, in San Roque, Cádiz province, where Berezovskiy had a residence.

It was in Sotogrande, *La Razón* reported, that Putin and Berezovskiy held at least five secret meetings in 1999 that appear to have been at least partially taped by Spanish intelligence. They contend that they were actually monitoring at the request of Interpol the activities of a member of the Russian mafia who happened to live next door to Berezovskiy in this quiet enclave by the sea. In early 1999 they only casually discovered Putin's presence when, in monitoring the movements of the Russian mafia figure, who was in the garden, they realized he was talking to Putin and Berezovskiy. It was then that they decided to inform the government of Spain, at which point surveillance was increased, since Putin was at that time secretary of the Russian Security Council and head of the FSB. Moreover he had not entered Spain legally, through passport control, but had flown into the British protectorate of Gibraltar, whose airstrip is under British military control, giving rise to never confirmed speculation that British intelligence had tracked Putin,[203] and transferred to a private boat, arriving at the private Sotogrande dock near Berezovskiy's house. CESID* reported that Putin was in Spain at the invitation of Berezovskiy to "plan the substitution of Yel'tsin." They claimed that British intelligence had monitored Putin's movements from Gibraltar and that he had made *at least* five trips in 1999 alone, including several when he was prime minister. While in Sotogrande, Putin restricted his activities and behaved with "great discretion"; the neighborhood's private security force noted only that during these periods there was a flurry of black luxury cars, but they were never informed who the visitor was. Berezovskiy, on the other hand, was more public, throwing a massive party with fireworks at the beach club for the area's growing Russian population soon after Putin was named prime minister.[204] The *Times* of London confirmed Spanish reports that Spanish police had monitored Putin, who had "flown to Gibraltar and sailed into Spain without declaring his presence on Spanish soil, as the law requires."[205]

---

*CESID was the primary Spanish intelligence agency until 2002, when it was reorganized and renamed Centro Nacional de Inteligencia.

The story published by *La Razón* stated that Spanish intelligence also knew of Putin's previous visits to Torrevieja, when he was a deputy mayor of St. Petersburg.[206] This concurs with allegations being made in St. Petersburg at the time by procurators that Putin had used false papers to travel frequently to Spain to supervise the building of apartments with money diverted from the Mayor's Contingency Fund.[207] A *Novaya gazeta* investigation based on the articles in *La Razón* and the *Times* found further details: that the mafia person being investigated was the leader of one of the St. Petersburg crime families; that Putin may have used false papers to enter Spain via the British base in Gibraltar; that he may have traveled to Gibraltar via London; that both MI5 and MI6 knew about his travels but did not share the information with Spanish officials—remembering that Putin was at this time the head of the FSB.[208]

In addition to Berezovskiy and Pavlovskiy, the Family needed not just to shape Putin's image; they needed to ensure that the Duma elections were won by a pro-Kremlin party. However, in the summer of 1999 such a party did not exist. The Our Home Is Russia Party, which had won sixty-five seats—more than any party but the Communists—in the 1995 Duma elections, under the leadership of Prime Minister Viktor Chernomyrdin, was no longer functional. With Primakov at the head of OVR, that party could be expected to win the lion's share of the seats and ally with the Communists to launch their own parliamentary investigations of the Family. They needed a party that could capture a sizable proportion of the seats. Berezovskiy is credited with the idea of creating such a party, but it was the job of Vladislav Surkov to realize it.

Surkov was born in Chechnya of a Chechen father and a Russian mother; brought up in southern Russia, he began the post-Soviet period as a publicist for Mikhayl Khodorkovskiy.[209] He became deputy head of the Presidential Administration when Sergey Zverev was fired in late July, although he had worked in the Kremlin for some months already. A brilliant tactician, he would succeed in the course of less than three months in organizing a founding congress on October 3 for the new pro-Putin party of power, Unity, and laying the groundwork for Unity to win 23.3 percent of the vote in the elections on December 19. Pavlovskiy subsequently stated, "Surkov was not just controlling the work, he was masterminding it; forming different political projects."[210] The combination of Putin's performance at the head of the "party of war," the growing and nontransparent power of his associates who followed him from St. Petersburg, Berezovskiy's intrigues, Pavlovskiy's PR skills, and Surkov's tactical genius resulted in a truly remarkable political team. And part of their strategy was to provide Prime Minister Putin with a platform that would focus the country on a strong response to the resurgence of Chechen terrorism and bombings, in which Putin would calm the people, prevent panic after a horrible wave of bombings, and become the actual and symbolic vehicle for the nation's demand for a strong and vengeful state response. A number of the St. Petersburg faithful were added to this team. Viktor Zolotov became head of Putin's personal security team, and Igor Sechin moved in as head of the new prime minister's Secretariat. Zolotov remained close to Tsepov in St. Petersburg but added his own close business connections with the Moscow-based oligarchs Roman Abramovich and Oleg Deripaska,[211] helping to extend Putin's ties beyond Petersburg.*

On August 23 Basayev announced that his Chechen forces had largely withdrawn from Dagestan, a date that coincided with Putin's self-imposed deadline to crush the uprising.[213] In late August Russia launched a major air campaign over Chechnya, designed (as evidently had been planned since March) to establish Russian preeminence over Chechen territory north of the Terek River. Then, between August 31 and September 16, five bombs exploded:

- On August 31 in the Okhotnyy Ryad underground mall underneath Manezh Square, just steps from the Kremlin, killing one person.[214]

---

*In 2013 the Russian press reported that Zolotov was in line to head a new unified team for the personal protection of Putin that would combine the support systems provided for presidential security from the FSO, the MVD, and the FSB.[212] But then Zolotov was moved instead in 2014 to become head of all Ministry of Interior troops.

- On September 4 in Buynaksk, Dagestan, via a car bomb in front of an apartment building housing Russian border guards, killing sixty-four.[215]
- On September 9 in Moscow's Pechatniki district on Gur'yanov Street, using a massive bomb planted in the ground floor of an apartment building, killing one hundred sleeping residents.[216]
- On September 13 on Moscow's Kashirskoye Highway, via a bomb planted in the basement of an apartment building, killing 118 sleeping residents.[217]
- September 16 in the southern Russian city of Volgodonsk, in which a massive truck bomb planted outside an apartment building killed eighteen sleeping residents.[218]

The bombing campaign came to a halt only when an FSB team that had evidently been involved in planting a bomb in the city of Ryazan was apprehended by local authorities.

Altogether 301 were killed and almost two thousand injured. Up to three additional bombs were allegedly located and defused in Moscow.[219] The government put out a nationwide call for vigilance, blamed the bombings on Chechen separatists, and appealed for help in finding a man who was using the stolen passport of a dead man named Mukhit Laypanov. The man was seen at the Pechatniki bombing scene, had leased space in the Moscow apartment buildings demolished by bomb attacks, and had rented a garage in which police found a cache of three tons of explosives disguised as seventy-six sacks of sugar.[220]

Beginning almost immediately, Russian investigative journalists began to analyze the evidence of responsibility for these bombings. Additional subsequent investigations by Western and Russian scholars, journalists, and participants expressed concern about government collusion or participation. Because of their similarity and high death toll, the apartment bombings in Moscow struck the most fear, but the botched effort in Ryazan produced the greatest debate about the identity of the actual perpetrators.

Whatever hopes there were to avoid a "storm in Moscow," it had definitely arrived. The horrors of the actions were almost immediately matched by discussion of the unthinkable: Had a group within the walls of the Kremlin been behind these bombings, and for what purpose? Certainly Luzhkov still needed to be defeated politically, and Putin's credibility as a security hawk and head of the "party of war" needed to be established not just in Kremlin corridors but in the public eye as well. Putin's public ratings when he was first appointed prime minister in August were in the low single digits, much lower than Luzhkov's, Primakov's, and the Communist leader Gennadiy Zyuganov's. The apartment bombings had the effect of creating panic in the country as a whole, but in Moscow in particular, Luzhkov's ability to display his control of events was undermined. Additionally Prime Minister Putin was on television nightly. The population was baying for vengeance, and Putin became their vehicle. Regional elites started to go over to the Putin camp. As retired KGB general Leonov subsequently wrote, "Putin's ratings were growing rapidly. Silent was the same Russian press that during the first Chechen war had waged a vicious anti-Russian campaign, defaming the army and all those who can be called 'statist patriots.' Now the moral and political climate in the country had changed completely. There was an awareness of the real risk of the collapse of the Russian state and the power of a united people." [221] On September 23 a group of twenty-four governors wrote President Yel'tsin, asking him to step down in favor of Putin.[222] That same day, according to Gessen, Yel'tsin signed a secret decree authorizing the military to renew combat in Chechnya; the next day Putin issued the same decree, although, as Gessen notes, "Russian law in fact gives the prime minister no authority over the military." [223] But Putin was to be the public face of the regime's fight against the Chechens, and it was on this day that he famously promised the country that he would indefatigably search for the Chechen bombers: "V sortire zamochim"— "We will wipe them out" (literally, "make wet" or "liquidate")—"in the outhouse and that will be the end of it." [224] His ratings began to rise, and having only narrowly achieved confirmation by the Duma in late August, he declared that discussion of the declaration of a state of emergency was simply fanciful talk designed to convince people that the federal authorities couldn't cope. His job was to reassure the Russian people that he was fully in charge and that Russian troops would prevail.[225]

By the end of September, after Yel'tsin gave him complete control over the war effort, Putin launched a ground offensive into Chechnya. Two months before the Duma elections, the Second Chechen War began. Within the month almost half of the total population of Chechnya would become refugees. The destruction inflicted on the capital city of Grozny—which was, after all, a city *within* Russia—was greater than any seen in Europe since World War II.

The heightened concern about a new Chechen war shaped Russian media coverage and blunted U.S. condemnation of the Yel'tsin Family at a time when the U.S. government's year-long investigation of a massive money-laundering scheme at the Bank of New York by Russian crime figures was becoming public.[226] Testimony given to a U.S. congressional committee in September 1999 claimed that there were two accounts at the bank's Cayman Islands branch worth $2.7 million in the name of Yel'tsin's son-in-law, Leonid D'yachenko. The committee also learned that one of the BNY employees who had allegedly facilitated the largest money-laundering operation *in U.S. history* (worth at least $10 billion) was the wife of Russia's former representative to the IMF, Konstantin Kagalovskiy. That one of the oldest financial institutions in the United States had been commandeered by Russian organized crime, with possible participation by elite Russian circles, went public in August. Vice President Al Gore's presidential campaign suffered from the revelations because he had been the point person for U.S. relations with the Kremlin under Clinton.[227] And the creditworthiness of the Russian regime was called into question. The fact that Undersecretary of State Strobe Talbott had met Putin in June and praised his performance most likely created the conditions for refraining from direct criticism of or legal action against the Family as they jockeyed to turn the government over to someone whose public persona was comparatively unblemished.[228]

Central to all of this was Boris Berezovskiy. He had the most to lose if OVR or the Communists came to power, and now even his backup plan to live abroad was in jeopardy, as these revelations suggested that he himself was a participant in several of these corrupt schemes. The financier George Soros, who knew Berezovskiy and followed his political career, provided the following trenchant analysis of the dilemma facing Berezovskiy as the

Mabetex and BNY scandals broke abroad and the personal attacks on him in the electoral campaign increased: "Berezovskiy and Yel'tsin's Family were looking for a way to perpetuate the immunity they enjoyed under the Yel'tsin administration. . . . Berezovskiy's situation turned desperate when the scandal broke over the laundering of Russian illegal money in U.S. banks in 1999, for he realized that he could no longer find refuge in the West. One way or the other he had to find a successor to Yel'tsin who would protect him. That is when the plan to promote Putin's candidacy was hatched."[229] Berezovskiy evidently thought it was in his interest to promote a general increase in tension in the country so that people's attention would be drawn to security threats and unifying the country against them, thus limiting the space for opposition politicians to attack the Kremlin. But presumably the Family continued to calculate that should the need arise, the elections could still be postponed under the guise of an antiterrorist campaign. Berezovskiy traveled to Washington in November, meeting with Talbott, who generally distrusted the Russian oligarch but was curious to see which new "product . . . he was selling." It was Putin, who Berezovsky wanted to assure Washington was a realist who would not oppose NATO expansion, unlike Primakov, and that Putin was concerned, as Washington should be, with fighting radical Islam in the northern Caucasus.[230]

In an interview with Masha Gessen ten years later, Berezovskiy put forward a slightly different view. Obviously he wasn't going to admit that he had been involved in such a monstrous act as blowing up apartment buildings. However, he did offer the following noteworthy appraisal of these events. At the time he discounted charges that the government was behind the bombings as mere political rhetoric during a campaign season: "It never occurred to me that there was a parallel game to ours—that someone else was doing what they thought was right to get Putin elected. Now I am convinced that was exactly what was going on." Gessen continues in her own words: "The 'someone else' would have been the FSB, and the 'parallel game' would have been the explosions, intended to unite Russians in fear and in a desperate desire for a new, decisive, even aggressive leader who would spare no enemy."[231]

FSB Team Arrested in Botched Ryazan Bombing

The idea that an elite team in the FSB was behind the bombings gained credence when, on September 22, 1999, two Ryazan residents noticed three people carrying sacks from a white car into the basement of an apartment building. The car's license plate was VAZ-2107; the code for Ryazan *oblast'*, 62, was written on a piece of paper and taped over the real code in the front, but the Moscow code was uncovered in the back, causing further suspicion. The residents were able to get a close enough look at the three, two men and one woman, to describe them to police, who created composite sketches showing three clearly Slavic, not Caucasian, individuals. The local militia and the bomb squad were called, and the bomb, whose contents were immediately identified by local authorities as hexogen (RDX) disguised in sugar bags (as at least one of the Moscow apartment bombs had been), was defused. Local residents were evacuated and thousands more throughout Ryazan took to the streets in panic.[232] Roadblocks were established to apprehend the terrorists, and Interior Minister Rushaylo praised his subordinates in Ryazan for finding a bomb.[233] Putin as well, going on television the next day to announce the beginning of the bombing of Grozny, stated, "If the sacks which proved to contain explosives were noticed, then there is a positive side to it." On September 24 he told his government, "We must not and we will not turn this government into a government of the state of emergency."[234]

But then the Ryazan story began to unravel:

- That evening a worker at the local telephone exchange listened in on a call from one of the three alleged bombers in which they were advised by a voice at the other end to "break up" and make their way back separately. The call was traced to FSB headquarters in Moscow.[235]
- But they did not break up, and they were captured by local police. When about to be formally detained, the three produced FSB identification cards, were subsequently released, and have never been charged. This became known to Russian journalists and analysts.

Boris Kagarlitskiy, who made a close study of the event, concluded, "FSB officers were caught red-handed while planting the bomb. They were arrested by the police and they tried to save themselves by showing FSB identity cards."[236]

- On the morning of September 24 government statements that a terrorist act had been averted were replaced by FSB director Patrushev's assertion that the entire event had been a civil defense exercise.[237] Yet the local FSB chief in Ryazan had rushed to the scene once the bomb was defused, and he had congratulated the residents for "being born again."[238] After Patrushev's statement, the local FSB in Ryazan responded with outrage to what they believed was an obvious canard: "This announcement [by Patrushev] came as a surprise to us and appeared at the moment when the [local] FSB had identified the places of residence in Ryazan of those involved in planting the explosive device and was prepared to detain them."[239] The local FSB station, having started an investigation, refused to stop it, even after Patrushev's statement. Major General Oleg Kalugin, a retired FSB official writing from the United States, went on record saying that in his opinion, the story that this was an FSB training exercise was "complete nonsense."[240] When one of the two residents of the targeted apartment building in Ryazan, Vladimir Vasil'yev, who had phoned in to the local police initially, heard that according to the FSB there had never been a bomb, he responded, "I heard the official version on the radio, when the press secretary of the FSB announced it was a training exercise. It felt extremely unpleasant."[241]

- Journalists noted the similarities between the Moscow apartment bombings and Ryazan, the "training exercise." This similarity became more sensitive when it was revealed that RDX, the material used in at least one of the Moscow bombs, as announced by Luzhkov,[242] and planted in Ryazan, was an explosive available only from a closed military installation in Perm. The FSB then announced that the sacks that had been "defused" in Ryazan had actually been filled with sugar, not hexogen. *Novaya gazeta*'s Pavel Voloshin conducted an extensive study on this detail and concluded, based on interviews with local FSB officials, the police, and the bomb squad, that "the Ryazantsi were not wrong. The technology and the people worked professionally. Inside the so-called 'training' bags was hexogen."[243] The local bomb squad, headed by Yuriy Tkachenko, stuck to their story that they had detected a bomb set to go off at 5.30 A.M., consisting of an armed detonator and three sacks of explosives. Tkachenko restated this on Russian television, and the picture of the detonator taken by police on September 23 was also released.[244] Faced with the sheer stubborn unwillingness of local authorities to concur that the substance had been sugar or that the detonator had been a fake, the FSB changed their story, now saying that it had been a mixture of a number of chemicals made at a fertilizer factory in Chechnya.[245]

Russian journalists investigating the Ryazan bombing quickly came to the conclusion that all the bombings may have been inspired by the government to deepen the anti-Chechen mood in the country as a prelude to launching a wider war in Chechnya, over which electoral politics and the need to boost Putin's image were paramount. "May God grant the federal troops victory," Aleksandr Zhilin wrote. "In this case it won't be necessary to conduct another series of blasts in Moscow and other cities, designed to lay the conditions for a state of emergency because the serious increase in Putin's ratings gives the 'Family' the chance to get out of the political stalemate without violating the constitution."[246] *Novaya gazeta* investigators found two conscripts on a base of the 137th Ryazan Paratroop Regiment who had been assigned to guard a warehouse full of fifty-kilogram bags marked "Sugar." When they opened one for tea, it tasted so bitter that they reported it to their superior, who had it tested. It came back positive for hexogen. The conscripts were berated for "divulging state secrets," and FSB officers arrived to advise them to forget what they had seen.[247]

Other aspects of the bombings became known and further strengthened the argument that the bombs were part of a centrally inspired plot. A liberal member of the Duma from St. Petersburg, Yuliy Rybakov, provided a transcript to Aleksandr Litvinenko of a September 13 Duma session in which Speaker Gennadiy Seleznyov interrupted the session to announce, "We have just received news that a residential building in Volgodonsk was blown up last night," when in fact that bombing was still three days away.[248] Later that week, when a parliamentarian asked Seleznyov why he had told them on Monday about a blast that did not happen until Thursday, the questioner's microphone was simply turned off, according to Duma member Mikhayl Trepashkin, a lawyer and former FSB agent.[249]

Other opposition lawmakers joined with Trepashkin in calling for a Duma investigation of this incident, and indeed of all the bombings. At the end of 2003 the remaining two of the nine suspects the Russians had sought for complicity in the bombings were due to go to trial. (Five of the nine had been killed, and two others had fled the country.) Trepashkin was certain that these remaining two were framed, and he intended to present evidence at their trial. As insurance, he gave *Moskovskiye novosti* all of his evidence, including the fact that in August 1999 he had recognized the man whose identikit picture had been posted by the authorities after the Moscow bombings. As the newspaper subsequently stated, he shared his own dated photo of the suspect, a person known as Vladimir Romanovich, whom Trepashkin had detained several years previously in connection with the criminal shakedown of the Sol'di Bank in Moscow by a group that included FSB officers—an investigation that Trepashkin maintains was stopped by Patrushev in 1995, when he was head of the FSB Directorate for Internal Security.[250] At that time Trepashkin believed that Romanovich, who was set free, must have had ties with the FSB. Now, in 1999, when he showed his own dated picture to his former superiors in the FSB, their only reaction was to change the identikit picture to lengthen the face and diminish the resemblance to Romanovich.[251]

Before Trepashkin could present his evidence in court supporting an FSB plot, he was arrested for illegal possession of a firearm. After a closed military trial, despite protests about due process from the International Commission of Jurists, he was convicted and served five years.[252] Needless to say, he was not able to testify in the defense of the two remaining suspects, and they were convicted. Many newspapers subsequently reported that Romanovich had fled to Cyprus, where he was killed by a hit-and-run driver in summer 2000.[253]

A parliamentary investigation was indeed launched, however. (At this time the Kremlin did not yet control the Duma.) Before his arrest, Trepashkin acted as a lawyer to the committee; the other three parliamentary leaders of the independent investigation were Sergey Kovalev, Yuriy Shchekochikhin, and Sergey Yushenkov. The investigation was not able to reach any conclusions because the government refused to cooperate with it. Rybakov, like Kovalev and other liberals, lost his seat in the 2003 elections, lamenting, "Now, as private figures, we will get only meaningless answers."[254] Kovalev told an Ekho Moskvy radio interviewer in 2002 that his commission had received testimony from the person held responsible for renting the space in Moscow where bombs had been placed—despite the fact that the FSB was still "searching for" this person.[255]

The person the FSB was searching for was Achemez Gochiyaev, an ethnic Karachai (not a Chechen) from the North Caucasus who served in the Russian Strategic Rocket Forces and who in 1999 lived in Moscow. He testified that he had used a fake passport of a deceased man to rent the spaces. He provided written and video testimony to *Novaya gazeta*[256] and the Russian historian Yuriy Felshtinskiy,[257] in which he confirmed that he had indeed rented the space in the Moscow buildings; that he had done so at the request of an FSB friend; and that when he realized he was going to be framed for these horrible acts, he was the one who called the police and alerted them to the location of the additional spaces that he had rented (at Borisovskiye Prudy and Kapotnya). He also categorically denied having anything to do with Ryazan.[258] Later, in 2003, however, the owner of the Moscow apartment space on Gur'yanov Street, Mark Blumenfeld, told *Moskovskiye novosti* that when he was shown a picture of Gochiyaev by the authorities while under interrogation in Lefortovo prison, he told them, "I have never seen this person. But they strongly recommended that I identify Gochiyaev. I understood what they wanted and never argued, and I signed the statement. But in fact, the man whose picture they showed me and who was called Gochiyaev, was not the man who came to me."[259] Despite considerable skepticism in the opposition press that Gochiyaev was in fact the person who rented the spaces used for the bombings, the FSB continued to blame him.

Kovalev stated that while the Duma's efforts to have a full investigation had been stymied, he had his own "interim" view of what happened in Ryazan: "In my opinion, the following version sounds quite trustworthy. The explosion of an apartment building was not planned, but a training exercise was also not planned. What was planned, we may say, was the following action, a propaganda action. First, to show the citizens that terrorists are active, that they have not abandoned their murderous plans, and at the same time, the second point was to show that the brave [security] organs perform their duties excellently, rescue citizens, and unmask these villainous plots. Why not this version? That plan, possibly, existed and failed. Honestly, I am very reluctant to believe that any sort of security services, obeying our supreme authorities, were capable of blowing up the sleeping inhabitants of their country." [260]

The fact remains that not only was Trepashkin sentenced to five years, but both Yushenkov and Shchekochikhin died in 2003. Yushenkov was assassinated outside his apartment building in Moscow on April 17, 2003, and Shchekochikhin, who had traveled to Ryazan in June 2003, came back suffering from a high fever, a sore throat, and a rash. He died in the Kremlin's Central Clinic on July 3; his father-in-law, a retired professor of pharmacology, stated in an interview, "He was very dangerous for the authorities. He penetrated into things he should not have." [261]

Similarly Artyom Borovik told Yabloko Party leaders that he was conducting an independent investigation of FSB involvement in the bombings for a series of articles in his journal *Sovershenno sekretno*; shortly afterward, in early 2000, he died in a plane crash. [262] By 2004 over a dozen men of "Caucasian nationality" had been sentenced *in camera* to extended periods in prison. Still dissatisfied with the government's failure to provide a public accounting of the events in 1999, *Novaya gazeta* published a list of questions for Putin and the other presidential candidates. They provide an apt summary of the issues raised by the troubling incident as the country entered the election season:

- Why did the authorities prevent the investigation of the events in Ryazan, where the FSB officers had been implicated in blowing up an apartment building?
- Why did Duma Speaker Gennadiy Seleznyov announce the explosion in the Volgodonsk apartment building three days before it happened?
- Why has the detection of RDX in sacks marked "sugar" on a military base in Ryazan in autumn 1999 not been investigated?
- Why was the investigation into the transfer by NII Roskonversvzryvtsentr* of RDX from military depots to front companies closed under pressure from the FSB?
- Trepashkin, who established the identity of the FSB agent who rented a room for planting [a bomb in an] apartment building on Gur'yanov Street—why was he arrested? [264]

Opposition politicians also began to question the government's version of events. Most were self-serving, but a pointed interview given to *Le Figaro* by the blunt nationalist general Aleksandr Lebed was picked up by the Russian press. He was quoted by Moscow's *Segodnya* saying, "As I understand it, an agreement was made with [Chechen rebel leader Shamil] Basayev, especially since he's a former KGB informant. I'm absolutely sure of this. [Lebed had been the Yel'tsin envoy that negotiated the end of the First Chechen War.] I think Basayev and the powers that be have a pact. Their objectives coincide. The President and the Family have become isolated. They don't have the political power to win the elections. So, seeing the hopelessness of its situation, the Kremlin has set itself just one goal: to destabilize the situation so the elections can be called off." When the general was asked whether he was sure that "the hand of power," as he put

---

* Scientific-Investigative Institute (Nauchno-Issledovatel'skiy Institut, NII) for the Disposal and Conversion of Explosive Materials (Roskonversvzryvtsentr) under the Ministry of Education. The letter from Minister of Education Vladimir Filippov to Procurator General Vladimir Ustinov complaining about the lack of progress in the investigation of the Institute's culpability in the transfer of RDX under Criminal Case No. 9271 was subsequently published. [263]

it, was behind the apartment bombings, he replied, "I'm all but convinced of it. Any Chechen field commander set on revenge would have started blowing up generals. Or he'd have started striking Internal Affairs Ministry and Federal Security Service buildings, military stockpiles or nuclear power plants. He wouldn't have targeted ordinary, innocent people. The goal is to sow mass terror and create conditions for destabilization, so as to be able to say when the time comes, 'You shouldn't go to the polls, or you'll risk being blown up along with the ballot box.'"[265]* Lebed continued to make troubling allegations of Kremlin involvement. He died in a helicopter crash in 2002.

Konstantin Borovoy, a Duma deputy, received a document warning of imminent terror attacks in September 1999, which he communicated to the FSB. He then received information about the FSB's involvement. In an interview on Ekho Moskvy in 2010 he recalled, "[Anatoliy] Sobchak asked me to support [Putin]; it was in the middle of 1999, but then there began the . . . bombings of the apartment houses. A member of the special services gave me as a [Duma] deputy a very serious document. As a deputy I held a press conference, during which I said that . . . the FSB is organizing these explosions. Putin immediately made a [sarcastic] declaration that this Borovoy should be sent out to defuse the bombs. Why was he lying? You understand that I grasped everything that had taken place in that September 1999. I wrote him a letter that I could not support him because it is wrong to resort to such methods. My relations with Putin came to an end, so to speak, in 1999."[267] Borovoy then added a critical detail: "When the bombings of the apartment houses took place in September 1999, I held a press conference. Into my possession there had come information, very serious information. . . . I began to transmit it to the Security Council. And the person who presented this witness's testimony, that the FSB was a participant, that person telephoned me after his meeting with the representative of the Security Council and said, 'Why did you send me to the FSB? Those are the very same FSB-shniki [FSB workers]. I was telling them what

---

* For the originals, see the series of articles by Mandeville.[266]

they were [already engaged in] doing.'"[268] Borovoy's warnings were the subject of newspaper articles in mid-September 1999, after the first Moscow bomb but before the second. An article on September 16 concluded, "For a long time [the special services] had information about imminent terrorist attacks but did not take any measures, so as 'not to sow panic.' . . . Inasmuch as one of the obligations of the special services is to check such information, the impression was formed that the special services intentionally did not conduct active operations and did not inform the government of Moscow concerning a terrorist act being prepared, since connivance was profitable to the Kremlin for its political goals. The enormous misfortune which befell the populace quickly squeezed off the front pages of newspapers and from television screens the theme of corruption in the presidential 'Family' and the scandal with the New York bank."[269]

While doubts and suspicions about the complicity of the security services continue to this day, the bombings were regarded at the time as absolutely critical in promoting Putin's candidacy.[270] Putin's approval ratings rose dramatically through the fall, from 2 percent in August to 45 percent by November.[271] In early spring Sergey Kovalev summed up the real political impact of the apartment bombings:

> Those explosions were a crucial moment in the unfolding of our current history. After the first shock passed, it turned out that we were living in an entirely different country, in which almost no one dared talk about a peaceful, political resolution of the crisis with Chechnya. How, it was asked, can you negotiate with people who murder children at night in their beds? War and only war is the solution! What we want—so went the rhetoric of many politicians, including Vladimir Putin—is the merciless extermination of the "adversary" wherever he may be, whatever the casualties, no matter how many unarmed civilians die in the process, no matter how many Russian soldiers must give up their lives for a military victory—just as long as we destroy the "hornets' nest of terrorists" once and for all. And it doesn't matter in the least who this "adversary" is—the fighters Basayev or [Ibn al-] Khattab, the elite guard of President [Aslan] Maskhadov [of

Chechnya] (who had nothing to do with the raid into Dagestan, or, of course, with blowing up apartment buildings in Russian towns), or simply a member of a local militia who is defending his native villagers from Russian troops that suddenly swoop down on them.

Russian politicians began to use a new language—the argot of the criminal world. The recently appointed prime minister was the first to legitimate this new language by publicly announcing that we would "bury them in their own crap." It was after saying this that Putin's rating in the polls began to rise astronomically: finally there was a "tough guy" at the wheel. . . . In fact, now, after three and a half months, more and more people recognize that the "Chechen terrorist" version of these crimes has not been confirmed by any facts at all. At least, no evidence, either direct or indirect, has yet been presented to the public to support the claim that the terrorists are to be found on "the Chechen trail." What little is known about the people suspected of having some responsibility for the explosions indicates that this is likely a false trail: the individuals in question are not even ethnic Chechens.

But the absence of evidence doesn't prevent the population from continuing to enthusiastically support the government's actions in the Caucasus. The explosions were needed only as an initial excuse for these actions.

While I do not believe Putin himself created this excuse, I have no doubt that he cynically and shamelessly used it, just as I have no doubt that the war was planned in advance. And not only in the headquarters of the Russian army, but, as I have suggested, in some political headquarters as well.

Which political headquarters? It is a question that is unpleasant even to contemplate. These plans do not bear the stamp of the older generation of Communists or the fanatic younger supporters of Great Russian Statehood, whose reactionary influence on the life of the country I so feared at one time. Instead, they are in keeping with the bold, dynamic, and deeply cynical style of a new political generation. It is unlikely that, after next March, President Putin will either resurrect Soviet power or resuscitate the archaic myths of Russian statehood. More likely he will build a regime which has a long tradition in Western history but is utterly new in Russia: an authoritarian-police regime that will preserve the formal characteristics of democracy, and will most likely try to carry out reforms leading to a market economy. This regime may be outspokenly anti-Communist, but it's not inconceivable that the Communists will be tolerated, as long as they don't "interfere." However, life will not be sweet for Russia's fledgling civil society.[272]

That the political group around Putin could have masterminded the apartment bombings is horrifying. It is virtually impossible to find such examples in modern history. Certainly many leaders have started wars abroad and killed "others" in their own quest for political power at home. Leaders like Hafez Assad in Syria and Saddam Hussein in Iraq brutally killed many of their citizens who dared to challenge their rule. But to blow up your own innocent and sleeping people in your capital city is an action almost unthinkable. Yet the evidence that the FSB was at least involved in planting a bomb in Ryazan is incontrovertible. This is not something that happens every day in a civilized or even an uncivilized country, and it strikes at the heart of the legitimacy of the Putin regime from its inception.

The claim to the regime's legitimacy was based, however, on the idea that the Russian state in the 1990s, under Yel'tsin, had ceased to be respected. Putin's objective, and the objective of those who came to power with him and helped to bring him to power, was to restore the idea of Russia as a Great Power (*derzhava*) and a state worthy of and demanding respect in international affairs. The evidence clearly lends support to the conclusion that Putin was not waiting passively throughout the 1990s. He was a player, and eventually a central player in the drama that did indeed bring to power an elite that was nontransparent, unrepresentative, and highly corrupt from its very inception.

Yet undoubtedly this group's desire to reestablish a strong Russian state, with themselves at its helm, responded to the desire of the general population to stop the disintegration of the country and its further slide into

collapse. The events that produced a rallying around Putin over his perceived strong hand in handling crises, even if they were shaped by a hidden Kremlin hand, played to the population's longing for an energetic and
steadfast leader. In his December 1999 Millennial Address, issued only two
days before he would become acting president, Putin called for the country
to rally around a unified state to prevent Russia from becoming a "third
tier country: Everything now depends entirely on our own ability to recognize the level of danger, to unify and rally ourselves and get ourselves
ready for prolonged and difficult labor." [273] It is impossible to avoid the conclusion, however, based on the available evidence, that this level of danger
was significantly increased by actions of the Kremlin itself, in promoting
renewed conflict in Chechnya so that Putin could benefit from a "small and
successful war" and then callously and cynically putting its own innocent
population in harm's way as FSB operatives sowed panic in Ryazan. It is
not plausible that Putin, as prime minister and former chief of the FSB,
would not have been aware of these actions, particularly since he was their
main beneficiary. By the end of September 1999, polls showed 45 percent
of Russians supported introducing a state of emergency to thwart further
terrorist acts;[274] by the end of October, Putin was the most favored presidential candidate.[275]

Chapter Five

———◆◆◆———

Putin Prepares to Take Over

From Prime Minister to Acting President, December 1999–May 2000

T HE CRITICAL PHASE of Putin's ascent to power occurred in December 1999, when he succeeded in destroying the chances of his main opponents to win elections. The fraud and abuse that were features of both the December Duma elections and the March 2000 presidential elections were a clear signal to rival politicians that those who provided early support would be rewarded and those who thought that elites could be ousted by democratic elections were both foolhardy and doomed. They would either be pushed from the scene or made into compliant Kremlin puppets, allowed to have their parties and their victories in return for playing the piper's tune. This period before Putin was formally inaugurated in May 2000 is marked by two fraud-filled elections and the leaking of a document that purported to be the Kremlin's strategy for reshaping the Presidential Administration's structure and staff in accord with Putin's plan to strengthen the presidency, undermine democracy, and fill the Kremlin's ranks with KGB "professionals." It is the contrast between Putin's open statements supporting democracy and his covert promotion of an authoritarian blueprint that is the key to his presidency and provides the core reason it is possible to see the shape and direction of his entire rule from this early period.

The Duma Elections, December 19, 1999

The Duma elections unfolded against the backdrop of the beginning of the Second Chechen War, an operation that former prime minister Sergey Stepashin was to declare had been planned since March 1999.[1] Putin's toughness, his promise to bring stability to the country, the overwhelming support he received from the oligarch-friendly media, its concomitant vilification of the Communists and OVR, and ad hominem attacks on Yevgeniy Primakov and Yuriy Luzhkov[2] ensured victory for Putin as Yel'tsin's heir apparent and for the latest Kremlin "party of power," Unity. Putin's emergence as the resolute leader of the "party of war" during a major national crisis produced a stunning increase in his popularity going into the elections. Starting at less than 5 percent in September (compared to more than 20 and 25 percent for Primakov and Gennadiy Zyuganov, respectively), Putin's approval rating rose to over 45 percent in late November (compared to less than 10 and 20 percent for Primakov and Zyuganov).[3]

The key to the Kremlin's strategy was not only to ensure a good showing for Unity but, even more crucially, to destroy the reputations of those candidates who had the greatest chance of beating Putin in the forthcoming presidential race: Luzhkov and Primakov. Putin's best chance of winning in the March elections was to limit the field of presidential candidates to those who were not positively perceived by the population as a whole: the head of the Communists, Gennadiy Zyuganov, and the head of the Liberal Democratic Party of Russia, Vladimir Zhirinovskiy. Luzhkov and Primakov's Fatherland–All Russia Party (OVR) occupied a center-left platform and commanded the loyalty of a large number of regional elites, including Putin's arch nemesis in St. Petersburg, Vladimir Yakovlev. And Primakov's ratings, though declining as Putin's grew, showed he was the real candidate to beat.

These regional leaders' opposition to the Kremlin under Yel'tsin, to his government, now headed by Prime Minister Putin, and to Unity marked the only time (before or since) that a viable opposition party of economic liberals and political conservatives had arisen to oppose the Kremlin. This development threw the Kremlin into a panic, according to Boris Berezovskiy: "The situation was bordering on catastrophe. We had lost time, and we had lost our positional advantage. Primakov and Luzhkov were organizing countrywide. Around fifty governors [out of eighty-nine] had already signed on to their political movement. And Primakov was a monster who wanted to reverse everything that had been accomplished in those years." [4] Primakov's call while he was prime minister to clear ordinary criminals out of Russian jails to make way for corrupt officials underlined his seriousness as a threat to the oligarchs. [5] And the presence in the election of so many OVR candidates for governor underlined the second main issue of this race: the choice between the continuation of a decentralized federal system or a reassertion of strong central control under a single unifying figure.

Alongside OVR, the Communist Party of the Russian Federation (CPRF) and the Liberal Democratic Party of Russia (LDPR), the liberals (with the exception of Grigoriy Yavlinskiy's Yabloko Party) succeeded in uniting various splinter parties into the Union of Right Forces.* However, the CPRF stood at the head of all parties in public opinion polls going into the fall election season, and the Kremlin had every reason to believe that Yel'tsin's unpopularity would only bolster the popularity of the other major non-Kremlin parties, all of whom vowed to continue the investigations of the Yel'tsin Family and the oligarchs around them. Yel'tsin's approval ratings dropped to 2 percent, and those around Yel'tsin became increasingly aware that their wealth, their positions, and perhaps even their freedom and lives were hanging in the balance. The campaign showed clear and, according to independent Western election observers, unfair advantage for Unity. Military units received handouts about the Duma elections that mentioned only Unity, and the army's chief deputy of the Main Administration of Educational Affairs publicly called on subordinates to promote Unity among the recruits. Similar reports emerged about special "Unity support

---

* Soyuz Pravykh Sil, or Union of Right Forces, included the Common Cause (headed by Irina Khakamada); Democratic Choice of Russia (headed by Yegor Gaidar); New Force (headed by Sergey Kiriyenko); Party of Economic Freedom (headed by Konstantin Borovoy); Republican Party (headed by Vladimir Lysenko); Russia's Voice (headed by Konstantin Titov); United Democrats (a group of social democratic parties headed by Aleksandr Yakovlev); Young Russia (headed by Boris Nemtsov); and some smaller groups.

committees" being formed within departments of the federal administration.[6]

In the days and weeks before the Duma election, the Kremlin took particular aim at Moscow's mayor Luzhkov: Yel'tsin fired the Moscow militia chief, a close associate of Luzhkov, for "unspecified shortcomings"; Moscow city government was assessed a fine of $140 million for violating unspecified foreign currency exchange laws; and, three days before the election, the Kremlin announced an investigation into the registration of OVR on the grounds that its activities may have exceeded its charter.[7] The fact that Putin's longtime right-hand man Vladimir Kozhin led the Federal Service for Currency and Export Control that imposed the fine left no doubt in the Luzhkov camp that Putin was behind the attacks.[8]

Putin was also directly involved in shaping the media's attacks on Primakov and Luzhkov. Even Russia's own Central Electoral Commission (CEC) called on the Kremlin to desist. The CEC singled out Sergey Dorenko, the host of ORT's popular prime-time news program, *Vremya*, for his continuous libelous attacks against Primakov and Luzhkov. Both candidates were offered prime-time airtime to rebut, which Primakov utilized. Luzhkov took Dorenko to court, and won, but Dorenko continued his attacks unabated. Russian analysts subsequently wrote about the emergence of units within the Presidential Administration that coordinated media attacks and used what they called "media killers" (like Dorenko) as "soldiers in the information war."[9] Dorenko himself freely admitted that he frequently met with Putin and took cues from him: "He often asked me in private to provoke a situation, for example, when I suggested that our army attack Chechnya, he said, 'Say it on the air.' I said I was going to anyway. *You* say it. He answered, 'No I want *you* to say it. We'll see how people react.'"[10] In its report on the Duma elections, the Parliamentary Assembly of the Council of Europe concluded that "the electoral campaign in the Russian media appeared to have been utterly unfair . . . often crossing the line to slander and libel."[11]

The results of the election showed that the single largest winner was the Communist Party of the Russian Federation, which got 24.3 percent of the votes to win 113 seats. But the biggest surprise was the emergence of Unity, which, after all, had been formed barely a month before the campaign began. It received seventy-three seats with 23.3 percent of the total vote, drawn overwhelmingly from the party list portion of the ballot. And it took these votes away from OVR, which earned only 13.3 percent of the votes for sixty-seven seats. Consequently the promise of OVR, and of its two main figures, Primakov and Luzhkov, faded, and Primakov announced he would not run in the presidential elections. The Union of Right Forces won almost 9 percent of the vote, led by former prime minister Sergey Kiriyenko running under the banner "Putin for President! Kiriyenko for the Duma!" Both Yabloko and the ultranationalist Liberal Democratic Party of Russia barely avoided falling below the threshold and scraped into the Duma with just over 5 percent each.

Charges of fraud emerged almost immediately. The most serious came from the Organization for Security and Co-operation in Europe, which had initially given the election results a "free and almost fair" rating, but in the subsequent full report of its Election Observation Mission (EOM) provided the following story, worth quoting in full:

> The EOM also encountered an incident that was never satisfactorily explained. In the early hours of 20 December, it already appeared from the results arriving from the east that Unity and the Communist party each had about 25% of the votes reported. Fatherland–All Russia was lagging behind below 10%. However, when results from Moscow City and Region started to flow in, the situation in the area showed a quite different picture: in the 15 districts of Moscow City, Fatherland–All Russia fared much better at over 40%; and in the 11 districts of the Moscow region, Fatherland–All Russia had gained over 27%, while in these areas Unity hardly reached 7 and 10%, respectively. Statements released through the media by high ranking officials explained that, in spite of their major showing in Moscow, Fatherland–All Russia's Federation-wide share remained below 10% because the results from the Moscow area were not yet entered in the overall tabulation as a result of irregularities that had appeared in the counting process in those regions. The EOM tried to learn more, but

its usual interlocutors at the CEC were not able to give any explanation except to confirm rumors that irregularities in the Moscow area were delaying integration of their results. The EOM tried to contact the Moscow Subject Election Commission, but was informed that *all officials were summoned to the Presidential Administration offices* [italics added]. For the whole day of 20 December, it was impossible to receive any clear information on the issue. On 21 December, the EOM again inquired about the Moscow results and whether they had been cleared. The surprising answer was that there was nothing more to be cleared, and that Moscow results were already part of the overall returns that had been progressively released. Telephone calls to Fatherland–All Russia headquarters and Yabloko confirmed that the parties had no concerns to raise. Some days later, Luzhkov was pronounced the winner of the Moscow Mayoral race and his victory in the local elections was publicly acknowledged by Prime Minister Putin. However, the results published on the web site of the CEC, through which it had been possible to follow the aggregation of results for each Subject of the Federation, were no longer available. It would be imprudent to read more into these events than they warrant. However, these are not the kinds of incident that are likely to promote public confidence.[12]

The inescapable conclusion from the European Election Observation Mission is that OVR's victory in Moscow was simply erased by Kremlin action, and in return Putin endorsed Luzhkov as the victor in the mayoral race. Parties and their leaders quickly came to the conclusion that the Unity victory was inevitable and that OVR would not be allowed to form a viable counter to it in the new Duma. Equally, Putin's bid to become president would be immeasurably assisted by this demonstration of Kremlin strength. Even Putin's erstwhile nemesis, Governor Yakovlev of St. Petersburg, signaled that he would get in line behind the Kremlin; on December 21 he announced, "The treaty concluded between Fatherland and All Russia is valid only until December 20." Clearly he would join other regional governors in making sure that his region was not going to be punished by any loss of Kremlin subsidy in the run-up to the presidential election.[13] The election results showed that Russian politics had become more fragmented, that regional elites had a considerable power base separate from the Kremlin, and that the mantra of the 1990s—that the choice was between the way back (the Communists) and the way forward (the forces around Yel'tsin and various "parties of power") no longer held. Instead the election results showed that the question of whether the center's power over the governors and the regions should be increased was not settled. Although the Communists, the LDPR, and Yabloko remained on the ballot in this election, their total vote counts did not significantly change between 1995 and 1999.

The main feature of the 1999 election was the battle between Fatherland–All Russia (OVR) and Unity for the regions' votes. And here the power of the governors and their political affiliation proved decisive. Where the governor was affiliated with OVR, Unity did not make inroads. But where the governor came over to Unity (sometimes after considerable political pressure or threats, as in the Republic of Kalmykiya, where the Kremlin first opened a criminal investigation against President Kirsan Ilyumzhinov and then dropped the case when he switched allegiance to Unity), the election results not only showed support for Unity but also signs of electoral fraud. Charges of fraud benefiting Unity were made at the time and were borne out by the quantitative evaluation of the returns by University of Oregon professor Mikhayl Myagkov, who plotted district (*rayon*)-level voting returns in Kalmykiya and Tuva, two regions where governors were both "notorious for their ability to rule as dictators" and supportive of Unity.[14] In these two regions, his quantitative analysis supported the conclusion that "local election officials simply added extra ballots to the ballot boxes, and all these 'additional' papers were marked for Unity."[15]

International observer missions expressed reservations and made a number of significant recommendations, including that due to its "vulnerability to manipulation," greater transparency in the electronic reporting of results via the State Automated System Vybory needed to be introduced. Their report noted, "Cynicism still lingers among those concerned about the lack of transparency surrounding the system. The CEC may want to explore measures that could be taken to increase general confidence in the system. Such measures might include the creation of an independent quality assurance working group to conduct independent tests of the software periodically in the pre-election and post-election period. This group could be appointed from recommendations of parties and blocs represented in the Duma, with strict technical qualifications requirements."[16]* Needless to say, the Kremlin never formed such a group.

So the Duma results set up the presidential race in important ways: by destroying OVR and its two leading political figures and by weakening the Communists, who officially received only 24 percent of the party list votes. Unity's strong official showing in the 1999 Duma elections against the Communists significantly disadvantaged the presidential chances of the Communist Party leader, Gennadiy Zyuganov. A very reliable opposition Duma member, whose identity is known to the author, spoke at a Washington-based think tank of a report that was then published by David Johnson's respected listserv early in 2000. The report claimed that the results had been substantially altered by the Kremlin (see Table 1).

Table 1. Report of Official and Actual Results of 1999 Duma elections

Party	Official Result %	Actual Result %
Communists	24	33
Unity	23	14
OVR	12	21
Union of Right Forces	9	3.4
Yabloko	6	12
Zhirinovskiy Bloc (LDPR)	6	4.5

Source: David Johnson, "Note on Election Results," *Johnson's List*, February 1, 2000. http://www.russialist.org/4082.html (accessed June 8, 2013).

---

*Wanting to be encouraging, the report issued by the Parliamentary Assembly of the Council of Europe in the immediate aftermath of the elections concluded meekly, and over the objection of rival Russian party leaders, "The Russians have been given the political freedom to elect their representatives and they have shown their determination to use it. This shows that Russia maintains its democratic course."[17]

If it is true, as alleged by this Duma member, that OVR had polled 7 percent higher than Unity and that the Communists' vote against the Kremlin party was actually 33 to 14 percent rather than the officially reported 24 to 23 percent, and if these results had been allowed to stand, then the momentum would have been with Zyuganov and OVR and not with Putin going into the presidential election. Given that Dmitriy Medvedev would subsequently acknowledge in a meeting with opposition leaders, "We all know that Boris Nikolayevich Yel'tsin did not win in 1996,"[18] it is certainly not beyond rational calculation to imagine that the Communists could have been denied fair results in 2000 as well.

The yearning of a broad cross section of the Russian people for stability and their support for Putin's aggressive stance against the Chechens in the Second Chechen War, which was ongoing at the time of the voting, were demonstrated in numerous public opinion polls.* This image was bolstered by the defection of many newly elected Duma deputies to the Unity faction. OVR broke apart, the Communists lost many of the independent Duma deputies to Unity, and as the presidential elections loomed, many of the high-profile candidates withdrew, including Luzhkov and Primakov. Many key elites and parties came out in favor of Putin—the momentum had shifted clearly in his favor.

Given that Luzhkov, Primakov, and other candidates were (not altogether fairly) pushed from the scene after the Duma elections, it is not known how Putin would have fared in the presidential election against stronger candidates, like Primakov, who were also identified with stability and a conservative national security outlook. What is clear is that the general *belief* among opposition elites that the election was rigged indicated that the presidential election results were also already decided. The Kremlin's signal was clear: resistance was not only pointless but perhaps even dangerous.

---

* See the many public opinion polls of the New Russia Barometer, conducted jointly by a team led by Richard Rose at the University of Aberdeen and the Levada Center since 1992, available at http://www.cspp.strath.ac.uk/catalog1_0.html.

Acting President, December 31, 1999

On the day before he was named acting president, a document attributed to Putin was posted on the government's website. In "Russia at the Turn of the Millennium," [19] Putin cautioned against the adoption of any new official ideology, yet at the same time blamed the slowness of necessary reform on the lack of societal cohesion characteristic of the 1990s. He called for building on people's embrace of universal rights implicit in rights to free speech, foreign travel, and property ownership by also recognizing Russians' unique, native, and traditional values. Among these he listed patriotism; *derzhavnost'* (Great Power–ism: "The funeral service for Russia as a great power is, to put it mildly, premature"); *gosudarstvennichestvo* (statism: "A strong state for the Russian is not an anomaly . . . but on the contrary, the source and guarantor of order, the initiator and main driving force of any change"); and *sotsial'naya solidarnost'* (social solidarity). He declared that a new Russian idea would be created as an "alloy" of these universal human rights and traditional Russian values.

He made it clear, however, that the resilience of this alloy would result from the creation of a strong state to defend it, and he provided an analysis of the rationale for and features of this stronger state. He planned to restructure the state's personnel policy, putting into place "the best professionals"; to restore the center's control over the regions; to launch a more aggressive fight against both crime and corruption; and to launch a national strategy for development.

He called for an increase in the role of the state in both the economy and the social sphere, recognizing that ultimately the state would withdraw and become only an arbiter. But in the meantime "the situation demands of us a greater degree of government influence on economic and social processes." Evidently in preparing for the withering away of the state, its role even under capitalism, once again, needed to be strengthened.*

---

* Stalin famously justified strengthening the state in a June 1930 address to the Sixteenth Party Congress when he called for "the highest development of state power with the object of preparing the conditions for the withering away of the state power—such is the Marxist formula. Is

On the day he became acting president, December 31, 1999, Putin gave an address to an expanded meeting of the Security Council in which he showed how he intended to implement some of these ideas. For example, in speaking about the law as stipulated in the Constitution and general rights, he noted, "Everything that is stipulated in the law, in the Constitution, must be strictly respected, especially civil and human rights. But we must not overlook the *rights of state institutions* and society as a whole either." He admonished the security services chiefs present, "I want you to maintain and even accelerate the pace you have gathered in the past few months." No other chiefs represented at the meeting were given such instructions.[21] Reflecting this special mission given to the security services to resurrect the state and its authority, retired KGB general Leonov gave an interview published in 2001 in which he stated, "The demand today is precisely for such tough, pragmatically thinking politicians. They are in command of operative information. . . . But at the same time, they are patriots and proponents of a strong state grounded in centuries-old tradition. History recruited them to carry out a special operation for the resurrection of our great power [*derzhava*], because there has to be balance in the world, and without a strong Russia the geopolitical turbulence will begin. . . . What is a KGB officer? He is, above all, a servant of the state. . . . Experience, loyalty to the state . . . an iron will—where else are you going to find cadres? . . . The only people that can bring order to the State are state people [*gosudarstvennyye lyudi*]."[22]

In line with this intention, Putin from his very first day as acting president paid enormous attention to personnel issues. After granting Yel'tsin permanent immunity from prosecution, one of the first items of business on his first afternoon in office was to appoint Igor Sechin and Dmitriy Medvedev as deputy directors of the Presidential Administration. Now working next to him were the two men he would send to head the oil and gas industries, the linchpins of his economic plans.

Putin had promised Yel'tsin not to change the top power ministries for a

this 'contradictory'? Yes, . . . but this contradiction is bound up with life, and it fully reflects Marxist dialectics."[20]

year, so he kept Voloshin as head of the Presidential Administration, but in a move that was popular in the country, and an ominous signal to Berezovskiy, he dismissed Yel'tsin's daughter Tat'yana D'yachenko as a presidential advisor in his first action after the New Year (Decree No. 7 2000).[23] The same week he appointed Viktor Ivanov as deputy head of the Presidential Administration for personnel. Ivanov shared with Putin the trifecta of experience: former KGB, business dealings in St. Petersburg, and work in Sobchak's office. Beginning in 2000 and for the next eight years, no one would get appointed to Putin's Presidential Administration without Ivanov's endorsement. These appointments complemented the close circle of key people from St. Petersburg: Nikolay Patrushev as director of the FSB (formerly Leningrad KGB); Sergey Ivanov as secretary of the Russian Security Council (KGB); Viktor Zolotov as head of Putin's personal security team (Baltik-Eskort security company, St. Petersburg); Leonid Reyman as minister of communications (St. Petersburg businessman); Aleksey Kudrin as deputy prime minister and minister of finance (first deputy mayor of St. Petersburg); German Gref (legal advisor to Sobchak's office on property and real estate); and Dmitriy Kozak as deputy head of the Presidential Administration (Sobchak administration). Two men unconnected with Putin's past who nonetheless emerged as central figures in his regime were Sergey Shoigu, named minister of emergency situations, and Vladislav Surkov, who remained as another deputy head of the Presidential Administration after his initial appointment in August 1999. With these appointments, the main figures that would drive the "Putin revolution" for the next decade were in place. Now he was ready to enter the presidential race—by refusing to campaign.

The Presidential Elections, March 26, 2000

Central to Putin's emergence was image building. As the eminent Russian journalist Andrey Kolesnikov (one of the journalists responsible for Putin's book *First Person*) commented in March 2000, "It is evidently not enough merely to show the acting chief of all Russians in the mass media. He must do something, pronounce almost rhymed words, sell his bright image on posters, and make himself agreeable to the Eurasian family of the peoples of Russia." Teams of young specialists were assembled, the so-called Generation P (for Putin): Gref took up leadership of the Strategic Research Center; Pavlovskiy of the Effective Policy Foundation; Mikhayl Margelov came into the Russian Information Center; Medvedev took over Putin's campaign staff; and Surkov stood over them all.[24]

In the period before the elections of March 2000, Putin positioned himself above the campaign, refusing to debate his opponents or participate in regular election events.[25] In a lecture to university students in Irkutsk in February, he showed clear disdain for the normal system of laws and checks and balances that stabilize and maintain a democratic regime over time: "You have to create a society and forms of leadership which will not strangle the most important thing, which is democracy, because without democratic processes, the real development of a government and society is impossible. . . . But there should be a clear institution which would guarantee the rights and freedoms of citizens independently of their social situation. . . . *This institution can only be the institution of the presidency*" (italics added).[26]

In his "Open Letter to the Voters" at the end of February 2000, he even proudly claimed, "There are no special electoral events on my calendar." In this letter Putin laid out the core of his platform: a unified national program to guide development and the strengthening of the executive branch of government so as to win the fight against crime and terrorism. He went on to state, "Modern Russian society does not identify a strong and effective state with a totalitarian state. . . . We have come to value the benefits of democracy, a law-based state, and personal and political freedom. At the same time, people are alarmed by the obvious weakening of state power. The public looks forward to the restoration of the guiding and regulating role of the state to a degree which is necessary."[27] The use of the words *restoration* and *guiding and regulating role of the state* is a clear harking back to Article 6 of the Soviet Constitution.* Putin further argued, "In an

---

* Article 6 of the Soviet Constitution, passed under Brezhnev, assigned to the Communist Party of the Soviet Union the role of "the leading and guiding force of Soviet society."

ungoverned, i.e. weak state, the individual is neither protected nor free. *The stronger the state, the freer is the individual [chem sil'nee gosudarstvo, tem svobodnee lichnost'—*italics added]. . . . But democracy is the dictatorship of the law [*zakona*]. . . . I know there are many today who are afraid of order. However, order is nothing more than rules [*pravila*]. And let those who are currently engaged in peddling substitutes, trying to pass off the absence of order for genuine democracy—let them stop selling us fool's gold and trying to scare us with the past. 'Our land is rich, but it lacks order,' they used to say in Russia. Nobody will ever say such things about us again." [28]

In this letter Putin also talked extensively about the protection and promotion of property rights, about the need to increase tax collection so that social benefits could be paid on time, but also to promote wealth creation: "I am absolutely convinced that a strong state needs wealthy people. So a key goal of our economic policy should be to make honest work more rewarding than stealing." [29]

How Putin Won the Presidential Election, March 26, 2000

Paving the Way for a Win

One of the purposes of getting Yel'tsin to resign on December 31, 1999, was so that the presidential elections that had been scheduled for June 2000 would have to be moved forward. The legal landscape dictated that the Putin camp's objectives from the very beginning were to have a high turnout and to win more than 50 percent of the vote in the first round.* The Kremlin sought a clear winner in the first round and hoped to avoid a run-

---

*The Russian Constitution stipulates in Article 92.2 that "presidential elections shall be held before the expiration of three months from the date of the early termination of presidential office." Article 72.4 of the December 1999 federal election law on the election of the president that Yel'tsin signed before he resigned also contains the provision that if fewer than half of all registered voters on the official lists take part in the ballot, the election will be declared not to have taken place and will be rescheduled for no more than four months later or three months after the day on which the election was declared not to have taken place.[30] Additionally the law mandates that the winner must garner a majority of votes actually cast, so that if there is no majority victor in round one, there is a possibility of a second-round runoff.

off with Zyuganov, given the continued strength of social justice issues in general among the population. Observers were concerned that the Kremlin would do whatever was necessary, including emergency changes to the Constitution, to prevent an opposition candidate from coming to power. The opposition's chances were significantly harmed by the move-up of Election Day, as it proved almost impossible to organize an effective counter to Putin in such a short period of time.

Moreover the results of the Duma elections had served their purpose of signaling the need for elites to get behind the Kremlin's candidate. The spirited contestation that had been a feature of the December Duma election season subsided, with many officials and parties coming out in favor of Putin. International observers commented on the bandwagoning that had occurred prior to the election: "The embryonic state of party politics in Russia exacerbates a tendency to fall back on traditional practices whereby demonstrations of loyalty to the 'party of power' are deemed necessary to political and administrative survival." [31]

In addition to the war in Chechnya, the campaign was dominated by debate over the reasons for the popularly held view that the country was neither stable nor cohesive. The opposition—both left and right—generally blamed the president (both Yel'tsin and Putin), and the forces around Putin blamed the emergence of greedy oligarchs and corrupt regional elites who were pulling the country apart for their own gain. When the 1993 Constitution was passed, regional leaders were appointed to the Federation Council, but over time Yel'tsin had made elections mandatory for governors as well. Now calls again were heard to return to the appointment of governors and members of the Federation Council as a way of reasserting central control and ending what Putin himself called the "threat of legal separatism," in which Moscow's authority had become "neglected, slack and lacking discipline." [32] In an open letter to Putin published in *Nezavisimaya gazeta*, the governors of Novgorod, Belgorod, and Kurgan *oblasts* espoused increasing the president's term from four to seven years. Under the circumstances, where regional elites were already beginning to operate as if a tribute system was taking shape, Putin's victory became inevitable, as international organizations noted. [33]

Putin's campaign enjoyed the usual privileges of having full Kremlin backing, referred to as "administrative resources." These evidently included the ability to lean on the Kremlin's allies inside and outside the country for campaign contributions. One such case came to light when a top official in the Ukrainian KGB* started to record the conversations of Ukrainian president Leonid Kuchma in 2000—unbeknown to him. These tapes covered many subjects, including Putin's involvement in illegal operations, such as SPAG, and his "request" to Kuchma for a significant campaign donation. These tapes were carried out of the country and published abroad, including by Radio Liberty's Ukrainian Service. They were authenticated by the U.S. government, given the charge by Washington that the tapes showed Kuchma had authorized the selling of a radar system to Iraq while at the same time receiving millions in aid.[35] Among the hundreds of hours that were recorded are conversations Kuchma had with the head of the State Tax Commission (and future prime minister) Mykola Azarov about Putin's calls to raise campaign cash. In the conversation Kuchma tells Azarov, "Putin telephoned, the fuck, during the election campaign: 'Leonid Danylovych [Kuchma], well, at least give us a bit of money.'" The tapes showed that Kuchma scrambled to find the money in the state coffers. Analysis of the tapes by Ukrainian scholar J. V. Koshiw concluded that Kuchma asked Ihor Bakai, the head of Naftogaz Ukraine, to take a total of $56 million in cash from two Ukrainian state banks, the Bank of Ukraine and Ukraine's Import-Export Bank, and transfer it to Putin.[36] His analysis of the tapes concluded, "Following his victory in March 2000, Putin graciously returned not only the donation but five times that sum—$250 million. According to Kuchma, Putin had taken the money from the state company Gazprom

---

* In his extensive discussion of this episode, Boris Volodarsky states that he was told by Alexander Litvinenko that the taping was ordered by Yevhen Marchuk (a Ukrainian KGB general, former prime minister, secretary of the National Security and Defense Council from 1999 to 2003, and himself a presidential contender) and carried out by Major Mykola Mel'nichenko, one of Kuchma's bodyguards, who subsequently received asylum in the United States.[34] The recordings convinced the U.S. government to cut off aid to Ukraine after the tapes revealed that Kuchma had authorized the sale of the advanced radar system Kolchuha to Saddam Hussein's Iraq.

and recommended that it be given to ITERA* to cover Ukraine's gas debts to Gazprom. While this was a nice gesture it wasn't legal even under Russian law. But the donation didn't pay Ukraine's gas debts. Instead, it went into Bakai's pocket, according to a discussion Kuchma had with Azarov."[38] So it appears Ukraine's president illegally took money from his state to fund Putin's campaign, Putin refunded the money by taking from Russian state coffers, and the money went into private Ukrainian hands—a perfect early example of collective kleptocracy.

As in the Duma elections, the finances of LDPR candidate Vladimir Zhirinovskiy were closely scrutinized; the CEC and then the Supreme Court denied him access to the ballot on the grounds that he had not registered an apartment that was owned by his son, as stipulated by law. Zhirinovskiy won the appeal on a technicality and was put back on the ballot, at more or less same time it was revealed that Putin also failed to disclose his family's ownership of a property, alleged to be on a six-hundred-square-meter plot in the Gdovskiy district of Pskov, 150 kilometers south of St. Petersburg, registered in the name of Lyudmila Putina. The amount paid was not verified because the person responsible for land registration had been taken to the hospital.[39] But Putin claimed that his house was "incomplete," and under the law only finished properties have to be registered. There was no mention of the Ozero dacha, nor of the bank account establishing the Ozero Cooperative, presumably because it was held by a cooperative association. He was not taken to court, unlike Zhirinovskiy,[40] whose successful appeal was protested by the procurator general, leading to speculation in the Russian press, and in the international observer report, that the Kremlin was trying to eliminate Zhirinovskiy as

---

*ITERA is a politically connected gas company established by Igor Makarov, registered in Jacksonville, Florida, which emerged as Russia's number-two gas company primarily by taking gas cheaply from Gazprom and selling it abroad for profit. Gazprom's loss of these profits became the subject of William Browder's own investigations when he sat as an independent director of Gazprom representing the interests of American investors through Hermitage Capital. Putin had promised to clean up this relationship when Gazprom's head Rem Vyakhirev was ousted in favor of Aleksey Miller, but the process of stripping Gazprom of assets via intermediate companies with close links to the Kremlin obviously continued and has been well documented.[37]

a candidate in order to help Putin garner more than 50 percent in the first round.[41]

Loopholes in the law were obviously exploited and interpreted to favor Putin, and initially to punish Zhirinovskiy. But as the Russian political commentator Andrey Ryabov noted in *Kommersant* on March 1, when it became known that Putin too had an undeclared house, the Supreme Court threw out the CEC's disbarment of Zhirinovskiy: "The CEC and the Supreme Court, who are very close, decided that it would be better for all participants to stop the scandal."[42] This situation led the international observer mission to comment, "In any election environment such ambiguities leave the door open for politically motivated decision-making and selective application of the law."[43] At the end of the day, there were eleven candidates left out of an original field of thirty-three.

Illegally Using the Administrative Resources of the State

Little by little regional governors lined up behind Putin's candidacy. Even Luzhkov, who had been a candidate, withdrew to support him. Despite this, the Kremlin signaled governors that their failure to support Putin would likely have very disastrous results. For example, the report on the elections by the Organization for Security and Co-operation in Europe noted that shortly before the election, the Ministry of Internal Affairs' Investigation Committee demanded all documents relating to housing construction in Moscow in 1999, an area where there had been numerous reports of corruption involving Luzhkov and his wife, Yelena Baturina.[44] If Kremlin officials were going to go after Luzhkov, they could go after anyone who showed independence.

Many dozens of top Kremlin officials took leaves of absence to work on the Putin campaign, bringing their administrative resources along with them. A notable example was the number of senior people from the country's Railways Ministry (the key transportation ministry in a country without a highway system), who helped Putin's campaign across Russia's eleven time zones. The International Election Observation Mission expressed concern about "the involvement of regional administration personnel in campaign activities. In some regions, campaign material for one candidate—Putin—was distributed to Territorial Election Commissions at the same time as election materials such as ballots and protocols. Senior staff of state and regional executives, including deputies to Governors, on leave of absence from their official positions served in large numbers as volunteers in the acting President's campaign organization. . . . In addition, such practice raises concern about potential abuses where subordinate State employees may feel compelled to 'volunteer.' "[45] Opposition elites similarly noted that Unity was promising positions in the future administration to campaign workers, and international observers found extensive evidence of the use of election commissions for the distribution of Putin election materials, in direct violation of Russian federal law banning the production and distribution of election materials by state officials.

Media Access

According to the 1999 electoral law, each candidate in the presidential election had to be offered eighty minutes of free nationwide television and radio airtime, half of which had to be used for debates. Candidates could also buy airtime on both private and state-run networks. Because the Duma elections in December had produced so many personal attacks on candidates, the Ministry of Internal Affairs intervened to warn candidates that this would not be allowed in the presidential campaign and that attacks on the Presidential Administration in particular would not be allowed. Putin's own campaign team went further, threatening "an asymmetrical response to acts of provocation" if the media attacked their candidate or damaged his character.[46] Consequently the media atmosphere surrounding these elections was much calmer, until about two days before the election, when the poll numbers of Grigoriy Yavlinskiy, the liberal party Yabloko's leader, started to rise and the Berezovskiy-controlled state TV channel ORT launched a slanderous personal attack on him.[47]

Although Putin declined to participate in televised debates or subject himself to interviews, his image dominated the airwaves, even his presence at a soccer match the night before polling. This led observers from the Parliamentary Assembly of the Council of Europe (PACE) to conclude that the media "failed to a large extent to provide impartial information about the election campaign and candidates." [48]

Balloting

The balloting on Election Day proceeded without significant complaints of violations in the main cities, but there were widespread and documented irregularities in Dagestan, Saratov, Tatarstan, Ingushetia, Bashkortostan, Kursk, Kabardino-Balkariya, Mordovia, Chechnya, Nizhniy Novgorod, and Kaliningrad, according to the results of an extensive investigation conducted by a group of journalists and reported in the *Moscow Times*. [49] As for the situation in Chechnya, where Duma elections had been suspended, returns in the presidential election showed Putin winning an extremely unlikely 50.63 percent—almost 200,000 votes. The *Moscow Times* pointed out that this return was from "a population made up of families whose homes and lives have been destroyed by the war and rank-and-file soldiers dropped into the middle of a bloody and terrifying guerrilla war. In other words, refugee camps and conscripts supposedly voted *en masse* in favor of Putin. Even otherwise timid international observers were not amused by this. They have refused to recognize results from Chechnya, which was under martial law on Election Day, and there were no observers there. With the exception of the federal government and the Central Elections Commission, almost no one sees the vote in Chechnya as legitimate." [50]

Did Fraud Ensure Putin's 2000 Electoral Victory?

There were a number of significant irregularities that cast doubt on whether Putin had won by a majority in the first round. The Central Electoral Commission announced that he won 52.94 percent of the vote, a margin of victory of 2.2 million votes. While some local counting discrepancies are present in every election, there were a number of actions that required extensive forethought and that have never been sufficiently explained.

The first piece of evidence concerns the inexplicable rise in the number of registered voters. The CEC reported that there were 108,073,956 registered voters for the December 1999 Duma elections—of which 66,667,682, or

61.69 percent, actually voted. Three months later, on March 26, the CEC
claimed that there were now 109,372,046 registered voters—of which
75,070,776, or 68.64 percent, participated. In other words, an additional
1.3 million voters appeared on the rolls. This occurred in a three-month
period when Russian demographic statistics showed a net loss of 182,000.
The head of the State Statistics Committee's department for national population rejected all the CEC explanations: "[The Central Elections Commis-
sion] is taking liberties with the truth when they explain such a figure with
a boost in the 18-year-old population and immigration."[51]

The second piece of evidence is the pattern of ballot stuffing and election fraud that occurred on the day. This increased number of "available
voters" still had to cast their ballots. And these imaginary voters turned
up in those regions whose governors had pledged their support to Putin
and where charges of irregularities were most numerous: Dagestan, Saratov,
Tatarstan, Ingushetia, and elsewhere. The pattern was typified in Tatarstan
by its capital Kazan's 372nd voting precinct, where three election observers and a precinct elections commission member claimed that "names of
voters were printed twice in the registration forms in a very large quantity,
while the same names were listed by different [passport] numbers." The
complaint quotes Zukhra Anisimova, the head of the precinct elections
commission, saying that the double-barreled lists were provided to her
by the local government. To accommodate these voters, extra completed
ballots were prepared and stuffed into the ballot boxes. When an inside
source alerted the Communist Party in Kazan that hundreds of thousands
of ballots had been illegally printed, the Party lodged a complaint. The
FSB arrived the next day, asking not about the additional ballots but for
the name of the source.[52] All over Russia, in districts loyal to the Kremlin,
phantom voters "registered" and "voted" for Putin.[53] The journalists who
investigated this issue at the time came to the conclusion that as many as
1.3 million votes of Putin's 2.2 million margin of victory were "acquired"
by a premeditated, and Kremlin-directed, plan to pad the voter rolls.

This conclusion was examined by several political scientists who special-
ize in electoral fraud. Their own conclusions support those of journalists on
the scene. Mikhayl Myagkov, as previously stated, had looked at the role of

regional governors favorable to Putin in manufacturing "dead souls" and then getting them to "cast their ballots" for Putin. With colleagues from the California Institute of Technology, he examined the 2000 Russian presidential election and found the same result, namely that regional governors were able to use a number of methods, including roll padding and ballot stuffing, "to direct the votes of their electorates in a nearly wholesale fashion." [54]* These authors conclude that a general trend in electoral fraud emerged in 1999–2000 in which pro-Putin regional governors, particularly in rural and ethnic regions, were mobilized (by a combination of intimidation and incentives) to deliver the votes. By 2008 this pattern had "moved into the cities" as well so that the entire country's electoral system was riven with fraud. [55]

The third piece of evidence is the extensive reports of intimidation by the vertical chain of command, in which the Kremlin put the squeeze on regional governors, and they obliged units below them all the way down to university rectors, military officers, and farm managers to turn out the vote for Putin. Village elders in particular, it was reported, often simply would not allow villagers to vote for other candidates, and they themselves cast villagers' votes for Putin over the objections of the voters. The *Moscow Times* charged, "In all of the above-named regions and also in Kursk, Mordovia, Kaliningrad and Nizhny Novgorod—nine regions where Putin won a total of 6.96 million votes—regional governors resorted to a vertical chain of bullying: Everyone from collective farm workers to college professors was forced to vote for Putin. Some critics have gone so far as to argue that on the eve of the 21st century, such bullying excluded villagers as a class from the democratic process." [56]

But sometimes local officials were so happy to comply with orders from above that they did not need to be intimidated; instead they happily described how they had "managed" the vote. Steven Fish reports in his own study of electoral fraud in 2000 that Vladimir Shevchuk, head of the Tatarstan

---

*See Myagkov et al. (2009). Using the same methodology, the authors conclude that fraud was present throughout the Putin period, beginning in 1999–2000, and in Ukraine in the first round of the 2004 presidential election. Also see Myagkov et al. (2008); and Hale (2003).

Elections-2000 Press Center, described to journalists how local officials had created a "caterpillar" to get the required votes: "There are people standing near the elections precincts and when they see a voter coming up, they offer him or her 50 rubles or a 100 rubles so that he or she takes a pre-filled-in ballot to drop in the box, and then returns with a blank ballot. Then [the fraudsters] fill in the new clean ballot and offer it to the next voter." As Fish notes, Tatarstan Governor Mintimer Shaimiev's personal spokesman, Irek Murtazin, confirmed the existence of the caterpillar with a chuckle and without embarrassment.[57] Aggregate studies of the variation among the eighty-nine regions in terms of the leaders' willingness to deliver the votes showed that on a 10-point scale of regional violation of electoral laws in federal elections in 2000, twelve regions scored favorably at 1 or 2, and eight scored 8 or below, indicating significant violations: Tatarstan, Kalmykiya, Mordovia, Bashkortostan, and the North Caucasus republics of Ingushetia, Dagestan, North Ossetia, and Kabardino-Balkariya.[58] As Nikolay Petrov from the Carnegie Foundation's Moscow Center found, while in most countries high turnout would be positively correlated with high levels of democratic competition, in Russia higher turnout occurs most often in those regions where there is a continuation of Soviet-era practices of controlling the votes of state farm and enterprise workers and "can be attributed to a higher level of administrative mobilization of participation in elections and a relatively lower level of freedom and institutionalized democracy."[59] In these eight regions, with their total population of almost 14 million people, Putin won 68 percent of the vote, or more than 15 percent above his total percentage of the national vote. The huge variation in support for Putin across regions showed a positive correlation between the support for Putin and voter turnout—the higher the support, the higher the turnout—further suggesting administrative "encouragement" of voting for the new leadership. This study also supports the basic conclusion of Mikhail Myagkov and Peter Ordeshook that regional bosses in 1999 and 2000, more so than in 1996, when Yel'tsin was reelected, moved votes from one candidate or party to another "as they sought to ally with the person they believed would eventually become president."[60] The point is that *they* moved the votes, not the voters.

The effect of this "abuse of administrative resources" on the vote tally is impossible to quantify exactly. But those who studied it and who spoke to the *Moscow Times* said bullying shifted several million votes from other candidates to Putin. Nearly all observers argued that it was far more influential than the crude falsifications discussed above. As the *Moscow Times* reported:

> In small villages where it is possible for someone to poll his neighbors and determine how they all voted, dishonesty turns up easily. Some villages have written open letters to the president and to other higher authorities to protest their votes being "stolen," and the *Moscow Times* has obtained such letters. In some cases, voters have testified to having the pens and ballots snatched out of their hands at the voting booth and filled in for them. In others, they have been bullied into voting for Putin with threats from local leaders that they will lose their jobs, or be denied state welfare support. . . . Those reluctant to vote "correctly" report being threatened with losing their jobs, being evicted or being denied their right to state support such as pensions. "Of course we were pressured from the top, and we pressured our people to vote for Putin," said one collective farm chief in an interview in Kazan, on condition of anonymity. "But it is forbidden to talk about it." [61]

A fourth piece of evidence is the switching of votes cast for other candidates to Putin after votes were counted, as indicated in the sample drawn up and published by the *Moscow Times*. Typically it appears that the votes were counted at individual precincts, passed up to the territorial or district level, and "corrected" there. As Table 2 demonstrates, in specific precincts in which all data were examined, the number of votes for Putin in the original precinct results was changed after the numbers were passed up to the territorial level. This kind of crude vote-rigging was the subject of a Duma investigation, the results of which were published in *Rossiyskaya gazeta* on April 27, 2000, which estimated that by this method alone, 700,000 votes were stolen. Added to the 1.3 million votes obtained by padding the electoral rolls, these two methods account for around 2 million of the 2.2 million needed to secure Putin's victory in the first round. And withholding the right of rural voters to a free vote was estimated to be even more influential than these two methods combined in swinging the vote to Putin.

Table 2. Evidence of Fabrication of Ballots

Polling precinct number as recorded in a copy of the protocol	Original precinct votes for Putin	Votes for Putin reported by the territorial commission	The difference in Putin's favor, as a number and as a percentage
In Bashkortostan:			
2,297	725	951	226 / 31.2%
1,026	777	909	132 / 17.0
411	672	794	122 / 18.1
In Dagestan:			
876	1,070	3,535	2,465 / 230.4%
903	480	1,830	1,350 / 281.3
896	1,110	2312	1,202 / 108.3
899	728	1,870	1,142 / 156.7
In Saratov:			
1,617	666	1,086	420 / 63.1%
1,797	667	995	328 / 49.2
1,591	822	1,012	190 / 23.1

Note: *Moscow Times* used copies of protocols and the official reports from territorial commissions.

Source: Table drawn from Yevgeniya Borisova, "And the Winner is?" *Moscow Times*, September 9, 2000, http://www.themoscowtimes.com/news/article/and-the-winner-is/258951.html.

The fifth piece of evidence relates to the transmission of results from the local, regional, and territorial commissions via the electronic reporting software State Automated System Vybory to the CEC in Moscow. Historically in Russia most people vote on their way to work in the morning, leaving the evening to watch prime-time television. The reporting of the turnout, however, which was a major Kremlin concern, proceeded in a highly dubious way. Despite the fact that the CEC reported at 6 P.M. that only 46.3 percent of the population had voted in the previous ten hours (not enough to satisfy the legal requirements for a legitimate election), in the next hour the number inexplicably jumped to 54 percent, as a result of which PACE observers concluded, "In view of that, the delegation considered that close observation of the electronic transmission of election results should be made in the future."[62] A typical example was reported in Dagestan, where an Interfax reporter voted thirty minutes before polls closed and observed that the registration form listing voters was only half full: "I just laughed upon hearing the next day that close to 100 percent of the people participated. They must have added people, but I have no facts to prove it." According to CEC data, 59.23 percent of Dagestan's registered voters had cast their ballots by 6 P.M. But two hours later turnout soared to 83.6 percent.[63] These observations were repeated by Marina Arbatskaya, whose work supported the subsequent quantitative finding of University of Michigan political scientists Walter Mebane and Kirill Kalinin that "the distribution of turnout throughout the day . . . can be attributed to the active interference of administrative elites with the electoral process."[64]

The sixth and final indication of fraud is the summary destruction of troublesome evidence. In Dagestan a militia officer, Abdulla Magomedov, guarding ballots in the aftermath of the election filed a complaint that election officials had taken away bags of votes for Zyuganov, the Communists' candidate, and burned them in front of his eyes in the street.[65] The *Moscow Times* team verified this report and saw scraps of the charred but clearly marked Zyuganov ballots still lying in the street.

In the six months after the elections, the *Moscow Times* investigative team, led by Yevgeniya Borisova, "met dozens of ordinary people like Magomedov. Federal elections authorities, foreign observers and the criminal justice system have all been dismissive of fraud allegations like his—admitting that fraud existed and lamenting it, but insisting it was insignificant (and apparently, punishing no one for it). But fraud was far from insignificant. *Given how close the vote was—Putin won with just 52.94 percent, or by a slim margin of 2.2 million votes—fraud and abuse of state power appear to have been decisive*" (italics added).[66] A Duma committee headed by the Communist deputy Aleksandr Saliy found that about 440 lawsuits were filed in courts across the nation charging fraud of one kind or another in the March 26 vote, and that various election commissions had received untold thousands of formal complaints. In August 2000, while these cases and complaints were still being settled, the CEC removed election data from its website, further complicating investigations into irregularities.[67]

All this led the *Moscow Times* to report, "The inescapable conclusion is that Putin would not have won outright on March 26 without cheating."[68] In a written reply to the *Moscow Times*, CEC chief Aleksandr Veshnyakov said that "investigations conducted by elections commissions of the Russian regions, by procurators, police organs and the Interior Ministry" had explored the allegations of fraud—and "did not find any documentary or other confirmation."[69]

Opposition leaders turned to the international observers for redress. But, as in every election, observers issued an interim report and, weeks later, a fuller report. In the Russian case, despite all the irregularities, immediately after the elections international observers determined that the voting had proceeded in a competent way on Election Day and that those irregularities that were found did not affect the overall result. On that basis, PACE declared that the election was free and that "the results should be understood as the free will of the Russian people, although the campaign cannot be considered to have been as fair as we would have liked to see it happen."[70] Only in the longer and fuller report, issued on May 19, were serious issues raised, without, however, in any way saying that Putin's election was illegitimate.

Results

Putin's ability to garner 52.94 percent of the votes and to turn out the vote so that almost 69 percent of all registered voters went to the polls was an impressive display of the fast-emerging power of what the Russians called "political technologies."* He was also, it must be emphasized, a viable and charismatic candidate who all conceded would have won against Zyuganov,

---

*Maksimov (1999) is a handbook for campaign workers on how to organize campaigns and how to distinguish between "clean" and "dirty" technologies. However, it is written in the language of battle, with descriptions of "frontal attacks," "partisan attacks," "security measures," "mass actions," and "operational groups."

whether in the first or the second round. The fact that the Communist leader Zyuganov officially came in a distant second at 29 percent, with a return that was less than his 1996 showing, showed the steady decline in the popularity of the Communist message, as well as the success of Kremlin-orchestrated political and media attacks against him. It is clearly the case as well that Unity's strong showing in the 1999 Duma elections against the Communists—results that may have been the consequence of significant electoral fraud—disadvantaged Zyuganov's presidential chances.

Immediately after the elections, Moscow became a swirl of reports about the coming turn to authoritarianism. *Nezavisimaya gazeta* published a report on March 30, 2000, that claimed legislation was actively being prepared that would eliminate local autonomy, making the regions dependent upon "the flourishes of Putin's pen." And regional leaders, including Moscow's mayor Luzhkov, smelling an inevitable loss of autonomy, fought to maintain free regional elections even as they jockeyed to rebrand themselves as the governor "most loyal" to both Putin and a reassertion of Kremlin control.[71] But nothing prepared anyone for the leaked document that appeared in May, only days before Putin's inauguration—much too late to stop the process that was now under way.

A Leaked Document Reveals Kremlin's Authoritarian Plans

If Putin's occasional paeans to democracy fooled anyone into thinking that his aim in running was to establish a system in which elites would rotate every four years, public revelation of his team's plans and strategies gave the lie to such naïveté. In the run-up to his May 2000 inauguration as president, Putin gave a lengthy interview to three journalists, which became his autobiography, *First Person*. In it he discusses the reasons he wanted to become president and the attractions for him of this lofty position. Looking at his Millennium message, discussed earlier, one can see the broader outlines of his public political purpose. But in *First Person*, perhaps unwittingly, he also reveals his personal reasons for seeking the presidency: only by becoming president can he "escape control," particularly the kind of strict control he had to endure as a line officer in the KGB. "I remember coming into the KGB building where I worked and feeling as if they were plugging me into an electrical outlet. . . . You couldn't even go out to a restaurant! . . . In the Kremlin, I have a different position. *Nobody controls me here. I control everybody else*" (italics added).[72] The means he was willing to use to achieve this purpose became very clear both in the actions undertaken during the first one hundred days after his inauguration and in the blueprint for the establishment of authoritarian rule that was leaked at this time.

Just before his inauguration in May 2000, this lengthy document, *Reform of the Administration of the President of the Russian Federation*, was leaked to the newspaper *Kommersant*. It seems that the leak came directly from the Kremlin's Presidential Administration, and it was the subject of three days of articles on May 3–5.[73] According to these articles, the document was accessible in its entirety through a link on the newspaper's website. However, it was later impossible to access the document through the archive section of *Kommersant*'s website, although it continued to exist on the Internet.[74]* While no one claimed that it had been approved by Putin, it was purported to be the very same strategic plan that Putin had been exhorting his team to write. The fact that subsequent policies pursued by Putin in the days immediately after his inauguration so closely followed this document speaks to its authenticity. The document's structure is outlined on the very first page. It is divided into "books" on the various departments within the Presidential Administration and their new functions.†

Published in excerpts over three days by *Kommersant*, and subsequently scrubbed from their site, the plan states that the president, "if he really wants to ensure social order and stability in the country during his rule, then the self-governing political system is not needed, instead he will need

---

*Given the sensitivity and importance of this document, and the persistent purging of the Internet of anti-Putin content, I have created a PDF of it, and provided an English translation, available at http://www.miamioh.edu/havighurstcenter/putins-russia. I have confirmed the authenticity of the document from multiple Russian sources.

† Of the seven books, only books 1 and 2 remained on the Internet in 2012, and of book 2, only 2.1, on the creation of a new Political Council (what would be the State Council, Gosudarstven-nyy Soviet), was included. The portion that remained consisted of approximately fourteen thousand words, or about forty-seven pages. The total size of the collected seven books, with their many classified appendixes, referred to but not published, must have been many times larger.

a political structure (authority) within his Administration, which will not only be able to forecast and create 'necessary' political situations in Russia, but really be able to manage social and political processes in the Russian Federation and in the countries of the near abroad."[75] Referring to the role of the FSB, the "intellectual, personnel, and professional potential, which the FSB has at its disposal, should be employed by the Political Directorate, which in its turn, will allow to achieve very quick, competent, and productive results, which are needed to 'jumpstart' the Directorate's work, and for the realization of long-term programs."[76] This is critical because society "at this time" rejects the use of any means to oppress the opposition. Therefore the Presidential Administration should use the public ("open and official") part of its work as a "shield" to "demonstrate" the positive side of the work of the office. At the same time the office should not only engage in "open" or "official" work but should also focus on "closed" and "basic" work so as to "*tangibly* and *concretely* influence all political processes that are occurring in society" (emphasis in original).[77]

What is so eye-opening about this document is that it presents an actual outline of the proposal to significantly increase the political control by the Kremlin's Presidential Administration. In explaining the objectives and tasks of these expanded presidential offices, the document refers both to the "open" or public role of the revitalized Presidential Administration and the "not publicized" functions. It is worth quoting in full all its edicts and instructions:

1. The formation of a *controlled* mass public *platform* for all politicians and public-political organizations of the Russian Federation, supporting the President of the R.F.
2. The continuing removal from the Russian political arena of the State Duma of the R.F. as a "political platform" for the forces in opposition to the President of the R.F., and affixing with it an exclusively lawmaking activity.
3. The establishment of an informational-political barrier between the President of the R.F and the entire spectrum of oppositional forces in the Russian Federation.

4. Introducing active agitation and propaganda throughout the entire territory of the Russian Federation in support of the President of the R.F., the Government of the R.F., and their policies.

5. Introducing constant information-analytical and political work in all means of mass media.

6. Introducing direct political counter-propaganda aimed at discrediting the opposition to the President, R.F.'s political leaders, and political public organizations.

7. Holding public gatherings (pickets, rallies, conferences, marches, and etc.) in support of the President of the R.F.

8. The organization and management of active political activity in all the regions of the Russian Federation in order to prevent attempts of governors, heads of *krais*, republics, and *oblasts* to conduct any activities aimed at dismembering Russia or weakening the powers of the center.

9. The creation and maintenance of our own sources of mass media.[78]

The very idea that there would be open discussion in a document of removing the legislature as a political actor, "discrediting political leaders," and "conducting active agitation" in support of the president is startling. And this was only 2000. The document also clearly reveals what the Kremlin actually meant by promising to rely on the work of "professionals." It explicitly states that the "FSB, FAPSI* and other security forces should be in charge of providing professionals to staff the offices of the Administration,"[79] and further that "all of the special and secret activities of the Directorate relating to counteracting the forces of opposition to the President of the R.F. . . . will be entirely in the hands and under the control of the special services [*spets. sluzhb*]."[80] These professionals would function on both an open and a closed basis but would have specific tasks in dealing with the press, the opposition, elections, and the regions.

---

* The Federal Agency of Government Communications and Information (Federal'noye Agentstvo Pravitel'stvennoy Svyazi i Informatsii, FAPSI) was responsible for electronic surveillance. It was the rough equivalent to the National Security Agency in the United States. It was reorganized in 2003 and largely absorbed into the FSB.

The Presidential Administration should not only be repackaging information in the mass media in a light more favorable to the president but should also be "taking control of different mass media outlets, using gathered special information, including that of a compromising character." Persistent opposition outlets should be driven to a "financial crisis." [81]

In relations with the opposition, the "open" function of the Presidential Administration is to "lock in constitutional norms" and "prevent the development in society of extremism," while the "closed" function is a "massive cascade of political actions against the opposition. . . . *It is necessary always to ruin coordinated plans of all opposition in general and each oppositionist personally.*" [82] As an example, the document proposes that "If there were a scandal with G. Seleznyov—beginning out of the publications in a St. Petersburg newspaper about his distant connection to the assassination of G. Starovoytova—developed and promoted by the 'Independent Commission for Public Enquiry into the Assassination of G. Starovoytova,' created with the help of the Administration, . . . sooner or later . . . he will begin looking for contacts within the Administration . . . and would be more 'compliant' in solving political questions than he is now." This is part of a whole section on the political uses of "independent public commissions" against the opposition. It explicitly states that such a commission on Starovoytova "will gradually reveal the 'communist trail' in the murder of Ms. Starovoytova, which will continue to use it as *the beginning of a large-scale campaign of struggle against the Communist Party.*" [83]

On elections, the role of the Presidential Administration is to ensure the election at all levels of "loyal to the 'Kremlin' (controlled) deputies [*loyalnyye 'Kremlyu' (upravlyayemykh) deputatov*]." [84] The maximum result for pro-Kremlin candidates at all levels is to be achieved; in particular the document promotes the targeting of anyone in favor of reducing the role of the "Center" in all aspects of life in the regions. As part of this effort, the document states that the Presidential Administration should take active measures to "disorient" the "protest electorate." As to what these measures might be, the document makes clear that the task at hand is to "start and to conduct a permanently increasing 'offensive' against the opposition." [85]

In the regions, it had long been known that Putin was concerned about the fissiparous tendencies in Russia, often expressing concern during the election that firm measures had to be taken to stop Russia's collapse. The document shows the awareness by Kremlin officials of the need to urgently deal with regional opposition to Putin's desire for central control: "Also, beginning in September 2000 electoral campaigns will be held in more than 40 regions of the Russian Federation, and for the new President of the R.F. strengthening his positions in regions of the Russian Federation and influencing these elections is a strategic necessity." [86] Efforts are to be made to obstruct the election of any leader whose actions might diminish the reassertion of the power of the Center on all aspects of life and governance in the regions, with details on the exact measures to be taken in controlling the regions contained in another classified document.

All in all, the document is a stunning foretaste of what the Kremlin *in fact* ended up doing. At the time there were still many who felt that Putin would decide not to take these measures, or that the opposition would succeed in obliging him to forgo them. In any case, the document appeared after Putin was already elected, although not inaugurated. A deputy press spokesperson was sent out to protest that this may have been one of dozens of proposals for reform circulating. [87] The journalist who followed the story, Nikolay Vardul', continued to stand by its authenticity and insisted he obtained the blueprint from a source inside the Presidential Administration: "Today they deny the plans, but tomorrow they will return to them. I'm interested in the fact they are proposing to bring the secret services into the administration. That needs to be written about and it's definitely going to happen." [88] Looking back a decade and a half later, it indeed happened—the plan was implemented to its last letter, and then some.

Putin's First Decisions as Acting President Target an Independent Media

Putin would start with the media. The independent media had known for months that, given their own harsh treatment of him, Putin would turn his attention on them the moment he was elected. On January 28, 2000, the radio station Ekho Moskvy conducted a lengthy interview with

Marina Sal'ye. She was the former St. Petersburg parliamentarian who led the investigation into Putin's corrupt business dealings, producing a city parliamentary resolution in 1992 that he be dismissed. She now charged that he was the head of a "corrupt oligarchy" who had worked in St. Petersburg with and through his "'partners' of the shadow economy, criminal and mafia structures, and front companies,"[89] and she once again brought up the untidy details of Putin's involvement in the food scandal.[90] Sal'ye's reaction to Putin's coming to power was symptomatic of the view of the liberal intelligentsia, who were largely in shock about the prospects of a KGB revanche.

A preeminent Russian journalist, Andrey Babitskiy, who had worked for Radio Liberty since 1989, had been relentlessly attacking Russian military actions endangering Chechen civilians. Russian troops captured him in Chechnya, charged him with being a Chechen agent, and ultimately exchanged him like a foreign spy for Russian soldiers held by the Chechens. This unprecedented treatment of an accredited journalist, and a Russian citizen, put the rest of the journalistic community on notice, particularly when Putin unabashedly declared, "What Babitskiy did is much more dangerous than firing a machine gun."[91] Putin's own detailed knowledge of the operation and involvement in the exchange became evident to Natalya Gevorkyan when she was interviewing Putin for *First Person*. As Masha Gessen subsequently reported, Gevorkyan wondered after the interview whether Babitskiy was even traded, or whether the whole exercise had actually been a special operation to demonstrate to journalists that they would be treated as foreign agents if necessary. Gevorkyan, who decided early on in Putin's tenure to move to France despite her very senior status in Russia, told Gessen, "The Babitskiy story made my life easier. . . . I realized that this was how [Putin] was going to rule. That this is how his fucking brain works. So I had no illusions. I knew this was how he understood the word *patriotism*—just the way he had been taught in all those KGB schools: the country is as great as the fear it inspires, and the media should be loyal."[92]

Alarmed by the growing atmosphere of intolerance from the Kremlin, thirty media organizations signed an open letter in the weekly *Obshchaya gazeta* on February 16, 2000, stating, "The threat to the freedom of speech in Russia has for the first time in the last several years transformed into its open and regular suppression." On the front page, the special edition of the newspaper posed a direct question to Putin: "Do you think that what is happening today and to freedom of speech is a worthy continuation of your course?" It continued, "It seems that the consolidation of ever more power in the hands of the president is not intended to implement some policy, since no policy unconnected with the consolidation of power itself has yet been announced, but has become an aim in itself." The paper printed and distributed free of charge over 500,000 copies of the special edition.[93]

At a funeral for Russian soldiers killed in Chechnya, Putin did not back down, stating even more broadly a recurring theme of his presidency: that whenever Russia is weak, "riff-raff" appear to destroy it. But "common Russian people" arise to sweep the "riff-raff away." And where do these elements get their money? An article in Moscow's *New Times* noted the strangely coincidental timing between Putin's speech and a financial report that just happened to be released by the FSB the same week, claiming that the "West" had injected "$1.5 billion" into certain Russian commercial banks "as a payment for the services of the journalists fighting against their own army on the side of the 'Chechen bandits.'" The author of the *New Times* article, the legendary Valeriya Novodvorskaya, who was herself forcibly committed to a Soviet psychiatric hospital for protesting the 1968 invasion of Czechoslovakia, lamented:

The daily allegations about money being paid to journalists for their work for the "Chechen bandits" and about Western special services hiring our mass media outlets and journalists in pursuit of their vile objectives involuntarily bring to mind the articles written by A. M. Yakovlev* in *Literaturnaya Gazeta*, in the seventies, in which he urged invoking not Article 70 (for anti-Soviet activities) but Article 64 (for high treason), which carried the death penalty, in judging dis-

---

*A.M. Yakovlev should not be confused with Aleksandr M. Yakovlev who was a legal specialist and a member of the Supreme Soviet. In 1994 Yel'tsin created the position of president's plenipotentiary representative in the Federal Assembly (*polnomochnyy predstavitel' prezidenta v Federal'nom Sobranii*) and named the latter Yakovlev to the post.[94]

sidents who supposedly worked for the West. All Lubyankas across the world repose upon foundations of lies. Therefore, above all, they seek to "rub out" the truth. And the press which dares to tell it.[95]

Dmitriy Medvedev, at that time the head of Putin's campaign, announced, "Wars, including information wars, are not the best way of settling relations. Quite honestly, Putin cares more for the mood of the voter than for attacks by his opponents."[96] On March 4, in a harbinger of his entire presidency, Putin's campaign issued an even stronger statement: "The press service of the election headquarters will continue to closely watch all facts or lies in respect of the candidate for the post of Russian President V. V. Putin, and reserves the right to use all means available in its arsenal for—as it has been stated more than once—an 'asymmetrical' answer to the provocations."[97] Arsenals? Asymmetrical responses? What did they have in mind by using this language of war?

One cannot debate the fact that by early spring both nationwide television channels had joined independent media in turning against Putin. Most notably, NTV carried a program only days before the March elections that directly blamed the FSB, and by implication Putin, for the summer 1999 apartment bombings in Russian cities.* For its part, the Kremlin's arsenal was unleashed in covert and illegal ways, including:

- Cyber attacks on *Novaya gazeta* for their investigation of the true culprits behind the attempted apartment bombings in Ryazan.[99]
- Personal pressure on NTV journalists, including attempts to blackmail them by threatening that if they did not work for the FSB, they or their families would face imprisonment on trumped-up charges. Such was the case with Eleonora Filina, who claimed in March 2000 that she was told if she did not act as a mole for the FSB inside NTV, a criminal case could be opened against her son.[100]

---

* The transcript of this program is presented as an appendix in Satter (2003). The NTV program was the centerpiece of a subsequent documentary, *Blowing Up Russia*, that presents all the evidence, including circumstantial, in support of this theory.[98]

- Failure to launch robust investigations of suspicious deaths that fueled rumors of Kremlin involvement, including in the crash of a chartered plane carrying the investigative journalist Artyom Borovik (who was investigating the Ryazan apartment bombings, federal casualties in Chechnya, and claims that Putin's publicized early childhood story was untrue*), which sent chills down the spine of independent media. Yevgeniy Primakov echoed the widespread belief that there had been foul play; at Borovik's funeral, he stated, "I don't understand how society and the government can possibly be indifferent to threats addressed against journalists. Why is there no reaction? Why are we so helpless? Why can't we twist these scoundrels' heads off?" [101]

- Mobilization of the mock intelligentsia to support the Kremlin. This feature, which became the Kremlin's modus operandi, first appeared in the spring of 2000: leading members of the administration at St. Petersburg State University, including their rector Lyudmila Verbitskaya, wrote to demand that those responsible for the popular television show *Kukly* be investigated for possible criminal malfeasance.

If all of this, and more, happened when Putin was only acting president, what would happen after he was inaugurated?

The media's desire to cover Chechnya in the same kind of open, robust, and critical way they had covered the First Chechen War brought them into conflict with a Kremlin determined not to have military operations constrained by media oversight—a sadly routine feature of Western media restrictions in war zones as well at this time. But in a much broader strategy, the Kremlin simply wanted to limit press scrutiny of all its actions. The real war against the press would start immediately after the inauguration, with independent television.

The political importance of nationwide television for cementing or loos-

---

*An alternative legend of Putin's early childhood can be found at many Internet sites critical of him. The argument is set out most clearly in Felshtinskiy and Pribylovskiy (2008).

ening the public's attachment to the Kremlin had never been overlooked by the political elite. The image of a young and vigorous president presiding over a victorious war against "bandits" vilified on TV only made Putin more popular. The nationwide state-owned ORT and RTR shaped their news coverage of Chechnya to maximize voter support for Putin. Gleb Pavlovskiy, the Kremlin's major spinmeister, subsequently openly admitted that the purpose of his PR campaign for Putin at this time was to reawaken in the Russian people the "habit of adoration of national leaders [*privychka k obozhaniyu*]," [102] which they had lost in the late Soviet and Yel'tsin eras.

But journalists and the independent media were having none of it. NTV, the only national independent television channel, owned by the oligarch Vladimir Gusinskiy, had openly challenged and mocked Putin (and Yel'tsin before him) in its popular show *Kukly* (Puppets). In one episode that Putin is reported to have been furious about, he is shown as an uncultured, foul-mouthed, whiney baby in the Kremlin Family whom bewitched villagers have been made to believe is beautiful. [103] Unlike Yel'tsin, who never interfered with the program despite its brutal portrayal of his faults, Putin and his team evidently had no intention of tolerating such insubordination. The creators of *Kukly* reported that they were instructed by the Kremlin to take Putin's puppet off the show. In response, the next week, in a program called "The Ten Commandments," Putin was depicted both as the burning bush and as a cloud calling down the Ten Commandments from atop Mount Sinai. The program's creator, Viktor Shenderovich, subsequently described the episode: "The ten commandments were like 'Don't kill anyone except people of Caucasian nationality,' 'Don't steal anything except federal property,' 'Don't create idols except the president, Vladimir Putin.' Technically we observed the conditions because we removed the Putin puppet. But that didn't make us any more loved." [104] The creators freely admitted they were testing the limits of Kremlin tolerance. [105]

On March 24, 2000, less than forty-eight hours before polls opened for the presidential election, NTV aired a damning talk show, *Independent Investigation*, that openly suggested the FSB had been behind the failed apartment bombings in the city of Ryazan in 1999. Reconstruction of the events that cast doubt on the official FSB story and interviews with residents, many of whom had backgrounds in military and police affairs, showed the FSB was intending to blow up the apartment building for the purpose of boosting the case for an attack on Chechnya, an attack that would increase Putin's electoral chances. NTV's general manager subsequently reported that Media Minister Mikhayl Lesin had warned him that by airing the show, NTV producers had "crossed the line" and were now "outlaws" in the Kremlin's eyes.[106] These threats were to translate into vigorous assaults against freedom of the press once Putin became president.

Putin Takes On the Oligarchs

It had not escaped the Kremlin's attention that NTV was owned by Vladimir Gusinskiy, so such threats were not just attacks against press freedom; they also signaled the beginning of the war against oligarchic independence from the Kremlin. The strategy unfolded against the backdrop of the deepening of the regime's commitment to continuing along the path toward a neoliberal authoritarian state.

Journalists immediately began to probe what was the "real" Putin agenda. In answering the question "Why Putin?," *Obshchaya gazeta*'s Dmitriy Furman focused not on Putin's own ambitions but on the obligations he had entered into with his backers and his circle. One of the major tasks Furman pointed to in a February 2000 article was to "achieve a general agreement on the results of privatization." This meant not giving in to the threats of Luzhkov and Primakov to undo the results of the "loans for shares" privatization of the 1990s.* But in addition, and more important, Putin decided to rein in the "predatory impulses" (*khishchnicheskikh impul'sov*) of the oligarchs, to dampen down and control their internal conflicts, which were seen as a threat to stability, and to focus on the creation not of a law-based

---

*The "loans for shares" scheme was hatched when the Kremlin, in desperate need of cash to pump into the economy prior to the 1996 elections, provided shares at below-market rates in the state's largest industrial and extractive enterprises in exchange for cash. Understanding that this scheme had a disputable legal basis, those oligarchs who benefited from it entered the Putin era with grave concerns that their financial gains could be overturned.

state but a "strong" one, one that could force the oligarchs to submit to the new rules of the game and avoid a bloody settling of accounts (*krovavym razborkam*).[107]

Other media outlets focused on rumors that Putin intended to increase state ownership in these entities as a means of bringing them under Kremlin control. On March 2 *Rossiyskaya gazeta* astutely observed that the Kremlin was now using "black PR" techniques in which compromising articles were planted in friendly outlets (*zakazukhi*). The newspaper lamented that this was turning people into *Homo zapiens*, without the ability to use the mass media to stay informed and instead becoming Pelevin-like* zombies who fall victim to manipulative technologies that "zap" them with false information.[108] The purpose of this strategy was "the establishment of an economy based on corporate entities . . . to replace the present economy based on individual entities."[109]

Indeed the monopolistic trend of Russian business continued at this time with Sibneft (owned by Berezovskiy and Abramovich) and Siberian Aluminum (owned by Deripaska) cooperating to establish Rusal, a company that would control over 80 percent of Russia's aluminum production and 7 percent of global production. This merger took place against the backdrop of the struggle between criminal and oligarchic interests, clans, and gangs in the Siberian city of Krasnoyarsk. These "aluminum wars" were indication of the inherent dangers of letting violence settle disputes. At one point the largest smelter in the former Soviet Union was being run by an alleged criminal enterprise that had won a pitched battle against the combined forces put together by the region's governor General Aleksandr Lebed, Oleg Deripaska, United Energy Systems chief Anatoliy Chubays, and the Alpha Group security forces. In early 2000 they had finally succeeded in arresting the leader of the gang, Anatoliy Bykov, and taking him to be tried in Moscow. Bykov sold his shares to Abramovich; then, on March 14, 2000, in London's Dorchester Hotel, Abramovich, Berezovskiy, and Badri Patarkatsishvili signed an agreement to the merger with

---

*Viktor Pelevin was a writer of novels such as *Generation P* and *Empire V* that provided thinly veiled critiques of the transition from Communism and the descent into authoritarianism.

Deripaska. At this time all four were on good terms with the Kremlin, so the arrangement, by suppressing local criminality and insubordination, received the center's blessing.[110]*

Meanwhile in Moscow, Putin's economic policy was being shaped by a specially formed committee. Clearly it was the liberal economists, working to put a growth-based economic strategy in place in the months before Putin's inauguration, that led many in the West to be optimistic about the chance for a deepening of the transition to both free-market capitalism and democracy. Under the leadership of the director of the Center for Strategic Research, German Gref, this group included First Deputy Finance Minister Aleksey Kudrin, presidential advisor Andrey Illarionov, the director of the Russian Government's Working Center for Economic Reforms Vladimir Mau, and former prime minister Yegor Gaidar. But the working group also included members who represented the interests of the oligarchs, including presidential chief of staff Aleksandr Voloshin and First Deputy Prime Minister Mikhayl Kas'yanov. This group was working on an economic plan for Putin that would overhaul the tax system, increase government revenue, provide a growth-based economic strategy, and reassure foreign investors that a law-based system would guarantee their investments. NTV reported in early April that a struggle for policy outcomes and posts had broken out between the oligarchs and representatives of the "St. Petersburg liberals," including members of this group and United Energy Systems chief Anatoliy Chubays.[112]

On April 25 it was announced that they had completed their first draft, just ahead of the inauguration. Clearly conflict was already breaking out about the future nature of economic policy, the division of economic spoils, and the coming appointments to key economic positions. Seeing that those with interests in big business were being outmaneuvered, Berezovskiy heaped scorn on what was called the Gref Plan as "unprofessional" and "naïve."[113] Boris Nemtsov, once one of the Kremlin's young reformers and

---

*Bykov was ultimately arrested for the death of a subordinate who ended up not being dead. Nevertheless he was sentenced to six and a half years in prison, a sentence that was suspended. Bykov then appealed to the European Court for Human Rights on the basis of wrongful imprisonment. For more on this episode see Hass (2011).[111]

a leader of the newly formed Union of Right Forces, criticized the draft report for not settling the divisions over economic policy: "There is a struggle going on over the strategy for Russia. Either it will be crony capitalism with tycoons, corruption, underground deals and social polarization, or it will be a Western-style economy." [114] Obviously Gref's preference to break up oligarchic control over the natural resources monopolies was going to be mightily resisted by the oligarchs, who wanted to continue the cozy relationship they had had with the Kremlin in the past. The Kremlin sided neither with the liberal economists nor with the oligarchs. Instead it exercised a third option: to strictly subordinate business interests to Kremlin needs, putting monopolistic trends second to the Kremlin's political interests, the economic needs of the Russian state, and the personal interests of the new elite coming to power. Central to this plan was the alliance between the Kremlin and those liberal economists, headed by Chubays, who understood from the "loans for shares" deal that oligarchs needed the Kremlin to protect their gains, and the Kremlin needed oligarchic money to win elections and oligarchic restraint to keep the budget afloat and the population satisfied. After the election, however, it began to dawn on the oligarchs that the Kremlin's interest in capturing revenues from these companies and in reasserting a strong state might diminish their own independence.

Chapter Six

---◦◎◦---

The Founding of the Putin System

His First Hundred Days and
Their Consequences, May–August 2000

Putin's Inauguration: The Embodiment of a Strong State

During the campaign Putin had declined to debate his opponents or to conduct meetings or rallies with voters. He was unwilling to submit to the kind of popular scrutiny normal in a democratic campaign. When prompted by an interviewer to address the belief that he would "change dramatically right after the elections," Putin had replied, "This is not something I will answer." [1] Now, during the inauguration on May 7, 2000, he made a virtue of his apparently unique right not to have to diminish his stature by indicating his plans for the next four years. Thus from the beginning of his tenure he built a metanarrative of being above politics, of framing politics as something dirty and beneath him, of creating an image of stability as solid and unassailable as the Kremlin walls themselves.

His inaugural ceremony as the second president of the Russian Federation was designed to underscore his main theme: the centrality for Russian history of a strong state located inside the Kremlin. He placed himself not among the Russian people, not in the vast open spaces of Russia, not in the democratic corridors of the newly revived federal assemblies. Putin deftly created a symbiosis between the Kremlin and his own power as president: "For today's solemn event we are gathered here, in the Kremlin, a place which is sacred for our people. The Kremlin is the heart of our national

266

memory. Our country's history has been shaped here, inside the Kremlin walls, over centuries. And we do not have the right to be heedless of our past. We must not forget anything. We must know our history, know it as it really is, draw lessons from it and always remember those who created the Russian state, championed its dignity and made it a great, powerful and mighty state." [2]

Identifying himself with the Kremlin and its past leaders allowed him to emerge as if out of a chrysalis from the position of deputy mayor of St. Petersburg, in ill-fitting suits and in Sobchak's shadow, to the presidency in less than four years. Putin's charisma was created over the course of his six months as acting president by PR specialists like Gleb Pavlovskiy and Vladislav Surkov for the purpose of embodying the power of the Kremlin walls in Putin himself.

The inauguration ceremony was carefully stage-managed as the founding event of the Putin presidency. Television cameras followed the arrival of his motorcade inside the Kremlin, the salute from the Kremlin's regimental commander, his long confident walk alone through the Kremlin's red-carpeted corridors into the halls where the Russian elite had been continuously shown standing and waiting for him behind cordons that would separate them from him. Foreign dignitaries and the diplomatic corps were excluded since this was, as the press secretary asserted, a "Russian internal event," signaling that the new president would not be beholden to any foreign pressure. The doddering Yel'tsin, whose painfully wobbly steps were followed fully and unnecessarily by television cameras, ascended the dais for the swearing-in and then descended the long Red Staircase to the Kremlin courtyard below, his bodyguard there to avert a possible fall. These shots of Putin and Yel'tsin underlined the contrast in the physical robustness of the two men, signifying that Russia's future was now in firmer hands.

Whereas the camera shots of all the speakers prior to Putin, including Yel'tsin, showed them against the backdrop of the dais's blue curtain, Putin, and Putin alone, was captured against the background of the gilded side doors, emerging godlike against a sky-blue background, interspersed with shots of a rapt audience straining to see him, to hear his every word; of the Russian Orthodox patriarch looking on approvingly; of the presidential standard being raised over the Kremlin; of the Kremlin clock marking the beginning of a new era. The camera shots looked up to him and down to the audience. This was not a "meet and greet" event, a celebration of a transition or of democracy; this was an occasion designed to herald the emergence of a single and indisputable leader of a renewed state.[3] Entering the Kremlin he had been pictured alone, but after the ceremony he walked out followed closely by the chief of his new presidential guard, Viktor Zolotov. As they left, again cordoned off from all onlookers, there was an artillery salute, the Kremlin bells started pealing, and Glinka's "Glory" from the opera *A Life for the Tsar* rang throughout the hall and via television throughout the land. It was intended to be and was undoubtedly quite a spectacle, and indeed marked the beginning of a presidency in which an actual relationship between the state and society, between the Kremlin and the country would constantly be mediated by images of Putin as the incarnation of Russia's aspirations, values, and history.*

Every frame of the inauguration had been carefully scripted to represent the founding event of Putin's spectacle-driven presidency. Pavlovskiy, the leader of his PR team, subsequently wrote about the aura around Putin they sought to create using state-controlled TV news, "TV news smelled of incense, holy oil poured on the work of the government and its leader."[4] But in addition those in the know understood the message behind the inclusion in the audience of the disgraced former KGB chief Vladimir Kryuchkov, who had been briefly imprisoned for his role in the abortive August 1991 coup: as ex-KGB general Oleg Kalugin commented, "No wonder the new Russian leader stalled the reforms, reversed the process of democratization, and introduced discredited Soviet practices."[5]

Following this remarkable performance, Putin was ready to take action. Within days he created seven superfederal districts to rule over, and rein in, the democratically elected governors of the eighty-nine federal units, and he launched an attack on independent TV and those oligarchs who had

---

*For more on this idea of the "society of the spectacle" in which authentic relationships are replaced by representation, as it applies to Putin, see Goscilo (2012).

opposed him. His people also swiftly took up their positions at the commanding heights of the state and the economy.

Putin Institutes a "Vertical of Power"

On May 13, four days after his inauguration, Putin issued an executive order, or *ukaz*, creating seven new superfederal regions that would supervise the work of the eighty-nine federal units, whose chiefs would all be appointed by, and beholden to, the president. The regional governors had been a major source of opposition to Putin during the election; now they were faced with the imposition of his "vertical of power." When Putin wrote in his February "Open Letter to Voters" that he was going to reintroduce the guiding and regulating power of the state,[6] this was a strong signal that he was going to reintroduce a top-down, centralized command structure familiar from Soviet times. He was trying to deal with the problems all federal-level officials have with the regions' resistance to subordination, but he had inherited a system in which the "parade of sovereignties" that Yel'tsin had encouraged had led to a significant weakening of central control.* Yet

---

*The Russian Justice Ministry had estimated that in 1997, of "44,000 regional legal acts, including laws, gubernatorial orders and similar documents, nearly half did not conform with the constitution or federal legislation."[7] This continued into the period when Putin came to power, when it was also calculated that only one republic (Udmurtia) had a constitution that was in accord with federal legislation.[8] Emblematic of this problem was the Far East's Primorskiy Krai, where the governor, Yevgeniy Nazdratenko, had so misruled affairs that the region had been thrown into darkness amid widespread power and heating outages in areas where average winter temperatures plummeted to below −30 Celsius. Local hospitals had been flooded with frostbite victims, some of whom needed amputations that had to be done without anaesthetic, which itself was in short supply.[9] Demonstrations broke out in Vladivostok in February against the government, and in response Putin sacked his own energy minister and sent an envoy who demanded that the governor and all deputy governors and heads of department submit their resignations. But Nazdratenko himself resigned only after being offered a federal position as head of the State Fisheries Committee. On the day Nazdratenko accepted the position, Putin signed an *ukaz* banning regional governors who had resigned from participating in future gubernatorial elections. Elsewhere the problems were much the same. Journalists reported that the governor of Mariy-El, Vyacheslav Kislitsyn, not having mines or energy wealth to exploit for his own personal use, started negotiations with Middle East governments behind the backs of the Ministry of Defense to sell them S-300 missile defense systems at a reduced rate for his personal profit.[10] It was clear from Putin's evaluation of the sorry state of these affairs that once he became president there would be a big shift in power away from the regions.

the way he introduced this vertical, by creating these superfederal regions, showed that he would disregard existing constitutional procedures if need be. This change was done by decree and was nowhere mentioned in the Constitution.

Thus in one bold stroke Putin ended the autonomy of the federal units. Additionally the career backgrounds of these seven plenipotentiaries showed that he trusted the power ministries to meet the challenge of creating this new "vertical of power." Five of the seven were generals, two veterans of the war in Chechnya and three from the security services: Georgiy Poltavchenko came out of the St. Petersburg KGB and became plenipotentiary of the newly established Central Federal District. Viktor Cherkesov, another close Putin associate and also from the St. Petersburg KGB, was appointed to the Northwestern Federal District. General Viktor Kazantsev had been a counterterrorism chief in the North Caucasus and now was named plenipotentiary to the North Caucasus District. Lieutenant General Pyotr Latyshev, who had been deputy minister of internal affairs, became the head of the Urals District, and General Konstantin Pulikovskiy, who had been commander of the federal forces in the First Chechen War, became the head of the Far Eastern District. Only Sergey Kiriyenko, a reformer and former prime minister who was named plenipotentiary to the Volga Federal District, and Leonid Drachevskiy, a former minister in the Commonwealth of Independent States who was sent to the new Siberian District, had no past security services involvement.[11] The *ukaz* gave them the power to coordinate all federal services to the regions and ensure regional compliance with federal legislation.[12]

In the federal legislature, the Kremlin worked with the Duma in a way the parties had not expected. Liberal parties thought the Kremlin would ally Unity with them, together ensuring a majority to promote a liberal economic and political agenda. Instead the Kremlin instructed Unity to ally with the Communists, giving them the lion's share of committee chairmanships, while benefiting from the decision of Yuriy Luzhkov (who was evidently hounded day and night by Putin's man Vladislav Surkov) and other leaders in Fatherland–All Russia to merge with Unity, thus forming United Russia. Surkov's major objective in the Duma was to stamp out the influence of those oligarchs who had been paying for votes. This he did with a combination of bullying and counterpayments. Surkov was the point man who now started to pay Duma deputies $5,000 per month on top of their salaries for their loyalty.[13]

Simultaneously, on May 17, Putin announced that he would introduce laws to weaken the power of the regions and the Federation Council. Initially the bills were vetoed by the Federation Council, but in July the laws were passed so overwhelmingly by the Duma that they could not procedurally be overridden by the upper chamber. They gave the president the right to fire provincial governors who broke federal laws or came under criminal investigation (which could be initiated by the president's office) and took away the governors' automatic immunity and membership in the Federation Council. Governors and local legislatures would henceforth choose full-time representatives to sit on the Federation Council, who would have to live in Moscow, thereby loosening their dependence on their regions.[14]

Boris Berezovskiy tried to rally regional governors to resist Putin, publicly stating, "Only the Federation Council is a guarantee that there will be no usurpation of power in Russia. If the Federation Council is destroyed, we will have one branch of power—authoritarian, a very tough totalitarian regime."[15] As the quintessential insider, Berezovskiy must have had more information than most about Putin's real intentions. He had supported Putin as a means of protecting the Family, including him, but now it was clear that Putin's dismissal of Yel'tsin's daughter and his attack on regional autonomy would also limit his own options. Some governors publicly protested as well; for example, the president of Bashkortostan Murtaza Rakhimov bluntly declared, "Russia has always had imperial ambitions and a desire for centralization. Putin is largely in line with this tradition." Yet, as *Vedomosti* noted, he had to give this interview outside the country, to the British newspaper the *Guardian*.[16] The Federation Council fought back and gained some concessions,[17] but by early summer Putin had succeeded in creating a Federation Council loyal only to him, shifting revenue streams to the federal level, and ultimately ending Yel'tsin's "parade of sovereignties" altogether. And in Chechnya, a republic where over 50 percent of the electorate had officially voted for Putin while under Russian bombardment,

Putin announced direct presidential rule on June 8, installing Ahmad Kadyrov as his representative on June 12, thereby belying the notion that the republic was becoming a beacon of stability—a continuous theme of his election campaign.

In early July Putin delivered his first annual address to the Federal Assembly (the combined membership of the Duma and the Federation Council). The speech focused on achieving progress by strengthening the state, rearranging center-regional relations to emphasize the "vertical of power," and removing restrictions on free economic activity. He spent by far the most time developing his justification for strengthening the *state*—a term mentioned ninety-one times, as compared with sixty-three for *Russia* or *Russians*, forty-nine for *economic* or *the economy*, forty-eight for *federal* or *federation*, thirty-four for *power*, thirty for *country*, and only twelve for *democracy* or *democratic*, twelve for *parties* or *party systems*, six for *civil society* or *liberties*, and four for *elections*—this last clearly a subject that occupied a very small corner of his political consciousness and that he had no desire to talk about for another four years.*

At the same time that Putin was diminishing the functions of the Federation Council and weakening the local and regional sources of governors' powers, he was preparing to announce a State Council, which would be an advisory body to the president whose members would be chosen entirely by him. This move was one of the measures proposed in the leaked Presidential Administration document published by *Kommersant* in early May,[18] and its announcement had obviously been delayed by the fierce resistance from the Federation Council. Nevertheless Putin signed a decree on September 1, 2000, establishing it in order to "provide for the coordinated functioning and interactions of organs of state power."[19] Governors and presidents of the eighty-nine federal districts would sit on the Coun-

---

* An analysis of word clouds in Putin's subsequent speeches, and those of Medvedev in 2008–12, shows that Putin continued to emphasize the state's needs, rights, and roles, while Medvedev's speeches deemphasized the state in preference for discussion of development, the people, and the country. Word clouds were generated by inserting the annual speeches into www.tocloud .com using a 20 percent tag, display frequencies, and linear interpolation.

cil, but the president could appoint others at his discretion. In response to these measures, Berezovskiy resigned his seat in the Duma, announcing that he did not want to be part of an emerging authoritarian regime.[20] From this point on the relationship between Putin and Berezovskiy was irreparable.

Putin began to implement the "vertical of power" during his first week in office. By May 20 *Kommersant* had already concluded, "There is yet another revolution in Russia. And once again from above."[21] *Obshchaya gazeta* on May 25 observed, "Appointments to the highest posts are being made on the basis of one principle: are any of them compromised, so as to make them instruments in the hands of the President. . . . The impression is being created that the consolidation of even more power in the hands of the president is not a means for implementing some policy (the president has not announced any clear political priorities unrelated to this consolidation of power) but an end in itself."[22]

Putin Takes On the Media and the Oligarchs

The week before Putin's inauguration, *Kommersant* had published the leaked document *Reform of the Administration of the President of the Russian Federation*, purporting to be the master plan that advocated the use of the FSB to "control the political process" and specifically to silence the opposition media by "driving them to financial crisis." The multipage section titled "The Information War with the Opposition" contained detailed examples of how to preempt, suppress, and discredit opposition exposés on issues such as "the purchase of property by representatives of the presidential structures" or any other issue to do with corruption, with the infamous statement "The Administration must make it clear to every opposition leader that as soon as he slings mud at the Presidential side, he will inevitably receive the same treatment"[23]

From his first days in office Putin made it clear that he would not allow media hostile to the Kremlin. The idea that a free media was intrinsic to a democracy meant nothing to a leader who had seen television used by oligarchs in their own battles with each other and with the Kremlin. For Putin that era was over, but his approach continued to be indirect.

His new relationship with the media and its owners was signaled immediately with the May 11 raid on Vladimir Gusinskiy's Media-Most company. *Segodnya*'s editor Mikhayl Berger had previously written to Putin appealing to him to guarantee freedom of the press after his inauguration. Referring to the masked special forces who swarmed the building and claimed to be from the tax police but whose credentials could not be verified, Berger now wrote, "Instead of an answer [from Putin] to this appeal, . . . we got gunmen."[24]

Gusinskiy was called to the Procurator's Office in mid-June as a witness in the investigation of the materials taken the previous month from the Media-Most headquarters. There he was unexpectedly taken into custody, without even the benefit of access to his attorney, under a provision that allows the procurator to imprison a person without formal charges. In a subsequent case at the European Court, Gusinskiy asserted that he took the manner of his detention to indicate that a "political contract" had been taken out against him.[25] He testified that Presidential Chief of Staff Aleksandr Voloshin had promised him millions to stop attacks on Putin, and when he turned down the offer, the Kremlin increased pressure both on Gusinskiy personally and on banks to dry up his line of credit.[26]

From prison Gusinskiy launched an international campaign lambasting the Kremlin, declaring, "This is a regime which has begun the move toward the creation of a totalitarian regime, whether it realizes it or not."[27] But three days later he agreed to leave the country and sell his shares in NTV to Gazprom at a price to be determined by Gazprom, in return for criminal charges being dropped. He signed an agreement that contained nondisclosure clauses presented to him directly by Media Minister Mikhayl Lesin that obligated him to agree to the "renunciation of all steps, including public statements or dissemination of information by the organizations, their shareholders and executives, which would damage the foundations of the constitutional regime and violate the integrity of the Russian Federation, undermine the security of the State, incite social, racial, national or religious discord or lead to the discrediting of the State institutions of the Russian Federation."* He was released from prison once he agreed to divest himself of his shares in Media-Most and accept the terms dictated not by the Procuracy but by Lesin, although the embezzlement charges against him were not dropped.[30]

Having forced Gusinskiy out of the country, Putin still had to deal with his and Berezovskiy's continued role, even from abroad, in their media companies. While admitting publicly that in theory a free press was necessary for the construction of a civil society, Putin warned in his first address to the Federal Assembly on July 8 that "the economic ineffectiveness of a significant part of the media makes it dependent on the commercial and political interests of its owners and sponsors." As such, many TV stations and newspapers were not independent but promoted the interests of their owners and engaged in "mass disinformation" and were "a means of struggle with the state."[31] According to Putin, not only should the state be strengthened as a practical matter, to prevent its disintegration, but "the authorities have the moral right to demand that norms established by the state are observed." Once again he returned to the idea that people can be free only if there is a strong state: "The debate about the ratio between force and freedom . . . continues to cause speculation on the themes of dictatorship and authoritarianism. But our position is very clear: only a strong, or effective if someone dislikes the word 'strong,' an effective state and a democratic state is capable of protecting civil, political and economic freedoms." Strong states encourage the development of strong civil societies and strong political parties. "A weak government benefits from having weak parties. It is easier and more comfortable for it to live by the rules of political bargaining. But a strong government is interested in strong rivals."

---

*Gusinskiy subsequently won a case against the Russian government in the European Court for Human Rights, which agreed that his criminal prosecution and imprisonment was an abuse of state power under Article 5 of the European Convention for Human Rights, to which Russia is a signatory.[28] The Parliamentary Assembly of the Council of Europe pronounced on this and similar cases in Russia, "Such predatory practices amount to an organized system of . . . takeovers . . . acting on behalf of private interests protected by the government, with the connivance or even on the instructions of the government . . . none of which would be possible without the cooperation of highly placed individuals."[29]

Naturally, therefore, until the Russian state became strong, it would not have an interest in allowing strong counterbalancing influences, including from the media, which he slammed precisely for being a too strong counterbalance to the state. He wanted the media to be free of economic influence, not to represent rival points of view, and he insisted that it could function only with something called "true independence." Without that independence, the media could turn into "a means of mass disinformation, a means of fighting the state."[32] Clearly for Putin, taking a stand against a state policy was equivalent to spewing disinformation.

The director general of NTV, Yevgeniy Kiselyev, issued a blistering rebuke to the president:

> Putin was throwing down the gauntlet to us: when he mentioned media which carry out anti-state activity, or more precisely fight against the state, he meant us, the NTV channel, first and foremost. We understand that perfectly well, and I am going to respond to this. The president has different ideas to ours about what the state is and what its interests are. I think Putin is trying to imitate Louis XIV, who said "the state is me." Putin's address yesterday made it clear that what he means by strengthening the state is strengthening his personal power. He didn't say a word in his address about developing parliamentarianism, nor developing local self-government, nor developing an independent judiciary, nor reforming the procurator's office, which has of late become the absolute shame of the Russian state—we'll have some more to say about that separately—nor about anything else. What we understand by the state is not a bureaucratic machine headed by a former member of the power structures and security services, but a democratic Russia with its people.[33]

The leaked internal document calling for the reform of the Presidential Administration, the raid on Media-Most, and Putin's statement justifying it, all clearly indicated that he understood, but had no intention of fostering, the press's role as a counter to the growth of state power. While 59 percent of the population polled supported NTV, there was no discernible mass public reaction to the crackdown on the station. The country was silent when Oleg Panfilov, director of the Center for Journalism in Extreme Situations, warned that "once all the media in the provinces and the capital are subdued, Putin will have total control of the entire information space."[34] In fact polls showed increased support for Putin. In early July 2000, 54 percent of citizens polled assessed his work positively.[35]

In the period immediately after his inauguration and throughout 2000, Putin was still constrained by projections that by 2003 half of the Russian budget would go for debt repayment to the Paris Club—a group of financial officials from the world's leading economies who assist in debt restructuring. Russian leaders needed "private" money, including that money oligarchs had received through the "loans for shares" deal under Yel'tsin—and they intended to get it, through more effective taxation but also through new arrangements with oligarchs that would provide more revenue for the state. The Russian state would no longer beg the oligarchs for loans from the profits they made in the companies the Kremlin had sold them on the cheap (the Yel'tsin model). Now the owners of those extractive industries sitting at the commanding heights of the economy were to exercise property rights only with state approval. In some cases the state's shares of these companies might increase, with oligarchs sharing their profits with the state and with Kremlin officeholders, including Putin, in return for a license to do business. Putin wanted the oligarchs to understand that they would have rents from these companies only as a reward for loyal state service. But for an oligarch loyal to Putin there would be no restrictions on the profits that could be realized.

Putin acted to limit the autonomy of all the oligarchs, not just those who had media holdings, whom he sought to destroy and drive from the country. On July 11 the procurator general demanded $140 million from Vladimir Potanin for underpaying the government when Norilsk Nickel was privatized; Potanin was co-owner of *Izvestiya* with Vagit Alekperov, owner of Lukoil, who was charged with tax evasion. Authorities also brought charges of tax evasion against AvtoVAZ in July for underpaying $600 million; this was the beginning of a series of moves against Berezovskiy. In response Duma member Boris Nemtsov organized a meeting between Putin and the oligarchs on July 28 seeking clarification of the new rules of the game. Nemtsov had been deputy prime minister under Yel'tsin, a member of Parliament at various times, and cofounder of the pro-business Union of Right Forces, and he was on good terms with the Yel'tsin oligarchs. Subsequent reports suggested that at that meeting Putin and the oligarchs agreed that the results of the 1990s privatizations would not be overturned and there would be no confiscation of assets, ill-gotten or otherwise, from those oligarchs who stayed out of opposition politics. Participants also say the oligarchs got an agreement that they would all be subject to the same rules and treated equally, an evident reference to the oligarchs who were not there: Berezovskiy and Gusinskiy, who were clearly on their way out, and Roman Abramovich, whose star was so ascendant that he didn't even attend the meeting. Anatoliy Chubays was strangely also absent, listed as being out of the country despite the fact that he had pushed for a meeting even earlier, saying, "Every issue should be clarified at that meeting. A question must be asked and answered as to whether the authorities have changed their mind or what is going to be done about the initiative of overzealous law enforcement officers," referring to the raids and arrests that had recently taken place.[36] After the meeting Nemtsov stated, "Today's meeting draws a line under ten years of the initial accumulation of capital. . . . The era of the oligarchs is over."[37] But this statement didn't apply to all oligarchs, and especially not to Abramovich, who later provided a very sanguine view of Putin's beneficence: "President Putin made it clear that he would support business to develop Russia's economy. In return for this support and business certainty, we needed to contribute taxes and act responsibly and transparently."[38] The statement from the Kremlin was more direct: "The president guarantees his support and comprehensive assistance to companies and banks proceeding in their activity guided by the government's interests."[39]

Abramovich, who previously had relied on Berezovskiy for access to the Yel'tsin Family, now himself could open the gates to the Kremlin, as revealed by the 2011 legal case between Berezovskiy and Abramovich in London. It became clear very early in 2000 that Abramovich enjoyed an excellent relationship with Putin and that he would get special treatment from the Kremlin in the future. Berezovskiy testified in London that after

Putin's October 1999 birthday party, to which Abramovich was the lone "big businessman" invited, Abramovich had approached Berezovskiy about contributing to the purchase of a yacht for Putin, the total cost of which would be $50 million. Berezovskiy claims to have declined (politically perhaps not a smart move), but the yacht, the *Olympia*, was ordered and was allegedly added to the presidential fleet in 2002.[40] *Novaya gazeta* ran a three-part investigative series on the yacht, confirming its existence and that it was commissioned in the Dutch shipyard of Papendrecht on April 25, 2002, according to Lloyd's Ship Register. In 2005 the newspaper estimated that over the previous five years the total amount spent on the "recreational presidential fleet" was $78 million to $84 million, while the amount budgeted during this period was $2.4 million.[41] The London courts heard testimony in 2010 from Dmitriy Skarga, who had worked for Gennadiy Timchenko (subsequently named in U.S. government sanctions for his financial links to Putin), Yevgeniy Malov, and Andrey Katkov at Kinex (one of the first companies to get an export license from Putin's Committee for Foreign Liaison in St. Petersburg). At age twenty-nine Skarga had been appointed to head Sovcomflot, Russia's state-owned and largest maritime shipping company.* In that capacity Skarga testified that he had met Christopher Bonehill in Geneva in 2002–3, where "they discussed a yacht which had been presented to Mr. Putin and was being managed by Unicom."[43] An investigation by *Novaya gazeta* revealed that the Lloyd's Shipping Register provided the following information: the yacht was initially owned by Ironstone Investments, registered in the Channel Islands, and then by Ironstone Marine Investments Ltd., registered in the British Virgin Islands. It was managed throughout by Unicom Management Services, registered in Cyprus.[44] Unicom, headed by presidential aide Igor Shuvalov, is a 100 percent state-owned subsidiary of Sovcomflot, and the yacht's cost

---

* Like many Soviet-era state corporations that dealt in foreign trade, Sovcomflot was characterized by some Russian analysts as a vehicle for KGB penetration abroad. Aleksandr Volskiy of the Higher School of Economics estimated that its staff was 85 percent KGB and 15 percent professionals.[42] As in other foreign trade enterprises, the professional staff was in charge of actually running the company, while the KGB watched the professional staff, used the company as a front for intelligence activities, and laundered massive amounts of KGB money abroad.

was $47.6 million, or equal to one-third of the annual budget for the entire city of Sochi.[45] It was guarded by Zolotov's Presidential Protection Service. *Novaya gazeta* concluded, "So, the mystery has been solved. *Olympia* is a presidential yacht."[46]

In the 2011 London trial, both Berezovskiy and Abramovich testified that the Kremlin message Abramovich brought to Berezovskiy was that if Berezovskiy didn't sell his shares in ORT, he would be subject to imprisonment. Abramovich had previously paid Berezovskiy to provide protection (*krysha*) and Kremlin access, but beginning in 2000 the roles were reversed: now it was Abramovich who acted as a Kremlin envoy, pressing Berezovskiy to comply with the new rules of the game. Berezovskiy insisted on meeting Putin directly, and when they met in the Kremlin in August, Berezovskiy understood that his only choice was to accept a buyout on Abramovich's (and the Kremlin's) terms or face prison. It was their final meeting; it was clear to Berezovskiy that he had to leave Russia.[47] Abramovich stated that he gave Berezovskiy $305 million not so much as a buyout but because "I wanted him to be able to establish himself properly abroad."[48]

This episode confirmed that under the Putin plan, the state would be strengthened not by breaking up the oligarchic system per se but by transforming an oligarchy independent of and more powerful than the state into a corporatist structure in which oligarchs served at the pleasure of state officials, who themselves gained and exercised economic control over these structures, both for the state and for themselves. This raises the prospect that state officials promoted the interests of a private economy, not just to serve some principle, not just to fill state coffers with tax revenue, but to help themselves. It was Abramovich who was sent to Berezovskiy to inform him of the new rules of the game, not Russian tax inspectors or the procurator general.

Putin's "Prime Personal Project": Gazprom

Intrinsic to Putin's desire to move beyond the influence of Yel'tsin's inner circle was the plan to take over Gazprom, which had served as a major source of revenue for the Kremlin in the 1990s. At that time Gazprom had received shares in oligarch-owned companies as surety against loans that the oligarchs never intended to repay. In this way Gazprom is estimated to have loaned over $1 billion to Gusinskiy alone, and as a result it ended up owning 30 percent of Gusinskiy's Media-Most company. This was not a problem under Yel'tsin, who allowed both independent media and independent oligarchic power. But in terms of corporate governance, it was not the best way to run one of the world's largest energy companies. As Ben Judah and many other keen observers of the energy sector observed, during the Yel'tsin period Gazprom "seemed to be investing in everything apart from its own pipelines and reserves. It was being used like a giant government slush fund and not a natural resource company." [49]

Under Yel'tsin Gazprom was led by Rem Vyakhirev as CEO and former prime minister Viktor Chernomyrdin as chairman of the board. Neither was particularly loyal to Putin, and there is considerable evidence that both were highly corrupt, including the fact that Gazprom steered $1 billion in contracts to Stroytransgaz, a company that was 50 percent owned by Gazprom managers and relatives, including Vyakhirev's daughter.[50] The second quality—personal accumulation of corruptly obtained wealth—would be allowable under Putin, but never the first, disloyalty.

Putin increased his influence over Gazprom's board of directors immediately upon being elected by removing Chernomyrdin, who was sent off to become ambassador to Ukraine. He was replaced as chairman by Dmitriy Medvedev, who had been Putin's legal advisor in Petersburg, headed his electoral campaign, and had become first deputy head of the Presidential Administration. Putin then began to move against Vyakhirev but was not able to remove him until 2001. Putin personally attended the Gazprom meeting on May 30, 2001, and in a six-minute address informed the startled board that he was instructing the five government-nominated directors to replace Vyakhirev with Aleksey Miller, a deputy minister of energy and Putin's St. Petersburg coworker; he suggested that the other six board members back Miller too.[51] Vyakhirev was temporarily kicked upstairs to become chairman of the board, with Medvedev becoming his deputy, but he soon was retired.[52] Medvedev remained chairman until he was elected Russia's president in 2008.

Within Putin's first years, more members of his clan would be placed on the Gazprom board. By 2008 eleven of the eighteen members of the board were people who had their career start in the St. Petersburg administration, the Petersburg Port Authority, other St. Petersburg companies, or the FSB. As Nemtsov and Milov (both former energy ministers) commented, "This is not the typical way in which global energy companies are run. Usually, leading positions are occupied by professionals with years of experience in top management in energy corporations. Former small-time regional bureaucrats, port and building company managers do not usually get given top management positions in major oil-and-gas corporations, especially in such numbers." [53] By all accounts, from the beginning Putin treated Miller as a mere adjutant and took a personal interest in the company's performance, its policies (particularly in terms of gas supply to Russia's neighbors), and the distribution of its profits. [54]

Installing Medvedev as chairman of the board gave Putin direct access to

His master's voice. Putin with his two energy lieutenants—both of whom rose with him from St. Petersburg—Aleksey Miller of Gazprom in the center and Igor Sechin of Rosneft on the right. Moscow 2009.
Photo by Sergey Karpukhin, Reuters

the board's decisions and deliberations. As early as 2000, the government and expert community began to discuss the need for Gazprom to buy back shares that had been divested to subsidiaries that had underperformed and dragged down share prices. These discussions resulted in the buyback of 4.8 percent of Gazprom shares from Stroytransgaz. Boris Nemtsov (minister of fuel and energy in the Yel'tsin government) and Vladimir Milov (deputy minister of energy in the first Putin term) subsequently claimed that, having been bought back, these shares "began to mysteriously disappear. The process was gradual but anyone who wishes to do so can see how it went by looking at Gazprom's Quarterly Reports prepared to international accounting standards. . . . 6.4% of Gazprom's shares have somehow fallen off its balance sheet. . . . Little by little . . . a large dollop of Gazprom shares has vanished from its subsidiaries' books. Where did they go? No one knows. . . . The market value of such a holding is in the region of $20 billion. . . . The dividends on such a holding, based on Gazprom's 2007 distribution, is over $170 million a year." [55]

The board also moved to strengthen its holdings in core Gazprom stock and to sell its shares in non-energy-related subsidiaries. But as with the buyback of shares from Stroytransgaz, transactions were often not transparent and did not always financially benefit Gazprom's bottom line. Thus SOGAZ, Gazprom's insurance company, was sold for $120 million to a consortium that included Bank Rossiya, despite its value being estimated as at least ten times higher.[56] Subsequently 51 percent was sold to a company called Abros, a 100 percent–owned subsidiary of Bank Rossiya, and another 12.5 percent to a company called Accept Ltd, which owned 3.93 percent of Bank Rossiya and was itself owned by Mikhayl Shelomov, the son of a cousin of Putin.[57] SOGAZ's income from premiums alone rose to $1.5 billion in 2007 as state-owned companies were put under "administrative pressure" to use SOGAZ for their insurance, including the Russian Railways, run by Vladimir Yakunin, who was one of the founders of the Ozero Cooperative.[58]

Gazprom is also alleged to have bought up Abramovich's share of stock at an inflated price, thus allowing the government to gain a majority interest (which they supported), but at a rate that cost the state $6.5 billion, an act that raised the question of whether this was not a "criminal waste of state funds."[59] Of greatest concern to global minority shareholders, such as Hermitage Capital's Bill Browder, was that certain business decisions appeared to benefit the personal interests of the board members, not the shareholders.

Particularly troubling to independent board members was the emergence of intermediary companies like ITERA, a gas trading company set up in the mid-1990s that also appeared to be stacked with Gazprom officials and family members and that received gas from Gazprom at low prices and sold it internationally at high prices, denying Gazprom and its shareholders a substantial profit. For example, in 1999 Gazprom sold ITERA a 32 percent stake in a gas-producing subsidiary, Purgaz, for only 32,000 rubles ($1,041), despite the fact that PricewaterhouseCoopers—Gazprom's own auditors—valued the deal at $200 million to $400 million. In June 2000 Putin himself acknowledged financial irregularities under the previous team: "We know that enormous amounts of money were misspent." Now the onus would be on Putin, Medvedev, and Miller to clean up Gazprom's act.[60] In 2001 Miller, who had started to clean out the stables, stated that Gazprom would exercise its option to buy back a 32 percent stake in Purgaz, giving markets hope that Putin and the new team at Gazprom would protect their investments more carefully.[61]

However, the objective problem for Russian leaders was that, as a result of this chronic mismanagement, Gazprom's stock price was depressed relative to its market valuation. So it needed to do something to improve its performance. It quickly moved to eliminate ITERA, but instead of selling gas directly to buyers overseas, a second intermediary company emerged, Eural Trans Gaz. Eventually allegations of corrupt practices and links with organized crime began to circulate, including in an anonymous document sent to governments in the Organisation for Economic Co-operation and Development (OECD).[62] The public version of the document criticized Gazprom for using intermediary companies like Eural Trans Gaz to "extract value from the company." This practice led to widespread claims by Russian and Western observers that Eural Trans Gaz, Putin's answer to ITERA, was "connected with Semyon Mogilevich, a major international organized criminal residing in Moscow, and top officials in Putin's adminis- tration," and that "the Putin administration had revealed itself. Its aim was not to clean up Russian business but to transfer the skimmed profits to its own people." [63] This practice began immediately after Miller and Medvedev took over Gazprom and was in full operation by 2003. Nemtsov and Milov estimated that asset stripping alone, which was meant to boost reserves in core holdings for exploration of future gas fields, actually cost the company $60 billion. [64]

Lest it appear that all big business throughout Russia was engaged in skimming and asset stripping at this time, Yukos (owned by Mikhayl Khodorkovskiy) and Sibneft (owned by Roman Abramovich) massively increased their assets during the same period, leading to the recovery of the oil sector. [65]

Evidently Putin's obsession with his image as an incorruptible leader did not get in the way of his helping his friends and Ozero colleagues to cap- ture the commanding heights of the economy. But how to keep the opposi- tion from publicizing this information? The media had to be silenced, and in the summer of 2000 his attention turned to Boris Berezovskiy.

The Sinking of the *Kursk* and the Takedown of Boris Berezovskiy

Putin's first months in office had seen an impressive display of adroit sur- prise attacks on his opponents. In August 2000, though he had earned a break, he was not to get it. In the first week a bomb planted in a metro underpass in central Moscow, killing eight, reminded the population that no number of antiterrorist actions in the Caucasus would entirely remove the threat they lived under.

Then, on the same day Putin departed for a vacation on the Black Sea in Sochi, naval exercises in the northernmost Barents Sea got under way. The pride of the Russian fleet, the recently commissioned nuclear-powered sub- marine *Kursk*, took part in the maneuvers, reportedly carrying aboard both dummy torpedoes and top-secret, experimental Shkval advanced torpe- does. In the course of the maneuvers, one of the dummy torpedoes appears to have misfired, leading to an even larger second explosion, possibly of a Shkval, sending the ship to the bottom with its full crew on board.* This was August 12.

Putin's clumsy and callous management of this tragedy taught him the harsh realities of presidential leadership, particularly the need for deft and sensitive handling of crises and the limits of imposing a strict "vertical of power" that paralyzes decision making at lower levels. He did not interrupt his vacation; he neither returned to Moscow nor flew to the control center in Murmansk to take charge of crisis management. While the dying men tapped out desperate messages from within the dark and disabled submarine that were picked up by Russian and foreign rescue vessels, Putin was pictured in short-sleeve shirts, relaxing and smiling in Sochi as he greeted visitors. The radio station Ekho Moskvy, allied with NTV, reported that 73 percent of listeners thought Putin should have flown to the scene of the rescue mission.[67] Marina Litvinovich worked for Gleb Pavlovskiy's Fund for Effective Politics at this time, the institute where Putin's "image" was created. She was also editor in chief of the Kremlin-connected Strana.ru. She recounts that she was "on call" that weekend and personally intervened to try to get Putin to interrupt his Sochi vacation because of the bad PR he was getting. She alleges that both of her superiors, Voloshin and Oleg Dobrodeyev, were drunk when they first got the news, so it fell on her to advocate for Putin going to Vidyayevo, the naval base where *Kursk* was based. In a subsequent interview, after falling out with the Fund and the Kremlin, she recounted:

> I worked for the President. The image that I had, I tried to advance. I was under the impression that the President is a man who cries when the people are crying, and when the people are happy, he is happy too. . . . But in those days of the *Kursk*, the whole country was cry-

---

*Detailed examination of the circumstances surrounding the *Kursk* disaster can be found in Truscott (2002) and Moore (2002). An examination of the controversy surrounding whether the *Kursk* could have been sunk by an accidental ramming from an American submarine shadowing the exercises is provided in the documentary *Kursk: A Submarine in Troubled Water* (2004).[66]

ing, not just the wives and mothers. . . . And the President, the main person in the country, sits in Sochi, when the whole country is crying. And if I, for example, had not come to this meeting, if I had not been invited, or been on vacation, in all likelihood he would not have gone [to Vidyayevo]. . . . And the moment he went everyone wrote: "Oh, at last he went, what a great guy, how he feels the pulse of the people." But few people knew that he doesn't have any empathy, that circumstances forced him to go there. I felt that he didn't give a damn, and this hit me hard. This was the "first moment" [that I saw him for what he is].[68]

In the meantime the military high command refused foreign offers of help but could not rescue the ship alone. Official Moscow went into a miasma of accusations: FSB director Nikolay Patrushev announced that two of the crewmen were Dagestanis, hinting at sabotage; many of the admirals claimed that U.S. submarines were in the area and had rammed the *Kursk*. Television showed Deputy Prime Minister Il'ya Klebanov sitting helplessly in front of family members so distraught that one had to be forcibly tranquilized, but not before she screamed out, referring to the lost sailors, "They earn $50 a month and now they're stuck in that tin can. . . . You better shoot yourself now." [69] Another personally attacked Putin: "Why was Putin away on holiday while our kids are dying here?" [70]

Putin did not appear on national TV until five days after the initial event and returned to Moscow only on day seven. It was not until the eighth day that the Russians accepted Norwegian offers to help rescue the sailors. On day nine, when divers finally reached the sub, it took them less than thirty minutes to open the hatch, but by then all the sailors had perished. Putin took personal blame for the accident, but after an official inquiry in 2001, he demoted Klebanov to be minister of industry, science and technology (the fellow St. Petersburg city administration employee would, however, become Putin's plenipotentiary to the Northwestern Federal District in 2003) and forcibly retired fourteen senior naval officers in one day. Russia had commissioned a world-class attack submarine but had no deep-sea rescue capability. Russia had innumerable senior military officers, but evidently none of them would tell the commander in chief that the situation was dire.

Also in August the country was left without nationwide television for hours when the Ostankino television tower in Moscow caught fire and no one would authorize the electricity to be turned off so that the firefighters could get into the tower. The request for authorization went all the way up the by now well-functioning "vertical of power" until Putin himself gave the order to turn off the electricity. Later in his presidency, analysts became used to speaking about the phenomenon of "manual control"—meaning Putin himself had to get involved to solve any issue—but clearly this hesitation to take personal responsibility, so much a feature of Soviet society, was once again fully on display.

Putin's major problem in 2000 was in combating the negative public reaction to his handling of these events, especially the *Kursk*, which led to a 10 percent drop in support for him in the polls. Andrey Kolesnikov noted, "You needn't be Gleb Pavlovskiy or anyone else to understand that vacationing at . . . [his residence in Sochi] during the national disaster would threaten the political health and rating of the president."[71] The contrast between state-owned and independent media coverage of Putin's reaction to the crisis could not have been starker. And foreign media overwhelmingly rebroadcast the negative views of the independent media, leading to a dip in international regard for Putin's leadership only months after his inauguration. The NTV journalist Vladimir Kara-Murza subsequently remarked that independent television's handling of the *Kursk* ended the lull in the fight between Putin and the media barons: "Putin was annoyed when NTV journalists took such a lively interest in the *Kursk* tragedy. It showed him that the media would report what they wanted unless they were put under control. The episode left Putin nervous of the media."[72]

In a subsequent meeting with journalists, Putin admitted, "I probably should have returned to Moscow, but nothing would have changed. I had the same level of communication both in Sochi and in Moscow, but from a PR point of view I could have demonstrated some special eagerness to return."[73] But in the immediate aftermath of the disaster, he was much less self-reflective about his own actions and much more vicious in blaming the press and the oligarchs, especially ORT and Berezovskiy, for the crisis. He stated publicly, "The people on television, who for ten years were destroying the army and the navy, where people are now dying, are the first among the army's defenders. . . . They want to influence the mass audience in order to show the military and political leadership that we need them, that we are on their hook and must fear and obey them, and let them further rob the country, the army and the navy." [74]

In his sworn written witness statement in the 2011–12 *Berezovskiy v. Abramovich* trial, Berezovskiy recounts a remarkable meeting with Putin at this time in which the oligarch defended ORT's coverage of the disaster as "entirely proper and that the openness of the coverage actually helped him [Putin] because it demonstrated that he was not seeking to censor the media. President Putin listened to what I had to say. After I had finished, he produced a file. He then read from it. I do not recall his exact words, but the gist of what he said was that both ORT and I were corrupt. He also accused me of hiring prostitutes to pose as the widows and sisters of sailors killed aboard the *Kursk* to attack him verbally. These allegations were completely untrue and I told President Putin this." Berezovskiy claimed that Putin told him point-blank to sell his shares or face imprisonment. [75] Presidential Administration Chief of Staff Voloshin confirmed in his own witness statement at the trial that the meeting between Putin and Berezovskiy had taken place and had failed to achieve a break in the impasse. [76] ORT's coverage had shown women who were truly the agonized relatives of sailors lost in the frigid northern seas, although to be sure, it also brutally counterposed those pictures with shots of Putin relaxing *on the water* in the subtropical south.

Against the backdrop of the intensely negative media coverage he received in August over his handling of the *Kursk* tragedy, Putin announced in September that in response to the "false information on the activities of the federal authorities," he was putting in place an Information Security Doctrine that would increase state control over the media. [77] "Information pollution" was undermining national security, and henceforth the state would have the right to limit the circulation not only of military and security data but also any political, economic, or environmental information deemed crucial to national security. It goes without saying that journalists circulating such information would be liable to espionage charges.

Putin's own role in the fight against the media was further indicated by the early involvement of Abramovich as his envoy, authorized to make Berezovskiy an offer he ultimately could not refuse. Initially Putin had been unable to wrest control of Berezovskiy's ORT television network even after Berezovskiy left the country, and Putin had to take the fight abroad. In an interview with French journalists in October he took advantage of his first trip to France, where Berezovskiy was living in exile, to threaten that if the oligarchs didn't give up their control of the mass media, the Russian state would swing a cudgel (*palitsa*) and "clinch the argument with one fell swoop. But we have not used it yet, we are simply holding it in our hands, and that has had some resonance already. But if we are provoked, we will have to use it."[78]

As 2000 drew to a close, Putin's first order of business was to work with and through Abramovich to get Berezovskiy to divest his shares in ORT. Abramovich's role was critical because Putin wanted to uphold the principle of private ownership in theory while ensuring that the next private owner would be wholly loyal to the Kremlin in practice. Thus Abramovich got the green light from Putin and worked with Voloshin to pressure Berezovskiy to sell his shares in ORT.

In the 2011 *Berezovskiy v. Abramovich* trial, the loyal Abramovich himself confirmed many details of Putin's involvement: "If the President would say that it's not recommended for me to buy the shares or if Mr. Voloshin would say that it's not recommended to buy the shares, I would not buy them. It's quite an explosive product, these ORT shares, I mean their impact, so that's why I didn't want to play any part in it at all. If I would have felt that someone is against it, I wouldn't touch it with a bargepole."[79] A number of failed meetings were held in late autumn; then, on December 6, after Berezovskiy's second-in-command in Russia, Nikolay Glushkov, was summoned to the Procurator General's Office and faced arrest, Berezovskiy again agreed to meet. This meeting, between Berezovskiy, his partner Badri Patarkatsishvili, and Abramovich, took place in Paris and was secretly recorded by Patarkatsishvili.* The transcript of the meeting was validated by both sides and entered into the record in the trial. In it, it is clear that Abramovich was Putin's agent. At the trial Abramovich was asked about the transcript: "This is you telling Mr. Patarkatsishvili that he doesn't have to be concerned about being arrested and you refer to a conversation you had with President Putin in which he said that Mr. Patarkatsishvili had nothing to fear and that he was free to visit Russia." Abramovich answered, "Yes I can see that and remember it."[82] Abramovich agreed that he "had spoken to President Putin and he has said that if the sale of ORT could be achieved quietly and he was kept out of it, then he would not stand in the way of money being paid to Mr. Berezovskiy." For Putin the issue was not money, but media control. As he told Abramovich, the financial arrangements were "nothing to do with me. Do it between yourselves. This is your private business." Taking his cue, Abramovich tried to get Berezovskiy to sign the agreement of divestiture promptly: "Should we sign then so that I could take it to Vladimir Vladimirovich [Putin], show it to him and say: here you are, the deal is done . . . ?"[83]

Despite this pressure, no written agreement was signed, and indeed the next day, December 7, Glushkov was arrested in Moscow. In response, a furious Berezovskiy spoke live to a Moscow radio station: "This is pure blackmail. Blackmail against me. And it is blackmail in the best KGB tradition, so to speak. In other words, the president said that he would bash my head with a cudgel. The cudgel turned out to be too short; he cannot reach me here. So he started hitting people close to me. In other words, it is in the

---

*Arkadiy "Badri" Patarkatsishvili was involved in Georgian and Russian politics and both licit and illicit business in his own right. He took credit for arranging for Putin to be hired by Pavel Borodin in 1996. He said that in 1996 Putin had called him twice a day to beg him to help get him a job in Moscow after Sobchak's defeat, and that he had gone to Borodin, asking for "this intelligent guy to be transferred to the financial-control administration." This conversation was recorded at the end of December 2007 between Patarkatsishvili and the Georgian interior minister and was part of a larger scandal that rocked Georgian politics in early 2008.[80] Patarkatsishvili remained on good terms with Putin until 2001, when he was accused of trying to organize the escape of Nikolay Glushkov from prison. Patarkatsishvili fled Russia at this time for Georgia, where he tried to enter politics, putting up a poor showing against Mikheil Saakashvili—not least because he campaigned entirely from abroad— in the January 2008 elections. He died of a heart attack at the age of fifty-two near London on February 12, 2008.[81]

very worst tradition: blackmailing someone by putting pressure on their relatives, their associates, their friends. . . . I believe it makes absolutely no sense to struggle on against such risks—not risks to me personally, but to my friends and family. Therefore I will decide within the next two . . . days."[84] Berezovskiy, Patarkatsishvili, and Abramovich met again, and this time they agreed on a deal that would transfer ownership to Abramovich. At the trial Abramovich made it very clear that Putin had no financial interest in the deal but only sought to get rid of Berezovskiy's influence over the media:

> Q[uestion]: The reason you were acquiring ORT was because President Putin wanted Mr. Berezovskiy to give up the shares in ORT and you were assisting President Putin in achieving that end?
> A[bramovich]: President Putin didn't want the shares. It was not the shares that he wanted. He wanted Mr. Berezovskiy and Mr. Patarkatsishvili to leave management of the company and relinquish control, stop influencing the content of the programmes. The papers [referring to the fact that Putin was willing to allow the newspapers owned by Berezovskiy to continue expressing an independent point of view] in themselves weren't that necessary.[85]

Later, on the same day, Abramovich clarified his role as an instrument of Putin's struggle against Berezovskiy:

> Q: You had promised President Putin to get the deal done by the end of the year; that's right, isn't it?
> A: . . . I promised that once the deal is closed, I would inform him. I don't remember if I told him that directly or via Mr. Voloshin. But I did say: when I finish the deal, I will inform.[86]

After Berezovskiy signed over his shares in ORT, Abramovich immediately transferred control to state-appointed executives. This campaign against NTV and ORT had started within forty-eight hours of Putin's inauguration; everything forecast in the secret document on the reform of the Presidential Administration had come to pass.

The Final Agenda Item: Putin's Escape from Prosecution

Putin's Kremlin in 2000 was involved in implementing plans to institute a "vertical of power" that would suppress opposition, control the mass media, diminish federalism, and remove the legislature as a source of independent activity. In addition 2000 was an extremely important year for Putin in suppressing prosecutions against him that still loomed. These have been dealt with extensively in a previous chapter, but it is worth revisiting what happened with these cases as Putin took over the presidency. Putin's emergence as acting president was like a call to arms for those democrats, procurators, and opposition politicians who knew him from his St. Petersburg days and sought to make last-ditch efforts to stymie his rise—all for naught.

Marina Sal'ye joined opposition forces in 2000 to call attention to Putin's behavior in the food scandal but was driven into hiding, where she remained for twelve years. Only after her death in 2012 were the documents about the scandal released, but by then Putin had begun a third, now six-year term. U.S. officials put Russia on an international money-laundering blacklist in 2000 allegedly as a result of Putin's links to SPAG. But he resigned from the board, and after the case finally went to court in Liechtenstein in 2003, his name was quietly forgotten.

The criminal investigation of Putin's involvement in Twentieth Trust (No. 144128), which allegedly used St. Petersburg city funds to build private residences in Spain, and Putin's personal involvement in supervising these constructions, exploded on to the Spanish, and then Russian media, during Putin's first trip there in 2000. By then, *Novaya gazeta* bemoaned, the Ministry of Finance documents verifying the activities of Twentieth Trust had been scooped up by "intelligence agencies who have tried to hide them from prying eyes," although the newspaper claimed it had "the most comprehensive" version available publicly (the paper has a reputation for extensive files it has threatened to publish if Kremlin pressure is used).[87]

But the investigative team was broken up in Russia, and when the Spanish authorities declined to pursue the case, it fizzled, at least until one of the investigators involved, Andrey Zykov, resurfaced in 2012.

The investigation of bribe-taking by the top leadership of the St. Petersburg city government, including Putin (Case No. 18/238278–95) was ended by order of the procurator general on August 30, 2000. Investigator Zykov's subsequent civil suit against Putin was rejected by the Kremlin, which asserted that a sitting president could not be party to a trial.

In the case of Mabetex, Putin had granted Yel'tsin and his family members immunity as his first presidential decree, but the role of others was still subject to legal scrutiny. The procurator general's case was very quietly dropped on December 13, 2000, "for lack of evidence" despite the nineteen thousand pages of documentation, including thousands of pages submitted by the Swiss.[88] Although the Swiss pursued the case and ultimately fined Borodin $177,000 for money laundering, he was allowed to return to Russia, where his lawyers announced he would not appeal his conviction since he did not "recognize the court's jurisdiction" anyway.[89] In 2000, Putin named him as the State Secretary of the Russian-Belarusian Union, giving him diplomatic immunity. The threats by Felipe Turover, the whistleblower in Switzerland who had started the whole Mabetex affair, to "turn the Yel'tsin-gate into Putin-gate"[90] did not materialize when the Russians issued an international arrest warrant for Turover for various petty crimes, including failure to pay his rent in Moscow.[91] Kremlin threats of an "asymmetrical response" to any attacks on the president were certainly fulfilled in these cases.

Kremlin, Inc. and the "Never-Ending Presidency"

After Putin's July 2000 meeting with the assembled oligarchs, Boris Nemtsov declared, "The era of the oligarchs is over."[92] In the period after this, the oligarchs did not know how to behave. They knew there were new rules, and they knew that Putin was establishing his power and authority over them, both by destroying Gusinskiy and then Berezovskiy as demonstration effects and by expecting them to pay tribute. Åslund writes, "Two oligarchs told me that when an oligarch was called to see one of the top figures in the

Kremlin, he was asked to put up $10 million or $20 million in 'donations,' either for Putin's reelection campaign or for some charitable purpose. In the Yel'tsin period, Mayor Luzhkov had persuaded the Moscow oligarchs to 'donate' $500 million to the reconstruction of the Christ the Savior Cathedral. Now, Putin attracted $300 million in 'donations' for the reconstruction of the Konstantinov Palace in St. Petersburg. . . . The Kremlin treated the oligarchs as its self-service boutiques. A few major businessmen were rumored to make large-scale payments of hundreds of millions of dollars to the corporations belonging to Putin's circle in St. Petersburg."[93] As a consequence many of the oligarchs began to spend more and more time abroad, according to Åslund, so as not to be called back to the Kremlin.

Among Putin's new circle were Sergey Kolesnikov and Dmitriy Gorelov, the owners of Petromed, the Petersburg-based medical supplies company established in the early 1990s, and Nikolay Shamalov, who was an Ozero Cooperative cofounder and the representative in northwestern Russia of Siemens, the giant German conglomerate. Since Putin had a relationship

Sergey Kolesnikov, on far right, with Nikolay Shamalov and Dmitriy Gorelov (center left and center right), whom he accused of using profits from state projects to help build a mansion later dubbed "Putin's palace." http://www.reuters.com/investigates/russia/#article/part1

with Petromed in the 1990s and this relationship flourished and grew in the 2000s, analyzing it provides a window into the way the Putin Kremlin has functioned.

Putin's Committee for Foreign Liaison had been a 51 percent co-owner of Petromed almost from the beginning, but the city government had withdrawn its support once Putin left for Moscow. Having established themselves with Petromed, Gorelov and Kolesnikov became major shareholders in Bank Rossiya as well as the Vyborg shipyards. Now that he was president, Putin wanted to work once again with Petromed and Shamalov, this time on a nationwide scale.

Kolesnikov subsequently left the country and became a whistleblower about Kremlin corruption, writing an open letter to President Medvedev asking him to intervene to stop the massive corruption that he maintains had led to the diversion of funds to build Putin a $1 billion palace in the south of the country. The story, which broke in the *Washington Post*,[94] went viral, as workers at the palace site also posted extensive images of the almost-finished construction, replete with pictures of a gilded double-headed eagle, the Russian state emblem, over the entry gates, and a worker sitting in what appears to be a replica of the presidential office.*

Russian and Western journalists took the investigation further, seeing the palace as a tangible sign of Putin's "crony capitalism." Kolesnikov provided extensive documents purporting to show how the scheme functioned. He explained that 2000 was a decisive year: early that year, Shamalov came to Petromed "with the offer from . . . Putin to provide funding for a number of major contracts in the field of public health. . . . Shamalov said that Putin had summoned him to his home to discuss certain business opportunities related to the fact that he, Putin, had become president. As Shamalov told Kolesnikov and Gorelov, the condition of the funding for these contracts which Putin was awarding was that 35% of

---

* Pictures originally appeared on the Russian Wikileaks site, RuLeaks.net,[95] but this site came under a denial-of-service attack. However, by that time, the pictures had spread throughout the Internet, and those presented here were posted on many sites on Google and Wikicommons.

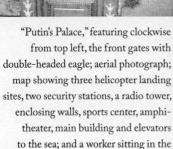

"Putin's Palace," featuring clockwise from top left, the front gates with double-headed eagle; aerial photograph; map showing three helicopter landing sites, two security stations, a radio tower, enclosing walls, sports center, amphitheater, main building and elevators to the sea; and a worker sitting in the office. Source: RuLeaks.net

the contract amount be put in foreign accounts. We were told that these contracts would be financed by oligarchs ready to make donations to the new president. The money accumulated in foreign accounts would come back and be invested in the Russian economy under the direct supervision of Putin."[96] They agreed—after all, in their understanding of the scheme, the money was coming not from the Russian state but from oligarchs who were told this would be the price of doing business from here on out. And the money was going to be rerouted for much-needed projects in Russia.

According to the contract provided by Kolesnikov,* Roman Abramovich was the first one asked; he pledged $203 million for the renovation of the Military Medical Academy in St. Petersburg but sought reassurances that the money would be used only for this purpose. Kolesnikov asked Abramovich directly whether Putin was behind this scheme, and Abramovich confirmed that the money had indeed been "donated" by him "on request."[97] Kolesnikov stated that Abramovich had himself confirmed the 35 percent rate with Putin, whom they referred to as "Mikhayl Ivanovich" among themselves.[98][†]

According to investigations by the *Financial Times* in 2012 and Reuters in 2014, equipment for the renovation was bought from Siemens, with

---

*I am in possession of the documents provided by Kolesnikov that were posted on his site Corruptionfreerussia.com before it was taken down and they can be viewed at www.miamioh .edu/havighurstcenter/putins-russia.

† Kolesnikov claims that within this tight circle, they all called each other by nicknames: Yuri Koval'chuk was known as Kosoy or "Cross-eyed"; Timchenko as Gangren or "Gangrene"; Miller as Soldat or "Soldier"; Kozhin as Tuzhurka or "Double-breasted Jacket"; Zolotov as Generalissimo; and Shamalov as Professor Preobrazhenskiy or "Professor of the Transfiguration," presumably after the central character in Bulgakov's *Heart of a Dog* who transforms a stray dog into a human. Of Putin's closest circle only Gorelov did not have a nickname.[99] As to the lifestyle of those within this group, Kolesnikov said in his interview with Al'bats that it was exactly as it had been described by Nataliya Vetlitskaya, a popular singer, who wrote in her LiveJournal blog of her experience singing before "the czar." In that account, which she calls a "fairytale," top artists were invited to perform free of charge, singing in front of only a handful of formally dressed guests who were waited on by servants in Catherine the Great–style costumes. When the performance was over, they were told to stay because the dinner group might like to sing with the performers. They were then each awarded prizes; one was given a People's Artist of Russia award, others were given a clock or jewelry. One was given an icon, and when the artist asked the tsar to sign it, he hesitated, thinking it might not be appropriate, but then decided that nothing could be more appropriate than the tsar signing an icon, and he signed. Vetlitskaya stated, "We 'wept' about what had just happened to put it mildly."[100] She didn't identify "the czar" as Putin, but when the "fairytale" exploded on the Internet, other commentators certainly did.[101] There was a similar account of a private 2009 concert given by a British ABBA cover band in an official compound in Valdai. The invitation referred to the host as "the #2 person in Russia," and the accompanying photograph showed a person who looked like Putin. With him were a "Miss X" in a long cream dress and only six other guests. While the band was obliged to perform behind a bizarre gauze curtain and were forbidden to have any conversation with the audience, they claimed that the eight exuberantly danced along with the songs. Their account was provided to the *Guardian* but was denied by the Kremlin.[102]

Shamalov as its representative, through U.K.-registered companies. The intermediary companies were co-owned directly or indirectly by Kolesnikov, Gorelov, and Shamalov. Equipment was sold by Siemens to the intermediary companies, where, according to Kolesnikov, "profits could be made," and only then delivered to Petromed, owned by Gorelov and Kolesnikov.[103] As was the case with intermediary companies in the gas industry, normally the existence of such companies suggests there is profit skimming all along the way. Kolesnikov claims that despite Abramovich's efforts to ensure transparency, providing funds only with the proper invoices from Siemens, $85 million nevertheless went to offshore companies. Kolesnikov insisted that these weren't kickbacks—"We were just able to buy for lower than the price list"—that they were taking advantage of deep discounts by the suppliers, but evidently they did not return to Abramovich the difference between the list price and the supplied price.[104] Since Siemens ultimately admitted to making corrupt payments to Russian officials for the purchase of medical devices, it appears that in order to achieve and maintain market share, Siemens was additionally willing to pay bribes.* According to bank transfers provided by Kolesnikov, in February 2002 EM&PS, a UK-domiciled company co-owned by Kolesnikov, Gorelov and Shamalov, transferred $85 million to Rollins International, registered in the British Virgin Islands. Kolesnikov claims that Gorelov and Shamalov used the money to buy a 12.6 percent stake in Bank Rossiya, but not before Rollins paid dividends on their investments of $22.3 million for Gorelov and $21.8 million for Shamalov, according to copies of the payments also referenced by the *Financial Times*.[106] Kolesnikov estimated that by 2007 almost $500 million had been gathered abroad just in Petromed-related offshore companies run by Shamalov, drawn from donors who were essentially paying tribute to Putin in return for being allowed to do business in Russia.[107] While this Petromed-related money was used also to fund development projects, and since it came from oligarchs who had paid their taxes,

---

* Shamalov was no longer retained by Siemens after the Siemens settlement under the U.S. Foreign Corrupt Practices Act.[105]

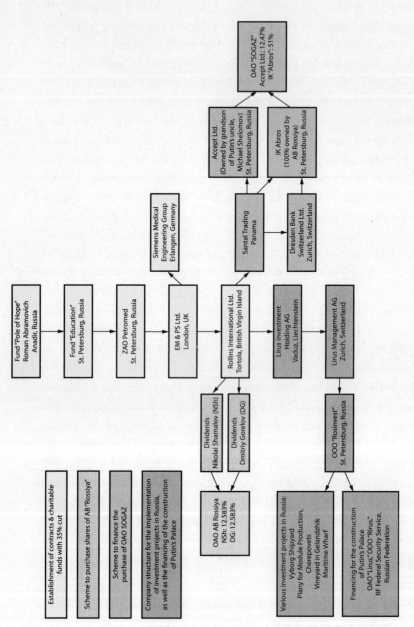

Cash Flow Scheme

Source: Sergey Kolesnikov

Note: OAO AB Rossiya is Bank Rossiya, and Dresden Bank, Switzerland Ltd., is Dresdner Bank.

Kolesnikov had no principled objection to it until the money began being diverted for "Putin's Palace."

Kolesnikov's documents indicated there were transfers from Rollins into another offshore company called Rosinvest. He alleged that Rosinvest "was set up in 2005 on Vladimir Putin's instructions conveyed through his friend Nikolay Shamalov." [108] Kolesnikov claimed that Putin owned 94 percent of the shares, and Shamalov, Gorelov, and Kolesnikov owned 2 percent each—all in bearer shares—in Rosinvest,* which was capitalized with an initial $200 million. [110] Kolesnikov said he was informed by Shamalov and Gorelov that they had given Putin his bearer shares and that Putin had placed these in a safe: "The situation was specially done in such a way that nowhere would be anyone's signatures." [111] After its founding in October 2005, the capital in Rosinvest rose, according to Kolesnikov, to 2 billion rubles in 2007 and 5 billion by 2009. [112] Rosinvest then made payments to another company, Lirus, which the *Financial Times* confirmed was named in a 2005 contract as a co-investor in "Putin's Palace," "together with the Kremlin's property department. Documents also show Lirus making payments to the presidential guard service for construction work on the same numbered contract." [113]

In a recording released by Kolesnikov, he and Shamalov are holding a meeting in 2009 in Rosinvest's office in Petersburg and are talking about Putin, whom they refer to as "Mikhayl Ivanovich," and his investments in Rollins (parentheses in the original):

---

*A bearer share is an equity security wholly owned by whoever holds the physical stock certificate. The issuing firm neither registers the owner of the stock, nor does it track transfers of ownership. The company disburses dividends to bearer shares when a physical coupon is presented to the firm. Bearer shares allow the greatest anonymity of ownership except for cash. Ownership can be transferred by simply handing the bearer shares to another party. In theory ownership of bearer shares is not subject to legal registration. However, OECD pressures have over time limited the free and anonymous transfer of bearer shares, so that by 2013 only Panama, Seychelles, Marshall Islands, and Antigua still offered true bearer shares. Thus, as one website specializing in tax havens suggested, "it is enough to incorporate an offshore corporation in a traditional tax haven and to register the yacht, the property, etc. in its name. If you want to sell it again, the buyer is just given the bearer shares, thereby changing the company's ownership and with it the asset in its name. It is an immediate transfer, and best of all, there are no records, notaries nor taxes to pay." [109]

Sergey Kolesnikov (hereafter—SK): In Rollins, what kind of money
        did they lay out?

Nikolay Shamalov (NS): Here's the list.

SK: Is this ours? Or Mikhayl Ivanovich's?

NS: Mikhayl's (Ivanovich) . . . (An argument breaks out
        about what part of the money lying in the Rollins' off-
        shore account in the British Virgin Islands belongs to
        "Mikhayl (Ivanovich)" and which part the other partners
        of Rosinvest).

NS: This is Mikhayl (Ivanovich's) money—this they know.

SK: Mikhayl (Ivanovich's) money is 439,968,000 (U.S.). This
        is Mikhayl (Ivanovich's) money.[114]

In an interview with the *Washington Post* Kolesnikov said that Putin was
briefed regularly on his hidden wealth: "Two or three times a year, during
8 years, at Shamalov's direction, I prepared financial summaries for him
to personally update President Putin on his investments. . . . Immediately
following each of these meetings, Shamalov would provide me with Putin's
comments and instructions for the use of funds."[115]

Petromed appears to have played a significant role in running Putin's tribute system, according to recordings made at Petromed offices in St. Petersburg and released to the *New Times* in 2012. In one conversation, which
Kolesnikov said was between Gorelov and Shamalov, they recount a meeting between Putin and Ziyad Manasir.* They say that Manasir had been
asked for a "gift" of "250 million," whether dollars or rubles is not known,
and that he had told Putin, "Vladimir Vladimirovich, if you say so, I will
give." Later, when they followed up with Manasir on the progress of his giving, he reassured them, "I want to give a gift, I want to give a gift." "Voice
one" (presumably Shamalov) tells Gorelov, "I said to him: 'Do it and it will
be engraved in gold letters that this was all from you! And the leadership will

---

* Manasir is a Jordanian-born businessman who heads Stroygazkonsalting, one of the main contractors of Gazprom. *Forbes* put his wealth at $2.5 billion as of March 2013, making him num-
ber 41 among the wealthiest people in Russia.[116]

know that you did all of this, all of this is from your money, your gift.'" The "Second Voice" (presumably Gorelov) says, "He has another idea: He will build it all for free, on the condition that he will receive other orders."[117]*

Kolesnikov continued to run Petromed, but ultimately he became a whistleblower against what he documented was a massive diversion of funds by the Kremlin to build "Putin's Palace." He told the *Washington Post* that the $1 billion cost came from a "combination of corruption, bribery and theft."[119] Construction of the Palace began in the early 2000s, and by 2005 it had become a $16 million project. But then "in 2006 we won the right to host the Olympics. And by then the entire perspective changed. Prior to 2006, an endless presidency had not been planned. The idea of finding ways and means to extend the leadership of the country was in general a project of the 2004–6 period." In line with this, the seaside mansion became a palace, one indeed fit for this "never-ending presidency." As part of the expansion, they made an order to transfer the land from protected forest to nonforest designation on October 4, 2005, in Order No. 1575-g; they then used federal money to upgrade roads and bridges, install high-voltage power lines and gas pipelines, and install secure governmental communication lines.[120] They added three helipads, a marina, private beach, summer house, guest and servant quarters, a winter theater, amphitheater, extensive recreational facilities, and a vineyard—twenty buildings in total within a massive private reserve. After the 2008 financial crisis, the amount of money left to spend on other projects shrank as all available funds were diverted to "Project South," as it came to be called. Despite the fact that Zolotov's Presidential Security Service was allegedly responsible for providing security and the Presidential Property Management Department for supervising the building,† the palace was formally

---

* This was not the first time Manasir was involved in building palaces. *Forbes* Russia revealed that in 2004 he built a 3,200-square-meter eighteenth-century-style palace on the outskirts of Moscow at the request of Gazprom for use in official and semiofficial events, but after the 2008 crisis it was abandoned and Manasir was left holding the property.[118]

† PPMD chief Kozhin ultimately admitted the Kremlin's involvement when he said in an interview that his office was contracted by Lirus to carry out the contract for the construction of the palace.[121]

in Shamalov's name. Whereas in the early period of building, the funds had largely come from "charitable contributions"—that is, tributes—from the offshore accounts of oligarchs like Abramovich eager to continue doing business with the Kremlin, the 2014 investigation by Reuters[122] showed that the burden of paying for the palace shifted to the taxpayer when the sums required exceeded even the ability of oligarchs to pay. Considering the fact that the palace was to be listed formally as a *private* residence, Russia had never before seen the skimming of state funds for private purposes on such a grand scale (see page 300).[123]

When the money was diverted to the palace, thousands of Petromed and RosModulStroy* workers in Russian factories building German-designed modular units for health clinics were put out of work. This was the final straw for Kolesnikov. He sums up the frustration many felt with the Putin presidency as it wore on: "It turns out that you worked for so many years and gave your strength, knowledge, energy and a whole part of your life— for what? For the sake of this building on the shore? That will be visited three, four, five times a year . . . ? It is such an insult."[126]

Closing the Circle

That such bold moves were taken within the first weeks of Putin's inauguration shows, in retrospect, that Putin had a clearly conceived strategy coming into the presidency for how he would deal with wayward press and

---

*One of the projects that Gorelov, Shamalov, Kolesnikov, and Rosinvest were involved in was the establishment of LLC RosModulStroy, founded in December 2006 to participate in the construction of fourteen regional centers for cardiovascular surgery. These centers were to be made of modules produced by the German company Cadolto, imported to Russia, and then assembled there at a plant in Cherepovets in a 1-billion-ruble plant. While reports suggested that a huge amount of money, in this case from federal and regional budgets, was spent, there were no reports of centers opening. After Kolesnikov left the country with documents about "Putin's Palace," RosModulStroy's board, chaired by Shamalov, voted to transfer their assets to another company, called ZERS, and then declared RosModulStroy's bankruptcy. Gorelov accused his opponents of creating an "artificial" debt and an unjustified initiation of bankruptcy.[124] They were then charged with "fraud on a large scale" under Part 4 of Article 159 of the Criminal Code.[125] If it is true, as Kolesnikov charged, that Putin himself owned 96 percent of the shares of Rosinvest, then he was able to personally benefit from the award of millions in state contracts.

disobedient oligarchs. As the phrase goes, "For our friends, anything; for our enemies, the law!" (famously attributed to Brazilian president Getulio Vargas, who ruled with military backing from 1930 to 1954). Putin's Ozero friends, St. Petersburg coworkers, and *siloviki* colleagues moved from a position of influence in one city to take up positions of influence throughout the economic and political structures of the country, and beyond. In the 1990s a major reason the excesses in privatization were allowed by the liberal reformers and their Western supporters was their belief that over time corrupt activities would give way to licit activities—initial ill-gotten gains would give way to the rule of law and ultimately good government as the new wealthy class sought to use law rather than violence to enforce contracts. Ordinary Russians voted for Putin precisely because they yearned for good government. But those who arrived with him pressured for and benefited from a new set of arrangements: not lawlessness, but not rule of law either—more like the rule of understandings or the rule of rules. And rule number one would be that the law would be applied only to someone who had broken the Kremlin's internal rules—the guarantee of impunity before the law was the primary benefit of maintaining loyalty.

While benefiting from this regime inside Russia, the same elite established bank accounts in every conceivable tax haven abroad where their gains could be safeguarded. In the years after Putin was elected it became apparent that the new Russian elite had concluded they could increase and sustain their gains by first maintaining weak rule of law in Russia, thus allowing them to maximize their profits through predation and raiding and then by investing these gains in strong rule-of-law regimes in the West. They further ensured their own and their families' personal security by keeping their children and their property in Europe. Inside Russia they could guarantee themselves immunity by becoming members of the Federation Council or the Duma or honorary consuls for a foreign government in Russia.*

---

*The status of honorary consul is governed by the Vienna Convention on Consular Relations of 1963, which lays out a consul's rights and responsibilities. In Russia businessmen and those around Putin have snatched up these positions because, as outlined on the website of the League of Honorary Consuls in Russia (Honoraryconsul.ru), Russian citizens who serve as honorary

When Putin became president in 2000, prosecutions against him were quietly dropped but not forgotten. Details became more widely known as his popularity was challenged in 2011 and 2012. For example, when the play *Berlusputin* opened in Moscow on February 14, 2012, the director Varvara Faer explained that one of the similarities between Berlusconi and Putin was their constant effort to escape criminal prosecution: "Putin was also under criminal investigation, which continued for half a year after he became president. But they decided that the president can't be under investigation, and the criminal case must be closed regardless of what Putin did and what happened when St. Petersburg was left without any food supply in the early 1990s and people were freezing and half starving. No one remembers this for some reason. And Berlusconi is also constantly slipping away from prosecution. . . . It's no accident that those two leaders are close friends." [129]*

Thus the kleptocratic aspects of the Putin regime were present from the outset and were part of the motivation to engage in such perilous activities. The entire period from late 1999 until summer 2000 was filled with the huge risk for the incoming elite that governors, journalists, outgoing elites, cultural and intellectual leaders, and big business would not accept this change of regime type. While there were undoubtedly levels of instability and uncertainty in the Yel'tsin era, there was also political, economic, and informational freedom, all of which was being brought under Putin's control. The extensive stories that started to appear in the Russian press immediately after Putin became acting president appear to have only heightened the sense of urgency to close down independent media. After

---

consuls are promised great benefits far in excess of the norm: "Consular officers are not subject to arrest or preventive detention. . . . [They have a] diplomatic passport and visa-free travel all over the world, . . . the right to bring three cars to the country without import duty, . . . the right to have a red diplomatic vehicle registration plate. . . . [The status] allows transfer of unlimited sums of money in cash across a border. . . . Luggage is not checked at customs." [127] The League's cofounders were close Putin associates and Ozero members Viktor Khmarin (who became honorary consul of the Seychelles in St. Petersburg), Sergey Fursenko (Bangladesh), Yuriy Koval'chuk (Thailand), and Taimuraz Bolloev (Brazil), who was head of St. Petersburg's Baltika brewery before taking over Olympstroy. [128]

*Wikileaks cables referenced not only Italy's strong interest in promoting Russia's energy interests but also close personal "and mutual commercial interests" between Putin and Berlusconi themselves. [130]

Putin presents a book about his rural lodge, Zavidovo, to Silvio Berlusconi, February 2003. Photo by Viktor Korotayev, AP

all, the *Reform of the Presidential Administration* document that was leaked in May 2000 has a clear directive about how to deal with journalists and opposition leaders who try to address Kremlin corruption: as noted earlier, the section "The Information War with the Opposition" contains detailed examples about how to preempt, suppress, and discredit opposition exposés about corruption in the Kremlin, with the threat that those who sling mud and start investigations against the president will "inevitably receive the same treatment."[131] One cannot find a pithier summary of the Kremlin's approach to such opposition forces as the anticorruption crusader Aleksey Navalnyy, who suffered a string of prosecutions beginning in 2012 on what he claimed were trumped-up charges, leading him to state, "I understand the logic of the authorities. They try to show everyone that if you do something not quite as they want, then they will terrorize you."[132]

Clearly Western governments were trying to decide what the bottom line on Putin was. On the one hand, he talked about rule of law; on the other, about dictatorship of the law. On the one hand, he criticized 1990s oligarchs in public; on the other, his own business activities were being monitored by the West, resulting in the United States placing Russia on a list of money-laundering countries as a result of their knowledge of his activities with SPAG. On the one hand, he talked about freedom of the press; on the other, he threatened to use cudgels to bring dissident voices into line. Needless to say, Western governments had a lot of information about the gap between Putin's global charm offensive and his private behavior and the behavior of his inner circle, as the Wikileaks documents and other sources of information have shown.

An example of the information the United States had about Putin's inner circle came from Sergey Tretyakov, who was the Russian foreign intelligence (SVR) station chief, or *rezident*, in New York City in 1995–2000 and who defected in late 2000. At the end of his first hundred days, Putin was looking forward to his first trip as president to the United Nations, and after the *Kursk* disaster he certainly did not want or need negative publicity. In August, in preparation for his UN speech, his security team flew to New York City. Yevgeniy Murov (director of the Federal Protection Service, Russia's Secret Service), Murov's deputy Aleksandr Lunkin, and Viktor Zolotov (head of Putin's presidential guard) personally went to approve the plans. There they met with Tretyakov, who was in charge of all SVR operations at the UN and in New York City. According to Tretyakov, Lunkin warned him to be wary of Murov and Zolotov: "They are common thugs." To illustrate, quoting from Tretyakov's account as told to the security affairs writer Pete Earley: "Lunkin said that he had been with both men in Moscow when Aleksandr Voloshin's name had been mentioned. Lunkin claimed that Murov and Zolotov had talked openly about Putin's feelings of jealousy toward Voloshin and the political power he wielded. Putin wanted to fire the 'Gray Cardinal,' but for political reasons couldn't. Lunkin told Sergey [Tretyakov] that Murov and Zolotov had suddenly begun discussing ways to murder Voloshin. One idea was to kill him and blame Chechen terrorists. Another was to make his execution appear to be a 'hit' by the Russian Mafia, the result of some sordid business deal gone bad. 'They were quite serious,' Lunkin assured Sergey. [But ultimately] they agreed that killing Voloshin would not end Putin's political problems. . . . Murov and Zolotov

Brighton Beach dinner, 2000. From the left, Viktor Zolotov, Yevgeniy Murov, Aleksandr Lunkin, Sergey Tretyakov. Earley, Pete. *Comrade J: The Untold Secrets of Russia's Master Spy in America After the End of the Cold War.* New York: G. P. Putnam's Sons, 2007, p. 299.

decided to make a list of politicians and other influential Muscovites whom they would need to assassinate to give Putin unchecked power. After the two men finished their list, Zolotov announced, *'There are too many. It's too many to kill—even for us.'* [133]

On the same trip, during a visit to a restaurant in Brighton Beach, Tretyakov claimed that Zolotov had boasted of the armaments and skills that the presidential guard possessed. Everyone was trained in advanced firearms and martial arts: "Without any warning, Zolotov suddenly swung his hand in the air and struck Sergey in his temple. The blow knocked him off his chair and unconscious on the café floor. Moments later, Sergey awoke with Murov and Zolotov standing over him. Murov was furious. 'You could have killed him!' he yelled. Zolotov began apologizing as he helped Sergey into a chair. 'Lunkin was correct,' Sergey said later after meeting Murov and Zolotov. 'They were dangerous. [At first] I didn't see a difference between Yel'tsin's people and these unsophisticates who were the president's closest friends.' " [134] Through Tretyakov, U.S. intelligence certainly had an early warning about the true nature of some of those surrounding Putin.

Zolotov's role would only increase under Putin. Anyone who watched the inauguration of Putin in 2012, when the Moscow streets were completely emptied of people and Zolotov's arrow-shaped phalanx, or *strelka*, of black armored cars carried the president through the eerily quiet city, understands the power that Zolotov possessed, the extent of the president's probably increased nervousness about his security after the 2011–12 demonstrations, and the obvious message from Putin to the residents of Moscow who had not voted for him as president: "This is my country and my city, and I can rule without you." [135] Zolotov was elevated to become the deputy minister of the interior in charge of the all internal troops and thus in a position to protect the regime. Tretyakov defected in October 2000, became a U.S. citizen, and died of a heart attack at the age of fifty-three at his home in Florida in 2010. [136] An FBI autopsy did not uncover any mysterious circumstances in his death. [137]

By the end of 2000 the major symbols of Russian statehood were in place. The tricolor had been adopted as the Russian flag, the tsarist double-headed eagle had been adopted as the state seal, and a slightly revised Soviet anthem had been approved as the new national hymn. But the fourth symbol had also been established: Putin himself. The Ministry of Defense ordered all military bases to display portraits of the president, a feature that had not been present under Yel'tsin. [138] Putinomania was stoked throughout the country, as state-owned media pictured Putin daily, meeting national and regional leaders and making an unprecedented number of foreign trips. Russia was once again a player on the international stage, to be respected and taken into account. If Putin wished it, cooperation with the United States would proceed, as occurred when the SALT II weapons treaty was finally ratified by the Duma on his recommendation. But if America pursued policies hostile to Russia, the Russian people could be assured that their president was ever-vigilant and would not allow decisions to be made on the international stage that did not take Russia's interests into account. In his speeches on foreign policy, Putin emphasized the trend toward competition with Western countries and with Western oil and gas companies in countries of the so-called near abroad, making it clear that Russia's influence would be exercised not only by the state but also by Russian oil and gas companies and marking the beginning of a major feature of Russian foreign policy in the Putin era.[139]

Putin also emerged as the hero and defender of Russia more broadly and of the security services in particular. He increased salaries of military and security service employees by 20 percent toward the end of the year. He gave medals to the pilots who buzzed the American aircraft carrier *Kitty Hawk* in October 2000, in the first such incident in what some called a new Cold War.[140] Counterintelligence services increased their surveillance and introduced the harassment of Americans inside Russia, resulting in the arrests in 2000 of Edmund Pope* on espionage charges and a Fulbright exchange student for marijuana possession. All of these activities were trumpeted in the Russian media and became part of Putin's allure, distracting attention from his slow implementation of economic measures and the continuing struggle in Chechnya. Poll figures showed that 48 percent of the population believed he had had an unsuccessful year generally, but this figure rose to 65 percent in the economic sphere. Yet he behaved as the undisputed Leader of the People. When a major national debate broke out in December 2000 over the choice of the new Russian anthem, Putin favored using the old Soviet version, with slightly updated words. Boris Yel'tsin came out of retirement to declare, "I am categorically against reinstating the USSR anthem as the state one."[142]† Putin was having none of it,

---

*Edmund Pope was a retired naval intelligence officer who was arrested in April 2000 in Moscow on charges of trying to obtain the blueprints for the Shkval torpedo (whose explosion evidently sank the *Kursk*). He was sentenced to twenty years in prison, the first American to be imprisoned in Russia for espionage in forty years. He was pardoned by Putin in December as "a present for the new president," George W. Bush, according to Vladimir Lukin, the former Russian ambassador to the United States.[141]

† Several writers have noted that Yel'tsin was completely absent from public life after his resignation. Irina Lesnevskaya, a noted television personality, said in an interview in 2007 that Yel'tsin was completely opposed not only to the introduction of the old anthem but also Putin's moves against the press, but had kept quiet, "perhaps out of a desire not to complicate the lives of his children and grandchildren."[143] Former prime minister Kas'yanov claimed that Putin had deliberately isolated Yel'tsin from his former staff and colleagues when he went into retirement and that he had been put into a "gilded cage." Initially he had taken an active interest in how things

justifying his preference by pointing to polls in which a majority of Russians supported the hymn. "Let's not forget that in this case we are talking about the majority of the people," he said, but slyly admitted, "I do allow that the people and I could be mistaken."[145] The Duma passed the package of symbols overwhelmingly.

Robust Kremlin measures against the media and opposition figures helped make Putin much more popular than any other contender—a strategy that has been used successfully since the beginning of his presidency. As the year ended, the new Russian Establishment, headed by Putin, had succeeded in promoting the key members of Putin's FSB and Petersburg circles to key positions to such an extent that astute observers were already calling it a "militocracy." The Russian sociologist Ol'ga Kryshtanovskaya estimated that over 58.3 percent of the Security Council and 32.8 percent of the government came from the *siloviki*, about 25 percent higher than the proportion of military and security elites in Yel'tsin's cohort in 1993.[146] In the meantime Putin had succeeded in chasing the powerful oligarchs Gusinskiy and Berezovskiy out of the country and erasing the investigations into his activities in the Russian courts. It had been a difficult but good year.

Putin's first year clearly demonstrated that the Kremlin, and the Kremlin alone, would be calling the shots. His close circle dominated all decision making, using whatever means necessary to constrain the oligarchs, stripping them of their assets and even imprisoning them if needed. Television was also firmly moving under Kremlin control. The regions had to submit to the seven presidential plenipotentiaries. Once these agenda items were achieved, the rest was relatively easy. And given that all of it was signaled and much of it accomplished in Putin's first hundred days, it should be registered as a singular achievement in the annals of authoritarian rule.

---

were going in the Kremlin and frequently invited former ministers to his dacha, Gorki-9. Then, according to Kas'yanov, at a meeting of the Security Council, Putin told them all, " 'Tell the members of the government not to unnecessarily bother Boris with visits. The doctors get angry, they say after these meetings he is worried, and he needs to rest, he still has a weak heart.' It was put in the form of a polite request, but in fact it was an order: don't go see Yel'tsin. . . . The last time I saw him was in the fall of 2006. . . . Boris advised me to constantly change my phones to avoid eavesdropping. 'Buy a lot of cheap phones. . . . Use one, and immediately dispose of it, take another, and then the next,' gesticulating excitedly, pretending to throw one from the car window."[144]

Chapter Seven

Russia, Putin, and the Future of Kleptocratic Authoritarianism

THE STORY of this book has been the emergence of the Putin cabal that took over Russia in 2000 and its structure, interests, and capabilities. It is by no means the wider story of Russia during that period, against whose background this group emerged. Nor is it the story of the Russian state as a whole, any more than a book about Nixon's White House can be read as an account of American politics in its entirety. Undoubtedly, however, the extensive and growing power of this group and the corruption that lies at the heart of the Russian state have had a singular effect on Russia's socio-economic development and on the nature of the Russian state. These issues and the phases that Putin's kleptocracy has gone through and its impact on the wider world are the subjects of this last chapter.

Corruption, Society, and the Economy

Russian society has had years of turbulence that produced decreased birth rates and increased mortality rates, especially among Russia's men. While Putin's early years brought greater social stability, this has eroded since the mid-2000s, so that by 2012 the 1.7 births per Russian woman, although slightly higher than previously (thanks to numbers from non-Russian republics like Chechnya, Dagestan, and Tuva), was still 20 percent below replacement level. Birth rates are not that different from European norms, but statistics on mortality rates are striking. The lack of adequate medical care produces five times more deaths from cardiovascular disease among women in Russia than in Europe. More Russian women die annually from domestic violence than the number of soldiers the USSR lost in the entire Afghan war. For Russian men, the situation is even grimmer. Poor workplace and road safety standards, plus high rates of suicide and homicide combine with the negative health effects of high alcohol consumption to make life especially precarious for Russian men. According to the World Health Organization, the life expectancy of a fifteen-year-old male is three years lower in Russia than in Haiti.[1] Added to these demographic maladies are the millions of Russians, mainly girls, that have been lost to sex trafficking. Russia's compliance with international conventions on human trafficking declined for nine straight years, and in 2013 the U.S. State Department finally gave Russia's compliance the lowest ranking possible, below Rwanda.[2]

These statistics are directly affected by corruption. When the health budget is raided and stolen, funds dry up for neonatal care, medicines to treat cancer, public health campaigns against HIV and drug-resistant tuberculosis, and improved emergency response. Russia committed to building its first eight-bed women's shelter in St. Petersburg, but by 2013 it still had not opened.[3] Despite receiving $1.6 trillion from oil and gas exports from 2000 to 2011, Russia was not able to build a single multi-lane highway during this time. There is still no interstate highway linking Moscow to the Far East; in contrast, China, another top-down authoritarian regime, has built 4,360 miles of modern highways annually for the last ten years—equivalent to two times around the circumference of the earth. The German-Russian Nord Stream (headed by Matthias Warnig, with Gerhard Schröder on the board) gas pipeline agreement signed in 2005 called for the construction of two pipelines linking Russia and Germany via deep-sea routes, bypassing troublesome states in central Europe. When the first pipeline was completed in July 2010, it was revealed that the construction cost was 2.1 million euros per kilometer on the German side and 5.8 million euros—three times higher—on the Russian side.[4] More than half of the $50 billion spent on the Sochi Olympics simply disappeared into the pockets of Putin's cronies, according to detailed analyses by multiple Russian experts.[5] *Forbes* Russia reported that over the two years prior to Sochi, when the Rotenberg brothers (Putin's childhood friends and judo partners) received 15 percent of all the contracts for the Olympics, the $2.5 billion increase in their personal wealth was achieved at the same time that the state announced it would cut health spending by 8.7 percent in 2013 and up to 17.8 percent by 2015.[6]

Russia scores high in overall education, but its economy is profoundly hamstrung by the relative lack of technological innovation. Despite the enormous reserve of talent in applied and theoretical sciences, Russia took home only 0.2 percent of the 1.3 million overseas patents awarded since 2000 by the U.S. Patent and Trademark Office, lagging behind the state of Alabama in total annual awards. Under the Patent Cooperation Treaty the number of Russian applications per university graduate was thirty-five times lower than Austria's.[7] The inability of well-trained young graduates to succeed as entrepreneurs and innovators in Russia has stimulated emigration and plans to emigrate. In 2011, during the more liberal Medvedev presidency, an online poll of 7,237 *Novaya gazeta* readers (what one might consider a microcosm of the country's educated, informed, and opposition-minded elite) found that 62 percent were considering leaving the country, the vast majority being under thirty-five, city dwellers, and fluent in a foreign language—a group that should be regarded as the cream of any country's population. Commenting on the results, the poll's author, Dmitriy Oreshkin, stated that this wave of Russian emigration is different from others in the past in that these young people could still come back because they are alienated from the regime, not the country: "If and when Russia will begin to comply with general law, and not only the rules of the KGB corporation, and accordingly there will be opportunities for self-realization, these people will return. They hated to leave. But here, they have nowhere to go, nothing to do, and nothing to hope for. For the last ten years, Russia has become a country only for those who are either the chief or a fool. And the transition from one category to another depends not on personal ability, but exclusively on loyalty."[8] Masha Gessen reported that the 2014 Ukraine events and the tightening of the domestic political noose so impacted educated Muscovites' sense of hopelessness that the new question was not whether or when to leave but "Which month?"[9]

This degradation of the socioeconomic situation was created by the political elite. When Transparency International announced in 2013 that Russia ranked 127th out of 177 countries in the level of corruption reported by respondents,[10] and when the Russian think tank Indem (Information Science for Democracy Fund) estimated already in 2005 that the amount paid annually in bribes is roughly equal to the size of the Russian budget, at approximately $300 billion,[11] it is fair to compare Russia with other super-corrupt countries. Looking only at one other major oil exporter, Nigeria, we see they are both near the bottom in the corruption perception index (see Table 3).

Table 3. Comparison of Russia's and Nigeria's Corruption and Human Development Indices

	Nigeria	Russia
Corruption Perceptions Index	144/177 Very corrupt	127/177 Very Corrupt
Control of Corruption Score	– .99	–1.07 Control of corruption worse in Russia than Nigeria
Bribe Payers Index	n/a	28/28 Last place among wealthiest countries
Human Development Index (HDI)	153/185 Low	55/185 High

Note: The Corruption Perceptions Index ranks countries based on how corrupt a country's public sector is perceived to be, based on expert and business surveys. The higher the number, the more corrupt the country is perceived to be by officials and experts in that country. The Control of Corruption score ranges from –2.5 to 2.5. Lower values correspond to worse governance outcomes. The Bribe Payers Index ranks the world's wealthiest countries according to the likelihood that their own firms will pay bribes abroad. Nigeria was not rich enough to be part of this cohort. Russia finished last. The Human Development Index is a composite measure of indicators along three dimensions: life expectancy, educational attainment, and command over the resources needed for a decent living.

Sources: United Nations, *Human Development Report* (United Nations Development Programme 2013); Transparency International, *Country Reports* for Nigeria and Russia (Transparency International 2013).

Both countries also rank low in the control of corruption, although shockingly the UN ranks Nigeria slightly better than Russia at controlling corruption. However, Russia ranks high in the Human Development Index, while Nigeria is low. This suggests that the country's slide into the abyss cannot be blamed on the Russian population. They have more than sufficient capabilities, as measured by the level of education and other socioeconomic indicators, to make substantial progress, but they are persistently hampered by elite predation that has dragged down economic growth, increased wealth inequality, and inhibited political freedoms.

It is a tragedy for Russia's talented population that the actions of their leaders have stymied development to the extent that they should be compared with much less developed countries. And average Russians know this. Transparency International's 2013 survey found that 77 percent of Russian respondents considered their government's anticorruption policies ineffective or very ineffective; 85 percent said that their government was run by a few big entities acting in their own best interests; 92 percent responded that corruption is a major problem in the public sector; and 89 percent felt that corruption in Russia had either stayed the same or gotten worse in the prior two years.[12]

When Putin gained the presidency a third time, in 2012, his first actions were not to reach out to those in society who might participate in the modernization of the country. Rather he cracked down on the freedoms required to build a civil society and an economy based on performance, not connections. The nonprofit sector was hit hard, with new laws requiring them to register as "foreign agents"; ordinary middle-class demonstrators with no previous record were imprisoned after the May 2012 Bolotnaya protests against electoral fraud; and new restrictions on the Internet threatened to completely eliminate the press freedoms that had largely already been driven from mainstream newspapers and television.

Perhaps the most surprising of the trends is the increase in the number of entrepreneurs arrested and imprisoned on tax evasion and other charges as part of a large-scale increase in the use of the corrupt criminal justice system as a vehicle for corporate raiding by regime insiders. In the ten years from 2002 to 2012, hundreds of thousands of businessmen were actually imprisoned, not just questioned or arrested, primarily as a result of rivals paying corrupt police, prosecutors, and judges to put away the competition.[13] Russian businessmen increasingly kept their money safe abroad, stimulating capital flight. Despite Putin's appointment of an ombudsman for business rights in 2012, the Kremlin's decision to proceed with the 2010 second trial of Mikhayl Khodorkovskiy on trumped-up charges that even the head of the Moscow Bar Association said were a "disgrace to justice" only added to this lack of business confidence.[14] Efforts by the new ombudsman, Boris Titov, to amnesty the 111,000 entrepreneurs who remained in prison in 2013 foundered on the Duma's insistence that no one amnestied could go free without paying damages or returning stolen property. But since most of the imprisoned claimed to have been framed and refused to pay what they said amounted to a further shakedown, all but 2,300 remained there.[15]

By 2014, as he marched into Crimea, Putin had clearly decided that he could maintain his power by ignoring the independent middle class, entrepreneurial interests, and the cultural elite. Instead he could rely on oil and gas extraction economically and on increased use of propaganda domestically to rally state workers and provincial populations. The main theme of this information war was anti-Americanism, the fight against "fascism" in Ukraine, the renewal of Russian greatness, and the distinctiveness of Russian values—as shown by the campaigns against Pussy Riot (the all-female punk rock band) and gay rights. The Kremlin has persistently portrayed the collapse of the Soviet Union as a defeat imposed on Russia by the West. And state-controlled media frames Putin not as the putative head of the party of "crooks and thieves," as the opposition politician Aleksey Navalnyy branded the ruling party United Russia prior to the 2011 Duma elections, but as the liberator of Russian lands and the head of a great civilization morally superior to gay-dominated and degraded Western culture.

As he reviewed the troops in Sevastopol, Crimea's capital, Putin set the tone by declaring that Crimea had seen three pivotal events in its history: its founding by Catherine the Great, its surviving 250 days of Nazi siege, and its rejoining Russia under his rule. In reunifying with Russia, Putin stated, Crimeans had expressed their loyalty to core values of "unity, fairness and togetherness . . . , thus remaining true to the historic truth and to our forefathers' memory." [16]

Putin's popularity in Russia soared above 80 percent as state-controlled television unleashed tirades against the West; public opinion polls showed that 90 percent of Russians considered the referendum in Crimea to be the result of the free will of the Crimean people,[17] despite evidence to the contrary. Putin endorsed the official results, that 83 percent of Crimean citizens turned out to vote and 97 percent voted in favor of annexation. These were the numbers trumpeted in the Russian media, although the president's own Council for the Development of Civil Society and Human Rights, headed by the human rights activist Mikhayl Fedotov, astonishingly declared that the actual numbers were quite different. The Council estimated that there was only a 30 to 50 percent turnout, and of those only 50 to 60 percent voted in favor of annexation. This provides a midpoint estimate of only 22.5 percent of registered voters favoring annexation. In other words, Putin's numbers showed 82 percent of Crimeans voting for annexation, while his own Human Rights Council's results showed only 22.5 percent voting in favor.[18] But this disparity did not make the headlines of Russia's state-controlled media, which was more than content to let the Kremlin simply create facts on the ground.

The country closed around Putin's promotion of revanchism abroad and conservatism at home. As for the urban middle class, the growth in the size of the state sector, ballooning to one-third of the entire Russian workforce, focused the country on the Kremlin's economic policy. In particular, young people were increasingly looking to the state for stable jobs; 36 percent of the entire workforce under the age of thirty had state jobs by 2009, as compared to 12 percent in OECD countries.[19] Those in the nonprofit sector who protested the turn toward authoritarianism in 2011–12 lost hope that they would be able to build any kind of free society and vibrant balanced economy in these conditions, and they started to pack their bags, spurred by news stories like that of the influential economist Sergey Guriyev, who fled to Paris. As head of the New Economic School, Guriyev was listed among the top one hundred experts connected to the Kremlin. Yet he was called in for repeated interrogations in early 2013, mainly over his testimony before the Human Rights Council that Khodorkovskiy's second trial had been politically motivated. The day before he was due to once again appear before the Investigative Committee of Putin's classmate Aleksandr Bastrykin, he "concluded that my next meeting with them could result in the loss of my freedom."[20] In an eerie echo of the 1930s, when the purges started, he stated, "A journalist from a state-owned news agency called and said that she had seen a press release about my arrest, dated the following day."[21] Putin's response to a question at a news conference about Guriyev's flight was classic: "[If Guriyev has] not violated anything, he is 100 percent safe. If he wants to come back, let him come back. If he wants to live in Paris, he's free to do so."[22] Such an admission that everyone is expendable stoked the numbers of people who expressed an interest in permanently leaving the country.[23]

By 2014 Russians had settled into a disturbing cycle. Only 5 percent felt that the Kremlin's new anticorruption efforts were serious or would succeed.[24] But at the same time, polls also showed a decrease in Russians' regard for Western-style democracy and institutions to 29 percent, following the spring events in Ukraine, which Putin and the Russian media portrayed as Western-inspired.[25] In 2014 Freedom House continued to negatively assess political rights and civil liberties in Russia that had started to slide as soon as Putin became president in 2000 (see Table 4).

Table 4. Freedom House Ratings of Freedom in Russia

	1999	2002	2006	2010	2014
Freedom	4.5	5.0	5.5	5.5	5.5
Civil Liberties	5	5	5	5	5
Political Rights	4	5	6	6	6
Status	Partly Free	Partly Free	Not Free	Not Free	Not Free

Notes: The ratings are based on a scale of 1 to 7, with 1 representing the highest level of democratic progress and 7 the lowest. Each score is an average of ratings for the subcategories tracked in a given year.

Source: Freedom House (2014).

This steady deterioration obviously did not come about accidentally but was the product of willful planning and steady execution from within the political elite. The rules governing elections have been changed bit by bit to become less inclusive of non-Kremlin-backed parties since Putin came to power. Alternative centers of power, whether parties, regions, or elites, have been relentlessly attacked and weakened. The media and the public space in general have become less and less tolerant of the free expression of ideas.

An increase in the sense of political hopelessness on the part of the vast majority occurred at the same time that Moscow vied with New York and London as the billionaire capital of the world. (Some of the New York and London billionaires were originally from Russia.)[26] In many countries the gap between rich and poor has grown in the past decade, but in Russia the gap is widest and the percentage of the country's wealth owned by the richest was the largest: 110 individuals, including Putin's cronies, control a staggering 35 percent of the country's wealth. Average household wealth has risen sevenfold since 2000, from $1,650 in 2000 to $11,900 in 2013, which sounds fabulous, but in 2013 median (midpoint) wealth in Russia was $871: that is, 50 percent of adults in Russia had total household wealth of $871 or lower. This was compared with median wealth of $90,252 in Canada—with one-quarter the population and roughly the same latitude as Russia, or $1,040 for India, which has a population almost ten times larger than Russia's and is an importer not exporter of oil.[27]

The increase in the gap between rich and poor has occurred at the same time that there has been an increase in the number of people seeking employment with the state. The growth in the size of the state, combined with a concomitant decline in the dynamic growth of the nonextractive sectors of the economy, has put a classic burden on the country. In states such as Saudi Arabia, where the economy relies on oil revenues, only a small percentage of the population is involved in the oil economy, and the state's coffers are the principal recipient of these revenues. Under such conditions, it is possible to see the inner workings of a sustainable nondemocratic political system: the government doesn't rely on taxes for its revenues, thereby decreasing the leverage the population has to demand change.

It is tempting to see Russia as one of these so-called rentier states. But is Russia really a classic rentier state?[28] Is the population so complacent? Typical rentier states do not have a vast pool of highly skilled professionals; most are nondiverse economies dependent on revenues from energy export. The Russian economy is becoming more dependent on energy exports as a percentage of the total, but between 25 and 35 percent of its export revenues still come from nonenergy sources—mainly military hardware—throughout the Putin period.[29] In Russia the percentage of the budget derived from oil and gas has certainly increased, from 30 to over 50 percent over the past decade, but it is still much less than the comparative figure of 92 percent in Saudi Arabia.

Russia is nevertheless tipping toward "the Dutch disease," in which an economy's overreliance on one source of income suppresses investment in other sectors. And this disease can also lead to a "resource curse," which the economist Guriyev described as "a trap, where democratic political and economic institutions do not develop because rents coming from natural resources provide incentives to the elite not to develop institutions."[30]

While Putin uses the revenues from oil and gas to fund large capital projects, from the multiple state residences to the Sochi Olympics, or allows his cronies to take it abroad, the population must contribute significantly to the budget through a combination of income taxes, high value-added taxes, and high duties on imported consumer goods. But the population also contributes a "tax" by paying bribes. Instead of cracking down on corruption, the state uses bribes both to feed the venality of the elites and as a way to supplement the insufficient salaries of low-paid workers. Instead of paying them from state coffers, the state allows low-level civil servants to supplement their meager incomes with petty bribes. This constitutes an additional tax on the population and a drag on the economy's overall efficiency. Over the long term this "corruption effect," equivalent to $2,000 per Russian and *equal* to the size of the Russian budget, can only slow economic growth and increase popular resentment, including among civil servants who feel degraded by the system. One policeman, Aleksey Dumovskiy, appealed on YouTube to Putin to do something to stop systemic corruption in which police had to meet their financial quotas from their bosses, leading them to "detect non-existent crimes and imprison people who are not guilty."

He was immediately arrested on fraud and corruption charges.[31] What he failed to understand is that everyone in Russia, except Putin, has to meet a quota.

The silver lining in the 2000s was that wealth from oil and gas flowed into Russia in staggering amounts, increasing from $30 billion in 1995 to approximately $175 billion annually only a decade later. However, a study by the former deputy minister of energy Vladimir Milov (who was obliged to resign after the study's release) showed that the imposition of state control and its concomitant lack of transparency gradually eroded efficiency and profitability even in the bloated energy sector.[32] Under such circumstances, it can be expected that prices and inefficiencies will increase, since rents and bribes become part of the cost of doing business, and inefficiency is not punished by the market, as the state protects and promotes this behavior. Preferential treatment of some firms over others and some sectors over others makes market entry for new firms more difficult, suppresses the desire or need for innovation as a way of gaining market share, and reinforces the tendency to invest in traditional and economically "reliable" sectors over other sectors that might promote the country's modernization but only in the long run.

Not only has corruption malformed Russia's society and its economy; it has also gradually distorted the state. The 1993 Russian Constitution created the broad institutional framework for a democratic system, with separation of powers, rotation of elites through elections, and guarantees of rights and freedoms. To be sure, even under Yel'tsin this system faced tough challenges. But elections were held in which influential candidates lost (including Anatoly Sobchak in 1996, for whom Putin was the campaign manager), and the individual rights and freedoms guaranteed in the Constitution were more or less upheld.

Certainly even in the 1990s, the oligarchs around Yel'tsin's Family sought to secure the wealth they had amassed through privatization schemes that largely excluded the average population. Popular hatred for individuals like Boris Berezovskiy and Anatoliy Chubays fueled the rise of Putin and his security elite, who were presented as incorruptible and willing to show a strong hand to those—like the Chechens—who would defy the Russian state. They launched a plan to remake the Presidential Administration and through it the Russian state from the earliest days of 2000. The leaked document *Reform of the Administration of the President of the Russian Federation* stated in writing what Putin ended up doing in practice: replacing the "self-regulating" nature of a democratic, market-driven, and rule-by-law system with manual control from the top. Written before he was even inaugurated, the document stated that the president did not need to rely on a self-regulating political system. He could control everything from the Kremlin, and he could achieve the best results by using "professionals" from the FSB. The results Putin achieved were indeed fast, and certainly not in a democratic direction.

The imbalance between state and society, in which society has not been able to countermobilize to prevent the strengthening in the power of the state over time, has been driven by Putin's desire from the beginning to control economic activity and to distribute profits to regime loyalists. Getting a position in the customs inspectorate, the tax office, or the presidential property administration became a more lucrative avenue for advancement than going into business. Massive companies that had previously flourished in the private sector, like Mikhayl Khodorkovskiy's Yukos, were raided and taken over by Kremlin insiders. And their economic performance suffered. They didn't become state companies so much as they became Putin's friends' companies. Putin gave loyalists directorships and memberships on the boards of these companies, like Gazprom and Rosneft, and these cronies then controlled the companies' activities and investments. Under Igor Sechin, Rosneft took over the most profitable parts of Yukos after it was raided in 2003, and yet Rosneft's market capitalization fell from $80 billion in 2006 to $69 billion in 2013. When Rosneft took over the well-performing TNK-BP in 2012, even the Putin ally Minister of Finance Aleksey Kudrin lamented that once again "an inefficient company absorbs an efficient one . . . [and] unfortunately, the company will be managed by the old Rosneft management."[33]

And Putin is directly involved in these companies. For instance, on March 3, 2009, he signed an executive order "on nominations of Russian Federation representatives and independent directors to the Boards of

Directors and Auditing Commissions" of sixteen joint-stock companies, including Gazprom, Transneft, United Aircraft, Russian Railways, Almaz-Antey, United Shipbuilding, and Aeroflot.[34] These are companies that may have controlling shares owned by the state but are publicly traded in New York and London, in which billions from Western pension funds are invested. The disregard for the rights of outside investors was underlined when Rosneft took over TNK-BP in 2012 and in response the price of the publicly traded TNK-BP stocks fell by 40 percent. Rosneft chief Sechin shot back at an investors' meeting that minority shareholders shouldn't expect to be treated equally and shouldn't expect such large dividends in the future, since Rosneft is "not a charity fund."[35]* But in truth it is such a fund for the Russian state and its elites. And the emergence of Rosneft as another largely state-owned company only strengthened the trend away from a market economy and toward state capitalism.[37]

This drag on economic performance caused by massive, systemic corruption makes prospects for economic development bleak, a remarkable situation considering that a decade of high oil revenues means that Russia has no sovereign debt. The Central Bank of Russia issued cautionary statements in 2014 predicting zero or negative growth if inflation and capital flight are not curbed. All this leads one to conclude that if rates of growth are not maintained and if something is not done about the high rate of income inequality in which those closest to the Kremlin become billionaires and ordinary citizens are pushed to the wall, then it is possible that analysts will repeat the nineteenth-century historian Vasiliy Klyuchevskiy's lament about Russian autocracy: "The state grew fat while the people grew thin." This was the path that ultimately led to revolution.

---

*By comparison, the Norwegian oil company Statoil, which is similarly largely owned by the state, operates on the principles that all shareholders will be treated equally and the board of directors will be independent, with no conflicts of interest between shareholders, the board, and the company's management.[36] Rosneft and Statoil are jointly exploring the Arctic, so their economic profile is similar, yet Statoil's share price grew almost 400 percent from 2010 to 2014 while Rosneft's declined 25 percent in the same period.

Putin's Home: Gazprom

In order to assess Putin's own role in this turn toward state control, it is worth looking more closely at his role in Gazprom, the publicly traded but majority-state-owned gas company. Gazprom is one of the largest companies worldwide, and its activities provided 8 percent of Russia's GDP in 2011. Mikhayl Krutikhin of RusEnergy, a consultancy firm, stated bluntly, "Gazprom has one manager: Putin." [38] And this assessment is no hyperbole. According to the websites of the Russian government and the Kremlin, Putin has met Gazprom chief Aleksey Miller, who served as Putin's deputy on the Committee for Foreign Liaison in St. Petersburg, over one hundred times—including dozens of one-on-one meetings, since Miller became head of Gazprom in 2001. By way of comparison, the number of times American and British government websites list President Obama or Prime Minister Cameron meeting one-on-one with the CEOs of Exxon or British Petroleum? Zero.

Financial analysts express concern that as much as 70 percent of Gazprom's capital investments are nontransparent, non-gas-related capital expenditures, and that such behavior is tantamount to "value destruction." [39] In the early years of Putin's presidency there were still independent members of boards of directors. One such was Bill Browder, an American with British citizenship who was chairman of Hermitage Capital Management. Browder had been a huge backer of Putin and had endorsed the arrest of Khodorkovskiy and the expropriation of Yukos assets. [40] He seemed like a perfect candidate to be on Gazprom's board. But there was a hitch: he happened to believe that greater transparency would allow minority shareholders to understand why the company was not producing better returns.

Hermitage became a major investor in Russia, investing $3.3 billion by 2005. [41] Browder bought millions in Gazprom shares, earning his company the right to vie for one of the independent slots on the board. He had started his company in the 1990s and correctly calculated that the profits from investing in Gazprom, even taking corruption into account, would be phenomenal. He, and his investors, became fabulously rich in the new

Russia. But believing that minority shareholders could press the company to reduce "inefficiencies," he became involved in trying to increase transparency and accountability to shareholders. As an activist shareholder, he lobbied for open disclosure of the reasons for the decline in the company's profitability. He had the temerity to suggest, as a major Gazprom investor, that Gazprom would be more profitable if it didn't rely so much on questionable intermediaries, like RosUkrEnergo.[42]

As a result, in 2005, as he was returning to Russia from the United Kingdom, he was barred from entry as a "threat to national security." Browder's companies were subjected to corporate raiding by an organized group of tax officials, police, and businessmen who reregistered the companies, declared them bankrupt, and then applied for, and received, a refund of the $230 million that Browder's companies had paid in taxes in 2006. The refund was the largest in Russian history, and they received it one day after applying. Browder's employees were subjected to arrest, illegal document seizures, and ultimately death when Sergey Magnitskiy, one of Hermitage's Moscow-based lawyers, died in 2009 in pretrial detention after being beaten and denied medical treatment.

Amid the international furor, Putin hit back, saying that Magnitskiy had died of heart failure: "Do you think no one dies in American jails? So what?"[43] The U.S. Congress passed a bill in 2012 putting those directly responsible for Magnitskiy's death and for the illegal seizure of Browder's assets in Moscow on a visa ban list. In an infantile knee-jerk reaction, Putin banned the adoption by Americans of Russian children. In 2013 both Browder (in absentia) and Magnitskiy (deceased) were put on trial in Moscow and sentenced to prison for tax evasion. This was regarded as the first conviction of a deceased person in Russian history.[44] Such was the fate of a truly independent member of the Gazprom board of directors.*

The use of intermediary firms as nontransparent, value-draining (and criminal) enterprises is legendary throughout the Russian economy, but Gazprom definitely gets the prize. A U.S. Embassy cable released through

---

*There is a vast literature on the Hermitage case, including a case study by Stanford Business School.[45]

Wikileaks concluded that RosUkrEnergo (RUE) was a money-making operation for the Kremlin. Gazprom itself owned 50 percent of RUE, and 50 percent was owned by two Ukrainian oligarchs, Dmitriy Firtash (45 percent) and Ivan Fursin (5 percent). But "the circle of true beneficiaries of RUE is wider and includes Semyon Mogilevich, a Russian organized crime boss wanted by the FBI and currently in custody in Russia." Mogilevich was soon released and took up residence in Moscow, where he lives freely. The Ukrainian government insisted that RUE be removed as a middleman, but the U.S. Embassy reported that another intermediary company had already been registered to take its place.[46]

Focus on RUE was important because it was seen in the West as a major vehicle for bringing together the Kremlin, business interests, and organized crime. Beginning in the mid-2000s the U.S. intelligence community provided a major assessment of the threat to U.S. national security posed, according to a Justice Department source, by the "growing nexus in Russian and Eurasian states among government, organized crime, intelligence services, and big business figures," including in the fields of energy and finance.[47] Without naming Russia or Putin specifically, Attorney General Michael Mukasey stated that of all the threats posed by international organized crime, the first was that "international organized criminals control significant positions in the global energy and strategic materials markets. . . . So-called 'iron triangles' of corrupt business leaders, corrupt government officials, and organized criminals exert substantial influence over the economies of many countries. . . . One of the most well-known recent examples is the case of Semyon Mogilevich [who] . . . is said to exert influence over large portions of the natural gas industry in parts of what used to be the Soviet Union."[48]

Mogilevich's relationship to Putin is of utmost interest but is not likely to be written about in open-source texts. However, their relationship was the subject of a conversation illicitly recorded by the security chief of the Ukrainian president Leonid Kuchma. The conversation is said to be between Leonid Derkach, the former head of the Ukrainian security services (SBU), and Kuchma on February 8, 2000:

Kuchma: Have you found Mogilevich?

Derkach: I found him.

Kuchma: So, are you two working now?

Derkach: We're working. We have another meeting tomorrow. He arrives incognito.

Later in the discussion Derkach revealed a few details about Mogilevich:

Derkach: He's on good terms with Putin. He and Putin have been in contact since Putin was still in Leningrad.

Kuchma: I hope we won't have any problems because of this.

Derkach: They have their own affairs.[49]*

In addition to RosUkrEnergo, an investigation by the anticorruption crusader Aleksey Navalnyy showed that Gazprom was buying gas from an independent producer, Novatek, through an intermediary, Transinvestgas. Police discovered that days before the purchase, Gazprom had turned down an offer to buy gas directly from Novatek, cutting out Transinvestgas, for 70 percent less. Transinvestgas transferred $10 million of the amount received to a "consulting company," which the police found had been registered using "two stolen passports."[51]

All these activities, plus asset stripping in which subsidiary companies were sold to Kremlin insiders at below-value prices, led the economist Anders Åslund to calculate that in 2011 alone, the total amount of waste and corruption in Gazprom may have reached $40 billion, as compared to $44.7 billion in profits—a situation that prompted him to conclude that the company resembled more an "organized crime syndicate" than a legal corporation.[52] Gazprom has more than one hundred wholly or majority-owned subsidiaries and affiliated companies registered in Russia as

---

*This conversation was quoted both in Kupchinskiy and in a classified document released by Wikileaks of key articles circulated within the U.S. government, lending it credibility.[50] For more on the Ukrainian tapes, see Kochiw (2013).

of 2014,[53] and another hundred subsidiaries were registered abroad already by 2007, including five in the Virgin Islands, nine in Cyprus, seven in Switzerland, and two in the Cayman Islands.[54] Undoubtedly other international oil companies have similar offshore registrations for their subsidiaries. The U.S. Securities and Exchange Commission lists twenty-two of Exxon's subsidiaries as being registered in the Bahamas alone, where corporate tax rates are lower.[55] As a publicly traded but private company, Exxon obviously seeks to maximize return to its investors. The difference is that it is not immediately clear why a state-owned company like Gazprom would be motivated to engage in asset stripping and then to allow these subsidiaries to register in tax havens and avoid paying state taxes. The rationale is simple: by stripping assets from the state-owned part of the company and selling them to insiders and relatives as subsidiaries, they can be registered abroad as private entities, operating in the world's tastiest tax havens for the personal benefit of their private owners, not Russian taxpayers. In any Western country, this would be called criminal malfeasance. In Russia it is called government.

Both the board of directors and the Management Committee of Gazprom are packed with Putin coworkers from the KGB and St. Petersburg who lack prior significant energy experience:

- Chairman of the Management Committee Aleksey Miller, Putin's deputy in St. Petersburg at the Committee for Foreign Liaison
- Chairman of the Board of Trustees Viktor Zubkov, deputy chairman of the agricultural subcommittee of Putin's KVS, head of the district where Putin's dacha was built
- Member of the Board Valeriy Musin, who was Putin's supervisor in the Law Faculty at Leningrad State University
- Member of the Board Andrey Akimov, who was a banker in Vienna at the time the CPSU and KGB money started to be sent abroad
- Deputy Chairman of the Management Committee Valeriy Golubev, formerly Leningrad KGB, St. Petersburg mayor's office, head of Vasileostrovskiy District when Putin moved into an apartment there
- Head of Gazprom's Investment and Construction Department Yaroslav Golko, said by Russian analysts to be a Rotenberg protégé

- Chief Accountant Elena Vasil'eva, who had worked with Miller in St. Petersburg's ports[56]
- Aleksandr Medvedev, another Vienna banker with an alleged KGB background
- Head of Gazprom's Department of Finance and Economics Andrey Kruglov, who was head of the Foreign Operations Department of Dresdner Bank when Matthias Warnig was its chief.[57]

Named in *Barron's* in 2014 as the "Worst-Managed Company on the Planet," Gazprom was trading in May 2014 at a 43 percent discount, compared to an average of 3 percent for other European energy companies.[58] Its share price had dropped from just under $16 in 2008 to just over $4 in late spring 2014, after the stock had rebounded from a $3 low during the Crimean crisis.

Despite the Russian state's obvious need for more financial inflows, when Gazprom signed a thirty-year gas deal with China in May 2014, it is telling that Putin sweetened the package by giving Gazprom a tax break. Such a move will deprive the Russian budget, according to the Russian economist Konstantin Sonin, "of most of the potential income from the deal."[59] Some analysts hope that companies close to the Kremlin will alter their ways and stop taking such a huge skim for personal and nonrelated state projects so that the companies can become more profitable. These analysts fail to understand the logic at the core of the system: profound access to riches is provided in return for absolute loyalty. Putin alone decides who and what will be profitable. There is no more important rule in today's Russia.

Kleptocracy's Development

The capture of the state and its financial reserves by the cronies around Putin has been a distinguishing feature of his entire rule.* *In this kleptoc-*

---

* The vast literature on captured states, where private firms pay public officials and politicians for preferential market entry, legal protection, and economic performance, is best reviewed in Hellman et al. (2003).

racy, the state nationalizes the risk but privatizes the reward. Access to this closed group required loyalty, discipline, and silence. Once within the group, officials could maraud the economy with impunity. Key to its successful functioning over time has been the unity of the key officials and their willingness to allow Putin to be the ultimate arbiter of any disputes, without using (and indeed undermining) the written law.

This kleptocracy has gone through several phases, although its aims have remained consistent. The first was the phase of primitive accumulation as the group emerged from their St. Petersburg roots, moved into positions of power in the Moscow bureaucracy, and removed or tamed the Yel'tsin oligarchs.

The second phase came after the takeover of Khodorkovskiy's company, Yukos, in 2003, when the company was seized and torn apart and its key assets reemerged as a new company, Rosneft, with Igor Sechin, the deputy head of Putin's administration, chairing its board of directors. In this phase, which lasted until 2011, beyond Dmitriy Medvedev's election as president in 2008 (with Putin moving over to become prime minister while retaining full actual powers), Putin allies within the government took up positions on the board of state-owned companies over which they simultaneously had supervisory powers. It was as if the U.K. minister of culture, media, and sport worked in her government office in the morning and made money as a BBC trustee in the afternoon. Except that in 2012 BBC trustees received on average $53,000 per year before taxes, after taking a cut from the previous year,[60] whereas Gazprom board members in 2012 received annual compensation in excess of $2 million each, after tax.[61]

This system provided enormous personal benefits to core elites: sitting as they did both on private boards of directors and in public office, they were able to steer state funds into their companies. When the economy almost collapsed in 2008, the Russian government bailed out state-supported banks first, to the tune of 5 trillion rubles (approximately $230 billion),* in a move in which government ministers who sat on boards (such as Finance

---

*Putin's own figures, as presented at the United Russia Interregional Conference on the Development Strategy for Central Russia through 2020, March 4, 2011, http://premier.gov.ru. He

Minister Kudrin, who sat on the board of VTB Bank) simply helped themselves to their own private stimulus package. But instead of using the money to stabilize the Russian ruble (which plummeted from 23RR/US$ to 36RR/US$) or the stock market (which lost 80 percent of its value), it only stimulated capital flight. Kudrin estimated that between October 2008 and January 2009, $200 billion was taken out of the country—i.e., virtually the entire stimulus.[62]

In addition the interlocking system of public officeholders with private interests allowed these place-holders to always act with impunity. Russia's long tradition of seeing the state itself as the source of law, based on the German idea of *Rechtsstaat* and its Russian equivalent, *pravovoe gosudarstvo*, gives great advantage to any firm or official enjoying state protection. In Russia historically, acts by state officeholders are typically not challenged in the politically compromised court system, while acts against or outside the state are vigorously prosecuted.[63]

This is not only a theoretical proposition, since the law provides immunity from prosecution for senators and Duma members and special consideration for those with state awards. All of Putin's cronies have received dozens of state awards—and as the oligarch Vladimir Gusinskiy happily discovered when his lawyer was able to get him released from prison in 2000, courts in Russia provide leniency in sentencing to those who have received state orders, which were reintroduced from tsarist times in spring 2000.[64] Gusinskiy had one such award. A cursory examination of Wikipedia reveals that Vladimir Yakunin, an Ozero cofounder and Russian Railways chief, has at least twenty-eight. And if this was not enough protection, members of the cabal could as already discussed become consuls of a foreign country in Russia, like Ozero members Viktor Khmarin, Sergey Fursenko, and Yuriy Koval'chuk, giving not only their persons inviolability but also their luggage, cars, and property.[65] * In these ways, their positions

---

referenced the fact that the state expects to be paid back with interest but had only received 200 billion rubles to date.

* Another notable close to the Kremlin is the conductor Valeriy Gergiev, who was named consul for Luxembourg.[66] Members of the Ozero group formed an association of honorary consuls in St.

close to Putin provide them with the ability to act with impunity, and their official positions provide them with immunity from effective prosecution.

While opposition elites long decried the emergence of corporatist tendencies, and with it the diminution of democracy, in this second phase it was not the subject of open discussion among insider elites themselves, who were content with public protestations of fealty to democracy but privately acknowledged unwritten "understandings" about how the inner structure actually worked. The discussion, however, was brought into the open by Viktor Cherkesov, at that time the head of the Federal Narcotics Control Service in Russia, when he lamented, apparently under pressure himself, that the stability of the ruling elite could be lost if people were to abandon the norms of the unity of the corporation and go over to an ethos of personal self-aggrandizement and war of "all against all." He wrote that Russia had three paths, the best being the thoroughgoing development of civil society and the worst being the slide into dictatorship. But there was also a middle option, a corporatist model that he preferred, because, at least in 2007, it bore the closest comparison with what actually existed at that time. Building an elite who consider themselves bound by corporatist principles is most likely, Cherkesov wrote, to "provide long-term stability and gradual escape from deep socio-cultural depression. I understand full well that in this scenario there are huge risks, including the danger of transforming a great country into a quagmire on the model of the worst Latin American dictatorships with their social closedness and neo-feudalism. But this is not a foregone conclusion. Besides negative, corporatism can also be positive. . . . As long as the stability of society to a significant degree relies on this force, the question of its quality is a question of the fate of the country."[67] Cherkesov's public criticism of the quality of some of those who were at the top, who had switched from being "warriors" to "traders," cost him his job.

The internal rules governing this elite were the subject of testimony before the U.S. Congress by Andrey Illarionov, who had been Putin's economic advisor for his first five years in office and was dismissed in 2005 for

Petersburg. The rights and responsibilities of these consuls is amply detailed in http://honorary consul.ru.

sounding alarm bells about the emergence of Russia as a corporate state. For Illarionov, this corporation came out of the traditions of the secret police and operated according to strict rules. As he said in his testimony, "The members of the Corporation do share strong allegiance to their respective organizations, strict codes of conduct and of honor, basic principles of behavior, including among others the principle of mutual support to each other in any circumstance and the principle of *omertà* [the mafia code of silence]. Since the Corporation preserves traditions, hierarchies, codes and habits of secret police and intelligence services, its members show a high degree of obedience to the current leadership, strong loyalty to each other, rather strict discipline. There are both formal and informal means of enforcing these norms. Violators of the code of conduct are subject to the harshest forms of punishment, including the highest form." [68]

Andrey Piontkovskiy, a lead researcher at the Institute for Systems Studies of the Russian Academy of Sciences, provided the following apt definition of this phenomenon:

The right to property in Russia is entirely conditional upon the property owner's loyalty to the Russian government. The system is tending to evolve not in the direction of freedom and a postindustrial society, but rather back toward feudalism, when the sovereign distributed privileges and lands to his vassals and could take them away at any moment. The only difference is that, in today's Russia, the things that Putin is distributing and taking away are not parcels of land, but gas and oil companies. Over the last decade, a mutant has evolved that is neither socialism nor capitalism, but some hitherto unknown creature. Its defining characteristics are the merging of money and political power; the institutionalization of corruption; and the domination of the economy by major corporations, chiefly trading in commodities, which flourish thanks to public resources. [69]

During this second phase, Putin appointed his core supporters into positions in the government and on the boards of key state-controlled companies (see Table 5).

Medvedev's Decree in 2009 forcing government ministers holding supervisory roles in the government to quit their board positions was welcomed by opposition activists and the international community, which had begun to loudly protest this flagrant violation of the basic principles of corporate governance and good government. Medvedev spoke against this system and signaled his desire to move Russia beyond such a state. But ministers immediately moved to shape the choice of their replacements on these boards; the Rosneft CEO even reassured jittery Russian markets that "Sechin will keep

Table 5. Interlocking Directorates:
Putin as Prime Minister, 2008–Spring 2011

	Government Position in 2008	Board Memberships 2009
Aleksey Kudrin	Deputy prime minister and minister of finance	VTB Bank ALROSA
Igor Levitin	Minister of transport	Sheremetyevo Airport Aeroflot
Igor Sechin	Deputy prime minister	Rosneft Rosneftgaz INTER RAO UES
Anatoliy Serdyukov	Defense minister (since 2007)	Oboronservis
Igor Shchegolev		Svyazinvest Channel One
Sergey Shmatko		RusHydro Gazprom Zarubezhneft
Yelena Skrynnik	Minister of agriculture	United Grain Company
Viktor Zubkov	First deputy prime minister	Gazprom (as of 2009) Russian Agricultural Bank Rosspirtprom Rosagroleasing

Notes: All the ministers listed here were forced to resign by July 1, 2011, from those companies for which they hold supervisory authority, as named in President Medvedev's Decree 1999. For a more complete list of government ministers and their board memberships, see Dawisha (2011).

Sources: http://www.gazprom.com/about/management/directors; http://eng.kremlin.ru/persons; http://government.ru/eng/gov/; http://eng.kremlin.ru/acts/1999.

control and . . . will even strengthen [Rosneft]."[70] These open efforts to undermine Medvedev's decree led Aleksey Navalnyy to lament that nothing had changed and that Medvedev's intentions were being undermined: "This problem is extremely serious because it creates a feudal regime. I'm skeptical that this decision to remove officials from state company boards will have an effect because all these companies under state control are turning into the personal property of these officials through their children." *

When Medvedev went after Sechin in particular, judged by most at that time to be the person closest to Putin, he won no awards from Putin.[72] Soon afterward Putin announced in a way designed to humiliate his partner that he would be running for a third term, eliminating Medvedev's chances of a second term. Out went Medvedev's calls for modernization, and in came the redistribution of board memberships and state contracts straight to Putin's cronies from Dresden and St. Petersburg (see Table 6). Once he was elected, and once he had weathered the storm of protests against election fraud in the 2011 Duma and 2012 presidential elections, Putin moved robustly to implement his third phase: direct control of the economy by his cronies. Of course, they had been getting rich throughout the 2000s, but now they were given public and visible positions controlling the state and the economy. Finally, we had a definitive answer to the question "Who owns Russia?"

When Putin's allies and cronies were sanctioned by the United States

---

* As the children of the top Kremlin elite enter their thirties, there has indeed been a clear tendency for parents to pass their positions on to their children and relatives. Putin's own nieces and nephews and other relatives have seen success: Igor Putin became vice president of Master Bank; Vera Putina became a member of the board of directors of Ganzakombank; Mikhayl Putin became the deputy director of SOGAZ. (Nemtsov, 2012) Other Kremlin insiders who have placed their sons in leading positions include Sergey Ivanov, whose thirty-one-year-old son became head of the supervisory board of the Russian Agricultural Banks, whose CEO was Dmitriy Patrushev, son of Security Council chief Nikolay Patrushev. Ivanov's other son, Aleksandr, became head of structured and credit financing at Vnesheconombank, where his father sat on the board in 2011.[71] Putin himself fatalistically addressed this issue at the Valdai meetings in 2007 (attended by the author) when he was asked about the growth of this phenomenon. In response he laughingly repeated the anecdote in which one guy complains to another that a minister's sons have been appointed to direct leading banks. The other responds by asking whether those sons could even be appointed to the army. The first retorts, "Never. After all, generals have their own sons."

Table 6. Who Owns Russia? Direct Control and Ownership of the Economy by Putin's Cronies, 2014

	Connection with Putin/KGB	Full or Partial Ownership, Board Memberships, Directorships 2014	2013 Alleged Net Worth (or annual compensation
Sergey Chemezov*	Dresden KGB with Putin	Aeroflot, Rostekh, AvtoVAZ, Kamaz, Oboronprom, National-Information Computing Systems, Novikombank, Uralkalia, United Aircraft Corporation, United Shipbuilding,* VSMPO-AVISMA	$800m net worth
Andrey Fursenko*	Ozero	Center for Strategic Research Northwest	Unknown
Sergey Fursenko*	Ozero	Lentransgaz, Gazprom Gas-Motor Fuel	Unknown
Yuriy Koval'chuk*	Ozero	Bank Rossiya (and its subsidiaries),* Center for Strategic Research Northwest	$1.4b net worth
Aleksey Miller	St. Petersburg government	Gazprom, Gazprombank*	$25m annual salary
Arkadiy Rotenberg*	St. Petersburg childhood	Stroygazmontazh,* Mostotrest, TPS Avia, SMP Bank,* Mineral Fertilizers InvestCapitalBank*	$4b net worth
Boris Rotenberg*	St. Petersburg childhood	Stroygazmontazh,* SMP Bank,* InvestCapitalBank*	$1.6b net worth
Igor Sechin*	St. Peterburg government	Rosneft,* United Shipping Corporation	$25m annual salary
Nikolay Shamalov	Ozero	Vyborg Shipyards, Bank Rossiya,* Gazprombank*	$500 million net worth
Vladimir Smirnov	Ozero, PTK	Tekhsnabeksport (nuclear materials)	Unknown
Gennadiy Timchenko*	Kinex, St. Petersburg	Gunvor (until spring 2014),* Aquanika,* Volga Group,* Avia Group,* Avia Group Nord,* Sakhatrans,* Stroytransgaz Group,* Transoil,* Novatek,* Russkoye Morye	$15.3b

(continued on next page)

	Connection with Putin/KGB	Full or Partial Ownership, Board Memberships, Directorships 2014	2013 Alleged Net Worth (or annual compensation
Nikolay Tokarev	Dresden	Sovcomflot, Transneft	$6m annual salary
Matthias Warnig	Stasi Dresden	Nord Stream, Bank Rossiya,* Gazprom, Rosneft,* Rusal, Transneft, Vneshtorgbank (VTB)*	Unknown
Vladimir Yakunin*	Ozero	Russian Railways	$15m annual salary

* Under sanction by United States as of August 1, 2014. The chart clearly indicates how targeted U.S. sanctions were on Putin's group. This table is by no means exhaustive but is meant to give the reader an indication of the material and political fortunes of those closest to Putin who were with him from the beginning. Wealth and compensation figures should be regarded as estimates and probably on the low side, given knowledge about the lifestyles of some of these figures.

Sources: Forbes.ru; Reuters.com; Russian corporate websites; http://www.treasury.gov/press-center/press-releases/Pages/jl23331.aspx; http://www.treasury.gov/ofac/downloads/ssi/ssi.pdf; Gertz (2014).

and the European Union following Russia's annexation of Crimea in spring 2014, Putin expressed first amusement, then shock, as the implications emerged of what had just happened. Banks that were subject to asset seizures, like Bank Rossiya, or owned even partially by those sanctioned could no longer conduct business in dollars. All of the assets of sanctioned individuals would be seized if they could not get them back to the Russian safe haven in time, so foreign assets were liquidated or buried deeper. Putin expressed his loyalty to his friends when speaking at the St. Petersburg Economic Forum in May 2014: "All the sanctions target my friends, people who are close to me personally. These sanctions are designed to bust them, as our intellectuals say, to punish them for God knows what. If I were in such a position I would have taken the matter to court a long time ago because they have nothing to do with the events in Ukraine or Crimea. And whom have they selected? Two Jews and one Ukrainian,* can you imagine?"[73]

---

* A possible reference to Timchenko and the Rotenbergs who were named in the sanctions list.

Russian Corruption and the International Community

When Putin says he would have "taken the matter to court a long time ago," one assumes he is referring to the European courts, where there are real judges and real judgments. This brings up an important point and the final one of this book: there has been a partner in this kleptocracy, and that partner is the West. Beginning in Yel'tsin's era, Western banks kept their vaults open for money launderers and scammers from Russia. The reluctance of these banks to bring Russia to account is fueled by the search for bonuses, commissions, bribes, and directorships. And Putin, as a former KGB officer, certainly knows the West's weak spots. Russian venality has a worthy partner among certain Western elites.

Since the KGB started to move money out of the USSR under Gorbachev, the Russians have had thirty years' experience, and even more, burying money in the West, using the West's institutions to their own advantage. This has, if anything, allowed Russia to delay needed reform at home. Russia depends on the public goods produced in the West, including a network of legal obligations and alliances that promote Russia's state interests and sustain its reputation and authority as a sovereign entity in international affairs. In Europe, for example, signing and appearing to live up to its obligations under the Council of Europe gave Russia the status of a legitimate and democratizing state long after the regime had taken the country in another direction. Its membership in the Parliamentary Assembly of the Council of Europe bought the regime time, at least until it annexed Crimea. Russian elites have long benefited from European public goods (rule of law, civil society, economic stability, property rights, relatively safe streets) while undermining the development of these goods in their own country.

Such free-riding behavior undermines not only Russia's development but also European societies themselves, which are subjected to behavior designed to extend private gain into geographic areas strongly governed by the production of public goods. And the behavior of Russia's foreign policy establishment abroad—whether in competing to get the Olympics or the World Cup, in contracting with BP in a deal that undermined BP's

Putin sizes up German Chancellor Gerhard Schröder. Berlin, June 2000. Photo by Fritz Reiss, AP

other contractual obligations in Russia, or in placing Russian representatives in international organizations like the European Bank for Reconstruction and Development who engage in fraudulent activity[74]—often shows that the Russian elite is in the business of maximizing short-term private gain, even if it corrupts not only Russian institutions but also international institutions of long-standing. Yet the 300,000 Russians who now reside in London, and those who own property there, depend on the surety that this property, along with the wives and children who live there, will be safeguarded while many of them continue to maraud their home country. In this social order, predatory elites rely on stable Western countries as a space in which to facilitate their own emergence into what Miami University professor Venelin Ganev has termed "a globally mobile, 'capital-flight' caste whose ultimate objective is to consume extracted resources in some of the nicer neighborhoods of the global village."[75]

The EU has worked hard to stanch the tide of corrupt behavior from Russia that is finding its way into the very heart of Europe and its institutions, but there are obviously politicians and public officials who are willing to partner with Russia in these transactions. Under its obligation as a member of the Council of Europe, Russia agreed to allow its citizens to appeal to the European Court in Strasbourg and to accept and implement the court's judgments. As Russian courts have become even more politically controlled, and with nongovernmental organizations and human rights activists increasingly subject to arbitrary arrest and detention, appeals from Russian citizens to Strasbourg have increased. By 2006 one in every five complaints to the court was made against Russian court decisions.

This pattern of verbal support for democracy combined with substantive resistance to it is repeated by Russia in many other European institutions. In 2005 the Parliamentary Assembly of the Council of Europe called for an investigation of the "obstacles encountered by the Russian authorities with regard to the ratification of Council of Europe conventions as, since accession 9 years ago, out of 200 conventions, the Russian Federation has ratified only 46 conventions and signed 15."[76] In 2007–8 PACE announced that because Russia had not provided conditions that would allow successful election monitoring, PACE could not send an observer team, and that Russia's decision to hold elections without European observers was in violation of its terms of membership. A group of states in the Council of Europe, led by Sweden, sought Russian expulsion after the 2008 invasion of Georgia. The EU at the same time also created the Eastern Partnership of Ukraine, Moldova, Belarus, Azerbaijan, Armenia, and Georgia to shape civil society and parliamentary cooperation with the goal of creating a visa-free regime that would extend the Schengen visa area (allowing free movement among the twenty-five European countries that signed the Schengen Agreement but restricting access to outsiders) to these countries, but pointedly not to Russia.[77]

Russia's problems mounted when in December 2010, the Council of Europe's Group of States against Corruption (GRECO) issued a report saying that Russia failed to implement almost two-thirds of the group's twenty-six recommendations. Specifically Russia had made no progress in taking action to criminalize corruption or create punishments for offenders. The head of the Duma's commission to draft anticorruption legislation avoided the issue of the impact of this noncompliance on democracy and on Russia's image by saying they would see how proposed measures would work in Russia, "taking into account our culture and traditions."[78] Two years later the follow-up compliance report noted that while it was encouraging that the Russians had carried out sociological and other research into the sources and nature of corruption,[79] "GRECO remains concerned that a large number of Russian officials continue to enjoy immunity from prosecution, including for corruption crimes. Furthermore, the strengthening of judicial independence—not only in law but also in practice—and of the operational independence of law enforcement agents remains an on-going challenge."[80]

In the borderlands between the EU and Russia and in the other newly independent states of the former Soviet Union, Russian money and muscle have their greatest clout. This is particularly noticeable in the energy sector. In 2008 in Serbia, a country 100 percent dependent on Russia for its oil and gas, Gazprom was "able" to purchase a controlling 51 percent stake in NIS, Serbia's largest oil refinery and its largest company, for 400 million euros, despite a market evaluation value of 2.2 billion euros and a number of higher bids from Austria, Hungary, Poland, and elsewhere. The Russian offer was made more attractive by the nonbinding promise of making Serbia a transit point in any future pipeline connecting Russia's Black Sea Coast and Western Europe.[81]

Beginning in Putin's second term, Russia increasingly used energy wars as a way of taming ungrateful and uncooperative neighbors whenever they sought independence from any line espoused in Moscow. However, quarrels with these states are also spawned by the personal interests of individuals who may hold a state position but who seek private advantage. Ukraine, Moldova, Georgia, and Belarus have all been subjected to the withdrawal or threat of withdrawal of energy deliveries at prices previously agreed upon (albeit lower than global levels). Two factors operate here. One is the state's interest in maximizing its influence over the domestic and foreign policy orientation of its neighbors; they are buying this influence for the state with subsidized energy. Another is the interest of elites in Gazprom or Rosneft or deputy ministers in foreign trade ministries (sometimes these are the same people) who are willing to negotiate these subsidized oil and gas deals but only in return for huge personal kickbacks through intermediary companies.

In addition to the establishment of intermediary companies, the pattern of using the power of the state to leverage public and private gain is particularly evident in Russian relations in the former Soviet countries. A pattern that has been widely used is Russian state involvement in debt-equity swaps, in which industrial infrastructure is leveraged by Russian state-connected firms at knockdown prices as payment for sovereign debt. Not having sufficient liquid assets to repay their debt to Russia, the debtor states give Russia an equity stake in their economic infrastructure, usually at deeply discounted prices. Russia has shown itself adept at leveraging increased control especially over the energy infrastructure of neighboring states. Russian companies are major beneficiaries: United Energy Systems and Gazprom have purchased gas, pipelines, nuclear facilities, and electricity grids as part of these debt-equity swaps.[82] Among many examples is Tajikistan's payment of its sovereign debt to Moscow with a 75 percent stake in the Sangtuda hydroelectric plant.[83] In 2005 United Energy Systems announced that Interenergo, its offshore subsidiary, had purchased 100 percent of the shares of Armenian Electricity Network for $73 million. Elsewhere in Armenia, Russia had already "secured" the Hrazdan thermal power plant, the largest such plant in Armenia, for $31 million.[84] Similar deals have been struck with virtually all non-energy-rich states in the Commonwealth of Independent States.[85]* In such negotiations the Russian state is owed the money, but it is often Russian firms close to the state, with Russian officials on their boards of directors, who reap the benefits. The officials suffer no risk for their investment while reaping all the rewards.

To the extent that Russia gets pushed back into its own region, the potential for putting enormous pressure on neighboring countries only

---

* In Kyrgyzstan the previous Bakiyev government promised Russian businessmen a controlling share in the country's second-largest company, the cell phone company Megacom, in return for the Russian state delivering fuel to the country tariff-free. The fuel was delivered, but when the Bakiyev regime was overthrown, the new government nationalized Megacom and denied Russian businessmen access to the company. This was a perfect example of Russian state assets (tariff-free fuel) being provided to leverage stock for Russian businessmen in a private company (Megacom).

increases. The story of the war with Georgia is a case in point. While the Kremlin presented it to the world as a conflict between two sovereign states, one of which was trying to repress its local non-Georgian population and join NATO, the facts about the nature of the local South Ossetian leadership suggest that there is also a parallel narrative. In this version, South Ossetia is seen as a wholly owned subsidiary of mafia-*siloviki* structures in Russia, who use the territory for offshore Russian counterfeiting and smuggling operations. After Georgian president Mikheil Saakashvili's election, he moved to stop Ossetia's use as a center for these operations, which are said to include the massive counterfeiting of $20 million in $100 bills.[86] The situation deteriorated, with Russian *silovik* officers moving to take up positions in South Ossetia's government.

By mid-2008 Anatoliy Baranov, who used to head the FSB in the Russian Republic of Mordovia, had become head of the local FSB. The new head of the South Ossetian Interior Ministry, Mikhayl Mindzayev, had served in the Interior Ministry of Russia's North Ossetia. The South Ossetian defense minister, Vasiliy Lunev, used to be military chief in Perm *oblast'*, and the secretary of South Ossetia's Security Council, Anatoliy Barankevich, was a former deputy military commissar of Stavropol Krai. This led Yuliya Latynina to observe, "South Ossetia is not a territory, not a country, not a regime. It is a joint venture of siloviki generals and Ossetian bandits for making money in a conflict with Georgia."[87] Other writers pointed to the links between South Ossetia's president Eduard Kokoity and St. Petersburg criminal elements.[88] Freedom House reported that Kokoity had been locked in a political battle with his prime minister, Vadim Brovtsev, a Russian businessman appointed by the Kremlin to oversee reconstruction funds. Analysts point out that much of the embezzlement occurs in Moscow before funds are even transferred, and since a reported 98 percent of the South Ossetian budget is a direct subsidy from Moscow, this extensive corruption is clearly responsible for the continued economic decline in the breakaway region.[89]

Similar stories could be written about the authorities in Transnistria, Moldova, a breakaway region located between the Dniester River and the eastern Moldovan border with Ukraine. The Russian military base in Trans-

nistria, sitting close to EU borders as it does, has been implicated in protecting officials and criminal forces that have created a haven and launch
point for smuggling in nuclear materials, drugs, trafficking in women, and
other illicit activities.*

But it is in Ukraine that Russian business has the greatest interest. Russian elites and their Ukrainian partners have long shared the spoils of the gas
trade by allowing a percentage of the gas supplied cheaply to the Ukrainian
domestic market to be re-exported at higher world prices, with both sides
sharing the proceeds. In addition Russian elites are significant landowners
in Crimea and have long held sway there. Putin himself was said to have
been the ultimate beneficiary of a sale by the pro-Russian Ukrainian regime
of Leonid Kuchma of the storied Dacha No. 1 (also called *Glitsynia* or Wis-
teria) on 20-hectare (50 acres) grounds on the Crimean Coast near Yalta to
Moscow's Vneshtorgbank for $15 million, as the "official residence of the
Russian President in Crimea." The terms were challenged by his successor
after the Orange Revolution, Viktor Yushchenko, but understanding how
much the property meant to the Kremlin, Yushchenko stated that "having
such a property as a vacation resort for members of the Russian government
is a question that deserves attention . . . We will propose an honest, public
and legal alternative, so that both sides can demonstrate their transparency
and openness and not base their relations on scandalous properties." [91] Putin
is said to have continued to visit the dacha, which formally was on Ukrainian
soil. Immediately after the annexation of Crimea by Russia, the Crimean
authorities announced that all Ukrainian state properties would now revert
to Russia, including "the state-owned dachas and resorts in Yalta." [92]

In Ukraine's eastern and southern regions Russian and Ukrainian arms
manufacturers collaborate to produce and ship, from the Oktyabrsk port

---

*A U.S. Senate report states, "Corruption within Transnistria's law enforcement institutions
and its absence of civil society watchdog groups have allowed Transnistria to fester as a source of
trafficking in persons, arms, and other illicit goods. In 2010, Moldovan authorities broke up a
criminal ring in Chisinau with reported ties to Transnistria that attempted to sell four pounds
of uranium-238, reportedly worth $11 million on the black market, that could be converted to
plutonium-239 (fissile material for nuclear weapons) or a dirty bomb. In the past, authorities
have seized weapons, including anti-tank grenade launchers without serial numbers (ideal for
trafficking) that were reportedly manufactured in Transnistria." [90]

in Odessa, military equipment for Syria, Algeria, India, Vietnam, and beyond. In 2012 Russia exported $17.6 billion worth of arms, and a significant percentage went out through Odessa. Russian and Ukrainian regional and national leaders are linked in a network that makes the business mutually beneficial. On the Russian side, according to a detailed study of "the Odessa Network," are companies linked to both Igor Levitin, who served as the Russian minister of transportation in 2004–12 and then as a personal advisor to Putin, and Sergey Chemezov, head of Rosoboroneksport and a key Putin ally.[93] Chemezov was added to the U.S. sanctions list in April 2014.[94] Russia has real and deep interests in this region that will not be compatible with a closer relationship between Ukraine and the EU. These interests include a long history of national collaboration as well as the personal interests of key Russian leaders. As Lev Gudkov, the director of the Levada Center, writes, "Putinism is a system of decentralized use of the institutional instruments of coercion . . . hijacked by the powers that be for the fulfillment of their private, clan-group interests."[95] The Russian leadership's attitude toward Ukraine is deeply affected by these interests.

Putin's Kleptocracy: What Now?

Whether, and how, the Russian government, or any government, so completely captured by these motivations can overcome them is a subject of significant importance. It is logical that as the Russian population at large begins to understand that the "public goods" produced by the state are not for public consumption, increasing amounts of coercion will be required to maintain the system. Additionally, reliance on Putin as an arbiter can be maintained only to the extent that he is interested in the increasing effort and risk required to play this role over time. The U.S. Embassy is only one of many players who observed that Putin's interest in putting in a full day's work has definitely declined.[96] As predation's rewards fall, the risks will become less attractive.

And there is an increasing risk that the country will be driven into a renewed hard authoritarian regime. In Putin's earliest career in St. Petersburg he declared, "However sad and frightening it may sound, . . . I think that in our country a return to a totalitarian past is possible. The danger is not from the organs of state power like the KGB, MVD, or even the army. It is a danger in the mentality of our people, our nation, our own particular mentality. We all think in this way . . . and I also sometimes think in this way that if only there was a firm hand to provide order we would all live better, more comfortably and in security." It is ironic that he went on to predict that any such illusions would be "short-lived, because a firm hand will be tight and very quickly strangle us."[97]

Once the state is captured, unity among the top elite is required. Yet while all know that unity is in their collective best interest, there is the classic "prisoner's dilemma," in which, in the absence of trust, each person's interest can be safeguarded only by caring only about his or her own fate and not about the group's. As an unattributed commentary posted as early as 2007 on the Russian website Gazeta.ru succinctly put it, "Attempts to safeguard one's children and oneself from possible persecution by former colleagues along the 'power vertical,' along with the desire to maximally enrich oneself while in power, has become practically the main purpose of all political and economic decisions."[98]

Putin's ability to rule with a charm offensive has been largely exhausted. Many Russians still admire his tough-guy approach against weaker neighbors, but the days when he could believably protest that he did not know Anna Politkovskaya, Sergey Magnitskiy, or any of the other regime targets are over. As Anders Åslund correctly observed already in 2007, "Putin reestablished the public lie as the standard as in the Soviet Union."[99] By 2014 the U.S. State Department was posting "lies" uttered by the Russian president on its website.

With a decline in both the economy and Putin's personal stature among the Russian middle class, maintaining control will more and more depend on coercion. The actions that Putin has taken since the beginning of his third term would appear to support this. The May 2014 promotion of Viktor Zolotov from the position of head of Putin's personal security detail to commander in chief of the 190,000 Interior Ministry troops does not bode well in this regard. He is the person who, according to local journalists, carried Putin's "black cash" (*chyornyy nal*) in Petersburg.[100] He was the one who, according to the account of Sergey Tretyakov, as discussed earlier, worked with General Yevgeniy Murov, director of the Federal Protection Service, "to make a list of politicians and other influential Muscovites whom they would need to assassinate to give Putin unchecked power." Tretyakov, who was resident in New York City from 1995 to 2000, reported, "After the two men finished their list, Zolotov announced, 'There are too many. It's too many to kill—even for us.' " [101] This man, who has been by Putin's side from the very beginning and, one assumes, is utterly loyal, is now in charge of all special forces troops.

Putin will not go gentle into the night. He shows himself to be less flexible and more bombastic in his public appearances, and those in his inner circle suggest that after the 2011–12 election demonstrations, there is also fear.[102] Gleb Pavlovskiy, his PR guru for over a decade, believes that Putin will never leave power and, indeed, is hampered by the idea that Russians will always decide matters by violence. Pavlovskiy says he heard Putin say, "We know ourselves . . . we know that as soon as we move aside, you will destroy us. He said that directly, you'll put us to the wall and execute us. And we don't want to go to the wall." [103]

Of course they do not want to be taken to the wall, given the obscene concentration of power and wealth in their hands. When all is said and done, this is the house that Vladimir Putin has built. Today's Russia is not the Russia of Leonid Brezhnev, Mikhayl Gorbachev, Boris Yel'tsin, or even Dmitriy Medvedev. It is the Russia of Vladimir Putin, built in his own image, subject to his will and whim, to his penchant for "manual control." When the new prime minister of a Central Asian state paid his first visit to Moscow, he met with Putin, and after the cameras had left the room, Putin is said to have loosened his tie, leaned forward, and in a menacing snarl told the startled leader, "Listen here (*slushay syuda*), I decide everything. Don't forget it." If he is willing to say this to the leader of a sovereign country, what does he say, and do, to his own Russian rivals? This is a man who thinks in zero-sum terms—your loss is his gain. Period. In an effort to live his life beyond the control of others, he has forced a whole people to submit. The most that can be said is that he will never reintroduce the gulag. Why should he? He just invites those who oppose him to leave the country.

And for those left behind, the gap between rich and poor has become the greatest in the world. To repeat the figures already cited in the book, the midpoint of wealth for Russians is only $871—as compared to the other BRIC countries—$5,117 for Brazil, $8,023 for China, and $1,040 for India, all energy importers. And on the other side, 35 percent of the total wealth in the country is owned by one hundred ten billionaires. Russia has become the country where the super-rich receive the greatest protection from the state. None of this would be possible without the personal involvement of Putin.

Nor has this come about by historical accident. The book has shown that the group now in power started out with Putin from the beginning. They are committed to a life of looting without parallel. This kleptocracy is abhorrent not just because of the gap between rich and poor that it has created, but because in order to achieve success this cabal has had to destroy any possibility of freedom. They have fed ordinary Russians pabulum of "unique culture" and "Russian values" to camouflage their throttling of civil society and the rule of law.

Putin responded to Western sanctions in 2014 by telling Russians it will be good for them, it will make them more self-reliant. It will stimulate business. But he's been in power fourteen years, and what has he done to stimulate business? What was he waiting for? The biggest threat to the success of ordinary Russians occurs not, as he claims, from Western business investments in Russia, but rather when Russia's all-powerful overlord, or one of his cronies, demolishes a village to build a palace, steals the money intended for health reforms, stymies innovation by maintaining state ownership of patents, or sends waves of tax, fire, and health inspectors as part of a shakedown. The only way for ordinary Russians to avoid state predation is to keep their heads down and believe in fate, or turn into cheerleaders of the system in order to gain insurance and a few crumbs from the table. Russians have a long history of great contributions to world culture, literature, and arts. They deserve better.

ACKNOWLEDGMENTS

T HIS BOOK has already had a rather storied past. I had submitted it to Cambridge University Press, which declined to publish it for fear of running afoul of libel laws in the U.K. This has become a growing trend in the book world, where the rich and the corrupt from many different countries use U.K. courts for libel tourism as a way of suppressing investigative work into their worlds. Some authors walk away and find another publisher. Others have gone ahead with publication in the U.K. and then have had to face a court case and the ultimate pulping of their books, sometimes over a single paragraph. I have never blamed CUP, with whom I have had a long relationship, for their decision, and the fact that Simon & Schuster also has decided not to publish this book in the U.K. underscores that the problem lies with U.K. libel laws, not with CUP.

In my own case, I decided to alert the academic and policy community to this sorry state of affairs by giving the exchange of correspondence to the *Economist*. The book in its present form would likely not have seen the light of day had it not been for Edward Lucas at the *Economist*, who not only brought the circumstances of its April 2014 rejection by CUP to light both in his blog and in the print edition of the *Economist* (www.economist.com /blogs/easternapproaches/2014/04/russia), but who also introduced me to Melanie Jackson, who became my agent. She moved quickly to find a publisher, and within literally thirty-six hours the deed was done.

At Simon & Schuster, I'm indebted to my editor, Alice Mayhew, for committing to the book so quickly and for her clear vision of the book's promise and potential. She has an able and nimble team who have worked hard, long, and fast to get the book to print, including associate editor Jonathan Cox and assistant editor Stuart Roberts, as well as Judith Hoover, Anthony Newfield, and Jay Schweitzer in copyediting. Navorn Johnson was the production editor, Jackie Seow art directed the great jacket design, Larry Hughes is in charge of publicity, and Stephen Bedford handles marketing. A special thanks also goes to Elisa Rivlin, who gave the whole manuscript a very thorough legal read.

For reading and providing invaluable comments on the whole manuscript or parts of it, I am indebted to Anders Åslund, Martin Dewhirst, John Dunlop, and Edward Lucas, and to several of my Russian friends, who shall go nameless.

For discussions and exchanges about the nature of Russian politics, I would like to thank Leon Aron, Sir Rodric Braithwaite, Ambassador James Collins, Cliff Gaddy, Helena Goscilo, Fiona Hill, Hon. Jan Kalicki, David J. Kramer, Steve LeVine, Ambassador Richard Miles, Steven Lee Myers, John Pepper, Ambassador Thomas Pickering, Arkady Ostrovsky, Peter Reddaway, Thomas Remington, Richard Sakwa, David Satter, Sandy Saunders, Louise Shelly, Angela Stent, and Elizabeth Teague. I also interviewed many other active and retired U.S. and British government officials who served in Moscow and St. Petersburg in the 1990s and who have had long careers in Russian analysis. I was greatly aided in my research by access to the files of Yuriy Felshtinskiy, whose work with Vladimir Pribylovskiy provided some of the earliest indication of the nature of the current regime.

At the Wilson Center and the Kennan Institute, I was fortunate to have fellowships in the first half of 2012 that allowed me not only to work full-time on the writing but also to meet many colleagues with shared interests, including Rob Litwak, William Pomeranz, Blair Ruble, Michael Van Dusen, and Sam Wells. Big thanks also go to the Kennan library staff, and to David Agranovich, who tirelessly and with great talent worked as my intern there.

At Miami, I was fortunate to have wonderful support both for this book and in the running of the Havighurst Center from the program coordinator, Lynn Stevens, who has developed the website for this book, helped by Kathryn Forrester, at www.miamioh.edu/havighurstcenter/putins-russia.

Readers will be able to find the entire bibliography and a timeline of Russian politics with live links, as well as all the documents used for this book from Russian and other sources, including many that have been scrubbed from Russian sites. Also, a huge thanks to Miami's Slavic librarian, Masha Stepanova, who helped me track down many books and articles on Russia, and to the library's Elias Tzoc Caniz for help with Spanish sources.

Many students over quite a few years now have helped in gathering and verifying information for this book, or have done research projects that ran parallel to the book. Many of them have now gone on to successful careers in journalism, government, and higher education—they include James Nealy, Victoria Kirnos, Peter Podkopaev, and several wonderful students from Russia, Ukraine, and central Asia whom I would have loved to thank by name. Thanks also to Angela Trubceac, who as a Muskie Fellow ably transcribed the testimonials by Lead Investigator Zykov that are referred to throughout the book and posted on the book's website. Sarah-Christin Müller's work in gathering and translating the Stasi archive documents referenced in the book and also included on the book's website was part of a joint project we did when she had a summer research scholarship at Miami, and is also greatly appreciated.

The Center has been able to host many top Russian academics, journalists, and analysts over the last decade, and I want to thank them for their contributions and insights, from which I learned so much. I have known many of them for decades, and it is a privilege to call them friends. I am full of admiration for the very high quality of work that they do under sometimes quite difficult circumstances.

Here at Miami, my own colleagues have been a great source of support and encouragement, reading multiple versions of various chapters in our research seminars. Special thanks for their support and friendship go to Venelin Ganev, Scott Kenworthy, Neringa Klumbytė, Steve Norris, Dan Prior, Ben Sutcliffe, and Zara Torlone.

For all of these contributions, I really am most grateful. It would not have been the book it is without the help and encouragement of so many people. Having said that, in no way do I assume any of them share my views on any of the subjects covered in the book.

Finally, my great thanks also go to my husband, Adeed Dawisha, who read every word of this manuscript several times, in the process learning much more about Putin than is healthy for a Middle East specialist. Our many discussions about the comparative trajectory of authoritarian regimes gives me hope that at some point in the future Russians will be able to have leaders whom they freely choose, in a society that truly values their unique and significant culture and history, a view of Russia that I hope I have passed on to my own children, Emile and Nadia, and to my many students in the U.K. and the U.S. over these last forty years of teaching.

Karen Dawisha
Oxford, Ohio
August 4, 2014

SELECTED BIBLIOGRAPHY

A full bibliography with live URLs, an annotated timeline, and key documents is available at www.miamioh.edu/havighurstcenter/putins-russia.

Albats, Yevgenia. *The State within a State*. New York: Farrar, Straus and Giroux, 1994.

Albats, Yevgenia. "Who Is Vladimir Putin?" *Frontline*. PBS. 2000. www.pbs.org/wgbh/pages/frontline/shows/yeltsin/putin/putin.html (accessed January 14, 2013).

Åslund, Anders. *Building Capitalism: The Transformation of the Former Soviet Bloc*. New York: Cambridge University Press, 2002.

Åslund, Anders. *Russia's Capitalist Revolution*. Washington, DC: Petersen Institute for International Economics, 2007.

Baker, Peter, and Susan Glasser. *Kremlin Rising*. Updated edition. Dulles, VA: Potomac, 2007.

Belton, Catherine. Various articles in *Financial Times, Moscow Times, and St. Petersburg Times*.

Blotskiy, Oleg. *Vladimir Putin: Doroga k vlasti* [Vladimir Putin: The path to power]. Book 2. Moscow: Mezhdunarodnyye otnosheniya, 2002.

Blowing Up Russia. Directed by Jean-Charles Deniau and Charles Gazelle. 2002.

Bonini, Carlo, and Giuseppe D'Avanzo. Various articles in *La Repubblica*.

Borogan, Irina, and Andrey Soldatov. Various articles at Agentura.ru.

Colton, Timothy J. *Yeltsin: A Life*. New York: Basic Books, 2008.

"Comrade Capitalism." Series by Roman Anin, Jason Bush, Douglas Busvine, Stephen Grey, Himanshu Ojha, Elizabeth Piper, Maria Tsvetkova and Brian Grow. Reuters. May 21–23, 2014.

Dawisha, Karen. "Is Russia's Foreign Policy That of a Corporatist-Kleptocratic Regime?" *Post-Soviet Affairs* 27, no. 4 (2011): 331–65.

Drozdov, Yuriy. *Nuzhnaya rabota* [Necessary work]. Moscow: VlaDar, 1994.

Drozdov, Yuriy. *Vymysel Isklyuchen* [Fiction excluded]. Moscow: Al'manakh "Vympel," 1996.

Drozdov, Yuriy, and Vasiliy Fartyshev. *Yuriy Andropov i Vladimir Putin: Na puti k vozrozhdeniyu* [Yuri Andropov and Vladimir Putin: On the path to renewal]. Moscow: Olma Press, 2001.

Drozdov, Yuriy, and A. G. Markin. *Operatsiya "Prezident": Ot kholodnoy voyny do perezagruzki* [Operation "President": From Cold War to reboot]. Moscow: Artstil'-poligrafiya, 2010.

Dunlop, John. *The Moscow Bombings of September 1999: Examinations of Russian Terrorist Attacks at the Onset of Vladimir Putin's Rule*. Stuttgart: Ibidem-Verlag, 2012.

Earley, Pete. *Comrade J: The Untold Secrets of Russia's Master Spy in America after the End of the Cold War.* New York: G. P. Putnam's Sons, 2007.

Felshtinskiy, Yuriy, and Vladimir Pribylovskiy. *The Age of Assassins: The Rise and Rise of Vladimir Putin.* London: Gibson Square, 2008.

Felshtinskiy, Yuriy, and Vladimir Pribylovskiy. *The Corporation: Russia and the KGB in the Age of President Putin.* New York: Encounter Books, 2008.

Felshtinskiy, Yuriy, and Vladimir Pribylovskiy. *Korporatsiya: Rossiya i KGB vo vremena Putina* [Corporation: Russia and the KGB in Putin's time]. Moscow: Terra–Knizhnyi klub, 2010.

Fish, M. Steven. *Democracy Derailed in Russia.* New York: Cambridge University Press, 2005.

Franchetti, Mark. Various articles in *Sunday Times (UK).*

Gaddy, Clifford G., and Barry W. Ickes. "Putin's Protection Racket." 2010. http://econ.la.psu.edu/~bickes/protection.pdf (accessed May 9, 2013).

Gertz, Bill. "Putin Corruption Network Revealed." *Washington (DC) Free Beacon,* April 7, 2014. http://freebeacon.com/national-security/putin-corruption-network-revealed/.

Gessen, Masha. *The Man without a Face: The Unlikely Rise of Vladimir Putin.* New York: Riverhead Books, 2012.

Goldman, Marshall I. *Petrostate: Putin, Power, and the New Russia.* New York: Oxford University Press, 2010.

Goldman, Marshall. *The Piratization of Russia: Russian Reform Goes Awry.* New York: Routledge, 2004.

Goscilo, Helena. ed. *Putin as Celebrity* and *Cultural Icon.* NY: Routledge, 2012.

Gustafson, Thane. *Wheel of Fortune: The Battle for Oil and Power in Russia.* Cambridge, MA: Belknap Press of Harvard University Press, 2012.

Hale, Henry E. "Explaining Machine Politics in Russia's Regions: Economy, Ethnicity, and Legacy." *Post-Soviet Affairs* 19, no. 3 (2003): 228–63.

Handelman, Stephen. *Comrade Criminal: Russia's New Mafiya.* New Haven, CT: Yale University Press, 1995.

Harding, Luke. Various articles in *Guardian (UK).*

Hellman, Joel S., Geraint Jones, and Daniel Kaufmann. "Seize the State, Seize the Day: State Capture and Influence in Transition Economies." *Journal of Comparative Economics* 31, no. 4 (2003): 751–73.

Hill, Fiona, and Clifford Gaddy. *Mr. Putin: Operative in the Kremlin.* Washington, DC: Brookings Institution Press, 2013.

Hosenball, Mark, and Christian Caryl. "A Stain on Mr. Clean: How a Money-Laundering Indictment in Europe Could Haunt Putin." *Newsweek,* September 3, 2001. http://russianlaw.org/newsweek$90301.htm (accessed April 7, 2012).

Ignatius, David. "Sergey Kolesnikov's Tale of Palatial Corruption, Russian Style." *Washington Post,* December 23, 2010. http://www.washingtonpost.com/wp-dyn/content/article/2010/12/22/AR2010122203770.html (accessed December 24, 2010).

Illarionov, Andrei. "Testimony." U.S. House Committee on Foreign Affairs. February 25, 2009. http://www.gpo.gov/fdsys/pkg/CHRG-111hhrg47667/html/CHRG-111hhrg47667.htm (accessed December 8, 2012).

In Search of Putin's Money. Directed by Sarah Spiller. 2012.

Ivanidze, Vladimir. Various articles in *Sovershenno sekretno, Novaya gazeta,* and Radio Free Europe/Radio Liberty.

Judah, Ben. *Fragile Empire: How Russia Fell in and out of Love with Vladimir Putin.* New Haven, CT: Yale University Press, 2013.

Kamyshev, Dmitriy. Various articles in *Kommersant.*

Kirilenko, Anastasia. Various articles at Radio Free Europe/Radio Liberty and Radio Svoboda websites.

Klebnikov, Paul. *Godfather of the Kremlin: The Decline of Russia in the Age of Gangster Capitalism.* New York: Harcourt, 2000.

Knight, Amy. *Spies without Cloaks: The KGB's Successors.* Princeton, NJ: Princeton University Press, 1996.

Kochiw, J. V. *Abuse of Power: Corruption in the Office of the President.* Reading, UK: Artemia Press, 2013.

Kolesnikov, Andrey I. Various books and articles, especially on Chubays.

Kolesnikov, Sergey. Documents on the building of "Putin's Palace," available at www .miamioh.edu/havighurstcenter/putins-russia.

Konstantinov, A. *Banditskiy Peterburg* [Bandit Petersburg]. St. Petersburg: Bibliopolis, 1995.

Konstantinov, Andrey, and Igor' Shusharin. *Banditskiy Peterburg: Dokumental'nye ocherki* [Bandit Petersburg: Documentary Study]. Vol. 2. St. Petersburg: Neva, 2004.

Kryshtanovskaya, Ol'ga. *Anatomiya rossiiskoy elity* [Anatomy of the Russian Elite]. Moscow: Zakharov, 2005.

Kryshtanovskaya, Olga, and Stephen White. "Putin's Militocracy." *Post-Soviet Affairs,* October–December 2003, 289–306.

Ledeneva, Alena V. *Can Russia Modernise? Sistema, Power Networks and Informal Governance.* New York: Cambridge University Press, 2013.

Ledeneva, Alena V. *How Russia Really Works.* Ithaca, NY: Cornell University Press, 2006.

Ledeneva, Alena V. *Russia's Economy of Favours: Blat, Networking and Informal Exchange.* New York: Cambridge University Press, 1998.

Leonov, Nikolay. "Krestnyy put' Rossii, gody 1991–2000 [The Way of the Cross of Russia, 1991–2000]." Gramotey.com. 2002. http://www.gramotey.com/?open_file=126 9069791.

Litvinenko, Alexander, and Yuri Felshtinsky. *Blowing Up Russia: The Secret Plot to Bring Back KGB Terror.* New York: Encounter Books, 2007.

Litvinovich, Marina. Election2012.ru. 2012.

Lucas, Edward. *Deception. The Untold Story of East-West Espionage Today.* London: Walker Books, 2012.

Lucas, Edward. *The New Cold War: Putin's Russia and the Threat to the West.* London: Palgrave, 2008.

Macrakis, Kristie. *Seduced by Secrets: Inside the Stasi's Spy-Tech World.* New York: Cambridge University Press, 2008.

Maksimov, Andrey A. *'Chistye' i 'Gryaznye' Tekhnologii Vyborov: Rossiyskiy opyt* ['Clean' and 'Gray' Electoral Technologies: The Russian Experiment]. Moscow: Delo, 1999.

Mandras, Marie. *Poutine: L'Envers du Pouvoir*. Paris: Editions Odile Jacob, 2008.

McFaul, Michael. *Russia's Unfinished Revolution*. Ithaca, NY: Cornell University Press, 2001.

Mikhaylov, Yuriy. *Delo Shutova: Politiko-kriminal'naya khronika Sankt-Peterburga* [The Shutov affair: A political-criminal chronicle of St. Petersburg]. St. Petersburg: Izdatel'skiy dom "Operativnoye prikrytiye," 2005.

Milov, Vladimir. Various writings on Putin's corruption at Putin-itogi.ru.

Moscow Times. Articles by Anna Badkhen, Yevgeniya Borosova, Simon Saradzhyan, Konstantin Sonin, Matt Taibbi.

Mukhin, Aleksey Alekseyevich. *Kto est' mister Putin i kto s nim prishel?: Dos'ye na Prezidenta Rossii i ego spetssluzhby* [Who is Mister Putin and who arrived with him? A dossier on the president of Russia and his special services]. Moscow: Gnom i D, 2002.

Myagkov, Mikhail, Peter C. Ordeshook, and Dimitry Shaikin. "Estimating the Trail of Votes in Russia's Elections and the Likelihood of Fraud." In R. Michael Alvarez, Thad E. Hall, and Susan D. Hyde, eds., *The Art and Science of Studying Election Fraud: Detection, Prevention, and Consequences*. Washington, DC: Brookings Institution, 2008.

Myagkov, Mikhail, Peter C. Ordeshook, and Dmitry Shaikin. *The Forensics of Election Fraud: Russia and Ukraine*. New York: Cambridge University Press, 2009.

Navalnyy, Aleksey. Various writings on elite corruption at Navalny.livejournal.com.

Nemtsov, Boris. "Putin's Clan in the Government and Business," *YouTube*, June 19, 2012, http://www.youtube.com/watch?v=hj5FdOiBnXk.

Nemtsov, Boris. Various writings on Putin's corruption at Putin-itogi.ru and Nemtsov.ru.

New Times. Articles by Yevgeniya Al'bats, Il'ya Barabanov, Andrey Kolesnikov, Valeriya Novodvorskaya, Vladimir Pribylovskiy.

New York Times. Articles by Celestine Bohlen, Andrew Kramer, Michael Wines.

New Yorker. Articles by Julia Ioffe, Masha Lipman, David Remnick, Michael Specter.

Novaya gazeta. Especially articles by Roman Anin, Vladimir Ivanidze, Yulia Latynina, Leonid Nikitinskiy, Roman Shleynov, and selected writings by Oleg Lur'ye.

Organized Crime and Corruption Reporting Project. www.reportingproject.net.

Ostrow, Joel M., Georgiy A. Satarov, and Irina M. Khakamada. *The Consolidation of Dictatorship in Russia: An Inside View of the Demise of Democracy*. Westport, CT: Praeger Security International, 2007.

Palmer, Richard L. "Statement on the Infiltration of the Western Financial System by Elements of Russian Organized Crime before the House Committee on Banking and Financial Services." American Russian Law Institute. September 21, 1999. http://www.russianlaw.org/palmer.htm (accessed April 6, 2012).

Parfitt, Tom. Various articles in *Guardian (UK)*.

Pavlovskiy, Gleb. *Genial'naya Vlast'! Slovar' Abstraktsi Kremlya* [The genius of power! A dictionary of Kremlin abstractions]. Moscow: Evropa, 2012.

Pitch, Iren. *Pikantnaya druzhba: Moya podruga Lyudmila Putina, eyo sem'ya i drugiye tovarishchi* [Piquant friendship: My friend Lyudmila Putina, her family and dear friends]. Moscow: Zakharov, 2002.

Pluzhnikov, Sergey. Various articles in *Sovershenno sekretno*.

Powell, Bill. "Follow the Money." *Newsweek,* March 28, 1999. http://www.newsweek
.com/follow-money-163696 (accessed April 10, 2012).

Pribylovskiy, Vladimir. Antikompromat.org.

Putin, Vladimir, Nataliya Gevorkyan, Natalya Timakova, and Andrei I. Kolesnikov. *First
Person.* New York: Public Affairs, 2000.

Reddaway, Peter. "The Silovik War of 2004–2010: What Does It Reveal about the Nature
and Direction of the Putin Regime?" Unpublished ms. October 1, 2012.

Reznik, Irina. Articles in *Vedomosti* and *Bloomberg.*

Sakwa, Richard. *Putin and the Oligarch.* London: I. B. Taurus, 2014.

Sal'ye Commission documents. Facebook. https://www.facebook.com/photo.php
?fbid=384728604885108&set=a.384728321551803.94156.273762169315086&
type=1&theater#!/media/set/?set=a.384728321551803.94156.273762169315086
&type=1 and at www.miamioh.edu/havighurstcenter/putins-russia.

Sal'ye, Marina. "Moy otvet Putinu [My answer to Putin]." Radio Svoboda, January 7,
2012. http://www.svobodanews.ru/content/blog/24444669.html (accessed April 13,
2012).

Sal'ye, Marina. "Nastal chered Putina—'Prezidenta' korrumpirovannogo klana [Putin's
turn—'President' of a corrupt clan]." Radio Svoboda, March 22, 2012. http://www
.svoboda.org/content/blog/24500639.html (accessed April 10, 2012).

Sal'ye, Marina. "V. Putin—'Prezident' korrumpirovannoy oligarkhii! [V. Putin—
'President' of a corrupt oligarchy!]" *Antikompromat,* March 2000.

Satter, David. *Darkness at Dawn: The Rise of the Russian Criminal State.* New Haven, CT:
Yale University Press, 2003.

Serio, Joseph. *Investigating the Russian Mafia.* Durham, NC: Carolina Academic Press,
2008.

Serrano, J. C., and E. Montánchez. "Los Viajes Secretos de Putin a Sotogrande" [The
Secret Travels of Putin to Sotogrande]. *La Razón (Madrid),* June 13, 2000, 16–17.

Shevtsova, Lilia. *Putin's Russia.* Revised and expanded edition. Washington, DC: Carnegie Endowment for International Peace, 2005.

Skuratov, Yuriy. *Variant drakona* [The Dragon Option]. Moscow: Detektiv-Press, 2000.

Sobchak, Anatolii. *Khozhdenie vo vlast'* [Walking in Power]. 2nd edition. Moscow:
Novosti. 2001

Soldatov, Andrei, and Irina Borogan. *The New Nobility: The Restoration of Russia's Security
State and the Enduring Legacy of the KGB.* New York: PublicAffairs, 2010.

Solnick, Stephen. *Stealing the State.* Cambridge MA: Harvard University Press, 1998.

Sonin, Konstantin. "Why the Rich May Favor Poor Protection of Property Rights." *Journal of Comparative Economics* 31, no. 4 (2003): 715–31.

Starobin, Paul. "The Accidental Autocrat." *Atlantic,* March 2005.

Talanov, Viktor. *Psikhologicheskiy portret Vladimira Putina* [Psychological portrait of
Vladimir Putin]. St. Petersburg: B&K, 2000.

Taylor, Brian D. *State Building in Putin's Russia: Policing and Coercion after Communism.*
New York: Cambridge University Press, 2011.

Timofeyev, Lev. *Russia's Secret Rulers.* New York: Knopf, 1992.

Tregubova, Elena. *Bayki Kremlyevskogo diggera* [Tales of a Kremlin digger]. Moscow: Izdatel'stvo Ad Marginem, 2003.

Treisman, Daniel. *The Return: Russia's Journey from Gorbachev to Putin.* New York: Free Press, 2011.

Vaksburg, Arkadi. *Toxic Politics: The Secret History of the Kremlin's Poison Laboratory.* Translated by Paul McGregor. Santa Barbara, CA: ABC-CLIO, 2011.

Varese, Frederico. *The Russian Mafia.* New York: Oxford University Press, 2001.

Volkov, Vadim. *Violent Entrepreneurs: The Use of Force in the Making of Russian Capitalism.* Ithaca, NY: Cornell University Press, 2002.

Volodarsky, Boris. *The KGB's Poison Factory.* Minneapolis, MN: Zenith Press, 2009.

Wikileaks.org.

NOTES

Introduction

1. OECD, "Economic Survey: Russian Federation 2006," in by Ariel Cohen, *Domestic Factors Driving Russia's Foreign Policy: Backgrounder #2084* (Washington, DC: Heritage Foundation, 2007).

2. Central Bank of Russia, "Net Inflows/Outflows of Capital by Private Sector in 2005–2013 and in the First Quarter of 2014," April 9, 2014, http://www.cbr.ru/eng/statistics/print.aspx ?file=credit_statistics/capital_new_e.htm&pid=svs&sid=itm_49171 (accessed May 4, 2014).

3. Credit Suisse, *Global Wealth Report 2013*, October 2013, https://publications.credit-suisse.com /tasks/render/file/?fileID=BCDB1364-A105-0560-1332EC9100FF5C83 (accessed November 1, 2013).

4. Mark Hosenball and Christian Caryl, "A Stain on Mr. Clean: How a Money-Laundering Indictment in Europe Could Haunt Putin," *Newsweek*, September 3, 2001, http://russianlaw.org /newsweek$90301.htm (accessed April 7, 2012).

5. White House, "President's Statement on Kleptocracy," August 2006, http://georgewbush -whitehouse.archives.gov/news/releases/2006/08/20060810.html (accessed May 4, 2014).

6. Peter Baker, "Sanctions Revive Search for Secret Putin Fortune," *New York Times.* April 27, 2014, http://www.nytimes.com/2014/04/27/world/sanctions-revive-search-for-secret-putin -fortune.html (accessed April 27, 2014).

7. Rob Evans, Luke Harding, and John Hooper, "WikiLeaks Cables: Berlusconi 'Profited from Secret Deals' with Putin," *Guardian.* December 2, 2010, http://www.theGuardian.com/world /2010/dec/02/wikileaks-cables-berlusconi-putin (accessed October 17, 2013).

8. Karen Dawisha, *Eastern Europe, Gorbachev and Reform*, 2nd ed. (New York: Cambridge University Press, 1990); Karen Dawisha and Bruce Parrott, *Russia and the New States of Eurasia: The Politics of Upheaval* (New York: Cambridge University Press, 1994); Karen Dawisha and Bruce Parrott, eds., *Authoritarianism and Democratization in Post-Communist Societies*, 4 vols. (New York: Cambridge University Press, 1997); Karen Dawisha and Bruce Parrott, series editors, *The International Politics of Eurasia,* 10 vols. (Armonk, NY: M.E. Sharpe, 1994–97).

9. Samuel Huntington, *The Third Wave: Democratization in the Late Twentieth Century* (Norman: University of Oklahoma Press, 1991); Mancur Olson, *Power and Prosperity* (New York: Oxford University Press, 2000).

10. Michael McFaul, *Russia's Unfinished Revolution* (Ithaca, NY: Cornell University Press, 2001); M. Steven Fish, *Democracy Derailed in Russia* (New York: Cambridge University Press, 2005); Richard Sakwa, *The Crisis of Russian Democracy: The Dual State, Factionalism and the Medvedev Succession* (New York: Cambridge University Press, 2011); Henry Hale, *Why Not Parties in Russia?* (New York: Cambridge University Press, 2007); Regina Smyth, *Candidate Strategies and Electoral Competition in the Russian Federation: Democracy without Foundation* (New York: Cambridge University Press, 2006); Brian D. Taylor, *State Building in Putin's Russia: Policing and Coercion after Communism* (New York: Cambridge University Press, 2011); Gulnaz Sharafutdinova, *Political Consequences of Crony Capitalism inside Russia* (South Bend, IN: University of Notre Dame Press,

2011); Thomas Remington, *The Politics of Inequality in Russia* (New York: Cambridge University Press, 2011); Michael Urban, *Cultures of Power in Post-Communist Russia* (New York: Cambridge University Press, 2010); Steven Levitsky and Lucan A. Way, *Competitive Authoritarianism: Hybrid Regimes After the Cold War* (New York: Cambridge University Press, 2010); Jennifer Gandhi, *Political Institutions under Dictatorship* (New York: Cambridge University Press, 2008); Jason Brownlee, *Authoritarianism in an Age of Democratization* (New York: Cambridge University Press, 2007).

11. Stephen Holmes, "Fragments of a Defunct State," *London Review of Books*, January 5, 2012, http://www.lrb.co.uk/v34/n01/stephen-holmes/fragments-of-a-defunct-state (accessed March 7, 2012).

12. Mancur Olson, *Power and Prosperity* (New York: Oxford University Press, 2000).

13. David Hearst, "Will Putinism See the End of Putin?," *Guardian*, February 27, 2012, http://www.theGuardian.co.uk/world/2012/feb/27/vladimir-putin-profile-putinism?INTCMP=SRCH (accessed April 28, 2013).

14. Masha Gessen, *The Man without a Face: The Unlikely Rise of Vladimir Putin* (New York: Riverhead Books, 2012), 259.

15. "Putin's Watch Collection Dwarfs His Declared Income," *Moscow Times*, June 8, 2012, http://www.themoscowtimes.com/news/article/putins-watch-collection-dwarfs-his-declared-income/460061.html (accessed June 10, 2012).

16. Maria Antonova, "Ex-IKEA Boss Bares Russia's 'Chaotic Reality,'" *Moscow Times*, March 25, 2010; Rupert Wingfield-Hayes, "Interview with IKEA Russia Manager Lennart Dahlgren," *BBC World Service*, May 10, 2010, http://www.bbc.co.uk/worldservice/news/2010/05/100514_russia_corruption_hayes.shtml?bw=nb&mp=wm&news=1&ms3=10&ms_javascript=true&bbcws=2 (accessed May 4, 2014).

17. American Embassy Moscow to U.S. Secretary of State, "The Kremlin's Luzhkov Dilemma," Wikileaks, February 12, 2010, http://www.wikileaks.org/plusd/cables/10MOSCOW317_a.html (accessed May 7, 2012).

Chapter One: The USSR at the Moment of Collapse

1. Nikolaus von Twickel, "Russia Implicated in Litvinenko Death," *Moscow Times*, December 13, 2012, www.themoscowtimes.com/mobile/article/russia-implicated-in-litvinenko-death/473102.html (accessed December 15, 2012).

2. Esther Addley, "Alexander Litvinenko Murder: British Evidence 'Shows Russia Involved,'" *Guardian*, December 13, 2012, http://www.theGuardian.co.uk/world/2012/dec/13/alexander-litvinenko-murder-british-evidence-russia?INTCMP=SRCH (accessed December 15, 2012).

3. "Ispanskiye SMI soobshchili ob obyske na ville deputata Gosdumy RF," Lenta.ru, October 19, 2008, http://old.lenta.ru/news/2008/10/19/ruso/ (accessed December 15, 2012).

4. Sergey Makarov. "The Corruption Rating of Russia's Ministries and Departments from Novaya Gazeta, June 11, 2011," Wikileaks, September 21, 2011, http://wikileaks.org/gifiles/docs/21/2186612_-os-russia-russian-paper-offers-rating-of-most-corrupt.html (accessed May 9, 2013).

5. Roman Shleynov, "Ptentsy gnezda Petrova [Chicks in Petrov's nest]," *Novaya gazeta*, November 2, 2009, http://dlib.eastview.com/browse/doc/20851285 (accessed July 18, 2012).

6. American Embassy Madrid to U.S. Secretary of State, "Spain Details Its Strategy to Combat the Russian Mafia," Wikileaks, February 8, 2010, https://wikileaks.org/cable/2010/02/10MADRID154.html (accessed April 23, 2012).

7. American Embassy Madrid to U.S. Secretary of State, "Spain Details Its Strategy to Combat the Russian Mafia."

8. American Embassy Madrid to U.S. Secretary of State, "Updates in Spain's Investigations of Russian Mafia," Wikileaks, August 31, 2009, http:/wikileaks.org/cable/2009/08/09MADRID869.html (accessed July 11, 2012).

9. A. Craig Copetas, *Bear-Hunting with the Politburo: A Gritty First-Hand Account of Russia's Young Entrepreneurs—and Why Soviet-Style Capitalism Can't Work* (New York: Simon & Schuster, 1991), 63.

10. Andrey Gromov, "Poglotiteli [Scavengers]," Slon.ru, December 2012, http://slon.ru/ipad /poglotiteli-861364.xhtml (accessed January 22, 2014).

11. Copetas, *Bear-Hunting with the Politburo.*

12. Richard L. Palmer, "Statement on the Infiltration of the Western Financial System by Elements of Russian Organized Crime before the House Committee on Banking and Financial Services," Russian Law Institute, September 21, 1999, http://www.russianlaw.org/palmer.htm (accessed April 6, 2012), 324.

13. Makarov Commission, "Results of the Work of the Special Commission of the General Pro-curacy of the Russian Federation on Investigation of Material Connected with the Corrup-tion of Officials," *Sovetskaya Rossiya,* September 4, 1993, in Foreign Broadcast Information Service Daily Report, FBIS-USR 93-122. http://infoweb.newsbank.com/iw-search/we/Hist Archive/?p_product=FBISX&p_theme=fbis&p_nbid=K6FW5AMVMTMzNTM4ODI4MC 40MTEwNDk6MToxNToyMDUuMjAxLjI0Mi4xMjY&p_action=doc&s_lastnonissuequery name=15&p_queryname=15&p_docref=v2:11C33B0D5F860D98@FBISX-1366DA7E231E 110 (accessed April 24, 2012).

14. Daniel Sneider, "Russia Goes after 'Party Gold,'" *Christian Science Monitor,* March 4, 1992, http://www.csmonitor.com/1992/0304/04021.html/(page)/2 (accessed April 25, 2013).

15. Celestine Bohlen, "U.S. Company to Help Russia Track Billions," *New York Times,* March 3, 1992, http://proquest.umi.com/pqdweb?index=2&did=116199933&SrchMode=1&sid=1&F mt=10&VInst=PROD&VType=PQD&RQT=309&VName=HNP&TS=1334093904&client Id=73174 (accessed April 8, 2012).

16. Marshall I. Goldman, *The Piratization of Russia: Russian Reform Goes Awry* (New York: Rout-ledge, 2004), 158.

17. Stephen Handelman, *Comrade Criminal: Russia's New Mafiya* (New Haven, CT: Yale Univer-sity Press, 1995); Paul Klebnikov, *Godfather of the Kremlin: The Decline of Russia in the Age of Gangster Capitalism* (New York: Harcourt, 2000); Robert I. Friedman, *Red Mafiya* (New York: Berkley Books, 2002); Frederico Varese, *The Russian Mafia* (New York: Oxford University Press, 2001); Jung Gerber, "On the Relationship between Organized and White-Collar Crime: Gov-ernment, Business, and Criminal Enterprise in Post-Communist Russia," *European Journal of Crime, Criminal Law and Criminal Justice* 8, no. 4 (2000): 327–42; Phil Williams, ed., *Rus-sian Organized Crime* (London: Frank Cass, 1997); and Louise Shelly, "Contemporary Russian Organised Crime," in *Organised Crime in Europe: Concepts, Patterns and Control Policies in the European Union and Beyond,* eds. Cyrille Fijnaut and Letizia Paoli. (Dordrecht, The Nether-lands: Springer, 2004), 563–85.

18. Vladimir Tikhomirov, "Capital Flight from Post-Soviet Russia," *Europe-Asia Studies* 49, no. 4 (1997): 592, http://www.jstor.org/stable/153715 (accessed April 1 2012, April).

19. Makarov Commission, "Results of the Work of the Special Commission of the General Procu-racy of the Russian Federation on Investigation of Material Connected with the Corruption of Officials."

20. Tikhomirov, "Capital Flight from Post-Soviet Russia," 592.

21. David E. Kaplan and Caryl Christian, "The Looting of Russia," *U.S. News & World Report,* August 3, 1998, 26, http://www.publicintegrity.org/1998/08/03/3349/looting-russia (accessed November 2, 2012); Mark Franchetti, "Panic Grips Kremlin in $180m Diamond Scandal," *Sunday Times (UK),* June 14, 1998, http://www.russialist.org/archives/2220.html##1 (accessed November 2, 2012); Thomas J. Kneir, Deputy Assistant Director, FBI Criminal Investiga-tive Division, *Testimony to House Banking, General Oversight and Investigations Subcommittee,* September 10, 1998, http://www.fas.org/irp/congress/1998_hr/98091006_clt.html (accessed November 2, 2012).

22. *Golden ADA, Inc. v. U.S.*, March 1, 1996, Leagle, http://www.leagle.com/xmlResult.aspx?page=7&xmldoc=19961275934FSupp341_11203.xml&docbase=CSLWAR2-1986-2006&SizeDisp=7 (accessed December 15, 2012).

23. FBI, "Organized Crime: Golden Ada Company. San Francisco, California," n.d., http://www.fbi.gov/about-us/investigate/organizedcrime/cases/golden-ada (accessed December 14, 2012).

24. Sergey Sokolov and Sergey Pluzhnikov, "Rassledovaniye: Zoloto KPSS. Desyat' let spustya [Investigation: Party Gold. Ten Years Later]," *Moskovskiye Novosti*, May 8, 2001, http://dlib.eastview.com/browse/doc/141444 (accessed July 3, 2013).

25. Alexander Rahr, *Putin Nach Putin: Das Kapitalistische Russland am Beginn einer neuen Weltordnung* (Berlin: Universitas Verlag, 2008), 75–79.

26. V. A. Ivashko, "Decree re Urgent Measures on the Organization of Commercial and Foreign Economic Activities of the Party," American Russian Law Institute, Appendix to Testimony by Richard Palmer, August 23, 1990, http://www.russianlaw.org/palmer.htm (accessed April 6, 2012).

27. Christopher Andrew and Vasili Mitrokhin, *The Sword and the Shield: The Mitrokhin Archive and the Secret History of the KGB* (New York: Basic Books, 1999), 568–69.

28. V. G. Veselovskiy, "Analytical Memorandum of Colonel of the KGB of the USSR, V. G. Veselovskiy, to Chief of the Executive Administration of the Central Committee of the CPSU, N. V. Kruchina, 1990," in Paul Klebnikov, *Godfather of the Kremlin: The Decline of Russia in the Age of Gangster Capitalism* (New York: Harcourt, 2000), 59.

29. Sergey Sokolov and Sergey Pluzhnikov, "Kak KGB svodil schyotu s KPSS [How the KGB settled scores with the CPSU]," Freelance Bureau, Agenstvo Federal'nykh Rassledovaniy [Agency of Federal Investigations], January 19, 1992, http://flb.ru/info/4895.html. (accessed April 7, 2012).

30. Palmer, "Statement on the Infiltration of the Western Financial System by Elements of Russian Organized Crime,", 317.

31. Nikolai Leonov, Eugenia Fediakova, and Joaquin Fermandois, "General Nikolay Leonov at the CEP," translated by Tim Ennis, *Estudios Públicos*, Summer 1999, 14, http://www.cepchile.cl/dms/archivo_1141_1464/rev73.leonov-interv_ing.pdf.

32. Bill Powell, "Follow the Money," *Newsweek*, March 28, 1999, http://www.newsweek.com/follow-money-163696 (accessed April 10, 2012).

33. Yevgenia Albats, *The State within a State* (New York: Farrar, Straus and Giroux, 1994), 248; U.S. Congress, House Committee on Banking and Financial Services, *Russian Money Laundering: Hearings before the Committee on Banking and Financial Services, 106th Congress, First Session, September 21–22, 1999*, vol. 4, http://books.google.com.pr/books?ei=ewvOUN7JK5OK9ASd2ICADA&id=80Pbegp2PCoC&dq=Leonid+Veselovsky&q=Leonid+Veselovsky (accessed December 16, 2012).

34. Alexander Yakovlev, *Sumerki* [Time of Darkness] (Moscow: Materik, 2003); Albats, *The State within a State*; Feliks Shemedlovskiy, *Ideolog mnogorazovogo ispol'zovaniya* [Ideologue for all seasons], March 4, 2005, http://flb.ru/infoprint/33789.html (accessed December 16, 2012); Andrey Grigor'yev, "Apolitichniy Gusinskiy [Apolitical Gusinskiy]," *Kompaniya Delovoy Ezhenedel'nik*, March 28, 2000, http://ko.ru/articles/1509 (accessed July 8, 2011); Conor O'Clery, *Moscow, December 25, 1991* (New York: PublicAffairs, 2011).

35. Catherine Belton, "Khodorkovsky's High Stakes Gamble," *Moscow Times*, May 16, 2005, http://mikhail_khodorkovsky_society_two.blogspot.com/ (accessed July 6, 2013); Martin Sixsmith, *Putin's Oil* (New York: Continuum, 2010).

36. Belton, "Khodorkovsky's High Stakes Gamble."

37. Belton, "Khodorkovsky's High Stakes Gamble."

38. TASS, November 14, 1991, in Amy Knight, *Spies without Cloaks: The KGB's Successors* (Princeton, NJ: Princeton University Press, 1996), 57.

39. Mark Deych, "Lyubanka: Vsyo na prodazhu? [The Lyubanka: Is everything for sale?]" *Literaturnaya gazeta*, June 24, 1992, 13.

40. "Kalugin Interview," in Lev Timofeev, *Russia's Secret Rulers* (New York: Knopf, 1992), 106–11; Albats, *The State within a State*, 249.

41. Oleg Kalugin, *Spymaster* (New York: Basic Books, 2009), 170.

42. Palmer, "Statement on the Infiltration of the Western Financial System by Elements of Russian Organized Crime," 318.

43. Leonid Berres, "Vozvrashchennyye den'gi KPSS rastracheny [Returned CPSU money siphoned off]," *Kommersant*, July 30, 1994, http://www.kommersant.ru/doc/85414/print (accessed April 28, 2013); Sokolov and Pluzhnikov, "Rassledovaniye: Zoloto KPSS. Desyat' let spustya [Investigation: Party Gold. Ten Years Later]"; Nikolay Leonov, "Krestnyy put' Rossii, gody 1991–2000 [The Way of the Cross of Russia, 1991–2000]," *Gramotey.com*, 2002, http://www.gramotey.com/?open_file=1269069791, p. 51.

44. Palmer, "Statement on the Infiltration of the Western Financial System by Elements of Russian Organized Crime," 317.

45. Susan Tifft and Yuriy Zarakhovich, "Desperately Seeking Rubles," *Time*, April 11, 1991, http://content.time.com/time/magazine/article/0,9171,974181-1,00.html (accessed July 4, 2013).

46. Lev Timofeyev, *Russia's Secret Rulers* (New York: Knopf, 1992); Anthony Jones and William Moskoff, *Ko-ops: The Rebirth of Entrepreneurship in the Soviet Union* (Bloomington: Indiana University Press, 1991).

47. Sokolov and Pluzhnikov, "Kak KGB svodil schyotu s KPSS [How the KGB settled scores with the CPSU]."

48. Aleksandr Borin, "KGB podstavil sobstvennyy proyekt, shtoby svalit' Gorbacheva [KGB established own project to topple Gorbachev]," *Novaya gazeta*, February 14, 2008, http://dlib.eastview.com/browse/doc/13431400 (accessed July 31, 2013).

49. Aleksandr Borin, "Zanyat' 'Oboronku' [To occupy 'Defense']," *Novaya gazeta*, February 7, 2008, http://dlib.eastview.com/browse/doc/13397267 (accessed July 21, 2013).

50. Borin, "Zanyat' 'Oboronku' [To occupy 'Defense']."

51. Vadim Belykh and Valery Rudnev, "The Party's Money," *Izvestiya*, February 10, 1992, http://dlib.eastview.com/browse/doc/13539206 (accessed June 20, 2012).

52. Carlo Bonini and Giuseppe D'Avanzo, "I Cekisti al Potere [The Checkists in power]," *La Repubblica*, July 15, 2001, http://ricerca.repubblica.it/repubblica/archivio/repubblica/2001/07/15/cekisti-al-potere.html (accessed April 4, 2012).

53. Carlo Bonini, Giuseppe d'Avanzo, and James Marcus, *Collusion* (New York: Melville House, 2007).

54. Leonov et al., "General Nikolay Leonov at the CEP," 14.

55. Vladimir Putin, Nataliya Gevorkyan, Natalya Timakova, and Andrei I. Kolesnikov, *First Person* (New York: Public Affairs, 2000), 80, 94.

56. Grigoriy Volchek, "Valeriy Shchukin: 'Sluzhba v KGB—plyus dlya politika' ['KGB service is a plus for a politician']," *Zvezda (Perm')*, June 15, 2000, www.nevod.ru/local/zvezda/archive.html (accessed May 4, 2013).

57. Gordon Bennett, "The SVR: Russia's Intelligence Service," UK Ministry of Defense, March 2000, http://www.fas.org/irp/world/russia/svr/c103-gb.htm (accessed April 11, 2012); Alan Cullison, Gregory L. White, and David Crawford, "In Putin's Past, Glimpses of Russia's Hardline Future," *Wall Street Journal*, December 21, 2007, http://online.wsj.com/article/SB119820263246543973.html (accessed April 17, 2012).

58. Nikolay Leonov, "Krestnyy put' Rossii, gody 1991–2000 [The Way of the Cross of Russia, 1991–2000]."

59. "Kalugin Interview," in Timofeev, *Russia's Secret Rulers*, 107.

60. Yuriy Drozdov and Vasiliy Fartyshev, *Yuriy Andropov i Vladimir Putin: na puti k vozrozhdeniyu* [Yuri Andropov and Vladimir Putin: On the path to renewal] (Moscow: Olma Press, 2001); Vladimir Usol'tsev, *Sosluzhivets: Neizvestnyye stranitsy zhizni prezidenta* [Colleague: Unknown Pages from the life of the President] (Moscow: Eksmo, 2004).

61. "Memorandum to the TsK KPSS from N. Kruchina, Administrator of the Administration of the TsK KPSS Affairs, re the deposit of 100,000,000 rubles into the account of the Kompartbank commercial bank, Reel 1.992 Opus 11(84), February 1991," in *Fond 89: Communist Part of the Soviet Union on Trial. Archives of the Communist Party and Soviet State. Guide to the Microfilm Collection in the Hoover Institution Archives, compiled by Lara Soroka* (Stanford, CA: Hoover Institution Press, 2001).

62. "Gavriil Popov Interview," in Timofeyev. *Russia's Secret Rulers*, 21.

63. Vadim Volkov, *Violent Entrepreneurs: The Use of Force in the Making of Russian Capitalism* (Ithaca, NY: Cornell University Press, 2002).

64. "Konstantin Maydanyk Interview," in Timofeyev, *Russia's Secret Rulers*, 75.

65. Boris Berezovskiy, interview by Karen Dawisha, Washington, DC, February 14, 2000.

66. Ivan Novikov, "Resolution on Aid to Foreign Banks Issued," *TASS*, February 10, 1992, 66.

67. "Agents in Power," *St. Petersburg Times*, February 12, 2008, http://www.sptimes.ru/index.php?story_id=25000&action_id=2 (accessed December 15, 2012); "Andrey Akimov," Gazprom, n.d., http://www.gazprom.com/about/management/directors/akimov/ (accessed April 28, 2013); Hans-Martin Tillack, "Liechtenstein contra Gazprom," Stern.de, October 10, 2007, http://www.stern.de/wirtschaft/2-finanzpruefung-liechtenstein-contra-gazprom-599892.html (accessed June 8, 2013); Roman Kupchinsky, "Bulgaria's 'Overgas,' a Russian Spy in Canada, and Gazprom," *Eurasia Daily Monitor*, February 13, 2009, http://www.jamestown.org/single/?no_cache=1&tx_ttnews%5Btt_news%5D=34511 (accessed May 8, 2013).

68. American Embassy Vienna to U.S. Secretary of State, "Raiffeisen on Ukraine-Russian Gas Deal," Wikileaks, February 6, 2006, http://wikileaks.org/cable/2006/02/06VIENNA350.html (accessed December 14, 2012).

69. Powell, "Follow the Money"; Celestine Bohlen, "Secrecy by Kremlin Financial Czars Raises Eyebrows," *New York Times*, July 30, 1999, http://www.nytimes.com/1999/07/30/world/secrecy-by-kremlin-financial-czars-raises-eyebrows.html (accessed April 10, 2012).

70. Powell, "Follow the Money."

71. Palmer, "Statement on the Infiltration of the Western Financial System by Elements of Russian Organized Crime," 339.

72. Bonini and D'Avanzo, "I Cekisti al Potere [The Checkists in power]."

73. Tifft and Zarakhovich, "Desperately Seeking Rubles."

74. Palmer, "Statement on the Infiltration of the Western Financial System by Elements of Russian Organized Crime."

75. Makarov Commission, "Results of the Work of the Special Commission of the General Procuracy of the Russian Federation on Investigation of Material Connected with the Corruption of Officials"; Palmer, "Statement on the Infiltration of the Western Financial System by Elements of Russian Organized Crime," 317.

76. Jones and Moskoff. *Ko-ops*, 92.

77. Klebnikov, *Godfather of the Kremlin*.

78. Hearst, "Will Putinism See the End of Putin?"

79. Yuriy Drozdov and A. G. Markin, *Operatsiya "Prezident": Ot kholodnoy voyny do perezagruzki* [Operation "President": From Cold War to reboot] (Moscow: Artstil'-poligrafiya, 2010); Nikolay Leonov, "Krestnyy put' Rossii, 1991–2000 [The way of the cross of Russia, 1991–2000]," Gramotey.com, 2002, 51, http://www.gramotey.com/?open_file=1269069791; Vladimir Putin, remarks at Körber-Stiftung conference, St. Petersburg, quoted from the transcript (at http://www.koerber-stiftung.de/fileadmin/bg/PDFs/bnd_101_de.pdf) by Timothy Garton Ash, "Putin's Deadly Doctrine," *New York Times*, July 18, 2014.

80. Timofeyev, *Russia's Secret Rulers*, 143.

81. Vladimir Putin, "Prime Minister Vladimir Putin Delivers His Report on the Government's Performance in 2011 to the State Duma," Premier.gov.ru, April 11, 2012.

82. Vyacheslav Shironin, *KGB-TsRU: Sekretnyye pruzhiny perestroiki* [KGB-CIA: The secret springs of perestroika] (Moscow: Yaguar, 1997).

Chapter Two: The Making of Money and Power

1. Clifford G. Gaddy and Barry W. Ickes, "Putin's Protection Racket," Center for Research on International Financial and Energy Security, September 23, 2010, http://crifes.psu.edu/papers /Putin's%20Protection%20Racket.pdf (accessed May 9, 2013).

2. Yuri Felshtinsky and Vladimir Pribylovsky, *The Corporation: Russia and the KGB in the Age of President Putin* (New York: Encounter Books, 2008); Andrey Illarionov, "The Rise of the Corporatist State in Russia," Institute of Economic Analysis, March 7, 2006, http://www.iea.ru /siloviki_model.php (accessed March 9, 2011).

3. Michael Specter, "Kremlin, Inc.," *New Yorker*, January 29, 2007, http://www.newyorker.com /reporting/2007/01/29/070129fa_fact_specter (accessed March 3, 2010).

4. Alena V. Ledeneva, *Can Russia Modernise? Sistema, Power Networks and Informal Governance* (New York: Cambridge University Press, 2013).

5. Karen Dawisha, "Is Russia's Foreign Policy That of a Corporatist-Kleptocratic Regime?," *Post-Soviet Affairs* 49, no. 4 (2011): 331–65.

6. Yevgeniy Gontmakher, "Rossiyskogo gosudarstva ne sushchestvuyet [A Russian state does not exist]," *Moskovskiy Komsomolets*, August 18, 2013, http://www.mk.ru/specprojects/free -theme/article/2013/08/18/901103-rossiyskogo-gosudarstva-ne-suschestvuet.html (accessed August 19, 2013).

7. Gontmakher, "Rossiyskogo gosudarstva ne sushchestvuyet [A Russian state does not exist]."

8. Credit Suisse, *Global Wealth Report 2013*, October 2013, 53, https://publications.credit-suisse .com/tasks/render/file/?fileID=BCDB1364-A105-0560-1332EC9100FF5C83 (accessed November 1, 2013).

9. Ted Koppel, "Acting President Putin Grants Interview," *Nightline*, March 24, 2000, http:// www.russialist.org/archives/4196.html (accessed April 28, 2013).

10. Ben Judah, "Last Cake with a Russian Agent," *Standpoint*, January/February 2010, 31, http:// standpointmag.co.uk/last-cake-with-a-russian-agent-features-jan-10-ben-judah-anton-surikov (accessed August 13, 2013).

11. Izvestiya Analytical Center, "Criminal Russia," *Izvestiya*, in Foreign Broadcast Information Service, *FBIS Report, Central Eurasia, FBIS-USR-94-123*, October 18-19, 1994, http://info web.newsbank.com/iw-search/we/HistArchive/?p_product=FBISX&p_theme=fbis&p_nbid =F6AI52KNMTMzNTY0MTg5MC4zODYxMjoxOjE1OjIwNS4yMDEuMjQyLjEyNg&p _action=doc&p_docref=v2:11C33B0D5F860D98@FBISX-12F1D7F7DDEA0138@24496 71-12F1D7FBE83A10B0-12F1D7FC15747650 (accessed April 28, 2012).

12. Gessen, *The Man without a Face*, 61–63; Usol'tsev, *Sosluzhivets* [Colleague], 186; Carlo Bonini and Giuseppe D'Avanzo, "Putin, le bugie sul KGB [Putin, lies about the KGB]," *La Repubblica*, July 11, 2001, http://ricerca.repubblica.it/repubblica/archivio/repubblica/2001/07/11/putin -le-bugie-sul-kgb.html (accessed April 11, 2012).

13. Pete Earley, *Comrade J: The Untold Secrets of Russia's Master Spy in America after the End of the Cold War* (New York: G. P. Putnam's Sons, 2007), 296.

14. Michael Wines, "Putin Was Once Decorated as a Spy: Few Agree on His Deeds," *New York Times*, January 10, 2000, http://www.nytimes.com/2000/01/10/world/putin-was-once -decorated-as-a-spy-few-agree-on-his-deeds.html (accessed May 7, 2013); Lorraine Millot, "Cinq ans en Allemagne sans (presque) laisser de traces [Five years in Germany without (almost) leaving any traces]," *Libération* (Paris), March 25, 2000, http://www.liberation.fr /evenement/0101329582-cinq-ans-en-allemagne-sans-presque-laisser-de-traces-de-1985-a-1990 -l-agent-du-kgb-vladimir-poutine-a-travaille-a-dresde-rda-en-toute-discretion (accessed June 4, 2013).

15. Andreas Förster, "Der getarnte Freund [The camouflaged friend]," *Berliner Zeitung*, January 8, 2000, http://www.berliner-zeitung.de/archiv/die-deutsche-vergangenheit-des-russischen-praes identen—stasi-berichte-legen-nahe—dass-der-kgb-mann-wladimir-putin-in-dresden-und-leip zig-eine-besondere-rolle-spielte-der-getarnte-freund,10810590,9755026.html.

16. Alexander Rahr, *Wladimir Putin* (Munich: Universitas Verlag in der F.A. Herbig Verlagsbuch-handlung, 2000), 56.

17. Alexander Mannheim and Daisy Sindelar, "A Spy in the House of Putin," Radio Free Europe Radio Liberty, November 7, 2011, http://www.rferl.org/content/putin_spy_affairs_wife_beat ing_philanderer/24383939.html; Joseph Fitsanakis, "Vladimir Putin 'Targeted by German Spy Agency' during His KGB Days," Intelnews.org, November 9, 2011, http://intelnews .org/2011/11/09/01-862 (accessed February 18, 2012).

18. Iren Pitch, *Pikantnaya druzhba: Moya podruga Lyudmila Putina, eyo sem'ya i drugiye tovarishchi* [Piquant friendship: My friend Lyudmila Putina, her family and dear friends] (Moscow: Zakha-rov, 2002).

19. Andrey Sharogradskiy, "Interv'yu s byvshim sosluzhivtsem Vladimira Putina [Interview with a former colleague of Vladimir Putin]," Radio Liberty, November 11, 2003, http://www.svo boda.org/content/article/24187711.html (accessed July 9, 2013).

20. Irina Borogan, "Erich Schmidt-Eenboom: 'The Downfall of Putin's Main Domestic Enemy Has Been a Success of German Foreign Intelligence,'" Agentura.ru, n.d., http://agentura.ru/english /experts/shmidt-eenboom/ (accessed August 20, 2013).

21. Sharogradskiy, "Interv'yu s byvshim sosluzhivtsem Vladimira Putina [Interview with a former colleague of Vladimir Putin]."

22. David Childs and Richard Popplewell, *The Stasi: The East German Intelligence and Security Service* (London: Macmillan, 1996), 82.

23. Chris Hutchins with Alexander Korobko, *Putin* (Leicester, UK: A&A Inform, 2012), 48.

24. Millot, "Cinq ans en Allemagne sans (presque) laisser de traces [Five years in Germany without (almost) leaving any traces]."

25. Wines, "Putin Was Once Decorated as a Spy."

26. Hutchins with Korobko, *Putin*, 42; David Hoffman, "Putin's Career Rooted in Russia's KGB," *Washington Post*, January 30, 2000, http://www.washingtonpost.com/wp-srv/inatl/longterm /russiagov/putin.htm (accessed May 9, 2013).

27. Steffen Winter, "Zoff um Auszeichung fuer Wladimir Putin [Trouble about the award of distinction for Vladimir Putin]," Spiegel Online, January 16, 2009, http://www.spiegel.de/politik /deutschland/saechsischer-dankesorden-zoff-um-auszeichnung-fuer-wladimir-putin-a-601656 -druck.html (accessed May 10, 2013).

28. Putin et al., *First Person*, 69.

29. Vladimir Putin, "Prime Minister Vladimir Putin Addresses the General Meeting of the Academy of Sciences," Government.ru, May 18, 2010, http://archive.government.ru/eng/docs /10609/ (accessed May 8, 2012).

30. Karen Dawisha, *The Kremlin and the Prague Spring* (Berkeley: University of California Press, 1984).

31. Putin et al., *First Person*, 69.

32. Richard C. S. Trahair and Robert Lawrence Miller, *Encyclopedia of Cold War Espionage, Spies, and Secret Operations*, 2nd ed. (New York: Enigma, 2012), 287.

33. Christopher Andrew and Vasili Mitrokhin, *The Sword and the Shield: The Mitrokhin Archive and the Secret History of the KGB* (New York: Basic Books, 1999), 271.

34. Andrew and Mitrokhin, *The Sword and the Shield*, 249–75.

35. "Protocol Guiding Cooperation between the Stasi and the KGB," Office of the Federal Commissioner for the Stasi Records (BStU), MfS, BdL/Dok. No. 001862, March 29, 1978, http:// digitalarchive.wilsoncenter.org/document/115716 (accessed May 9, 2013).

36. Leonid Nikitinskiy and Yuriy Shpakov, "Putin v razvedke" [Putin in Intelligence]," Freelance Bureau, January 20, 2000, http://flb.ru/info/3508.html (accessed June 9, 2013); Ulrich Hey-den, "Was trieb Putin in den 80er Jahren als KGB-Mann in Dresden? [What did Putin do in the 80s as a KGB man in Dresden?]," *Sächsische Zeitung*, February 23, 2008, http://www .sz-online.de/nachrichten/kultur/was-trieb-putin-in-den-80er-jahren-als-kgb-mann-in-dresden -2266496.html (accessed March 8, 2012).

37. "Stasi Note on Meeting between Minister Mielke and KGB Chairman Andropov," Office of the Federal Commissioner for the Stasi Records (BStU), MfS, ZAIG 5382, July 11, 1981, http://digitalarchive.wilsoncenter.org/document/115717 (accessed May 6, 2013).
38. "Stasi Note on Meeting between Minister Mielke and Head of the KGB 5th Directorate Abramov," Office of the Federal Commissioner for the Stasi Records (BStU), MfS, ZAIG 5387, September 26, 1987, http://digitalarchive.wilsoncenter.org/document/115722 (accessed May 6, 2013).
39. Karen Dawisha, *Eastern Europe, Gorbachev and Reform*, 2nd ed. (New York: Cambridge University Press, 1990).
40. Putin et al., *First Person*, 73.
41. Nikitinskiy and Shpakov. "Putin v razvedke" [Putin in Intelligence]."
42. Vladislav Kramar, "Vladimir Shirokov: 'Gruppa v Drezdene byla nebol'shaya, no moshchnaya' [Vladimir Shirokov: 'The Dresden group was small but powerful']," *Voenno-Promyshlennyy Kur'er*, December 14, 2005, http://vpk-news.ru/articles/3728 (accessed March 9, 2013).
43. Mark Franchetti, "Germans Flush Out Putin's Spies: Fears That KGB Ring Is Still Active," *Sunday Times* (UK), January 16, 2000, http://www.russialist.org/archives/4040.html (accessed June 10, 2013).
44. Franchetti, "Germans Flush Out Putin's Spies."
45. Oleg Blotskiy, *Vladimir Putin: Doroga k vlasti* [Vladimir Putin: The path to power], book 2 (Moscow: Mezhdunarodnyye otnosheniya, 2002), 263.
46. Putin et al., *First Person*, 76.
47. Putin et al., *First Person*, 79–81.
48. Kramar, "Vladimir Shirokov."
49. Putin et al., *First Person*, 70.
50. Michael Wines, "Path to Power: A Political Profile. Putin Steering to Reform, but with Soviet Discipline," *New York Times*, February 20, 2000, http://www.nytimes.com/2000/02/20/world/path-power-political-profile-putin-steering-reform-but-with-soviet-discipline.html?pagewanted=all&src=pm (accessed May 8, 2013).
51. Franchetti, "Germans Flush Out Putin's Spies."
52. Sergey Kolesnikov, "Interview with Masha Gessen et al.: 'Pochemy Ya rasskazal pro Dvorets Putina. My pereshli granitsy mezhdy dobrom i zlom v 2009 gody' [Why I spoke out about Putin's Palace. 'We crossed the line between good and evil in 2009]," *Snob.ru*, June 23, 2011, http://www.snob.ru/selected/entry/37367 (accessed June 30, 2012).
53. Roger Witten, William R. McLucas, Andrew B. Weissman, Kimberly A. Parker, and Jay Holtmeier, "Siemens Agrees to Record-Setting $800 Million in FCPA Penalties," *Wilmerhale Publications*, December 22, 2008, http://www.wilmerhale.com/pages/publicationsandnewsdetail.aspx?NewsPubId=95919 (accessed October 8, 2013).
54. Kalugin, *Spymaster*, 198.
55. Andrew and Mitrokhin, *The Sword and the Shield*, 392.
56. John C. Schmeidel, "My Enemy's Enemy: Twenty Years of Co-operation between West Germany's Red Army Faction and the GDR Ministry for State Security," *Intelligence and National Security* 8, no. 4 (1993): 59–72.
57. Pyotr A. Abrasimov, *Vospominaya proshedshiye gody: Chetvert veka poslom Sovetskogo Soyuza* [Memories of past years: A quarter of a century as a Soviet ambassador] (Moscow: Mezhdunarodnyye otnosheniya, 1992); CIA. "The Soviet Presence in Berlin," *Special Report*. Office of Current Intelligence. Central Intelligence Agency. SC no. 00595/63B, June 7, 1963, http://www.foia.cia.gov/sites/default/files/document_conversions/89801/DOC_0000422398.pdf (accessed June 4, 2013).
58. Kalugin, *Spymaster*, 250.
59. Childs and Popplewell, *The Stasi*. 138.
60. John Schmeidel, "My Enemy's Enemy: Twenty Years of Cooperation between West Germany's Red Army Faction and the GDR Ministry of State Security," *Intelligence and National Security* 8, no. 4 (1993): 59–72.

61. Gessen, *The Man without a Face*, 257–60.
62. "Kraft: Putin Stole Bowl Ring," *New York Post*, June 15, 2013, http://pagesix.com/2013/06/15/kraft-putin-stole-bowl-ring/ (accessed April 8, 2014).
63. Associated Press, "Putin Offers to Replace Patriots Owner Robert Kraft's 'Stolen' Super Bowl Ring," *Guardian*, June 17, 2013, http://www.theGuardian.com/sport/2013/jun/17/putin-patriots-kraft-super-bowl-ring (accessed April 18, 2014).
64. Kristie Macrakis, *Seduced by Secrets: Inside the Stasi's Spy-Tech World* (New York: Cambridge University Press, 2008), 46.
65. Macrakis, *Seduced by Secrets*.
66. Mark Franchetti, "Agent Reveals Young Putin's Spy Disaster," *Sunday Times (UK)*, March 20, 2000, https://groups.google.com/forum/#!msg/alt.current-events.russia/q4Bt_9UbMcY/Hpx pyXiVmEQJ.
67. Zuchold's Personnel Card (Kaderkarteikarte) confirms he was sworn into the Stasi on August 29, 1975, and assigned to work in Dresden. Stasi Archive, Zuchold-Personnel Card, n.d.
68. Letter from Major Kultsch to Colonel Anders, Information zur Aussprache mit dem Genossen Maxim Samarin der sowjetischen Militäraufklärung, Dienststelle Dresden, Kamenz: BStU MfS BV Dresden 1. Stellvertr. D. LTR3 page 000054, March 15, 1989; Letter from Major General Böhm to Major General Shirokov, March 29, 1989. About the illegal recruitment among NVA reservists with radio training by an employee of the Soviet Army, Maxim Samarin, see Dresden: BStU MfS BV Dresden 1.Stellvertr. d.LTR. 3, pp. 000048-000049.
69. Letter from Putin to Major General Böhm, Brief von Putin an Generalmajor Böhm: Über die Neuinstallation einer Telefonverbindung für mögliche FIM, Dresden: BStU MfS BV Dresden 1.Stellvertr. d.LTR. 3, September 07, 1989.
70. Mark Franchetti, "Agent Reveals Young Putin's Spy Disaster," *Sunday Times (UK)*, March 20, 2000, https://groups.google.com/forum/#!msg/alt.current-events.russia/q4Bt_9UbMcY/Hpxpy XiVmEQ.
71. (Matthias Warnig's alias) "Hans-Detleff's statement of commitment [Verplichtungserklärung] created by the Stasi," February 2, [19]74, Senftenberg: BStU MfS AIM 6367/75 Teil 1, p.000010, [19]74.
72. Note to Matthias Warnig's alias Hans-Detleff's file, Aktenvermerk zu Matthias Warnig von Oberstleutnant Halla, BStU MfS AIM 6367/75 Teil 1, 42, November 27, 1974.
73. Warnig-Personnel Card, Kaderkarteikarte Warnig, Matthias, geb. 26.09.1955. Bestätigung seiner Entwicklung vom IMS, zum Leutnant, zum Oberstleutnant und später zum Hauptmann. Kaderkarteikarte, Stasi Archive, BStU, MfS KKK Warnig, Matthias 26.09.1955.
74. Warnig's National People's Army medal of merit in silver, Warnig's Verdienstmedaille der Nationalen Volksarmee in Silber, Berlin: BStU, MfS-HA KuSch, Nr. 124, p. 000001, October 7, 1984.
75. Macrakis, *Seduced by Secrets*, 49.
76. Putin National People's Army Medal in Bronze, Befehl Nr. K 114/88 Putin Verdienstmedaille der Nationalen Volksarmee in Bronze, Berlin: BStU HA KuSch 186 pages 000261 and 000296, February 8, 1988.
77. Andreas Nölting and Arne Stuhr, "Der Präsident, die Stasi und der Banker [The president, the Stasi and the banker]," *Manager-Magazin.de*, February 23, 2005, http://www.manager-magazin.de/unternehmen/artikel/a-343332.html (accessed June 7, 2012).
78. Guy Chazan and David Crawford, "In From the Cold: A Friendship Forged in Spying Pays Dividends in Russia Today: Top Dresdner Banker's Ties to Putin Go Back to Days When They Were Agents," *Wall Street Journal*, February 23, 2005 (accessed April 26, 2012).
79. Pitch, *Pikantnaya druzhba* [Piquant friendship].
80. Chazan and Crawford. "In From the Cold."
81. "Report Links Putin to Dresdner," *St. Petersburg Times*, March 1, 2005, http://www.sptimes.ru/index.php?action_id=2&story_id=2858 (accessed June 15, 2012).
82. "Matthias Warnig," *VTB*, 2012, http://www.vtb.com/we/today/management/council/warnig/.

83. Chazan and Crawford, "In From the Cold."
84. Felshtinsky and Pribylovsky, *The Corporation*, 62.
85. Chazan and Crawford, "In From the Cold"; "Report Links Putin to Dresdner"; Pitch, *Pikantnaya druzhba* [Piquant friendship], 171.
86. Rachel Katz, "Ex-Finance Chief Optimistic," *St. Petersburg Times*, July 8–17, 1996, http://www.friends-partners.org/oldfriends/spbweb/times/175-176/exfinan.html (accessed June 23, 2012).
87. Chazan and Crawford, "In From the Cold"; Richard Sakwa, *The Quality of Freedom: Khodorkovsky, Putin, and the Yukos Affairs* (New York: Oxford University Press, 2009); David Rothnie, "DrKW Sets Yukos Valuation at $17bn," *Financial News*, October 11, 2004, http://www.efinancialnews.com/story/2004-10-11/drkw-sets-yukos-valuation-at?ea9c8a2de0ee111045601a b04d673622 (accessed January 7, 2014).
88. Jethro Wookey, "Rusal Appoints Another New Chairman," *Metal Bulletin Daily Alerts*, October 1, 2012, http://www.lexisnexis.com.proxy.lib.muohio.edu/hottopics/lnacademic/?verb=sr&csi=332263 (accessed May 5, 2013); Rusal, "Matthias Warnig Nominated to UC RUSAL's Board of Directors as Independent Non-Executive Director," Rusal.ru, May 14, 2012, http://www.rusal.ru/en/press-center/news_details.aspx?id=7007&ibt=13 (accessed June 15, 2012); "Rusal Hires 'Former Stasi Agent' Matthias Warnig as Chairman," *Telegraph (London)*, October 2, 2012, http://www.lexisnexis.com.proxy.lib.muohio.edu/hottopics/lnacademic/?verb=sr&csi=332263 (accessed May 7, 2013).
89. E. Grishkovets, K. Mel'nikov, and D. Belikov, "Igor Sechin podobral smenshchikov [Igor Sechin picked new candidates]," *Kommersant*, May 11, 2011, http://dlib.eastview.com.proxy.lib.muohio.edu/browse/doc/24740685 (accessed June 9, 2013).
90. Vladimir Pribylovskiy, "Proiskhozhdeniye putinskoy oligarkhii [Origins of Putin's oligarchy]," *Antikompromat*, n.d., http://www.anticompromat.org/oligarhi/ppo.html (accessed May 4, 2012); Vladimir Milov and Boris Nemtsov, "Putin: What 10 Years of Putin Have Brought," Putin-itogi.ru, 2010, http://www.putin-itogi.ru/putin-what-10-years-of-putin-have-brought/ (accessed June 15, 2012); Roman Kupchinsky, "Nord Stream, Matthias Warnig (code name 'Arthur') and the Gazprom Lobby," Jamestown Foundation, June 15, 2009, http://www.jamestown.org/single/?no_cache=1&tx_ttnews%5Btt_news%5D=35128 (accessed March 19, 2012); "A Profile of Vladimir Putin." Gazeta.ru, February 28, 2012. http://www.gazeta.ru/2001/02/28/AProfileofVl.shtml (accessed March 15, 2012); Vladimir Milov, Boris Nemtsov, Vladimir Ryzhkov, and Ol'ga Shorina, "Putin: Corruption. An Independent White Paper," Putin-Itogi.ru, 2011, http://www.putin-itogi.ru/putin-corruption-an-independent-white-paper/ (accessed June 8, 2013).
91. Roman Shleynov, "Revizor iz 'razvedochnoy partii' [Inspector from 'prospecting party']," *Vedomosti*, February 11, 2013, http://dlib.eastview.com.proxy.lib.muohio.edu/browse/doc/28616081 (accessed March 9, 2013).
92. Vera Surzhenko and Irina Reznik, "'Vsyo ravno, skol'ko stoyat aksii': Nikolay Tokarev, prezident Transneft ['No matter how much the shares are worth': Nikolay Tokarev, president of Transneft]," *Vedomosti*, February 18, 2008, http://dlib.eastview.com.proxy.lib.muohio.edu/browse/doc/13505924 (accessed March 7, 2013).
93. "Nikolay Tokarev," *Forbes.ru*, August 27, 2012, http://www.forbes.ru/sobytiya-slideshow/vlast/101007-sputniki-prezidenta/slide/6 (accessed August 25, 2013).
94. Tai Adelaja, "Grand Theft Pipeline," *Russia Profile*, November 18, 2010, http://russiaprofile.org/business/a1290102813/print_edition/ (accessed August 25, 2013).
95. Usol'tsev, *Sosluzhivets* [Colleague].
96. Andrey Vandenko, "Ot Pervogo Litsa: Chelovek vo vseoruzhii [From the first person: An armed man]," *Itogi*, October 31, 2005, http://dlib.eastview.com.proxy.lib.muohio.edu/browse/doc/8502730 (accessed July 1, 2012); "Sergey Chemezov," Novikombank Board of Directors website, n.d., http://novikom.ru/ru/about/managment/committee_of_directors/chemezov/ (accessed June 19, 2013).
97. Vandenko, "Ot Pervogo Litsa [From the first person]"; "Sergey Chemezov."

98. Vandenko, "Ot Pervogo Litsa [From the first person]"; Rahr, *Putin Nach Putin*, 92.

99. Pavel Sedakov and Aleksandr Levinskiy, " 'Zavkhoz' iz Drezdena: Kak Vladimir Putin soshelsya s Sergeem Chemezovym ['Manager' from Dresden: How Vladimir Putin became friends with Sergey Chemezov]," *Forbes.ru*, May 20, 2013, http://www.forbes.ru/sobytiya/obshchestvo/239270-zav hoz-iz-drezdena-kak-vladimir-putin-soshelsya-s-sergeem-chemezovym (accessed June 10, 2013).

100. Phil Berger, "Getting to the Main Event Becomes a Main Event," *New York Times*, November 25, 1989, http://www.nytimes.com/1989/11/25/sports/getting-to-the-main-event-be comes-a-main-event.html?src=pm (accessed June 8, 2013).

101. Jeff Jacobs, "It Took Musician to Bring Soviets to NHL," *Los Angeles Times*, October 8, 1989, http://articles.latimes.com/1989-10-08/sports/sp-499_1_soviet-union/2 (accessed June 8, 2013).

102. "Tinker, Tailor, Cyclist, Spy," *INRNG: The Inner Ring Cycling Blog*, December 29, 2011, http://inrng.com/2011/12/tinker-tailor-cyclist-spy/ (accessed May 8, 2013).

103. Marshall I. Goldman, *Petrostate: Putin, Power, and the new Russia* (New York: Oxford University Press, 2010), 227.

104. Vandenko, "Ot Pervogo Litsa [From the first person]."

105. Vandenko, "Ot Pervogo Litsa [From the first person]."

106. "Shkolov, Yevgeniy M.," *Kommersant*, November 22, 2007, http://www.kommersant.ru/doc /828190 (accessed June 16, 2013); "V Kremle poyavilsya upolnomochennyy po antikorrupt-sionnym proverkam [The implementor of anticorruption measures appears in the Kremlin]," *Lenta.ru*, June 7, 2013, http://lenta.ru/news/2013/06/07/corrupt/ (accessed June 16, 2013).

107. "Geburtstage der sowjetischen Genossen einschliesslich Ehepartner [The birthdays of the Soviet comrades and their spouses]," BStU 42-010 09.95. MfS BV Dresden, Abt.II No. 10448, Dresden: Archiv der Aussenstelle Dresden, December 22, 1988.

108. Putin et al., *First Person*, 72.

109. Gessen, *The Man without a Face*, 97.

110. "Rudolf Abel's Liberation: Interview with KGB Gen. Yuriy Drozdev," *RIA Novosti*, February 10, 2012, http://en.rian.ru/video/20120210/171253628.html (accessed April 12, 2012); Yuriy Drozdov, "Interview about Rudolf Abel," YouTube, April 20, 2012, http://www.youtube.com /watch?v=xaY3TxR3wLQ (accessed June 22, 2013).

111. Frank Rafalko, *A Counterintelligence Reader*, 4 vols. (Washington, DC: Federation of American Scientists, 2004), 4: 179.

112. Rodric Braithwaite, *Afgantsy: The Russians in Afghanistan, 1979–1989* (New York: Oxford University Press, 2011), 99.

113. Andrei Soldatov and Irina Borogan, *The New Nobility: The Restoration of Russia's Security State and the Enduring Legacy of the KGB* (New York: Public Affairs, 2010), 200.

114. Dima Beliakov, "Veterans of Russia's Spetsnaz," Flickr, 2012, http://www.flickr.com/photos /dimabelyakov/6828920659/ (accessed April 12, 2012).

115. Soldatov and Borogan, *The New Nobility*; Boris Volodarsky, "License to Kill," *Wall Street Journal*, December 20, 2006, http://global.factiva.com.proxy.lib.muohio.edu/ha/default.aspx (accessed April 27, 2012); Konstantin Preobrazhensky, *KGB/FSB's New Trojan Horse* (Liberty, TN: St. John of Kronstadt Press, 2008).

116. Rustam Arifdzhanov, "A gorod ne znal, chto uchen'ya idut [The town did not know that training was taking place]," *Sovershenno sekretno*, no. 6 (June 1, 2002), http://www.sovsekretno.ru /articles/id/830/ (accessed April 12, 2012).

117. Alexander Litvinenko and Yuri Felshtinsky, *Blowing Up Russia: The Secret Plot to Bring Back KGB Terror* (New York: Encounter Books, 2007); David Satter, *Darkness at Dawn: The Rise of the Russian Criminal State* (New Haven, CT: Yale University Press, 2003); *Blowing Up Russia*, directed by Jean-Charles Deniau and Charles Gazelle, 2002; Mark Ulensh, "On the Actual Trails?." Russian Military and Security Media Coverage #2906, December 17, 2003, http:// groups.yahoo.com/group/RMSMC/message/3005 (accessed June 5, 2013).

118. Blotskiy, *Vladimir Putin*, 301.

119. Putin et al., *First Person*, 86–91.

120. Kramar, "Vladimir Shirokov."
121. Albats, *The State within a State.*
122. Yevgeniya Al'bats, "Materialy Komissii VS SSSR po rassledovaniyu obstoyatel'stv gosudarstven-nogo perevorot v SSSR [Materials from the USSR Supreme Soviet Commission to Investigate the Circumstances of the Coup d'Etat in the USSR]," in Albats, *The State within a State*, 235.
123. Felshtinsky and Pribylovsky, *The Corporation*; Knight, *Spies without Cloaks*; Soldatov and Boro-gan. *The New Nobility.*
124. Drozdov and Fartyshev, *Yuriy Andropov i Vladimir Putin.*
125. Bonini and D'Avanzo, "I Cekisti al Potere [The Checkists in power]."
126. A. A. Zykov, "Part 1," Rutube, April 10, 2010, http://rutube.ru/video/129581c30ae127d4ff02 caf4a88f3163/?ref=relroll (accessed May 31, 2013).
127. Oleg Mukhin, "Byvshiy sledovatel' po osobo vazhnym delam Andrey Zykov: Nam skazali, chto v otnoshenii prezidenta ugolovnoye delo ne vedetsya [Former investigator for especially important cases Andrey Zykov: They told us with the president, criminal cases do not proceed]." Zaks.ru. September 6, 2011, http://www.zaks.ru/new/archive/view/83713 (accessed April 24, 2012).
128. Nataliya Gevorkyan, "Special Services: The Organs Are Strong through Their Ties to the People," *Moskovskiye Novosti*, September 3–10, 1995, http://infoweb.newsbank.com.proxy.lib.muohio .edu/iw-search/we/HistArchive/?p_product=FBISX&p_theme=fbis&p_nbid=W4FU49IBM TQwNTI2NDQ5NC42MDUwMjoxOjExOjEzNC41My4yNC4y&p_action=doc&s_last nonissuequeryname=6&p_queryname=6&p_docref=v2:11C33B0D5F860D98@FBISX-124 F722D1242D9B8@2450015-124F722E4124D4D8@5-124F722E7950F170@KGB%20 Successors%20Said%20Mum%20on%20File%20of%20Agents&p_docnum=12 (accessed May 5, 2012).
129. Anna Shcherbakova, "Interview: Mikhayl Klishin, Gendirector of Bank Rossiya," *Vedomosti*, March 1, 2005, http://www.vedomosti.ru/newspaper/article/2005/03/01/88331 (accessed July 11, 2012).
130. "Memorandum to the TsK KPSS from N. Kruchina re allocation of 1,500,000 rubles for the KPSS Leningradskaya obkom to invest in the Rossiia commercial bank, Reel 1.996, Opus 21(13), July 1990," in *Fond 89.*
131. Pribylovskiy, "Proiskhozhdeniye putinskoy oligarkhii [Origins of Putin's oligarchy]."
132. "Memorandum to the TsK KPSS from N. Kruchina, Administrator of the Administration of the TsK KPSS Affairs, re the deposit of 100,000,000 rubles into the account of the Kompart-bank commercial bank, Reel 1.992, Opus 11(84), February 1991."
133. Pribylovskiy, "Proiskhozhdeniye putinskoy oligarkhii [Origins of Putin's oligarchy]."
134. White House Office of the Press Secretary, "Background Briefing on Ukraine by Senior Ad-ministration Officials," Whitehouse.gov, March 20, 2014, http://www.whitehouse.gov/the -press-office/2014/03/20/background-briefing-ukraine-senior-administration-officials (accessed March 20, 2014).
135. Pribylovskiy, "Proiskhozhdeniye putinskoy oligarkhii [Origins of Putin's oligarchy]."
136. Shcherbakova, "Interview: Mikhayl Klishin."
137. "Chancery," Netherlands Consulate-General in St. Petersburg, n.d., http://stpetersburg.nlcon sulate.org/organization/chancery (accessed April 5, 2013).
138. "Chancery."
139. Suzanna Andrews, "The Widow and the Oligarchs," *Vanity Fair*, October 2009, http://www .vanityfair.com/politics/features/2009/10/oligarchs200910 (accessed May 8, 2012).
140. Masha Gessen, "Dead Soul: Vladimir Putin," *Vanity Fair*, October 2008, www.vanityfair.com (accessed June 6, 2013).
141. Pribylovskiy, "Proiskhozhdeniye putinskoy oligarkhii [Origins of Putin's oligarchy]."
142. Felshtinsky and Pribylovsky, *The Corporation*, 62.
143. U.S. Department of the Treasury, "Treasury Sanctions Russian Officials, Members of the Rus-sian Leadership's Inner Circle, and an Entity for Involvement in the Situation in Ukraine,"

March 20, 2014, http://www.treasury.gov/press-center/press-releases/Pages/jl23331.aspx (accessed March 20, 2014).

144. Russia Report, "Twelve Who Have Putin's Ear," Radio Free Europe Radio Liberty, October 15, 2007, http://www.rferl.org/content/article/1078952.html (accessed May 8, 2013).

145. Irina Reznik and Ol'ga Petrova, "Pomoshchniki 'Rossii' [Helpers of 'Rossiya']," *Vedomosti*, July 24, 2008, http://dlib.eastview.com.proxy.lib.muohio.edu/browse/doc/18660105 (accessed June 4, 2012).

146. Pribylovskiy, "Proiskhozhdeniye putinskoy oligarkhii [Origins of Putin's oligarchy]."

147. Elena Tofanyuk, "Zamorozhennyy Milliard na Kipre: U banka 'Druzey Putina' zavisli den'gi v prizis [Frozen billion in Cyprus: At the bank of 'Putin's friends' they placed money in the crisis]," *Forbes.ru*, June 27, 2013, http://www.forbes.ru/finansy/igroki/241394-zamorozhennyi-milliard-na-kipre-u-banka-druzei-putina-zavisli-dengi-v-krizis (accessed August 5, 2013).

148. Putin et al., *First Person*, 92.

149. Evgenia Pismennaya and Irina Reznik, "Putin Filmmaker Says Lonely Leader Scared to Loosen Grip," *Bloomberg*, August 27, 2013, http://www.bloomberg.com/news/2013-08-27/putin-filmmaker-says-lonely-leader-scared-to-loosen-grip.html (accessed August 15, 2013).

150. Pismennaya and Reznik, "Putin Filmmaker Says Lonely Leader Scared to Loosen Grip."

151. Marina Litvinovich, "Fursenko, Andrey Aleksandrovich," Election2012.ru, 2012, http://eng.election2012.ru/reports/1/4.html (accessed June 8, 2013).

152. Roman Shleynov, " 'Rossiya' i K° ['Rossiya' and Co.]," *Novaya gazeta*, May 13, 2009, http://old.novayagazeta.ru/data/2009/048/00.html (accessed July 12, 2012).

153. U.S. Department of the Treasury, "Treasury Sanctions Russian Officials."

154. "Bank Rossiya Discloses Timchenko Stake," Interfax, March 16, 2010, http://www.silobreaker.com/bank-rossiya-discloses-timchenko-stake-5_2263339487188746240 (accessed May 21, 2012).

155. "Bank Rossiya Discloses Timchenko Stake."

156. Reuters, "New Bank in Leningrad," *New York Times*, October 15, 1990, http://www.nytimes.com/1990/10/15/business/new-bank-in-leningrad.html (accessed July 11, 2012).

157. Fiona Govan, "Russian Politician Investigated in Spain over Mafia Connections," *Daily Telegraph (UK)*, October 19, 2008, http://www.telegraph.co.uk/news/worldnews/europe/spain/3226931/Russian-politician-investigated-in-Spain-over-Mafia-connections.html (accessed October 5, 2012).

158. American Embassy Madrid to U.S. Secretary of State, "Updates in Spain's Investigations of Russian Mafia."

159. Andreu Manresa, Francisco Mercado, Juana Viudez, and Arturo Ruiz, "Un desembarco con dinero del KGB,"*El País*, June 14, 2008, http://elpais.com/diario/2008/06/14/espana/1213394402_850215.html (accessed December 15, 2012).

160. Luis Gomez, "La Audiencia dicta orden de captura para un diputado del partido de Putin [The National Court seeks warrant for Putin party deputy]," *El País*, October 19, 2008, http://elpais.com/diario/2008/10/19/espana/1224367203_850215.html (accessed June 8, 2013; Francisco Mercado, "Apresados en España los jefes de la principal organización mafiosa rusa [Bosses arrested in Spain's main Russian mafia organization]," *El País*, June 14, 2008, http://elpais.com/diario/2008/06/14/espana/1213394401_850215.html (accessed June 8, 2012); Luis Gomez, "¿Vuelven los rusos poco recomendables? [Do unsavory Russians return?]," *El País*, February 1, 2013, http://politica.elpais.com/politica/2013/02/01/actualidad/1359737015_052785.html (accessed June 15, 2013).

161. Milov et al., "Putin: Corruption."

162. U.S. Department of the Treasury, "Ukraine Related Designations," April 28, 2014, http://www.treasury.gov/resource-center/sanctions/OFAC-Enforcement/Pages/20140428.aspx.

163. Peter Hobson, "Sanctioned Bank Rossiya to Service $36B in Domestic Electricity Market," *Moscow Times*, April 14, 2014, http://www.themoscowtimes.com/business/article/sanctioned-bank-rossiya-to-service-36bln-domestic-electricity-market/498012.html (accessed April 18, 2014).

164. Vadim Nesvizhskiy, "Staryye druz'ya [Old friends]," *Segodnya*, January 10, 2001, http://dlib .eastview.com/browse/doc/1994890 (accessed July 16, 2012).

165. Russia Report, "Twelve Who Have Putin's Ear."

166. Vladimir Sungorkin and Viktor Baranets, "Interview with Sergey Ivanov," *Komsomol'skaya Pravda*, March 4, 2013, http://archive.constantcontact.com/fs156/1102820649387/archive /1112756080578.html (accessed May 1, 2013).

167. Henry Plater-Zyberk, "The Russian Decisionmakers in the Chechen Conflict," 2000, www .da.mod.uk/CSRC/documents/Caucasus/P31/P31.ch6 (accessed May 9, 2013).

168. "Vladimir Strzhalkovskiy," *Russia Monitor*, 2001, http://www.russiamonitor.net/en/main.asp ?menu_id=1_a_1040_25 (accessed May 9, 2013).

169. Nadia Popova, "Norilsk Nickel Chooses Strzhalkovsky as New CEO," *St. Petersburg Times*, August 12, 2008, http://www.sptimesrussia.com/index.php?action_id=2&story_id=26822 (accessed August 28, 2013).

170. Andrew E. Kramer, "Mining Executive Receives Payout of $100 Million, Russia's Largest Ever," *New York Times*, December 17, 2012, http://www.nytimes.com/2012/12/18/business/global /norilsk-nickel-pays-strzhalkovsky-100-million-severance.html?_r=0 (accessed August 28, 2013).

171. Peter Reddaway, "The Silovik War of 2004–2010: What Does It Reveal about the Nature and Direction of the Putin Regime?," unpublished ms., October 1, 2012, 7.

172. Reddaway, "The Silovik War of 2004–2010," 12.

173. Matt Bivens and Jen Tracy, "Profile: Putin's Patronage Lifts Ex-Dissident Persecutor," *Moscow Times*, February 24, 2000, http://www.themoscowtimes.com/news/article/profile-putins -patronage-lifts-ex-dissident-persecutor/266308.html (accessed April 19, 2014).

174. Bivens and Tracy, "Profile: Putin's Patronage."

175. Nesvizhskiy, "Staryye druz'ya [Old friends]."

176. Vladimir Kovalyev, "Dark Rumors Surround City FSB Shuffle," *St. Petersburg Times*, January 12, 2001, http://sptimes.ru/index.php?action_id=2&story_id=13968 (accessed June 7, 2013).

177. Hill and Gaddy, *Mr. Putin*.

178. Leonid Nikitinskiy, "Litso vlasti: Svyaznoy s proshlym [A person of power: Consistent with the past]," *Novaya gazeta*, March 28, 2005, http://dlib.eastview.com.proxy.lib.muohio.edu/browse /doc/7523007 (accessed January 17, 2013).

179. Reddaway, "The Silovik War of 2004–2010," 8.

180. Felshtinsky and Pribylovsky, *The Corporation*, 227.

181. Marina Litvinovich, "Murov, Yevgeniy Alekseyevich," Election2012.ru, 2012, http://elec tion2012.ru/reports/1/12.html (accessed March 7, 2013).

182. Afsati Dzhusoyti and Aleksey Dospekhov, "General Murov prinimaet komandovaniye rossiys-kim boksom [General Murov takes command of Russian boxing]," *Kommersant*, June 9, 2007, http://dlib.eastview.com.proxy.lib.muohio.edu/browse/doc/12130375 (accessed February 26, 2013).

183. Donald N. Jensen, "Putin's 'Praetorian Guard,'" Institute of Modern Russia, October 10, 2013, http://imrussia.org/en/politics/572-putins-praetorian-guard?utm_source=Institute+of+Modern +Russia+newsletter&utm_campaign=23210c707b-Newsletter+10%2F11%2F2013_English &utm_medium=email&utm_term=0_279627583b-23210c707b-295510881 (accessed October 11, 2013).

184. U.S. Department of the Treasury, "Ukraine Related Designations," April 28, 2014, http://www .treasury.gov/resource-center/sanctions/OFAC-Enforcement/Pages/20140428.aspx.

185. "Poema bez geroyev [Poem without heroes]," *Kommersant*, July 8, 1995, http://kommersant.ru /doc/112827 (accessed June 5, 2012).

186. Roman Shleynov, "Ptentsy gnezda Petrova [Chicks in Petrov's nest]," *Novaya gazeta*, November 2, 2009, http://dlib.eastview.com/browse/doc/20851285 (accessed July 18, 2012).

187. A.A. Zykov, "Case #144128: 'Putin's Case,' Part 4," YouTube, July 17, 2013, http://www.you tube.com/watch?v=z2rlO8EhkMU (accessed July 25, 2013).

188. Nabi Abdullaev, "Interior Minister Disbands RUBOP," *St. Petersburg Times*, August 14, 2001, http://www.sptimes.ru/?action_id=2&story_id=5055 (accessed April 7, 2014).

189. Reddaway, "The Silovik War of 2004–2010," 9; Yuriy Felshtinskiy and Vladimir Pribylovskiy, *Korporatsiya: Rossiya i KGB vo vremena Putina* [Corporation: Russia and the KGB in Putin's time] (Moscow: Terra—Knizhnyi klub, 2010), 263.

190. Viktor Kostyukovskiy, "Roman Tsepov 'pomogal khot' chertu': Kto pomog emu umeret'? [Roman Tsepov even helped the devil: Who helped him die?]," *Russkiy kur'er*, September 27, 2004, http://dlib.eastview.com.proxy.lib.muohio.edu/browse/doc/6783024 (accessed February 22, 2013).

191. Nikitinskiy, "Litso vlasti [A Person of Power]."

192. Nikitinskiy, "Litso vlasti [A Person of Power]."

193. Andrey Petrov, "Skol'ko stoit Gubernator [How much does a governorship cost?]," *Russkiy Kur'er*, September 21, 2004, http://dlib.eastview.com.proxy.lib.muohio.edu/browse/doc/6758419 (accessed February 22, 2013).

194. Andrey Konstantinov and Igor' Shusharin, *Banditskiy Peterburg: Dokumental'nye ocherki* [Bandit Petersburg: Documentary study]. vol. 2 (St. Petersburg: Neva, 2004), 191.

195. Criminal Code of the Russian Federation, June 5, 1996, http://www.russian-criminal-code.com/PartII/SectionVIII/Chapter21.html (accessed February 20, 2013).

196. Petrov, "Skol'ko stoit Gubernator [How much does a governorship cost?]."

197. Petrov, "Skol'ko stoit Gubernator [How much does a governorship cost?]."

198. Petrov, "Skol'ko stoit Gubernator [How much does a governorship cost?]."

199. Petrov, "Skol'ko stoit Gubernator [How much does a governorship cost?]."

200. Igor' Korol'kov, "Yadovitaya ataka [Toxic attack]," *Moskovskiye novosti*, March 18, 2005, http://dlib.eastview.com.proxy.lib.muohio.edu/sources/article.jsp?id=7488301 (accessed March 6, 2013).

201. Kostyukovskiy, "Roman Tsepov 'pomogal khot' chertu' [Roman Tsepov even helped the devil]."

202. Reddaway, "The Silovik War of 2004–2010," 15–17.

203. Nabi Abdullaev, "Interior Minister Disbands RUBOP," *St. Petersburg Times*, August 14, 2001, http://www.sptimes.ru/?action_id=2&story_id=5055 (accessed April 7, 2014).

204. Andrey Tsyganov, "Otravlen okhrannik Smol'nogo [The poisoned guard of Smolny]," *Kommersant*, September 25, 2004, http://dlib.eastview.com.proxy.lib.muohio.edu/browse/doc/6778065 (accessed February 20, 2013).

205. Charles Gurin, "Roman Tsepov, R.I.P.," Jamestown Foundation, September 26, 2004. http://www.jamestown.org/single/?no_cache=1&tx_ttnews%5Bswords%5D=8fd5893941d69d0be3f378576261ae3e&tx_ttnews%5Bany_of_the_words%5D=tsepov&tx_ttnews%5Btt_news%5D=26907&tx_ttnews%5BbackPid%5D=7&cHash=4425ca26c859c2dd2f694781570becf2 (accessed February 21, 2013).

206. Nikitinskiy, "Litso vlasti [A Person of Power]."

207. Arkadi Vaksburg, *Toxic Politics: The Secret History of the Kremlin's Poison Laboratory*, translated by Paul McGregor (Santa Barbara, CA: ABC-CLIO, 2011), 185–87.

208. Drozdov and Fartyshev, *Yuriy Andropov i Vladimir Putin*, 104.

209. Matt Bivens, "A Wonkish, Wary Debut," *Moscow Times*, March 4, 2000, http://dlib.eastview.com/browse/doc/225408 (accessed May 8, 2012).

210. Yevgenia Albats, "Who Is Putin?," *Frontline*, 2000, www.pbs.org/wgbh/pages/frontline/shows/yeltsin/putin/putin.html (accessed January 14, 2013).

211. John Pepper, *Russian Tide: Procter & Gamble Enters Russia* (Cincinnati, OH: Procter & Gamble, 2012), 23.

212. Y. Gilinskiy, "Organised Crime: The Russian and World Perspective," in Kauko Aromaa, ed., *The Baltic Region: Insights in Crime and Crime Control* (Oslo: Pax Forlag, 1997), 168–82.

213. Cullison et al., "In Putin's Past, Glimpses of Russia's Hardline Future."

214. V. S. Sokolov, "Otchet o rezul'tatakh proverki zakonnosti prodazhi Rossiyskim fondom federal'nogo imyshchestva v 1994 gody paketa aktsiy Kotlasskogo tsellyulozno-bumazhnogo

kombinata zakrytomu aktsionernomu obshchestvu 'Ilim Palp Enterprayz,' " [Report on the results of verifying the legality of the 1994 sale from the Russian federal property fund of stakes in the Kotlas Pulp and Paper Mill Joint Stock company to the closed stock company Ilim Pulp Enterprise], *Byulleten Schetnoy Palat* [Bulletin of the Accounting Chamber], April 7, 2000, http://www.rospres.com/corruption/5849 (accessed June 15, 2012).

215. Sokolov, "Otchet" [Report]

216. Victor Yasmann and Donald Jensen, "Putin's Choice: A Profile of Dmitry Medvedev," Radio Free Europe Radio Liberty, March 25, 2008, http://www.rferl.org/content/article/1347769.html (accessed June 18, 2012).

217. Nikolay Svanidze and Marina Svanidze, *Medvedev* (St. Petersburg: Amphora, 2008), 173; Daniel Treisman, *The Return: Russia's Journey from Gorbachev to Putin* (New York: Free Press, 2011), 132–34.

218. Mukhin, "Byvshiy sledovatel' po osobo vazhnym delam Andrey Zykov [Former investigator for especially important cases Andrey Zykov]."

219. Hill and Gaddy, *Mr. Putin*, 347.

220. Putin et al., *First Person*.

221. Yuri Zarakhovich, "Inside the Yukos Endgame," *Time*, August 22, 2004, http://www.time.com/time/magazine/article/0,9171,685965,00.html (accessed September 8, 2012).

222. Hill and Gaddy, *Mr. Putin*, 324.

223. Marina Litvinovich, "Zubkov, Viktor Alekseyevich," Election2012.ru, 2012, http://eng.election2012.ru/reports/1/21.html (accessed June 16, 2013); Max Delany, "An Inside Track to President Putin's Kremlin," *St. Petersburg Times*, October 2, 2007, http://www.sptimes.ru/index.php?action_id=2&story_id=23175 (accessed June 12, 2012).

224. Roman Shleynov, "V teni prezidenta [In the shadow of the president]," *Novaya gazeta*, September 17, 2007, http://www.novayagazeta.ru/politics/34024.html (accessed July 31, 2013).

225. Yuriy Mikhaylov, *Delo Shutova: Politiko-kriminal'naya khronika Sankt-Peterburga* [The Shutov affair: A political-criminal chronicle of St. Petersburg] (St. Petersburg: Izdatel'skiy dom 'Operativnoye prikrytiye,' 2005) 252-55.

226. Anatoly Medetsky, "Siloviki's Pyramid of Power Revealed," *St. Petersburg Times*, January 20, 2004, http://www.sptimes.ru/archive/pdf/936.pdf (accessed June 5, 2013).

227. Andrey Piontkovsky, "Who Is in the Minority?," *Moscow Times*, September 5, 2005, http://dlib.eastview.com.proxy.lib.muohio.edu/search/pub/doc?art=27&id=5231717 (accessed December 9, 2013).

228. Medetsky, "Siloviki's Pyramid of Power Revealed"; "Viktor Ivanov Biography," Federal Drug Control Service of the Russian Federation, n.d., http://fskn.gov.ru/pages/eng/Victor_Ivanov/index.shtml (accessed April 26, 2012).

229. "Kto takoy Naryshkin [Who is Naryshkin]," *Gazeta.ru*, February 15, 2007, http://www.gazeta.ru/2007/02/15/oa_231787.shtml (accessed October 5, 2013).

230. Miriam Elder, "Discreet with a Deceptively Shy Grin," *Moscow Times*, October 26, 2007, http://www.themoscowtimes.com/special_report/article/discreet-with-a-deceptively-shy-grin/193370.html (accessed December 8, 2013); "Sergey Naryshkin," *Moscow Times*, n.d., http://www.themoscowtimes.com/mt_profile/sergei_naryshkin/434258.html (accessed June 15, 2012).

231. RIA-Novosti, "Medvedev Loses Another Official," *Vedomosti*, December 24, 2012, http://en.rian.ru/papers/20121224/178370614.html (accessed June 16, 2013); "The Friends of Vladimir," *BusinessWeek*, December 3, 2000, http://www.businessweek.com/stories/2000-12-03/the-friends-of-vladimir (accessed June 16, 2013).

232. "Sergey Naryshkin."

233. Aleksey Alekseyevich Mukhin, *Nevskiy-Lubyanka-Kreml': Proyekt 2008* [Nevsky-Lubyanka-Kremlin: Project 2008] (Moscow: Tsentr politicheskoy informatsii, 2005), 194.

234. "Prominent Russians: Dmitriy Kozak," Russian Television Russiapedia, n.d., http://russiapedia.rt.com/prominent-russians/politics-and-society/dmitry-kozak/ (accessed June 15, 2012).

235. Oleg Sukhov, "From Olympics to Crimea, Putin Loyalist Kozak Entrusted with Kremlin Mega-Projects," *Moscow Times*, March 28, 2014, http://www.themoscowtimes.com/news /article/from-olympics-to-crimea-putin-loyalist-kozak-entrusted-with-kremlin-mega-projects /497007.html (accessed March 29, 2014).

236. U.S. Department of the Treasury, "Ukraine Related Designations," April 28, 2014, http://www .treasury.gov/resource-center/sanctions/OFAC-Enforcement/Pages/20140428.aspx.

237. "Vladimir Kozhin," *Peoples.ru*, n.d., http://www.peoples.ru/state/poltiics/vladimir_kozhin/ (accessed June 16, 2012).

238. Oleg Lur'ye, "VIP-Infitsirovannyye: Zavkhoz vlasti i ego vesyolyy barabanshchik [VIP-infected: The superintendent of power and his happy drummer]," *Novaya gazeta*, December 10, 2001, http://dlib.eastview.com.proxy.lib.muohio.edu/browse/doc/3468311 (accessed June 16, 2012).

239. Andrey Kamakin, "Kolybel' Konstitutsii [Cradle of the Constitution]," *Itogi*, December 3, 2007, http://dlib.eastview.com/browse/doc/13053834 (accessed June 16, 2012).

240. Roman Anin, "Upravleniye 'del'tsov' prezidenta [The administration of 'hustlers' of the president]," *Novaya gazeta*, May 28, 2012, http://www.novayagazeta.ru/inquests/52799.html (accessed June 17, 2012).

241. Pavel Korobov and Oleg Kashin, "Interview with Vladimir Kozhin: 'Vot chego-chego, a kontrolyorov u nas khvataet' ['We have enough inspectors there']," *Kommersant*, April 20, 2011, http://www.kommersant.ru/Doc/1625310 (accessed June 22, 2013).

242. Vladimir Voronov, "Bol'shiye podryady [Large contracts]," *Sovershenno sekretno*, August 1, 2010, http://www.sovsekretno.ru/articles/id/2561/ (accessed January 2, 2014).

243. U.S. Department of the Treasury. "Treasury Sanctions Russian Officials."

244. Vladimir Pribylovskiy, "Shamalov, Nikolay Terent'evich," *Antikompromat*, n.d., http://anti compromat.org/shamalovy/shamal01bio.html (accessed January 26, 2012).

245. "Company News," *Kommersant*, November 21, 1992, http://www.kommersant.ru/doc/30636 (accessed May 23, 2013).

246. Kolesnikov, "Interview with Masha Gessen et al."

247. David Ignatius, "Sergey Kolesnikov's Tale of Palatial Corruption, Russian Style," *Washington Post*, December 23, 2010, http://www.washingtonpost.com/wp-dyn/content/article/2010 /12/22/AR2010122203770.html (accessed December 24, 2010).

248. "Vladimir Churov Biography," Central Electoral Commission of the Russian Federation, n.d., http://cikrf.ru/eng/aboutcik/biografy/churov.html (accessed May 4, 2012).

249. Marina Sal'ye, "Moy otvet Putinu [My answer to Putin]," Radio Liberty, January 7, 2012, http://www.svobodanews.ru/content/blog/24444669.html (accessed April 13, 2012).

250. Yegor Mostovshchikov and Konstantin Novikov, "Zolotoy vypusk [Gold edition]," *New Times*, May 31, 2010, http://newtimes.ru/articles/detail/21934/ (accessed September 15, 2012).

251. Olesia Yakhno, "Noch' chekista [Night of a Checkist]," Glavred.ru, November 9, 2007, http://www.kartina-ua.info/print_form.phtml?art_id=184273&print_action=article (accessed March 4, 2013).

252. Masha Lipman, "Heckling Russia's J. Edgar Hoover," *New Yorker*, November 30, 2013, http:// www.newyorker.com/online/blogs/newsdesk/2013/11/heckling-russias-j-edgar-hoover.html (accessed April 3, 2014).

253. Andrew E. Kramer, "Putin Aide Said to Hold Secret Assets in Europe," *New York Times*, July 26, 2012, http://www.nytimes.com/2012/07/27/world/europe/in-russia-aleksei-navalny-accuses -chief-investigator-of-secret-european-holdings.html (accessed March 8, 2013).

254. Howard Amos, "Russian Official Made Death Threats to Journalist in Forest, Claims Newspaper," *Guardian*, June 13, 2012, http://www.theGuardian.com/world/2012/jun/13/russian -official-death-threats-journalist-forest (accessed April 8, 2014).

255. "A Student Tells Bastrykin 'You're a Criminal!,'" YouTube, n.d., http://www.youtube.com /watch?v=rHQHJZvHt3M (accessed April 5, 2014); Marie Jégo, "Alexandre Bastrykine Sifflé à La Sorbonne [Aleksandr Bastrykin is hissed at the Sorbonne]," *Le Monde*, November 21,

2013, http://www.lemonde.fr/europe/article/2013/11/21/alexandre-bastrykine-siffle-a-la-sor bonne_3518268_3214.html (accessed April 8, 2014).

256. Boris Nemtsov and Leonid Martynyuk, "Nezavisimyy Ekspertnyy doklad: Zimnyaya olim-piada v subtropikakh [Independent expert report: The Winter Olympics in the subtropics]," Nemtsov.ru, 2013, http://www.nemtsov.ru/?id=718789 (accessed June 23, 2013).
257. U.S. Department of the Treasury. "Treasury Sanctions Russian Officials."
258. Catherine Belton, "Rotenberg Defends His Rising Fortune," *Financial Times*, Novem-ber 12, 2012, http://www.ft.com/intl/cms/s/0/ee6ce89a-2824-11e2-afd2-00144feabdc0.html #axzz2bV2ojDs4 (accessed March 8, 2013).
259. Roman Shleynov, "Druzya Prem'era [Friends of the premier]," *Novaya gazeta*, December 23, 2009, http://dlib.eastview.com.proxy.lib.muohio.edu/browse/doc/21096860 (accessed May 7, 2011).
260. Shleynov, "Druzya Prem'era [Friends of the premier]."
261. U.S. Department of the Treasury, "Treasury Sanctions Russian Officials."
262. Nemtsov and Martynyuk, "Nezavisimyy Ekspertnyy doklad [Independent expert report]."
263. "2013 List of Richest Billionaires in Russia," Forbes.ru, June 21, 2013, http://www.forbes.ru /rating/200-bogateishih-biznesmenov-rossii-2013/2013?full=1&table=1 (accessed June 21, 2013).
264. Aleksandr Levinskiy, "Arkadiy Rotenberg: 'Yesli by menya ne piarili kak druga Putina, biznes byl by pokhuzhe' ['If they had not promoted me as a friend of Putin, business would have been worse']," Forbes.ru, July 23, 2012, http://www.forbes.ru/sobytiya/lyudi/84415-esli-menya-ne -piarili-kak-druga-putina-tak-i-biznes-byl-pohuzhe (accessed June 25, 2013).
265. Hill and Gaddy. *Mr. Putin*, 351.
266. *In Search of Putin's Money*, directed by Sarah Spiller, 2012.
267. Zykov, "Case #144128: 'Putin's Case,' Part 4."
268. Putin et al., *First Person*, 121–22.
269. A. A. Zykov, "Ozero Cooperative. Part 5," Rutube, 2012, http://rutube.ru/video/0d2ff0aec39d 3b909a83(f)554590bc49f/.
270. "Polnyy Spisok Uchrediteley Koopererativa 'Ozero' [Complete list of founders of the 'Ozero' Cooperative]," Anticompromat.org, n.d., http://www.anticompromat.org/putin/ozero.html (accessed April 28, 2012).
271. Rimma Akhmirova, "Zabor Putina [Putin's fence]," Sobesednik.ru, September 14, 2010, http:// sobesednik.ru/incident/sobes_35_10_dacha (accessed July 23, 2012).
272. Jones and Moskoff, *Ko-ops*.
273. Jones and Moskoff, *Ko-ops*.
274. Viktor Yushkin, "Lyudi kak teni [People like shadows]," *Postimees*, September 20, 2007, http:// rux.postimees.ee/200907/glavnaja/mnenie/22618.php (accessed June 8, 2012); "2013 List of Richest Billionaires in Russia."
275. Mukhin, "Byvshiy sledovatel' po osobo vazhnym delam Andrey Zykov [Former investigator for especially important cases Andrey Zykov]."
276. Milov et al., "Putin: Corruption."
277. Milov et al., "Putin: Corruption."
278. Milov et al., "Putin: Corruption."
279. Shleynov, "Druzya Prem'era [Friends of the premier]."
280. Milov et al., "Putin: Corruption."
281. Delany, "An Inside Track to President Putin's Kremlin."
282. Delany, "An Inside Track to President Putin's Kremlin"; "Vladimir Yakunin's Biography," Rus-sian Railways, 2013, http://eng.rzd.ru/factorye/public/en?STRUCTURE_ID=11&layer_id=4 506&refererLayerId=4523&id=21 (accessed June 22, 2013).
283. Delany, "An Inside Track to President Putin's Kremlin."
284. Delany, "An Inside Track to President Putin's Kremlin."
285. Anatoly Medetsky, "Putin Promises $13.6 Bln in Infrastructure Spending," *Moscow Times*, June 21, 2013, http://www.themoscowtimes.com/business/article/putin-promises-136bln-in-infra

structure-spending/482057.html (accessed June 22, 2013); Andrey I. Kolesnikov, "Eto gibkoye slovo 'Svoboda' ['Freedom' is a flexible word]," *Russkiy Pioneer*, June 21, 2013, http://www.ruspioner.ru/profile/blogpost/482/view/4141/ (accessed June 22, 2013).

286. David M. Herszenhorn and Andrew E. Kramer, "Putin Puts Pensions at Risk in $43 Billion Bid to Jolt Economy," *New York Times*, June 22, 2013, http://www.nytimes.com/2013/06/22/world/europe/russia-to-tap-reserve-funds-for-infrastructure-projects.html?ref=europe&_r=0 (accessed June 22, 2013).

287. Aleksey Navalnyy, "Dacha Yakunina [Yakunin's dacha]," Navalny.livejournal.com, June 1, 2013, http://navalny.livejournal.com/804492.html (accessed June 8, 2013).

288. "Grease My Palm," *Economist*, November 27, 2008, http://www.economist.com/node/12628030 (accessed July 7, 2012).

289. "200 bogateyshikh biznesmenov Rossii—2013 [200 wealthiest businessmen in Russia—2013]," Forbes.ru, April 18, 2013, http://www.forbes.ru/rating/200-bogateishih-biznesmenov-rossii-2013/2013?full=1&table=1 (accessed May 8, 2013).

290. Vladimir Milov, Boris Nemtsov, Vladimir Ryzhkov, and Ol'ga Shorina, "The Nemtsov White Paper, Part V: Putin the Thief," *La Russophobe*, April 3, 2011, http://larussophobe.wordpress.com/2011/04/03/special-extra-the-nemtsov-white-paper-part-v-putin-the-thief/ (accessed February 6, 2012).

291. Kolesnikov, "Interview with Masha Gessen et al."

292. "Vlast' i den'gi—2013: Reyting dokhodov federal'nykh chinovnikov [Power and money—2013: Rating of the incomes of federal officials]," Forbes.ru, June 18, 2013, http://www.forbes.ru/rating/vlast-i-dengi-2013-reiting-dohodov-federalnyh-chinovnikov/2013 (accessed July 6, 2013).

293. "Reiting 25 camykh dorogikh top-menedzherov—2012 [Top 25 best-paid top managers—2012]," Forbes.ru, November 19, 2012, http://www.forbes.ru/sobytiya-photogallery/lyudi/210627-reiting-25-samyh-dorogih-top-menedzherov-2012/photo/11 (accessed May 9, 2013).

294. "Reyting Rossiyskikh milliyarderov 2011 [Ratings of Russian billionaires 2011]," *Finance Magazine*, February 2011, http://m2011.finansmag.ru/ (accessed May 6, 2013).

295. Andrew E. Kramer and David M. Herszenhorn, "Midas Touch in St. Petersburg: Friends of Putin Glow Brightly," *New York Times*, March 1, 2012, http://www.nytimes.com/2012/03/02/world/europe/ties-to-vladimir-putin-generate-fabulous-wealth-for-a-select-few-in-russia.html (accessed June 5, 2013).

296. Hill and Gaddy, *Mr. Putin*.

297. Milov et al., "Putin: Corruption."

298. High Court of Justice, "Judgment by Mr. Justice Andrew Smith, Fiona Trust & Holding Corporation and Others vs. Privalov and Others," England and Wales High Court (Commercial Court) Decisions, December 10, 2010, para. 581, http://www.bailii.org/ew/cases/EWHC/Comm/2010/3199.html (accessed June 8, 2013).

299. "Vlast' i den'gi [Power and money]."

300. Aleksey Boyarskiy et al., "Tayna za sem'yu zaborami [Secret behind family fences]," *Kommersant-den'gi*, January 31, 2011, http://www.kommersant.ru/doc/1576415 (accessed April 8, 2013).

301. Kramer and Herszenhorn, "Midas Touch in St. Petersburg."

302. Tom Parfitt, "Russia's Rich Double Their Wealth, but Poor Were Better Off in the 1990s," *Guardian*, April 11, 2011, http://www.thetheGuardian.com/world/2011/apr/11/russia-rich-richer-poor-poorer (accessed August 31, 2013).

Chapter Three: Putin in St. Petersburg, 1990–1996

1. Roman Shleynov, "Nepravitel'stvennyy doklad: Ugolovnyye dela, v kotorykh upominalsya Vladimir Putin, ob'yasnyayut kadrovuyu politiku prezidenta [Nongovernmental report: Criminal cases that mention Vladimir Putin, explaining the personnel policy of the president],"

Novaya gazeta, October 3, 2005, http://dlib.eastview.com.proxy.lib.muohio.edu/browse/doc /8335194 (accessed May 4, 2012).

2. Anders Åslund, *Russia's Capitalist Revolution* (Washington, DC: Petersen Institute for International Economics, 2007), 201.
3. Anu Nousiainen, "Putin Knows the Finns Well Enough, but Do Any of Us Really Know Him?," *Helsingen Sanomat*, January 9, 2000, http://www2.hs.fi/english/archive/thisweek/02022000 .html (accessed January 18, 2012).
4. Åslund, *Russia's Capitalist Revolution*, 201.
5. A. Konstantinov, *Banditskiy Peterburg* (St. Petersburg: Bibliopolis, 1995); A. Konstantinov and M. Dikselius, *Banditskaya Rossiya* (St. Petersburg: Bibliopolis, 1997); Louise Shelly, "Contemporary Russian Organised Crime." In Cyrille Fijnaut and Letizia Paoli, eds., *Organised Crime in Europe: Concepts, Patterns and Control Policies in the European Union and Beyond* (Dordrecht: Springer, 2004), 563–85.
6. Pitch, *Pikantnaya druzhba* [Piquant friendship], 265.
7. "Interview with Aleksandr Belyayev," *Russpress*, March 24, 2012, http://www.russpress .net/?p=2214 (accessed March 26, 2012).
8. Maureen Orth, "Russia's Dark Master," *Vanity Fair*, October 2000, http://www.vanityfair.com/ politics/features/2000/10/putin200010 (accessed April 1, 2012).
9. Vladimir Ivanidze, "Spasaya podpolkovnika Putina: Vtoraya popytka [Saving Lieutenant Colonel Putin: The second attempt]," Radio Svoboda, March 16, 2010, http://www.svobodanews .ru/articleprintview/1983851.html (accessed April 28, 2012).
10. Oleg Lur'ye, "Kolbasa dlya Pitera [Sausage for Piter]," *Novaya gazeta*, March 13, 2000, http:// dlib.eastview.com/browse/doc/3464053 (accessed June 15, 2013).
11. Gessen, *The Man without a Face*, 118.
12. "Ushli iz zhizni 'babushka russkoy demokratii' Marina Sal'ye [The 'grandmother of Russian democracy' Marina Sal'ye dies]," RBK.ru, March 21, 2012, http://top.rbc.ru/society /21/03/2012/642799.shtml (accessed January 28, 2014).
13. Vladimir Ivanidze, "Nerazborchivyye svyazi severnoy stolitsy [The indecipherable connections of the northern capital]," *Sovershenno sekretno*, August 2000, http://www.sovsekretno.ru /magazines/article/514 (accessed March 23, 2012); Oleg Lur'ye. "Kolbasa dlya Pitera: Kak V. Putin pytalsya spasti svoy gorod ot goloda [Sausage for St. Pete: How Vladimir Putin tried to avert famine]," *Novaya gazeta*, March 13, 2000, http://www.novayagazeta.ru/society/11313 .html (accessed March 20, 2012); Marina Sal'ye, "V. Putin—'Prezident' korrumpirovannoy oligarkhii! [V. Putin—'President' of a corrupt oligarchy!]," *Antikompromat*, March 2000, http:// anticompromat.org/putin/salie.html (accessed March 21, 2012).
14. Sal'ye Commission, "Ye. Gaidar to P. Aven, EG-5-03444," January 28, 1992, http://www.face book.com/photo.php?fbid=384728604885108&set=a.384728321551803.94156.27376216 9315086&type=1&theater#!/photo.php?fbid=384729264885042&set=a.384728321551803 .94156.273762169315086&type=1&permPage=1 (accessed March 27, 2012).
15. Gessen, *The Man without a Face*, 123.
16. Sal'ye Commission, "Letter from A. N. Belyaev to V. V. Putin, Doc. No. 300010," January 13, 1992, http://www.facebook.com/photo.php?fbid=384728604885108&set=a.384728321551 803.94156.273762169315086&type=1&theater#!/photo.php?fbid=384734771551158&set =a.384728321551803.94156.273762169315086&type=1&permPage=1 (accessed March 27, 2012).
17. "Interview with Aleksandr Belyayev."
18. St. Petersburg City Council of People's Deputies, "Resheniye ot 08.05.92 No. 88 Ob otchete deputatskoy gruppy po voprosu realizatsii Komitetom vneshnikh svyazey pri mere kvot na syr'ye i materialy," [Decision from 08.05.92 No. 88 on the Report of the parliamentary group on questions about the Implementation of the Committee for Foreign Liaison of the mayor's office about the quotas for raw materials], Anticompromat.org, May 8, 1992, section 2.2, http://anticompromat.org/putin/salie92.html (accessed March 14, 2012).

19. St. Petersburg City Council of People's Deputies, "Resheniye ot 08.05.92 No. 88 Ob otchete deputatskoy gruppy po voprosu realizatsii Komitetom vneshnikh svyazey pri mere kvot na syr'ye i materialy," table 2.

20. St. Petersburg City Council of People's Deputies, "Resheniye ot 08.05.92 No. 88 Ob otchete deputatskoy gruppy po voprosu realizatsii Komitetom vneshnikh svyazey pri mere kvot na syr'ye i materialy," section 5.5.1.

21. St. Petersburg City Council of People's Deputies, "Resheniye ot 08.05.92 No. 88 Ob otchete deputatskoy gruppy po voprosu realizatsii Komitetom vneshnikh svyazey pri mere kvot na syr'ye i materialy," section 5.6.

22. St. Petersburg City Council of People's Deputies, "Resheniye ot 08.05.92 No. 88 Ob otchete deputatskoy gruppy po voprosu realizatsii Komitetom vneshnikh svyazey pri mere kvot na syr'ye i materialy," section 7.4.

23. St. Petersburg City Council of People's Deputies, "Resheniye ot 08.05.92 No. 88 Ob otchete deputatskoy gruppy po voprosu realizatsii Komitetom vneshnikh svyazey pri mere kvot na syr'ye i materialy," section 7.4.

24. St. Petersburg City Council of People's Deputies, "Resheniye ot 08.05.92 No. 88 Ob otchete deputatskoy gruppy po voprosu realizatsii Komitetom vneshnikh svyazey pri mere kvot na syr'ye i materialy," table 2.

25. Sal'ye, "V. Putin—'Prezident' korrumpirovannoy oligarkhii! [V. Putin—'President' of a corrupt oligarchy!]"; Yuriy Felshtinskiy and Vladimir Pribylovskiy, *The Age of Assassins: The Rise and Rise of Vladimir Putin* (London: Gibson Square, 2008), 58.

26. Richard Torrence, "Social Life in St. Petersburg," in Joyce Lasky Reed and Blair Ruble, eds., *St. Petersburg, 1993–2003: A Dynamic Decade* (Washington, DC: St. Petersburg Conservancy, 2010), 62. For Torrence's biography, see http://www.circlesinternet.org/torrence/page0/page0 .html.

27. St. Petersburg City Council of People's Deputies. "Resheniye ot 08.05.92 No. 88 Ob otchete deputatskoy gruppy po voprosu realizatsii Komitetom vneshnikh svyazey pri mere kvot na syr'ye i materialy." section 6.2.

28. Sal'ye Commission, "Agreement No. 1 between V. V. Putin and G. M. Miroshnik," December 25, 1991, http://www.facebook.com/photo.php?fbid=384734771551158&set=a.3847 28321551803.94156.273762169315086&type=1&permPage=1#!/photo.php?fbid=38473 7841550851&set=a.384728321551803.94156.273762169315086&type=1&permPage=1 (accessed April 25, 2012).

29. "To the Chairman of the Russian Federation Supreme Soviet R. I. Khasbulatov on the Abuses in the ZGV in the Sphere of Trade and the Sales of Military Equipment and Property," *Literaturnaya gazeta*, May 13, 1992, http://www.dtic.mil/cgi-bin/GetTRDoc?Location=U2&doc=Get TRDoc.pdf&AD=ADA334747 (accessed May 3, 2012).

30. Oleg Lur'ye. "Kolbasa dlya Pitera [Sausage for St. Pete]."

31. Pitch, *Pikantnaya druzhba* [Piquant friendship], 171.

32. Oleg Lur'ye, "Kolbasa dlya Pitera [Sausage for St. Pete]."

33. Vladimir Pribylovskiy, "Georgiy Miroshnik," http://www.anticompromat.org/putin/miro shnik.html.

34. Hill and Gaddy, *Mr. Putin*, 345–46.

35. Andrew Higgins, Guy Chazan, and Alan Cullison, "Secretive Associate of Putin Emerges as Czar of Russian Oil Trading," *Wall Street Journal*, June 11, 2008, https://global.factiva.com .proxy.lib.muohio.edu/ha/default.aspx?ftx=andrew%20higgins#./!?&_suid=14052703733210 37987486994825304 (accessed April 17, 2012).

36. Catherine Belton and Neil Buckley, "On the Offensive: How Gunvor Rose to the Top of Russian Oil Trading," *Financial Times*, May 14, 2008, http://www.ft.com/intl/cms/s/c3c5c012-21e9 -11dd-a50a-000077b07658,Authorised=false.html?_i_location=http%3A%2F%2Fwww.ft .com%2Fcms%2Fs%2F0%2Fc3c5c012-21e9-11dd-a50a-000077b07658.html&_i_referer =#axzz1pyls8joc (accessed March 23, 2012).

37. U.S. Department of the Treasury, "Treasury Sanctions Russian Officials."

38. Higgins et al., "Secretive Associate of Putin Emerges as Czar of Russian Oil Trading."

39. "Grease My Palm."

40. "Grease My Palm."

41. Edward Lucas, "Private Eye Piece about *Economist* Libel Case," *Private Eye*, August 7, 2009, http://www.edwardlucas.com/2009/08/07/private-eye-piece-about-economist-libel-case/#respond (accessed August 4, 2013).

42. Luke Harding, "Russian Billionaire Drops Libel Case against *Economist*," *Guardian*, July 30, 2009, http://www.theGuardian.com/world/2009/jul/30/russian-billionaire-timchenko-libel -economist (accessed August 8, 2013).

43. Harding, "Russian Billionaire Drops Libel Case against *Economist*."

44. Vsevolod Bel'chenko, "Kuznets svoego 'Gazproma' [Blacksmith of his own 'Gazprom']," *Ogonek*, March 29, 2010, http://dlib.eastview.com.proxy.lib.muohio.edu/browse/doc/21614 432 (accessed January 28, 2014).

45. "Vladimir Putin Talked with Writers," *ITAR-TASS*, September 29, 2011, http://www.itar-tass .com/en/c142/236108.html (accessed March 14, 2012).

46. Higgins et al., "Secretive Associate of Putin Emerges as Czar of Russian Oil Trading."

47. Brian Whitmore, "Inside the Corporation: Russia's Power Elite," Radio Free Europe/Radio Liberty, October 15, 2007, http://www.rferl.org/content/article/1078958.html (accessed June 21, 2012).

48. Thane Gustafson, *Wheel of Fortune: The Battle for Oil and Power in Russia* (Cambridge, MA: The Belknap Press of Harvard University Press, 2012), 45.

49. Higgins et al., "Secretive Associate of Putin Emerges As Czar of Russian Oil Trading."

50. Anastasiya Kirilenko, "Sled Timchenko v 'doklade Sal'ye' [The footprints of Timchenko in the Sal'ye document]," Radio Svoboda, March 11, 2010, http://www.svobodanews.ru/articleprint view/1979833.html (accessed April 28, 2012).

51. Sal'ye Commission, Nevskiy Dom and Kirishinefteorgsintez, "Application 001: For the Supply of 150 Thousand Tons of Diesel and Oil Products," March 31, 1992, http://www.facebook .com/media/set/?set=a.384728321551803.94156.273762169315086&type=3#!/photo.php?f bid=384740611550574&set=a.384728321551803.94156.273762169315086&type=3&the ater (accessed April 14, 2012).

52. Sal'ye Commission, "From Vladimir Putin to P. O. Aven: Document No. 200245," December 4, 1991, http://www.facebook.com/media/set/?set=a.384728321551803.94156.2737621 69315086&typ.

53. St. Petersburg City Council of People's Deputies, "Resheniye ot 08.05.92 No. 88 Ob otchete deputatskoy gruppy po voprosu realizatsii Komitetom vneshnikh svyazey pri mere kvot na syr'ye i materialy."

54. Anders Åslund, *How Russia Became a Market Economy* (Washington, DC: Brookings Institution, 1995), 42; Alexander Vorobyov and Stanislav Zhukov, "Russia: Globalization, Structural Shifts and Inequality," Working Paper No. 19, Center for Economic Policy Analysis, New School University, February 2000, 14, http://www.newschool.edu/scepa/publications/work ingpapers/archive/cepa0119.pdf (accessed April 28, 2012).

55. Copetas, *Bear-Hunting with the Politburo*.

56. Belton and Buckley, "On the Offensive."

57. Quirin Schiermeier, "Russian Science Academy Rejects Putin Ally," *Nature*, June 4, 2008, http://www.nature.com/news/2008/080604/full/453702a.html (accessed June 23, 2013).

58. Yuliya Latynina, "Reforms Spell the End for Russian Sciences," *Moscow Times*, September 25, 2013, http://www.themoscowtimes.com/opinion/article/reforms-spell-the-end-for-russian-sci ences/486560.html (accessed September 25, 2013).

59. Ivan Rybkin, "Ivan Rybkin protiv Vladimira Putina [Ivan Rybkin against Vladimir Putin]," *Kommersant*, February 2, 2004, http://http://dlib.eastview.com.proxy.lib.muohio.edu/browse /doc/5864150 (accessed June 18, 2013).

60. Luke Harding, "Putin, the Kremlin Power Struggle and the $40bn Fortune," *Guardian*, December 20, 2007, http://www.theGuardian.co.uk/world/2007/dec/21/russia.topstories3 (accessed March 20, 2012).

61. Higgins et al., "Secretive Associate of Putin Emerges As Czar of Russian Oil Trading."

62. Roman Shleynov, "Kto Tretiy Vladelets 'Gunvora'? [Who is the third owner of 'Gunvor'?]," *Novaya gazeta*, October 12, 2009, http://dlib.eastview.com/browse/doc/20752073 (accessed July 31, 2013).

63. U.S. Department of the Treasury, "Treasury Sanctions Russian Officials."

64. Belton and Buckley. "On the Offensive."

65. Kramer and Herszenhorn, "Midas Touch in St. Petersburg."

66. Belton and Buckley. "On the Offensive."

67. "2013 List of Richest Billionaires in Russia."

68. Sal'ye Commission, "Report of the Working Group of Deputies: Table 2," January 10, 1992, http://www.facebook.com/media/set/?set=a.384728321551803.94156.273762169315086& type=3#!/photo.php?fbid=384741341550501&set=a.384728321551803.94156.273762169 315086&type=3&theater (accessed June 6, 2012).

69. Sal'ye Commisssion, "Report of the Working Group of Deputies: Table 3," January 10, 1992, https://www.facebook.com/photo.php?fbid=384741664883802&set=a.384728321551803.94 156.273762169315086&type=3&permPage=1 (accessed June 9, 2012); Kirilenko, "Sled Timchenko v 'doklade Sal'ye' [The footprints of Timchenko in the Sal'ye document]."

70. Sal'ye, "V. Putin—'Prezident' korrumpirovannoy oligarkhii! [V. Putin—'President' of a corrupt oligarchy!]."

71. St. Petersburg City Council of People's Deputies, "Resheniye ot 08.05.92 No. 88 Ob otchete deputatskoy gruppy po voprosu realizatsii Komitetom vneshnikh svyazey pri mere kvot na syr'ye i materialy," section 6.6.2.

72. "Putin, Vladimir Vladimirovich," Anticompromat, n.d., http://www.anticompromat.org /putin/ (accessed February 1, 2012).

73. Usol'tsev, *Sosluzhivets* [Colleague], 182–83.

74. Mariya Abakumova, "Dolya professora: Kak odnokursnik Putina Il'gam Ragimov okazalsya sovladel'tsem dorogoy Moskovskoy nedvizhemosti [The share of a professor: How Putin classmate Ilham Rahimov became the owner of expensive Moscow property]," *Forbes.ru*, October 2012, http://www.anticompromat.org/putin/ragimov_i04.html (accessed February 9, 2014).

75. "Letter from V. V. Putin to V. B. Stepanov, Head of Petersburg Customs," Sal'ye Commission, January 27, 1992, http://gdb.rferl.org/B4B76202-5FA4-4EE7-BEE0-4F371F1927C2.jpg (accessed November 23, 2013).

76. Sal'ye Commission, "Agreement No. 19/92 between Tamigo and the Committee for Foreign Liaison of St. Petersburg," January 14, 1992, https://www.facebook.com/photo.php?fbid=3847 38378217464&set=a.384728321551803.94156.273762169315086&type=3&permPage=1 (accessed June 8, 2013).

77. Matt Bivens, "Waiting for Vladimir Putin," *Moscow Times*, March 4, 2000, http://dlib.eastview .com/browse/doc/225405 (accessed June 7, 2013).

78. Zykov, "Testimony, Part 3."

79. St. Petersburg City Council of People's Deputies, "Resheniye ot 08.05.92 No. 88 Ob otchete deputatskoy gruppy po voprosu realizatsii Komitetom vneshnikh svyazey pri mere kvot na syr'ye i materialy," section 7.5.

80. St. Petersburg City Council of People's Deputies, "Resheniye ot 08.05.92 No. 88 Ob otchete deputatskoy gruppy po voprosu realizatsii Komitetom vneshnikh svyazey pri mere kvot na syr'ye i materialy," section 8.2.

81. St. Petersburg City Council of People's Deputies, "Resheniye ot 08.05.92 No. 88 Ob otchete deputatskoy gruppy po voprosu realizatsii Komitetom vneshnikh svyazey pri mere kvot na syr'ye i materialy," section 8.4.

82. Irina Bobrova, Mariya Markina, Sergey Bychkov, Mikhail Rostovskiy, Aleksandr Khinshteyn, and Ekaterina Deyeva, "7 Mgnovenii iz Zhizni 'Preyemnika' [Seven moments from the life of the 'successor']," *Moskovskiy Komsomolets*, August 18, 1999, http://dlib.eastview.com/browse /doc/107921 (accessed May 8, 2013).

83. Sal'ye Commission, "Letter from Yu. Boldyrev to P. O. Aven," March 31, 1992, http://www .facebook.com/media/set/?set=a.384728321551803.94156.273762169315086&type=1#! /photo.php?fbid=384728604885108&set=a.384728321551803.94156.273762169315086 &type=1&theater (accessed March 27, 2012); Carlo Bonini and Giuseppe D'Avanzo, "Lo Scandalo della fame a Petroburgo [The scandal of hunger in St. Petersburg]," *La Repubblica*, July 13, 2001, http://ricerca.repubblica.it/repubblica/archivio/repubblica/2001/07/13/lo -scandalo-della-fame-pietroburgo.html?ref=search (accessed June 3, 2013).

84. Anastasiya Kirilenko, "Kak Sobchak i Putin khodili na kovyor [How Sobchak and Putin were brought to account]," Radio Liberty, March 9, 2010, http://www.svobodanews.ru/articleprint view/1978453.html (accessed April 28, 2012).

85. Sal'ye Commission, "Letter from Yu. Boldyrev to P. O. Aven."

86. Bonini and D'Avanzo, "Lo Scandalo della fame a Petroburgo [The scandal of hunger in St. Petersburg]."

87. "#223 Pyotr Aven," *Forbes*, May 16, 2014, http://www.forbes.com/profile/pyotr-aven / (accessed May 16, 2014).

88. Kirilenko, "Kak Sobchak i Putin khodili na kovyor [How Sobchak and Putin were brought to account]."

89. Boris Vishnevskiy, "Ten', znayushchaya svoyo mesto [A shadow, knowing its place]." *Moscow News*, September 24, 2004, http://www.compromat.ru/page_11389.htm (accessed January 28, 2014).

90. Yuliya Latynina, "Russia's Squandered Billions," *The Other Russia*, March 26, 2010, http:// www.theotherrussia.org/2010/03/26/yulia-latynina-on-russias-squandered-billions/ (accessed March 26, 2012); Natalya Alyakrinskaya and Vladimir Pribylovskiy, "Prem'er v krugu 'Sem'i'— Gazprom [The premier in the circle of the 'Family'—Gazprom]," *New Times*, April 19, 2010, http://newtimes.ru/articles/detail/20011 (accessed March 26, 2012).

91. Ivanidze, "Spasaya podpolkovnika Putina [Saving Lieutenant Colonel Putin]."

92. Felshtinskiy and Pribylovskiy, *The Age of Assassins*, 60–61.

93. Robert Orttung, *From Leningrad to St. Petersburg* (New York: St. Martin's Press, 1995), 206–12.

94. Gessen, *The Man without a Face*, 124; Arsen Rstaki and Sergey Borisov, "Delo Putina [The Putin affair]," *Novaya gazeta*, March 23, 2000, http://old.novayagazeta.ru/data/2000/20/02 .html (accessed February 12, 2012).

95. Vladimir Pribylovskiy, "Valeriy Golubev," *Antikompromat*, n.d., http://www.anticompromat .org/golubev/golubbio.html (accessed June 15, 2012).

96. Shleynov, "Druzya Prem'era [Friends of the premier]."

97. "Golubev, Valeriy," Gazprom, n.d., http://ir.gazprom-neft.com/corporate-governance/board -of-directors/valery-golubev/ (accessed April 29, 2012).

98. Mukhin, "Byvshiy sledovatel' po osobo vazhnym delam Andrey Zykov [Former investigator for especially important cases Andrey Zykov]."

99. Sergey Buntman, "Interview with Marina Sal'ye," Ekho Moskvy, January 28, 2000, http://echo .msk.ru/programs/beseda/10742 (accessed March 13, 2012).

100. St. Petersburg City Council of People's Deputies, "Resheniye ot 08.05.92 No. 88 Ob otchete deputatskoy gruppy po voprosu realizatsii Komitetom vneshnikh svyazey pri mere kvot na syr'ye i materialy."

101. Mark Franchetti, "Putin Caught in Food Scandal," *Sunday Times (UK)*, March 12, 2000, http:// www.russialist.org/archives/4163.html (accessed March 18, 2012).

102. Franchetti, "Putin Caught in Food Scandal."

103. Sal'ye, "V. Putin—'Prezident' korrumpirovannoy oligarkhii! [V. Putin—'President' of a corrupt oligarchy!]."

104. Kirilenko, "Kak Sobchak i Putin khodili na kovyor [How Sobchak and Putin were brought to account]."

105. Vladimir Baburin, "Interview with Sergey Yushenkov," Radio Svoboda, March 13, 2002, http://archive.svoboda.org/programs/hr/2002/hr.031302.asp (accessed March 26, 2012).

106. Mikhail Vinogradov, Konstantin Getmanskiy, Vladimir Denchenko, Roman Kirillov, and Aleksandr Sadchikov, "Ubit Sergey Yushenkov [Sergey Yushenkov is killed]," *Izvestiya*, April 19, 2003, http://dlib.eastview.com.proxy.lib.muohio.edu/browse/doc/4868651 (accessed January 28, 2014); Julie A. Corwin, "Requiem for a Political Heavyweight: Sergei Yushenkov," Radio Free Europe, April 25, 2003, http://www.rferl.org/content/article/1344349.html (accessed January 28, 2014).

107. "Pered smert'yu Yushenkovu peredali kompromat na FSB po Nord-Ostu [Before his death, Yushenkov passed kompromat on the FSB's role in Nord-Ost]," Newsru.com, April 28, 2003, http://www.newsru.com/russia/28apr2003/basaev.html (accessed January 28, 2014); "Litvinenko: Yushenkova ubili za rassledovaniye terakta v 'Nord-Oste' [Litvinenko: They killed Yushenkov for investigating the terrorist attack on 'Nord-Ost']," Lenta.ru, April 25, 2003, http://lenta.ru/russia/2003/04/25/litvinenko/ (accessed March 26, 2012).

108. Putin et al., *First Person*, 98–99.

109. Kirilenko, "Kak Sobchak i Putin khodili na kovyor [How Sobchak and Putin were brought to account]"; Anastasiya Kirilenko and Yuriy Timofeev, "Pochemy Marina Sal'ye molchala o Putine 10 let? [Why was Marina Sal'ye silent about Putin for 10 years?]," Radio Svoboda, February 3, 2012, http://www.svoboda.org/content/article/1972366.html (accessed March 23, 2012).

110. Sal'ye Commission, "Dokumenty Mariny Sal'ye [Documents of Marina Sal'ye]," April 2012, http://www.facebook.com/media/set/?set=a.384728321551803.94156.273762169315086&type=3 (accessed April 20, 2012).

111. Putin et al., *First Person*, 98.

112. "On the Regulation of the Activities of Enterprises that Derive an Income from the Gambling Business in the St. Petersburg Free Enterprise Zone, Order No. 753-r." in Felshtinsky and Pribylovsky, *The Age of Assassins*, 303.

113. Vladimir Putin, "Speech at Law Enforcement Conference," YouTube, 1991, http://www.youtube.com/watch?NR=1&v=Or17Un5Go0k&feature=endscreen (accessed March 9, 2013).

114. Putin et al., *First Person*, 101–2.

115. Felshtinskiy and Pribylovskiy, *The Age of Assassins*, 65.

116. "Dossier on Putin in St. Petersburg," *Ruspress*, January 15, 2010, http://www.rospres.com/hearsay/5833/ (accessed June 5, 2013).

117. Vladimir Ivanidze, "Komy Neva dala shans [To whom Neva gave a chance]," *Novaya gazeta*, February 8, 2012, http://www.novayagazeta.ru/society/50920.html (accessed April 2, 2012).

118. Yakhno, "Noch' chekista [Night of a Chekist]."

119. Manfred Quiring, "Interview with Stanislav Belkovskiy: Warum Putin gar nicht Präsident bleiben will [Why Putin doesn't want to stay president]," *Die Welt*, November 12, 2007, http://www.welt.de/politik/article1352592/Warum-Putin-gar-nicht-Praesident-bleiben-will.html (accessed February 6, 2013).

120. Ali Nassor, "Politician Killed in Car Wreck," *St. Petersburg Press*, 1995, http://www.friends-partners.org/oldfriends/spbweb/sppress/137/politic.html (accessed April 27, 2012); Ali Nassor, "Savitsky's driver dies, police may close case," *St. Petersburg Press*, 1995, http://www.friends-partners.org/oldfriends/spbweb/sppress/141/savitsky.html (accessed April 8, 2011); Associated Press, "Murder Alleged in Wreck," *Star News*, December 15, 1995, http://news.google.com/newspapers?nid=1454&dat=19951212&id=f60sAAAAIBAJ&sjid=IxUEAAAAIBAJ&pg=6019,4567297 (accessed April 27, 2012); "Deputy's Death," *St. Petersburg Press*, 1995, http://www.friends-partners.org/oldfriends/spbweb/sppress/137/what.html (accessed April 27, 2012); Matt Taibbi, "Campaign Violence: Politics or Business?" *Moscow Times*, December 14, 1995, http://www.themoscowtimes.com/news/article/campaign-violence-politics-or-business/331191.html (accessed April 27, 2012); *St. Petersburg Times*, "Investigation Complete," *St. Peters-*

burg Times, October 8, 2004, http://www.sptimes.ru/index.php?action_id=100&story_id =1791 (accessed April 27, 2012).

121. Yuliya Shum, "K skandalu preveli deystviya Minfina [Activities of the Ministry of Finance produce a scandal]," *Kommersant*, September 4, 1993, http://www.kommersant.ru/doc/58602 (accessed May 23, 2013).

122. Dmitriy Kamyshev, "Desyat' let pri Putine [The ten years under Putin]," *Kommersant-Vlast'*, August 3, 2009, http://dlib.eastview.com.proxy.lib.muohio.edu/browse/doc/20445310 (accessed July 23, 2012); Shum, "K skandalu preveli deystviya Minfina [Activities of the Ministry of Finance produce a scandal]."

123. Caroline Humphrey, *The Unmaking of Soviet Life* (Ithaca, NY: Cornell University Press, 2002), 99–127; Alena V. Ledeneva, *How Russia Really Works* (Ithaca, NY: Cornell University Press, 2006).

124. Vladimir Ivanidze, "Kto takoy V. V. Kiselyev, kotoryy vyvel na stsenu V. V. Putina? [Who is this V. V. Kiselyev, who brought V. V. Putin up on stage?]," *Novaya gazeta*, August 29, 2011, http:// old.novayagazeta.ru/data/2011/095/00.html (accessed April 3, 2012).

125. Ivanidze, "Komy Neva dala shans [To whom Neva gave a chance]."

126. Ivanidze, "Kto takoy V.V. Kiselyev? [Who is this V. V. Kiselyev?]."

127. Viktor Seslavin, "Kremlinskiy Massovik-zateynik [Kremlin's organizer of mass amusements]," *Leningradskaya pravda*, March 8, 2001, http://www.lenpravda.ru/today/251369.html (accessed April 4, 2012).

128. Ivanidze, "Komy Neva dala shans [To whom Neva gave a chance]."

129. Ivanidze, "Komy Neva dala shans [To whom Neva gave a chance]."

130. Ivanidze, "Komy Neva dala shans [To whom Neva gave a chance]."

131. Åslund, *Russia's Capitalist Revolution*, 201.

132. Zykov, "Testimony, Part 1."

133. Gomez, "La Audiencia dicta orden de captura para un diputado del partido de Putin [The National Court seeks warrant for Putin party deputy]"; Gomez, "¿Vuelven los rusos poco recomendables? [Do unsavory Russians return?]."

134. Korobov and Kashin, "Interview with Vladimir Kozhin."

135. Julia Ioffe, "Dead Souls," *New Yorker*, July 12, 2011, http://www.newyorker.com/online/blogs /newsdesk/2011/07/dead-souls.html (accessed April 10, 2012).

136. Ivanidze, "Kto takoy V. V. Kiselyev? [Who is this V. V. Kiselyev?]"; Julia Ioffe, "Vladimir Putin and the Guy Code," *New Yorker*, November 6, 2011, http://www.newyorker.com/online/blogs /newsdesk/2011/11/vladimir-putin-and-the-guy-code.html (accessed April 4, 2012).

137. "Putin vnov' poyavilsya na kontserte skandal'nogo fonda 'Federatsiya' [Putin again appears at a concert of the scandal-ridden 'Federation' Fund]," Newsru.com, November 3, 2011, http:// www.newsru.com/russia/03nov2011/patzany.html (accessed April 4, 2012); Daniil Turovskiy, " 'Patsany! Vam eto ne nado!' Fond 'Federatsiya' ustraivayet antinarkoticheskiy kontsert s Putinym [Come on fellas, quit drugs! Federation Fund organizes an antinarcotics concert with Putin]," Afisha.ru, November 11, 2011, http://gorod.afisha.ru/archive/come-on-fellas-quit -drugs/ (accessed May 24, 2013).

138. Putin et al., *First Person*, 101–2.

139. Nikitinskiy, "Litso vlasti [A Person of Power]."

140. Petrov, "Skol'ko stoit Gubernator [How much does a governorship cost?]."

141. Agathe Duparc, "Le nom de M. Poutine apparaît en marge des affaires de blanchiment au Liechtenstein [The name of Mr. Putin appears in the margin of money-laundering cases in Liechtenstein]," *Le Monde*, May 26, 2000, http://global.factiva.com/hp/printsavews.aspx ?pp=Print&hc=Publication (accessed April 7, 2012).

142. Ivanidze, "Nerazborchivyye svyazi severnoy stolitsy [The indecipherable connections of the northern capital]."

143. Andrew Jack, *Inside Putin's Russia: Can There Be Reform without Democracy?* (New York: Oxford University Press, 2006); Hosenball and Caryl, "A Stain on Mr. Clean."

144. Hosenball and Caryl, "A Stain on Mr. Clean"; Vladimir Ivanidze, "Gryaznaya zona Evropu [Europe's gray zone]," *Sovershenno sekretno*, July 2000, http://www.sovsekretno.ru/magazines /article/502 (accessed April 7, 2012).

145. Jack, *Inside Putin's Russia*, 73.

146. Ivanidze, "Nerazborchivyye svyazi severnoy stolitsy [The indecipherable connections of the northern capital]."

147. Felshtinsky and Pribylovsky, *The Age of Assassins*, 2008.

148. Catherine Belton, "Putin's Name Surfaces in German Probe," *Moscow Times*, May 19, 2003, www.themoscowtimes.com/sitemap/free/2003/5/article/putins-name-surfaces-in-german-probe /238432.html.

149. Boris Berezovskiy, "Novyy peredel: Chto delat'? [New repartition: What is to be done?]," *Kommersant*, July 24, 2003, http://www.kommersant.ru/doc/398799 (accessed April 19, 2012).

150. Sal'ye, "V. Putin—'Prezident' korrumpirovannoy oligarkhii! [V. Putin—'President' of a corrupt oligarchy!]."

151. "Bank 'Sankt-Peterburg' okazalsya v tsentre vnimaniya [The Bank of St. Petersburg in the spotlight]," *Delovoy Peterburg*, October 7, 2003, http://www.dp.ru/a/2003/10/07/Bank_Sankt -Peterburg_ok/ (accessed May 23, 2013).

152. Pavel Sergeyevskiy, "Vneshtorgbank, Mal'tiyskiye kresty i granatovyye braslety [Vneshtorgbank, the Maltese Cross and the pomegranate bracelet]," Freelance Bureau, May 17, 2005, http://flb .ru/info/34169.html (accessed May 3, 2012).

153. Tikhomirov, "Capital Flight from Post-Soviet Russia."

154. Ivanidze, "Nerazborchivyye svyazi severnoy stolitsy [The indecipherable connections of the northern capital]."

155. Andrey Tsyganov, "Delo ob Otmyvanii: 'My reshili, chto nam vygodnee stroit' benzokolonki' [The money-laundering case: 'We decided that building gas stations would be more profitable']," *Kommersant*, April 5, 2004, http://dlib.eastview.com/browse/doc/6110130 (accessed April 7, 2012).

156. Jack, *Inside Putin's Russia*, 77; Ivanidze, "Nerazborchivyye svyazi severnoy stolitsy [The indecipherable connections of the northern capital]."

157. Hosenball and Caryl. "A Stain on Mr. Clean."

158. Jürgen Roth, *Gangster aus dem Osten* [Gangster from the East], vol. 1 (Hamburg: Europa Verlag, 2003).

159. "Analysis of SPAG," Wallstreet-online, December 13, 2000, http://www.wallstreet-online.de /diskussion/315662-1-10/analyse-spag-st-petersburg-immobilien-ag (accessed April 20, 2012).

160. Hosenball and Caryl. "A Stain on Mr. Clean."

161. Belton, "Putin's Name Surfaces in German Probe."

162. Catherine Belton, "New Book Poses Question of Putin's Links with Underworld," *St. Petersburg Times*, October 7, 2003, http://www.sptimes.ru/index.php?action_id=100&story_id=11164 (accessed June 7, 2013).

163. Duparc, "Le nom de M. Poutine apparaît en marge des affaires de blanchiment au Liechtenstein [The name of Mr. Putin appears in the margin of money-laundering cases in Liechtenstein."

164. Belton, "Putin's Name Surfaces in German Probe."

165. Mark Franchetti, "Russia's 'Al Capone' Sneers at His Trial," *Sunday Times (UK)*, May 31, 2009, http://www.thesundaytimes.co.uk/sto/news/world_news/article170555.ece (accessed May 20, 2012).

166. Milov et al., "Putin: Corruption."

167. "Analysis of SPAG."

168. Ivanidze, "Nerazborchivyye svyazi severnoy stolitsy [The indecipherable connections of the northern capital]."

169. Tsyganov, "Delo ob Otmyvanii [The money-laundering case]."

170. Roman Shleynov, "Posazhenyye ottsy [Sponsoring fathers]," *Novaya gazeta*, Feburary 7, 2005, http://2005.novayagazeta.ru/nomer/2005/09n/n09n-s26.shtml (accessed April 22, 2012).

171. Hosenball and Caryl, "A Stain on Mr. Clean."

172. Ivanidze, "Nerazborchivyye svyazi severnoy stolitsy [The indecipherable connections of the northern capital]."

173. J. V. Koshiw, "Kuchma's 'Parallel Cabinet': The Center of President Kuchma's Authoritarian Rule Based on the Melnychenko Recordings," Third Annual Danyliw Research Seminar on Contemporary Ukraine, 2007, www.ukrainianstudies.uottawa.ca/pdf/P_Koshiw_Danyliw07.pdf (accessed April 20, 2012).

174. Koshiw, "Kuchma's 'Parallel Cabinet.'"

175. Hosenball and Caryl, "A Stain on Mr. Clean"; Elizabeth Olson, "Liechtenstein: Money-Laundering Charges," *New York Times*, July 20, 2001, http://proquest.umi.com/pqdweb?index=0&did=366510482&SrchMode=1&sid=3&Fmt=10&VInst=PROD&VType=PQD&RQT=309&VName=HNP&TS=1333837773&clientId=73174 (accessed April 7, 2012); Belton, "Putin's Name Surfaces in German Probe."

176. Yuliya Latynina, "The Geopolitics of Accounts Receivable," *St. Petersburg Times*, March 30, 2007, http://www.sptimes.ru/index.php?action_id=2&story_id=21150 (accessed April 23, 2012).

177. Shleynov, "Posazhenyye ottsy [Sponsoring fathers]."

178. Jochen Kummer, "Was weiß der Kanzler über seinen Freund Putin? [What does the chancellor do to help his friend Putin?]," *Die Welt*, August 31, 2003, http://www.welt.de/print-wams/article99908/Was-weiss-der-Kanzler-ueber-seinen-Freund-Putin.html (accessed August 6, 2013).

179. Belton, "Putin's Name Surfaces in German Probe."

180. "Spiegel Interview with Ex-Chancellor Gerhard Schröder," *Der Spiegel*, October 23, 2006, http://www.spiegel.de/international/spiegel/spiegel-interview-with-ex-chancellor-gerhard-schroeder-i-m-anything-but-an-opponent-of-america-a-444069.html (accessed June 21, 2012).

181. Jürgen Roth, *Gangster aus dem Osten* [Gangster from the East]; "Putin bei Schröder 'Offener Dialog' und Milliarden-Deals [The Putin Schröder 'Open Dialogue' and Billions in Deals]," *Frankfurter Allgemeine Zeitung*, December 21, 2004, http://www.faz.net/aktuell/politik/putin-bei-schroeder-offener-dialog-und-milliarden-deals-1191842.html.

182. Borogan, "Erich Schmidt-Eenboom."

183. Andrey Musatov and Gleb Krampets, "Stockmann Purchases a Retail Complex," *St. Petersburg Times*, May 27, 2005, http://www.sptimes.ru/archive/pdf/1073.pdf (accessed April 13, 2012).

184. Thomson Reuters Business Description, "St. Petersburg Immobilien & Beteiligungen AG (SPAG)," Alacra: Premium Business Information Source, April 13, 2012, http://www.alacrastore.com/company-snapshot/St_Petersburg_Immobilien_Beteiligungen_AG_SPAG-2518437 (accessed April 13, 2012).

185. "SPAG St. Petersburg Immobilien und Beteiligungs AG," Amiculum.de, Das Borsenmantel-Portal, n.d., http://www.amiculum.de/SPAG.html (accessed April 13, 2012).

186. "Glazkov, Vadim Petrovich," Personalities of St. Petersburg, n.d., http://www.ceo.spb.ru/eng/business/glazkov.v.p/index.shtml (accessed May 16, 2014); Reddaway, "The Silovik War of 2004–2010," 11.

187. Hosenball and Caryl, "A Stain on Mr. Clean."

188. Vladimir Pribylovskiy, "Khmarin, Viktor Nikolayevich," *Antikompromat*, n.d. www.anticompromat.org/putin/hmarinbio.html (accessed June 21, 2012).

189. Petersburg Fuel Company, "Istoriya kompanii 1994 god [History of the company in 1994]," 2012, http://www.ptk.ru/files/1994_god_1.pdf (accessed June 4, 2013).

190. Petersburg Fuel Company, "Istoriya kompanii 1995 god [History of the company in 1995]." 2012, http://www.ptk.ru/about/istoriya-kompanii/istoriya-kompanii (accessed April 7, 2012).

191. Roman Anin, "Druz'ya—ne razley neft' [Friends—don't spill the oil]," *Novaya gazeta*, April 14, 2011, http://www.novayagazeta.ru/inquests/6222.html (accessed April 17, 2012); Petersburg Fuel Company, "Istoriya kompanii 1995 god [History of the company in 1995]"; Felshtinsky and Pribylovsky, *The Corporation*; Ivanidze, "Gryaznaya zona Evropu [Europe's gray zone]."

192. Ivanidze, "Nerazborchivyye svyazi severnoy stolitsy [The indecipherable connections of the northern capital]."

193. Valeriy Beresnev, "Grand Operation," *Novaya gazeta*, June 19, 2008, http://dlib.eastview.com .proxy.lib.muohio.edu/sources/article.jsp?id=17635783 (accessed April 26, 2012). For an extensive discussion of Traber's activities as reported by the Russian media see http://www .rumafia.com/person.php?id=64.

194. Gustafson, *Wheel of Fortune*, 126.

195. Roman Shleynov, "Ptentsy gnezda Petrova [Chicks in Petrov's s nest]," *Novaya gazeta*, November 2, 2009, http://dlib.eastview.com/browse/doc/20851285 (accessed July 18, 2012).

196. Anin, "Druz'ya—ne razley neft' [Friends—don't spill the oil]"; Roman Anin, "Malen'kaya prachechnaya prem'er-klassa [A small laundry of the premier class]," *Novaya gazeta*, April 10, 2011, http://novayagazeta.ru/inquests/6287.html (accessed April 17, 2012).

197. Anin, "Druz'ya—ne razley neft' [Friends—don't spill the oil]."

198. Yuliya Panfilova, "Privatizatsiya 'Rosgosstrakha' nachinaetsya snachala [Privatization of Rosgosstrakh Starts all over Again]," *Kommersant*, February 5, 1998, http://dlib.eastview.com .proxy.lib.muohio.edu/browse/doc/3745405 (accessed April 24, 2012).

199. Igor' Pylayev, "Vladislav Reznik podchishchaet banki [Vladislav Reznik cleans up banks]," *RBK daily*, November 10, 2006, http://rbcdaily.ru/finance/562949979054436 (accessed April 25, 2012).

200. American Embassy Madrid to U.S. Secretary of State, "Spain Details Its Strategy to Combat the Russian Mafia."

201. "Spain Releases 'Gangster,'" *Moscow Times*, February 4, 2010, http://www.themoscowtimes .com/news/article/spain-releases-gangster/399001.html (accessed February 7, 2014).

202. Franchetti, "Russia's 'Al Capone' Sneers at His Trial"; Michael Schwirtz, "A Mobster Trial, and a Flash of a Violent Past," *New York Times*, May 19, 2009, http://www.nytimes.com/2009/05/14 /world/europe/14mobster.html?_r=0 (accessed May 31, 2013).

203. Boris Gryzlov, "'Boy s organizovannoy prestupnost'yu my proigryvayem' [We are losing the fight against organized crime]," *SPB Vedomosti*, August 9, 2001, http://dlib.eastview.com.proxy .lib.muohio.edu/browse/doc/2150075 (accessed June 8, 2013).

204. Leonid Nikitinskiy, "Delo Putina [The Putin case]," *Novaya gazeta*, March 23, 2000, http:// www.novayagazeta.ru/society/11232.html (accessed April 10, 2012).

205. Zykov, "Case #144128: 'Putin's Case,' Part 4"; Mukhin, "Byvshiy sledovatel' po osobo vazhnym delam Andrey Zykov [Former investigator for especially important cases Andrey Zykov]."

206. Nikitinskiy, "Delo Putina [The Putin case]."

207. Mukhin, "Byvshiy sledovatel' po osobo vazhnym delam Andrey Zykov [Former investigator for especially important cases Andrey Zykov]."

208. OCCRP, "Russia: Abuse of Criminal Prosecution," Organized Crime and Corruption Reporting Project, July 13, 2009, http://www.reportingproject.net/prosecution//index.php?option=com _content&task=view&id=8&Itemid=1 (accessed April 23, 2012).

209. Shleynov, "Nepravitel'stvennyy doklad [Nongovernmental report]."

210. Mukhin, "Byvshiy sledovatel' po osobo vazhnym delam Andrey Zykov [Former investigator for especially important cases Andrey Zykov]."

211. Anton Ivanitskiy, "Operatsiya 'XX Trest' [Operation Twentieth Trust]," *Novaya gazeta*, September 11, 2000, http://dlib.eastview.com.proxy.lib.muohio.edu/browse/doc/3464992 (accessed October 7, 2013).

212. Anna Badkhen, "Spanish Villa Was Putin's Getaway," *Moscow Times*, June 24, 2000, www.the moscowtimes.com/news/article/spanish-villa-was-putins-getaway/261585.html (accessed June 5, 2012); Giles Tremlett, "Leader's Secret Holidays to Spain," *Times (UK)*, June 15, 2000, http:// www.russialist.org/archives/4379.html (accessed August 18, 2012); J. C. Serrano and E. Montánchez, "Los Viajes Secretos de Putin a Sotogrande [The Secret Travels of Putin to Sotogrande]," *La Razón (Madrid)*, June 13, 2000, 16–17; Juan Pablo Duch, "Encarcelan Gusinski, Principal Accionista de Media-Most [Gusinskiy jailed, the main shareholder of Media-Most],"

La Jornada, June 14, 2000, http://www.jornada.unam.mx/2000/06/14/mun5.html (accessed June 5, 2013).

213. Shleynov, "Nepravitel'stvennyy doklad [Nongovernmental report]"; Nikitinskiy, "Delo Putina [The Putin case]"; Sergey Pluzhnikov, "Nekhoroshiye kvartiry [Bad apartments]," *Sovershenno sekretno*, February 1998, http://www.sovsekretno.ru/magazines/article/138 (accessed April 24, 2012).
214. Serrano and Montánchez. "Los Viajes Secretos de Putin a Sotogrande [The Secret Travels of Putin to Sotogrande]."
215. Mukhin, "Byvshiy sledovatel' po osobo vazhnym delam Andrey Zykov [Former investigator for especially important cases Andrey Zykov]."
216. Shleynov, "Nepravitel'stvennyy doklad [Nongovernmental report]."
217. Shleynov, "Nepravitel'stvennyy doklad [Nongovernmental report]."
218. Zykov, "Case #144128: 'Putin's Case,' Part 4."
219. Nikitinskiy, "Delo Putina [The Putin case]"; Orth, "Russia's Dark Master"; Zykov, "Case #144128: 'Putin's Case,' Part 4."
220. Il'ya Barabanov, "Ptentsy gnezda Petrova [Chicks in Petrov's nest]," *New Times*, June 15, 2007, http://newtimes.ru/articles/detail/12341/ (accessed December 23, 2012).
221. Pravoslavie.ru, "Interview with Igumenia Georgia (Shchukina), the Mother Superior of the Gornensky Monastery in the Holy Land," *Troparion Bulletin*. July 4, 2010, http://www.troparion.com/bulletin2a.htm (accessed January 2, 2014).
222. Nikitinskiy, "Delo Putina [The Putin case]."
223. "Twentieth Trust Company," EInforma Directory: Reports of all Companies in Spain, 2013, http://www.einforma.com/servlet/app/prod/DATOS_DE/EMPRESA/TWENTIETH-TRUST-COMPANY-SL-C_QjAzOTU5NDY3_de-ALICANTE.html (accessed June 1, 2013).
224. Ivanitskiy, "Operatsiya 'XX Trest' [Operation Twentieth Trust]."
225. Zykov, "Case #144128: 'Putin's Case,' Part 4."
226. Nikitinskiy, "Delo Putina [The Putin case]."
227. Alessandra Stanley, "In St. Petersburg, a Struggle for Room at the Top," *New York Times*, April 6, 1994, http://www.nytimes.com/1994/04/06/world/in-st-petersburg-a-struggle-for-room-at-the-top.html?pagewanted=1 (accessed June 8, 2012).
228. Ioffe, "Dead Souls"; Nikitinskiy, "Delo Putina [The Putin case]."
229. Nikitinskiy, "Delo Putina [The Putin case]."
230. Matt Bivens, "Waiting for Putin (Continued)," *Moscow Times*, March 4, 2000, http://dlib.eastview.com.proxy.lib.muohio.edu/browse/doc/225406 (accessed June 5, 2013).
231. Barabanov, "Ptentsy gnezda Petrova [Chicks in Petrov's nest]."
232. Barabanov, "Ptentsy gnezda Petrova [Chicks in Petrov's nest]."
233. Vitaliy Kamyshev and Andrey Kolesnikov, "Prezident Olbanskiy Federatsii: Who Is Mr. Medvedeff? [President of the Albanian Federation: Who is Mr. Medvedev?]," *New Times*, May 21, 2007, http://dlib.eastview.com.proxy.lib.muohio.edu/browse/doc/15052744 (accessed April 10, 2012).
234. Shleynov, "Nepravitel'stvennyy doklad [Nongovernmental report]."
235. Marina Litvinovich, "Kudrin, Aleksey Leonidovich," Election2012.ru, 2012, http://election2012.ru/reports/1/8.html (accessed June 8, 2013).
236. OCCRP, "Russia: Abuse of Criminal Prosecution."
237. Zykov, "Part 1."
238. Zykov, "Case #144128: 'Putin's Case,' Part 4."
239. Anatoly Sobchak, "Glava 1—Istoriya odnoy provokatsii ili tak nazuvayemoye 'delo' Sobchaka [Part 1—The history of a provocation, or the so-called 'Sobchak affair']," in *Dyuzhina nozhey v spiny: Poychitel'naya istoriya o rossiyskikh politicheskikh nravakh* [A dozen knives in my back: An instructive history of Russian political customs], 1999, http://sobchak.org/rus/main.php3?fp=f02080000_fl000093 (accessed May 7, 2012); Marina Sal'ye, "Nastal chered Putina—'Prezidenta' korrumpirovannogo klana [Putin's turn—'President' of a corrupt clan],"

Radio Svoboda, March 22, 2012, http://www.svoboda.org/content/blog/24500639.html (accessed April 10, 2012); Pluzhnikov, "Nekhoroshiye kvartiry [Bad apartments]."

240. Zykov, "Case #144128: 'Putin's Case,' Part 4."
241. "Figuranty po kvartirnomu delu No.18/238278-95 [Persons involved in the apartment affair No. 18/238278-95]," *Sovershenno sekretno*, February 4, 1997, http://www.compromat.ru/page _10200.htm (accessed July 6, 2013).
242. Andrey Evdokimov, "Avstriyskaya ploshchad' ili peterburgskiye igry [Austrian Square or Petersburg games]," Modernlib.ru. 2000, http://modernlib.ru/books/evdokimov_andrey/avstriys kaya_ploschad_ili_peterburgskie_igri/read/.
243. Zykov, "Case #144128: 'Putin's Case,' Part 4."
244. Putin et al., *First Person*, 112.
245. Jane Croft and Neil Buckley, "Berezovsky loses against Abramovich," *Financial Times*, August 31, 2012, http://www.ft.com/intl/cms/s/0/8eec8602-f34d-11e1-9c6c-00144feabdc0 .html#axzz3764qzNEa (accessed July 8, 2014).
246. Pribylovskiy, "Proiskhozhdeniye putinskoy oligarkhii [Origins of Putin's oligarchy]"; David Crawford, "Germany Steps Up Russian Money Laundering Probe," *Wall Street Journal*, December 14, 2011, http://online.wsj.com/article/SB1000142405297020433610457709655049544 44844.html (accessed January 17, 2013).
247. Crawford, "Germany Steps Up Russian Money Laundering Probe."
248. David Crawford, "Germany Ends Probe Implicating Russian Corruption," *Wall Street Journal*, April 12, 2012, http://www.flarenetwork.org/learn/europe/article/germany_ends_probe _implicating_russian_corruption.htm (accessed June 21, 2013).
249. World Bank, "Leonid Reiman and Jeffrey Galmond/IPOC Case," n.d., http://star.worldbank .org/corruption-cases/node/18539 (accessed January 17, 2013).
250. World Bank, "Leonid Reiman and Jeffrey Galmond/IPOC Case."
251. World Bank, "Leonid Reiman and Jeffrey Galmond/IPOC Case."
252. Yelena Rudneva, Gleb Krampets, Igor' Tsuknov, and Anna Nikolayeva, "Vlast'/Den'gi: Nemtsy napali na Putinykh [Power/money: Germans attack the Putins]," *Vedomosti*, July 28, 2005, http://dlib.eastview.com.proxy.lib.muohio.edu/browse/doc/8013910 (accessed June 5, 2013); Greg Walters, "Germans See Shady City Link," *St. Petersburg Times*, July 29, 2005. http:// sptimes.ru/index.php?action_id=2&story_id=310 (accessed January 17, 2013).
253. Tana Group, "InfoCom-2002," 2002 http://www.tana.ru/News/2002/21_2510.htm.
254. "Lyudmila Putina Opens International Book Festival for Children," *ITAR-TASS*, October 10, 2007, http://en.trend.az/regions/world/russia/1041081.html (accessed January 17, 2013).
255. Stephen Fidler, Arkady Ostrovsky, and Neil Buckley, "A Disputed Stake Pits an Oligarch against a Putin Ally," *Financial Times*, April 23, 2006, http://www.ft.com/intl/cms/s/1/a47d51d2 -d2f1-11da-828e-0000779e2340.html#axzz2ILLXJ1PT (accessed January 17, 2013).
256. Timofey Dzyadko, "Leonid Reyman: Svyazist, ministr, podozrevayemyy [Signalman, minister, suspect]," *Forbes.ru*, February 17, 2012, http://www.forbes.ru/sobytiya/lyudi/79318-leonid -reiman-dose-svyazista (accessed June 8, 2012).
257. Yuriy Shutov, *"Sobchach'ye serdtse" ili Zapiski pomoshchnika khodivshego vo vlast'* ["Heart of a dog," or notes of an assistant who was walking in the corridors of power] (St. Petersburg, Russia, 1991) http://www.gramotey.com/?open_file=1269035051.
258. Yuriy Shutov, *Anatoliy Sobchak: Tayny khozhdeniya vo vlast'* [Secrets of walking in the corridors of power] (Moscow: Algoritm, 2005); Yuriy Shutov, *Krestnyy otets 'peterskikh'* [The godfather of Petersburg] (Moscow: Algoritm, 2011).
259. Felshtinskiy and Pribylovskiy, *The Age of Assassins*, 273–77.
260. Wines, "Path to Power."
261. Charles Digges, "Probe Targets Sobchak Government," *St. Petersburg Times*, 1996, http://www .friends-partners.org/oldfriends/spbweb/times/177-178/probe.html (accessed June 8, 2012).
262. Digges, "Probe Targets Sobchak Government."

263. Evdokimov, "Avstriyskaya ploshchad' ili peterburgskiye igry [Austrian Square or Petersburg games]."
264. Zykov, "Case #144128: 'Putin's Case,' Part 4."
265. A. Kirilenko, "Podpolkovnik Putin nezakonno vozglavil FSB [Lieutenant Colonel Putin illegally became head of the FSB]," *Yuridicheskiy Peterburg Segodnya* [Juridical Petersburg Today], August 12, 1998, 5.
266. Vadim Nesvizhskiy, "Piterskiye zhurnalisty ishchut ubiyts Anatoliya Levina-Utkina [St. Petersburg journalists search for the killers of Anatoliy Levin-Utkin]," *Segodnya*, August 26, 1998, http://dlib.eastview.com.proxy.lib.muohio.edu/browse/doc/2049348 (accessed August 8, 2013).
267. Anna Badkhen, "Petersburg Journalist Beaten to Death," *Moscow Times*, August 28, 1998, http://dlib.eastview.com.proxy.lib.muohio.edu/searchresults/article.jsp?pager.offset=2 (accessed June 9, 2012).
268. Oleg Panfilov, "Levin-Utkin, Anatoliy," Memorium, Center for Journalists in Extreme Situations, 1999, http://www.memorium.cjes.ru/?pid=2&id=112 (accessed June 9, 2012).
269. Olson, *Power and Prosperity*.
270. Sal'ye, "Nastal chered Putina [Putin's turn]."
271. Wolfgang Krach and Georg Mascolo, "Shares for the Candy Fund," *Der Spiegel*, July 23, 2001.
272. Putin et al., *First Person*, 95.
273. Oleg Kalugin, "Open Letter to Putin," in Preobrazhensky, *KGB/FSB's New Trojan Horse*.
274. Financial Action Task Force on Money Laundering, "Review to Identify Non-Cooperative Countries or Territories: Increasing the World-wide Effectiveness of Anti–Money Laundering Measures," June 22, 2000, http://www.fatf-gafi.org/media/fatf/documents/reports/1999%20 2000%20NCCT%20ENG.pdf (accessed May 24, 2013).
275. Yevgeniya Borisova and Robin Munro, "Report: Blacklist Because of Putin," *Moscow Times*, August 29, 2001, http://www.themoscowtimes.com/news/article/report-blacklist-because-of-putin/251891.html.
276. Hill and Gaddy, *Mr. Putin*, 165.

Chapter Four: Putin in Moscow, 1996–1999

1. Putin et al., *First Person*, 113.
2. Richard Sakwa, *Putin: Russia's Choice* (New York: Routledge, 2008), 103.
3. Aleksey Alekseyevich Mukhin, *Kto est' mister Putin i kto s nim prishel? Dos'ye na Prezidenta Rossii i ego spetssluzhby* [Who is Mister Putin and who arrived with him? A dossier on the president of Russia and his special services] (Moscow: Gnom i D, 2002).
4. Hill and Gaddy, *Mr. Putin*, 166.
5. Il'ya Milshtein, "Vladimir Putin Is 50," *New Times*, January 11, 2002, http://dlib.eastview.com/browse/doc/4505342 (accessed July 22, 2012).
6. "Perechen' Svedeniy o Dokhodakh za 1998–1999 gody [A list of information about incomes for 1998–1999]," *Kommersant*, February 22, 2000, http://kommersant.ru/doc/140817 (accessed June 23, 2012).
7. Putin et al., *First Person*, 122.
8. Milov et al., "Putin: Corruption."
9. Putin et al., *First Person*, 122; Zarakhovich, "Inside the Yukos Endgame."
10. "Putin, V. V.," in Vladimir Pribylovskiy, *Vlast'—2010: 60 Biografiy* [Power—2010: 60 biographies] (Moscow: Tsentr Panorama, 2010), 135.
11. Pavel Zhavoronkov, "Piterskiye: Zhizn' na dva goroda [The Petersburg group: Life in two cities]," *Kompaniya*, March 28, 2005, http://www.compromat.ru/page_16491.htm (accessed January 24, 2014).
12. Putin et al., *First Person*, 126; Peter Baker and Susan Glasser, *Kremlin Rising*, updated ed. (Dulles, VA: Potomac, 2007), 48.

13. Leonov, "Krestnyy put' Rossii, gody 1991–2000 [The way of the cross of Russia, 1991–2000]," 36–37.
14. Leonov, "Krestnyy put' Rossii, gody 1991–2000 [The way of the cross of Russia, 1991–2000]," 55.
15. Hill and Gaddy, *Mr. Putin*, 205.
16. Putin et al., *First Person*, 126.
17. Putin et al., *First Person*, 127; Pierre Lorrain, *La Mystérieuse Ascension de Vladimir Poutine* (Paris: Éditions du Rocher, 2000), 378.
18. Viktor Talanov, *Psikhologicheskiy portret Vladimira Putina* [Psychological portrait of Vladimir Putin] (St. Petersburg: B&K, 2000), 23.
19. Kit Vladmirov, "President's Office Seizes U.S. Firm's Headquarters," *St. Petersburg Press*, October 17–23, 1995, http://www.friends-partners.org/oldfriends/spbweb/sppress/128/pres.html (accessed July 23, 2012).
20. Vladmirov, "President's Office Seizes U.S. Firm's Headquarters."
21. James Kimer, "Franz Sedelmayer: Leading the Fight against Sovereign Immunity," *Corporate Foreign Policy*, February 1, 2012, http://corporateforeignpolicy.com/democracy/franz-sedelmayer-leading-the-fight-against-sovereign-immunity (accessed July 23, 2012).
22. Arbitration Institute of the Stockholm Chamber of Commerce SCC Institute, "Franz Sedelmayer vs. The Russian Federation through the Procurement Department of the President of the Russian Federation," Arbitrations.ru, July 8, 1998, http://www.arbitrations.ru/userfiles/file/Case%20Law/Investment%20arbitration/Russia/Sedermayer/sedelmayer%20award.pdf (accessed July 23, 2012); Decision of the Swedish Supreme Court, "The Russian Federation vs. Franz Sedelmeyer, Case No. Ö 170-10," SCC Institute, July 1, 2011, http://www.sccinstitute.com/filearchive/4/41226/Case170_10ENG.pdf (accessed July 23, 2012); "Russian in Berlin Property Intact," *Kommersant*, May 22, 2006, http://www.kommersant.com/page.asp?idr=530&id=675176 (accessed July 22, 2012); "Mr. Franz Sedelmayer vs. The Russian Federation," British Institute of International and Comparative Law, n.d., http://www.biicl.org/damages/sedelmayer/.
23. Riksdagen press release, "Utrikesministerns agerande med anledning av ett ärende hos Kronofogden om att genomföra ett beslut om försäljning av utländsk egendom [Foreign Minister's statement in connection with the implementation of the decision on the sale of foreign property]," June 4, 2013, http://www.riksdagen.se/sv/Start/Press-startsida/pressmeddelanden/201213/KUs-granskning-av-regeringen-klar/ (accessed May 7, 2014); "Sedelmayer Concludes Four Auctions within 5 Months," *Rolfsgriechenlandblog*, February 25, 2014, http://rolfsgriechenlandblog.blogspot.com/2014/02/sedelmayer-concludes-4-auctions-within.html (accessed May 7, 2014); "Russia Vows Reaction to Auction of Its Trade Mission Building in Sweden," Russian Legal Information Agency, February 18, 2014, http://rapsinews.com/news/20140218/270745888.html (accessed May 9, 2014).
24. Baker and Glasser, *Kremlin Rising*, 48.
25. Anders Åslund, *Building Capitalism: The Transformation of the Former Soviet Bloc* (New York: Cambridge University Press, 2002), 216.
26. "Ukaz 797. Ukaz Prezidenta RF ot 02.08.95 N 797 (red. ot 11.12.96) 'Ob upravlenii delami Prezidenta Rossiyskoy Federatsii' [Decree of the president of RF from 02.08.95 No. 797 'On the Property Management Department of the president of the RF']," *Zakonprost*, August 2, 1995. http://www.zakonprost.ru/content/base/14700 (accessed April 8, 2013).
27. Mariya Kakturskaya and Sergey Shakhidzhanyan, "Neizvestnyye fakty iz zhizni Vladimira Putina [Some unknown facts from the life of Vladimir Putin]," *Argumenty i Fakty*, January 19, 2000, http://dlib.eastview.com.proxy.lib.muohio.edu/browse/doc/2545586 (accessed January 4, 2012); Felshtinsky and Pribylovsky, *The Age of Assassins*, 81.
28. Andrey Bandenko, "Ot Pervogo Litsa: Chelovek vo vseoruzhii [In the first person: A man fully armed]," *Itogi*, October 31, 2005, http://dlib.eastview.com/browse/doc/8502730 (accessed July

30, 2012); Oleg Lur'ye, "Putin lyubit luzhi: Nu i pri chem zdes' Pugachev? [Putin likes skiing: So what does Pugachev have to do with it?]," *Novaya gazeta*, November 26, 2001, http://www .novayagazeta.ru/society/12090.html (accessed March 12, 2012).

29. Igor Sedykh, "How Russia Made and Broke Behgjet Pacolli," *Moscow News*, September 8, 1999, http://dlib.eastview.com.proxy.lib.muohio.edu/browse/doc/223897 (accessed July 23, 2012).

30. Bobrova et al., "7 Mgnovenii iz Zhizni 'Preyemnika' [Seven moments from the life of the 'successor']."

31. Oleg Lur'ye, "Turover's List: File on Corrupt Russians Revealed," *Novaya gazeta*, December 27, 1999, http://russialist.org/4023.html#8 (accessed July 25, 2012).

32. Oksana Yablokova, "Skuratov: 'Turover List' Is Real," *Moscow Times*, December 29, 1999, http://www.themoscowtimes.com/news/article/skuratov-turover-list-is-real/268363 (accessed July 24, 2012).

33. Felshtinsky and Pribylovsky, *The Age of Assassins*, 94.

34. Oleg Lur'ye, "Yesli Ya Priyedu, poluchu pulyu v aeroportu [If I return, I will receive a bullet in the airport]," *Novaya gazeta*, October 23, 2000, http://dlib.eastview.com.proxy.lib.muohio .edu/browse/doc/3465306 (accessed July 23, 2012).

35. Matt Taibbi, "On the Trail of Star Witness Felipe Turover," *eXile*, February 10–17, 2000, http:// exiledonline.com/old-exile/vault/feature/feature83.html (accessed October 9, 2012).

36. Julia Wishnevsky, "Poltoranin Exonerated," *RFE/RL*, No. 206, October 26, 1993, http://www .friends-partners.org/friends/news/omri/1993/10/931026.html.

37. Lur'ye, "Turover's List."

38. Taibbi, "On the Trail of Star Witness Felipe Turover."

39. Ulrika Lomas, "Swiss Authorities Push for Russian Cooperation," Tax-news.com, Brussels, September 19, 2000, http://www.tax-news.com/news/Swiss_Authorities_Push_For_Russian _Cooperation_Over_Mabetex_Case____868.html (accessed June 23, 2013).

40. "Borodin vs. Ashcroft," Leagle, March 21, 2001, http://www.leagle.com/xmlResult.asp x?page=7&xmldoc=2001261136FSupp2d125_1250.xml&docbase=CSLWAR2-1986-2006 &SizeDisp=7 (accessed February 15, 2012).

41. Igor Semenenko, "Book Is Closed on Probe of Mabetex," *Moscow Times*, December 14, 2000, http://www.themoscowtimes.com/business/article/book-is-closed-on-probe-of-mabetex/2566 69.html (accessed July 23, 2012).

42. Simon Saradzhyan, "Warrant Issued for Borodin Witness," *Moscow Times*, March 6, 2001, http://www.themoscowtimes.com/news/article/warrant-issued-for-borodin-witness/254821 .html (accessed July 26, 2012).

43. Leonid Berres, "Filipp Turover: Mozhno ustroit' Putingayt [Filipp Turover: It is possible to build a Putingate]," *Kommersant-Daily*, March 3, 2001, http://dlib.eastview.com.proxy.lib.muohio .edu/browse/doc/3717182 (accessed July 24, 2012).

44. Vladimir Shurov, "Informator khochet stat' svidetelem: Felipe Turover podal v sud na Shveyt-sariyu [The informer wants to meet: Felipe Turover files a suit in Switzerland]," *Vremya novostei*, January 14, 2002, http://dlib.eastview.com.proxy.lib.muohio.edu/browse/doc/2451681 (accessed July 24, 2012).

45. Bandenko, "Ot Pervogo Litsa [In the first person]."

46. "Igor' Sechin," Government of the Russian Federation, n.d., http://government.ru/eng/per sons/8/ (accessed December 12, 2012).

47. "Presidential Control Directorate," Kremlin, n.d., http://eng.state.kremlin.ru/administration/ division (accessed October 3, 2012).

48. Andrey V. Kolesnikov, "Aleksey Kudrin zaveshchal svoyo kreslo Vladimiru Putinu [Aleksey Kudrin bequethed his seat to Vladimir Putin]," *Segodya*, March 28, 1997, http://dlib.eastview .com.proxy.lib.muohio.edu/browse/doc/2021827 (accessed June 22, 2013).

49. "Ukaz 1536. 'O Merakh po sovershenstvovaniyu organizatsii kontrolya i proverki ispolneniya porucheniy Prezidenta RF' ['Measures for the improvement of the organization of control and

accountability for carrying out the tasks of the president of the RF']," Kremlin, November 6, 1996, http://document.kremlin.ru/doc.asp?ID=79722&PSC=1&PT=1&Page=1 (accessed June 6, 2013).

50. Putin et al., *First Person*, 129.
51. Gessen, *The Man without a Face*, 124.
52. Sal'ye Commission, "Letter from Yu. Boldyrev to P. O. Aven," March 31, 1992, http://www.facebook.com/media/set/?set=a.384728321551803.94156.273762169315086&type=1#!/photo.php?fbid=384728604885108&set=a.384728321551803.94156.273762169315086&type=1&theater (accessed March 27, 2012).
53. Yuriy Boldyrev, "Na Materialakh o Putine grifa sekretnosti ne bylo [The materials about Putin were not classified]," *Novaya gazeta*, February 9, 2004, http://old.novayagazeta.ru/data/2004/09/32.html (accessed April 8, 2013).
54. Yevgeniya Borisova, "Boldyrev Calls Audit Chamber Putin's Tool," *Moscow Times*, February 2, 2001, http://www.themoscowtimes.com/news/article/boldyrev-calls-audit-chamber-putins-tool/255575.html (accessed March 19, 2012).
55. Anastasiya Kirilenko, "'Delo Putina' umerlo v arkhive? [Did the 'Putin affair' die in the archive?]," Radio Liberty, April 18, 2012, http://www.svoboda.org/content/article/24552575.html (accessed January 28, 2014).
56. Pluzhnikov, "Nekhoroshiye kvartiry [Bad apartments]."
57. Pluzhnikov, "Nekhoroshiye kvartiry [Bad apartments]."
58. Pluzhnikov, "Nekhoroshiye kvartiry [Bad apartments]."
59. Roy Medvedev, *Vladimir Putin: Chetyre goda v Kremle* [Four years in the Kremlin] (Moscow: Vremya, 2004), 32–46.
60. Putin et al., *First Person*, 117.
61. Baker and Glasser, *Kremlin Rising*, 49, 404n.
62. Yelena Masyuk, "Lyudmila Narusova: 'Eto moyo politicheskoye zaveshchaniye' ['This is my political testament']," *Novaya gazeta*, November 9, 2012, http://www.novayagazeta.ru/politics/55331.html (accessed November 20, 2012).
63. Igor' Korol'kov, "Chornaya lesnitsa [Backstairs]," *Izvestiya*, April 2, 1998, http://dlib.eastview.com/browse/doc/3164172 (accessed June 22, 2013). Also see Mikhaylov, *Delo Shutova* [The Shutov Affair], 135.
64. Shutov, *"Sobchach'ye serdtse"* ["Heart of a Dog"].
65. "'Nuzhno deystvovat' ochen' zhestko.' Deputat Gosdumy Lyudmila Narusova yasno dayet ponyat': Nado ustranit' meshayushchego cheloveka ['We need to act very tough.' State Duma Deputy L. Narusova makes clear: It is necessary to remove this interfering person]," *Novaya gazeta*, May 25, 1998, http://dlib.eastview.com/browse/doc/3471273 (accessed June 22, 2013).
66. Shutov, *"Sobchach'ye serdtse"* ["Heart of a Dog"]; Yuriy Shutov, *Sobchach'ya prokhindiada, ili, Kak vsekh obokrali* [Sobchak's prokhindiada, or how everyone stole] (St. Petersburg: "Artik" po zakazy TOO "Eva," 1994); "Interview with Marina Sal'ye." Ekho Moskvy, January 28, 2000, http://www.echo.msk.ru/programs/beseda/10742/ (accessed January 24, 2012).
67. "Shutov (III) vs. Russia," European Court for Human Rights, September 14, 2010, http://europeancourt.ru/spisok-kommunicirovannyx-zhalob-protiv-rossii/zhaloby-kommunicirovannye-rossijskoj-federacii-v-sentyabre-2010-goda#20922/08 (accessed June 2, 2013).
68. Tat'yana Vostroilova and Nadezhda Zaytseva, "Chubays raskryl ubiystvo Manevicha [Chubays exposed the murder of Manevich]," Fontanka.ru, November 29, 2006, http://www.fontanka.ru/2006/11/29/181097/ (accessed June 3, 2013).
69. Boris Yeltsin, *Midnight Diaries* (New York: Public Affairs, 2000), 234.
70. Yevgenia Borisova, "And the Winner Is?," *Moscow Times*, September 19, 2000, http://www.moscowtimes.ru/article/1008/49/258951.htm (accessed August 17, 2009); "Prosecutors Close Case on Sobchak," *Moscow Times*, November 23, 1999, http://dlib.eastview.com/browse/doc/236075 (accessed June 17, 2012); *The Putin System*, directed by Jean-Michel Carré, 2007, http://www.youtube.com/watch?v=h9gGjECn21c&feature=related (accessed April 2, 2011).

71. Putin et al., *First Person*, 117–18.

72. "Figuranty po kvartirnomu delu No.18/238278-95 [Persons involved in the apartment affair No. 18/238278-95]"; Gessen, *The Man without a Face*, 124.

73. Pribylovskiy, "Proiskhozhdeniye putinskoy oligarkhii [Origins of Putin's oligarchy]."

74. American Embassy Madrid to U.S. Secretary of State, "Spain Details Its Strategy to Combat the Russian Mafia"; Govan, "Russian Politician Investigated in Spain over Mafia Connections."

75. Zykov, "Case #144128: 'Putin's Case,' Part 4."

76. Felshtinsky and Pribylovsky, *The Corporation*, 65.

77. Oleg Lur'ye and Inga Savel'eva, "Chetyre voprosa nasledniku prestola [Four questions for the heir to the throne]," *Versiya*, August 17-23, 1999, http://www.compromat.ru/page_11188.htm (accessed May 4, 2013).

78. Gessen, *The Man without a Face*, 156–64.

79. Ol'ga Levicheva, "My sprashivayem u vas na ulitse: 'Kak vy otnosites' k migalkam? [We ask you on the street: 'How do you feel about migalkas?']," *Novaya gazeta*, December 6, 1999, http://dlib.eastview.com.proxy.lib.muohio.edu/browse/doc/3473728 (accessed January 15, 2012).

80. David Satter, "Is Russia Becoming a Free Market Law Based Democracy?," Hudson Institute, August 1, 2002. http://www.hudson.org/index.cfm?fuseaction=publication_details&id=2090 (accessed December 18, 2012).

81. Chapter 27, Russian Criminal Code, June 13, 1996, http://www.russian-criminal-code.com /PartII/SectionIX/Chapter27.html (accessed October 24, 2012).

82. Levicheva, "My sprashivayem u vas na ulitse [We ask you on the street]."

83. Nikolay Fedyanin, "Ubiytsy Soprovozhdeniya 2: V tom samom dzipe yekhal Putin [Killer escorts 2: Putin traveled in the same Jeep]," *Novaya gazeta*, February 14, 2000, http://www .novayagazeta.ru/society/11535.html (accessed January 8, 2012).

84. Fedyanin, "Ubiytsy Soprovozhdeniya 2 [Killer escorts 2]."

85. "Vozvrashchayas' k napechatannomy [Returning to previously published]," *Novaya gazeta*, February 19, 2001, http://www.novayagazeta.ru/society/14130.html (accessed June 9, 2012).

86. Felshtinsky and Pribylovsky, *The Age of Assassins*, 87.

87. Ger P. Van Den Berg, "Power-Sharing Compacts under Russian Constitutional Law," in Robert S. Sharlet and Ferdinand Feldbrugge, eds., *Public Policy and Law in Russia* (Leiden: Brill, 2005), 51–52.

88. Putin et al., *First Person*, 129–30.

89. Gessen, *The Man without a Face*, 26.

90. Putin et al., *First Person*, 136.

91. Bobrova et al., "7 Mgnovenii iz Zhizni 'Preyemnika' [Seven moments from the life of the 'successor']."

92. Yakhno, "Noch' chekista [Night of a Checkist]."

93. Boris Yel'tsin, *Prezidentskiy Marafon* [Presidential marathon] (Moscow: Act, 2000), 359.

94. Yuriy Shchekochikhin, "Bratva plashcha i kinzhala 3 [The brotherhood of the cloak and dagger 3]," *Novaya gazeta*, May 25, 1998, http://dlib.eastview.com/browse/doc/3471267 (accessed June 20, 2013).

95. Andrei Soldatov, "Organized Crime in Russia: How to Struggle in Favor of Legality?," Agentura .ru, June 10, 2005, http://studies.agentura.ru/english/listing/organizedcrime/ (accessed May 7, 2014).

96. Scott Anderson, "Vladimir Putin's Dark Rise to Power," *GQ*, September 6, 2009, http://www .kavkazcenter.com/eng/content/2009/09/06/10979.shtml (accessed July 1, 2013).

97. Yakhno, "Noch' chekista [Night of a Checkist]."

98. Richard Sakwa, *Russian Politics and Society*, 4th ed. (New York: Routledge, 2008), 98; Soldatov and Borogan, *The New Nobility*, 18–19.

99. Aleksandr Khinshteyn, "Okhota na ved'm [Witch hunt]," *Moskovskiy Komsomolets*, April 10, 1999. http://dlib.eastview.com.proxy.lib.muohio.edu/browse/doc/104491 (accessed April 7, 2012).

100. Reddaway, "The Silovik War of 2004–2010."
101. "Sergey Ivanov," Lenta.ru, April 4, 2012, http://lenta.ru/lib/14160049/full.htm (accessed October 5, 2012).
102. Brian D. Taylor, "Security Sector Reform and Patrimonial Administration in Russia." Paper presented to International Studies Association Annual Conference, February 2010, http://citation .allacademic.com//meta/p_mla_apa_research_citation/4/1/6/1/9/pages416192/p416192-1.php (accessed January 19, 2013).
103. Zarakhovich, "Inside the Yukos Endgame."
104. Khinshteyn, "Okhota na ved'm [Witch hunt]."
105. "Kozak, Dmitriy," Lenta.ru, 2013, http://lenta.ru/lib/14160279/ (accessed June 23, 2013).
106. Hill and Gaddy, *Mr. Putin*, 208; "Zubkov, Viktor," Lenta.ru, 2013, http://lenta.ru/lib /14174946/ (accessed June 23, 2013).
107. Putin et al., *First Person*, 133–34.
108. Oksana Yablokova, "Purse-Snatching Takes FSB to NTV," *Moscow Times*, March 14, 2000, http://www.themoscowtimes.com/sitemap/free/2000/3/article/purse-snatching-takes-fsb-to-ntv /265592.html (accessed May 4, 2013).
109. Yeltsin, *Midnight Diaries*, 112.
110. Michael Wines, "Yeltsin Swings His Ax. Then Retreats to His Hospital Bed," *New York Times*, December 8, 1998, http://www.nytimes.com/1998/12/08/world/yeltsin-swings-his-ax-then -retreats-to-his-hospital-bed.html (accessed December 2, 2012).
111. William H. Cooper and John P. Hardt, "Russian Capital Flight, Economic Reforms, and U.S. Interests," CRS Report for Congress, March 10, 2000, http://www.fas.org/man/crs/RL30394 .pdf (accessed June 7, 2012).
112. Analytical Center of Yuriy Levada, *Russian Public Opinion 2010–2011* (Moscow: Levada-Center, 2012), http://en.d7154.agava.net/sites/en.d7154.agava.net/files/Levada2011Eng .pdf.
113. Timothy J. Colton. *Yeltsin. A Life*. New York: Basic Books, 2008, 415–418; Ryan Barilleaux and Jody Baumgartner, "Victims or Rogues? The Impeachment of Presidents Clinton and Yeltsin in Comparative Perspective," in Robert W. Watson, ed., *White House Studies Compendium*, vol. 4 (Hauppauge, NY: Nova Science, 2006), 281–99.
114. Tat'yana Yumasheva, "Kak Lyzhkov chut' ne stal prezidentom Rossii [How Luzhkov just about became president of Russia]," January 25, 2010, http://t-yumasheva.livejournal.com/11039 .html (accessed October 1, 2012).
115. Tatyana Yumasheva, "Kak Primakov pytalsya uvolut' Putina [How Primakov tried to dismiss Putin]," March 15, 2010, http://t-yumasheva.livejournal.com/19015.html (accessed December 15, 2012).
116. Yumasheva, "Kak Primakov pytalsya uvolut' Putina [How Primakov tried to dismiss Putin]."
117. Yekaterina Zapodinskaya, "Nesostoyavsheyesya ubiystvo Berezovskogo [The never-committed murder of Berezovskiy]," *Kommersant*, November 13, 1998, http://dlib.eastview.com.proxy.lib .muohio.edu/browse/doc/3760094 (accessed November 8, 2012).
118. Zapodinskaya, "Nesostoyavsheyesya ubiystvo Berezovskogo [The never-committed murder of Berezovskiy]."
119. Alexander Litvinenko, "Why I Believe Putin Wanted Me Dead," *Daily Mail on Sunday (UK)*, November 25, 2006, http://www.mailonsunday.co.uk/news/article-418652/Why-I-believe -Putin-wanted-dead-.html (accessed November 4, 2012).
120. Baker and Glasser, *Kremlin Rising*, 52.
121. *La Prise Du Pouvoir par Vladimir Poutine* [How Putin came to power], directed by Tania Rakhmanova and Paul Mitchell, Arte France, Wilton Films, Quark Productions, 2007.
122. *La Prise Du Pouvoir par Vladimir Poutine* [How Putin came to power].
123. Powell, "Follow the Money."
124. Peter Truscott, *Putin's Progress* (London: Pocket Books, 2005), 93.

125. *La Prise Du Pouvoir par Vladimir Poutine* [How Putin came to power].
126. *La Prise Du Pouvoir par Vladimir Poutine* [How Putin came to power].
127. Yuriy Skuratov, *Variant drakona* [The Dragon Option] (Moscow: Detektiv-Press, 2000), 235.
128. Skuratov, *Variant drakona* [The Dragon Option], 147.
129. Leonov, "Krestnyy put' Rossii, gody 1991–2000 [The way of the cross of Russia, 1991–2000]," 160.
130. Jack, *Inside Putin's Russia*, 83.
131. Denis Babichenko, "Vladimir Putin stal dvazhdy silovikom [Vladimir Putin becomes silovik twice over]," *Segodnya*, March 30, 1999, http://dlib.eastview.com/browse/doc/2061161 (accessed June 1, 2012); Baker and Glasser, *Kremlin Rising*, 51.
132. "1990–2004: Khronologiya zakhvatov i vzryvov v Rossii [Chronology of hostage-takings and explosions in Russia]," BBC Russian Service, September 2, 2004, http://news.bbc.co.uk/hi/russian/russia/newsid_3621000/3621314.stm#6 (accessed August 11, 2012).
133. Yevgeniy Krutikov, "Vzryv v bazarnyy chas [Explosion at market time]," *Izvestiya*, March 20, 1999, http://dlib.eastview.com.proxy.lib.muohio.edu/browse/doc/3172821 (accessed June 1, 2012).
134. Celestine Bohlen, "Midday Bomb in Caucasus Market Kills 62 and Hurts 100," *New York Times*, March 20, 1999, http://www.nytimes.com/1999/03/20/world/midday-bomb-in-caucasus-market-kills-62-and-hurts-100.html (accessed April 15, 2012).
135. Lorrain, *La Mystérieuse Ascension de Vladimir Poutine*, 418.
136. Sergey Pravosudov, "Sergey Stepashin: 'Bloka OVR voobshche moglo i ne byt' ['OVR bloc might not have been']," *Nezavisimaya gazeta*, January 14, 2000, http://dlib.eastview.com.proxy.lib.muohio.edu/browse/doc/267285 (accessed January 2, 2013).
137. Pravosudov, "Sergey Stepashin."
138. Barilleaux and Baumgartner, "Victims or Rogues?," 281–99.
139. Khinshteyn, "Okhota na ved'm [Witch hunt]."
140. Anatoliy Stasovskiy, "27 Marta—den' vnytrennikh voysk MVD Rossii [27 March—the day of Interior Forces of the Russian MVD]," *Krasnaya zvezda*, March 27, 1999, http://dlib.eastview.com.proxy.lib.muohio.edu/browse/doc/3348362 (accessed December 24, 2012).
141. Yevgeniy Primakov, *Vosem' mesyatsev plyus* [Seven months more] (Moscow: Mysl', 2001), 204–5.
142. Yuriy Shchekochikhin, "Nado perenosit' prezidenta, a ne vybory: 13 Maya etogo goda v Rossii dolzhny byli [It's necessary to support the president, not the elections: On 13 May of this year in Russia it might have been]," *Novaya gazeta*, July 5, 1999, http://dlib.eastview.com.proxy.lib.muohio.edu/browse/doc/3473000 (accessed March 5, 2012).
143. Patrick Cockburn, "Russia 'Planned Chechen War before Bombings,'" *Independent (UK)*, January 29, 2000, http://archive.today/4BRsR (accessed May 23, 2013).
144. Dzhul'etto K'eza, "Terroristy tozhe raznyye [Terrorists are also varied]," *Literaturnaya gazeta*, June 16, 1999, http://dlib.eastview.com.proxy.lib.muohio.edu/browse/doc/9615 (accessed May 10, 2012).
145. Dzhul'etto K'eza, *Russkaya ruletka: Chto sluchitsya v mire, yesli Rossiya raspadetsya* [Russian roulette: What happens in the world if Russia collapses] (Moscow: Izdatel'stvo Prava cheloveka, 2000), 206–7.
146. Yevgeniy Krutnikov, "Internal Affairs Ministry and Federal Security Service Divide Up North Caucasus 'Field,'" *Izvestiya*, May 20, 1999, http://dlib.eastview.com/browse/doc/20079596 (accessed June 1, 2012).
147. Yevgeniy Krutikov, "Za predstavitel'stvom MVD Ichkerii v Moskve stoit 'Chechenskaya mafiya'[Internal Affairs Ministry mission for Ichkeria in Moscow is 'Chechen mafia']," *Izvestiya*, May 20, 1999, http://dlib.eastview.com.proxy.lib.muohio.edu/browse/doc/3174186 (accessed June 1, 2012).
148. Putin et al., *First Person*, 139–43.
149. Quiring, "Interview with Stanislav Belkovskiy."

150. Mukhin, "Byvshiy sledovatel' po osobo vazhnym delam Andrey Zykov [Former investigator for especially important cases Andrey Zykov]."

151. Mostovshchikov and Novikov, "Zolotoy vypusk [Gold edition]."

152. Mukhin, "Byvshiy sledovatel' po osobo vazhnym delam Andrey Zykov [Former investigator for especially important cases Andrey Zykov]."

153. Ellen Barry, "Scathing Report Issued on Russian Lawyer's Death," *New York Times*, December 28, 2009, http://www.nytimes.com/2009/12/29/world/europe/29russia.html?_r=0 (accessed August 25, 2013).

154. Lyudmila Alekseyeva, "Letter to Aleksandr Bastrykin from the Moscow Helsinki Group," Russian Untouchables.com, March 26, 2010, http://russian-untouchables.com/docs/Alekseyeva-Complaint-Eng29Mar2010.pdf (accessed June 8, 2013).

155. U.S. Department of the Treasury, "Magnitsky Sanctions Listings," April 12, 2013, http://www.treasury.gov/resource-center/sanctions/OFAC-Enforcement/Pages/20130412.aspx (accessed June 7, 2013).

156. Kremlin, "Kadrovyye izmeneniya v Ministerstve vnutrennikh del [Personnel changes in the Ministry of Internal Affairs]," June 11, 2011, http://kremlin.ru/acts/11536 (accessed November 15, 2012).

157. Andrey Piontkovskiy, "Season of Discontent: Primakov Is Our Amazing Mediocrity," *Moscow Times*, July 22, 1999, http://www.russialist.org/archives/3402.html (accessed August 5, 2012).

158. *Guardian* interview with Gleb Pavlovskiy, January 2012, in Hill and Gaddy, *Mr. Putin*, 20.

159. Baker and Glasser, *Kremlin Rising*, 51–52.

160. Andrey V. Kolesnikov, *Anatoliy Chubays: Biographiya* [Anatoliy Chubays: A biography] (Moscow: Izdatel'stvo ACT, 2008), 182.

161. Brian Whitmore, "Sobchak Stages Flamboyant Return," *St. Petersburg Times*, July 13, 1999, http://www.russialist.org/archives/3393.html (accessed August 15, 2012).

162. Vaksburg, *Toxic Politics*, 182.

163. Vaksburg, *Toxic Politics*, 182.

164. Dmitriy Volchek, "Neozhidannoye razvitiye dela rassledovanii obstoytel'stv smerti Anatoliya Sobchaka [Unexpected development in the investigation into the cause of death of Anatoliy Sobchak]," *Radio Liberty*, July 30, 2000, http://sobchak.org/rus/main.php3?fp=f02110200_fl000260 (accessed March 26, 2013).

165. Vaksburg, *Toxic Politics*, 180.

166. Nikolay Vardul', "Zhukov uspel ne srabotat'sya s Aksenenko [Zhukov didn't have time to work with Aksenenko]," *Kommersant*, May 21, 1999, http://dlib.eastview.com.proxy.lib.muohio.edu/browse/doc/3768627 (accessed December 1, 2012).

167. Kolesnikov, *Anatoliy Chubays*, 182.

168. Yeltsin, *Midnight Diaries*, 290.

169. Yeltsin, *Midnight Diaries*, 294–95.

170. Aleksandr Zhilin, "Burya v Moskve [Storm in Moscow]," *Moskovskaya pravda*, July 22, 1999, http://dlib.eastview.com.proxy.lib.muohio.edu/browse/doc/210398 (accessed March 3, 2012).

171. Aleksandr Zhilin, "Opasnyye igry v kremlevskikh zastenkakh [Dangerous games in the Kremlin torture chambers]," *Moskovskaya pravda*, August 25, 1999, http://dlib.eastview.com.proxy.lib.muohio.edu/browse/doc/211578 (accessed March 13, 2012).

172. Zhilin, "Opasnyye igry v kremlevskikh zastenkakh [Dangerous games in the Kremlin torture chambers]."

173. Mark A. Smith, *A Russian Chronology July–September 1999* (London: Ministry of Defense, Conflict Studies Research Centre, 1999), 31.

174. Zhilin, "Opasnyye igry v kremlevskikh zastenkakh [Dangerous games in the Kremlin torture chambers]."

175. "Perspectives," *Newsweek*, March 25, 2001, http://archive.is/Fo3A (accessed May 23, 2013).

176. Kolesnikov, *Anatoliy Chubays*, 182; Baker and Glasser, *Kremlin Rising*, 53; Yeltsin, *Midnight Diaries*, 332; Leonov, "Krestnyy put' Rossii, gody 1991–2000 [The way of the cross of Russia, 1991–2000]," 181.

177. Gessen, *The Man without a Face*, 20.

178. "'Tayna' otstavki S. Zvereva [The 'secret' of the resignation of S. Zvereva]," *SPB Vedomosti*, August 5, 1999, http://dlib.eastview.com/browse/doc/2179788 (accessed January 17, 2013).

179. "'Tayna' otstavki S. Zvereva [The 'secret' of the resignation of S. Zvereva]."

180. Yelena Dikun, "Zverev ne ugovoril Voloshina podat' v otstavku [Zverev didn't talk Voloshin into resigning]," *Obshchaya gazeta*, August 5, 1999, http://dlib.eastview.com/browse/doc/3562283 (accessed January 17, 2012).

181. Vasiliy Ustyuzhanin, "Sergey Zverev: Moyo pis'mo prezidenty rano ili posdno 'vystrelit' [My letter to the president sooner or later will hit its mark]," *Komsomol'skaya pravda*, August 5, 1999, http://dlib.eastview.com/browse/doc/3254802 (accessed January 17, 2012).

182. "Moskovskiye vzryvy gotovilis' v Kremle? [Were Moscow explosions prepared in the Kremlin?]," *Moskovskiy Komsomolets*, September 14, 1999, http://dlib.eastview.com/browse/doc/108572 (accessed June 3, 2013).

183. Boris Kagarlitskiy, "S terroristami ne razgovarivaem: No pomogayem? [With terrorists we don't negotiate: But do we help them?]," *Novaya gazeta*, January 24, 2000, http://old.novayagazeta.ru/data/2000/5/08.html (accessed Januray 6, 2013).

184. John Dunlop, *The Moscow Bombings of September 1999: Examinations of Russian Terrorist Attacks at the Onset of Vladimir Putin's Rule* (Stuttgart: Ibidem-Verlag, 2012), 70–71.

185. Kagarlitskiy, "S terroristami ne razgovarivaem [With terrorists we don't negotiate]."

186. Smith, *A Russian Chronology July–September 1999*, 30.

187. Boris Karpov, *Vnutrenniye voyska: Kavkazskiy krest-2* [Internal Forces: The Caucasian Cross 2] (Moscow: Delovoy ekspress, 2000), 47.

188. Bakhtiyar Akhmedkhanov, "Voyna po obe storony gory [War on both sides of the mountain]," *Vremya MN*, August 1, 2003, http://dlib.eastview.com/sources/article.jsp?id=5146351 (accessed August 4, 2012).

189. "Chechen Deputy Premier's Death in Prison Confirmed," *RFE/RL Newsline*, August 23, 2002, http://www.hri.org/news/balkans/rferl/2002/02-08-23.rferl.html (accessed June 3, 2013); "Chechen Field Commander Says He Gave Putin Advance Warning of Invasion of Dagestan," *RFE/RL Newsline*, November 29, 2001, http://www.hri.org/news/balkans/rferl/2001/01-11-29.rferl.html#28 (accessed June 8, 2013).

190. Dunlop, *The Moscow Bombings of September 1999*.

191. "Text of President Yeltsin's Speech," BBC, August 9, 1999, http://news.bbc.co.uk/2/hi/not_in_website/syndication/monitoring/415278.stm (accessed March 15, 2012).

192. "Stepashin's Statement to Government," BBC, August 9, 1999, http://news.bbc.co.uk/2/hi/not_in_website/syndication/monitoring/415134.stm (accessed March 15, 2012).

193. Elena Tregubova, *Bayki Kremlyevskogo diggera* [Tales of a Kremlin digger] (Moscow: Izdatel'stvo Ad Marginem, 2003), section 9.7; Andrey V. Kolesnikov, "The Unknown Chubays: Putin Dislikes but Values Him," *Moscow News*, November 12, 2003, http://dlib.eastview.com/browse/doc/5535195 (accessed July 21, 2012); Kolesnikov, *Anatoliy Chubays*, 182–83.

194. Yel'tsin, *Prezidentskiy Marafon* [Presidential marathon], 356.

195. Yel'tsin, *Prezidentskiy Marafon* [Presidential marathon], 381–82.

196. Vladimir Putin, "Putin Pledged Order and Continuity." BBC Monitoring, August 16, 1999, http://news.bbc.co.uk/2/hi/world/monitoring/422089.stm (accessed August 8, 2012).

197. "Russian Duma Confirms Putin as Prime Minister," CNN, August 16, 1999, http://articles.cnn.com/1999-08-16/world/9908_16_russia.putin.03_1_dagestan-conflict-duma-members-233to84?_s=PM:WORLD (accessed August 9, 2012).

198. "Primakov to Head New Russian Bloc," BBC, August 17, 1999, http://news.bbc.co.uk/2/hi/europe/422813.stm (accessed May 12, 2012).

199. Yelena Masyuk, "Gleb Pavlovskiy: 'What Putin Is Most Afraid of Is to Be Left Out,'" *Novaya gazeta*, November 6, 2012, http://en.novayagazeta.ru/politics/55288.html?print=1 (accessed January 8, 2013).

200. Orth, "Russia's Dark Master"; Yevgeniya Al'bats, "Gleb Pavlovskiy: Privychka k obozhaniyu u Putina voznikla ran'she [Gleb Pavlovskiy: The habit of adoration of Putin arose earlier]," *New Times*, March 26, 2012, http://www.newtimes.ru/articles/print/51401/ (accessed August 5, 2012).

201. Gessen, *The Man without a Face*, 20.

202. Ben Judah, *Fragile Empire: How Russia Fell In and Out of Love with Vladimir Putin* (New Haven, CT: Yale University Press, 2013), 27.

203. Ivanitskiy, "Operatsiya 'XX Trest' [Operation Twentieth Trust]."

204. Serrano and Montánchez, "Los Viajes Secretos de Putin a Sotogrande [The Secret Travels of Putin to Sotogrande]."

205. Tremlett, "Leader's Secret Holidays to Spain."

206. Serrano and Montánchez, "Los Viajes Secretos de Putin a Sotogrande [The Secret Travels of Putin to Sotogrande]."

207. Zykov, "Case #144128: 'Putin's Case,' Part 4"; Mukhin, "Byvshiy sledovatel' po osobo vazhnym delam Andrey Zykov [Former investigator for especially important cases Andrey Zykov]."

208. Ivanitskiy, "Operatsiya 'XX Trest' [Operation Twentieth Trust]."

209. Karen Dawisha, "Vladislav Surkov," in Stephen M. Norris and Willard Sunderland, eds., *Russia's People of Empire* (Bloomington: Indiana University Press, 2012), 339–51.

210. "Russia's 'Grey Cardinal' Given Social Policy Job," *Russia Briefing*, January 12, 2012, http://russia-briefing.com/news/russias-grey-cardinal-given-social-policy-job.html/ (accessed August 4, 2012).

211. Yakhno, "Noch' chekista [Night of a Chekist]."

212. "Eshchyo odna slyzhba okhrany? [Another security service?]," *Argumenty Nedeli*, August 15, 2013, http://argumenti.ru/politics/n401/275839 (accessed August 25, 2013).

213. Steve Harrigan, "Rebels Say They're out of Dagestan," CNN.com, August 23, 1999, http://edition.cnn.com/WORLD/europe/9908/23/dagestan.withdraw/ (accessed March 25, 2012).

214. "Russia Mourns Blast Victims," BBC, September 9, 1999, http://news.bbc.co.uk/2/hi/europe/443161.stm (accessed May 9, 2012).

215. "1990–2004: Khronologiya zakhvatov i vzryvov v Rossii [Chronology of hostage-takings and explosions in Russia]"; "Dozens Dead in Moscow Blast," BBC, September 13, 1999, http://news.bbc.co.uk/2/hi/europe/445529.stm (accessed May 9, 2012).

216. Dunlop, *The Moscow Bombings of September 1999*, 78.

217. "1990–2004: Khronologiya zakhvatov i vzryvov v Rossii [Chronology of hostage-takings and explosions in Russia]"; "Dozens Dead in Moscow Blast."

218. Michael Gordon, "Another Bombing Kills 18 in Russia," *New York Times*, September 17, 1999, http://www.nytimes.com/1999/09/17/world/another-bombing-kills-18-in-russia.html (accessed May 10, 2012); "1990–2004: Khronologiya zakhvatov i vzryvov v Rossii [Chronology of hostage-takings and explosions in Russia]."

219. Dunlop, *The Moscow Bombings of September 1999*; Satter, *Darkness at Dawn*; Felshtinskiy and Pribylovskiy, *The Age of Assassins*.

220. Gordon, "Another Bombing Kills 18 in Russia."

221. Leonov, "Krestnyy put' Rossii, gody 1991–2000 [The way of the cross of Russia, 1991–2000]."

222. Gessen, *The Man without a Face*, 26.

223. Gessen, *The Man without a Face*, 26.

224. Paul Starobin, "The Accidental Autocrat," *Atlantic Monthly*, March 2005; Vladimir Putin, "V Sortire zamochim! [We will wipe them out in the outhouse]," Youtube, September 23, 1999. http://www.youtube.com/results?search_query=Putin+and+%22v+sortire+zamochim%22 (accessed May 8, 2012).

225. Yelena Yevstigneyeva, "Kabinet ministrov zanyalsya ekonomikoy [The Cabinet of Ministers concerns itself with economics]," *Nezavisimaya gazeta*, September 24, 1999, http://www.ng.ru/politics/1999-09-24/kabinet.html (accessed August 17, 2012).

226. Raymond Bonner, "Activity at Bank Raises Suspicions of Russia Mob Tie," *New York Times*, August 19, 1999, http://femch.s5.com/52.html#524 (accessed March 18, 2012).

227. J. Michael Waller, "Gore's Embrace," *Insight* 15, no. 36 (September 27, 1999), https://global.factiva.com.proxy.lib.muohio.edu/ha/default.aspx#./!?&_suid=14052825177280845048520 7140446.

228. Strobe Talbott, *The Russia Hand: A Memoir of Presidential Diplomacy* (New York: Random House, 2002), ch. 14; Strobe Talbott, "Testimony before the Senate Appropriations Committee Subcommittee on Foreign Operaitons," *Frontline*, April 4, 2000, http://www.pbs.org/wgbh/pages/frontline/shows/yeltsin/putin/talbott00.html (accessed June 6, 2012).

229. George Soros, *Open Society: Reforming Global Capitalism* (New York: Public Affairs, 2000) 260.

230. Talbott, *The Russia Hand*, 365.

231. Gessen, *The Man without a Face*, 41.

232. Sergey Topol' and Nadezhda Kurbacheva, "Taymer ostanovili za sem' chasov do vzryva: Terakt predotvratil voditel' avtobusa [They stopped the timer seven hours before the explosion: Bus driver prevented terror act]," *Kommersant*, September 24, 1999, http://kommersant.ru/doc/226161 (accessed May 5, 2012).

233. Simon Saradzhyan, "There Was No Ryazan Bomb—It Was a Test," *Moscow Times*, September 25, 1999, http://www.themoscowtimes.com/news/article/there-was-no-ryazan-bomb—it-was-a-test/272001.html (accessed July 8, 2012).

234. Yevstigneyeva, "Kabinet ministrov zanyalsya ekonomikoy [The Cabinet of Ministers concerns itself with economics]."

235. Satter, *Darkness at Dawn*, 28.

236. John Sweeney, "Take Care Tony, That Man Has Blood on His Hands: Evidence Shows Secret Police Were Behind 'Terrorist' Bomb," *Observer (UK)*, March 12, 2000, http://www.theGuardian.co.uk/world/2000/mar/12/chechnya.johnsweeney (accessed August 7, 2012).

237. "Ryazan 'Bomb' Was Security Service Exercise," BBC, September 24, 1999, http://news.bbc.co.uk/2/hi/europe/456848.stm (accessed May 18, 2012).

238. Gessen, *The Man without a Face*, 38.

239. Edward Lucas, *The New Cold War: Putin's Russia and the Threat to the West* (London: Palgrave, 2008), 25.

240. "The FSB Bombing According to Former KGB," Gazeta.ru in Chechnya List, March 23, 2000, http://groups.yahoo.com/group/chechnya-sl/message/7484 (accessed January 7, 2013).

241. Sweeney, "Take Care Tony."

242. Gessen, *The Man without a Face*, 38.

243. Pavel Voloshin, "Chto Bylo v Ryazani: Sakhar ili Geksogen? [What was it in Ryazan: Sugar or Hexagon?]," *Novaya gazeta*, February 14, 2000, http://old.novayagazeta.ru/data/2000/11/01.html (accessed August 14, 2012).

244. *Blowing Up Russia*.

245. Aleksey Gerasimov and Fyodor Maksimov, "Dva pozhiznennykh sroka za 246 ubiystv [Two life sentences for the murders of 246]," *Kommersant*, January 13, 2004, http://kommersant.ru/doc/440000 (accessed May 18, 2012).

246. Aleksandr Zhilin, "Voyna i my. Kavkaz: Voyna na dva fronta [War and us. The Caucasus: War on two fronts]," *Novaya gazeta*, October 18, 1999, http://dlib.eastview.com.proxy.lib.muohio.edu/browse/doc/3473480 (accessed March 7, 2012).

247. "RDX.FSB.Ryazan," *Novaya gazeta*, March 13, 2000, http://www.novayagazeta.ru/society/11303.html (accessed April 5, 2012).

248. Gessen, *The Man without a Face*, 203.

249. Anderson, "Vladimir Putin's Dark Rise to Power."

250. Anderson, "Vladimir Putin's Dark Rise to Power."
251. Igor' Korol'kov, "Izbiratel': Fotorobot ne pervoy svezhesti [Voter: The Identikit is not fresh]," *Moskovskiye Novosti*, November 11, 2003, http://dlib.eastview.com.proxy.lib.muohio.edu /browse/doc/5529815 (accessed 7 May).
252. "Mezhdunarodnaya komissiya yuristov zhelaet prokontrolirovat' khod dela Trepashkina," [The International Commission of Jurists wants to ensure due process for Trepashkin] Grani.ru, December 16, 2003, http://grani.ru/Politics/Russia/FSB/m.54089.html (accessed June 9, 2012).
253. Anatoly Medetsky, "For Trepashkin, Bomb Trail Leads to Jail," *Moscow Times*, January 14, 2004, http://www.russialist.org/8014-18.php (accessed May 10, 2012); *Disbelief*, directed by Andrey Nekrasov, 2004.
254. Douglas Birch, "Putin Critic Loses Post, Platform for Inquiry," *Baltimore Sun*, December 11, 2003, http://groups.yahoo.com/group/RMSMC/message/3005 (accessed June 1, 2012).
255. Tat'yana Pelipeyko, "Interview with Sergey Kovalev: 'Svedeniya Litvinenko o vzryvakh zhilykh domov v Moskve' [Information from Litvinenko about the apartment bombings in Moscow]," Ekho Moskvy, July 25, 2002, http://echo.msk.ru/programs/beseda/19169/ (accessed May 7, 2012).
256. "Geksogenovyy sled 4 [Hexogen track 4]," *Novaya gazeta*, March 3, 2003, http://2003.novaya gazeta.ru/nomer/2003/16n/n16n-s17.shtml (accessed August 7, 2013).
257. Felshtinskiy and Pribylovskiy, *The Age of Assassins*.
258. Achemez Gochiyaev, "Pokazaniya Achemeza Gochiyaeva, predstavlennyye na zasedanii Obshchestvennoy komissii 25 Iyulya 2002 goda [Testimony of Achemez Gochiyaev, presented at the meeting of the Public Commission, July 25, 2002]," Terror-99.ru, July 25, 2002, http:// terror99.ru/documents/doc36.htm (accessed May 10, 2012).
259. Korol'kov, "Izbiratel' [Voter]."
260. Pelipeyko, "Interview with Sergey Kovalev."
261. Birch, "Putin Critic Loses Post, Platform for Inquiry."
262. Grigoriy Yavlinskiy, "Interv'yu Grigoriya Yavlinskogo programme 'Nedelya' [Interview with Grigoriy Yavlinskiy on the program 'Nedelya']," Yavlinsky.ru, March 11, 2000, http://yavlinsky .ru/news/index.phtml?id=29 (accessed May 19, 2012).
263. V. M. Filippov, "Letter from Minister of Education V. M. Filippov to Procurator General V. V. Ustinov," *Gazeta.ru*, March 5, 2002, http://www.gazeta.ru/2002/03/05/pisjmominist.shtml (accessed January 3, 2014).
264. "Prezidentskiye vybory—Nash posledniy shans uznat' pravdy [Presidential elections—Our last chance to know the truth]," *Novaya gazeta*, January 15, 2004, http://www.novayagazeta.ru /society/25103.html (accessed May 19, 2012).
265. Kirill Privalov, "I tut Lebed—ves' v belom! [And here's Lebed (the swan), all in white!]," *Segodya*, September 30, 1999, http://dlib.eastview.com.proxy.lib.muohio.edu/browse/doc/2070729 (accessed May 8, 2012).
266. Laure Mandeville, "Alexandre Lebed: 'Le pouvoir veut déstabiliser la Russie,'" *Le Figaro*, September 29, 1999; Laure Mandeville, "Attentats de Moscou: Lebed accuse le Kremlin," *Le Figaro*, September 29, 1999; Laure Mandeville, "Les eaux troubles du Kremlin," *Le Figaro*, October 11, 1999, http://recherche.lefigaro.fr/recherche/access/lefigaro_fr.php?archive=BszTm8dCk78Jk8 uwiNq9T8CoS9GECSHiCTfu%2B2AH52iXZVSLRBCXlbdsfHEuMFCuRdGhGvsif3qZy 6BaSOXVcw%3D%3D.
267. Konstantin Borovoy, "Osoboye mneniye [Personal opinion]," Ekho Moskvy, August 19, 2010, http://www.echo.msk.ru/programs/personalno/703727-echo.html (accessed January 12, 2013).
268. Konstantin Borovoy, "Osoboye mneniye [Personal opinion]." Ekho Moskvy, September 9, 2010, http://www.echo.msk.ru/programs/personalno/709194-echo/#element-text (accessed January 12, 2013).
269. Yelena Tokareva, "Spetssluzhby znali o gotovyashchikhsya teraktakh [Intelligence agencies were aware of imminent terrorist attacks]," *Obshchaya gazeta*, September 16, 1999, http://dlib.east view.com/browse/doc/3562653 (accessed July 1, 2013).

270. Steve LeVine, *Putin's Labyrinth* (New York: Random House, 2008).

271. Timothy J. Colton and Michael McFaul, *Popular Choice and Managed Democracy: The Russian Elections of 1999 and 2000* (Washington, DC: Brookings Institution, 2003), 173.

272. Sergei Kovalev, "Putin's War," *New York Review of Books*, February 10, 2000, http://www .nybooks.com/articles/archives/2000/feb/10/putins-war/?pagination=false (accessed September 1, 2012).

273. Vladimir Putin, "Rossiya na rubezhe tycyacheletniy [Russia at the turn of the millennium]," *Nezavisimaya gazeta*, December 30, 1999, http://www.ng.ru/politics/1999-12-30/4_millenium.html (accessed 01 20, 2012).

274. Valeriy Vyzhutovich, "Bombit', Vydvoryat', Arestovyvat'! [Bomb, deport, arrest!]," *Izvestiya*, September 28, 1999, http://dlib.eastview.com.proxy.lib.muohio.edu/browse/doc/3177610 (accessed December 8, 2013).

275. Colton and McFaul, *Popular Choice and Managed Democracy*.

Chapter Five: Putin Prepares to Take Over

1. Pravosudov, "Sergey Stepashin."

2. Jack, *Inside Putin's Russia*, 148; Henry Hale, *Why Not Parties in Russia? Democracy, Federalism, and the State* (New York: Cambridge University Press, 2007), 226.

3. Hale, *Why Not Parties in Russia?*, 226.

4. "Interview with Boris Berezovskiy," in Gessen, *The Man without a Face*, 21.

5. Simon Saradzhyan, "Primakov to Clear Jails for Corrupt," *Moscow Times*, February 2, 1999, http://www.themoscowtimes.com/news/article/primakov-to-clear-jails-for-corrupt/280826.html (accessed May 5, 2013).

6. OSCE, ODIHR, *Russian Federation: Elections to the State Duma (19 December 1999). Final Report* (Warsaw: ODIHR, February 2000), 13.

7. "Luzhkov Cozies Up to KPRF as He Declares Russian Democracy Dean," Jamestown Monitor, December 13, 1999, http://www.jamestown.org/single/?no_cache=1&tx_ttnews%5Btt _news%5D=11539&tx_ttnews%5BbackPid%5D=213 (accessed May 2, 2013).

8. Igor' Chernyak, "Lyudi Putina: Kto est' kto [Putin's people: Who is who]," *Komsomol'skaya pravda*, January 26, 2000, http://dlib.eastview.com.proxy.lib.muohio.edu/browse/doc/32197 13 (accessed May 2, 2013).

9. Aleksey Alekseyevich Mukhin, *Media-Imperii Rossii* [Media empires of Russia] (Moscow: Algorithm Books, 2005), 6–9.

10. *The Putin System.*

11. Parliamentary Assembly, Council of Europe, *Report of the Ad Hoc Committee to Observe the Parliamentary Elections in Russia (19 December 1999)*, January 24, 2000, http://assembly.coe.int /main.asp?Link=/documents/workingdocs/doc00/edoc86 (accessed May 24, 2012), 5.

12. OSCE, ODIHR, *Russian Federation*.

13. Sarah Karush, "Putin Predicts Friendly Duma," *Moscow Times*, December 22, 1999, http:// www.themoscowtimes.com/news/article/putin-predicts-friendly-duma/268571.html (accessed May 4, 2013).

14. Mikhail Myagkov, "The 1999 Duma Election in Russia: A Step toward Democracy or the Elites' Game?," in Vicki L. Hesli and William M. Reisinger, eds., *The 1999–2000 Elections in Russia: Their Impact and Legacy* (New York: Cambridge University Press, 2003), 155.

15. Myagkov, "The 1999 Duma Election in Russia," 156.

16. OSCE, ODIHR, *Russian Federation*, 31.

17. Parliamentary Assembly, Council of Europe, *Report of the Ad Hoc Committee to Observe the Parliamentary Elections in Russia (19 December 1999)*, 5.

18. Simon Shuster, "Rewriting Russian History: Did Boris Yeltsin Steal the 1996 Presidential Election?," *Time*, February 24, 2012, http://www.time.com/time/world/article/0,8599,2107 565,00.html (accessed June 3, 2013).

19. Putin, "Rossiya na rubezhe tycyacheletniy [Russia at the turn of the millennium]."

20. Philip Boobbyer, *The Stalin Era* (New York: Routledge, 2000), 83.

21. Vladimir Putin, "Address at an Expanded Meeting of the Russian Security Council," Kremlin, December 31, 1999, http://archive.kremlin.ru/appears/1999/12/31/0002_type63374type633 78_59568.shtml (accessed January 21, 2012).

22. Pavel Yevdokimov, "Russkaya pravda Generala Leonova [The Russian truth of General Leonov]," *Spetznaz Rossii,* as quoted in Fiona Hill and Clifford G. Gaddy, *Mr. Putin: Operative in the Kremlin* (Washington, DC: Brookings Institution Press, 2013), 38.

23. "Putin Sacks Yeltsin's Daughter," BBC, January 3, 2000, http://news.bbc.co.uk/2/hi/europe /589498.stm (accessed September 10, 2011).

24. Andrey V. Kolesnikov, "Generation 'P,' " *New Times,* March 1, 2000, in *Current Digest of the Soviet Press,* March 29, 2000, http://dlib.eastview.com.proxy.lib.muohio.edu/browse/doc/ (accessed January 25, 2012).

25. Paul Goble, "Russia: Analysis from Washington—toward Totalitarian Democracy?," Radio Free Europe Radio Liberty, February 10, 2000, http://www.rferl.org/content/article/1093335.html (accessed February 10, 2012).

26. Vladimir Putin, "Vstrecha so studentami Irkutskogo gosudarstvennogo universiteta [Meeting with students of Irkukst State University]," Kremlin, February 18, 2000, http://archive.krem lin.ru/appears/2000/02/18/0004_type63376_122112.shtml (accessed May 7, 2013).

27. Vladimir Putin, "Okrytoe pis'mo Vladimira Putina k rossiyskim izbiratelyam [An open letter by Vladimir Putin to Russian voters]," *Kommersant,* February 25, 2000, http://www.kommersant .ru/Doc/141144 (accessed March 2, 2012); Michael Wines, "Yeltsin Resigns," *New York Times,* January 1, 2000, http://www.nytimes.com/2000/01/01/world/yeltsin-resigns-man-top-still -mystery-vladimir-vladimirovich-putin.html?src=pm (accessed November 3, 2011).

28. Putin, "Okrytoe pis'mo Vladimira Putina k rossiyskim izbiratelyam [An open letter by Vladimir Putin to Russian voters]."

29. Putin, "Okrytoe pis'mo Vladimira Putina k rossiyskim izbiratelyam [An open letter by Vladimir Putin to Russian voters]."

30. Federal Law #228-FZ, "On the Election of the President of the Russian Federation," Demokratiya.ru, December 31, 1999, http://www.democracy.ru/english/library/laws/preside lect_eng/index.html (accessed April 18, 2013).

31. OSCE, ODIHR, *Russian Federation,* 8.

32. OSCE, ODIHR, *Russian Federation,* 9.

33. OSCE, ODIHR, *Russian Federation,* 9.

34. Boris Volodarsky, *The KGB's Poison Factory* (Minneapolis, MN: Zenith Press, 2009), 63.

35. Wade Boese, "U.S. Says Ukrainian President Approved Arms Sale to Iraq," *Arms Control Today,* October 2002, https://www.armscontrol.org/act/2002_10/ukraineoct02 (accessed July 10, 2014).

36. Koshiw, "Kuchma's 'Parallel Cabinet,' "18; J. V. Koshiw, *Abuse of Power: Corruption in the Office of the President* (Reading, UK: Artemia Press, 2013), 56.

37. Goldman, *Petrostate*; Vladimir Milov and Boris Nemtsov, "Putin and Gazprom: An Independent Expert Report," *European Energy Review,* 2008, http://www.europeanenergyreview.eu /data/docs/Viewpoints/Putin%20and%20Gazprom_Nemtsov%20en%20Milov.pdf (accessed June 8, 2012); Paul Starobin and Catherine Belton, "Gazprom: Russia's Enron?," *Business Week,* February 17, 2002, http://www.businessweek.com/stories/2002-02-17/gazprom-russias-enron (accessed June 9, 2012); Anders Åslund, "Why Gazprom Resembles a Crime Syndicate," *Moscow Times,* February 28, 2012, http://www.themoscowtimes.com/opinion/article/why-gaz prom-resembles-a-crime-syndicate/453762.html (accessed March 12, 2012).

38. Koshiw, "Kuchma's 'Parallel Cabinet,' "18.

39. Anastasiya Telegina, "Strashnaya tayna Vladimira Putina [The terrible secret of Vladimir Putin]," *Kommersant,* March 1, 2000, http://dlib.eastview.com.proxy.lib.muohio.edu/browse /doc/3691534 (accessed March 8, 2010); Vladimir Novikov, "Tayna rokovogo domika [The

secret of the fatal house]," *Moskovskiy Komsomolets*, March 7, 2000, http://dlib.eastview.com .proxy.lib.muohio.edu/browse/doc/68127 (accessed May 6, 2013).

40. Konstantin Katanyan, "Sud dramy i komedii [The court of drama and comedy]," *Izvestiya*, February 26, 2000, http://dlib.eastview.com.proxy.lib.muohio.edu/browse/doc/3042233 (accessed May 24, 2013), 3; Novikov, "Tayna rokovogo domika [The secret of the fatal house]."

41. Konstantin Katanyan, "U Zhirinovskogo vnov' yest' povod dlya bespokoystva [Zhirinovskiy again has reason to worry]," *Izvestiya*, March 11, 2000, http://dlib.eastview.com.proxy.lib.muohio.edu/browse/doc/3042645 (accessed May 2, 2013); Marina Volkova, "Bitva za protsenty [Fight for percentages]," *Nezavisimaya gazeta*, February 29, 2000, http://dlib.eastview.com .proxy.lib.muohio.edu/browse/issuetext?issue=8921 (accessed February 8, 2013); OSCE, ODIHR, *Russian Federation*, 20.

42. Pamela Johnson, "Zhirinovsky's Return Seen as Avoiding Putin Scandal," *Russia Journal*, March 13–19, 2000, http://russiajournal.com/archive/The_Russia_Journal/2000/March/13 .03.2000/Analysis/Mar.13-05.pdf (accessed August 8, 2009).

43. OSCE, ODIHR, *Russian Federation*, 21.

44. "Next—The Mayor's Office," *Izvestiya*, March 10, 2000, 3, http://www.osce.org/odihr/elections/russia/16275 (accessed September 7, 2009).

45. Parliamentary Assembly, Council of Europe, *Report of the Ad Hoc Committee to Observe the Russian Presidential Election (26 March 2000).* (Strasbourg, France: Council of Europe, April 3, 2000).

46. OSCE, ODIHR, *Russian Federation*, 28.

47. Michael McFaul, "Testimony before the U.S. Senate Committee on Foreign Relations, Washington, D.C.," Carnegie Endowment, April 12, 2000, http://carnegieendowment.org /2000/04/01/russia-s-2000-presidential-elections-implications-for-russian-democracy-and-u.s .-russian-relations/4ova (accessed July 3, 2013).

48. Parliamentary Assembly, Council of Europe, *Report of the Ad Hoc Committee to Observe the Russian Presidential Election (26 March 2000).*

49. Borisova, "And the Winner Is?"

50. Borisova, "And the Winner Is?"

51. Yevgeniya Borisova, "Baby Boom or Dead Souls?," *Moscow Times*, September 9, 2000, www .moscowtimes.ru/stories/2000/09/09/116.html (accessed April 1, 2013).

52. Borisova, "Baby Boom or Dead Souls?"

53. Yevgeniya Borisova, "Hot Off the Press: Extra Ballots," *Moscow Times*, September 9, 2000, http://www.moscowtimes.ru/article/1008/49/258955.htm (accessed April 18, 2013).

54. Mikhail Myagkov and Peter C. Ordeshook, "The Trail of Votes in Russia's 1999 Duma and 2000 Presidential Elections," *Communist and Post-Communist Studies* 34, no. 3 (2001): 353.

55. Walter R. Mebane Jr. and Kirill Kalinin, "Electoral Fraud in Russia: Vote Counts Analysis Using Second-Digit Mean Tests," Paper presented at Annual Meeting of the Midwest Political Science Association, Chicago, 2010.

56. Yevgeniya Borisova, "And the Winner Is? Part 2," *Moscow Times*, September 9, 2000, http:// www.themoscowtimes.com/news/article/and-the-winner-is—-part-2/258950.html.

57. M. Steven Fish, *Democracy Derailed in Russia* (New York: Cambridge University Press, 2005), 42–43.

58. Nikolai Petrov, "Federalism," in Michael McFaul, Nikolai Petrov, and Andrei Ryabov, eds., *Between Dictatorship and Democracy* (Washington, DC: Carnegie Endowment, 2004), 213–38.

59. Petrov, "Federalism," 249.

60. Myagkov and Ordeshook, "The Trail of Votes in Russia's 1999 Duma and 2000 Presidential Elections," 24.

61. Borisova, "And the Winner Is?"; Borisova, "And the Winner Is? Part 2."

62. Parliamentary Assembly, Council of Europe, *Report of the Ad Hoc Committee to Observe the Russian Presidential Election (26 March 2000).*

63. Borisova, "Baby Boom or Dead Souls?"
64. Marina Arbatskaya, *Skol'ko zhe izbirateley v Rossii?* [How many voters are there in Russia?] (Irkutsk: Siberian Branch of Academy of Sciences, Institute of Geography, 2004).
65. Borisova, "And the Winner Is?"
66. Borisova, "And the Winner Is?"
67. Yevgeniya Borisova, "And the Winner Is? Part 3," *Moscow Times*, September 9, 2000, http://www.moscowtimes.ru/article/1008/49/258949.htm.
68. Borisova, "And the Winner Is?"
69. Borisova, "And the Winner Is? Part 3."
70. Parliamentary Assembly, Council of Europe. *Report of the Ad Hoc Committee to Observe the Russian Presidential Election (26 March 2000).*
71. Ekaterina Grigor'yeva, "Kreml' ishchet liniyu vlasti: Putin nesomnenno budet strog k glavam regionov [The Kremlin seeks power line: Putin is sure to be strict with regional leaders]," *Nezavisimaya gazeta*, March 30, 2000, http://dlib.eastview.com.proxy.lib.muohio.edu/browse/doc/270450 (accessed June 7, 2012).
72. Putin et al., *First Person*, 131.
73. Nikolay Vardul', "Politicheskiy sovet prezidentu: Kak Putin budet upravlyat' stranoy 3 [A political council to the president: How Putin will run the country—part 3]," *Kommersant*, May 5, 2000, http://kommersant.ru/doc/147181 (accessed 01 20, 2012).
74. "Reformirovaniye Administratsii RF Prezidenta [Reform of the Administration of the RF President]," *Kommersant*, May 5, 2000, http://www.kommersant.ru/include/inc-archive /materials/archive-material-newWind.asp?textPath=/documents/reforma.htm&textTitle=%20 %C4%CE%CA%D3%CC%C5%CD%D2%20&id_arcdoc=10&year=2000 (accessed January 20, 2012).
75. "Reformirovaniye Administratsii RF Prezidenta [Reform of the Administration of the RF President]," 11. All page numbers refer to the translated version available at www.muohio.edu/havighurstcenter/putins-russia.
76. "Reformirovaniye Administratsii RF Prezidenta [Reform of the Administration of the RF President]," 12.
77. "Reformirovaniye Administratsii RF Prezidenta [Reform of the Administration of the RF President]," 14.
78. "Reformirovaniye Administratsii RF Prezidenta [Reform of the Administration of the RF President]," 37.
79. "Reformirovaniye Administratsii RF Prezidenta [Reform of the Administration of the RF President]," 30.
80. "Reformirovaniye Administratsii RF Prezidenta [Reform of the Administration of the RF President]," 31.
81. "Reformirovaniye Administratsii RF Prezidenta [Reform of the Administration of the RF President]," 23.
82. "Reformirovaniye Administratsii RF Prezidenta [Reform of the Administration of the RF President]," 13.
83. "Reformirovaniye Administratsii RF Prezidenta [Reform of the Administration of the RF President]," 26.
84. "Reformirovaniye Administratsii RF Prezidenta [Reform of the Administration of the RF President]," 20.
85. "Reformirovaniye Administratsii RF Prezidenta [Reform of the Administration of the RF President]," 16.
86. "Reformirovaniye Administratsii RF Prezidenta [Reform of the Administration of the RF President]," 4-5.
87. Catherine Belton, "Kremlin, KGB May Unite," *Moscow Times*, May 5, 2000, http://www.the moscowtimes.com/news/article/report-kremlin-fsb-may-unite/263489.html (accessed January 23, 2012).

88. Belton, "Kremlin, KGB May Unite."

89. "Interview with Marina Sal'ye."

90. Franchetti, "Putin Caught in Food Scandal"; Hoffman, "Putin's Career Rooted in Russia's KGB."

91. Putin et al., *First Person*, 173.

92. Gessen, *The Man without a Face*, 36.

93. Andrei Zolotov, "Papers Unite to Defend Babitsky, Free Speech," *Moscow Times*, February 17, 2000, http://dlib.eastview.com/searchresults/article.jsp?art=1&id=225111 (accessed January 2012); Gareth Jones, "Journalists Say Russia Press Freedom at Risk," Reuters, February 16, 2000, http://www.russialist.org/archives/4113.html (accessed January 25, 2012).

94. "Yeltsin Reorganizes, Strengthens Presidential Structures," *Rossiyskaya gazeta*, Foreign Broadcast Information Service, March 9, 1994, http://nlg.csie.ntu.edu.tw/courses/IR/project2005/FB396001 (accessed January 5, 2014).

95. Valeriya Novodvorskaya, "The First Seal," *New Times*, March 1, 2000, http://dlib.eastview.com.proxy.lib.muohio.edu/browse/doc/3496749 (accessed January 25, 2012).

96. "Putin's Campaign Staff Ready to Rebuff Opponents' Attacks—Medvedev," Interfax, February 16, 2000, http://www.cdi.org/russia/johnson/4113.html#4 (accessed January 25, 2012).

97. *ITAR-TASS*, "A Covert War on the Media?," March 4, 2000, NIS Observed, edited by Jonathan Solomon, March 21, 2000, http://www.bu.edu/iscip/digest/vol5/ed0505.html#media (accessed June 3, 2013).

98. *Blowing Up Russia.*

99. Sarah Karush, "Hackers Attack Novaya Gazeta," *Moscow Times*, March 16, 2000, http://www.themoscowtimes.com/sitemap/free/2000/3/article/hackers-attack-novaya-gazeta/265485.html (accessed October 30, 2013).

100. Yablokova, "Purse-Snatching Takes FSB to NTV."

101. Anna Badkhen, "Borovik Laid to Rest at Novodevichy," *Moscow Times*, March 14, 2000.

102. Al'bats, "Gleb Pavlovskiy."

103. "Kukly—Story of Putin: Parody of E. T. A. Hoffmann's novella 'Klein Zaches,'" YouTube, 2000, http://www.youtube.com/watch?v=eZJx9bgwdv0&feature=related (accessed January 25, 2012).

104. Baker and Glasser, *Kremlin Rising*, 93–94.

105. Michael Wines, "TV's Impious Puppets: On Kremlin's Hit List?," *New York Times*, June 18, 2000, http://www.nytimes.com/2000/06/18/world/tv-s-impious-puppets-on-kremlin-s-hit-list.html?pagewanted=all&src=pm (accessed January 25, 2012); Viktor Shenderovich, "Zdec' bylo NTB, TV-6, TVS [Here was NTV, TV-6, TVS]," *Svetlana Sorokina: Transmission, Interviews, Publications*, 2003, http://tvoygolos.narod.ru/klio/text1.htm (accessed January 25, 2012).

106. Miriam Lanskoy, "Caucasus Ka-Boom," NIS Observed, November 8, 2000, http://www.cdi.org/russia/johnson/4630.html##3 (accessed February 3, 2012).

107. Dmitriy Furman, "Ot pozdnego Yel'tsina k rannemu Putinu [From late Yel'tsin to early Putin]," *Obshchaya gazeta*, February 10, 2000, http://dlib.eastview.com/sources/article.jsp?id=3551396 (accessed January 31, 2012).

108. Nataliya Kanatikova, "Cherniy piar deystvuyet [Black PR acts]," *Rossiyskaya gazeta*, March 2, 2000, http://dlib.eastview.com/browse/doc/1810011 (accessed June 5, 2013).

109. Jonathan Solomon, "A Covert War on the Media?," NIS Observed, March 21, 2000, http://www.bu.edu/iscip/digest/vol5/ed0505.html#media (accessed November 11, 2011).

110. Satter, *Darkness at Dawn*, 182–97; Roman Abramovich, "Third Witness Statement of Roman Arkadievich Abramovich," High Court of Justice, May 30, 2011, http://www.scribd.com/doc/71158207/Third-Witness-Statement-of-Roman-Abramovich?secret_password=27q4ccv9z5lnrepjvnko (accessed February 3, 2012).

111. Jeffrey K. Hass, *Power, Culture, and Economic Change in Russia* (New York: Routledge, 2011).

112. NTV, "Russian President-Elect Looks Set to Oust Oligarchs from Government," BBC Monitoring, April 2, 2000, http://russialist.org/4222.html##5 (accessed June 6, 2013).

113. Celestine Bohlen, "Putin's Team Hammers Out a Plan to Untwist, Level and Streamline Russia's Economy," *New York Times*, April 4, 2000, http://www.nytimes.com/2000/04/02/world /putin-s-team-hammers-out-a-plan-to-untwist-level-and-streamline-russia-s-economy.html?scp =7&sq=Illarionov&st=nyt&pagewanted=1 (accessed November 2, 2011).

114. Bohlen, "Putin's Team Hammers Out a Plan to Untwist, Level and Streamline Russia's Economy."

Chapter Six: The Founding of the Putin System

1. Nataliya Gevorkyan and Andrey Kolesnikov, "Interview with Vladimir Putin," *Kommersant*, March 10, 2000, http://dlib.eastview.com.proxy.lib.muohio.edu/browse/doc/3692017 (accessed May 23, 2013).

2. Vladimir Putin, "Inaugural Speech," BBC, May 7, 2000, http://news.bbc.co.uk/2/hi/world /monitoring/media_reports/739432.stm (accessed November 3, 2011).

3. Vladimir Putin, "Vstupleniya v dolzhnost' Prezidenta Rossii [The accession to office of the President of Russia]," YouTube, May 7, 2000, http://www.youtube.com/watch?v=hcKCYBC fpM4&feature=watch_response_rev (accessed January 26, 2012); Guy Debord, *Society of the Spectacle*, New York: Zone Books, 1994; Helena Goscilo, ed., *Putin as Celebrity and Cultural Icon*, New York: Routledge, 2012.

4. Gleb Pavlovskiy, *Genial'naya Vlast'! Slovar' Abstraktsi Kremlya* [The genius of power! A Dictionary of Kremlin abstractions] (Moscow: Evropa, 2012), 84.

5. Kalugin, *Spymaster*, 292.

6. Putin, "Okrytoe pis'mo Vladimira Putina k rossiyskim izbiratelyam [An open letter by Vladimir Putin to Russian voters]."

7. Dmitriy Dokuchayev, "Tsentr ob"yavil voynu ekonomicheskomu separatizmu regionov [Center has declared war on the economic separatism of the regions]," *Izvestiya*, November 4, 1997, http://dlib.eastview.com/browse/doc/3153229 (accessed May 8, 2013).

8. Lilia Shevtsova, *Putin's Russia*, revised and expanded ed. (Washington, DC: Carnegie Endowment for International Peace, 2005), 92.

9. "Putin Fires Energy Minister," BBC, February 5, 2000, http://news.bbc.co.uk/2/hi/europe /1153941.stm (accessed January 31, 2012).

10. NTV, "TV Recalls Mess in Russian Regions in 1990s, Notes Putin's Role in Combating It," BBC Monitoring, Johnson's Russia List, #33, February 22, 2012. http://www.russialist.org/archives /johnsons-russia-list-newsletter-table-contents-2012.php (accessed February 24, 2012).

11. Eugene Huskey, "Political Leadership and the Center-Periphery Struggle: Putin's Administrative Reforms," in Archie Brown and Lilia Shevstova, eds., *Gorbachev, Yeltsin, and Putin: Political Leadership in Russia's Transition* (Washington, DC: Carnegie Endowment, 2001), 113–43.

12. Matthew Hyde, "Putin's Federal Reforms and Their Implications for Presidential Power in Russia," *Europe-Asia Studies* 53, no. 5 (2001).

13. Baker and Glasser, *Kremlin Rising*, 85.

14. Dmitriy Kamyshev, "Tri Putinskikh udara [Putin's three strikes]," *Kommersant*, May 20, 2000, http://dlib.eastview.com.proxy.lib.muohio.edu/browse/doc/3697207 (accessed May 23, 2013); Thomas Remington, "The Russian Federal Assembly, 1994–2004," *Journal of Legislative Studies* 13, no. 1 (2007): 130.

15. "Russia: Duma Deputy Says Putin Trying to Create 'Authoritarianism,'" Interfax, July 7, 2000, http://toolkit.dialog.com/intranet/cgi/present?STYLE=739318018&PRESENT=DB=985,AN =118950910,FM=9,SEARCH=MD.GenericSearch (accessed February 4, 2012).

16. Aleksey Germanovich, "Doloy Knyazey [Down with the princes]," *Vedomosti*, May 16, 2000, http://dlib.eastview.com.proxy.lib.muohio.edu/browse/doc/9436266 (accessed May 9, 2013).

17. Thomas Remington, "Majorities without Mandates: The Russian Federation Council since 2000," *Europe-Asia Studies* 55, no. 5 (2003): 672.

18. Vardul', "Politicheskiy sovet prezidentu [A political council to the president]"; "Reformirovaniye Administratsii RF Prezidenta [Reform of the Administration of the RF President]." 31-50.
19. "Ukaz 1602: O Gosydarstvennom sovete Rossiyskoy Federatsii [On the State Council of the RF]," Kremlin, September 1, 2000, http://graph.document.kremlin.ru/page.aspx?661745 (accessed June 5, 2013).
20. Patrick Cockburn, "Berezovsky Quits Duma at 'Ruining of Russia,'" *Independent (UK)*, July 18, 2000, http://www.independent.co.uk/news/world/europe/berezovsky-quits-duma-at-ruining-of-russia-707942.html (accessed May 8, 2013).
21. Il'ya Bulavin, Nikolay Vardul', and Azer Mursaliyev, "Vsya vlast'—Sovetu: Bezopasnosti [All power—to the soviets: The Security Council]," *Kommersant*, May 20, 2000, http://dlib.east view.com/browse/doc/3697257 (accessed May 23, 2013).
22. Editorial, "Diktatura razrushit strany [Dictatorship destroys the country]," *Obshchaya gazeta*, May 25-31, 2000, http://dlib.eastview.com/sources/article.jsp?id=3552081 (accessed January 30, 2012).
23. "Reformirovaniye Administratsii RF Prezidenta [Reform of the Administration of the RF President]," 25. 21.
24. "Putin Sacks Yeltsin's Daughter."
25. "Gusinskiy vs. Russia," European Court of Human Rights, May 19, 2004, para. 19, http://cmiskp.echr.coe.int/tkp197/view.asp?item=1&portal=hbkm&action=html&highlight=70276/01&sessionid=85933970&skin=hudoc-en (accessed February 3, 2012).
26. David Hoffman, "Probers Jail Top Russian Media Mogul," *Washington Post*, June 14, 2000, http://www.washingtonpost.com/wp-srv/WPcap/2000-06/14/060r-061400-idx.html (accessed January 25, 2012).
27. Vladimir Gusinskiy, "Vlast' nachala dvizheniye k totalitarizmu [Power has begun a move toward totalitarianism]," *Segodya*, June 16, 2000, http://www.segodnya.ru/w3s.nsf/Archive/2000_128_polit_text_segodnya1.html (accessed January 31, 2012).
28. "Gusinskiy vs. Russia."
29. Parliamentary Assembly, Council of Europe, "Allegations of Politically Motivated Abuses of the Criminal Justice System in Council of Europe Member States," September 29, 2009, http://assembly.coe.int/Documents/WorkingDocs/Doc09/EDOC12038.pdf (accessed February 3, 2012).
30. Aleksandr Arkhangel'skiy, "Protokol N. 6. Aktsii v obmen na svobodu: takovo usloviye sdelki mezhdu 'Gazprom-Media' i gr. Gusinskim [Protocol No. 6. Shares for freedom: That was the deal struck between Gazprom-Media and citizen Gusinskiy]," *Izvestiya*, September 20, 2000, http://dlib.eastview.com.proxy.lib.muohio.edu/browse/doc/3049720 (accessed May 9, 2013).
31. Vladimir Putin, "Annual Address to the Federal Assembly of the Russian Federation," Kremlin, July 8, 2000, http://archive.kremlin.ru/eng/speeches/2000/07/08/0000_type70029type82912_70658.shtml (accessed February 21, 2012).
32. Putin, "Annual Address to the Federal Assembly of the Russian Federation."
33. Yevgeniy Kiselyev, "Itogi Commentary," BBC Monitoring, July 9, 2000, http://russialist.org/4396##14 (accessed May 8, 2013).
34. Romesh Ratnesar, "Putin's Media Blitz," *Time*, April 30, 2001, http://www.time.com/time/magazine/article/0,9171,107338,00.html (accessed February 3, 2012).
35. "Putin's Approval Rating Still Solid," Interfax, July 6, 2000, http://toolkit.dialog.com/intranet/cgi/present?STYLE=739318018&PRESENT=DB=985,AN=118900828,FM=9,SEARCH=MD.GenericSearch (accessed February 2012).
36. "Chubays Says Putin, Big Businessmen Must Sit," Interfax, July 14, 2011, http://toolkit.dialog.com/intranet/cgi/present?STYLE=739318018&PRESENT=DB=985,AN=119300730,FM=9,SEARCH=MD.GenericSearch (accessed February 4, 2012).
37. Charles Clover, Fiona Fleck, and Arkady Ostrovsky, "Putin Says There Is to Be No Review of Privatizations," *Financial Times*, July 29, 2000.

38. Abramovich, "Third Witness Statement of Roman Arkadievich Abramovich," para. 179.

39. "Putin: Businesses Can Play Positive Role in Strengthening Russia," Interfax, July 28, 2000, http://toolkit.dialog.com/intranet/cgi/present?STYLE=739318018&PRESENT=DB=985,AN =120000859,FM=9,SEARCH=MD.GenericSearch (accessed February 4, 2012).

40. Milov et al., "Putin: Corruption."

41. "Yakhty dlya prezidenta: Chast' III [Yachts for the president: Part III]," *Novaya gazeta*, June 6, 2005, http://www.novayagazeta.ru/inquests/27211.html (accessed June 1, 2013).

42. Gromov, "Poglotiteli [Scavengers]."

43. High Court of Justice, "Judgment by Mr. Justice Andrew Smith, Fiona Trust & Holding Corporation and Others vs. Privalov and Others," para. 581.

44. "Yakhty dlya prezidenta [Yachts for the president]," *Novaya gazeta*, May 30, 2005, http://www .novayagazeta.ru/economy/27278.html (accessed June 5, 2013).

45. "Yakhty dlya prezidenta: Chast' II [Yachts for the president: Part II]," *Novaya gazeta*, June 2, 2005, http://www.novayagazeta.ru/economy/27242.html (accessed June 6, 2013).

46. "Yakhty dlya prezidenta [Yachts for the president]."

47. Luke Harding, "Abramovich v Berezovsky: What Have We Learned So Far?," *Guardian*, November 7, 2011, http://www.theGuardian.co.uk/world/2011/nov/07/abramovich-berezov sky (accessed February 1, 2012).

48. Sarah Lyall, "A Clash of Titans Exposes Russia's Seamy Underside," *New York Times*, November 9, 2011, http://www.nytimes.com/2011/11/10/world/europe/berezovsky-v-abramovich -offers-peek-into-post-soviet-russia.html?pagewanted=all (accessed February 1, 2012).

49. Judah, *Fragile Empire*, 42.

50. Starobin and Belton, "Gazprom: Russia's Enron?"

51. "Miller Rising," *Economist*, May 31, 2001, http://www.economist.com/node/639683 (accessed June 7, 2011).

52. "Gazprom History, 2001," Gazprom, n.d., http://www.gazprom.ru/about/history/chronicle /2001/ (accessed May 8, 2011).

53. Boris Nemtsov and Vladimir Milov, "Putin and Gazprom," translated by Dave Essel, 2008, http://www.europeanenergyreview.eu/data/docs/Viewpoints/Putin%20and%20Gazprom_Nem tsov%20en%20Milov.pdf (accessed March 12, 2012), 5.

54. Åslund, "Why Gazprom Resembles a Crime Syndicate."

55. Nemtsov and Milov, "Putin and Gazprom," 11.

56. Irina Reznik, " 'Nado byt' gotovym k tomu, chto uzhalyat': Dmitriy Lebedev predsedatel' pravleniya Bank Rossiya [We must be prepared moreover, for a sting: Dmitriy Lebedev chairman of Bank Rossiya]," *Vedomosti*, June 17, 2008, http://dlib.eastview.com.proxy.lib.muohio.edu /browse/doc/17617809 (accessed May 9, 2013).

57. Nemtsov and Milov, "Putin and Gazprom," 13.

58. Reznik and Petrova, "Pomoshchniki 'Rossii' [Helpers of 'Rossiya']."

59. Nemtsov and Milov, "Putin and Gazprom," 12.

60. Starobin and Belton. "Gazprom: Russia's Enron?"

61. Jeanne Whalen, "Gazprom Buys Back Itera's Stake in Purgaz: Company's Vote Signals an End to Old Ways," *Wall Street Journal*, December 18, 2001, http://online.wsj.com/article /SB1008623557630055240.html (accessed October 10, 2012).

62. Jonathan P. Stern, *The Future of Russian Gas and Gazprom* (New York: Oxford University Press, 2005), 93.

63. Åslund, *Russia's Capitalist Revolution*, 230.

64. Nemtsov and Milov, "Putin and Gazprom," 17.

65. Andrei Shleifer, *A Normal Country: Russia after Communism* (Cambridge, MA: Harvard University Press, 2005), 167–68.

66. Peter Truscott, *Putin's Progress*, London: Pocket Books, 2005; Robert Moore, *A Time to Die: The Kursk Disaster*, New York: Doubleday, 2002; Carré, Jean-Michel, dir., *Kursk—A Submarine in Troubled Waters*, 2004.

67. Patrick Jackson, "Media Struggles for *Kursk* Truth," BBC News, August 21, 2000, http://news .bbc.co.uk/2/hi/europe/886016.stm (accessed February 26, 201).

68. Nataliya Rostova, "Interview with Marina Litvinovitch," *Slon.ru*, May 31, 2011, http://slon.ru /russia/kogda_poyavilsya_putin_komanda_elcina_vospryala_d-591758.xhtml.

69. Jean-Michel Carré, "*Kursk*: A Submarine in Troubled Waters," 2004, http://www.youtube.com /watch?v=985zeVQLnDc.

70. Carré, "*Kursk*."

71. Shevtsova, *Putin's Russia*, 117–20.

72. Tina Burrett, *Television and Presidential Power in Putin's Russia* (New York: Routledge, 2011), 41.

73. Stephen Dalziel, "Spectre of *Kursk* Haunts Putin," BBC, August 12, 2001, http://news.bbc .co.uk/2/hi/europe/1487112.stm (accessed February 25, 2012).

74. Vladimir Putin, "Interview on Vesti, RTR, August 23, 2000," in Burrett, *Television and Presidential Power in Putin's Russia*, 40.

75. "Boris Berezovsky's Witness Statement," *Guardian*, November 2, 2011, http://www.theGuard ian.co.uk/world/interactive/2011/nov/02/boris-berezovsky-witness-statement-full (accessed February 23, 2012).

76. Testimony in the Berezovsky vs. Abramovich Trial, November 7, 2011, 56, http://pravo.ru /store/interdoc/doc/307/Day_21.pdf (accessed February 23, 2012).

77. Burrett, *Television and Presidential Power in Putin's Russia*, 49.

78. Vladimir Putin, "Interview with *Le Figaro*," Kremlin, October 26, 2000, http://archive.krem lin.ru/eng/speeches/2000/10/26/0000_type82916_134301.shtml (accessed February 23, 2012).

79. Testimony in the Berezovsky vs. Abramovich Trial, 58.

80. Vladimir Novikov, "Difficulties of a Georgian Translation," *Kommersant Vlast*, February 11, 2008, http://www.kommersant.ru/doc/851013 (accessed February 26, 2012).

81. Tom Parfitt, "Badri Patarkatsishvili: Georgian Billionaire and Promoter of Putin Latterly Exiled to London," *Guardian*, February 14, 2008, http://www.theGuardian.co.uk/world/2008 /feb/15/georgia.russia (accessed February 26, 2012).

82. Testimony in the Berezovsky vs. Abramovich Trial, 25.

83. Testimony in the Berezovsky vs. Abramovich Trial, 105–6.

84. Testimony in the Berezovsky vs. Abramovich Trial, November 8, 2011, 135–36, http://pravo .ru/store/interdoc/doc/308/Day_22.pdf (accessed February 23, 2012).

85. Testimony in the Berezovsky vs. Abramovich Trial, November 8, 2011, 83.

86. Testimony in the Berezovsky vs. Abramovich Trial, November 8, 2011, 90.

87. Rstaki and Borisov, "Delo Putina [The Putin affair]."

88. Semenenko, "Book Is Closed on Probe of Mabetex."

89. World Bank, "Pavel Borodin," Stolen Asset Recovery Initiative, 2013, http://star.worldbank .org/corruption-cases/node/18561 (accessed May 18, 2014).

90. Berres, "Filipp Turover."

91. Saradzhyan, "Warrant Issued for Borodin Witness."

92. Clover et al., "Putin Says There Is to Be No Review of Privatizations."

93. Åslund, *Russia's Capitalist Revolution*, 228.

94. Ignatius, "Sergey Kolesnikov's Tale of Palatial Corruption, Russian Style."

95. "Fotographii 'dvortsa Putina' v Praskoveevke na Chyornom more [Photos of 'Putin's Palace' in the Black Sea Praskoveevka]," RuLeaks, January 18, 2011, http://ruleaks.net/1901 (accessed January 8, 2012).

96. Rinat Sagdiyev and Irina Reznik, "Kakimi proyektami, krome dvortsa v Praskoveevke, zanimalis' druz'ya Putina [What other projects besides the palace in Praskoveevka are Putin's friends engaged in]," *Vedomosti*, April 4, 2011, http://www.vedomosti.ru/library/news/1387741/kak imi_proektami_krome_dvorca_v_praskoveevke_zanimalis?full#cut (accessed May 5, 2012).

97. Kolesnikov, "Interview with Masha Gessen et al."

98. Yevgeniya Al'bats, "Chisto konkretnyy kandidat [A very specific candidate]," *New Times*, February 27, 2012, http://dlib.eastview.com.proxy.lib.muohio.edu/searchresults/article.jsp?art=6&id=26696471 (accessed February 28, 2012).

99. Al'bats, "Chisto konkretnyy kandidat [A very specific candidate]."

100. Nataliya Vetlitskaya, "Skazka [Fairy tale]," LiveJournal.com, August 15, 2011, http://n-vetlitskaya.livejournal.com/72068.html?thread=2321028#t2321028 (accessed October 18, 2013).

101. "Pevitsa Vetlitskaya rasskazala v bloge 'skazku,' kak uchastvovala v 'sverkhsekretnom korporative dlya tsarya' [Singer Vetlitskaya tells the 'fairy tale' in her blog how she participated in a 'top-secret corporate party for the tsar']," News.ru, August 17, 2011, http://www.newsru.com/russia/17aug2011/vetlitskaya.html (accessed October 8, 2013).

102. Luke Harding, "Concert Raises Questions about Putin's Alleged Love for Abba," *Guardian*, February 6, 2009, http://www.theGuardian.com/world/2009/feb/06/vladimir-putin-russia-abba-tribute-concert (accessed May 9, 2013).

103. Stephen Grey, Jason Bush, and Roman Anin, "Billion-Dollar Medical Project Helped Fund 'Putin's Palace' on the Black Sea," Reuters, May 21, 2014, http://www.reuters.com/investigates/russia/#article/part1 (accessed May 21, 2014).

104. Catherine Belton, "A Realm Fit for a Tsar," *Financial Times*, November 11, 2011, http://www.ft.com/intl/cms/s/0/69d1db86-1aa6-11e1-ae14-00144feabdc0.html?siteedition=intl#axzz2hhM6rWb1 (accessed November 12, 2011).

105. Al'bats, "Chisto konkretnyy kandidat [A very specific candidate]"; and Witten, et al., "Siemens Agrees to Record-Setting $800 Million in FCPA Penalties."

106. Belton, "A Realm Fit for a Tsar."

107. Kolesnikov, "Interview with Masha Gessen et al."

108. Anin, "Upravleniye 'del'tsov' prezidenta [The administration of 'hustlers' of the president]."

109. "Bearer Shares," *Tax Haven Guide*, October 13, 2013, http://www.taxhavensguide.com/bearer-shares.php (accessed October 13, 2013).

110. Kolesnikov, "Interview with Masha Gessen et al."

111. Jason Bush, Elizabeth Piper, Stephen Grey, and Maria Tsvetkova, "When Putin Ordered Up New Hospitals, His Associates Botched the Operation," Reuters, May 22, 2014, http://www.reuters.com/investigates/russia/#article/part2 (accessed May 22, 2014).

112. Al'bats, "Chisto konkretnyy kandidat [A very specific candidate]."

113. Belton, "A Realm Fit for a Tsar."

114. Al'bats, "Chisto konkretnyy kandidat [A very specific candidate]."

115. Ignatius, "Sergey Kolesnikov's Tale of Palatial Corruption, Russian Style."

116. "Ziyad Manasir," Forbes.com, 2013, http://www.forbes.com/profile/ziyad-manasir/ (accessed October 18, 2013).

117. Al'bats, "Chisto konkretnyy kandidat [A very specific candidate]."

118. Pavel Sedakov, "Pamyatnik epokhe: Dvorets podryadchika 'Gazproma' [Monument to the epoch: Palace contracted by 'Gazprom']," *Forbes.ru*, December 17, 2010, http://www.forbes.ru/ekonomika/nedvizhimost/61256-pamyatnik-epohe-neftyanogo-raya (accessed October 8, 2013).

119. Ignatius, "Sergey Kolesnikov's Tale of Palatial Corruption, Russian Style."

120. Sergey Kolesnikov, "Bor'ba s korruptsiyey: Prizrak dvortsa [The struggle with corruption: The specter of the palace]," *Vedomosti*, May 24, 2011, http://dlib.eastview.com.proxy.lib.muohio.edu/browse/doc/24806636 (accessed October 18, 2013).

121. Korobov and Kashin, "Interview with Vladimir Kozhin."

122. Grey et al., "Billion-Dollar Medical Project Helped Fund 'Putin's Palace' on the Black Sea"; Bush et al., "When Putin Ordered Up New Hospitals, His Associates Botched the Operation."

123. Anin, "Upravleniye 'del'tsov' prezidenta [The administration of 'hustlers' of the president]"; Yevgeniy Titov, "Prem'ernoye povedeniye [Premiere behavior]," *Novaya gazeta*, February 14, 2011, http://dlib.eastview.com.proxy.lib.muohio.edu/browse/doc/24209635 (accessed May 9, 2012).

124. " 'Putin's Friends' Have Falling Out in Cherepovets," Olgaskaspb.com, April 17, 2012, http://oglaskaspb.com/bank/a43/ (accessed June 9, 2012).

125. "Businessmen 'Friends of Putin' Brought under Criminal Investigation," Oglaskaspb.com, July 10, 2012, http://oglaskaspb.com/eng/bank/a59/ (accessed June 9, 2013).

126. Kolesnikov, "Interview with Masha Gessen et al."

127. "Honorary Consulate and Diplomatic Passport," Honoraryconsul.ru, n.d., http://www.honoraryconsul.ru/index.php?an=dip_pass (accessed March 9, 2013).

128. Roman Shleynov, Vlad Lavrov, Aleksandr Bozinovski, and Stevan Dojčinović, "Honorary Consuls: Wealth Can Beget Wealth," Organized Crime and Corruption Reporting Project, November 29, 2009, http://reportingproject.net/visa/index.php?option=com_content&view=article&id=56:honorary-consul&catid=34:visa&Itemid=53 (accessed October 8, 2013).

129. Alexander Kulygin, "Political Monster 'Berlusputin' Menaces Moscow Theatergoers," RFE/RL Russian Service, February 2012, http://www.youtube.com/watch?v=qNhVZc6KCbo (accessed February 26, 2012).

130. Evans et al., "WikiLeaks Cables."

131. "Reformirovaniye Administratsii RF Prezidenta [Reform of the Administration of the RF President]," 25.21.

132. Reuters, "Navalny Hit with New Theft Charges," *Moscow Times*, October 30, 2013, http://www.themoscowtimes.com/news/article/navalny-hit-with-new-theft-charges/488709.html (accessed October 30, 2013).

133. Earley, *Comrade J*, 299.

134. Earley, *Comrade J*, 301.

135. "Vladimir Putin's Presidential Inauguration," RT, May 7, 2012, http://www.youtube.com/watch?v=TNiWnSOsAnE (accessed May 7, 2012).

136. William Grimes, "Sergei Tretyakov, Spy Who Fled to U.S., Dies at 53," *New York Times*, July 9, 2010, http://www.nytimes.com/2010/07/10/world/europe/10tretyakov.html?_r=0 (accessed June 8, 2013); "Afterwords with Pete Earley and Sergei Tretyakov," C-SPAN, January 28, 2008, http://www.c-spanvideo.org/program/Tret (accessed May 8, 2012).

137. Stratfor, "Re: [CT] Contradictory Quotes about Tretyakov Autopsy," Wikileaks, September 7, 2010, http://wikileaks.org/gifiles/docs/1168958_re-ct-contradictory-quotes-about-tretyakov-autopsy-.html (accessed October 11, 2013).

138. Shevtsova, *Putin's Russia*, 123.

139. Dale R. Herspring and Jacob Kipp, "Understanding the Elusive Mr. Putin," *Problems of Post-Communism* 48, no. 5 (2001): 13; Carol R. Saivetz, "Putin's Caspian Policy," Belfer Center for Science and International Affairs, Harvard University, October 2000, http://belfercenter.ksg.harvard.edu/publication/3101/putins_caspian_policy.html (accessed September 11, 2011).

140. Lucas, *The New Cold War*.

141. Sabrina Tavernise, "American Jailed as Spy in Moscow Is Freed on Putin's Orders," *New York Times*, December 15, 2000, http://www.nytimes.com/2000/12/15/world/american-jailed-as-spy-in-moscow-is-freed-on-putin-s-orders-us-welcomes-gesture.html?pagewanted=print&src=pm (accessed June 3, 2013).

142. Shevtsova, *Putin's Russia*, 145.

143. "Lesnevskaya: Yel'tsin pri Putine molchal, opasayas' za detey i vnukov [Lesnevskaya: Under Putin, Yel'tsin remained silent out of fear for his children and grandchildren]," Sobesednik.ru, No. 168, 2007, http://www.newsru.com/russia/27jun2007/lesnevskaya.html.

144. Mikhayl Kas'yanov and Yevgeniy Kiselev, "Mikhayl Kas'yanov: Yel'tsin sam soglasilsya na nesvobodu' [Yel'tsin himself agreed to a lack of freedom]," *New Times*, September 21, 2009, http://dlib.eastview.com.proxy.lib.muohio.edu/browse/doc/20645756 (accessed July 9, 2013).

145. Shevtsova, *Putin's Russia*, 157–58.

146. Olga Kryshtanovskaya and Stephen White, "Putin's Militocracy," *Post-Soviet Affairs*, October–December 2003, 294.

Chapter Seven: Russia, Putin, and the Future of Kleptocratic Authoritarianism

1. Nicholas Eberstadt, "Putin's Hollowed-out Homeland," *Wall Street Journal*, May 8, 2014, http://rbth.com/articles/2013/01/12/russian_authorities_plan_to_cut_health_spending_in _2013_21817.html (accessed May 8, 2014).

2. U.S. Department of State, "Trafficking in Persons Report 2013: Russia," Washington, DC, 2013, 310–12.

3. U.S. Department of State, "Trafficking in Persons Report 2013: Russia," 310–12.

4. Yuliya Latynina, "Russia: A Superpower If Measured in Mansions and Yachts," unpublished mimeo, Putin's Russia Symposium, Havighurst Center, Miami University, Oxford, Ohio, 2011.

5. Nemtsov and Martynyuk, "Nezavisimyy Ekspertnyy doklad [Independent expert report]"; Aleksandr Sokolov, "Zatraty na Olimpiadu Sochi-2014 rekordnyye za vsyu Istoriyu Olimpi- yskikh igr [Cost for the Sochi 2014 Olympics is a record in the history of the Olympic Games]," *Initsiativnaya gruppa po provedeniyu referenduma*, August 16, 2012, http://igpr.ru/articles/ zatraty_na_olimpiadu_v_sochi (accessed August 8, 2013).

6. Varvara Petrenko, "Russian Authorities Plan to Cut Health Spending in 2013," *Russia beyond the Headlines*, January 12, 2013, http://rbth.com/articles/2013/01/12/russian_authorities _plan_to_cut_health_spending_in_2013_21817.html (accessed May 7, 2014).

7. Eberstadt, "Putin's Hollowed-out Homeland."

8. Dmitriy Oreshkin, "Beg: Pochemu uyezhayut iz Rossii? [Running: Why leave Russia?]," *Novaya gazeta*, January 30, 2011, http://old.novayagazeta.ru/data/2011/010/00.html (accessed May 8, 2014).

9. Masha Gessen, "The Living Ghosts of Moscow," *New York Times*, May 29, 2014, http://www .nytimes.com/2014/05/29/opinion/gessen-the-living-ghosts-of-moscow.html?ref=opinion&_r =0 (accessed May 29, 2014).

10. Transparency International, *Corruption Perceptions Index 2013*, 2014, http://cpi.transparency .org/cpi2013/ (accessed April 9, 2014).

11. Indem Fund, *Corruption Process in Russia: Level, Structure, Trends* (Moscow: Indem Fund, 2005).

12. Transparency International, "Russia," *Global Corruption Barometer 2013*, 2014, http://www .transparency.org/gcb2013/country/?country=russia (accessed May 3, 2014).

13. Rebecca Kesby, "Why Russia Locks Up So Many Entrepreneurs," BBC World Service, July 4, 2012, http://www.bbc.com/news/magazine-18706597 (accessed November 27, 2013).

14. Elena Masyuk, "Henry Reznik: Our Court Is a Stranger to Doubts," *Novaya gazeta*, January 14, 2014, http://en.novayagazeta.ru/politics/61770.html (accessed January 24, 2014).

15. "Russia's Lower House Adopts Bill on Economic Amnesty," Russian Legal Information Agency, July 3, 2013, http://rapsinews.com/legislation_news/20130703/268004684.html (accessed March 28, 2014).

16. V. V. Putin, "Speech at Naval Parade, Sevastopol," Kremlin, May 9, 2014, http://kremlin.ru /transcripts/20992 (accessed May 25, 2014).

17. Levada Center, "Mozhet, zavtra voyna [Perhaps tomorrow there will be war]," May 6, 2014, http://www.levada.ru/06-05-2014/mozhet-zavtra-voina (accessed May 11, 2014).

18. Presidential Council, "Problemy zhiteley Kryma [Problems of Crimean residents]," Presidential Council for the Development of Civil Society and Human Rights, May 7, 2014, http://www .president-sovet.ru/structure/gruppa_po_migratsionnoy_politike/materialy/problemy_zhiteley _kryma.php?print=Y (accessed May 11, 2014).

19. OECD, Human Resources Management Country Profiles, "Russian Federation," Decem- ber 6, 2012, http://www.oecd.org/gov/pem/OECD%20HRM%20Profile%20-%20Russia .pdf (accessed February 23, 2014).

20. Sergei Guriev, "Why I Am Not Returning to Russia," *New York Times*, June 5, 2013, http://www.nytimes.com/2013/06/06/opinion/global/sergei-guriev-why-i-am-not-returning-to-russia.html?pagewanted=all (accessed June 6, 2013).

21. Yulia Ponomareva, "New Wave of Russian Emigration: Leave or Stay?," *Russia beyond the Headlines*, June 10, 2013, http://rbth.com/society/2013/06/10/new_wave_of_russian_emigration_leave_or_stay_26923.html (accessed May 7, 2014).

22. Ponomareva, "New Wave of Russian Emigration."

23. Interfax, "Number of Russians Eager to Leave the Country Almost Doubled since 2009," *Russia beyond the Headlines*, June 6, 2013, http://rbth.com/news/2013/06/06/number_of_russians_eager_to_leave_the_country_almost_doubled_since_2009_26799.html (accessed May 9, 2014).

24. Freedom House, "Russia: Freedom in the World 2014," 2014, http://www.freedomhouse.org/report/freedom-world/2014/russia-0#.U4N7NvldWSo (accessed May 27, 2014).

25. Levada Center, "On the Growth of Social and Political Infantilism in Russia," May 16, 2014, http://www.levada.ru/16-05-2014/o-roste-sotsialno-politicheskogo-infantilizma-v-rossii (accessed May 27, 2014).

26. "London Has the Most Billionaires in the World," *al Jazeera*, May 11, 2014, http://www.aljazeera.com/news/europe/2014/05/london-most-billionaires-world-201451101120149236.html (accessed May 27, 2014).

27. Credit Suisse, *Global Wealth Report 2013.*

28. Hazem Beblawi, "The Rentier State in the Arab World," in Giaccomo Luciani, ed., *The Arab State* (London: Routledge, 1990), 85.

29. U.S. Energy Information Administration, "Russia," November 26, 2013; Olga Oliker, Keith Crane, and Lowell H. Schwartz, *Russian Foreign Policy: Sources and Implications* (Santa Monica, CA: RAND, 2009), 77.

30. Henry Meyer and Agnes Lovasz, "Russia Faces Economy Trap as Oil Decline Looms, EBRD Says," Bloomberg.com, December 14, 2012, http://www.bloomberg.com/news/2012-12-13/russia-at-risk-from-dwindling-oil-reserves-european-bank-says.html (accessed November 4, 2013).

31. Samuel Bakowski, "Courage to Face Down Corruption: Russia's Endemic Problems," Transparency International, January 29, 2010, http://blog.transparency.org/2010/01/29/courage-to-face-down-corruption-%E2%80%93-russia%E2%80%99s-endemic-problems/ (accessed November 22, 2013); Aleksey Dumovskiy, "Russian Police Officer, Pt. 1," YouTube, November 6, 2009, http://www.youtube.com/watch?v=R4vB2a15dOU (accessed November 22, 2013).

32. Vladimir Milov, Leonard L. Coburn, and Igor Danchenko, "Russia's Energy Policy, 1992–2005," *Eurasian Geography and Economics*, 2006: 285–313.

33. Anders Åslund, "How Rosneft Is Turning into Another Gazprom," *Moscow Times*, June 21, 2013, http://www.themoscowtimes.com/opinion/article/how-rosneft-is-turning-into-another-gazprom/482022.html (accessed June 22, 2013).

34. Vladimir Putin, "Press Service Announcements," Archive of the Official Site of the 2008–2012 Prime Minister of the Russian Federation Vladimir Putin, March 3, 2009, http://archive.premier.gov.ru/eng/events/messages/3519 (accessed May 23, 2013); Vladimir Putin, "Press Service Announcements," Archive of the Official Site of the 2008–12 Prime Minister, February 16, 2011, http://archive.premier.gov.ru/eng/events/messages/14163/ (accessed January 23, 2012).

35. Åslund, "How Rosneft Is Turning into Another Gazprom."

36. "Annual Report," Statoil, 2012, http://www.statoil.com/annualreport2012/en/Download%20Center%20Files/01%20Key%20downloads/11%20Annual%20Report%20on%20Form%2020-F%202012/AnnualreportonForm20-F.pdf (accessed April 9, 2014).

37. Sergei Guriev and Aleh Tsyvinski, "Rosneft Delivers a Blow to Market Economy," *Moscow Times*, October 30, 2012, http://www.themoscowtimes.com/opinion/article/rosneft-delivers-a-blow-to-market-economy/470615.html (accessed January 30, 2014).

38. "Russia's Wounded Giant," *Economist*, March 23, 2013, http://www.economist.com/news /business/21573975-worlds-biggest-gas-producer-ailing-it-should-be-broken-up-russias-wounded -giant (accessed February 21, 2014).

39. Milov and Nemtsov, "Putin and Gazprom."

40. Matthew Kaminski, "The Man Who Stood Up to Putin," *Wall Street Journal*, May 9, 2014, http://online.wsj.com/articles/SB10001424052702304885404579552120262256240 ?mg=reno64-wsj&url=http%3A%2F%2Fonline.wsj.com%2Farticle%2FSB1000142405270 23048854045795521202622562340.html (accessed May 10, 2014).

41. "William F. Browder," Hermitage Capital Management, 2008, http://web.archive.org/web /20080727055246/http://www.hermitagefund.com/index.pl/asset_management/ceo.html.

42. Andrew E. Kramer, "At Gazprom, Investors in Battle for the Board," *International Herald Tribune*, June 27, 2006, http://www.nytimes.com/2006/06/27/business/worldbusiness/27 iht-gazprom.2066786.html?_r=0 (accessed January 8, 2012).

43. Vladimir Putin, "News Conference on Magnitskiy," *60 Minutes*, CBS News, February 16, 2014, http://www.cbsnews.com/news/americans-fight-to-expose-corruption-in-russia/ (accessed March 7, 2014).

44. "Russia Finds Magnitsky Posthumously Guilty of Fraud," BBC World News, July 11, 2013, http://www.bbc.com/news/world-europe-23265423 (accessed July 12, 2013).

45. John McMillan and James Twiss, *Gazprom and Hermitage Capital: Shareholder Activism in Russia*. Case Study. (Palo Alto, CA: Stanford Graduate School of Business, 2002); Edward Lucas, *Deception: The Untold Story of East-West Espionage Today* (London: Walker Books, 2012), 23–51; and a Web page devoted to the Magnitskiy case, http://russian-untouchables.com/eng/.

46. American Embassy Kyiv to U.S. Secretary of State, "Ukraine: Too Early to Write Off Ros-UkrEnergo in 2009," Wikileaks, October 30, 2008, http://wikileaks.ch/cable/2008/10/08KY IV2173.html (accessed November 23, 2011).

47. Glenn R. Simpson, "U.S. Identifies Russian 'Nexus' of Organized Crime," Main Justice. International Assessment and Strategy Center, February 10, 2010, http://www.strategycenter.net /research/pubID.223/pub_detail.asp (accessed May 29, 2014).

48. Michael B. Mukasey, "Remarks Prepared for Delivery by Attorney General Michael B. Mukasey on International Organized Crime at the Center for Strategic and International Studies," Justice.gov, April 23, 2008, http://www.justice.gov/ag/speeches/2008/ag_speech_080423.html (accessed May 29, 2014).

49. Roman Kupchinsky, "The Strange Ties between Semyon Mogilevich and Vladimir Putin," *Eurasia Daily Monitor* 6, no. 57 (2009).

50. U.S. Government, "Russia 090326: Basic Political Developments," Wikileaks, March 26, 2009, https://www.google.com/url?sa=t&rct=j&q=&esrc=s&source=web&cd=4&ved=0CDs QFjAD&url=http%3A%2F%2Fwikileaks.org%2Fgifiles%2Fattach%2F60%2F60052_Russia %2520090326.doc&ei=H56HU9zVIM2uyASDmYKYCQ&usg=AFQjCNHtoazuo0ZQJU FGIW_rSXIHByxHew (accessed May 29, 2014).

51. Julia Ioffe, "Net Impact: One Man's Cyber-Crusade against Russian Corruption," *New Yorker*, April 4, 2011, www.newyorker.com/reporting/2011/04/04/110404fa_fact_ioffe (accessed Feburary 6, 2012).

52. Åslund, "Why Gazprom Resembles a Crime Syndicate."

53. "Companies with Gazprom Participation and Other Affiliated Entities," Gazprom, 2014, http://www.gazprom.com/about/subsidiaries/list-items/ (accessed May 28, 2014).

54. Andreas Heinrich, "Gazprom's Expansion Strategy in Europe and the Liberalization of EU Energy Markets," *Russian Analytical Digest*, February 2008, 8–14.

55. "Exxon: Subsidiaries of the Registrant," Securities and Exchange Commission, December 31, 2010, http://www.sec.gov/Archives/edgar/data/34088/000119312511050134/dex21.htm (accessed May 27, 2014).

56. "Gazprom—New Russian Weapon," *Kommersant*, January 30, 2008, www.kommersant.com /p845604/Gazprom_Business_Gas/.

57. Mikhayl Zygar and Valeriy Panyushkin, "Gazprom: New Russian Weapon," *Kommersant*, January 30, 2008, http://www.kommersant.com/p845604/Gazprom_Business_Gas/ (accessed December 4, 2013); "Gazprom Management Board," Gazprom, 2014, http://www.gazprom .com/about/management/board/ (accessed May 29, 2014); "Gazprom Board of Directors," Gazprom, 2014, http://www.gazprom.com/about/management/directors/ (accessed May 29, 2014); Alyakrinskaya and Privylovskiy, "Prem'er v krugu 'Sem'i' [The premier among the circle of 'the Family']"; Roman Shleynov, "Dzhyudo: Svoikh ne brosayut [Judo: They don't throw their own]," *Novaya gazeta*, June 29, 2009. http://www.novayagazeta.ru/inquests/44531.html (accessed May 29, 2014).

58. Brendan Conway, "Grant on Gazprom: 'Worst-Managed Company on the Planet' Is a Buy," *Barron's*, May 5, 2014, http://blogs.barrons.com/focusonfunds/2014/05/05/grant-on-gazprom -worst-managed-company-on-the-planet-is-a-buy/ (accessed May 5, 2014).

59. Konstantin Sonin, "Gas Deal Profit Depends on Costs of Corruption," *Moscow Times*, May 28, 2014, http://www.themoscowtimes.com/opinion/article/gas-deal-profit-depends-on-costs-of -corruption/501102.html (accessed May 28, 2014).

60. "Suzanna Taverne Appointed as New BBC Trustee," BBC Trust, December 15, 2011, http:// www.bbc.co.uk/bbctrust/news/press_releases/2011/suzanna_taverne.html (accessed May 8, 2014).

61. "Compensation and Liability Insurance of Members of the Board of Directors, Members of the Management Committee and Chairman of the Management Committee of OAO Gazprom," Gazprom, 2012, http://www.gazprom.com/f/posts/94/225493/directors-management-remu neration-insurance-2012-en.pdf (accessed May 23, 2014).

62. "Capital Flight from Russia Reaches $40 Billion in January—Minister," *RIA-Novosti*, February 26, 2009, http://en.rian.ru/russia/20090226/120317628.html. (accessed September 8, 2012).

63. Kathryn Hendley, "Varieties of Legal Dualism: Making Sense of the Role of Law in Contemporary Russia," *Wisconsin Journal of International Law*, 29, no. 2 (2011): 233–363.

64. Masyuk, "Henry Reznik: Our Court Is a Stranger to Doubts."

65. Shleynov et al., "Honorary Consuls."

66. "Consulate of Luxembourg in St. Petersburg," Embassy Pages, September 27, 2013, http:// www.embassypages.com/missions/embassy1392/ (accessed May 25, 2014).

67. Viktor Cherkesov, "Nel'zya dopustit' chtoby voiny prevratilis' v torgovtsev [We must not allow warriors to turn into traders]," *Kommersant*, October 9, 2009, http://dlib.eastview.com.proxy .lib.muohio.edu/browse/doc/12708486 (accessed January 7, 2011).

68. Andrei Illarionov, "Testimony," House Committee on Foreign Affairs, February 25, 2009, http://foreignaffairs.house.gov/111/ill022509.pdf (accessed December 8, 2012).

69. Andrei Piontkovsky, "The Dying Mutant," *Journal of Democracy* 20, no. 2 (April 2009): 52.

70. John Helmer, "Medvedev Reelection Fight Leads to Punchup on Russian Shipbuilder Board," *Business Insider*, May 13, 2011, http://www.businessinsider.com/medvedev-reelection-fight -leads-to-punchup-on-russian-shipbuilder-board-2011-5?utm_source=feedburner&utm_me dium=feed&utm_campaign=Feed%3A+businessinsider+%28Business+Insider%29.

71. Henry Meyer and Il'ya Arkhipov, "Fathers, Sons, and Russian Power Games: The Sons of Putin Allies Land in Key Positions in State Companies, to Medvedev's Chagrin," *Bloomberg Businessweek*, May 19, 2011, http://www.businessweek.com/magazine/content/11_22 /b4230014956456.htm. (accessed April 7, 2013); Boris Nemtsov, *Putin's Clan in the Government and Business*, YouTube, June 19, 2012, http://www.youtube.com/watch?v=hj5FdOiBnXk.

72. Aleh Tsyvinski and Sergei Guriev, "The Purge of the Kremlin Chairmen," *Moscow Times*, April 13, 2011, http://www.themoscowtimes.com/opinion/article/the-purge-of-the-kremlin-chair men/434935.html (accessed January 3, 2014).

73. Vladimir Putin, "St. Petersburg International Economic Forum," Kremlin, May 23, 2014, http://eng.kremlin.ru/news/7230 (accessed May 24, 2014).

74. Louise Armitstead, "UK Police Investigate Russian Fraud at European Bank for Reconstruction and Development," *Telegraph (UK)*, January 19, 2011, http://www.telegraph.co.uk/finance

/newsbysector/banksandfinance/8267716/UK-police-investigate-Russian-fraud-at-European
-Bank-for-Reconstruction-and-Development.html (accessed January 23, 2013).

75. Venelin I. Ganev, "Post-Communism as an Episode of State Building: A Reversed Tillyan Per-spective," *Communist and Post-Communist Studies* 48, no. 4 (2005): 441.

76. Parliamentary Assembly, the Council of Europe, "Recommendation 1710: Honoring of Obli-gations and Commitments by the Russian Federation," 2005, http://assembly.coe.int/Mainf
.asp?link=/Documents/AdoptedText/ta05/EREC1710.htm (accessed December 8, 2011).

77. American Embassy Stockholm to Secretary of State, Washington, DC, "Sweden on the EU Partnership and Nordstream," Wikileaks, November 28, 2008, http://wikileaks.ch/cable
/2008/11/08STOCKHOLM792.html (accessed April 15, 2012).

78. Irina Filatova and Khristina Narizhnaya, "Russia Faces Pressure after Report on Graft," *Moscow Times*, January 12, 2011, http://www.cdi.org/russia/johnson/russia-corruption-europe-greco
-report-jan-153.cfm (accessed January 13, 2011).

79. Parliamentary Assembly, Council of Europe, "Recommendation 1710: Honoring of Obliga-tions and Commitments by the Russian Federation."

80. GRECO Secretariat, Council of Europe, "Addendum to the Compliance Report on the Rus-sian Federation," December 3, 2012, http://www.coe.int/t/dghl/monitoring/greco/evaluations
/round2/GrecoRC1&2(2010)2_Add_RussianFederation_EN.pdf (accessed March 8, 2014).

81. "Serbia Approves Sale of NIS to Gazprom," *RIA-Novosti*, January 23, 2008, http://en.rian.ru
/analysis/20080123/97600280.html (accessed February 15, 2012).

82. Igor Torbakov, "Russian Policymakers Air Notion of 'Liberal Empire' in Caucasus, Central Asia," Eurasianet.org, October 27, 2003, http://www.eurasianet.org/departments/insight/arti
cles/eav102703.shtml (accessed January 16, 2010).

83. "Russian, Tajik Presidents Unveil Joint-Venture Power Plant," Radio Free Europe Radio Lib-erty, March 14, 2011, http://www.rferl.org/content/Russian_Tajik_Presidents_Unveil_Joint_
Venture_Power_Plant/1789915.html (accessed January 17, 2012).

84. Samvel Martyrosyan, "Armenia: Answers Demanded on UES Deal," Eurasianet.org, July 13, 2005, http://www.eurasianet.org/departments/business/articles/eav071405.shtml (accessed January 7, 2012).

85. For Georgia, see Zeyno Baran, "Deals Give Russian Companies Influence over Georgia's Energy Infrastructure," Eurasianet.org, August 17, 2003, http://www.eurasianet.org/departments
/business/articles/eav081803.shtml. For Kyrgyzstan, see Cholpon Orozobekova, "Kyrgyz-stan: Moscow, Riled over Nationalization, Fires Shot across Bishkek's Bow," Eurasianet.org, March 14, 2011, http://www.eurasianet.org/node/63068.

86. Peter Finn, "Probe Traces Global Reach of Counterfeiting Ring; Fake $100 Bills in Mary-land Tied to Organized Crime in Separatist Enclave," *Washington Post*, November 26, 2006, http://www.washingtonpost.com/wp-dyn/content/article/2006/11/25/AR2006112500963.
(accessed March 23, 2011).

87. Yulia Latynina, "South Ossetia Crisis Could Be Russia's Chance to Defeat Siloviki," Radio Free Europe/Radio Liberty, August 8, 2008, http://www.rferl.org/content/South_Ossetia_Crisis
_Could_Be_Russian_Chance_To_Defeat_Siloviki/1189525.html.

88. "South Ossetia: Recent Developments," Global Security, 2008, http://www.globalsecurity.org
/military/world/war/south-ossetia-2.htm (accessed December 8, 2011).

89. Freedom House, "South Ossetia: 2011," http://www.freedomhouse.org/modules/mod_call
_dsp_country-fiw.cfm?year=2011&country=8193. Also see Russian Expert Group, Black Sea Peacebuilding Network, Carnegie Moscow Center, *South Ossetia: Aftermath and Outlook*, rap-porteur, Alexander Skakov, Report No. 2011/1, 2011, http://www.carnegieendowment.org
/files/Report_ossetia_eng_2011.pdf.

90. U.S. Senate Foreign Relations Committee, "Will Russia End Eastern Europe's Last Frozen Con-flict?," 112th Congress, 1st Session, February 8, 2011 (Washington, DC: U.S. Government Printing Office, 2011). http://www.gpo.gov/sfsys.

91. Tom Warner, "Dubious dacha sale raises tricky questions over Ukrainians fleeing to Moscow," *Financial Times,* May 6, 2005, http://www.ft.com/intl/cms/s/0/5e6356c4-bdda-11d9-87aa -00000e2511c8.html#axzz3764qzNEa (accessed July 11, 2014).

92. Harriet Salem and Ludmila Makarova, "Crimean Annexation Brings Dacha Prize Closer for Putin," *Guardian,* March 28, 2014, http://www.theGuardian.com/world/2014/mar/28 /crimean-annexation-dacha-vladimir-putin-russian-president (accessed May 3, 2014).

93. Tom Wallace and Farley Mesko, "The Odessa Network: Mapping Facilitators of Russian and Ukrainian Arms Transfer," C4ADS, September 2013, http://www.globalinitiative.net/down load/arms-trafficking/arms(2)/C4ads%20-%20The%20Odessa%20Network%20Mapping %20facilitators%20of%20Russian%20and%20Ukranian%20Arms%20Transfers%20-%20Sept %202013.pdf (accessed May 4, 2014).

94. U.S. Department of the Treasury, "Ukraine Related Designations," April 28, 2014, http://www .treasury.gov/resource-center/sanctions/OFAC-Enforcement/Pages/20140428.aspx.

95. Anatoliy Karlin, "The Kremlinologist Catechism," Sublime Oblivion, August 27, 2010, www .sublimeoblivion.com (accessed February 15, 2012).

96. American Embassy Moscow to U.S. Secretary of State, "Questioning Putin's Work Ethic," Wikileaks, March 4, 2009, http://wikileaks.ch/cable/2009/03/09MOSCOW532.html (accessed April 8, 2010).

97. Vladimir Putin, "Interview," Lenta TV, 1996, http://www.youtube.com/watch?feature=player _embedded&v=DvAYV6-ZN0I (accessed June 6, 2013).

98. "Right of Ownership to a Country," Gazeta.ru, June 18, 2007, in Johnson's Russia List, no.137, June 19, 2007 (accessed by email listserve April 1, 2013).

99. Åslund, *Russia's Capitalist Revolution,* 211.

100. Nikitinskiy, "Litso vlasti [A Person of Power]."

101. Earley, *Comrade J,* 299.

102. Masyuk, "Gleb Pavlovskiy: 'What Putin Is Most Afraid of Is to Be Left Out.'"

103. *Guardian* interview with Gleb Pavlovskiy, January 2012, in Hill and Gaddy, *Mr. Putin,* 20.

INDEX

Page numbers in *italics* refer to picture captions.

Baader-Meinhof Group, 10
Babitskiy, Andrey, 257
Bachmann, Peter, 116–17
Baikal Finance Group, 55*n*
Bakai, Ihor, 239–40
Baltic Bunker Company, 143*n*
Baltic Shipping Company, 75, 76
Baltik-Eskort, 74, 76, 77, 127–28, 131–32,
    235
Balyasnikov, Andrey, 64, 179
Banca del Gottardo, 170, 170*n*
Bankers War, 167
Bank Menatep, 25, 140
Bank of New York (BNY), 210–11, 220
Bank of St. Petersburg, 133–34
Bank of Ukraine, 239
Bank Rossiya, 3, 31, 55–56, 63–70, 84, 88,
    90, 94, 150, 179, 296, 299, 340
  Gazprom and, 283
  Petersburg Fuel Company (PTK) and,
    142, 143
  Putin and, 3, 64–70
banks, 9, 31–32, 55, 185, 258, 340
Barankevich, Anatoliy, 345
Baranov, Anatoliy, 345
Barents Sea, 285
Barron's, 331
Barsukov, Mikhayl, 152
Barsukov, Vladimir (Vladimir Kumarin), 73,
    79, 98, 127, 165, 177, 178
  Petersburg Fuel Company (PTK) and,
    141–42, 143–44
  St. Petersburg Real Estate Holding Co.
    and, 132, 134–37
  Twentieth Trust and, 151
Basayev, Shamil, 200–201, 204, 207, 218,
    220
Bashkortostan, 243, 246, 248
Bastrykin, Aleksandr, 91, 195*n*, 320
Baturina, Yelena, 241
BBC, 332
bearer shares, 301*n*
Belarus, 14, 343, 344
Belgium, 151
Belgorod, 238
Belkovskiy, Stanislav, 6, 113, 115, 127*n*, 194
Belton, Catherine, 135

Belyayev, Aleksandr, 106, 108–9, 160
Berezovskiy, Boris, 31, 65*n*, 122*n*, 133, 146,
    154, 156, 170, 183, 184, 186–88,
    191, 192, 194, 197–200, 206, 207,
    210–11, 225–26, 235, 242, 263–64,
    273, 275, 277–80, 290–92, 294,
    312, 323
  Abramovich and, 278–79, 280, 289–92
  Federation Council and, 271
  Kursk submarine disaster and, 289
  Putin's meetings with, 204–5
  resignation of, 273
Berger, Mikhayl, 274
Beria, Lavrentiy, 24
Berliner Zeitung, 40
Berlin Wall, 43, 45, 47, 50, 51, 53, 63
Berlusconi, Silvio, 6, 141, 306, *307*
Berlusputin, 306
Beryozka, 199
Beslan hostage crisis, 60*n*
bespredel, 3
Beyrle, John, 12
Bezrukov, Sergey, 59
Bikfin, 66*n*, 67
billionaires, 37, 101, 103, 321
birth rates, 313
Bivens, Matt, 150
Black Sea, 344
Blomgren, Jan, 192
Blowing Up Russia, 259*n*
Blumenfeld, Mark, 216
BMW, 75
BND (Bundesnachrichtendienst), the
    German Federal Intelligence Agency,
    41, 42, 48, 132, 134, 137–38, 140
Bobkov, Filipp, 23, 24–25, 45, 45*n*
Böhm, Horst, 46, 51
Boldyrev, Yuriy, 118–19, 121, 124, 174–75
Bolloev, Taimuraz, 306*n*
Bolotnaya demonstrations, 91, 317
Bolshakov, Aleksey, 167
bombings, 122*n*, 208–9, 211, 285
  FSB and, 212–23, 259, 262
  Ryazan, 208, 212–23, 259–62
Bonehill, Christopher, 279
Bonini, Carlo, 28, 61
Bonner, Yelena, 73

ABOUT THE AUTHOR

Karen Dawisha has been the director of the Havighurst Center for Russian and Post-Soviet Studies, and, since 2000, the Walter E. Havighurst Professor of Political Science at Miami University. She received her Ph.D. from the London School of Economics.

She has served as an advisor to the British House of Commons Foreign Affairs Committee and as an International Affairs Fellow of the Council on Foreign Relations, and was a member of the Policy Planning Staff and the Bureau of Political-Military Affairs of the U.S. State Department (1985–87). Until the summer of 2000, she was a Distinguished Research Professor in the Department of Government and Politics at the University of Maryland and the director of its Center for the Study of Post-Communist Societies. She has had extensive overseas experience, living abroad from 1969 to 1983 in England and from 1990 to 1991 in Egypt, and having undertaken more than three dozen research trips to Russia, central and eastern Europe, and central Asia, and has traveled widely in Europe and the Middle East.

Professor Dawisha has received fellowships from the MacArthur Foundation, the Council on Foreign Relations, the British Council, the Rockefeller Foundation, and the Fulbright-Hays Program. She has served on the national boards of the American Association for the Advancement of Slavic Studies, the British Association for Slavonic and East European Studies, the Kennan Institute, and the Social Science Research Council's Eurasia Program and its Committee on International Peace and Security.